BEN JONSON

BEN JONSON

BEN JONSON

Selected Works

EDITED, AND WITH AN INTRODUCTION, BY

HARRY LEVIN, OF HARVARD UNIVERSITY

RANDOM HOUSE · NEW YORK

CONTENTS

v

CONTENTS

CONTENTS

CONTENTS

CONTENTS

INTRODUCTION

Introduction

BEN JONSON'S position, three hundred years
after his death, is more than secure; it might
almost be called impregnable. He is still the greatest
unread English author. It is partly his fault and
partly his misfortune that we find Jonson's volumes
so uninviting. It was his fault because, like James
Joyce, his extraordinary equipment for observing
people and for handling words ended by taking him
farther in the direction of experiment than all but
a devoted few cared to follow, and by encumbering
his collected works with what Dryden called 'dot-
ages.' It was his misfortune, and the fault of his
editors, to pile Pelion on Ossa; Jonson has always
had more attention from antiquarians than from
critics, and has too often served as a cadaver over
which to read a lecture on the lore of language and
custom. Surely, after three hundred years, the misfortune of being over-edited has atoned for the fault
of over-writing. Today, it is hoped, the core of
Jonson can be easily discriminated and conveniently
presented.

The purpose of the present volume is to make
Jonson's most valuable and typical works as accessible as Shakespeare's. This has meant the preparation of an independent text. Jonson has not been
fully edited since 1816, and it is becoming increas-
ingly difficult to consider William Gifford's edition
a modern one. The critical edition of C. H. Herford
and Percy Simpson, like all monuments, has been
slow in getting under way; even when completed, it

is not likely to be within reach of the general literary public. Happily, the modern editor is faced with a task of restoration, rather than emendation. He need only appeal from those who have reprinted Gifford, with varying degrees of inaccuracy, to Jonson himself. He can confidently depend upon the first folio for definitive versions of the bulk of Jonson's work, for everything written before 1616 with the exception of *Bartholomew Fair*. For that, and for what remains, he must continue with the second folio, which Jonson started to supervise in 1631 and which finally appeared in 1640 under the presumable care of Kenelm Digby. If he goes beyond these sources, it is only to garner four sets of commendatory verses from the books of Jonson's friends, and to profit by the transcription of Drummond's record of Jonson's *Conversations*. The quartos occasionally supply a more vivid or, rarely, a more distinct turn of phrase.

Where it does no violence to the sound or the sense, the regularization of Jonson's spelling and punctuation has proceeded along the lines indicated by our dictionaries and grammars. Jonson's own usages are so elaborately consistent that it seems a pity not to adopt them, but they would undoubtedly prove obtrusive and retard the pace in reading. Jonson's articulation of scenes, in the French manner, at the entrance of new characters, has been discarded for the more usual division based on changes of place. Stage directions are reduced to a normalized minimum, because attempts of the editorial imagination to vie with Jonson can only defeat themselves. The business of communicating Volpone's will, for example, is more than adequately described by no less a person than the deceased. The absence of footnotes has its consolation in the fact that Jonson ordinarily tells us what he wants us to know—'officers, the Saffi.' The reader is under no further sense of obligation to the editor who informs him that 'Banks's horse was a remarkable horse of the period which belonged to an individual by the name of Banks.' Clearly, Bobadil's duelling vocabulary and Subtle's alchemical hocus-pocus were intended to bedazzle and intimidate their listeners in the audience, as well as on the stage.

No single book, perhaps, can encompass the range and richness of an author like Jonson. Yet it can demonstrate his versatility, it can illustrate the development of his art, and it can show the high quality of his craftsmanship persisting through other forms than that with which his name is associated. It can stimulate a fresh insight into the life of the period or into the technique of the theatre. It can furnish materials for the re-estimate of Jonson which must be rendered soon, unless students of literature are willing to shelve the most brilliant and vigorous of English comic dramatists. The only service this part of the book can perform is to clear the way for such a re-estimate, by meeting some of the stock arguments and suggesting a few possible approaches.

1. TRADITION

In the history of literature, Ben Jonson has gone down as a figure, rather than as a writer. Critics call him by his first name upon very slight acquaintance. The strength of this impression is a testimony to the malice of one of his friends, William Drummond of Hawthornden. The eighteenth century contributed to the confusion by producing a Johnson whose opinions were quite as emphatic and even more notorious. The nineteenth century, with its prefer-ence for personalities above achievements, put the final stamp on what was left of Ben Jonson's reputation. His unique personal prestige, the extraordinary number of his articulate friends and enemies, the fact that we know more about him than we need to know—these are the accidents that constrain him into playing the part of eccentric. What is actually eccentric is the development of English literature. By the standards of his time, Jonson never deviates from his defined intentions and assured technique, which constituted the nearest approximation England had yet made to an organized culture and an academic style. Saint-Evremond expressed the mind of the Restoration when he singled Jonson out for the select company of Aristotle, Horace, Corneille, Boileau, and other literary law-givers. A succession of revolutions has impaired their authority.

For the last two centuries Jonson's principal function has been to serve as a stalking-horse for Shakespeare. Others abide our question, Shakespeare transcends it; and if you would understand, point for point, the limitations he transcends, go read Jonson. Often an attempt is made to settle the problem on a quantitative basis—Shakespeare's characters are considered three-dimensional, Jonson's are reproached with incurable flatness. The retort to this kind of criticism is a stubborn insistence that, strictly speaking, no literary creation has any dimensions at all. Another chapter in the history of taste and of studies has been compiled since the days when Jonson was damned by the canons of Shakespearean pantheism. Scholarship talks less about nature and more about the theatre. Aesthetics requires a measure of abstraction. The old impatience with limitation has been replaced by a new appreciation of convention, which we take to be not only the form, but also the essence, of art.

No dramatist could have strayed very far from the crude psychology and constricting conditions that hedged in the Elizabethan stage. It is true that Shakespeare had an artifice against artifice, an unequalled capacity for conveying the impression that he was not subject to such limitations. So successful are his occasional touches of nature that we are still surprised when his personages act according to the exigencies of the plot, and not according to motives which we ourselves should acknowledge in their place. But this trick of transcendence is not to be reckoned with; all that can be said is that it succeeds sporadically, even in Shakespeare. Webster catches it now and then, Dekker and Heywood handle it rather inexpertly, and if Jonson is really responsible for the painter's scenes in *The Spanish Tragedy*, he had mastered it, too. There is no reason to condemn his usual method of characterization for dealing with encounters instead of experiences and appealing to judgment instead of sympathy. Jonson's characters move in the same world as those of Marlowe and Middleton, Nashe and Donne, lampooning courtiers and pamphleteering journalists. In this as in other respects, Jonson is closer than Shakespeare to the literature of his day, and by no means preoccupied with the literature of the past.

Jonson is commonly conceived as a man who wrote comedies because he had a theory about why comedies ought to be written. This formidable misconception is buttressed by Jonson's own words, in a tireless series of prefaces, prologues, and asides. To accept them is to take an author's rationalizations about his own work too seriously and to ignore the historical circumstances that they were designed to meet. The comedy of humours was not arrived at as a descriptive formulation for purely critical purposes; it was seized upon as a polemical weapon to answer the Puritan attacks on the stage. Jonson, Chapman, and other dramatists were exploiting a psychological novelty which had appeared at the turn of the sixteenth century, in order to ward off popular resentment against the satirical sharpness of their 'wormwood comedies.' The induction to *Every Man out of his Humour* sets forth the full argument for comedy as a social purgative. It is perhaps as relevant to Jonson's work as psycho-analysis is to the dramas of Eugene O'Neill.

Like Aristotle's doctrine of katharsis which it strikingly resembles, Jonson's theory of humours is less analytic than apologetic, less a system of liter-ary criticism than an exercise in ethical justification. Had Jonson regarded it as more than a convenient metaphor, he would have become entangled in the contradiction which brought the Spanish philos-opher Huerte before the Inquisition. If you under-take to reform society by confronting it with its own picture, and that picture is so darkly deterministic that it precludes all possibility of reform, what then? Do you curb your reforming zeal? Do you moderate your behaviourism? Are you obliged to choose be-tween philanthropy and misanthropy? Or are you simply a hard-working playwright, with a hard-headed and somewhat doctrinaire view of humanity, trying to protect your vested interests by beating the moralists at their own game? O cursèd spite!

If Jonson's too ample protestations can be con-strued to show him as a reformer, he does nothing to discourage the assumption that he is a pedant as well. Here the incentive may be a private one. We must bear in mind the bricklayer's apprentice who lived to receive an honorary degree from Oxford, the second-rate actor and patcher of second-hand plays who forged for himself the position of *arbiter elegantiarum* of English letters. Jonson was a dramatist before he was a scholar. Poetry was too literally its own reward, and he envied the status of acquaintances who had fallen back on the gospel or the law—Donne and Bacon, for example. The wars of the theatres, his repeated retirements from the loathèd stage, and the petulance and paralysis of his old age left him no solace but his books. As his audiences grew smaller, his own orientation widened; he improved his relations with the ancients and began to invoke posterity. Practical disappointments could only confirm him in the theoretical principles of a self-made humanist.

Gathering manuscripts and accumulating commentaries, enjoying the friendship of Camden, Cotton, Savile, and Selden, he sought to fit into a better regimen for a literary life than the Bohemian purlieus of the theatre afforded. The *Discoveries* are chiefly remarkable as an evidence of this phase of Jonson's activity, as an armoury of maxims and a storehouse of ideas, as a link between Jonson and his masters in rhetoric, Seneca and Quintilian, Vossius and Heinsius. The very titles of his occasional collections of verse and prose—*Underwoods, The Forest, Timber*—glance at the *Sylvae* of the polymaths of humanism. His failures, never clapperclawed by the palms of the vulgar, were dressed up in annotated editions to catch the eye of the learned. The thin quarto of *Sejanus*, with its marginal freight of Latin citations, must have formed a curious item on an Elizabethan bookstall. Derisive echoes make us wonder at Jonson's presumption in daring to gather his plays into a folio volume and publish them under the insufferable designation of *Works*.

The cultivation of these outward and visible marks of erudition accomplished far more than its calculated effect. It persuaded readers that the *Works* smelled exclusively of the lamp and desensitized their perception against a swarm of other odours—fragrant, pungent, savoury, and rank, as the case may be. Jonson does speak with much conviction when he is paraphrasing the classics, but it is doubtful if an indefinite number of hours in a library could have taught him to sketch in his detail so casually as this:

> 'Ha' not I
> Known him, a common rogue, come fiddling in
> To th' ostería, with a tumbling whore,
> And, when he has done all his forced tricks, been
>   glad
> Of a poor spoonful of dead wine, with flies in't?'

It would be strange if signs of Jonson's vast reading had not crept into his writing; it would be stranger if the Tyburn brand on his thumb, his military career in the Low Countries, his religious conversion, his dubious activities as a spy, and all his duels and amours had not given him opportunities for observation that are assimilated in the things he wrote. Next to extreme bookishness, undue realism is the quality for which Jonson has been most bitterly censured. At Saint John's College, Cambridge, he was looked down upon as 'a meere Empirick, one that getts what he hath by obseruation, and makes only nature priuy to what he indites.' He put down everything he read, according to one side, everything he saw according to the other.

These vicissitudes of opinion are resolved by a single consideration—Jonson, first and last, was preeminently a craftsman, planning and constructing his verse and prose as solidly as he had learned to lay bricks. That is why he has been mistaken for both a pedant and a reformer, why he has been miscalled an arrant translator and a mere empiric. The fact is that, like a good workman, he felt the weight of literary tradition while remaining within the current of contemporary life. He differs from his fellow writers not in aims and methods, but in being more conscious of the task of adaptation they jointly performed and in going about it more systematically. England had, for the first time, a legislator of Parnassus, to sit in the chair later occupied by Dryden, Pope, and Samuel Johnson. All of a sudden, it had seemed, there were not enough forms and concepts, not enough phrases and words, in the native stock, to express all the possibilities of which people were becoming aware. There had ensued a stage of borrowing and engrafting, of translation and experiment. What was now needed, and what Jonson definitely represented, was a vernacular classicism.

In this light, we are struck by the straightforward and pragmatic nature of Jonson's classical program. The efforts of scholars at the Universities, lawyers in the Inns of Court, and friends of the Countess of Pembroke had failed to revive tragedy in its pristine purity; schoolmasters, critics, and divines united to deplore the way in which Paul's Churchyard flouted the rules of rhetoric; English poets had abandoned the chase after the chimaera of quantitative metres. Ben Jonson entered the field as a professional man of letters. As one who thoroughly grasped and had extensively practised most of the bastard forms which had sprung up, he knew how they could be clarified and made supple. As the first of a line of neo-classicists, he wanted not to surrender to Greece and Rome, but to rival them, to wed ancient form to modern substance. He had hoped to achieve a perfect embodiment of this ideal in the pastoral fragment of *The Sad Shepherd*, where his pro-claimed purpose was to garner

'. . . such wool
  As from mere English flocks his Muse can pull,'

and therewith to fashion

'. . . a fleece
  To match or those of Sicily or Greece.'

It is characteristic of the culture of the Renais-sance at its ripest, that it should seek to give classical precedent a local habitation and a name. Horace's *fons Bandusiae* is transformed into Ronsard's *fon-taine Bellerie*. The tropes of Catullus,

> *Quam magnus numerus Libyssae harenae*
> *Lasarpiciferis iacet Cyrenis,*
> *Oraclum Iovis inter aestuosi*
> *Et Batti veteris sacrum sepulcrum;*
> *Aut quam sidera multa, cum tacet nox,*
> *Furtivos hominum vident amores,*

suffer a sea-change, in Jonson's paraphrase:

> 'All the grass that Rumney yields,
>   Or the sands in Chelsea fields,
>   Or the drops in silver Thames,
>   Or the stars that gild his streams,
>   In the silent summer nights,
>   When youths ply their stol'n delights.'

Sedate dignitaries from the pantheon of Natalis Comes are jostled out of Jonson's masques by English worthies from Captain Cox's library; the same blend of refined commonplace and homely folklore tinctures the lyrics of Jonson's disciple, Herrick. The tribe of Ben was responsible for fastening his favourite measure, the heroic couplet, upon English poetry, where it prevailed with the tenacity of neoclassicism itself until, further straitened by an enforced sojourn in France, it became the cell in which Pope was condemned to pace out his existence, five steps down and five steps back.

We can distinguish between what is classical and what is native in the traditions available to Jonson, but we have no means of measuring the extent to which they make themselves felt in his work. It would be futile to try to determine the preponderating element or to weigh them both in the clumsy balance of form and content. The norms of dramatic structure, in comedy and in tragedy, Jonson had obviously generalized from Latin models, more precisely from Plautus, Terence, and Seneca. Of the profound significance of the Roman satirists for the late Elizabethan mentality, particularly after downright imitation had been prohibited and the pent-up gall had burst forth on the stage, Jonson's 'comical satires' are our main witness. Yet more than the materials of his plays is indigenous. The conventions of the English morality are respected in Jonson's casts and plots, in the *redende Namen* of his characters, in the beast-fable of *Volpone* or the gaping Hell-mouth of *The Devil is an Ass*. And beneath his writing runs a broad substratum of journalism, of all the tracts, broadsides, and jest-books that had granted literary recognition to the London underworld before Jonson came along.

Finally, there is a plane upon which these opposing forces reach an equilibrium. The extremes of
rhetoric and pamphleteering, the old and the new,
foreign and domestic, and erudite and popular meet
in an illusory half-world, wherein the *fallax servus*
borrows the lath dagger of the Vice and Cato shakes
his finger at Til Eulenspiegel. The whole farago of
types and themes becomes intelligible, from this
distant vantage point, as the outside of a large,
heterogeneous cultural movement. Across Europe,
along the drift from Renaissance to Reformation,
from Italy to Germany, stride two gigantic protag-
onists, the rogue and the fool. In the conflicts of
humanistic learning and empirical experience, the
war between theology and science, a literature is
evolved which has the expansiveness of the picar-
esque and the inclusiveness of satire. It is the age
of Erasmus, Brandt, Rabelais, and Cervantes. It is
the time to cry 'Ducdame' and call all fools into a
circle.

Against the background of the Reformation, then,
rather than that of the Renaissance, Jonson may be
seen at his best. He was by birth and apprenticeship an Elizabethan, but the succeeding years are
those he dominates, and the elegies of his lamenting 'sons' would have been more impressive if they
had not been issued in the year of the Bishops'
War. For it is Jonson's career which most strongly
marks the transition in English literature from
sonnet to satire, from comedy of the court to comedy
of the city, from poets who celebrated imaginary
mistresses to poets who dedicated themselves to detraction, from the virtuous conduct of Castiglione's
Courtier to the gross etiquette of Dedekind's Gro-
bian. Jonson is the legitimate heir of the Renais-

sance, of the Elizabethan age, and of Christopher
Marlowe—it took a third poetic craftsman, T. S.
Eliot, to discern that. When we come to examine
the texture of Jonson's verse, we shall be grateful
for this discernment. We must recognize this formal
continuity, if only to appreciate how sharply it reverses its intellectual bearing. Marlowe belongs to
one century and Jonson to another, and their
respective attitudes toward human nature are as far
apart as More's *Utopia* and Hobbes' *Leviathan*.

2. SATIRE

The richness of the Renaissance, about which
so much has been said, is more than a metaphor. In
what was, after all, the heroic age of mercantile
enterprise, it should not astonish us to find a lustre
reflecting the influx of wealth from the Indies and
of gold from the Americas. We breathe the glitter-
ing atmosphere of the Mediterranean, ever the
centre of fashion and luxury, in *The Jew of Malta,
Othello,* and *Volpone,* while *Eastward Ho, The
Tempest,* and *The Fair Maid of the West* have in
them something of the saltier air of British adventure. Economic expansion, in England, is accompanied by an intensely universal feeling of nation-
wide participation, which finds cultural expression
in the collections of the voyagers, in the Tudor
translations, in the chronicle plays, in the idealized
figure of the Virgin Queen. This exaltation and
confidence, which suggests comparison with the
American Dream, seems to lose its bloom in the last
decade of Elizabeth's reign, just as the freshness of
our own national ideals withered after the Civil
War.

In the latter half of the sixteenth century, there

was time for a new English aristocracy to grow up, and for a popular monarchy to leave off fostering democratic notions and assume more or less absolute pretensions. By the turn of the century, a mercantilist economy had dammed up the enormous flow of resources, and it was no longer easy to believe that all things were possible to any man. Patents and monopolies still changed hands; the great companies were setting out to establish the new plantations; projectors flourished, and made the court a hotbed of promotion and intrigue. Step by step, through the literature of these crucial years, we can watch the sentiment of expectation change to a sense of wariness, depression, and disillusionment. With increasing introspection, everything is anatomized. Newer and more analytic forms, such as the character and the essay, are devised; ancient modes, like satire and epigram, are borrowed to fit modern instances. The native hue of Elizabethan resolution is sicklied o'er with the pale cast of Jacobean melancholy. Nature, it is felt, is in decay; the times are out of joint; *difficile est satyram non scribere.*

That Ben Jonson should have viewed this change in the light of the historic contrast between the Roman Republic and the Roman Empire was inevitable. Exasperated by the demands of the groundlings, exhausted by the rivalry of Marston, Dekker, and other poetasters and professionals, he was led to adopt the idiom of the Silver Age and to address himself, in the tone of Martial and Tacitus, to the imperial theme. *Sejanus,* with its acid depiction of the caprice of princes and the folly of favourites, greeted the accession of the leading apologist for the divine right of kings, the future patron of Somerset and Buckingham. Small wonder that it brought Jonson to the Star Chamber. It is no accident that Shakespeare, in his Roman tragedies, and Chapman, in his French histories, were dwelling upon the problem of authority, or that the issues of *Coriolanus* and of *Sejanus* seem even more pregnant today. The concentrated indignation of Jonson's Roman elders, the glimpses of espionage and repression, the episodes of judicial murder, the mood of flattery and fear evoke as many echoes in our ears as the cry, 'Lictors, resume the fasces!'

Significantly, both Jonson's tragic heroes are villains, so confirmed in their villainy that they need no motive; Sejanus resolves to debauch Livia before her husband has struck him, and Catiline does not wait for the election of Cicero to hatch his plot. If their efforts do not achieve the fullness of tragedy, it is Jonson's fault, for failing to counterweight them with anything but appeals to principles and exercises in rhetoric. Cicero, not Catiline, is remiss. It would be rash to conclude that the satiric spirit is hostile to tragedy. On the contrary, Jonson's tragedies come most to life when his courtiers are fawning or when his women, whose psychology is never more than cosmetic-deep, are gossiping. The very satire which called the story of Sejanus to Jonson's attention, Juvenal's tenth, is almost mediaeval in its stress upon tragic reversal of fortune. The tragedian of an age of satire, Seneca, was the unavoidable model for every Elizabethan dramatist who aspired to the buskin. Shakespeare himself was forced to describe the Trojan War and Homeric heroes as 'Nothing but lechery! all incontinent varlets!' His Cleopatra gives more than a hint of how Jonson would have treated her:

> '. . . the quick comedians
> Extemporally will stage us, and present
> Our Alexandrian revels. Antony
> Shall be brought drunken forth, and I shall see
> Some squeaking Cleopatra boy my greatness
> I' the posture of a whore.'

The genius of tragedy is essentially the same as that of comedy, as someone mumbled through a haze of wine fumes, very early one morning in the house of Agathon. Of the tragedy of the Renaissance, disposed as it was to leave so little to fate, this is particularly true. Tragic suffering can be, and in the more remote past has been, blind and passive; comic matters notoriously involve human agency. The slings and arrows of an outrageous fortune are not to be endured, revenge is sweet, revenge ripens into conspiracy, conspiracy passes over into intrigue, and the gap is bridged; the Elizabethans have proved at least that a similar dramatic technique will serve for tragedy and for comedy. Thus Tiberius and Sejanus, the Jew of Malta and his blackamoor, the arch-plotter Volpone and the parasite Mosca, are respectively related.

If tragedy can scoff, comedy can scorn. The comical satires are of the 'biting' variety, not the 'toothless.' Professing to sport with human follies, not with crimes, Jonson too often took it upon himself to dispense poetic justice, to regulate his comical satires by a more rigorous ethic than life itself ever provides, to conjure up an inferno of punishments for his personal enemies. Some high-minded malcontent—an Asper or a Crites—like the melancholy Jacques and not unlike the sort of madman that Hamlet pretended to be, figures as Jonson's accredited representative, and is entrusted with the

responsibility of scourging vice, untrussing affectation, and reconciling humours all around. Jonsonian
comedy invariably tends in the direction of an
arraignment; it must enact a trial and achieve an
official resolution of the comic knot, whether by
royal Cynthia or imperial Augustus, by court or
Senate, or merely by a nonchalant interloper or
humane jurist of the Bridlegoose breed.

In the riper comedies, the rules become more flexible. The final court-room scene in *Volpone*, it is
true, reverses the venal decision of the fourth act,
but by that time our faith in lawyers and judges
and Venetians and human beings has become cor-
roded, and we sense the hollowness of the categorical
imperative. In *Epicene*, the pretense is acknowledged, and we are invited to hear a false canon
lawyer and a mock doctor of divinity hold a sham
disputation. This discrepancy between law and life
is the condition which governs *Bartholomew Fair*.
'Think to make it as lawful as you can,' pleads
Dame Purecraft, and Rabbi Busy discovers scrip-
tural sanction for the eating of pig. The bumpkin
Cokes, while being edified by a ballad on the
wretched end which befalls pickpockets, is robbed
of his purse. In this select company of gamblers and
bawds, only the half-witted Troubleall would insist
upon warrant for what is done; in the very sink of
enormities, the pompous Justice Overdo can find no
one to expose but his own wife; in the topsy-turvy
jurisdiction of Pie-powders, it is the reforming element—Overdo, the puritan Busy, and the angry
man, Wasp—who land side by side in the stocks.
Jonson could go no farther in reducing his own
legalism to absurdity, except by haling into *The
Staple of News* the trial of dogs which Aristophanes
had originated and Racine would improve. These

names are worth recalling, if they convey the generalization that parody of justice has always been a premise for comedy.

His object all sublime Jonson gradually relinquished to the genuine doctors and divines. With a more incisive perception of the conflict between interests and ideals, 'the space between the breast and lips,' he gave up the attempt to discipline his characters and they profited by their freedom. His uncompromising attitude toward his fellow men persisted, but he no longer described men as good and bad; they were simply fools and knaves, or, in Elizabethan parlance, gulls and coney-catchers. The eschatology of *The Alchemist* is based on this simplified scheme; after the three knaves have cozened their victims, one of them outwits the other two, who thereupon assume the status of fools, while the arch-knave is pardoned and permitted to baffle the one honest man of the piece. *The Devil is an Ass,* as its name implies, is a study in comparative ethics, demonstrating that what is religiously regarded as the absolute in evil can only bungle along by contrast with what goes on above ground. 'Hell is a grammar-school to this!' exclaims the chastened fiend, and departs on the back of the Vice, setting off an ineffectual fire-cracker, and leaving the field to Protagoras and Jeremy Bentham.

Because Jonson was enough of an Aristotelian to rank knowledge above virtue, and enough of a Machiavellian to delight in ingenuity for its own sake, it does not follow that he ever succeeded in banishing morality from his stage. In comedy, as well as tragedy, there must be a context of good and evil, but it can be defined socially rather than theologically. Pity and terror, accordingly, give way to insouciance and curiosity, and sometimes to contempt and cynicism. Comic writers start by making certain devastating assumptions about human nature, by questioning every man's honesty and every woman's virtue, even though they seldom push them to such drastic conclusions as *Mandragola, The Country Wife, Turcaret,* and *Volpone.* 'Interpreteth best sayings and deeds often to the worst,' says Drummond. These assumptions inhere in the tradition of classical comedy, as part of that perfectly Euclidean realm where there are so many coincidences and no surprises, where old men exist to leave legacies, clever parasites to get around them, beautiful orphans to be shipwrecked, and young men to go a-whoring.

Jonson had assimilated the latent antagonisms of this early comedy—fathers versus sons, philistines against poets, the city as opposed to the universities. When he came to print *Every Man in his Humour* in folio, he heightened the asperity of the elder generation by assigning Old Knowell a speech out of Juvenal on the depraving of youth through luxury and trade, and weakened the position of the younger generation by omitting Lorenzo Junior's defense of poetry. The Ovid of *Poetaster* becomes virtually the 'marked man' of later romanticism, condemned first by his father to the study of law, and then by the Emperor to banishment. When Jonson came to composition with his audience, however, in *Epicene* and *Bartholomew Fair,* youth could expect indulgence and pantaloons or serious asses might tremble in apprehension of the fate of Malvolio. His scholars, dropping their academic accent, set up for wits; the city became the town, and they found their way around it without difficulty. It might have comforted the banished Ovid to learn that he had furnished the very language

for this elegant new coterie of Truewits and Cleri-
monts.

Epicene, the most brittle of Jonson's comedies,
was the most likely to win Pepys' plaudits and fit
Dryden's canons. Frankly a thing of veneer, explicitly discouraging attempts to glance beneath its
polished contours, it stands at an interesting half-
way point between Plautine and Restoration
comedy. Its courtly air and its emphasis on the
relations between the sexes remind us that it was
written for the boy-actors who had performed Lyly's
plays, whereas Jonson's apprenticeship was served in
the theatre that had employed Marlowe, while
Sejanus and *Volpone* were produced by Shakespeare's company. But the action of *Epicene* is not
presided over by any Meredithian comic spirit. If it
were not farce, it would be pathology. Was there
ever a more disillusioned cavalier than Sir Dauphine
Eugenie, setting out to win the collective favours
of a bevy of women he totally despises? And in the
attitude of the wits toward their monomaniac vic-
tim, there is more than a touch of sadism, of the
'comedy of affliction.'

For all its artificiality, *Epicene* was definitely set
in London. From that time forth, Jonson cast aside
the *fabula palliata* and took up the *fabula togata.*
The change is merely a matter of nomenclature,
since Jonson always followed the standard comic
practice—from Menander to Minsky—of conceiving
the comic stage as an intersection of city streets.
Within this convention there is dramatic unity, as
well as room for considerable movement. All that
is needed are a few doors and windows, which
Jonson, revising *Every Man in his Humour,* had no
trouble in labelling 'Moorfields' and 'The Old
Jewry.' He never returned to the 'fustian countries'

where he had dallied before, or to the Rome which he had tried to use as a looking-glass for England. Italy, to an English eye the incarnate breeding-place of corruption, had seemed the appropriate setting for *Volpone*; it is a grim chauvinism which insists on laying the scene for *The Alchemist* at home:

'Our scene is London, 'cause we would make known, No country's mirth is better than our own.'

The demands of realism are most fully satisfied by *Bartholomew Fair*. Although the most meticulously local of Jonson's plays, it is also the most broadly universal; for is not all the world a fair—paraphrasing Seneca, Jonson develops the conceit in his *Discoveries*—and do not men seek gilded roofs and marble pillars, even as children are attracted to cockleshells and hobby-horses? Under this more genial dispensation, humours diffuse into vapours, and vapours evaporate *in fumo*. Like a pilgrimage, a fair forms a comprehensive natural background against which all types and classes may be exhibited; like Chaucer, Jonson allows his characters to step out of the proscenium. Ursula, the pig-woman, challenges an odorous comparison with the Wife of Bath herself, let alone Elinor Rumming or Marion Tweedy Bloom. Here as always, realism thrives upon the implicit contrast between the way things are presented and the way literature has been in the habit of presenting those same things. What, then, could be a crueller falling-off than for Leander, having swum the Hellespont from Sestos to Abydos, to let a foul-mouthed ferryman row him across the Thames from the Bankside to Puddle Wharf?

The plots of *Eastward Ho, Volpone,* and *The Alchemist* are more highly wrought, but not so far-fetched as we might believe. Amid the traffic and speculation of the Renaissance, treasure-trove, legacy hunting, and alchemy were considered legitimate alternatives in the general pursuit of riches. If this crass afterthought robs Jonson's comedies of their fantasy, it binds them much more firmly to the life of their time. For they have a single theme, which may be underscored as the leading-motive of Jonsonian drama, and which is enunciated by its most authoritative spokesman in the mystic words, 'Be rich!' Even through the disembodied parables of his final period, Jonson was playing with such subjects as the pursuit of the Lady Pecunia; and in the projector Merecraft, he created a prototype for the Mr. Micawbers and Robert Macaires and Mulberry Sellerses of bourgeois literature.

Gold is the core of Jonson's comedy, getting and spending are the chains which bind it together, and luxury furnishes the ornaments which cover its surfaces. It is further stipulated, by Volpone himself, that such gold must not be the reward of any productive endeavour. Both *Volpone* and *The Alchemist* hinge upon some monstrous device, a will or the Philosophers' Stone, but Jonson can bring to bear upon almost any situation a suspiciously circumstantial familiarity with all the ruses of craft and quackery. Insofar as it would be the nature of Volpone or Subtle to plot, whether on or off the stage, the motive of chicane becomes the determining factor in the strategy of Jonson's plays. In *Volpone,* perhaps even more than in *The Alchemist,* he has erected his most imposing hierarchies of collusion. In the later play he relaxes the two-edged ironies of fathers who disinherit sons and husbands who prostitute wives, in order to admit a procession of more earth-bound appetites, ranging from the petty desires of a lawyer's clerk to cut a figure, to the intransigent gluttony of Sir Epicure Mammon.

This fat knight is a Falstaff who has suddenly begun to babble like a Faustus. Hankering after fleshpots, his lordly talk is 'all in gold'; 'Silver I care not for.' Out of the boundless opulence which his insatiate libido has already summoned up, he is even prepared to make an occasional benefaction—'And now and then a church.' The limit of his lust is only measured by his gullibility; he observes Hapsburg and Medici traits in Doll Common, and addresses her in the language which Faustus reserved for Helen of Troy. 'Tis pity she's a whore! Before he takes her upstairs, he is warned not to arouse her fanaticism by introducing topics of biblical controversy. 'We think not on 'em,' he replies. And their departure gives Face and Subtle the excuse to bring experiments to a fiasco and blame it upon Sir Epicure's impatient sensuality. 'O my voluptuous mind!' he cries.

Marlowe consistently presented the voluptuary as a hero; to Jonson, he is always either a villain like Volpone or a dupe like Sir Epicure Mammon. Taking up, at Eliot's suggestion, Sir Epicure's moist-lipped recital of the delights he hopes to enjoy, and placing it alongside Gaveston's announcement of the entertainments he has prepared for Edward II, we can observe in each case a texture woven with equal richness and a comparable barrage of sensuous appeal. Jonson's accumulation of images is even denser and more various than Marlowe's, and its effect is utterly subversive. Jonson could not have expressed his reservations more explicitly, nor hit upon a more elaborate contrivance for turning to dust and ashes all the lovely fruit of the Renaissance imagination. Nothing has been neglected, but the intonation has changed, for he is consciously dealing in illusion. Marlowe to Jonson is as Hyperion to a satyr. Sir Philip Sidney had pimples, Jonson told Drummond, and advanced an appalling explanation of Queen Elizabeth's best-known trait.

The luxurious trappings of Jonson's verse are to be viewed, but not touched; they will either vanish away or taint whoever is brash enough to reach out for them. The limping jig of Volpone's deformed chorus rehearses the tale of Lucian's cock, whose crowing awoke its indigent master from dreams of banquets and visions of riches. The plague hangs over the house in which *The Alchemist* operates; brightness falls from the air. Sooner or later, of course, Jonson would rally to the cause of the expiring Renaissance, and the Ghost of Dionysius would bawl down Zeal-of-the-Land Busy in Leatherhead's puppet-show. He would have *Pleasure Reconciled to Virtue* in a masque, at any rate. Perhaps Jonson's asperity was due to the fact that he was a satirist by vocation and a Stoic by philosophical inclination. But vocation and inclination are the result of temperament; if Jonson had not been a scholar, he might have called himself a Puritan. And if he had never existed, there still would have been the Puritans, and other poets would have found it difficult not to write satire. Sir Toby Belch's question was a little beside the point. Malvolio was virtuous precisely because there were no more cakes and ale.

Jonson raised one question which neither Mandeville nor Rousseau would settle. Like his author, the miser of *The Staple of News* is a disciple of Seneca:

'Who can endure to see
The fury of men's gullets and their groins?
What stews, ponds, parks, coops, garners, magazines,
What velvets, tissues, scarfs, embroideries,
And laces they might lack? They covet things
Superfluous still, when it were much more honour
They could want necessary. What need hath Nature
Of silver dishes or gold chamber-pots?
Of perfumed napkins, or a numerous family
To see her eat? Poor and wise, she requires
Meat only; hunger is not ambitious.'

Here, in his Stoic doctrine of nature, he is at vari-
ance with King Lear:

'O, reason not the need; our basest beggars
Are in the poorest thing superfluous.
Allow not nature more than nature needs,
Man's life is cheap as beast's. Thou art a lady;
If only to go warm were gorgeous,
Why, nature needs not what thou gorgeous wear'st,
Which scarcely keeps thee warm.'

Jonson takes more for granted than Shakespeare
does. He presupposes that life is fundamentally a
compact, rational affair, needlessly complicated by
impulse and artifice. To Shakespeare, all experience,
however variegated, is of the same baseless fabric.
The two poets, who worked so closely together, were
as far apart as Heraclitus and Parmenides. Jonson
adopts the attitude of society, Shakespeare the view-
point of the individual, which is finally more real.
Jonson's instrument is logic, Shakespeare's psychology; Jonson's method has been called mechanical,
Shakespeare's organic. That is why we must criticize
Shakespeare in terms of movement and warmth,
Jonson in terms of pattern and colour.

3. RHETORIC

It was an inescapable irony which compelled Jonson to spend his last twenty years as a purveyor of magnificence to the court. It was ironic that a Stoic should be a party to such an extreme form of conspicuous consumption as the masque; that a poet should be forced into competition not only with Inigo Jones, but—as *Neptune's Triumph* dramatizes the issue—with the cook, and at a far lower stipend than the dancing-master; that Ben Jonson should be called upon to provide what he himself ruefully brands

> '. . . the short bravery of the night,
> . . . the jewels, stuffs, the pains, the wit
> There wasted, some not paid for yet!'

But it was inescapable because Jonson had been overlooked by popular success; because he had to get what comfort he could from his official position as poet laureate; because his talent for decoration, his penchant for symbolism, his command of poetic convention, his play of allusion, his knowledge of the classics, and his interest in folklore needed an occasion to converge upon. Shakespeare's career proceeded, according to Edward Dowden's formula, out of the workshop into the world; Jonson's career went in the other direction.

All of his conscientious craftmanship was insufficient to impose coherence on so synthetic a medium. To gather some slight conception of what it was all about, we find ourselves trying to envisage an aristocratic revue or an erudite Silly Symphony. Spain and France, in the persons of their ambassadors, quarrelled over invitations, precedence, and the

King's right ear; Lanière and Ferrabosco contributed galliards and corrantos; the Queen, the Prince,
the Lady Arabella, and other mummers disguised
themselves as gipsies or heathen deities or parts of
speech, and mounted the musicians' gallery to descend in some grandiose machine. From state papers,
viola da gamba scores, and architects' elevations,
we emerge as confused as Pocahontas must have
seemed at the performance of *The Vision of Delight*. Thumbing through Jonson's part in these
evanescent entertainments is like visiting a cos-
tumer's shop strewn with a musty assortment of
bent farthingales, second-hand armour, faded wigs,
and limp dominos.

If there is any special significance in the masque,
it is apparent in the frequency with which a pastoral note is sounded, with which golden ages and
happier eras are restored, or we are whisked away
to unreal Arcadias and remote Hesperides. Behind
the frivolity and superficiality of the *genre* lay at
least one meaning—that the court and the city no
longer shared any literary conventions, that there
was less and less of the community of interest which
had permitted the Globe and Blackfriars to present
the same plays. Structurally, the relation between
Jonson's masques and comedies is close, too close to
have pleased the spectators of his last comedies.
Yet Jonson's comedies, from first to last, have a
tendency to crystallize, whenever opportunity offers,
into a series of games, ceremonies, shows, songs,
litanies, orations, and every sort of masque-like
invention. The rites conducted by Sejanus, Volpone's medicine-show, Morose's invective against his
barber, Dapper's interview with the Queen of Faery,
Justice Clement's merry assizes, Littlewit's redaction
of *Hero and Leander*—these episodes, besides ful-

filling their dramatic function in the plays to which they belong, are independently reducible to formal pattern.

Beyond these internal harmonies, Jonson invites scrutiny as an engineer of plots. We have noticed that the recurrent trials point a moral; we must recognize that they also adorn a play, by supplying an external framework for the action and a ritual for some of the scenes. If we admit the parallel between promoting a confidence game and spinning a comic intrigue, we can appreciate the way Jonson utilized the get-rich-quick motive and the scheme of a hoax in his most successful comedies. His others are less so because they sacrifice situation to character. The lists of *dramatis personae*, in *Every Man out of his Humour* or *The New Inn*, read like pages out of Earle and Overbury. The stage becomes so overloaded with sharply defined, carefully delineated supernumeraries, who have been called into being only to have their legs pulled, that it becomes all but impossible for a plot to get under way.

The difficulty of introducing his characters in a natural sequence of encounters was met by Jonson with a great deal of ingenuity. The plan of *Volpone*, turned to account again in *The Alchemist*, enables them to make their entrances one after another, without monotony or stiffness. The opening scene of *The Alchemist*, wherein the thieves, having fallen out, bespatter each other with abuse until the spectators have learned the past history, crimes, misdemeanours, and unendearing foibles of all three, is a triumph of exposition. The complicated intermarriages, the awkward progresses from house to house, and the Mephistophelian servants that comic dramatists allowed themselves in order to hold their plots together, Jonson was never quite ready to give up. But he did devise, in *Bartholomew Fair*, a new unity, which incorporates the three old ones into a more manageable partnership, based solely upon local colour. The critical dialogue in which he sought warrant for his innovation in Horace's *Art of Poetry* did not survive the conflagration of his library, but we have today in the films ample evidence of the breadth and diversity of this method. Particularly in the journalistic milieu of *The Staple of News*, with his gift for recreating an atmosphere, Jonson seems to be striving toward a comic institution around which to build his play—a thinking-shop or a school for scandal.

Occasionally the hand of the puppeteer appears, the situation is obviously manipulated, and we smell a device. If Jonson had been less fond of those who are witty in themselves, he might have done more convincing portraits of those who are the cause that wit is in others. There are not enough fools positive and too many fools contingent. The dramatist relies upon the assistance of his characters to bring off his practical jokes. It is the difference between Socrates' basket and Falstaff's; Socrates is made a fool by Aristophanes, Falstaff by Mistress Ford and Mistress Quickly. It would not have occurred to Jonson to let well enough alone and allow circumstances to force Sganarelle to practise medicine. His ironies must be overseen by his personal representatives, ever alert to persuade the jealous Corvino to lend his wife to another, or to stir up a reluctant duel between Sir John Daw and Sir Amorous La Foole. Sometimes his fools are conscious of their folly and have good reasons for persisting. Captain Otter, as a creature of humours, is a palpable fraud; he is a realistically drawn, thoroughly unpleasant broken-down gambler, who affects certain mannerisms which we have come to associate with the name of Jonson's pupil, Dickens, to ingratiate himself with his rich wife and her fine friends.

Because Jonsonian comedy can only succeed by subordinating parts to whole, its cast of characters is not its outstanding feature. Each has only his characteristic move, as in chess, and the object of the game is to see what new combinations have been brought about. Between the abstract idea of the plot and the concrete detail of the language is a hiatus. Nothing is lacking, but the various components can be distinguished without much trouble. In Corvino's phrase, it is too manifest. After the large masses have been sketched out in baroque symmetry, decoration is applied to the surfaces. What is said, frequently, does not matter, so long as something is said, and then Jonson is at special pains to make what is said interesting for its own sake. Surly's school-book Spanish and Doll's memorized ravings are simply blocked in. But when Mosca reads the inventory, or when Subtle puts Face through the alchemists' catechism, they too are saying something where—in the dramatic economy— they mean nothing, and their speeches take on the aspect of incantation. It is a trick which reaches its logical limit in *Epicene*, where everything spoken has a high nuisance value and the words themselves become sheer filigree. Beyond that point, they have the force of Molière's comic refrains. Lady Would-be's uncontrollable flow of recipes, prescriptions, literary opinions, and philosophical speculations, at cross-purposes with Volpone, demonstrates how conveniently this talking-machine technique bears out Bergson's theory of laughter.

To linger over the elements of pure design in Jonson's dialogue is to ignore its expressiveness as representation. The language itself is completely idiomatic, uninhibited by the formality of plot and characterization or the complexity of scenes and speeches. Because 'Spenser writ no language,' Jonson refused to tolerate him, and he could spare Marston nothing but a prescription to purge unnatural diction. His own occasional verse moves, like his drama, on the social plane and speaks in the familiar tones of human intercourse. Even self-communion, with Jonson, takes the form of a public address. Ode, epigram, elegy, epistle—nearly every poem is composed on something or to somebody, brandishing precepts and eliciting examples in the injunctive mood of Roman poetry. A poetic style suitable for these purposes had to be fittest for discourse and nearest prose. Whatever the restraints Jonson chose to accept, his handling of words never lost its flexibility; throughout the most tortuous stanzas his phrasing remains as English as Purcell's.

It would be hard to derive an inference about Jonson's dramatic verse from the comedies he wrote in prose, since *Epicene* and *Bartholomew Fair* are farther from one another than from any of the remaining plays. Neither the enamelled elegance of the one nor the rough-and-ready realism of the other accomplishes anything that Jonson has not been able to achieve in metre with the help of two fertile resources, enjambment and the broken line. He is so unwilling to pause every time five iambs have elapsed, that he now and then revives the classical stratagem of concluding a line in the midst of a word. And he is so fond of crisp dialogue that he often divides a single pentameter among three speakers, as in the staccato asides that punctuate the harangues of Tiberius or Voltore. Longer

speeches strike up a syncopation between the shifting colloquial rhythms and the sustained stresses
of blank verse. Face's praise of Spaniards is rendered in a string of four-foot clauses, so that the
iterated phrase leaps across the page and then
creeps back again:

'Ask from your courtier to your inns-of-court man,
To your mere milliner. They will tell you all,
Your Spanish jennet is the best horse; your Spanish
Stoop is the best garb; your Spanish beard
Is the best cut; your Spanish ruffs are the best
Wear; your Spanish pavan the best dance;
Your Spanish titillation in a glove
The best perfume. And for your Spanish pike
And Spanish blade, let your poor Captain speak.'

The cadence is individualized to catch the breath-
lessness of Celia's appeal for mercy or reverberate
with the finality of Volpone's revelation.

It is typical of Jonson, as of Dryden and the
baroque in general, that rhythmic arrangement
should take precedence over actual sound. High,
astounding terms are relatively rare. Already a
rationalistic bias is perceptible; writers seem less
eager to use words for their own sake and more
anxious to employ them for what they signify. Jonson had the custom of setting down everything
he proposed to say in prose and versifying it in
a subsequent operation. Hence his poetry is prima-
rily pictorial and only then musical, it addresses
the visual rather than the auditory instincts, it
appeals—as the writing of a poet who gave up the
stage for the printing-press—to the eye instead of
the ear. Like his personifications of Fancy and
Wonder in *The Vision of Delight*, Jonson's eye
had the power to summon up an infinite variety

of vistas. Like a good apothecary, he was never without an ounce of civet with which he might sweeten his imagination at will. 'He hath consumed a whole night in lying looking to his great toe,'— if we are to believe Drummond—'about which he hath seen Tartars and Turks, Romans and Carthaginians, fight in his imagination.'

Graphic speech is the generic trait with which even Jonson's ugliest ducklings are well endowed. The stolid Corvino indulges in unsuspected flights of conceit and the sullen Ananias reveals a flamboyant strain of polemical eloquence. Kitely's jealousy of his wife prompts him to deliver an exhaustive survey of the wiles of amorous deception. To dismiss the threat of punishment, Voltore invokes a swarm of luridly ridiculous tortures upon the prostrate person of his client. In introducing Drugger as an honest tobacconist, Face cannot resist the temptation to add some dozen or sixteen lines covering the various sharp practices of dishonest tobacconists that Drugger utterly eschews. Dramatic action is supplemented by the potential drama of these three speeches. In each instance a set of images picks up the situation where the business leaves off, and projects it to the most extravagant bounds of possibility. Uniformly Jonson's style is stamped with the brilliance of his iconoplastic talents.

The imagery surprises us by being so tangible, by presenting its objects not as fanciful comparisons but as literal descriptions. They are seldom glimpsed through the magic casement of metaphor, through the intervention of rhetoric. The rich jewel in the Ethiop's ear belonged to Juliet only by metaphysical parallel; Jonson would have slashed off the ear, conveyed the jewel to Volpone's coffers, and dangled it before Celia as the price of her virtue. Heaping up sensuous detail in thorough-going Elizabethan fashion, he ordinarily contrives to bring it within the immediate grasp of his tan-talized characters. The result is that the theme of his plays and their poetic realization are more closely knit together. Examining the content of Jonson's images, Caroline Spurgeon has discovered that the largest single category is drawn from the usages and conditions of society and that he returns more consistently than any of his rivals to the subject of money. A further consequence of this restriction of materials is a kind of heightening of the commonplace, more proper to the humorous than to the lyrical imagination. Deprived of other figures of speech, Jonson relies much on hyperbole. That is not the only quality of style he shares with Aristophanes and Rabelais.

The poetry of misplaced concreteness and solid specification is an instrument of the satirist; he is adept at mastering the tricks of a trade and enu-merating technical data; his swift, disintegrating glance takes in all the ingredients of Goody Trash's gingerbread. A profusion of images is not the best way to communicate feeling. Selection is more likely to produce the poignant response; accumulation bewilders at first and invites analysis in the end. When Jonson's intention is not satirical, his 'wit's great overplus' dilutes the effect of his verse. In one line,

'Ditch-delivered by a drab,'

Shakespeare can concentrate an impact that Jonson laboured through the long and learned *Masque of Queens* without quite attaining. Ultimately his facility at image-making becomes self-conscious and, as it were, poetical. It carries him into the region of the conventionally beautiful and leaves him among the curlèd woods and painted meads. It ominously foreshadows the time when poets will work with a repertory of standard items and critics will ponder the distinction between imagination and fancy.

Satirists are well aware that appearances deceive, yet it is with appearances that satirists are chiefly concerned. Jonson delights in exhibiting façades, because they both impress us and make us uneasy about what lies behind them. Every once in a while a masochistic fascination leads him to explore the obverse of beauty, to give way to the fly-blown fancies of *The Famous Voyage*, to betray a revulsion worthy of Swift.

> 'Though art's hid causes are not found,
>   All is not sweet, all is not sound.'

It is never simple for literature to report the senses directly. In the Renaissance especially, it was hard to reconcile perceptions and principles; attempts oscillate from the sheer apprehension of Marlowe to the sublimated allegory of Spenser. Between these poles there is room for voluptuousness, scientific curiosity, asceticism, prurience—all the degrees and mixtures of intellectualized sensibility that we see in *Ovid's Banquet of Sense*, *The Metamorphosis of Pygmalion's Image*, *Nosce Teipsum*, or *The Ecstasy*. As an Elizabethan, Jonson too had been perplexed by the problem. As a Stoic and satirist, he was able to make his own rejection. As a professional man of letters, he had to keep on writing through a period when immanent emotions and confident attitudes were being reduced to questions of literary technique.

In his fecundity and in his artificiality, in his virtues and in his faults, Jonson remains the craftsman. When he appraises the idle apprentice Shakespeare, he speaks with the authority of a fellow craftsman, and—after a few precise couplets of prefatory remarks, acknowledgments, and qualifications —deliberately turns on the lyric strain:

'I therefore will begin. Soul of the age!
   The applause, delight, the wonder of our stage!'

And he proceeds to a workmanlike and reasonably impassioned estimate. Because he was in the habit of discussing his craft concretely, he could not fail to be interested in Plutarch's comparison of poetry and painting. It is no mere chance that any effort to describe his own work falls repeatedly into the vocabulary of the fine arts. If we are looking for a single impression of Ben Jonson, it is of the Flemish painters that we are finally mindful—of crowded street scenes and rich interiors, of sharp portraiture and lavish ornament, of the gloss and the clarity and the tactile values that are the tokens of mastery.

I. TRAGEDY

Sejanus, His Fall

TIBERIUS

DRUSUS SENIOR

NERO

DRUSUS JUNIOR

CALIGULA

LUCIUS ARRUNTIUS

CAIUS SILIUS

TITIUS SABINUS

MARCUS LEPIDUS

CREMUTIUS CORDUS

ASINIUS GALLUS

REGULUS

TERENTIUS

GRACINUS LACO

EUDEMUS

RUFUS

SEJANUS

LATIARIS

VARRO

SERTORIUS MACRO

COTTA

DOMITIUS AFER

HATERIUS

SANQUINIUS

POMPONIUS

JULIUS POSTHUMUS

FULCINIUS TRIO

MINUTIUS

SATRIUS SECUNDUS

PINNARIUS NATTA

OPSIUS

AGRIPPINA

LIVIA

SOSIA

FLAMEN

NUNTIUS

PRAECONES

LICTORES

TRIBUNI

MINISTRI

TUBICINES

TIBICINES

SERVI, &C.

The Scene: ROME

39

THE ARGUMENT

Aelius Sejanus, son to Seius Strabo, a gentleman
of Rome, and born at Vulsinium,—after his long
service in court, first under Augustus, afterward,
Tiberius—grew into that favour with the latter, and
won him by those arts, as there wanted nothing but
the name to make him a co-partner of the Empire.
Which greatness of his, Drusus, the Emperor's son,
not brooking, after many smothered dislikes, it one
day breaking out, the prince struck him publicly on
the face. To revenge which disgrace, Livia, the wife
of Drusus (being before corrupted by him to her
dishonour, and the discovery of her husband's counsels) Sejanus practiseth with, together with her physician, called Eudemus, and one Lygdus, an eunuch,
to poison Drusus. This their inhuman act having
successful and unsuspected passage, it emboldeneth
Sejanus to farther and more insolent projects, even
the ambition of the Empire; where finding the lets
he must encounter to be many and hard, in respect
of the issue of Germanicus (who were next in hope
for the succession), he deviseth to make Tiberius'
self his means, and instils into his ears many doubts
and suspicions, both against the princes and their
mother Agrippina; which Caesar jealously hearkening to, as covetously consenteth to their ruin, and
their friends'. In this time, the better to mature and
strengthen his design, Sejanus labours to marry
Livia, and worketh with all his engine to remove
Tiberius from the knowledge of public business,
with allurements of a quiet and retired life; the latter of which, Tiberius (out of a proneness to lust,
and a desire to hide those unnatural pleasures which

he could not so publicly practise) embraceth; the former enkindleth his fears, and there gives him first cause of doubt or suspect towards Sejanus. Against whom he raiseth in private a new instrument, one Sertorius Macro, and by him underworketh; discovers the other's counsels, his means, his ends; sounds the affections of the senators; divides, distracts them. At last, when Sejanus least looketh, and is most secure, with pretext of doing him an unwonted honour in the Senate he trains him from his guards, and with a long, doubtful letter, in one day hath him suspected, accused, condemned, and torn in pieces by the rage of the people.

SEJANUS, HIS FALL

ACT ONE

The Palace

Enter SABINUS *and* SILIUS, *followed by* LATIARIS.

SABINUS. Hail, Caius Silius!

SILIUS.   Titius Sabinus, hail!
You're rarely met in court.

SABINUS.   Therefore well met.

SILIUS. 'Tis true. Indeed, this place is not our
   sphere.

SABINUS. No, Silius, we are no good engineers;
We want the fine arts, and their thriving use
Should make us graced, or favoured of the times.
We have no shift of faces, no cleft tongues,
No soft and glutinous bodies, that can stick,
Like snails on painted walls, or, on our breasts,
Creep up, to fall from that proud height to which
We did by slavery, not by service, climb.
We are no guilty men, and then no great;
We have no place in court, office in state,
That we can say we owe unto our crimes.
We burn with no black secrets which can make
Us dear to the pale authors, or live feared
Of their still waking jealousies, to raise
Ourselves a fortune by subverting theirs.
We stand not in the lines that do advance
To that so courted point.

Enter SATRIUS *and* NATTA.

SILIUS.   But yonder lean
A pair that do.

43

SABINUS. —Good cousin Latiaris.

SILIUS. Satrius Secundus and Pinnarius Natta,
The great Sejanus' clients—there be two,
Know more than honest counsels; whose close breasts,
Were they ripped up to light, it would be found
A poor and idle sin, to which their trunks
Had not been made fit organs.   These can lie,
Flatter, and swear, forswear, deprave, inform,
Smile, and betray; make guilty men; then beg
The forfeit lives, to get the livings; cut
Men's throats with whisp'rings; sell to gaping suitors
The empty smoke that flies about the Palace;
Laugh when their patron laughs; sweat when he sweats;
Be hot and cold with him; change every mood,
Habit, and garb, as often as he varies;
Observe him, as his watch observes his clock;
And, true as turquoise in the dear lord's ring,
Look well or ill with him, ready to praise
His lordship, if he spit, or but piss fair,
Have an indifferent stool, or break wind well;
Nothing can 'scape their catch.

SABINUS.   Alas! these things
Deserve no note, conferred with other vile
And filthier flatteries, that corrupt the times:
When, not alone our gentries chief are fain
To make their safety from such sordid acts,
But all our consuls, and no little part
Of such as have been praetors, yea, the most
Of senators, that else not use their voices,
Start up in public Senate, and there strive
Who shall propound most abject things, and base;
So much, as oft Tiberius hath been heard,
Leaving the court, to cry, 'O race of men,
Prepared for servitude!'—which showed that he,

Who least the public liberty could like,
As loathly brooked their flat servility.
    SILIUS. Well, all is worthy of us, were it more,
Who with our riots, pride, and civil hate,
Have so provoked the justice of the gods.
We, that, within these fourscore years, were born
Free, equal lords of the triumphèd world,
And knew no masters but affections;
To which betraying first our liberties,
We since became the slaves to one man's lusts;
And now to many: every minist'ring spy
That will accuse and swear, is lord of you,
Of me, of all our fortunes and our lives.
Our looks are called to question, and our words,
How innocent soever, are made crimes;
We shall not, shortly, dare to tell our dreams,
Or think, but 'twill be treason.
    SABINUS.   Tyrants' arts
Are to give flatterers grace, accusers power,
That those may seem to kill whom they devour.

Enter CORDUS *and* ARRUNTIUS.

Now, good Cremutius Cordus.
    CORDUS.   Hail to your lordship!
    NATTA. *Whispers.* Who's that salutes your cousin?
    LATIARIS.   'Tis one Cordus,
A gentleman of Rome; one that has writ
Annals of late, they say, and very well.
    NATTA. Annals? of what times?
    LATIARIS.   I think of Pompey's,
And Caius Caesar's, and so down to these.
    NATTA. How stands he affected to the present state?
Is he or Drusian, or Germanican,
Or ours, or neutral?
    LATIARIS.   I know him not so far.

NATTA. Those times are somewhat queasy to be
    touched.
Have you or seen or heard part of his work?
    LATIARIS. Not I; he means they shall be public
        shortly.
    NATTA. Oh. Cordus do you call him?
    LATIARIS.   Ay.
    SABINUS.   But these our times
Are not the same, Arruntius.
    ARRUNTIUS.   Times! the men,
The men are not the same! 'Tis we are base,
Poor, and degenerate from th' exalted strain
Of our great fathers. Where is now the soul
Of godlike Cato? he that durst be good,
When Caesar durst be evil; and had power,
As not to live his slave, to die his master?
Or where's the constant Brutus, that, being proof
Against all charm of benefits, did strike
So brave a blow into the monster's heart
That sought unkindly to captive his country?
O, they are fled the light! Those mighty spirits
Lie raked up with their ashes in their urns,
And not a spark of their eternal fire
Glows in a present bosom. All's but blaze,
Flashes and smoke, wherewith we labour so,
There's nothing Roman in us; nothing good,
Gallant, or great. 'Tis true, that Cordus says,
'Brave Cassius was the last of all that race.'

DRUSUS *passes over the stage.*

    SABINUS. Stand by! Lord Drusus.
    HATERIUS.   Th' Emp'ror's son! Give place.
    SILIUS. I like the Prince well.
    ARRUNTIUS.   A riotous youth,
There's little hope of him.

SABINUS.   That fault his age
Will, as it grows, correct. Methinks he bears
Himself each day more nobly than other,
And wins no less on men's affections,
Than doth his father lose. Believe me, I love him;
And chiefly for opposing to Sejanus.

  SILIUS. And I, for gracing his young kinsmen so,
The sons of Prince Germanicus. It shows
A gallant clearness in him, a straight mind,
That envies not, in them, their father's name.

  ARRUNTIUS. His name was, while he lived, above all
          envy;
And, being dead, without it. O, that man!
If there were seeds of the old virtue left,
They lived in him.

  SILIUS.   He had the fruits, Arruntius,
More than the seeds. Sabinus and myself
Had means to know 'im within, and can report him;
We were his followers—he would call us friends.
He was a man most like to virtue; in all
And every action, nearer to the gods
Than men, in nature; of a body as fair
As was his mind; and no less reverend
In face than fame. He could so use his state,
Temp'ring his greatness with his gravity,
As it avoided all self-love in him,
And spite in others. What his funerals lacked
In images and pomp, they had supplied
With honourable sorrow, soldiers' sadness,
A kind of silent mourning, such as men
Who know no tears but from their captives, use
To show in so great losses.

  CORDUS.   I thought once,
Considering their forms, age, manner of deaths,
The nearness of the places where they fell,

T' have paralleled him with great Alexander:
For both were of best feature, of high race,
Yeared but to thirty, and, in foreign lands,
By their own people, alike made away.

   SABINUS. I know not, for his death, how you might
     wrest it;
But, for his life, it did as much disdain
Comparison with that voluptuous, rash,
Giddy, and drunken Macedon's, as mine
Doth with my bondman's. All the good in him,
His valour and his fortune, he made his.
But he had other touches of late Romans,
That more did speak him: Pompey's dignity,
The innocence of Cato, Caesar's spirit,
Wise Brutus' temperance; and every virtue,
Which, parted unto others, gave them name,
Flowed mixed in him. He was the soul of goodness;
And all our praises of him are like streams
Drawn from a spring, that still rise full, and leave
The part remaining greatest.

   ARRUNTIUS.   I am sure
He was too great for us, and that they knew
Who did remove him hence.

   SABINUS.   When men grow fast
Honoured and loved, there is a trick in state,
Which jealous princes never fail to use,
How to decline that growth, with fair pretext,
And honourable colours of employment,
Either by embassy, the war, or such,
To shift them forth into another air,
Where they may purge, and lessen. So was he;
And had his seconds there, sent by Tiberius
And his more subtle dam, to discontent him;
To breed and cherish mutinies; detract
His greatest actions; give audacious check

To his commands; and work to put him out
In open act of treason. All which snares
When his wise cares prevented, a fine poison
Was thought on, to mature their practices.

Enter SEJANUS *with* TERENTIUS.

CORDUS. Here comes Sejanus.

SILIUS.   Now observe the stoops,
The bendings, and the falls.

ARRUNTIUS.   Most creeping base!

SEJANUS. I note 'em well. No more. Say you?

SATRIUS.   My lord,
There is a gentleman of Rome would buy——

SEJANUS. How call you him you talked with?

SATRIUS.   Please your lordship,
It is Eudemus, the physician
To Livia, Drusus' wife.

SEJANUS.   On with your suit.
Would buy, you said——

SATRIUS.   A tribune's place, my lord.

SEJANUS. What will he give?

SATRIUS.   Fifty sestertia.

SEJANUS. Livia's physician, say you, is that fellow?

SATRIUS. It is, my lord. Your lordship's answer.

SEJANUS.   To what?

SATRIUS. The place, my lord. 'Tis for a gentleman
Your lordship will well like of, when you see him;
And one you may make yours, by the grant.

SEJANUS. Well, let him bring his money, and his
    name.

SATRIUS. Thank your lordship. He shall, my lord.

SEJANUS.   Come hither.
Know you this same Eudemus? Is he learned?

SATRIUS. Reputed so, my lord, and of deep practice.

SEJANUS. Bring him in to me, in the gallery,

And take you cause to leave us there together.
I would confer with him about a grief.—On.

Exeunt SEJANUS, SATRIUS, *and* TERENTIUS.

ARRUNTIUS. So! yet another? yet? O desperate state
Of grov'lling honour! Seest thou this, O sun,
And do we see thee after? Methinks day
Should lose his light, when men do lose their shames,
And for the empty circumstance of life,
Betray their cause of living.

SILIUS.   Nothing so.
Sejanus can repair, if Jove should ruin.
He is the now court-god; and, well applied
With sacrifice of knees, of crooks and cringe,
He will do more than all the house of heav'n
Can for a thousand hecatombs. 'Tis he
Makes us our day or night. Hell and Elysium
Are in his look. We talk of Rhadamanth,
Furies, and firebrands, but 'tis his frown
That is all these; where, on the adverse part,
His smile is more than e'er yet poets feigned
Of bliss and shades, nectar——

ARRUNTIUS.   A serving-boy!
I knew him, at Caius' trencher, when for hire
He prostituted his abusèd body
To that great gormand, fat Apicius,
And was the noted pathic of the time.

SABINUS.   And now, the second face of the
    whole world!
The partner of the Empire, hath his image
Reared equal with Tiberius, borne in ensigns;
Commands, disposes every dignity—
Centurions, tribunes, heads of provinces,
Praetors, and consuls—all that heretofore
Rome's general suffrage gave, is now his sale.

The gain, or rather spoil, of all the earth,
One, and his house, receives.

    SILIUS.   He hath of late
Made him a strength, too, strangely, by reducing
All the praetorian bands into one camp,
Which he commands; pretending that the soldier,
By living loose and scattered, fell to riot;
And that if any sudden enterprise
Should be attempted, their united strength
Would be far more than severed; and their life
More strict, if from the city more removed.

    SABINUS. Where now he builds what kind of forts
      he please;
Is heard to court the soldier by his name;
Woos, feasts the chiefest men of action,
Whose wants, not loves, compel them to be his.
And though he ne'er were liberal by kind,
Yet to his own dark ends, he's most profuse,
Lavish, and letting fly he cares not what
To his ambition.

    ARRUNTIUS.   Yet hath he ambition?
Is there that step in state can make him higher,
Or more, or anything he is, but less?

    SILIUS. Nothing but Emperor.

    ARRUNTIUS.   The name Tiberius,
I hope, will keep, howe'er he hath foregone
The dignity and power.

    SILIUS.   Sure, while he lives.

    ARRUNTIUS. And dead, it comes to Drusus. Should
      he fail,
To the brave issue of Germanicus;
And they are three. Too many—ha?—for him
To have a plot upon?

    SABINUS.   I do not know
The heart of his designs, but sure their face
Looks farther than the present.

ARRUNTIUS.   By the gods,
If I could guess he had but such a thought,
My sword should cleave him down from head to
    heart,
But I would find it out; and with my hand
I'd hurl his panting brain about the air,
In mites as small as atomi, t'undo
The knotted bed——
    SABINUS.   You are observed, Arruntius.
    ARRUNTIUS. Death! I dare tell him so, and all his
    spies. *Turns to* LATIARIS *and* NATTA.
You, sir, I would! Do you look? And you!
    SABINUS.   Forbear.

The scene opens.
Enter SATRIUS *with* EUDEMUS.

    SATRIUS. Here he will instant be; let's walk a turn.
You're in a muse, Eudemus?
    EUDEMUS.   Not I, sir—
I wonder he should mark me out so! Well,
Jove and Apollo form it for the best.
    SATRIUS. Your fortune's made unto you now,
        Eudemus,
If you can but lay hold upon the means.
Do but observe his humour, and—believe it—
He is the noblest Roman, where he takes—
Here comes his lordship.

Enter SEJANUS.

    SEJANUS.   Now, good Satrius.
    SATRIUS. This is the gentleman, my lord.
    SEJANUS.   Is this?
Give me your hand, we must be more acquainted.
Report, sir, hath spoke out your art and learning;
And I am glad I have so needful cause,

However in itself painful and hard,
To make me known to so great virtue.—Look,
Who's that, Satrius? *Exit* SATRIUS. I have a grief, sir,
That will desire your help. Your name's Eudemus?

EUDEMUS. Yes.

SEJANUS. Sir?

EUDEMUS. It is, my lord.

SEJANUS. I hear you are
Physician to Livia, the Princess.

EUDEMUS. I minister unto her, my good lord.

SEJANUS. You minister to a royal lady, then.

EUDEMUS. She is, my lord, and fair.

SEJANUS. That's understood
Of all their sex, who are or would be so.
And those that would be, physic soon can make 'em;
For those that are, their beauties fear no colours.

EUDEMUS. Your lordship is conceited.

SEJANUS. Sir, you know it,
And can, if need be, read a learnèd lecture
On this, and other secrets. Pray you, tell me,
What more of ladies, besides Livia,
Have you your patients?

EUDEMUS. Many, my good lord.
The great Augusta, Urgulania,
Mutilia Prisca, and Plancina, divers——

SEJANUS. And all these tell you the particulars
Of every several grief? how first it grew,
And then increased; what action causèd that,
What passion that; and answer to each point
That you will put 'em?

EUDEMUS. Else, my lord, we know not
How to prescribe the remedies.

SEJANUS. Go to,
You are a subtle nation, you physicians!
And grown the only cabinets in court,
To ladies' privacies. Faith, which of these

Is the most pleasant lady in her physic?
Come, you are modest now.

    EUDEMUS.   'Tis fit, my lord.

    SEJANUS. Why, sir, I do not ask you of their urines,
Whose smell's most violet, or whose siege is best,
Or who makes hardest faces on her stool?
Which lady sleeps with her own face a-nights?
Which puts her teeth off, with her clothes, in court?
Or which her hair, which her complexion,
And in which box she puts it? These were questions
That might, perhaps, have put your gravity
To some defence of blush. But I inquired
Which was the wittiest, merriest, wantonest?
Harmless interr'gatories, but conceits.
Methinks Augusta should be most perverse,
And froward in her fit.

    EUDEMUS.   She's so, my lord.

    SEJANUS. I knew it. And Mutilia the most jocund?

    EUDEMUS. 'Tis very true, my lord.

    SEJANUS.   And why would you
Conceal this from me, now? Come, what is Livia?
I know she's quick, and quaintly spirited,
And will have strange thoughts, when she is at
    leisure—
She tells 'em all to you?

    EUDEMUS.   My noblest lord,
He breathes not in the Empire, or on earth,
Whom I would be ambitious to serve,
In any act that may preserve mine honour,
Before your lordship.

    SEJANUS.   Sir, you can lose no honour
By trusting aught to me. The coarsest act
Done to my service, I can so requite,
As all the world shall style it honourable.
Your idle, virtuous definitions

Keep honour poor, and are as scorned as vain;
Those deeds breathe honour that do suck in gain.
  EUDEMUS. But, good my lord, if I should thus be-
    tray
The counsels of my patient, and a lady's
Of her high place and worth, what might your lord-
    ship,
Who presently are to trust me with your own,
Judge of my faith?
  SEJANUS.   Only the best, I swear.
Say now that I should utter you my grief,
And with it the true cause: that it were love,
And love to Livia; you should tell her this—
Should she suspect your faith? I would you could
Tell me as much from her; see if my brain
Could be turned jealous.
  EUDEMUS.   Happily, my lord,
I could in time tell you as much and more,
So I might safely promise but the first
To her from you.
  SEJANUS.   As safely, my Eudemus,—
I now dare call thee so—as I have put
The secret into thee.
  EUDEMUS.   My lord——
  SEJANUS.   Protest not,
Thy looks are vows to me; use only speed,
And but affect her with Sejanus' love,
Thou art a man made to make consuls. Go.
  EUDEMUS. My lord, I'll promise you a private
    meeting
This day, together.
  SEJANUS.   Canst thou?
  EUDEMUS.   Yes.
  SEJANUS.   The place?
  EUDEMUS. My gardens, whither I shall fetch your
    lordship.

SEJANUS. Let me adore my Aesculapius.
Why, this indeed is physic, and outspeaks
The knowledge of cheap drugs, or any use
Can be made out of it! more comforting
Than all your opiates, juleps, apozems,
Magistral syrups, or——Begone, my friend,
Not barely stylèd, but created so;
Expect things greater than thy largest hopes,
To overtake thee. Fortune shall be taught
To know how ill she hath deserved thus long,
To come behind thy wishes. Go, and speed.

Exit EUDEMUS.

Ambition makes more trusty slaves than need.
These fellows, by the favour of their art,
Have still the means to tempt, oft-times the power.
If Livia will be now corrupted, then
Thou hast the way, Sejanus, to work out
His secrets, who, thou know'st, endures thee not,
Her husband, Drusus; and to work against them.
Prosper it, Pallas, thou that better'st wit;
For Venus hath the smallest share in it.

Enter TIBERIUS *and* DRUSUS, *attended.*

TIBERIUS. *To one who kneels to him.* We not en-
dure these flatteries. Let him stand.
Our empire, ensigns, axes, rods, and state
Take not away our human nature from us.
Look up on us, and fall before the gods.

SEJANUS. How like a god speaks Caesar!

ARRUNTIUS.   —There, observe!
He can endure that second, that's no flattery!
O, what is it proud slime will not believe
Of his own worth, to hear it equal praised
Thus with the gods?

CORDUS.   He did not hear it, sir.

ARRUNTIUS. He did not! Tut, he must not; we
    think meanly.
'Tis your most courtly known confederacy,
To have your private parasite redeem
What he, in public subtlety, will lose,
To making him a name.

    HATERIUS.   Right mighty lord——

    TIBERIUS. We must make up our ears 'gainst these
    assaults
Of charming tongues; we pray you use no more
These contumelies to us. Style not us
Or lord or mighty, who profess ourself
The servant of the Senate, and are proud
T' enjoy them our good, just, and favouring lords.

    CORDUS. —Rarely dissembled!

    ARRUNTIUS.   Prince-like to the life.

    SABINUS. When power that may command, so
    much descends,
Their bondage, whom it stoops to, it intends.

    TIBERIUS. Whence are these letters?

    HATERIUS.   From the Senate.

    TIBERIUS.   So.
Whence these?

    LATIARIS.   From thence, too.

    TIBERIUS.   Are they sitting now?

    LATIARIS. They stay thy answer, Caesar.

    SILIUS.   —If this man
Had but a mind allied unto his words,
How blest a fate were it to us, and Rome!
We could not think that state for which to change,
Although the aim were our old liberty.
The ghosts of those that fell for that, would grieve
Their bodies lived not now, again to serve.
Men are deceived, who think there can be thrall
Beneath a virtuous prince. Wished liberty
Ne'er lovelier looks, than under such a crown.

But when his grace is merely but lip-good,
And that no longer than he airs himself
Abroad in public—there to seem to shun
The strokes and stripes of flatterers, which within
Are lechery unto him, and so feed
His brutish sense with their afflicting sound,
As, dead to virtue, he permits himself
Be carried like a pitcher by the ears,
To every act of vice—this is a case
Deserves our fear, and doth presage the nigh
And close approach of blood and tyranny.
Flattery is midwife unto princes' rage;
And nothing sooner doth help forth a tyrant
Than that, and whisp'rers' grace, who have the
    time,
The place, the power, to make all men offenders.

  ARRUNTIUS. He should be told this, and be bid dis-
  semble
With fools and blind men. We that know the evil,
Should hunt the palace-rats, or give them bane;
Fright hence these worse than ravens, that devour
The quick, where they but prey upon the dead.
He shall be told it.

  SABINUS.   Stay, Arruntius,
We must abide our opportunity,
And practise what is fit, as what is needful.
It is not safe t' enforce a sovereign's ear;
Princes hear well, if they at all will hear.

  ARRUNTIUS. Ha, say you so? Well. In the meantime,
  Jove,—
Say not but I do call upon thee now—
Of all wild beasts preserve me from a tyrant;
And of all tame, a flatterer.

  SILIUS.   'Tis well prayed.

  TIBERIUS. Return the lords this voice: we are their
  creature,

And it is fit a good and honest prince,
Whom they, out of their bounty, have instructed
With so dilate and absolute a power,
Should owe the office of it to their service,
And good of all and every citizen.
Nor shall it e'er repent us, to have wished
The Senate just and favouring lords unto us,
Since their free loves do yield no less defence
T' a prince's state, than his own innocence.
Say then, there can be nothing in their thought
Shall want to please us, that hath pleasèd them;
Our suffrage rather shall prevent, than stay
Behind their wills. 'Tis empire to obey,
Where such, so great, so grave, so good, determine.
Yet, for the suit of Spain, t' erect a temple
In honour of our mother and ourself,
We must, with pardon of the Senate, not
Assent thereto. Their lordships may object
Our not denying the same late request
Unto the Asian cities. We desire
That our defence for suffering that be known
In these brief reasons, with our after purpose:
Since deified Augustus hindered not
A temple to be built at Pergamum,
In honour of himself and sacred Rome,
We, that have all his deeds and words observed
Ever, in place of laws, the rather followed
That pleasing precedent, because with ours
The Senate's reverence, also, there was joined.
But as, t' have once received it, may deserve
The gain of pardon, so to be adored
With the continued style and note of gods,
Through all the provinces, were wild ambition,
And no less pride; yea, even Augustus' name
Would early vanish, should it be profaned
With such promiscuous flatteries. For our part,

We here protest it, and are covetous
Posterity should know it: we are mortal,
And can but deeds of men; 'twere glory enough,
Could we be truly a prince. And they shall add
Abounding grace unto our memory,
That shall report us worthy our forefathers,
Careful of your affairs, constant in dangers,
And not afraid of any private frown
For public good. These things shall be to us
Temples and statues, rearèd in your minds,
The fairest and most during imag'ry;
For those of stone or brass, if they become
Odious in judgment of posterity,
Are more contemned as dying sepulchres,
Than ta'en for living monuments. We then
Make here our suit, alike to gods and men:
The one, until the period of our race,
T' inspire us with a free and quiet mind,
Discerning both divine and human laws;
The other to vouchsafe us, after death,
An honourable mention, and fair praise,
T' accompany our actions and our name.
The rest of greatness princes may command,
And therefore may neglect; only a long,
A lasting, high, and happy memory
They should, without being satisfied, pursue.
Contempt of fame begets contempt of virtue.

    NATTA. Rare!

    SATRIUS.   Most divine!

    SEJANUS.   The oracles are ceased,
That only Caesar, with their tongue, might speak.

    ARRUNTIUS. —Let me be gone, most felt and open
      this!

    CORDUS. Stay.

    ARRUNTIUS.   What, to hear more cunning and
      fine words,

With their sound flattered ere their sense be meant?

TIBERIUS. Their choice of Antium, there to place
  the gift
Vowed to the Goddess for our mother's health,
We will the Senate know, we fairly like;
As also of their grant to Lepidus,
For his repairing the Aemilian place,
And restoration of those monuments.
Their grace, too, in confining of Silanus
To th' other isle Cythera, at the suit
Of his religious sister, much commends
Their policy, so tempered with their mercy.
But for the honours which they have decreed
To our Sejanus, to advance his statue
In Pompey's theatre,—whose ruining fire
His vigilance and labour kept restrained
In that one loss—they have therein outgone
Their own great wisdoms, by their skilful choice,
And placing of their bounties on a man
Whose merit more adorns the dignity,
Than that can him; and gives a benefit,
In taking, greater than it can receive.
Blush not, Sejanus, thou great aid of Rome,
Associate of our labours, our chief helper.
Let us not force thy simple modesty
With offering at thy praise, for more we cannot,
Since there's no voice can take it. No man here
Receive our speeches as hyperboles;
For we are far from flattering our friend,
Let envy know, as from the need to flatter.
Nor let them ask the causes of our praise;
Princes have still their grounds reared with them-
  selves,
Above the poor, low flats of common men;
And who will search the reasons of their acts,

Must stand on equal bases.—Lead, away.
Our loves unto the Senate.

Exeunt TIBERIUS, SEJANUS, NATTA, LATIARUS
and Attendants.

ARRUNTIUS.   Caesar!
SABINUS.   —Peace.
CORDUS. Great Pompey's theatre was never ruined
Till now, that proud Sejanus hath a statue
Reared on his ashes.
ARRUNTIUS.   Place the shame of soldiers
Above the best of generals? Crack the world,
And bruise the name of Romans into dust,
Ere we behold it!
SILIUS.   Check your passion,
Lord Drusus tarries.
DRUSUS.   Is my father mad?
Weary of life and rule, lords? thus to heave
An idol up with praise! make him his mate,
His rival in the Empire!
ARRUNTIUS.   O, Good Prince!
DRUSUS. Allow him statues, titles, honours, such
As he himself refuseth!
ARRUNTIUS.   Brave, brave Drusus!
DRUSUS. The first ascents to sovereignty are hard;
But, entered once, there never wants or means
Or ministers, to help th' aspirer on.
ARRUNTIUS. True, gallant Drusus.
DRUSUS.   We must shortly pray
To Modesty, that he will rest contented——
ARRUNTIUS. Ay, where he is, and not write Em-
    peror.

Re-enter SEJANUS *with* LATIARIS *and other Clients.*

SEJANUS. There is your bill.—And yours.—Bring
    you your man.—

I have moved for you, too, Latiaris.

DRUSUS.   What!

Is your vast greatness grown so blindly bold,

That you will over us?

SEJANUS.   Why, then give way.

DRUSUS. Give way, Colossus! Do you lift? Advance
     you?

Take that!   *Strikes him.*

ARRUNTIUS. Good! brave! excellent, brave Prince!

DRUSUS. Nay, come, approach. What, stand you
     off? at gaze?

It looks too full of death for thy cold spirits.

Avoid mine eye, dull camel, or my sword

Shall make thy brav'ry fitter for a grave,

Than for a triumph. I'll advance a statue

O' your own bulk, but 't shall be on the cross,

Where I will nail your pride at breadth and length,

And crack those sinews, which are yet but stretched

With your swol'n fortune's rage.

ARRUNTIUS.   A noble prince!

ALL. A Castor! a Castor! a Castor! a Castor!

                 Exeunt all but SEJANUS.

SEJANUS. He that, with such wrong moved, can
     bear it through

With patience, and an even mind, knows how

To turn it back. Wrath, covered, carries fate.

Revenge is lost, if I profess my hate. ·

What was my practice late, I'll now pursue

As my fell justice. This hath styled it new.   *Exit.*

Chorus of Musicians.

ACT TWO. SCENE ONE

The gardens of Eudemus

Enter SEJANUS, LIVIA, *and* EUDEMUS.

SEJANUS. Physician, thou art worthy of a province,
For the great favours done unto our loves;
And, but that greatest Livia bears a part
In the requital of thy services,
I should alone despair of aught, like means,
To give them worthy satisfaction.

LIVIA. Eudemus, I will see it, shall receive
A fit and full reward for his large merit.
But for this potion we intend to Drusus,
No more our husband now, whom shall we choose
As the most apt and abled instrument
To minister it to him?

EUDEMUS.   I say Lygdus
SEJANUS. Lygdus? what's he?

LIVIA.   An eunuch Drusus loves.
EUDEMUS. Ay, and his cup-bearer.

SEJANUS.   Name not a second.
If Drusus love him, and he have that place,
We cannot think a fitter.

EUDEMUS.   True, my lord,
For free access and trust are two main aids.

SEJANUS. Skilful physician!

LIVIA   But he must be wrought
To th' undertaking, with some laboured art.

SEJANUS. Is he ambitious?

LIVIA.   No.

SEJANUS.   Or covetous?

LIVIA. Neither.

EUDEMUS. Yet gold is a good general charm.

SEJANUS. What is he, then?

LIVIA. Faith, only wanton, light.

SEJANUS. How! is he young and fair?

EUDEMUS. A delicate youth.

SEJANUS. Send him to me, I'll work him.—Royal
lady,
Though I have loved you long, and with that height
Of zeal and duty, like the fire, which more
It mounts it trembles, thinking nought could add
Unto the fervour which your eye had kindled;
Yet now I see your wisdom, judgment, strength,
Quickness, and will, to apprehend the means
To your own good and greatness, I protest
Myself through rarefied, and turned all flame
In your affection. Such a spirit as yours
Was not created for the idle second
To a poor flash, as Drusus; but to shine
Bright as the moon among the lesser lights,
And share the sovereignty of all the world.
Then Livia triumphs in her proper sphere,
When she and her Sejanus shall divide
The name of Caesar, and Augusta's star
Be dimmed with glory of a brighter beam;
When Agrippina's fires are quite extinct,
And the scarce seen Tiberius borrows all
His little light from us, whose folded arms
Shall make one perfect orb.—Who's that? Eudemus,
Look 'tis not Drusus! *Exit Eudemus.* Lady, do not
fear.

LIVIA. Not I, my lord. My fear and love of him
Left me at once.

SEJANUS. Illustrious lady, stay——

EUDEMUS. I'll tell his lordship.

Re-enter EUDEMUS.

SEJANUS. Who is't, Eudemus?

EUDEMUS. One of your lordship's servants brings
you word
The Emp'ror hath sent for you.

SEJANUS. Oh! where is he?
With your fair leave, dear Princess, I'll but ask
A question, and return. *Exit.*

EUDEMUS. Fortunate Princess!
How are you blest in the fruition
Of this unequalled man, this soul of Rome,
The Empire's life, and voice of Caesar's world!

LIVIA. So blessèd, my Eudemus, as to know
The bliss I have, with what I ought to owe
The means that wrought it. How do I look today?

EUDEMUS. Excellent clear, believe it. This same
fucus
Was well laid on.

LIVIA. Methinks 'tis here not white.

EUDEMUS. Lend me your scarlet, lady. 'Tis the sun,
Hath giv'n some little taint unto the ceruse.
You should have used of the white oil I gave you.
Sejanus for your love! his very name
Commandeth above Cupid or his shafts——

LIVIA. Nay, now you've made it worse.

EUDEMUS. I'll help it straight——
And but pronounced, is a sufficient charm
Against all rumour, and of absolute power
To satisfy for any lady's honour.

LIVIA. What do you now, Eudemus?

EUDEMUS. Make a light fucus,
To touch you o'er withal. Honoured Sejanus!
What act, though ne'er so strange and insolent,
But that addition will at least bear out,
If't do not expiate?

LIVIA. Here, good physician.

EUDEMUS. I like this study to preserve the love
Of such a man, that comes not every hour
To greet the world.—'Tis now well, lady, you should
Use of the dentifrice I prescribed you, too,
To clear your teeth, and the prepared pomatum,
To smooth the skin.—A lady cannot be
Too curious of her form, that still would hold
The heart of such a person, made her captive,
As you have his; who, to endear him more
In your clear eye, hath put away his wife,
The trouble of his bed and your delights,
Fair Apicata, and made spacious room
To your new pleasures.

LIVIA. Have not we returned
That, with our hate of Drusus, and discovery
Of all his counsels?

EUDEMUS. Yes, and wisely, lady.
The ages that succeed, and stand far off
To gaze at your high prudence, shall admire,
And reckon it an act without your sex;
It hath that rare appearance. Some will think
Your fortune could not yield a deeper sound,
Than mixed with Drusus; but, when they shall hear
That and the thunder of Sejanus meet—
Sejanus, whose high name doth strike the stars,
And rings about the concave; great Sejanus,
Whose glories, style, and titles are himself,
The often iterating of Sejanus—
They then will lose their thoughts, and be ashamed
To take acquaintance of them.

Re-enter SEJANUS.

SEJANUS. I must make
A rude departure, lady. Caesar sends
With all his haste both of command and prayer.

Be resolute in our plot; you have my soul,
As certain yours as it is my body's.—
And, wise physician, so prepare the poison,
As you may lay the subtle operation
Upon some natural disease of his.
Your eunuch send to me.—I kiss your hands,
Glory of ladies, and commend my love
To your best faith and memory.

    LIVIA.   My lord,
I shall but change your words. Farewell. Yet, this
Remember for your heed, he loves you not.
You know what I have told you: his designs
Are full of grudge and danger; we must use
More than a common speed.

    SEJANUS.   Excellent lady,
How you do fire my blood!

    LIVIA.   Well, you must go?
The thoughts be best, are least set forth to show.

                    Exit SEJANUS.
    EUDEMUS. When will you take some physic, lady?
    LIVIA.   When
I shall, Eudemus. But let Drusus' drug
Be first prepared.

    EUDEMUS.   Were Lygdus made, that's done;
I have it ready. And tomorrow morning
I'll send you a perfume, first to resolve,
And procure sweat, and then prepare a bath
To cleanse and clear the cutis; against when,
I'll have an excellent new fucus made,
Resistive 'gainst the sun, the rain, or wind,
Which you shall lay on with a breath, or oil,
As you best like, and last some fourteen hours.
This change came timely, lady, for your health,
And the restoring your complexion,
Which Drusus' choler had almost burnt up;

Wherein your fortune hath prescribed you better
Than art could do.

LIVIA.   Thanks, good physician,
I'll use my fortune, you shall see, with reverence.
Is my coach ready?

EUDEMUS.   It attends your highness.

Exeunt.

ACT TWO. SCENE TWO

The Palace

Enter SEJANUS.

If this be not revenge, when I have done
And made it perfect, let Egyptian slaves,
Parthians, and barefoot Hebrews brand my face,
And print my body full of injuries.
Thou lost thyself, child Drusus, when thou
        thought'st
Thou couldst outskip my vengeance, or outstand
The power I had to crush thee into air.
Thy follies now shall taste what kind of man
They have provoked, and this thy father's house
Crack in the flame of my incensèd rage,
Whose fury shall admit no shame or mean.
Adultery? It is the lightest ill
I will commit. A race of wicked acts
Shall flow out of my anger, and o'erspread
The world's wide face, which no posterity
Shall e'er approve, nor yet keep silent; things
That for their cunning, close, and cruel mark,
Thy father would wish his, and shall, perhaps,

Carry the empty name, but we the prize.
On, then, my soul, and start not in thy course;
Though heav'n drop sulphur, and hell belch out
  fire,
Laugh at the idle terrors. Tell proud Jove,
Between his power and thine there is no odds.
'Twas only fear first in the world made gods.

Enter TIBERIUS *attended.*

TIBERIUS. Is yet Sejanus come?
SEJANUS.   He's here, dread Caesar.
TIBERIUS. Let all depart that chamber, and the
  next.   *Exeunt Attendants.*
Sit down, my comfort. When the master prince
Of all the world, Sejanus, saith he fears,
Is it not fatal?
SEJANUS.   Yes, to those are feared.
TIBERIUS. And not to him?
SEJANUS.   Not if he wisely turn
That part of fate he holdeth, first on them.
TIBERIUS. That nature, blood, and laws of kind
  forbid.
SEJANUS. Do policy and state forbid it?
TIBERIUS.   No.
SEJANUS. The rest of poor respects, then, let go by.
State is enough to make th' act just, them guilty.
TIBERIUS. Long hate pursues such acts.
SEJANUS.   Whom hatred frights,
Let him not dream of sovereignty.
TIBERIUS.   Are rites
Of faith, love, piety, to be trod down,
Forgotten, and made vain?
SEJANUS.   All for a crown.
The prince who shames a tyrant's name to bear,
Shall never dare do anything but fear;
All the command of sceptres quite doth perish,

If it begin religious thoughts to cherish.
Whole empires fall, swayed by those nice respects.
It is the licence of dark deeds protects
Ev'n states most hated, when no laws resist
The sword, but that it acteth what it list.

TIBERIUS. Yet so, we may do all things cruelly,
Not safely.

SEJANUS. Yes, and do them thoroughly.

TIBERIUS. Knows yet Sejanus whom we point at?

SEJANUS.   Ay,
Or else my thought, my sense, or both do err:
'Tis Agrippina?

TIBERIUS.   She, and her proud race.

SEJANUS. Proud? dangerous, Caesar. For in them
     apace
The father's spirit shoots up. Germanicus
Lives in their looks, their gait, their form, t' upbraid
     us
With his close death, if not revenge the same.

TIBERIUS. The act's not known.

SEJANUS.   Not proved. But whisp'ring fame
Knowledge and proof doth to the jealous give,
Who, than to fail, would their own thought believe.
It is not safe, the children draw long breath,
That are provokèd by a parent's death.

TIBERIUS. It is as dangerous to make them hence,
If nothing but their birth be their offence.

SEJANUS. Stay, till they strike at Caesar; then their
     crime
Will be enough, but late and out of time
For him to punish.

TIBERIUS.   Do they purpose it?

SEJANUS. You know, sir, thunder speaks not till
     it hit.
Be not secure; none swiftlier are oppressed,
Than they whom confidence betrays to rest.

Let not your daring make your danger such.
All power's to be feared, where 'tis too much.
The youths are, of themselves, hot, violent,
Full of great thought; and that male-spirited dame,
Their mother, slacks no means to put them on,
By large allowance, popular presentings,
Increase of train and state, suing for titles;
Hath them commended with like prayers, like vows,
To the same Gods, with Caesar; days and nights
She spends in banquets and ambitious feasts
For the nobility, where Caius Silius,
Titius Sabinus, old Arruntius,
Asinius Gallus, Furnius, Regulus,
And others of that discontented list,
Are the prime guests. There, and to these, she tells
Whose niece she was, whose daughter, and whose
    wife.
And then must they compare her with Augusta,
Ay, and prefer her too; commend her form,
Extol her fruitfulness, at which a shower
Falls for the memory of Germanicus;
Which they blow over straight with windy praise
And puffing hopes of her aspiring sons,
Who, with these hourly ticklings, grow so pleased,
And wantonly conceited of themselves,
As now they stick not to believe they're such
As these do give 'em out; and would be thought
More than competitors, immediate heirs.
Whilst to their thirst of rule they win the rout,
That's still the friend of novelty, with hope
Of future freedom, which, on every change,
That greedily, though emptily expects.
Caesar, 'tis age in all things breeds neglects,
And princes that will keep old dignity
Must not admit too youthful heirs stand by;
Not their own issue, but so darkly set

As shadows are in picture, to give height
And lustre to themselves.

    TIBERIUS.   We will command
Their rank thoughts down, and with a stricter hand
Than we have yet put forth, their trains must 'bate,
Their titles, feasts, and factions.

    SEJANUS.   Or your state.
But how, sir, will you work?

    TIBERIUS.   Confine 'em.

    SEJANUS.   No.
They are too great, and that too faint a blow
To give them now; it would have served at first,
When with the weakest touch, their knot had burst.
But now your care must be, not to detect
The smallest cord or line of your suspect.
For such who know the weight of princes' fear,
Will, when they find themselves discovered, rear
Their forces, like seen snakes, that else would lie
Rolled in their circles, close. Nought is more high,
Daring, or desperate, than offenders found;
Where guilt is, rage and courage both abound.
The course must be to let 'em still swell up,
Riot, and surfeit on blind fortune's cup;
Give 'em more place, more dignities, more style;
Call 'em to court, to Senate; in the while,
Take from their strength some one or twain, or more
Of the main fautors—it will fright the store—
And by some by-occasion. Thus, with sleight
You shall disarm them first; and they, in night
Of their ambition, not perceive the train,
Till in the engine they are caught and slain.

    TIBERIUS. We would not kill, if we knew how to
        save;
Yet, than a throne, 'tis cheaper give a grave.
Is there no way to bind them by deserts?

SEJANUS. Sir, wolves do change their hair, but not
    their hearts.
While thus your thought unto a mean is tied,
You neither dare enough, nor do provide.
All modesty is fond, and chiefly where
The subject is no less compelled to bear,
Than praise his sovereign's acts.

    TIBERIUS.   We can no longer
Keep on our mask to thee, our dear Sejanus.
Thy thoughts are ours in all, and we but proved
Their voice, in our designs, which by assenting
Hath more confirmed us, than if heart'ning Jove
Had, from his hundred statues, bid us strike,
And at the stroke clicked all his marble thumbs.
But who shall first be struck?

    SEJANUS.   First, Caius Silius;
He is the most of mark, and most of danger,
In power and reputation equal strong,
Having commanded an imperial army
Seven years together, vanquished Sacrovir
In Germany, and thence obtained to wear
The ornaments triumphal. His steep fall,
By how much it doth give the weightier crack,
Will send more wounding terror to the rest,
Command them stand aloof, and give more way
To our surprising of the principal.

    TIBERIUS. But what, Sabinus?

    SEJANUS.   Let him grow a while,
His fate is not yet ripe. We must not pluck
At all together, lest we catch ourselves.
And there's Arruntius, too; he only talks.
But Sosia, Silius' wife, would be wound in
Now, for she hath a fury in her breast
More than hell ever knew, and would be sent
Thither in time. Then is there one Cremutius
Cordus, a writing fellow, they have got

To gather notes of the precedent times,
And make them into annals; a most tart
And bitter spirit, I hear, who, under colour
Of praising those, doth tax the present state;
Censures the men, the actions; leaves no trick,
No practice unexamined; parallels
The times, the governments; a professed champion
For the old liberty——
   TIBERIUS.   A perishing wretch!
As if there were that chaos bred in things,
That laws and liberty would not rather choose
To be quite broken, and ta'en hence by us,
Than have the stain to be preserved by such.
Have we the means to make these guilty first?
   SEJANUS. Trust that to me: let Caesar, by his
      power,
But cause a formal meeting of the Senate,
I will have matter and accusers ready.
   TIBERIUS. But how? Let us consult.
   SEJANUS.   We shall misspend
The time of action. Counsels are unfit
In business, where all rest is more pernicious
Than rashness can be. Acts of this close kind
Thrive more by execution than advice.
There is no ling'ring in that work begun,
Which cannot praisèd be, until through done.
   TIBERIUS. Our edict shall forthwith command a
      court.
While I can live, I will prevent earth's fury:
Ἐμοῦ θανόντος γαῖα μιχθήτω πυρί.   *Exit.*

    Enter JULIUS POSTHUMUS.
   POSTHUMUS. My lord Sejanus——
   SEJANUS.   Julius Posthumus,
Come with my wish! What news from Agrippina's?

POSTHUMUS. Faith, none. They all lock up them-
selves o' late,
Or talk in character. I have not seen
A company so changed. Except they had
Intelligence by augury of our practice.
    SEJANUS. When were you there?
    POSTHUMUS.   Last night,
    SEJANUS.   And what guests found you?
    POSTHUMUS. Sabinus, Silius,—the old list—Arrun-
tius,
Furnius, and Gallus.
    SEJANUS.   Would not these talk?
    POSTHUMUS.   Little.
And yet we offered choice of argument.
Satrius was with me.
    SEJANUS.   Well, 'tis guilt enough
Their often meeting. You forgot t' extol
The hospitable lady?
    POSTHUMUS.   No, that trick
Was well put home, and had succeeded, too,
But that Sabinus coughed a caution out;
For she began to swell.
    SEJANUS.   And may she burst!
Julius, I would have you go instantly
Unto the palace of the great Augusta,
And, by your kindest friend, get swift access.
Acquaint her with these meetings: tell the words
You brought me, th' other day, of Silius;
Add somewhat to 'em. Make her understand
The danger of Sabinus, and the times,
Out of his closeness. Give Arruntius' words
Of malice against Caesar; so, to Gallus;
But, above all, to Agrippina. Say,
As you may truly, that her infinite pride,
Propped with the hopes of her too fruitful womb,
With popular studies gapes for sovereignty,

And threatens Caesar. Pray Augusta then,
That for her own, great Caesar's, and the pub-
Lic safety, she be pleased to urge these dangers.
Caesar is too secure, he must be told,
And best he'll take it from a mother's tongue.
Alas! what is't for us to sound, t' explore,
To watch, oppose, plot, practise, or prevent,
If he, for whom it is so strongly laboured,
Shall, out of greatness and free spirit, be
Supinely negligent? Our city's now
Divided as in time o' th' Civil War,
And men forbear not to declare themselves
Of Agrippina's party. Every day
The faction multiplies; and will do more,
If not resisted—you can best enlarge it,
As you find audience. Noble Posthumus,
Commend me to your Prisca, and pray her,
She will solicit this great business,
To earnest and most present execution,
With all her utmost credit with Augusta.

   posthumus. I shall not fail in my instructions.

Exit.

   sejanus. This second, from his mother, will well
      urge
Our late design, and spur on Caesar's rage,
Which else might grow remiss. The way to put
A prince in blood, is to present the shapes
Of dangers greater than they are, like late
Or early shadows; and, sometimes, to feign
Where there are none, only to make him fear.
His fear will make him cruel; and once entered,
He doth not easily learn to stop, or spare
Where he may doubt. This have I made my rule,
To thrust Tiberius into tyranny,
And make him toil to turn aside those blocks
Which I alone could not remove with safety.

Drusus once gone, Germanicus' three sons
Would clog my way, whose guards have too much
 faith
To be corrupted, and their mother known
Of too, too unreproved a chastity
To be attempted, as light Livia was.
Work then, my art, on Caesar's fears, as they
On those they fear, till all my lets be cleared,
And he in ruins of his house, and hate
Of all his subjects, bury his own state;
When, with my peace and safety, I will rise,
By making him the public sacrifice.   *Exit.*

ACT TWO. SCENE THREE

Before Agrippina's house

Enter SATRIUS *and* NATTA.

SATRIUS. They're grown exceeding circumspect and
 wary.

NATTA. They have us in the wind. And yet Arruntius
Cannot contain himself.

SATRIUS.   Tut, he's not yet
Looked after; there are others more desired,
That are more silent.

NATTA.   Here he comes. Away.

            Exeunt.

Enter SABINUS, ARRUNTIUS, *and* CORDUS.

SABINUS. How is it that these beagles haunt the
 house
Of Agrippina?

ARRUNTIUS.   O, they hunt, they hunt!
There is some game here lodged, which they must rouse,
To make the great ones sport.

CORDUS.   Did you observe
How they inveighed 'gainst Caesar?

ARRUNTIUS.   Ay, baits, baits,
For us to bite at! Would I have my flesh
Torn by the public hook, these qualified hangmen
Should be my company.

CORDUS.   Here comes another.

DOMITUS AFER passes by.

ARRUNTIUS. Ay, there's a man, Afer the orator!
One that hath phrases, figures, and fine flowers
To strew his rhetoric with, and doth make haste
To get him note or name, by any offer
Where blood or gain be objects; steeps his words,
When he would kill, in artificial tears.
The crocodile of Tiber! him I love,
That man is mine! He hath my heart and voice
When I would curse, he, he!

SABINUS.   Contemn the slaves,
Their present lives will be their future graves.

                             Exeunt.

ACT TWO. SCENE FOUR

Within Agrippina's house

Enter SILIUS, AGRIPPINA, NERO, *and* SOSIA.

SILIUS. May't please your highness not forget yourself;
I dare not, with my manners, to attempt
Your trouble farther.

AGRIPPINA. Farewell, noble Silius!

SILIUS. Most royal Princess.

AGRIPPINA. Sosia stays with us?

SILIUS. She is your servant, and doth owe your
grace
An honest, but unprofitable love.

AGRIPPINA. How can that be, when there's no gain
but virtue's?

SILIUS. You take the moral, not the politic sense.
I meant, as she is bold, and free of speech,
Earnest to utter what her zealous thought
Travails withal, in honour of your house;
Which act, as it is simply borne in her,
Partakes of love and honesty, but may,
By th' over-often and unseasoned use,
Turn to your loss and danger. For your state
Is waited on by envies, as by eyes;
And every second guest your tables take
Is a fee'd spy, t' observe who goes, who comes;
What conference you have, with whom, where,
when,
What the discourse is, what the looks, the thoughts
Of every person there, they do extract,
And make into a substance.

AGRIPPINA. Hear me, Silius:
Were all Tiberius' body stuck with eyes,
And every wall and hanging in my house
Transparent as this lawn I wear, or air;
Yea, had Sejanus both his ears as long
As to my inmost closet, I would hate
To whisper any thought, or change an act,
To be made Juno's rival. Virtue's forces
Show ever noblest in conspicuous courses.

SILIUS. 'Tis great, and bravely spoken, like the
spirit
Of Agrippina; yet your highness knows

There is nor loss nor shame in providence.
Few can, what all should do, beware enough.
You may perceive with what officious face,
Satrius, and Natta, Afer, and the rest
Visit your house, of late, t' inquire the secrets;
And with what bold and privileged art, they rail
Against Augusta, yea, and at Tiberius;
Tell tricks of Livia and Sejanus—all
T' excite, and call your indignation on,
That they might hear it at more liberty.

AGRIPPINA. You're too suspicious, Silius.

SILIUS.   Pray the gods
I be so, Agrippina, but I fear
Some subtle practice. They that durst to strike
At so examp'less and unblamed a life
As that of the renowned Germanicus,
Will not sit down with that exploit alone.
He threatens many that hath injured one.

NERO. 'Twere best rip forth their tongues, sear out
   their eyes,
When next they come.

SOSIA.   A fit reward for spies.

Enter DRUSUS JUNIOR.

DRUSUS JUNIOR. Hear you the rumour?

AGRIPPINA.   What?

DRUSUS JUNIOR.   Drusus is dying.

AGRIPPINA. Dying!

NERO.   That's strange!

AGRIPPINA.   Y' were with him yesternight.

DRUSUS JUNIOR. One met Eudemus the physician,
Sent for but now, who thinks he cannot live.

SILIUS. Thinks! if it be arrived at that, he knows,
Or none.

AGRIPPINA. This's quick! What should be his disease?

SILIUS. Poison, poison——

AGRIPPINA. How, Silius!

NERO. What's that?

SILIUS. Nay, nothing. There was late a certain blow
Given o' the face.

NERO. Ay, to Sejanus.

SILIUS. True.

DRUSUS JUNIOR. And what of that?

SILIUS. I'm glad I gave it not.

NERO. But there is somewhat else?

SILIUS. Yes, private meetings
With a great lady, at a physician's,
And a wife turned away—

NERO. Ha!

SILIUS. Toys, mere toys!
What wisdom's now i' th' streets, i' th' common
　　mouth?

DRUSUS JUNIOR. Fears, whisp'rings, tumults, noise,
　　I know not what;
They say the Senate sit.

SILIUS. I'll thither straight,
And see what's in the forge.

AGRIPPINA. Good Silius, do.
Sosia and I will in.

SILIUS. Haste you, my lords,
To visit the sick prince; tender your loves
And sorrows to the people. This Sejanus,
Trust my divining soul, hath plots on all.
No tree that stops his prospect, but must fall.

Exeunt.

Chorus of Musicians.

ACT THREE. SCENE ONE

The Senate

Enter SEJANUS, VARRO, LATIARIS, COTTA, AFER,
PRAECONES *and* LICTORS.

SEJANUS. 'Tis only you must urge against him,
    Varro.
Nor I nor Caesar may appear therein,
Except in your defence, who are the Consul;
And, under colour of late enmity
Between your father and his, may better do it,
As free from all suspicion of a practice.
Here be your notes, what points to touch at. Read,
Be cunning in them. Afer has them too.
    VARRO. But is he summoned?
    SEJANUS.   No. It was debated
By Caesar, and concluded as most fit
To take him unprepared.
    AFER.   And prosecute
All under name of treason.
    VARRO.   I conceive.

Enter SABINUS, GALLUS, LEPIDUS, *and* ARRUNTIUS.

SABINUS. Drusus being dead, Caesar will not be
    here.
    GALLUS. What should the business of this Senate
    be?
    ARRUNTIUS. That can my subtle whisp'rers tell
    you: we
That are the good, dull, noble lookers-on,
Are only called to keep the marble warm.
What should we do with those deep mysteries

Proper to these fine heads? Let them alone.
Our ignorance may, perchance, help us be saved
From whips and furies.

   GALLUS.   See, see, see their action!
   ARRUNTIUS. Ay, now their heads do travail, now
     they work.
Their faces run like shuttles; they are weaving
Some curious cobweb to catch flies.

   SABINUS.   Observe,
They take their places.

   ARRUNTIUS.   What! so low?
   GALLUS.   O yes,
They must be seen to flatter Caesar's grief,
Though but in sitting.

   VARRO.   Bid us silence.
   PRAECONES.   Silence!
   VARRO. 'Fathers Conscript, may this our present
     meeting
Turn fair, and fortunate to the commonwealth!'

Enter SILIUS *and other* SENATORS.

   SEJANUS. See, Silius enters.
   SILIUS.   Hail, grave fathers!
   LICTOR.   Stand.
Silius, forbear thy place.

   SENATORS.   How!
   PRAECO.   Silius, stand forth,
The Consul hath to charge thee.

   LICTORS.   Room for Caesar!
   ARRUNTIUS. Is he come too? Nay, then expect a
     trick.
   SABINUS. Silius accused? Sure, he will answer
     nobly.

Enter TIBERIUS *attended.*

   TIBERIUS. We stand amazèd, fathers, to behold
This general dejection. Wherefore sit

Rome's consuls thus dissolved, as they had lost
All the remembrance both of style and place?
It not becomes. No woes are of fit weight
To make the honour of the Empire stoop;
Though I, in my peculiar self, may meet
Just reprehension, that so suddenly
And in so fresh a grief, would greet the Senate;
When private tongues, of kinsmen and allies,
Inspired with comforts, loathly are endured,
The face of men not seen, and scarce the day,
To thousands that communicate our loss.
Nor can I argue these of weakness, since
They take but natural ways; yet I must seek
For stronger aids, and those fair helps draw out
From warm embraces of the commonwealth.
Our mother, great Augusta's struck with time,
Our self impressed with agèd characters,
Drusus is gone, his children young and babes.
Our aims must now reflect on those that may
Give timely succour to these present ills,
And are our only glad surviving hopes,
The noble issue of Germanicus,
Nero and Drusus. Might it please the Consul
Honour them in—they both attend without.
I would present them to the Senate's care,
And raise those suns of joy that should drink up
These floods of sorrow in your drownèd eyes.

    ARRUNTIUS. —By Jove, I am not Oedipus enough
To understand this Sphinx.

    SABINUS.   The princes come.

Enter NERO *and* DRUSUS JUNIOR.

    TIBERIUS. Approach you, noble Nero, noble Drusus.
These princes, fathers, when their parent died,
I gave unto their uncle, with this prayer,
That though h' had proper issue of his own,
He would no less bring up, and foster these,

Than that self-blood; and by that act confirm
Their worths to him, and to posterity.
Drusus ta'en hence, I turn my prayers to you,
And 'fore our country and our gods, beseech
You take and rule Augustus' nephew's sons,
Sprung of the noblest ancestors; and so
Accomplish both my duty, and your own.
Nero, and Drusus, these shall be to you
In place of parents, these your fathers, these,
And not unfitly; for you are so born,
As all your good or ill's the commonwealth's.
Receive them, you strong guardians; and blest gods,
Make all their actions answer to their bloods;
Let their great titles find increase by them,
Not they by titles. Set them, as in place,
So in example, above all the Romans;
And may they know no rivals but themselves.
Let Fortune give them nothing, but attend
Upon their virtue; and that still come forth
Greater than hope, and better than their fame.
Relieve me, fathers, with your general voice.

  SENATORS. 'May all the gods consent to Caesar's
   wish,
And add to any honours that may crown
The hopeful issue of Germanicus!'

  TIBERIUS. We thank you, reverend fathers,
   in their right.

  ARRUNTIUS. —If this were true now! But the space,
   the space
Between the breast and lips—Tiberius' heart
Lies a thought farther than another man's.

  TIBERIUS. My comforts are so flowing in my joys,
As in them all my streams of grief are lost,
No less than are land waters in the sea,
Or show'rs in rivers; though their cause was such
As might have sprinkled ev'n the gods with tears.

Yet, since the greater doth embrace the less,
We covetously obey.

ARRUNTIUS.   —Well acted, Caesar.

TIBERIUS. And now I am the happy witness made
Of your so much desired affections
To this great issue, I could wish the fates
Would here set peaceful period to my days.
However, to my labours, I entreat
And beg it of this Senate, some fit ease.

ARRUNTIUS. —Laugh, fathers, laugh! Ha' you no
  spleens about you?

TIBERIUS. The burden is too heavy I sustain
On my unwilling shoulders; and I pray
It may be taken off, and reconferred
Upon the consuls, or some other Roman,
More able, and more worthy.

ARRUNTIUS.   —Laugh on still.

SABINUS. Why, this doth render all the rest suspected!

GALLUS. It poisons all.

ARRUNTIUS.   O, do you taste it then?

SABINUS. It takes away my faith to anything
He shall hereafter speak.

ARRUNTIUS.   Ay, to pray that
Which would be, to his head, as hot as thunder—
'Gainst which he wears that charm—should but the
  court
Receive him at his word.

GALLUS.   Hear!

TIBERIUS.   For myself,
I know my weakness; and so little covet,
Like some gone past, the weight that will oppress
  me,
As my ambition is the counter-point.

ARRUNTIUS. —Finely maintained, good still!

SEJANUS.   But Rome, whose blood,
Whose nerves, whose life, whose very frame relies
On Caesar's strength, no less than heav'n on Atlas,
Cannot admit it but with general ruin.

ARRUNTIUS. —Ah! are you there to bring him off?

SEJANUS.   Let Caesar
No more then urge a point so contrary
To Caesar's greatness, the grieved Senate's vows,
Or Rome's necessity.

GALLUS.   —He comes about.

ARRUNTIUS. More nimbly than Vertumnus.

TIBERIUS.   For the public,
I may be drawn to show I can neglect
All private aims, though I affect my rest.
But if the Senate still command me serve,
I must be glad to practise my obedience.

ARRUNTIUS. —You must and will, sir. We do know it.

SENATORS.   'Caesar,
Live long and happy, great and royal Caesar;
The gods preserve thee and thy modesty,
Thy wisdom, and thy innocence!'

ARRUNTIUS.   —Where is't?
The prayer's made before the subject.

SENATORS.   'Guard
His meekness, Jove, his piety, his care,
His bounty——'

ARRUNTIUS.   —And his subtlety, I'll put in.
Yet he'll keep that himself, without the gods.
All prayers are vain for him.

TIBERIUS.   We will not hold
Your patience, fathers, with long answer; but
Shall still contend to be what you desire,
And work to satisfy so great a hope.
Proceed to your affairs.

ARRUNTIUS.   —Now, Silius, guard thee;
The curtain's drawing. Afer advanceth.

PRAECONES.   Silence!

AFER. Cite Caius Silius.

PRAECONES.   Caius Silius!

SILIUS.   Here.

AFER. The triumph that thou hadst in Germany
For thy late victory on Sacrovir,
Thou hast enjoyed so freely, Caius Silius,
As no man it envied thee; nor would Caesar
Or Rome admit that thou wert then defrauded
Of any honours thy deserts could claim
In the fair service of the commonwealth.
But now, if, after all their loves and graces,
Thy actions and their courses being discovered,
It shall appear to Caesar and this Senate,
Thou hast defiled those glories with thy crimes——

SILIUS. Crimes!

AFER.   Patience, Silius.

SILIUS.   Tell thy mule of patience;
I'm a Roman. What are my crimes? Proclaim them.
Am I too rich, too honest for the times?
Have I or treasure, jewels, land, or houses
That some informer gapes for? Is my strength
Too much to be admitted, or my knowledge?
These now are crimes.

AFER.   Nay, Silius, if the name
Of crime so touch thee, with what impotence
Wilt thou endure the matter to be searched?

SILIUS. I tell thee, Afer, with more scorn than fear:
Employ your mercenary tongue and art.
Where's my accuser?

VARRO.   Here.

ARRUNTIUS.   —Varro? The Consul!
Is he thrust in?

VARRO.   'Tis I accuse thee, Silius.
Against the majesty of Rome, and Caesar,
I do pronounce thee here a guilty cause,

First of beginning and occasioning,
Next, drawing out the war in Gallia,
For which thou late triumph'st; dissembling long
That Sacrovir to be an enemy,
Only to make thy entertainment more,
Whilst thou and thy wife, Sosia, polled the province;
Wherein, with sordid, base desire of gain,
Thou hast discredited thy actions' worth
And been a traitor to the state.

    SILIUS.   Thou liest.

    ARRUNTIUS. —I thank thee, Silius, speak so still and
    often.

    VARRO. If I not prove it, Caesar, but unjustly
Have called him into trial, here I bind
Myself to suffer what I claim 'gainst him;
And yield, to have what I have spoke confirmed
By judgment of the court, and all good men.

    SILIUS. Caesar, I crave to have my cause deferred,
Till this man's consulship be out.

    TIBERIUS.   We cannot,
Nor may we grant it.

    SILIUS.   Why? shall he design
My day of trial? Is he my accuser,
And must he be my judge?

    TIBERIUS.   It hath been usual,
And is a right that custom hath allowed
The magistrate, to call forth private men,
And to appoint their day; which privilege
We may not in the Consul see infringed,
By whose deep watches and industrious care
It is so laboured, as the commonwealth
Receive no loss, by any oblique course.

    SILIUS. Caesar, thy fraud is worse than violence.

    TIBERIUS. Silius, mistake us not, we dare not use
The credit of the Consul to thy wrong;
But only do preserve his place and power,

So far as it concerns the dignity
And honour of the state.

    ARRUNTIUS.   Believe him, Silius.

    COTTA. Why, so he may, Arruntius.

    ARRUNTIUS.   I say so.
And he may choose, too.

    TIBERIUS.   By the Capitol.
And all our gods, but that the dear republic,
Our sacred laws, and just authority
Are interes'd therein, I should be silent.

    AFER. Please Caesar to give way unto his trial.
He shall have justice.

    SILIUS.   Nay, I shall have law,
Shall I not, Afer? Speak.

    AFER.   Would you have more?

    SILIUS. No, my well-spoken man, I would no more,
Nor less, might I enjoy it natural,
Not taught to speak unto your present ends,
Free from thine, his, and all your unkind handling,
Furious enforcing, most unjust presuming,
Malicious and manifold applying,
Foul wresting, and impossible construction.

    AFER. He raves, he raves.

    SILIUS.   Thou durst not tell me so,
Hadst thou not Caesar's warrant. I can see
Whose power condemns me.

    VARRO.   This betrays his spirit.
This doth enough declare him what he is.

    SILIUS. What am I? Speak.

    VARRO.   An enemy to the state.

    SILIUS. Because I am an enemy to thee,
And such corrupted ministers o' the state,
That here art made a present instrument
To gratify it with thine own disgrace.

    SEJANUS. This, to the Consul, is most insolent,
And impious!

SILIUS. Ay, take part. Reveal yourselves.
Alas! I scent not your confed'racies,
Your plots and combinations! I now know
Minion Sejanus hates me; and that all
This boast of law, and law, is but a form,
A net of Vulcan's filing, a mere engine,
To take that life by a pretext of justice,
Which you pursue in malice! I want brain
Or nostril to persuade me that your ends
And purposes are made to what they are,
Before my answer! O you equal gods,
Whose justice not a world of wolf-turned men
Shall make me to accuse—howe'er provoke—
Have I for this so oft engaged myself?
Stood in the heat and fervour of a fight,
When Phoebus sooner hath forsook the day
Than I the field, against the blue-eyed Gauls,
And crispèd Germans? when our Roman eagles
Have fanned the fire with their labouring wings,
And no blow dealt, that left not death behind it?
When I have charged alone into the troops
Of curled Sicambrians, routed them, and came
Not off with backward ensigns of a slave,
But forward marks, wounds on my breast and face,
Were meant to thee, O Caesar, and thy Rome?
And have I this return? Did I, for this,
Perform so noble and so brave defeat
On Sacrovir? O Jove, let it become me
To boast my deeds, when he whom they concern
Shall thus forget them!
AFER. Silius, Silius,
These are the common customs of thy blood,
When it is high with wine, as now with rage.
This well agrees with that intemperate vaunt
Thou lately mad'st at Agrippina's table,
That, when all other of the troops were prone

To fall into rebellion, only thine
Remained in their obedience. Thou wert he
That sav'dst the Empire, which had then been lost,
Had but thy legions there rebelled or mutinied.
Thy virtue met and fronted every peril.
Thou gav'st to Caesar, and to Rome their surety.
Their name, their strength, their spirit, and their
     state,
Their being was a donative from thee.

    ARRUNTIUS. —Well worded, and most like an
      orator.

    TIBERIUS. Is this true, Silius?

    SILIUS.   Save thy question, Caesar.
Thy spy of famous credit hath affirmed it.

    ARRUNTIUS. —Excellent Roman!

    SABINUS.   He doth answer stoutly.

    SEJANUS. If this be so, there needs no farther cause
Of crime against him.

    VARRO.   What can more impeach
The royal dignity and state of Caesar,
Than to be urgèd with a benefit
He cannot pay.

    COTTA.   In this, all Caesar's fortune
Is made unequal to the courtesy.

    LATIARIS. His means are clean destroyed, that
      should requite.

    GALLUS. Nothing is great enough for Silius' merit.

    ARRUNTIUS. —Gallus on that side too!

    SILIUS.   Come, do not hunt,
And labour so about for circumstance,
To make him guilty, whom you have foredoomed.
Take shorter ways, I'll meet your purposes.
The words were mine, and more I now will say:
Since I have done thee that great service, Caesar,
Thou still hast feared me; and, in place of grace,
Returned me hatred. So soon all best turns,

With doubtful princes, turn deep injuries
In estimation, when they greater rise
Than can be answered. Benefits, with you,
Are of no longer pleasure than you can
With ease restore them; that transcended once,
Your studies are not how to thank, but kill.
It is your nature to have all men slaves
To you, but you acknowledging to none.
The means that make your greatness must not come
In mention of it; if it do, it takes
So much away, you think; and that which helped
Shall soonest perish, if it stand in eye,
Where it may front, or but upbraid the high.

    COTTA. Suffer him speak no more.

    VARRO.   Note but his spirit.

    AFER. This shows him in the rest.

    LATIARIS.   Let him be censured.

    SEJANUS. He hath spoke enough to prove him Cae-
        sar's foe.

    COTTA. His thoughts look through his words.

    SEJANUS.   A censure.

    SILIUS.   Stay,
Stay, most officious Senate, I shall straight
Delude thy fury. Silius hath not placed
His guards within him, against Fortune's spite,
So weakly but he can escape your gripe
That are but hands of Fortune; she herself,
When virtue doth oppose, must lose her threats.
All that can happen in humanity,
The frown of Caesar, proud Sejanus' hatred,
Base Varro's spleen, and Afer's bloodying tongue,
The Senate's servile flattery, and these
Mustered to kill, I'm fortified against,
And can look down upon. They are beneath me.
It is not life whereof I stand enamoured,
Nor shall my end make me accuse my fate.

The coward and the valiant man must fall,
Only the cause, and manner how, discerns them;
Which then are gladdest, when they cost us dearest.
Romans, if any here be in this Senate,
Would know to mock Tiberius' tyranny,
Look upon Silius, and so learn to die.

Stabs himself.

VARRO. O desperate act!

ARRUNTIUS.   —An honourable hand!

TIBERIUS. Look, is he dead?

SABINUS.   —'Twas nobly struck, and home.

ARRUNTIUS. —My thought did prompt him to it.
    Farewell, Silius.
Be famous ever for thy great example.

TIBERIUS. We are not pleased in this sad accident,
That thus hath stallèd and abused our mercy,
Intended to preserve thee, noble Roman,
And to prevent thy hopes.

ARRUNTIUS.   —Excellent wolf!
Now he is full, he howls.

SEJANUS.   Caesar doth wrong
His dignity and safety, thus to mourn
The deserved end of so professed a traitor;
And doth, by this his lenity, instruct
Others as factious, to the like offence.

TIBERIUS. The confiscation merely of his state
Had been enough.

ARRUNTIUS.   —O, that was gaped for then?

VARRO. Remove the body.

SEJANUS.   Let citation
Go out for Sosia.

GALLUS.   Let her be proscribed.
And for the goods, I think it fit that half
Go to the Treasure, half unto the children.

LEPIDUS. With leave of Caesar, I would think that
    fourth

Part, which the law doth cast on the informers,
Should be enough; the rest go to the children.
Wherein the prince shall show humanity,
And bounty, not to force them by their want—
Which in their parent's trespass they deserved—
To take ill courses.

   TIBERIUS.   It shall please us.

   ARRUNTIUS   —Ay.
Out of necessity. This Lepidus
Is grave and honest, and I have observed
A moderation still in all his censures.

   SABINUS. And bending to the better——Stay, who's
this?

Enter SATRIUS *and* NATTA, *with* CREMUTIUS CORDUS,
guarded.

Cremutius Cordus! What! is he brought in?

   ARRUNTIUS. More blood into the banquet! Noble
     Cordus,
I wish thee good. Be as thy writings, free
And honest.

   TIBERIUS.   What is he?

   SEJANUS.   For th' annals, Caesar.

   PRAECO. Cremutius Cordus!

   CORDUS.   Here.

   PRAECO.   Satrius Secundus,
Pinnarius Natta, you are his accusers.

   ARRUNTIUS. —Two of Sejanus' bloodhounds,
     whom he breeds
With human flesh, to bay at citizens.

   AFER. Stand forth before the Senate, and confront
     him.

   SATRIUS. I do accuse thee here, Cremutius Cordus,
To be a man factious and dangerous,
A sower of sedition in the state,
A turbulent and discontented spirit;

Which I will prove from thine own writings, here,
The annals thou hast published; where thou bit'st
The present age, and with a viper's tooth,
Being a member of it, dar'st that ill
Which never yet degenerous bastard did
Upon his parent.

  NATTA.   To this I subscribe;
And, forth a world of more particulars,
Instance in only one: comparing men,
And times, thou praisest Brutus, and affirm'st
That Cassius was the last of all the Romans.

  COTTA. How! what are we then?

  VARRO.   What is Caesar? Nothing?

  AFER. My lords, this strikes at every Roman's private,
In whom reigns gentry and estate of spirit,
To have a Brutus brought in parallel,
A parricide, an enemy of his country,
Ranked, and preferred to any real worth
That Rome now holds. This is most strangely invective,
Most full of spite and insolent upbraiding.
Nor is 't the time alone is here disprized,
But the whole man of time, yea, Caesar's self
Brought in disvalue; and he aimed at most,
By oblique glance of his licentious pen.
Caesar, if Cassius were the last of Romans,
Thou hast no name.

  TIBERIUS.   Let's hear him answer. Silence!

  CORDUS. So innocent I am of fact, my lords,
As but my words are argued, yet those words
Not reaching either prince or prince's parent;
The which your law of treason comprehends.
Brutus and Cassius I am charged t' have praised;
Whose deeds, when many more besides myself
Have writ, not one hath mentioned without honour.

Great Titus Livius, great for eloquence
And faith amongst us, in his history,
With so great praises Pompey did extol,
As oft Augustus called him a Pompeian;
Yet this not hurt their friendship. In his book
He often names Scipio, Afranius,
Yea, the same Cassius, and this Brutus too,
As worthiest men; not thieves and parricides,
Which notes upon their fames are now imposed.
Asinius Pollio's writings quite throughout
Give them a noble memory; so Messala
Renowned his general Cassius—yet both these
Lived with Augustus, full of wealth and honours.
To Cicero's book, where Cato was heaved up
Equal with heav'n, what else did Caesar answer,
Being then Dictator, but with a penned oration,
As if before the judges? Do but see
Antonius' letters; read but Brutus' pleadings,
What vile reproach they hold against Augustus,
False, I confess, but with much bitterness.
The epigrams of Bibaculus and Catullus
Are read, full stuffed with spite of both the Caesars;
Yet deified Julius, and no less Augustus,
Both bore them, and contemned them. I not know,
Promptly to speak it, whether done with more
Temper or wisdom, for such obloquies
If they despisèd be, they die suppressed;
But if with rage acknowledged, they are confessed.
The Greeks I slip, whose licence not alone,
But also lust did 'scape unpunishèd;
Or where someone, by chance, exception took,
He words with words revenged. But, in my work,
What could be aimed more free, or farther off
From the time's scandal, than to write of those
Whom death from grace or hatred had exempted?
Did I, with Brutus and with Cassius,

Armed, and possessed of the Philippi fields,
Incense the people in the civil cause,
With dangerous speeches? Or do they, being slain
Seventy years since, as by their images—
Which not the conqueror hath defaced—appears,
Retain that guilty memory with writers?
Posterity pays every man his honour.
Nor shall there want, though I condemnèd am,
That will not only Cassius well approve,
And of great Brutus' honour mindful be,
But that will also mention make of me.

ARRUNTIUS. —Freely and nobly spoken!

SABINUS.   With good temper.
I like him, that he is not moved with passion.

ARRUNTIUS. He puts 'em to their whisper.

TIBERIUS.   Take him hence;
We shall determine of him at next sitting.

Exit CORDUS *guarded.*

COTTA. Meantime, give order, that his books be
    burnt,
To the aediles.

SEJANUS.   You have well advised.

AFER. It fits not such licentious things should live
T' upbraid the age.

ARRUNTIUS.   If th' age were good, they might.

LATIARIS. Let 'em be burnt.

GALLUS.   All sought, and burnt today.

PRAECONES. The court is up. Lictors, resume the
    fasces.   *Exeunt all but* ARRUNTIUS, SABINUS,
                    and LEPIDUS.

ARRUNTIUS. Let 'em be burnt! O how ridiculous
Appears the Senate's brainless diligence,
Who think they can, with present power, extinguish
The memory of all succeeding times!

SABINUS. 'Tis true; when, contrary, the punish-
    ment

Of wit, doth make th' authority increase.
Nor do they aught, that use this cruelty
Of interdiction, and this rage of burning,
But purchase to themselves rebuke and shame,
And to the writers an eternal name.

LEPIDUS. It is an argument the times are sore,
When virtue cannot safely be advanced,
Nor vice reproved.

ARRUNTIUS.   Ay, noble Lepidus,
Augustus well foresaw what we should suffer
Under Tiberius, when he did pronounce
The Roman race most wretched, that should live
Between so slow jaws, and so long a bruising.

Exeunt.

ACT THREE. SCENE TWO

The Palace

Enter TIBERIUS *and* SEJANUS.

TIBERIUS. This business hath succeeded well, Se-
janus,
And quite removed all jealousy of practice
'Gainst Agrippina and our nephews. Now
We must bethink us how to plant our engines
For th'other pair, Sabinus and Arruntius,
And Gallus too—howe'er he flatter us,
His heart we know.

SEJANUS.   Give it some respite, Caesar.
Time shall mature and bring to perfect crown,
What we, with so good vultures, have begun.
Sabinus shall be next.

TIBERIUS.　　　　　Rather Arruntius.

SEJANUS. By any means, preserve him. His frank tongue
Being lent the reins, would take away all thought
Of malice, in your course against the rest.
We must keep him to stalk with.

TIBERIUS.　　　　　　　　Dearest head,
To thy most fortunate design I yield it.

SEJANUS. Sir, I have been so long trained up in grace—
First with your father, great Augustus; since,
With your most happy bounties so familiar—
As I not sooner would commit my hopes
Or wishes to the gods, than to your ears.
Nor have I ever yet been covetous
Of over-bright and dazzling honours; rather
To watch and travail in great Caesar's safety,
With the most common soldier.

TIBERIUS.　　　　　　　　'Tis confessed.

SEJANUS. The only gain, and which I count most fair
Of all my fortunes, is that mighty Caesar
Hath thought me worthy his alliance. Hence
Begin my hopes.

TIBERIUS.　　　Hmh?

SEJANUS.　　　　　　I have heard Augustus,
In the bestowing of his daughter, thought
But even of gentlemen of Rome. If so—
I know not how to hope so great a favour—
But if a husband should be sought for Livia,
And I be had in mind, as Caesar's friend,
I would but use the glory of the kindred.
It should not make me slothful, or less caring
For Caesar's state; it were enough to me
It did confirm and strengthen my weak house,
Against the now unequal opposition

Of Agrippina. And for dear regard
Unto my children, this I wish; myself
Have no ambition farther than to end
My days in service of so dear a master.

   TIBERIUS. We cannot but commend thy piety,
Most loved Sejanus, in acknowledging
Those bounties; which we, faintly, such remember.
But to thy suit. The rest of mortal men,
In all their drifts and counsels, pursue profit.
Princes alone are of a different sort,
Directing their main actions still to fame.
We therefore will take time to think and answer.
For Livia, she can best, herself, resolve
If she will marry, after Drusus, or
Continue in the family; besides,
She hath a mother and a grandam yet,
Whose nearer counsels she may guide her by.
But I will simply deal. That enmity
Thou fear'st in Agrippina, would burn more,
If Livia's marriage should, as 'twere in parts,
Divide th' imperial house; an emulation
Between the women might break forth, and discord
Ruin the sons and nephews on both hands.
What if it cause some present difference?
Thou art not safe, Sejanus, if thou prove it.
Canst thou believe that Livia, first the wife
To Caius Caesar, then my Drusus, now
Will be contented to grow old with thee,
Born but a private gentleman of Rome;
And raise thee with her loss, if not her shame?
Or say that I should wish it, canst thou think
The Senate or the people, who have seen
Her brother, father, and our ancestors,
In highest place of Empire, will endure it?
The state thou hold'st already, is in talk;
Men murmur at thy greatness; and the nobles

Stick not in public, to upbraid thy climbing
Above our father's favours or thy scale;
And dare accuse me, from their hate to thee.
Be wise, dear friend. We would not hide these
    things,
For friendship's dear respect; nor will we stand
Adverse to thine or Livia's designments.
What we have purposed to thee, in our thought,
And with what near degrees of love to bind thee,
And make thee equal to us, for the present,
We will forbear to speak. Only, thus much
Believe, our loved Sejanus, we not know
That height in blood or honour, which thy virtue
And mind to us, may not aspire with merit.
And this we'll publish, on all watched occasion
The Senate or the people shall present.

    SEJANUS. I am restored, and to my sense again,
Which I had lost in this so blinding suit.
Caesar hath taught me better to refuse,
Than I knew how to ask. How pleaseth Caesar
T' embrace my late advice for leaving Rome?

    TIBERIUS. We are resolved.

    SEJANUS.   Here are some motives more,
Which I have thought on since, may more confirm.

    TIBERIUS. Careful Sejanus! we will straight peruse
    them.
Go forward in our main design, and prosper. *Exit.*

    SEJANUS. If those but take, I shall. Dull, heavy
    Caesar!
Wouldst thou tell me thy favours were made crimes,
And that my fortunes were esteemed thy faults,
That thou for me wert hated, and not think
I would with wingèd haste prevent that change,
When thou might'st win all to thyself again
By forfeiture of me? Did those fond words
Fly swifter from thy lips, than this my brain,

This sparkling forge, created me an armour
T' encounter chance and thee? Well, read my
    charms,
And may they lay that hold upon thy senses,
As thou hadst snuffed up hemlock, or ta'en down
The juice of poppy and of mandrakes. Sleep,
Voluptuous Caesar, and security
Seize on thy stupid powers, and leave them dead
To public cares, awake but to thy lusts,
The strength of which makes thy libidinous soul
Itch to leave Rome! And I have thrust it on:
With blaming of the city business,
The multitude of suits, the confluence
Of suitors, then their importunacies,
The manifold distractions he must suffer,
Besides ill rumours, envies and reproaches;
All which a quiet and retired life
Larded with ease and pleasure, did avoid;
And yet for any weighty and great affair,
The fittest place to give the soundest counsels.
By this I shall remove him both from thought
And knowledge of his own most dear affairs;
Draw all dispatches through my private hands;
Know his designments, and pursue mine own;
Make mine own strengths by giving suits and places,
Conferring dignities and offices;
And these that hate me now, wanting access
To him, will make their envy none, or less.
For when they see me arbiter of all,
They must observe, or else with Caesar fall.   *Exit.*

ACT THREE. SCENE THREE

Another room in the Palace

Enter TIBERIUS.

TIBERIUS. To marry Livia! Will no less, Sejanus,
Content thy aims? no lower object? well!
Thou know'st how thou art wrought into our trust,
Woven in our design; and think'st we must
Now use thee, whatsoe'er thy projects are.
'Tis true. But yet with caution and fit care.
And, now we better think—Who's there within?

Enter SERVUS.

SERVUS. Caesar!

TIBERIUS.   To leave our journey off were sin
'Gainst our decreed delights; and would appear
Doubt, or, what less becomes a prince, low fear.
Yet doubt hath law, and fears have their excuse,
Where princes' states plead necessary use,
As ours doth now—more in Sejanus' pride,
Than all fell Agrippina's hates beside.
Those are the dreadful enemies, we raise
With favours, and make dangerous with praise.
The injured by us, may have will alike,
But 'tis the favourite hath the power to strike.
And fury ever boils more high and strong,
Heat' with ambition, than revenge of wrong.
'Tis then a part of supreme skill, to grace
No man too much; but hold a certain space
Between th' ascender's rise and thine own flat,
Lest, when all rounds be reached, his aim be that.
'Tis thought—Is Macro in the palace? See.

If not, go seek him, to come to us. *Exit* SERVUS. He
Must be the organ we must work by now,
Though none less apt for trust. Need doth allow
What choice would not. I've heard that aconite,
Being timely taken, hath a healing might
Against the scorpion's stroke; the proof we'll give,
That, while two poisons wrestle, we may live.
He hath a spirit too working, to be used
But to th' encounter of his like. Excused
Are wiser sovereigns then, that raise one ill
Against another, and both safely kill.
The prince that feeds great natures, they will sway
    him;
Who nourisheth a lion, must obey him.—

Re-enter SERVUS *with* MACRO.

Macro, we sent for you.
    MACRO.   I heard so, Caesar.
    TIBERIUS. Leave us a while. *Exit* SERVUS. When
    you shall know, good Macro,
The causes of our sending, and the ends,
You will then hearken nearer, and be pleased
You stand so high both in our choice and trust.
    MACRO. The humblest place in Caesar's choice or
    trust
May make glad Macro proud, without ambition,
Save to do Caesar service.
    TIBERIUS.   Leave your courtings.
We are in purpose, Macro, to depart
The city for a time, and see Campania;
Not for our pleasures, but to dedicate
A pair of temples, one to Jupiter
At Capua, th' other at Nola, to Augustus;
In which great work, perhaps our stay will be
Beyond our will produced. Now, since we are
Not ignorant what danger may be born

Out of our shortest absence, in a state
So subject unto envy, and embroiled
With hate and faction; we have thought on thee,
Amongst a field of Romans, worthiest Macro,
To be our eye and ear: to keep strict watch
On Agrippina, Nero, Drusus, ay,
And on Sejanus—not that we distrust
His loyalty, or do repent one grace,
Of all that heap we have conferred on him;
For that were to disparage our election,
And call that judgment now in doubt, which then
Seemed as unquestioned as an oracle—
But greatness hath his cankers. Worms and moths
Breed out of too much humour, in the things
Which, after, they consume, transferring quite
The substance of their makers int' themselves.
Macro is sharp, and apprehends. Besides,
I know him subtle, close, wise, and well-read
In man and his large nature. He hath studied
Affections, passions; knows their springs, their ends;
Which way, and whither they will work. 'Tis proof
Enough of his great merit that we trust him.
Then, to a point:—because our conference
Cannot be long without suspicion—
Here, Macro, we assign thee both to spy,
Inform, and chastise; think, and use thy means,
Thy ministers, what, where, on whom thou wilt;
Explore, plot, practise. All thou dost in this
Shall be as if the Senate or the laws
Had giv'n it privilege, and thou thence styled
The saviour both of Caesar and of Rome.
We will not take thy answer but in act;
Whereto, as thou proceed'st, we hope to hear
By trusted messengers. If't be inquired
Wherefore we called you, say you have in charge

To see our chariots ready, and our horse.
Be still our loved and, shortly, honoured Macro.
                           Exit.

   MACRO. I will not ask why Caesar bids do this,
But joy that he bids me. It is the bliss
Of courts to be employed, no matter how;
A prince's power makes all his actions virtue.
We whom he works by, are dumb instruments,
To do, but not inquire. His great intents
Are to be served, not searched. Yet, as that bow
Is most in hand, whose owner best doth know
T' affect his aims; so let that statesman hope
Most use, most price, can hit his prince's scope.
Nor must he look at what or whom to strike,
But loose at all; each mark must be alike.
Were it to plot against the fame, the life
Of one with whom I twinned; remove a wife
From my warm side, as loved as is the air;
Practise away each parent; draw mine heir
In compass, though but one; work all my kin
To swift perdition; leave no untrained engine,
For friendship, or for innocence; nay, make
The gods all guilty—I would undertake
This, being imposed me, both with gain and ease.
The way to rise is to obey and please.
He that will thrive in state, he must neglect
The trodden paths that truth and right respect;
And prove new, wilder ways, for virtue there
Is not that narrow thing she is elsewhere.
Men's fortune there is virtue; reason, their will;
Their licence, law; and their observance, skill.
Occasion is their foil; conscience, their stain;
Profit their lustre; and what else is, vain.
If then it be the lust of Caesar's power,
T' have raised Sejanus up, and in an hour
O'erturn him, tumbling down, from height of all;

We are his ready engine; and his fall
May be our rise. It is no uncouth thing
To see fresh buildings from old ruins spring. *Exit.*

Chorus of Musicians.

ACT FOUR. SCENE ONE

Agrippina's house

Enter GALLUS *and* AGRIPPINA.

GALLUS. You must have patience, royal Agrippina.

AGRIPPINA. I must have vengeance first, and that
    were nectar
Unto my famished spirits. O my Fortune,
Let it be sudden thou prepar'st against me;
Strike all my powers of understanding blind,
And ignorant of destiny to come!
Let me not fear, that cannot hope.

GALLUS.   Dear Princess,
These tyrannies on yourself are worse than Caesar's.

AGRIPPINA. Is this the happiness of being born
    great?
Still to be aimed at, still to be suspected?
To live the subject of all jealousies?
At least the colour made if not the ground
To every painted danger? Who would not
Choose once to fall than thus to hang forever?

GALLUS. You might be safe if you would——

AGRIPPINA.   What, my Gallus!
Be lewd Sejanus' strumpet, or the bawd
To Caesar's lusts, he now is gone to practise?
Not these are safe, where nothing is. Yourself

While thus you stand but by me, are not safe.
Was Silius safe, or the good Sosia safe?
Or was my niece, dear Claudia Pulchra, safe,
Or innocent Furnius? they that latest have,
By being made guilty, added reputation
To Afer's eloquence? O foolish friends,
Could not so fresh example warn your loves,
But you must buy my favours with that loss
Unto yourselves; and when you might perceive
That Caesar's cause of raging must forsake him,
Before his will? Away, good Gallus, leave me.
Here to be seen is danger; to speak, treason;
To do me least observance is called faction.
You are unhappy in me, and I in all.
Where are my sons, Nero and Drusus? We
Are they be shot at. Let us fall apart;
Not, in our ruins, sepulchre our friends.
Or shall we do some action like offence,
To mock their studies that would make us faulty,
And frustrate practice by preventing it?
The danger's like; for what they can contrive,
They will make good. No innocence is safe,
When power contests. Nor can they trespass more,
Whose only being was all crime before.

Enter NERO, DRUSUS, *and* CALIGULA.

NERO. You hear Sejanus is come back from Caesar?
GALLUS. No. How? Disgraced?
DRUSUS.   More gracèd now than ever.
GALLUS. By what mischance?
CALIGULA.   A fortune like enough
Once to be bad.
DRUSUS.   But turned too good to both.
GALLUS. What was't?
NERO.   Tiberius sitting at his meat
In a farm-house they call Spelunca, sited

By the seaside, among the Fundane hills,
Within a natural cave; part of the grot
About the entry, fell, and overwhelmed
Some of the waiters; others ran away.
Only Sejanus, with his knees, hands, face,
O'erhanging Caesar, did oppose himself
To the remaining ruins, and was found
In that so labouring posture by the soldiers
That came to succour him. With which adventure,
He hath so fixed himself in Caesar's trust,
As thunder cannot move him, and is come
With all the height of Caesar's praise to Rome.

  AGRIPPINA. And power to turn those ruins all on
    us,
And bury whole posterities beneath them.
Nero, and Drusus, and Caligula,
Your places are the next, and therefore most
In their offence. Think on your birth and blood,
Awake your spirits, meet their violence.
'Tis princely when a tyrant doth oppose,
And is a fortune sent to exercise
Your virtue, as the wind doth try strong trees,
Who by vexation grow more sound and firm.
After your father's fall, and uncle's fate,
What can you hope, but all the change of stroke
That force or sleight can give? Then stand upright;
And though you do not act, yet suffer nobly.
Be worthy of my womb, and take strong cheer;
What we do know will come, we should not fear.

             Exeunt.

ACT FOUR. SCENE TWO

A street

Enter MACRO.

MACRO. Returned so soon! renewed in trust and
    grace!
Is Caesar then so weak? or hath the place
But wrought this alteration with the air,
And he, on next remove, will all repair?
Macro, thou art engaged; and what before
Was public, now must be thy private, more.
The weal of Caesar fitness did imply;
But thine own fate confers necessity
On thy employment; and the thoughts borne
    nearest
Unto ourselves, move swiftest still, and dearest.
If he recover, thou art lost; yea, all
The weight of preparation to his fall
Will turn on thee, and crush thee. Therefore strike
Before he settle, to prevent the like
Upon thyself. He doth his vantage know,
That makes it home, and gives the foremost blow.
        Exit.

ACT FOUR. SCENE THREE

Agrippina's house

Enter LATIARIS, RUFUS, *and* OPSIUS.

LATIARIS. It is a service great Sejanus will
See well requited, and accept of nobly.
Here place yourselves, between the roof and ceiling;
And when I bring him to his words of danger,
Reveal yourselves, and take him.

RUFUS.   Is he come?

LATIARIS. I'll now go fetch him.   *Exit.*

OPSIUS.   With good speed. I long
To merit from the state, in such an action.

RUFUS. I hope it will obtain the consulship
For one of us.

OPSIUS.   We cannot think of less,
To bring in one so dangerous as Sabinus.

RUFUS. He was a follower of Germanicus,
And still is an observer of his wife
And children, though they be declined in grace;
A daily visitant, keeps them company
In private and in public, and is noted
To be the only client of the house.
Pray Jove, he will be free to Latiaris.

OPSIUS. He's allied to him, and doth trust him
   well.

RUFUS. And he'll requite his trust!

OPSIUS.   To do an office
So grateful to the state, I know no man
But would strain nearer bands than kindred——

RUFUS.   List,
I hear them come.

OPSIUS.   Shift to our holes with silence.

Re-enter LATIARIS *with* SABINUS.

LATIARIS. It is a noble constancy you show
To this afflicted house: that not like others,
The friends of season, you do follow fortune,
And, in the winter of their fate, forsake
The place whose glories warmed you. You are just,
And worthy such a princely patron's love,
As was the world's renowned Germanicus,
Whose ample merit when I call to thought,
And see his wife and issue, objects made
To so much envy, jealousy, and hate,
It makes me ready to accuse the gods
Of negligence, as men of tyranny.
  SABINUS. They must be patient, so must we.
  LATIARIS.   O Jove,
What will become of us or of the times,
When to be high or noble are made crimes,
When land and treasure are most dangerous faults?
  SABINUS. Nay, when our table, yea, our bed, assaults
Our peace and safety? when our writings are
By any envious instruments, that dare
Apply them to the guilty, made to speak
What they will have, to fit their tyrannous wreak?
When ignorance is scarcely innocence;
And knowledge made a capital offence?
When not so much, but the bare empty shade
Of liberty is reft us; and we made
The prey to greedy vultures and vile spies,
That first transfix us with their murdering eyes?
  LATIARIS. Methinks the genius of the Roman race
Should not be so extinct, but that bright flame
Of liberty might be revived again—
Which no good man but with his life should lose—
And we not sit like spent and patient fools,

Still puffing in the dark at one poor coal,
Held on by hope till the last spark is out.
The cause is public, and the honour, name,
The immortality of every soul
That is not bastard or a slave in Rome,
Therein concerned; whereto, if men would change
The wearied arm, and for the weighty shield
So long sustained, employ the facile sword,
We might have soon assurance of our vows.
This ass's fortitude doth tire us all.
It must be active valour must redeem
Our loss, or none. The rock and our hard steel
Should meet t' enforce those glorious fires again,
Whose splendour cheered the world, and heat gave
    life,
No less than doth the sun's.

SABINUS.   'Twere better stay
In lasting darkness, and despair of day.
No ill should force the subject undertake
Against the sovereign, more than hell should make
The gods do wrong. A good man should and must
Sit rather down with loss, than rise unjust.
Though, when the Romans first did yield themselves
To one man's power, they did not mean their lives,
Their fortunes and their liberties should be
His absolute spoil, as purchased by the sword.

LATIARIS.   Why, we are worse, if to be slaves, and
    bond
To Caesar's slave, be such, the proud Sejanus!
He that is all, does all, gives Caesar leave
To hide his ulcerous and anointed face
With his bald crown at Rhodes, while he here
    stalks
Upon the heads of Romans, and their princes,
Familiarly to empire.

SABINUS. Now you touch
A point indeed, wherein he shows his art,
As well as power.
    LATIARIS. And villainy in both.
Do you observe where Livia lodges? how
Drusus came dead? what men have been cut off?
    SABINUS. Yes, those are things removed. I nearer
       looked
Into his later practice, where he stands
Declared a master in his mystery.
First, ere Tiberius went, he wrought his fear
To think that Agrippina sought his death;
Then put those doubts in her; send her oft word,
Under the show of friendship, to beware
Of Caesar, for he laid to poison her;
Drave them to frowns, to mutual jealousies,
Which now in visible hatred are burst out.
Since, he hath had his hired instruments
To work on Nero, and to heave him up;
To tell him Caesar's old, that all the people,
Yea, all the army, have their eyes on him;
That both do long to have him undertake
Something of worth, to give the world a hope;
Bids him to court their grace. The easy youth
Perhaps gives ear, which straight he writes to Caesar,
And with this comment: 'See yon dangerous boy;
Note but the practice of the mother there;
She's tying him, for purposes at hand,
With men of sword.' Here's Caesar put in fright
'Gainst son and mother. Yet he leaves not thus.
The second brother, Drusus, a fierce nature,
And fitter for his snares, because ambitious
And full of envy, him he clasps and hugs;
Poisons with praise; tells him what hearts he wears;
How bright he stands in popular expectance;

That Rome doth suffer with him, in the wrong
His mother does him, by preferring Nero.
Thus sets he them asunder, each 'gainst other,
Projects the course that serves him to condemn,
Keeps in opinion of a friend to all,
And all drives on to ruin.

LATIARIS.   Caesar sleeps,
And nods at this?

SABINUS.   Would he might ever sleep,
Bogged in his filthy lusts!

OPSIUS *and* RUFUS *rush in.*

OPSIUS.   Treason to Caesar!

RUFUS. Lay hands upon the traitor, Latiaris,
Or take the name thyself.

LATIARIS.   I am for Caesar.

SABINUS. Am I then catched?

RUFUS.   How think you, sir? You are.

SABINUS. Spies of this head, so white, so full of
     years!
Well, my most reverend monsters, you may live
To see yourselves thus snared.

OPSIUS.   Away with him!

LATIARIS. Hale him away.

RUFUS.   To be a spy for traitors
Is honourable vigilance.

SABINUS.   You do well,
My most officious instruments of state,
Men of all uses. Drag me hence, away.
The year is well begun, and I fall fit
To be an off'ring to Sejanus. Go!

OPSIUS. Cover him with his garments, hide his face.

SABINUS. It shall not need. Forbear your rude
     assault.
The fault's not shameful, villainy makes a fault.

                           Exeunt.

ACT FOUR. SCENE FOUR

Before Agrippina's house

Enter MACRO *and* CALIGULA.

MACRO. Sir, but observe how thick your dangers
    meet
In his clear drifts! Your mother and your brothers,
Now cited to the Senate! Their friend Gallus,
Feasted today by Caesar, since committed!
Sabinus here we meet, hurried to fetters!
The senators all struck with fear and silence,
Save those whose hopes depend not on good means,
But force their private prey from public spoil!
And you must know, if here you stay, your state
Is sure to be the subject of his hate,
As now the object.
    CALIGULA.   What would you advise me?
    MACRO. To go for Capreae presently, and there
Give up yourself entirely to your uncle.
Tell Caesar—since your mother is accused
To fly for succours to Augustus' statue,
And to the army, with your brethren—you
Have rather chose to place your aids in him,
Than live suspected, or in hourly fear
To be thrust out by bold Sejanus' plots;
Which you shall confidently urge to be
Most full of peril to the state and Caesar,
As being laid to his peculiar ends,
And not to be let run with common safety.
All which, upon the second, I'll make plain,
So both shall love and trust with Caesar gain.
    CALIGULA. Away then, let's prepare us for our
    journey.   *Exeunt.*

ACT FOUR. SCENE FIVE

A street

Enter ARRUNTIUS.

ARRUNTIUS. Still dost thou suffer, Heaven? Will
    no flame,
No heat of sin, make thy just wrath to boil
In thy distempered bosom, and o'erflow
The pitchy blazes of impiety,
Kindled beneath thy throne? Still canst thou sleep,
Patient, while vice doth make an antic face
At thy dread power, and blow dust and smoke
Into thy nostrils? Jove, will nothing wake thee?
Must vile Sejanus pull thee by the beard,
Ere thou wilt open thy black-lidded eye,
And look him dead? Well! Snore on, dreaming
    gods,
And let this last of that proud giant race
Heave mountain upon mountain 'gainst your state—
Be good unto me, Fortune and you powers,
Whom I, expostulating, have profaned.
I see, what's equal with a prodigy,
A great, a noble Roman, and an honest,
Live an old man!

Enter LEPIDUS.

          O Marcus Lepidus,
When is our turn to bleed? Thyself and I,
Without our boast, are almost all the few
Left to be honest in these impious times.
   LEPIDUS. What we are left to be, we will be, Lucius,
Though tyranny did stare as wide as death,
To fright us from it.

ARRUNTIUS.   'T hath so, on Sabinus.

LEPIDUS. I saw him now drawn from the Gemonies,
And—what increased the direness of the fact—
His faithful dog, upbraiding all us Romans,
Never forsook the corpse, but, seeing it thrown
Into the stream, leaped in, and drowned with it.

ARRUNTIUS. O act to be envied him of us men!
We are the next the hook lays hold on, Marcus.
What are thy arts, good patriot, teach them me,
That have preserved thy hairs to this white dye,
And kept so reverend and so dear a head
Safe on his comely shoulders?

LEPIDUS.   Arts, Arruntius?
None, but the plain and passive fortitude
To suffer and be silent; never stretch
These arms against the torrent; live at home,
With my own thoughts and innocence about me,
Not tempting the wolf's jaws—these are my arts.

ARRUNTIUS. I would begin to study 'em, if I
    thought
They would secure me. May I pray to Jove
In secret and be safe? Ay, or aloud,
With open wishes, so I do not mention
Tiberius or Sejanus? Yes I must,
If I speak out. 'Tis hard that. May I think,
And not be racked? What danger is't to dream,
Talk in one's sleep, or cough? Who knows the law?
May I shake my head, without a comment? say
It rains, or it holds up, and not be thrown
Upon the Gemonies? These now are things
Whereon men's fortune, yea, their fate depends.
Nothing hath privilege 'gainst the violent ear.
No place, no day, no hour, we see, is free,
Not our religious and most sacred times,
From some one kind of cruelty; all matter,
Nay, all occasion pleaseth. Madmen's rage,

The idleness of drunkards, women's nothing,
Jester's simplicity, all, all is good
That can be catched at. Nor is now th' event
Of any person, or for any crime,
To be expected; for 'tis always one:
Death, with some little difference of place,
Or time——What's this? Prince Nero, guarded!

Enter LACO *and* NERO *with* LICTORS.

LACO. On, lictors, keep your way. My lords, for-
bear.
On pain of Caesar's wrath, no man attempt
Speech with the prisoner.

NERO.　　　　　　Noble friends, be safe.
To lose yourselves for words, were as vain hazard,
As unto me small comfort. Fare you well.
Would all Rome's sufferings in my fate did dwell!

LACO. Lictors, away.

LEPIDUS.　　　　　Where goes he, Laco?

LACO.　　　　　　　　　　　　Sir,
He's banished into Pontia by the Senate.

ARRUNTIUS. —Do I see, and hear, and feel? May I
trust sense,
Or doth my fancy form it?

LEPIDUS.　　　　　Where's his brother?

LACO. Drusus is prisoner in the Palace.

ARRUNTIUS.　　　　　　　　　—Ha!
I smell it now; 'tis rank.—Where's Agrippina?

LACO. The princess is confined to Pandataria.

ARRUNTIUS. —Bolts, Vulcan, bolts for Jove!
Phoebus, thy bow;
Stern Mars, thy sword; and, blue-eyed maid, thy
spear;
Thy club, Alcides—all the armoury
Of heaven is too little!—ha! to guard
The gods, I meant. Fine, rare dispatch! This same

Was swiftly borne! Confined, imprisoned, banished?
Most tripartite!—The cause, sir?

LACO.   Treason.

ARRUNTIUS.   —O!
The complement of all accusings, that
Will hit when all else fails!

LEPIDUS.   This turn is strange!
But yesterday, the people would not hear,
Far less objected, but cried Caesar's letters
Were false and forged; that all these plots were
    malice;
And that the ruin of the Prince's house
Was practised 'gainst his knowledge. Where are now
Their voices, now that they behold his heirs
Locked up, disgraced, led into exile?

ARRUNTIUS.   Hushed,
Drowned in their bellies. Wild Sejanus' breath
Hath, like a whirlwind, scattered that poor dust,
With this rude blast. *Turns to* LACO *and the rest.*
    We'll talk no treason, sir,
If that be it you stand for. Fare you well.
We have no need of horse-leeches. Good spy,
Now you are spied, begone.

                    Exeunt LACO, NERO, *and* LICTORS.

LEPIDUS.   I fear you wrong him.
He has the voice to be an honest Roman.

ARRUNTIUS. And trusted to this office? Lepidus,
I'd sooner trust Greek Sinon than a man
Our state employs. He's gone; and being gone,
I dare tell you, whom I dare better trust,
That our night-eyed Tiberius doth not see
His minion's drifts; or, if he do, he's not
So arrant subtle, as we fools do take him:
To breed a mongrel up, in his own house,
With his own blood, and, if the good gods please,
At his own throat flesh him to take a leap.

I do not beg it, Heav'n, but if the fates
Grant it these eyes, they must not wink.

    LEPIDUS.   They must
Not see it, Lucius.

    ARRUNTIUS.   Who should let 'em?

    LEPIDUS.   Zeal
And duty, with the thought he is our prince.

    ARRUNTIUS. He is our monster, forfeited to vice
So far, as no racked virtue can redeem him;
His loathèd person fouler than all crimes,
An Emp'ror only in his lusts. Retired,
From all regard of his own fame or Rome's,
Into an obscure island, where he lives,
Acting his tragedies with a comic face,
Amidst his rout of Chaldees; spending hours,
Days, weeks, and months, in the unkind abuse
Of grave astrology, to the bane of men,
Casting the scope of men's nativities,
And having found aught worthy in their fortune,
Kill, or precipitate them in the sea,
And boast he can mock fate. Nay, muse not, these
Are far from ends of evil, scarce degrees.
He hath his slaughter-house at Capreae,
Where he doth study murder as an art;
And they are dearest in his grace, that can
Devise the deepest tortures. Thither, too,
He hath his boys and beauteous girls ta'en up
Out of our noblest houses, the best formed,
Best nurtured, and most modest; what's their good,
Serves to provoke his bad. Some are allured,
Some threatened; others, by their friends detained,
Are ravished hence like captives, and, in sight
Of their most grievèd parents, dealt away
Unto his spintries, sellaries, and slaves,
Masters of strange and new commented lusts,
For which wise nature hath not left a name.

To this—what most strikes us, and bleeding Rome—
He is, with all his craft, become the ward
To his own vassal, a stale catamite,
Whom he, upon our low and suffering necks,
Hath raised from excrement to side the gods,
And have his proper sacrifice in Rome;
Which Jove beholds, and yet will sooner rive
A senseless oak with thunder than his trunk!

Re-enter LACO, *with* POMPONIUS *and* MINUTIUS.

LACO. These letters make men doubtful what t'
     expect,
Whether his coming or his death.
     POMPONIUS.   Troth, both;
And which comes soonest, thank the gods for.
     ARRUNTIUS.   —List,
Their talk is Caesar; I would hear all voices.
     MINUTIUS. One day he's well, and will return to
     Rome;
The next day sick, and knows not when to hope it.
     LACO. True; and today one of Sejanus' friends
Honoured by special writ, and on the morrow
Another punished——
     POMPONIUS.   By more special writ.
     MINUTIUS. This man receives his praises of Sejanus,
A second but slight mention, a third none,
A fourth, rebukes; and thus he leaves the Senate
Divided and suspended, all uncertain.
     LACO. These forkèd tricks, I understand 'em not;
Would he would tell us whom he loves or hates,
That we might follow without fear or doubt.
     ARRUNTIUS. —Good Heliotrope! Is this your honest
     man?
Let him be yours so still. He is my knave.
     POMPONIUS. I cannot tell, Sejanus still goes on,
And mounts, we see: new statues are advanced,

Fresh leaves of titles, large inscriptions read,
His fortune sworn by, himself new gone out
Caesar's colleague in the fifth consulship;
More altars smoke to him than all the gods.
What would we more?

    ARRUNTIUS. —That the dear smoke would choke
      him,
That would I more.

    LEPIDUS.   Peace, good Arruntius.

    LATIARIS. But there are letters come, they say,
      ev'n now,
Which do forbid that last.

    MINUTIUS.   Do you hear so?

    LACO.   Yes.

    POMPONIUS. By Pollux, that's the worst!

    ARRUNTIUS.   —By Hercules, best!

    MINUTIUS. I did not like the sign, when Regulus,
Whom all we know no friend unto Sejanus,
Did, by Tiberius' so precise command,
Succeed a fellow in the consulship.
It boded somewhat.

    POMPONIUS.   Not a mote. His partner,
Fulcinius Trio, is his own, and sure.
Here comes Terentius. He can give us more.

             Enter TERENTIUS. *They whisper with him.*

    LEPIDUS. I'll ne'er believe but Caesar hath some
      scent
Of bold Sejanus' footing. These cross-points
Of varying letters and opposing consuls,
Mingling his honours and his punishments,
Feigning now ill, now well, raising Sejanus
And then depressing him, as now of late
In all reports we have it, cannot be
Empty of practice. 'Tis Tiberius' art.
For having found his favourite grown too great,
And with his greatness strong; that all the soldiers

Are, with their leaders, made at his devotion;
That almost all the Senate are his creatures,
Or hold on him their main dependences,
Either for benefit, or hope, or fear;
And that himself hath lost much of his own,
By parting unto him; and, by th' increase
Of his rank lusts and rages, quite disarmed
Himself of love, or other public means,
To dare an open contestation—
His subtlety hath chose this doubling line,
To hold him even in: not so to fear him,
As wholly put him out, and yet give check
Unto his farther boldness. In meantime,
By his employments, makes him odious
Unto the staggering rout, whose aid in fine
He hopes to use, as sure; who, when they sway,
Bear down, o'erturn all objects in their way.

ARRUNTIUS. You may be a Lynceus, Lepidus; yet I
See no such cause, but that a politic tyrant,
Who can so well disguise it, should have ta'en
A nearer way: feigned honest, and come home
To cut his throat by law.

LEPIDUS.   Ay, but his fear
Would ne'er be masked, albe his vices were.

POMPONIUS. His lordship then is still in grace?

TERENTIUS.   Assure you,
Never in more, either of grace or power.

POMPONIUS. The gods are wise and just.

ARRUNTIUS.   —The fiends they are,
To suffer thee belie 'em.

TERENTIUS.   I have here
His last and present letters, where he writes him,
The 'partner of his cares' and 'his Sejanus'——

LACO. But is that true, it is prohibited
To sacrifice unto him?

TERENTIUS.   Some such thing

Caesar makes scruple of, but forbids it not,
No more than to himself; says he could wish
It were forborne to all.

LACO.   Is it no other?

TERENTIUS. No other, on my trust. For your more
  surety,
Here is that letter too.

ARRUNTIUS.   —How easily
Do wretched men believe what they would have!
Looks this like plot?

LEPIDUS.   Noble Arruntius, stay.

LACO. He names him here without his titles.

LEPIDUS.   —Note!

ARRUNTIUS. Yes, and come off your notable fool.
  I will.

LACO. No other than Sejanus.

POMPONIUS.   That's but haste
In him that writes. Here he gives large amends.

MARCUS. And with his own hand written?

POMPONIUS.   Yes.

LACO.   Indeed?

TERENTIUS. Believe it, gentlemen, Sejanus' breast
Never received more full contentments in,
Than at this present.

POMPONIUS.   Takes he well th' escape
Of young Caligula, with Macro?

TERENTIUS.   Faith,
At the first air it somewhat troubled him.

LEPIDUS. —Observe you?

ARRUNTIUS.   Nothing. Riddles. Till I see
Sejanus struck, no sound thereof strikes me.
                        Exeunt ARRUNTIUS *and* LEPIDUS.

POMPONIUS. I like it not. I muse h' would not
  attempt
Somewhat against him in the consulship,
Seeing the people 'gin to favour him.

TERENTIUS. He doth repent it now; but h' has employed
Pagonianus after him; and he holds
That correspondence there, with all that are
Near about Caesar, as no thought can pass
Without his knowledge, thence, in act to front him.

POMPONIUS. I gratulate the news.

LACO. But how comes Macro
So in trust and favour with Caligula?

POMPONIUS. O, sir, he has a wife, and the young Prince
An appetite; he can look up and spy
Flies in the roof, when there are fleas i' bed;
And hath a learnèd nose t' assure his sleeps.
Who, to be favoured of the rising sun,
Would not lend little of his waning moon?
It is the saf'st ambition. Noble Terentius!

TERENTIUS. The night grows fast upon us. At your service. *Exeunt.*

Chorus of Musicians.

ACT FIVE. SCENE ONE

Sejanus' house

Enter SEJANUS.

SEJANUS. Swell, swell, my joys, and faint not to declare
Yourselves as ample as your causes are.
I did not live till now: this my first hour,
Wherein I see my thoughts reached by my power.

But this, and gripe my wishes! Great and high,
The world knows only two, that's Rome and I.
My roof receives me not; 'tis air I tread;
And, at each step, I feel my advancèd head
Knock out a star in heav'n! Reared to this height,
All my desires seem modest, poor, and slight,
That did before sound impudent. 'Tis place,
Not blood, discerns the noble and the base.
Is there not something more than to be Caesar?
Must we rest there? It irks t' have come so far,
To be so near a stay. Caligula,
Would thou stood'st stiff, and many in our way!
Winds lose their strength, when they do empty fly,
Unmet of woods or buildings; great fires die,
That want their matter to withstand them. So,
It is our grief, and will be our loss, to know
Our power shall want opposites; unless
The gods, by mixing in the cause, would bless
Our fortune with their conquest. That were worth
Sejanus' strife, durst fates but bring it forth.

Enter TERENTIUS.

TERENTIUS. Safety to great Sejanus!
SEJANUS.   Now, Terentius?
TERENTIUS. Hears not my lord the wonder?
SEJANUS.   Speak it; no.
TERENTIUS. I meet it violent in the people's
      mouths,
Who run in routs to Pompey's theatre,
To view your statue, which, they say, sends forth
A smoke, as from a furnace, black and dreadful.
   SEJANUS. Some traitor hath put fire in.—You, go
      see,
And let the head be taken off, to look
What 'tis. Some slave hath practised an imposture,
To stir the people.—How now! why return you?

Enter SATRIUS *and* NATTA.

SATRIUS. The head, my lord, already is ta'en off,
I saw it; and, at op'ning, there lept out
A great and monstrous serpent.

SEJANUS.   Monstrous! why?
Had it a beard, and horns? no heart? a tongue
Forkèd as flattery? Looked it of the hue,
To such as live in great men's bosoms? Was
The spirit of it Macro's?

NATTA.   May it please
The most divine Sejanus, in my days—
And by his sacred fortune, I affirm it—
I have not seen a more extended, grown,
Foul, spotted, venomous, ugly——

SEJANUS.   O the fates!
What a wild muster's here of attributes,
T' express a worm, a snake!

TERENTIUS.   But how that should
Come there, my lord!

SEJANUS.   What, and you too, Terentius!
I think you mean to make 't a prodigy
In your reporting.

TERENTIUS.   Can the wise Sejanus
Think Heav'n hath meant it less?

SEJANUS.   O superstition!
Why, then the falling of our bed, that brake
This morning, burdened with the populous weight
Of our expecting clients, to salute us;
Or running of the cat betwixt our legs,
As we set forth unto the Capitol,
Were prodigies.

TERENTIUS.   I think them ominous;
And would they had not happened! As, today,
The fate of some your servants: who declining
Their way, not able, for the throng, to follow,

Slipped down the Gemonies, and brake their necks!
Besides, in taking your last augury,
No prosperous bird appeared; but croaking ravens
Flagged up and down, and from the sacrifice
Flew to the prison, where they sat all night,
Beating the air with their obstreperous beaks!
I dare not counsel, but I could entreat
That great Sejanus would attempt the gods
Once more with sacrifice.

SEJANUS.   What excellent fools
Religion makes of men! Believes Terentius,
If these were dangers—as I shame to think them—
The gods could change the certain course of fate?
Or, if they could, they would now, in a moment,
For a beef's fat, or less, be bribed t' invert
Those long decrees? Then think the gods, like flies,
Are to be taken with the steam of flesh,
Or blood, diffused about their altars; think
Their power as cheap as I esteem it small.
Of all the throng that fill th' Olympian hall,
And, without pity, lade poor Atlas' back,
I know not that one deity, but Fortune,
To whom I would throw up, in begging smoke,
One grain of incense; or whose ear I'd buy
With thus much oil. Her I indeed adore;
And keep her grateful image in my house,
Sometimes belonging to a Roman king,
But now called mine, as by the better style.
To her I care not if, for satisfying
Your scrupulous fancies, I go offer. Bid
Our priest prepare us honey, milk, and poppy,
His masculine odours, and night-vestments. Say
Our rites are instant, which performed, you'll see
How vain, and worthy laughter, your fears be.

                           Exeunt.

ACT FIVE. SCENE TWO

Before Sejanus' house

Enter COTTA *and* POMPONIUS.

COTTA. Pomponius, whither in such speed?

POMPONIUS.   I go
To give my lord Sejanus notice——

COTTA.   What?

POMPONIUS. Of Macro.

COTTA.   Is he come?

POMPONIUS.   Entered but now
The house of Regulus.

COTTA.   The opposite Consul!

POMPONIUS. Some half hour since.

COTTA.   And by night, too! Stay, sir,
I'll bear you company.

POMPONIUS.   Along, then——

                                              Exeunt.

ACT FIVE. SCENE THREE

Regulus' house

Enter MACRO, REGULUS, *and* SERVUS.

MACRO. 'Tis Caesar's will to have a frequent
    Senate;
And therefore must your edict lay deep mulct
On such as shall be absent.

REGULUS.   So it doth.—
Bear it my fellow Consul to adscribe.

MACRO. And tell him it must early be proclaimed,
The place Apollo's temple.   *Exit* SERVUS.

REGULUS.   That's remembered.

MACRO. And at what hour?

REGULUS.   Yes.

MACRO.   You do forget
To send one for the Provost of the Watch.

REGULUS. I have not. Here he comes.

Enter LACO.

MACRO.   Gracinus Laco,
You are a friend most welcome; by and by,
I'll speak with you.—You must procure this list
Of the praetorian cohorts, with the names
Of the centurions, and their tribunes.

REGULUS.   Ay.

MACRO. —I bring you letters, and a health from
    Caesar.

LACO. Sir, both come well.

MACRO.   —And hear you? with your note,
Which are the eminent men, and most of action.

REGULUS. That shall be done you, too.

MACRO.   Most worthy Laco,
Caesar salutes you. *Exit* REGULUS. Consul! Death
    and furies!
Gone now? The argument will please you, sir.
Ho! Regulus! The anger of the gods
Follow his diligent legs, and overtake 'em,
In likeness of the gout!

Re-enter REGULUS.

          O, good my lord,
We lacked you present; I would pray you send
Another to Fulcinius Trio, straight,

To tell him you will come and speak with him.
The matter we'll devise, to stay him there,
While I with Laco do survey the watch.—
What are your strengths, Gracinus?

LACO.   Seven cohorts.

                                        Exit REGULUS.

MACRO. You see what Caesar writes, and—Gone
    again!
H' has sure a vein of mercury in his feet.
Know you what store of the praetorian soldiers
Sejanus holds about him, for his guard?

LACO. I cannot the just number, but I think
Three centuries.

MACRO.   Three? Good.

LACO.   At most, not four.

MACRO. And who be those centurions?

LACO.   That the Consul
Can best deliver you.

MACRO.   When he's away?
Spite on his nimble industry! Gracinus,
You find what place you hold, there, in the trust
Of royal Caesar?

LACO.   Ay, and I am——

MACRO.   Sir,
The honours there proposed are but beginnings
Of his great favours.

LACO.   They are more——

MACRO.   I heard him,
When he did study what to add.

LACO.   My life
And all I hold——

MACRO.   You were his own first choice;
Which doth confirm as much as you can speak,
And will, if we succeed, make more——Your guards
Are seven cohorts, you say?

LACO.   Yes.

MACRO. Those we must
Hold still in readiness and undischarged.

LACO. I understand so much. But how it can——

MACRO. Be done without suspicion, you'll object?

Re-enter REGULUS.

REGULUS. What's that?

LACO. The keeping of the watch in arms,
When morning comes.

MACRO. The Senate shall be met, and set
So early in the temple, as all mark
Of that will be avoided.

REGULUS. If we need,
We have commission to possess the Palace,
Enlarge Prince Drusus, and make him our chief.

MACRO. —That secret would have burnt his rever-
end mouth,
Had he not spit it out now. By the gods,
You carry things too——Let me borrow a man
Or two, to bear these——That of freeing Drusus,
Caesar projected as the last and utmost;
Not else to be remembered.

Enter SERVI.

REGULUS. Here are servants.

MACRO. These to Arruntius, these to Lepidus;
This bear to Cotta, this to Latiaris.
If they demand you of me, say I have ta'en
Fresh horse and am departed. *Exeunt* SERVI. You,
my lord,
To your colleague, and be you sure to hold him
With long narration of the new, fresh favours,
Meant to Sejanus, his great patron; I,
With trusted Laco, here, are for the guards;
Then to divide. For night hath many eyes,
Whereof, though most do sleep, yet some are spies.
Exeunt.

ACT FIVE. SCENE FOUR

A shrine in Sejanus' house

Enter PRAECONES, FLAMEN, TUBICINES, TIBICINES,
MINISTRI, SEJANUS, TERENTIUS, SATRIUS, NATTA, *&c.*

PRAECONES. 'Be all profane far hence; fly, fly far
   off!
Be absent far; far hence be all profane!'
   TUBICINES *and* TIBICINES *sound while the* FLAMEN
   washeth.
   FLAMEN. 'We have been faulty, but repent us now;
And bring pure hands, pure vestments, and pure
   minds.'
   1ST MINISTER. 'Pure vessels.'
   2ND MINISTER.   'And pure off'rings.'
   3RD MINISTER.   'Garlands pure.'
   FLAMEN. 'Bestow your garlands, and, with rever-
   ence, place
The vervain on the altar.'
   PRAECONES.   'Favour your tongues.'
   FLAMEN. 'Great mother Fortune, queen of human
   state,
Rectress of action, arbitress of fate,
To whom all sway, all power, all empire bows,
Be present, and propitious to our vows!'
   PRAECONES. 'Favour it with your tongues.'
   MINISTRI. 'Be present, and propitious to our vows!'
   While they sound again, the FLAMEN *takes of the
   honey with his finger, and tastes; then ministers
   to all the rest. So of the milk, in an earthen
   vessel he deals about. Which done, he sprinkleth
   upon the altar milk, then imposeth the honey*

and kindleth his gums, and after censing about
the altar, placeth his censer thereon, into which
they put several branches of poppy, and the
music ceasing, say all:

'Accept our off'ring, and be pleased, great goddess.'

TERENTIUS. See, see, the image stirs!

SATRIUS.   And turns away!

NATTA. Fortune averts her face!

FLAMEN.   Avert, you gods,
The prodigy. Still! still! Some pious rite
We have neglected. Yet, Heav'n, be appeased.
And be all tokens false and void, that speak
Thy present wrath!

SEJANUS.   Be thou dumb, scrupulous priest;
And gather up thyself, with these thy wares,
Which I, in spite of thy blind mistress, or
Thy juggling mystery, religion, throw
Thus scornèd on the earth! *Overturns the statue.*

                              Nay, hold thy look
Averted till I woo thee turn again,
And thou shalt stand to all posterity,
Th' eternal game and laughter, with thy neck
Writhed to thy tail, like a ridiculous cat.
Avoid these fumes, these superstitious lights,
And all these coz'ning ceremonies; you,
Your pure and spicèd conscience!

      Exeunt FLAMEN, PRAECONES, TUBICINES, TIBICINES,
      MINISTRI, &c.

                              I, the slave
And mock of fools, scorn on my worthy head!
That have been titled, and adored a god;
Yea, sacrificed unto, myself, in Rome,
No less than Jove; and I be brought to do
A peevish giglot rites! Perhaps the thought
And shame of that, made Fortune turn her face,
Knowing herself the lesser deity,

And but my servant. Bashful queen, if so,
Sejanus thanks thy modesty.—Who's that?

Enter POMPONIUS *and* MINUTIUS.

POMPONIUS. His fortune suffers, till he hears my
    news.
I've waited here too long.—Macro, my lord——
    SEJANUS. Speak lower and withdraw.
    TERENTIUS.   Are these things true?
    MINUTIUS. Thousands are gazing at it in the streets.
    SEJANUS. What's that?
    TERENTIUS.   Minutius tells us here, my lord,
That, a new head being set upon your statue,
A rope is since found wreathed about it! And
But now, a fiery meteor, in the form
Of a great ball, was seen to roll along
The troubled air, where yet it hangs unperfect,
Th' amazing wonder of the multitude!
    SEJANUS. No more. That Macro's come is more
    than all!
    TERENTIUS. Is Macro come?
    POMPONIUS.   I saw him.
    TERENTIUS.   Where? With whom?
    POMPONIUS. With Regulus.
    SEJANUS.   Terentius—
    TERENTIUS.   My lord.
    SEJANUS. Send for the tribunes; we will straight
    have up
More of the soldiers for our guard. *Exit* TERENTIUS.
    Minutius,
We pray you go for Cotta, Latiaris,
Trio the Consul, or what senators
You know are sure, and ours. *Exit* MINUTIUS. You,
    my good Natta,
For Laco, Provost of the Watch. *Exit* NATTA. Now,
    Satrius,

The time of proof comes on. Arm all our servants,
And without tumult. *Exit* SATRIUS. You, Pomponius,
Hold some good correspondence with the Consul;
Attempt him, noble friend. *Exit* POMPONIUS. These
    things begin
To look like dangers, now, worthy my fates.
Fortune, I see thy worst. Let doubtful states,
And things uncertain hang upon thy will;
Me surest death shall render certain still.
Yet, why is now my thought turned toward death,
Whom fates have let go on so far in breath,
Unchecked or unreproved? I, that did help
To fell the lofty cedar of the world,
Germanicus; that, at one stroke, cut down
Drusus, that upright elm; withered his vine;
Laid Silius and Sabinus, two strong oaks,
Flat on the earth; besides those other shrubs,
Cordus and Sosia, Claudia Pulchra,
Furnius and Gallus, which I have grubbed up;
And since, have set my axe so strong and deep
Into the root of spreading Agrippine;
Lopped off and scattered her proud branches, Nero,
Drusus, and Caius too, although replanted.
If you will, Destinies, that after all,
I faint now ere I touch my period,
You are but cruel; and I already have done
Things great enough. All Rome hath been my slave;
The Senate sat an idle looker-on
And witness of my power, when I have blushed
More to command, than it to suffer. All
The fathers have sat ready and prepared
To give me empire, temples, or their throats,
When I would ask 'em; and, what crowns the top,
Rome, Senate, people, all the world have seen
Jove but my equal, Caesar but my second.
'Tis then your malice, Fates, who—but your own—
Envy and fear t' have any power long known. *Exit.*

ACT FIVE. SCENE FIVE

A hall in Sejanus' house

Enter TERENTIUS *and* TRIBUNES.

TERENTIUS. Stay here. I'll give his lordship you are
come.

Enter MINUTIUS, *with* COTTA *and* LATIARIS.

MINUTIUS. Marcus Terentius, pray you tell my
lord,
Here's Cotta and Latiaris.

TERENTIUS. Sir, I shall. *Exit.*

COTTA. *Conferring their letters.* My letter is the
very same with yours;
Only requires me to be present there,
And give my voice to strengthen his design.

LATIARIS. Names he not what it is?

COTTA. No, nor to you.

LATIARIS. 'Tis strange and singular doubtful!

COTTA. So it is.
It may be all is left to lord Sejanus.

Enter NATTA *and* LACO.

NATTA. Gentlemen, where's my lord?

TRIBUNE. We wait him here.

COTTA. The provost Laco! What's the news?

LATIARIS. My lord——

Enter SEJANUS.

SEJANUS. Now, my right dear, noble, and trusted
friends,
How much I am a captive to your kindness!

Most worthy Cotta, Latiaris; Laco,
Your valiant hand; and, gentlemen, your loves.
I wish I could divide myself unto you;
Or that it lay within our narrow powers,
To satisfy for so enlargèd bounty.
Gracinus, we must pray you, hold your guards
Unquit, when morning comes. Saw you the Consul?

MINUTIUS. Trio will presently be here, my lord.

COTTA. They are but giving order for the edict,
To warn the Senate

SEJANUS.　　　　How! the Senate?

LACO.　　　　　　　　　Yes.
This morning in Apollo's temple——

COTTA.　　　　　　　　We
Are charged by letter to be there, my lord.

SEJANUS. By letter? Pray you let's see!

LATIARIS.　　　　　　Knows not his lordship?

COTTA. It seems so!

SEJANUS. A Senate warned, without my knowledge,
And on this sudden? Senators by letters
Required to be there! Who brought these?

COTTA.　　　　　　　　Macro.

SEJANUS. Mine enemy! And when?

COTTA.　　　　　　This midnight.

SEJANUS.　　　　　　　Time,
With every other circumstance, doth give
It hath some strain of engine in 't!—How now?

Enter SATRIUS.

SATRIUS. My lord, Sertorius Macro is without,
Alone, and prays t' have private conference
In business of high nature with your lordship,
He says to me, and which regards you much.

SEJANUS. Let him come here.

SATRIUS.　　　　Better, my lord, withdraw.

You will betray what store and strength of friends
Are now about you, which he comes to spy.

SEJANUS. Is he not armed?

SATRIUS. We'll search him.

SEJANUS. No, but take
And lead him to some room, where you concealed
May keep a guard upon us. *Exit* SATRIUS. Noble
Laco,
You are our trust; and till our own cohorts
Can be brought up, your strengths must be our
guard.
Now, good Minutius, honoured Latiaris,
Most worthy and my most unwearied friends,
I return instantly.

Salutes TRIBUNES *humbly, and exit.*

LATIARIS. Most worthy lord!

COTTA. His lordship is turned instant kind, methinks;
I've not observed it in him heretofore.

1ST TRIBUNE. 'Tis true, and it becomes him nobly.

MINUTIUS. I
Am rapt withal.

2ND TRIBUNE. By Mars, he has my lives,
Were they a million, for this only grace.

LACO. Ay, and to name a man!

LATIARIS. As he did me!

MINUTIUS. And me!

LATIARIS. Who would not spend his life
and fortunes
To purchase but the look of such a lord?

LACO. He that would nor be lord's fool, nor the
world's. *The scene closes.*

ACT FIVE. SCENE SIX

An inner room in Sejanus' house

Enter SEJANUS, MACRO, *and* SATRIUS.

SEJANUS. Macro! most welcome, as most coveted
friend!
Let me enjoy my longings. When arrived you?
MACRO. About the noon of night.
SEJANUS.   Satrius, give leave.
                           Exit SATRIUS.

MACRO. I have been, since I came, with both the
Consuls,
On a particular design from Caesar.
SEJANUS. How fares it with our great and royal
master?
MACRO. Right plentifully well, as with a prince
That still holds out the great proportion
Of his large favours, where his judgment hath
Made once divine election; like the god
That wants not, nor is wearied to bestow
Where merit meets his bounty, as it doth
In you, already the most happy, and ere
The sun shall climb the south, most high Sejanus.
Let not my lord be amused. For to this end
Was I by Caesar sent for, to the isle,
With special caution to conceal my journey;
And thence had my dispatch as privately
Again to Rome; charged to come here by night,
And only to the Consuls make narration
Of his great purpose, that the benefit
Might come more full and striking, by how much
It was less worked for or aspired by you,
Or least informèd to the common thought.

SEJANUS. What may this be? Part of myself, dear
    Macro,
If good, speak out, and share with your Sejanus.
    MACRO. If bad, I should for ever loathe myself
To be the messenger to so good a lord.
I do exceed my instructions to acquaint
Your lordship with thus much, but 'tis my venture
On your retentive wisdom; and because
I would no jealous scruple should molest
Or rack your peace of thought. For I assure
My noble lord, no senator yet knows
The business meant; though all by several letters
Are warnèd to be there, and give their voices,
Only to add unto the state and grace
Of what is purposed.
    SEJANUS.   You take pleasure, Macro,
Like a coy wench, in torturing your lover.
What can be worth this suffering?
    MACRO.   That which follows:
The tribunicial dignity and power,
Both which Sejanus is to have this day
Conferred upon him, and by public Senate.
    SEJANUS. Fortune, be mine again! th'hast satisfied
For thy suspected loyalty.
    MACRO.   My lord,
I have no longer time; the day approacheth,
And I must back to Caesar.
    SEJANUS.   Where's Caligula?
    MACRO. That I forgot to tell your lordship. Why,
He lingers yonder about Capreae,
Disgraced; Tiberius hath not seen him yet.
He needs would thrust himself to go with me,
Against my wish or will; but I have quitted
His forward trouble, with as tardy note
As my neglect or silence could afford him.
Your lordship cannot now command me aught,
Because I take no knowledge that I saw you;

But I shall boast to live to serve your lordship.
And so take leave.
 SEJANUS.   Honest and worthy Macro,
Your love and friendship.—Who's there? Satrius,
Attend my honourable friend forth. *Exit* MACRO. O,
How vain and vile a passion is this fear!
What base, uncomely things it makes men do!
Suspect their noblest friends, as I did this,
Flatter poor enemies, entreat their servants,
Stoop, court, and catch at the benevolence
Of creatures unto whom, within this hour,
I would not have vouchsafed a quarter-look,
Or piece of face! By you that fools call gods,
Hang all the sky with your prodigious signs,
Fill earth with monsters, drop the scorpion down
Out of the zodiac, or the fiercer lion,
Shake off the loosened globe from her long hinge,
Roll all the world in darkness, and let loose
Th' enragèd winds to turn up groves and towns!
When I do fear again, let me be struck
With forkèd fire, and unpitied die!
Who fears, is worthy of calamity.   *Exit.*

ACT FIVE. SCENE SEVEN

A hall in Sejanus' house

TERENTIUS, MINUTIUS, LACO, COTTA, LATIARIS, *as before. Enter* POMPONIUS, REGULUS, *and* TRIO.

 POMPONIUS. Is not my lord here?
 TERENTIUS.   Sir, he will be straight.
 COTTA. What news, Fulcinius Trio?

TRIO. Good, good tidings,
But keep it to yourself. My lord Sejanus
Is to receive this day, in open Senate,
The tribunicial dignity.

COTTA. Is't true?

TRIO. No words—not to your thought—but, sir,
believe it.

LATIARIS. What says the Consul?

COTTA. —Speak it not again.—
He tells me that today my lord Sejanus——

TRIO. —I must entreat you, Cotta, on your honour
Not to reveal it.

COTTA. On my life, sir.

LATIARIS. Say.

COTTA. Is to receive the tribunicial power.
But, as you are an honourable man,
Let me conjure you not to utter it;
For it is trusted to me with that bond.

LATIARIS. I am Harpocrates.

TERENTIUS. Can you assure it?

POMPONIUS. The Consul told it me, but keep it
close.

MINUTIUS. Lord Latiaris, what's the news?

LATIARIS. I'll tell you,
But you must swear to keep it secret——

Enter SEJANUS.

SEJANUS. I knew the Fates had on their distaff left
More of our thread, than so.

REGULUS. Hail, great Sejanus!

TRIO. Hail, the most honoured!

COTTA. Happy!

LATIARIS. High Sejanus!

SEJANUS. Do you bring prodigies, too?

TRIO. May all presage

Turn to those fair effects, whereof we bring
Your lordship news.

REGULUS. May't please my lord withdraw.

SEJANUS. Yes. *To some that stand by.* I will speak
    with you anon.

TERENTIUS. My lord,
What is your pleasure for the tribunes?

SEJANUS. Why,
Let 'em be thanked and sent away.

MINUTIUS. My lord——

LACO. Will't please my lordship to command
    me——

SEJANUS. No.
You're troublesome.

MINUTIUS. The mood is changed.

1ST TRIBUNE. Not speak!

2ND TRIBUNE. Nor look!

LACO. Ay. He is wise, will make him friends
Of such who never love but for their ends. *Exeunt.*

ACT FIVE. SCENE EIGHT

Before the Temple of Apollo

Enter ARRUNTIUS *and* LEPIDUS, *divers other* SENATORS
passing by them.

ARRUNTIUS. Ay, go, make haste, take heed you be
    not last
To tender your all-hail in the wide hall
Of huge Sejanus. Run a lictor's pace;
Stay not to put your robes on; but away,
With the pale, troubled ensigns of great friendship

Stamped i' your face!—Now, Marcus Lepidus,
You still believe your former augury?
Sejanus must go downward? You perceive
His wane approaching fast?

    LEPIDUS.   Believe me, Lucius,
I wonder at this rising.

    ARRUNTIUS.   Ay, and that we
Must give our suffrage to it? You will say
It is to make his fall more steep and grievous?
It may be so. But think it, they that can
With idle wishes 'say to bring back time.
In cases desperate, all hope is crime.
See, see! what troops of his officious friends
Flock to salute my lord, and start before
My great, proud lord, to get a lord-like nod!
Attend my lord unto the Senate House!
Bring back my lord! like servile ushers, make
Way for my lord! proclaim his idol lordship,
More than ten criers, or six noise of trumpets!
Make legs, kiss hands, and take a scattered hair
From my lord's eminent shoulder!

    SANQUINIUS *and* HATERIUS *pass over the stage.*
                          See, Sanquinius,
With his slow belly, and his dropsy! look,
What toiling haste he makes! Yet here's another,
Retarded with the gout, will be afore him.
Get thee Liburnian porters, thou gross fool,
To bear thy obsequious fatness, like thy peers.
They're met! The gout returns, and his great car-
    riage.

    LICTORS, REGULUS, TRIO, SEJANUS, SATRIUS *and*
    other SENATORS *pass over the stage.*

    LICTORS. Give way, make place, room for the
Consul!

SANQUINIUS. Hail,
Hail, great Sejanus!

HATERIUS. Hail, my honoured lord!

ARRUNTIUS. —We shall be marked anon, for our
not-hail.

LEPIDUS. That is already done.

ARRUNTIUS. It is a note.
Of upstart greatness, to observe, and watch
For these poor trifles, which the noble mind
Neglects and scorns.

LEPIDUS. Ay, and they think themselves
Deeply dishonoured where they are omitted,
As if they were necessities that helped
To the perfection of their dignities;
And hate the men that but refrain 'em.

ARRUNTIUS. O,
There is a farther cause of hate. Their breasts
Are guilty, that we know their obscure springs
And base beginnings; thence the anger grows.
On. Follow.

Enter MACRO *and* LACO.

MACRO. When all are entered, shut the temple
doors,
And bring your guards up to the gate.

LACO. I will.

MACRO. If you shall hear commotion in the
Senate,
Present yourself, and charge on any man
Shall offer to come forth.

LACO. I am instructed. *Exeunt.*

ACT FIVE. SCENE NINE

The Temple of Apollo

Enter HATERIUS, TRIO, SANQUINIUS, COTTA, REGULUS, SEJANUS, POMPONIUS, LATIARIS, LEPIDUS, ARRUNTIUS, *other* SENATORS, PRAECONES *and* LICTORS.

HATERIUS. How well his lordship looks today!

TRIO. As if
He had been born or made for this hour's state.

COTTA. Your fellow Consul's come about, methinks?

TRIO. Ay, he is wise.

SANQUINIUS. Sejanus trusts him well.

TRIO. Sejanus is a noble, bounteous lord.

HATERIUS. He is so, and most valiant.

LATIARIS. And most wise.

SANQUINIUS. He's everything.

LATIARIS. Worthy of all, and more
Than bounty can bestow.

TRIO. This dignity
Will make him worthy.

POMPONIUS. Above Caesar.

SANQUINIUS. Tut,
Caesar is but the rector of an isle;
He of the Empire.

TRIO. Now he will have power
More to reward than ever.

COTTA. Let us look
We be not slack in giving him our voices.

LATIARIS. Not I.

SANQUINIUS. Nor I.

COTTA. The readier we seem
To propagate his honours, will more bind
His thoughts to ours.

HATERIUS. I think right with your lordship.
It is the way to have us hold our places.

SANQUINIUS. Ay, and get more.

LATIARIS. More office and more titles.

POMPONIUS. I will not lose the part I hope to share
In these his fortunes, for my patrimony.

LATIARIS. See how Arruntius sits, and Lepidus!

TRIO. Let 'em alone; they will be marked anon.

1ST SENATOR. I'll do with others.

2ND SENATOR. So will I.

3RD SENATOR. And I.
Men grow not in the state but as they are planted
Warm in his favours.

COTTA. Noble Sejanus!

HATERIUS. Honoured Sejanus!

LATIARIS. Worthy and great Sejanus!

ARRUNTIUS. —Gods! how the sponges open, and
        take in,
And shut again! Look, look, is not he blest
That gets a seat in eye-reach of him? more,
That comes in ear-, or tongue-reach? O, but most
Can claw his subtle elbow, or with a buzz
Fly-blow his ears?

PRAETOR. Proclaim the Senate's peace,
And give last summons by the edict.

PRAECO. Silence!
In the name of Caesar and the Senate, silence!

'Memmius Regulus and Fulcinius Trio, Consuls,
these present kalends of June, with the first light,
shall hold a Senate in the temple of Apollo Palatine.
All that are fathers, and are registered fathers, that
have right of entering the Senate, we warn or com-

mand you be frequently present; take knowledge
the business is the commonwealth's. Whosoever is
absent, his fine or mulct will be taken; his excuse
will not be taken.'

TRIO. Note who are absent, and record their
names.

REGULUS. Fathers Conscript, may what I am to
utter
Turn good and happy for the commonwealth!
And thou, Apollo, in whose holy house
We here are met, inspire us all with truth
And liberty of censure, to our thought!
The majesty of great Tiberius Caesar
Propounds to this grave Senate the bestowing
Upon the man he loves, honoured Sejanus,
The tribunicial dignity and power.
Here are his letters, signèd with his signet.
What pleaseth now the fathers to be done?

SENATORS. Read, read 'em; open, publicly read
'em.

COTTA. Caesar hath honoured his own greatness
much
In thinking of this act.

TRIO.   It was a thought
Happy, and worthy Caesar.

LATIARIS.   And the lord
As worthy it, on whom it is directed!

HATERIUS. Most worthy!

SANQUINIUS.   Rome did never boast the virtue
That could give envy bounds, but his: Sejanus——

1ST SENATOR. Honoured and noble!

2ND SENATOR.   Good and great Sejanus!

ARRUNTIUS. —O most tame slavery and fierce flattery!

PRAECO. Silence!

The epistle is read.

'Tiberius Caesar to the Senate, greeting:

If you, Conscript Fathers, with your children, be in health, it is abundantly well; we, with our friends here, are so. The care of the commonwealth, howsoever we are removed in person, cannot be absent to our thought; although oftentimes, even to princes most present, the truth of their own affairs is hid, than which nothing falls out more miserable to a state, or makes the art of governing more difficult. But since it hath been our easeful happiness to enjoy both the aids and industry of so vigilant a Senate, we profess to have been the more indulgent to our pleasures, not as being careless of our office, but rather secure of the necessity. Neither do these common rumours, of many and infamous libels published against our retirement, at all afflict us; being born more out of men's ignorance than their malice; and will, neglected, find their own grave quickly, whereas, too sensibly acknowledged, it would make their obloquy ours. Nor do we desire their authors, though found, be censured, since in a free state, as ours, all men ought to enjoy both their minds and tongues free.'

ARRUNTIUS. The lapwing, the lapwing!

PRAECO. 'Yet in things which shall worthily and more near concern the majesty of a prince, we shall fear to be so unnaturally cruel to our own fame, as to neglect them. True it is, Conscript Fathers, that we have raised Sejanus from obscure and almost unknown gentry—'

SENATORS. How! how!

PRAECO. 'To the highest and most conspicuous point of greatness, and, we hope, deservingly; yet not without danger: it being a most bold hazard in that sovereign who, by his particular love to one, dares adventure the hatred of all his other subjects.'

ARRUNTIUS. —This touches, the blood turns.

PRAECO. 'But we affy in your loves and understandings, and do no way suspect the merit of our Sejanus to make our favours offensive to any.'

SENATORS. Oh! good, good.

PRAECO. 'Though we could have wished his zeal had run a calmer course against Agrippina and our nephews, howsoever the openness of their actions declared them delinquents; and that he would have remembered no innocence is so safe, but it rejoiceth to stand in the sight of mercy. The use of which in us he hath so quite taken away toward them, by his loyal fury, as now our clemency would be thought but wearied cruelty, if we should offer to exercise it.'

ARRUNTIUS. —I thank him, there I looked for 't. A good fox!

PRAECO. 'Some there be that would interpret this his public severity to be particular ambition, and that, under a pretext of service to us, he doth but remove his own lets; alleging the strengths he hath made to himself, by the praetorian soldiers, by his faction in court and Senate, by the offices he holds himself and confers on others, his popularity and dependents, his urging and almost driving us to this our unwilling retirement, and lastly, his aspiring to be our son-in-law.'

SENATORS. This 's strange!

ARRUNTIUS. —I shall anon believe your vultures, Marcus.

PRAECO. 'Your wisdoms, Conscript Fathers, are able to examine and censure these suggestions. But

were they left to our absolving voice, we durst pronounce them, as we think them, most malicious.'

SENATORS. O, he has restored all, list!

PRAECO. 'Yet are they offered to be averred,
and on the lives of the informers. What we should
say, or rather what we should not say, lords of the
Senate, if this be true, our gods and goddesses confound us if we know! Only we must think we have
placed our benefits ill; and conclude that, in our
choice, either we were wanting to the gods, or the
gods to us.'

The SENATORS *shift their places.*

ARRUNTIUS. —The place grows hot; they shift.

PRAECO. 'We have not been covetous, honourable fathers, to change; neither is it now any new
lust that alters our affection, or old loathing, but
those needful jealousies of state that warn wiser
princes hourly to provide their safety, and do teach
them how learned a thing it is to beware of the
humblest enemy—much more of those great ones,
whom their own employed favours have made fit
for their fears.'

1ST SENATOR. Away.

2ND SENATOR.   Sit farther.

COTTA.   Let's remove——

ARRUNTIUS. —Gods! how the leaves drop off, this
little wind!

PRAECO. 'We therefore desire that the offices he
holds be first seized by the Senate, and himself suspended from all exercise of place or power——'

SENATORS. How!

SANQUINIUS.   By your leave.

ARRUNTIUS. —Come, porpoise. Where's Haterius?
His gout keeps him most miserably constant.
Your dancing shows a tempest.

SEJANUS.   Read no more.

REGULUS. Lords of the Senate, hold your seats.—
Read on.

SEJANUS. These letters they are forged.

REGULUS.   A guard! Sit still.

Enter LACO *with the* LICTORS.

ARRUNTIUS. There's change!

REGULUS.   Bid silence, and read forward.

PRAECO. Silence—'And himself suspended from
all exercise of place or power, but till due and mature trial be made of his innocency, which yet we
can faintly apprehend the necessity to doubt. If,
Conscript Fathers, to your more searching wisdoms,
there shall appear farther cause—or of farther pro-
ceeding, either to seizure of lands, goods, or more—
it is not our power that shall limit your authority,
or our favour that must corrupt your justice; either
were dishonourable in you, and both uncharitable
to ourself. We would willingly be present with your
counsels in this business, but the danger of so potent
a faction—if it should prove so—forbids our attempting it, except one of the Consuls would be entreated
for our safety, to undertake the guard of us home;
then we should most readily adventure. In the meantime, it shall not be fit for us to importune so judicious a Senate, who know how much they hurt the
innocent, that spare the guilty; and how grateful a
sacrifice to the gods is the life of an ungrateful person. We reflect not in this on Sejanus,—notwithstanding, if you keep an eye upon him—and there
is Latiaris, a senator, and Pinnarius Natta, two of
his most trusted ministers, and so professed, whom
we desire not to have apprehended, but as the necessity of the cause exacts it.'

REGULUS. A guard on Latiaris!

ARRUNTIUS.   —O, the spy,

The reverend spy is caught! Who pities him?
Reward, sir, for your service: now, you ha' done
Your property, you see what use is made!

Exeunt LATIARIS *and* NATTA *guarded.*

Hang up the instrument.

SEJANUS. Give leave.

LACO. Stand, stand!
He comes upon his death, that doth advance
An inch toward my point.

SEJANUS. Have we no friends here?

ARRUNTIUS. Hushed! Where now are all the hails
and acclamations?

Enter MACRO.

MACRO. Hail to the Consuls, and this noble Senate!

SEJANUS. —Is Macro here? O, thou art lost, Sejanus!

MACRO. Sit still, and unaffrighted, reverend
fathers.
Macro, by Caesar's grace, the new-made provost,
And now possessed of the praetorian bands,
An honour late belonged to that proud man,
Bids you be safe; and to your constant doom
Of his deservings, offers you the surety
Of all the soldiers, tribunes, and centurions,
Received in our command.

REGULUS. Sejanus, Sejanus,
Stand forth, Sejanus!

SEJANUS. Am I called?

MACRO. Ay, thou,
Thou insolent monster, art bid stand.

SEJANUS. Why, Macro,
It hath been otherwise between you and I!
This court, that knows us both, hath seen a differ-
ence,
And can, if it be pleased to speak, confirm
Whose insolence is most.

MACRO. Come down, Typhoeus.
If mine be most, lo, thus I make it more—
Kick up thy heels in air, tear off thy robe,
Play with thy beard and nostrils! Thus 'tis fit—
And no man take compassion of thy state—
To use th' ungrateful viper, tread his brains
Into the earth.

REGULUS. Forbear.

MACRO. If I could lose
All my humanity now, 'twere well to torture
So meriting a traitor. Wherefore, fathers,
Sit you amazed and silent? and not censure
This wretch, who, in the hour he first rebelled
'Gainst Caesar's bounty, did condemn himself?
Phlegra, the field where all the sons of earth
Mustered against the gods, did ne'er acknowledge
So proud and huge a monster.

REGULUS. Take him hence.
And all the gods guard Caesar!

TRIO. Take him hence.

HATERIUS. Hence!

COTTA. To the dungeon with him!

SANQUINIUS. He deserves it.

SENATORS. Crown all our doors with bays.

SANQUINIUS. And let an ox
With gilded horns and garlands, straight be led
Unto the Capitol.

HATERIUS. And sacrificed
To Jove, for Caesar's safety.

TRIO. All our gods
Be present still to Caesar!

COTTA. Phoebus!

SANQUINIUS. Mars!

HATERIUS. Diana!

SANQUINIUS. Pallas!

SENATORS.   Juno, Mercury,
All guard him!
 MACRO.   Forth, thou prodigy of men.
       Exit SEJANUS, *guarded.*
 COTTA. Let all the traitor's titles be defaced.
 TRIBUNES. His images and statues be pulled down.
 HATERIUS. His chariot-wheels be broken.
 ARRUNTIUS.   And the legs
Of the poor horses, that deservèd naught,
Let them be broken too!
  Exeunt LICTORS, PRAECONES, MACRO, REGULUS,
   TRIO, HATERIUS, *and* SANQUINIUS.
 LEPIDUS.   O violent change,
And whirl of men's affections!
 ARRUNTIUS.   Like as both
Their bulks and souls were bound on Fortune's
  wheel,
And must act only with her motion!
 LEPIDUS. Who would depend upon the popular
  air,
Or voice of men, that have today beheld
That which, if all the gods had foredeclared,
Would not have been believed, Sejanus' fall?
He that this morn rose proudly as the sun,
And, breaking through a mist of clients' breath,
Came on, as gazed at and admired as he,
When superstitious Moors salute his light!
That had our servile nobles waiting him
As common grooms, and hanging on his look
No less than human life on destiny!
That had men's knees as frequent as the gods,
And sacrifices more than Rome had altars—
And this man fall! Fall? Ay, without a look
That durst appear his friend, or lend so much
Of vain relief, to his changed state, as pity!

ARRUNTIUS. They that before, like gnats, played in
    his beams,
And thronged to circumscribe him, now not seen,
Nor deign to hold a common seat with him!
Others, that waited him unto the Senate,
Now inhumanely ravish him to prison!
Whom but this morn they followed as their lord,
Guard through the streets, bound like a fugitive!
Instead of wreaths give fetters, strokes for stoops,
Blind shame for honours, and black taunts for
    titles!
Who would trust slippery chance?
LEPIDUS.   They that would make
Themselves her spoil; and foolishly forget,
When she doth flatter, that she comes to prey.
Fortune, thou hadst no deity, if men
Had wisdom; we have placèd thee so high,
By fond belief in thy felicity.
    SENATORS *shout within.* The gods guard Caesar!
        All the gods guard Caesar!

Re-enter MACRO, REGULUS, *and divers* SENATORS.

MACRO. Now, great Sejanus, you that awed the
    state,
And sought to bring the nobles to your whip;
That would be Caesar's tutor, and dispose
Of dignities and offices; that had
The public head still bare to your designs,
And made the general voice to echo yours;
That looked for salutations twelve score off,
And would have pyramids, yea, temples, reared
To your huge greatness; now you lie as flat
As was your pride advanced!
REGULUS.   Thanks to the gods!
    SENATORS. And praise to Macro, that hath savèd
        Rome!

Liberty, liberty, liberty! Lead on,
And praise to Macro, that hath savèd Rome!

Exeunt all but ARRUNTIUS *and* LEPIDUS.

ARRUNTIUS. I prophesy, out of this Senate's flattery,
That this new fellow, Macro, will become
A greater prodigy in Rome than he
That now is fall'n.

Enter TERENTIUS.

TERENTIUS.   O you whose minds are good,
And have not forced all mankind from your breasts;
That yet have so much stock of virtue left,
To pity guilty states, when they are wretched:
Lend your soft ears to hear, and eyes to weep,
Deeds done by men, beyond the acts of furies.
The eager multitude—who never yet
Knew why to love or hate, but only pleased
T' express their rage of power—no sooner heard
The murmur of Sejanus in decline,
But with that speed and heat of appetite,
With which they greedily devour the way
To some great sports, or a new theatre,
They filled the Capitol, and Pompey's Cirque;
Where, like so many mastiffs biting stones,
As if his statues now were sensitive
Of their wild fury, first, they tear them down;
Then fast'ning ropes, drag them along the streets,
Crying in scorn, 'This, this was that rich head
Was crowned with garlands, and with odours! this
That was in Rome so reverencèd!' Now
The furnace and the bellows shall to work,
The great Sejanus crack, and piece by piece
Drop i' the founder's pit.

LEPIDUS.   O popular rage!

TERENTIUS. The whilst the Senate, at the Temple
    of Concord,

Make haste to meet again, and thronging cry,
'Let us condemn him, tread him down in water,
While he doth lie upon the bank. Away!'
Where some, more tardy, cry unto their bearers,
'He will be censured ere we come. Run, knaves!'
And use that furious diligence, for fear
Their bondmen should inform against their slack-
    ness,
And bring their quaking flesh unto the hook.
The rout, they follow with confusèd voice,
Crying they're glad, say they could ne'er abide him;
Inquire what man he was, what kind of face,
What beard he had, what nose, what lips? protest
They ever did presage h' would come to this,
They never thought him wise nor valiant; ask
After his garments, when he dies, what death?
And not a beast of all the herd demands
What was his crime, or who were his accusers,
Under what proof or testimony he fell?
There came, says one, a huge, long-worded letter
From Capreae against him. Did there so?
O, they are satisfied; no more.

  LEPIDUS.   Alas!
They follow Fortune, and hate men condemned,
Guilty or not.

  ARRUNTIUS. But had Sejanus thrived
In his design, and prosperously oppressed
The old Tiberius, then, in that same minute,
These very rascals, that now rage like furies,
Would have proclaimed Sejanus Emperor.

  LEPIDUS. But what hath followed?

  TERENTIUS.   Sentence by the Senate,
To lose his head; which was no sooner off,
But that and the unfortunate trunk were seized
By the rude multitude; who not content
With what the forward justice of the state

Officiously had done, with violent rage
Have rent it limb from limb. A thousand heads,
A thousand hands, ten thousand tongues and voices,
Employed at once in several acts of malice!
Old men not staid with age, virgins with shame,
Late wives with loss of husbands, mothers of chil-
    dren,
Losing all grief in joy of his sad fall,
Run quite transported with their cruelty!
These mounting at his head, these at his face,
These digging out his eyes, those with his brain
Sprinkling themselves, their houses and their friends;
Others are met, have ravished thence an arm,
And deal small pieces of the flesh for favours;
These with a thigh; this hath cut off his hands,
And this his feet; these fingers, and these toes;
That hath his liver, he his heart; there wants
Nothing but room for wrath, and place for hatred!
What cannot oft be done, is now o'erdone.
The whole, and all of what was great Sejanus,
And, next to Caesar, did possess the world,
Now torn and scattered, as he needs no grave—
Each little dust covers a little part—
So lies he nowhere, and yet often buried!

Enter NUNTIUS.

ARRUNTIUS. More of Sejanus?

NUNTIUS.   Yes.

LEPIDUS.   What can be added?
We know him dead.

NUNTIUS.   Then there begin your pity.
There is enough behind to melt ev'n Rome
And Caesar into tears; since never slave
Could yet so highly offend, but tyranny,
In torturing him, would make worth lamenting.
A son and daughter to the dead Sejanus—

Of whom there is not now so much remaining
As would give fast'ning to the hangman's hook—
Have they drawn forth for farther sacrifice,
Whose tenderness of knowledge, unripe years,
And childish, silly innocence was such,
As scarce would lend them feeling of their danger:
The girl so simple, as she often asked
Where they would lead her? for what cause they
    dragged her?
Cried she would do no more; that she could take
Warning with beating. And because our laws
Admit no virgin immature to die,
The wittily and strangely cruel Macro
Delivered her to be deflow'red and spoiled
By the rude lust of the licentious hangman,
Then to be strangled with her harmless brother.

    LEPIDUS. O act most worthy hell, and lasting
      night,
To hide it from the world!

    NUNTIUS.   Their bodies thrown
Into the Gemonies—I know not how,
Or by what accident returned—the mother,
Th' expulsèd Apicata, finds them there;
Whom when she saw lie spread on the degrees,
After a world of fury on herself,
Tearing her hair, defacing of her face,
Beating her breasts and womb, kneeling amazed,
Crying to heaven, then to them; at last,
Her drownèd voice gat up above her woes.
And with such black and bitter execrations
As might affright the gods, and force the sun
Run backward to the east—nay, make the old
Deformèd chaos rise again, t' o'erwhelm
Them, us, and all the world—she fills the air;
Upbraids the heavens with their partial dooms;
Defies their tyrannous powers; and demands,

What she, and those poor innocents have trans-
gressed,
That they must suffer such a share in vengeance,
Whilst Livia, Lygdus, and Eudemus live,
Who, as she says, and firmly vows to prove it
To Caesar and the Senate, poisoned Drusus?

LEPIDUS. Confederates with her husband!

NUNTIUS.   Ay.

LEPIDUS.   Strange act!

ARRUNTIUS. And strangely opened! What says now
my monster,
The multitude? They reel now, do they not?

NUNTIUS. Their gall is gone, and now they 'gin to
weep
The mischief they have done.

ARRUNTIUS.   I thank 'em, rogues!

NUNTIUS. Part are so stupid, or so flexible,
As they believe him innocent; all grieve.
And some, whose hands yet reek with his warm
blood,
And gripe the part which they did tear of him,
Wish him collected and created new.

LEPIDUS. How Fortune plies her sports, when she
begins
To practise 'em! pursues, continues, adds,
Confounds with varying her impassioned moods!

ARRUNTIUS. Dost thou hope, Fortune, to redeem
thy crimes,
To make amends for thy ill placèd favours
With these strange punishments? Forbear, you
things
That stand upon the pinnacles of state,
To boast your slippery height; when you do fall,
You pash yourselves in pieces, ne'er to rise,
And he that lends you pity is not wise.

TERENTIUS. Let this example move the insolent
man
Not to grow proud and careless of the gods.
It is an odious wisdom to blaspheme,
Much more to slighten, or deny their powers.
For whom the morning saw so great and high,
Thus low and little, 'fore the even doth lie.

Exeunt.

II. COMEDY

II. COMEDY

Volpone, or the Fox

VOLPONE, *a magnifico*

MOSCA, *his parasite*

VOLTORE, *an advocate*

CORBACCIO, *an old gentleman*

CORVINO, *a merchant*

BONARIO, *son to* CORBACCIO

SIR POLITIC WOULDBE

PEREGRINE, *a gentleman traveller*

NANO, *a dwarf*

CASTRONE, *an eunuch*

ANDROGYNO, *an hermaphrodite*

GREGE, *or mob*

COMMENDATORI, *officers of justice*

MERCATORI, *three merchants*

AVOCATORI, *four magistrates*

NOTARIO, *the register*

LADY WOULDBE, SIR POLITIC'S *wife*

CELIA, CORVINO'S *wife*

Servitori, Women, &c.

The Scene: VENICE

THE ARGUMENT

V olpone, childless, rich, feigns sick, despairs,
O ffers his state to hopes of several heirs,
L ies languishing. His parasite receives
P resents of all, assures, deludes, then weaves
O ther cross-plots, which ope themselves, are told.
N ew tricks for safety are sought; they thrive; when, bold,
E ach tempts the other again, and all are sold.

PROLOGUE

Now luck God send us, and a little wit
    Will serve to make our play hit;
According to the palates of the season,
    Here is rhyme not empty of reason.
This we were bid to credit from our poet,
    Whose true scope, if you would know it,
In all his poems still hath been this measure,
    To mix profit with your pleasure;
And not as some, whose throats their envy failing,
    Cry hoarsely, all he writes is railing;
And when his plays come forth, think they can flout
    them
    With saying he was a year about them.
To these there needs no lie but this his creature,
    Which was two months since no feature.
And though he dares give them five lives to mend it,
    'Tis known, five weeks fully penned it,
From his own hand, without a coadjutor,
    Novice, journeyman, or tutor.
Yet thus much I can give you as a token
    Of his play's worth: no eggs are broken,
Nor quaking custards with fierce teeth affrighted,
    Wherewith your rout are so delighted;
Nor hales he in a gull, old ends reciting,
    To stop gaps in his loose writing;
With such a deal of monstrous and forced action,
    As might make Bedlam a faction.
Nor made he his play for jests stol'n from each
    table,
    But makes jests to fit his fable;
And so presents quick comedy, refined
    As best critics have designed.

The laws of time, place, persons he observeth;
  From no needful rule he swerveth.
All gall and copperas from his ink he draineth;
  Only a little salt remaineth,
Wherewith he'll rub your cheeks till, red with
    laughter,
  They shall look fresh a week after.

VOLPONE, or THE FOX

ACT ONE

Volpone's house

Enter VOLPONE *and* MOSCA.

VOLPONE. Good morning to the day; and next, my
    gold!—
Open the shrine, that I may see my saint.—
Hail the world's soul, and mine! More glad than is
The teeming earth to see the longed-for sun
Peep through the horns of the celestial ram,
Am I, to view thy splendour darkening his;
That lying here, amongst my other hoards,
Show'st like a flame by night, or like the day
Struck out of chaos, when all darkness fled
Unto the centre. O thou son of Sol,
But brighter than thy father, let me kiss,
With adoration, thee, and every relic
Of sacred treasure in this blessèd room,
Well did wise poets, by thy glorious name,
Title that age which they would have the best;
Thou being the best of things; and far transcending
All style of joy, in children, parents, friends,
Or any other waking dream on earth.
Thy looks when they to Venus did ascribe,
They should have giv'n her twenty thousand Cupids;
Such are thy beauties and our loves! Dear saint,
Riches, the dumb god, that giv'st all men tongues!
That canst do nought, and yet mak'st men do all
    things.
The price of souls! even hell, with thee to boot,
Is made worth heaven! Thou art virtue, fame,

Honour, and all things else. Who can get thee,
He shall be noble, valiant, honest, wise——
  MOSCA. And what he will, sir. Riches are in
    fortune
A greater good than wisdom is in nature.
  VOLPONE. True, my beloved Mosca. Yet I glory
More in the cunning purchase of my wealth,
Than in the glad possession, since I gain
No common way. I use no trade, no venture;
I wound no earth with ploughshares, fat no beasts
To feed the shambles; have no mills for iron,
Oil, corn, or men, to grind 'em into powder;
I blow no subtle glass, expose no ships
To threat'nings of the furrow-facèd sea;
I turn no monies in the public bank,
Nor usure private——
  MOSCA.   No sir, nor devour
Soft prodigals. You shall ha' some will swallow
A melting heir as glibly as your Dutch
Will pills of butter, and ne'er purge for 't;
Tear forth the fathers of poor families
Out of their beds, and coffin them alive
In some kind, clasping prison, where their bones
May be forthcoming when the flesh is rotten.
But your sweet nature doth abhor these courses;
You loathe the widow's or the orphan's tears
Should wash your pavements, or their piteous cries
Ring in your roofs, and beat the air for vengeance.
  VOLPONE. Right, Mosca, I do loathe it.
  MOSCA.   And, besides, sir,
You are not like the thresher that doth stand
With a huge flail, watching a heap of corn,
And, hungry, dares not taste the smallest grain,
But feeds on mallows and such bitter herbs;
Nor like the merchant who hath filled his vaults
With Romagnía, and rich Candian wines,

Yet drinks the lees of Lombard's vinegar.
You will not lie in straw, whilst moths and worms
Feed on your sumptuous hangings and soft beds.
You know the use of riches, and dare give now
From that bright heap, to me, your poor observer,
Or to your dwarf, or your hermaphrodite,
Your eunuch, or what other household trifle
Your pleasure allows maint'nance——
VOLPONE.   Hold thee, Mosca,
Take of my hand; thou strik'st on truth in all,
And they are envious term thee parasite.
Call forth my dwarf, my eunuch, and my fool,
And let 'em make me sport! *Exit* MOSCA. What
        should I do
But cocker up my genius, and live free
To all delights my fortune calls me to?
I have no wife, no parent, child, ally,
To give my substance to; but whom I make
Must be my heir, and this makes men observe me.
This draws new clients daily to my house,
Women and men of every sex and age,
That bring me presents, send me plate, coin, jewels,
With hope that when I die—which they expect
Each greedy minute—it shall then return
Tenfold upon them; whilst some, covetous
Above the rest, seek to engross me whole,
And counter-work the one unto the other,
Contend in gifts, as they would seem, in love.
All which I suffer, playing with their hopes,
And am content to coin 'em into profit,
And look upon their kindness, and take more,
And look on that; still bearing them in hand,
Letting the cherry knock against their lips,
And draw it by their mouths, and back again.—
How now!

Re-enter MOSCA *with* NANO, ANDROGYNO, *and*
        CASTRONE.

NANO. 'Now, room for fresh gamesters, who do
    will you to know,
They do bring you neither play nor university show;
And therefore do entreat you that whatsoever they
    rehearse
May not fare a whit the worse for the false pace of
    the verse.
If you wonder at this, you will wonder more ere we
    pass,
For know, here is enclosed the soul of Pythagoras,
That juggler divine, as hereafter shall follow:
Which soul, fast and loose, sir, came first from
    Apollo,
And was breathed into Aethalides, Mercurius's son,
Where it had the gift to remember all that ever was
    done.
From thence it fled forth, and made quick trans-
    migration
To goldy-locked Euphorbus, who was killed in good
    fashion
At the siege of old Troy, by the cuckold of Sparta.
Hermotimus was next—I find it in my charta—
To whom it did pass, where no sooner it was missing,
But with one Pyrrhus of Delos it learned to go
    a-fishing;
And thence did it enter the Sophist of Greece.
From Pythagore, she went into a beautiful piece,
Hight Aspasia the Meretrix; and the next toss of
    her
Was again of a whore she became a philosopher,
Crates the Cynic, as itself doth relate it.
Since, kings, knights, and beggars, knaves, lords, and
    fools gat it,

Besides ox and ass, camel, mule, goat, and brock,
In all which it hath spoke, as in the cobbler's cock.
But I come not here to discourse of that matter,
Or his one, two, or three, or his great oath, "By
    Quater!"
His musics, his trigon, his golden thigh,
Or his telling how elements shift. But I
Would ask how of late thou hast suffered transla-
    tion,
And shifted thy coat in these days of reformation?'
    ANDROGYNO. 'Like one of the reformèd, a fool, as
      you see,
Counting all old doctrine heresy.'
    NANO. 'But not on thine own forbid meats hast
      thou ventured?'
    ANDROGYNO. 'On fish, when first a Carthusian I
      entered.'
    NANO. 'Why, then thy dogmatical silence hath left
      thee?'
    ANDROGYNO. 'Of that an obstreperous lawyer be-
      reft me.'
    NANO. 'O wonderful change! When Sir Lawyer
      forsook thee,
For Pythagore's sake, what body then took thee?'
    ANDROGYNO. 'A good dull mule.'
    NANO.   'And how! by that means
Thou wert brought to allow of the eating of beans?'
    ANDROGYNO. 'Yes.'
    NANO. 'But from the mule into whom didst thou
      pass?'
    ANDROGYNO. 'Into a very strange beast, by some
      writers called an ass;
By others a precise, pure, illuminate brother,
Of those devour flesh, and sometimes one another;
And will drop you forth a libel, or a sanctified lie,
Betwixt every spoonful of a nativity-pie.'

NANO. 'Now quit thee, 'fore Heaven, of that profane nation,
And gently report thy next transmigration.'

ANDROGYNO. 'To the same that I am.'

NANO.   'A creature of delight,
And, what is more than a fool, an hermaphrodite!
Now, pr'ythee, sweet soul, in all thy variation,
Which body wouldst thou choose to take up thy
station?'

ANDROGYNO. 'Troth, this I am in; even here would
I tarry.'

NANO. ' 'Cause here the delight of each sex thou
canst vary?'

ANDROGYNO. 'Alas, those pleasures be stale and
forsaken.
No, 'tis your fool wherewith I am so taken,
The only one creature that I can call blessèd;
For all other forms I have proved most distressèd.'

NANO. 'Spoke true as thou wert in Pythagoras still.
This learned opinion we celebrate will,
Fellow eunuch, as behoves us, with all our wit and
art,
To dignify that whereof ourselves are so great and
special a part.'

VOLPONE. Now, very, very pretty! Mosca, this
Was thy invention?

MOSCA.   If it please my patron,
Not else.

VOLPONE. It doth, good Mosca.

MOSCA.   Then it was, sir.

SONG.

'Fools they are the only nation
   Worth men's envy or admiration,

Free from care or sorrow taking,
Selves and others merry making.
All they speak or do is sterling.
Your fool he is your great man's darling,
And your ladies' sport and pleasure;
Tongue and bauble are his treasure.
E'en his face begetteth laughter,
And he speaks truth free from slaughter.
He's the grace of every feast,
And sometimes the chiefest guest;
Hath his trencher and his stool,
When wit waits upon the fool.
   O, who would not be
    He, he, he?'

                        One knocks without.

VOLPONE. Who's that? Away!—Look, Mosca.—Fool,
  begone!

     Exeunt NANO, CASTRONE, *and* ANDROGYNO.

MOSCA. 'Tis Signior Voltore, the advocate;
I know him by his knock.

VOLPONE.   Fetch me my gown,
My furs, and nightcaps; say my couch is changing;
And let him entertain himself a while
Without i' th' gallery. *Exit* MOSCA. Now, now my
  clients
Begin their visitation! Vulture, kite,
Raven, and gorcrow, all my birds of prey,
That think me turning carcase, now they come.
I am not for 'em yet. *Re-enter* MOSCA. How now!
  the news?

MOSCA. A piece of plate, sir.

VOLPONE.   Of what bigness?

MOSCA.   Huge,
Massy, and antique, with your name inscribed
And arms engraven.

VOLPONE. Good! and not a fox
Stretched on the earth, with fine delusive sleights,
Mocking a gaping crow? ha, Mosca?
    MOSCA. Sharp, sir.
    VOLPONE. Give me my furs. Why dost thou laugh
      so, man?
    MOSCA. I cannot choose, sir, when I apprehend
What thoughts he has, without, now as he walks:
That this might be the last gift he should give;
That this would fetch you; if you died today,
And gave him all, what he should be tomorrow;
What large return would come of all his ventures;
How he should worshipped be, and reverenced;
Ride with his furs and foot-cloths, waited on
By herds of fools and clients; have clear way
Made for his mule, as lettered as himself;
Be called the great and learned advocate;
And then concludes there's nought impossible.
    VOLPONE. Yes, to be learnèd, Mosca.
    MOSCA. O no, rich
Implies it. Hood an ass with reverend purple,
So you can hide his two ambitious ears,
And he shall pass for a cathedral doctor.
    VOLPONE. My caps, my caps, good Mosca. Fetch
      him in.
    MOSCA. Stay, sir, your ointment for your eyes.
    VOLPONE. That's true;
Dispatch, dispatch. I long to have possession
Of my new present.
    MOSCA. That and thousands more
I hope to see you lord of.
    VOLPONE. Thanks, kind Mosca.
    MOSCA. And that, when I am lost in blended dust,
And hundred such as I am, in succession——
    VOLPONE. Nay, that were too much, Mosca.
    MOSCA. You shall live
Still to delude these harpies.

VOLPONE.   Loving Mosca!
'Tis well; my pillow now, and let him enter.
                                        Exit MOSCA.
Now, my feigned cough, my phthisic, and my gout,
My apoplexy, palsy, and catarrhs,
Help, with your forcèd functions, this my posture,
Wherein this three year I have milked their hopes.
He comes; I hear him—Uh! uh! uh! uh! O!

            Re-enter MOSCA *with* VOLTORE.

  MOSCA. You still are what you were, sir. Only you,
Of all the rest, are he, commands his love;
And you do wisely to preserve it thus
With early visitation, and kind notes
Of your good meaning to him, which, I know,
Cannot but come most grateful.—Patron! sir!
Here's Signior Voltore is come——
  VOLPONE.   What say you?
  MOSCA. Sir, Signior Voltore is come this morning
To visit you.
  VOLPONE. I thank him.
  MOSCA.   And hath brought
A piece of antique plate, bought of Saint Mark,
With which he here presents you.
  VOLPONE.   He is welcome.
Pray him to come more often.
  MOSCA.   Yes.
  VOLTORE.   What says he?
  MOSCA. He thanks you, and desires you see him
    often.
  VOLPONE. Mosca.
  MOSCA.   My patron!
  VOLPONE.   Bring him near; where is he?
I long to feel his hand.
  MOSCA.   The plate is here, sir.
  VOLTORE. How fare you, sir?

VOLPONE. I thank you, Signior Voltore.
Where is the plate? mine eyes are bad.

VOLTORE. I'm sorry
To see you still thus weak.

MOSCA. —That he is not weaker.

VOLPONE. You are too munificent.

VOLTORE. No, sir, would to Heaven,
I could as well give health to you, as that plate!

VOLPONE. You give, sir, what you can. I thank you.
Your love
Hath taste in this, and shall not be unanswered.
I pray you see me often.

VOLTORE. Yes, I shall, sir.

VOLPONE. Be not far from me.

MOSCA. Do you observe that, sir?

VOLPONE. Hearken unto me still. It will concern
you.

MOSCA. You are a happy man, sir; know your
good.

VOLPONE. I cannot now last long——

MOSCA. —You are his heir, sir.

VOLTORE. Am I?

VOLPONE. I feel me going—Uh! uh! uh! uh!
I'm sailing to my port—Uh! uh! uh! uh!
And I am glad I am so near my haven.

MOSCA. Alas, kind gentleman! Well, we must all
go——

VOLTORE. But, Mosca——

MOSCA. Age will conquer.

VOLTORE. Pray thee, hear me.
Am I inscribed his heir for certain?

MOSCA. Are you!
I do beseech you, sir, you will vouchsafe
To write me i' your family. All my hopes
Depend upon your worship. I am lost,
Except the rising sun do shine on me.

VOLTORE. It shall both shine and warm thee,
Mosca.

MOSCA.   Sir,
I am a man that hath not done your love
All the worst offices: here I wear your keys,
See all your coffers and your caskets locked,
Keep the poor inventory of your jewels,
Your plate, and monies; am your steward, sir,
Husband your goods here.

VOLTORE.   But am I sole heir?

MOSCA. Without a partner, sir, confirmed this
morning;
The wax is warm yet, and the ink scarce dry
Upon the parchment.

VOLTORE.   Happy, happy me!
By what good chance, sweet Mosca?

MOSCA.   Your desert, sir;
I know no second cause.

VOLTORE.   Thy modesty
Is loath to know it; well, we shall requite it.

MOSCA. He ever liked your course, sir; that first
took him.
I oft have heard him say how he admired
Men of your large profession, that could speak
To every cause, and things mere contraries,
Till they were hoarse again, yet all be law;
That, with most quick agility, could turn
And re-turn, make knots and undo them,
Give forkèd counsel, take provoking gold
On either hand, and put it up. These men,
He knew, would thrive with their humility.
And, for his part, he thought he should be blest
To have his heir of such a suffering spirit,
So wise, so grave, of so perplexed a tongue,
And loud withal, that would not wag, nor scarce
Lie still, without a fee; when every word

Your worship but lets fall, is a sequine!

         Another knocks.

—Who's that? One knocks; I would not have you
  seen, sir.

And yet—pretend you came and went in haste;

I'll fashion an excuse. And, gentle sir,

When you do come to swim in golden lard,

Up to the arms in honey, that your chin

Is borne up stiff with fatness of the flood,

Think on your vassal; but remember me.

I ha' not been your worst of clients.

  VOLTORE.   Mosca—

  MOSCA. When will you have your inventory
   brought, sir?

Or see a copy of the will?—Anon!—

I'll bring 'em to you, sir. Away, begone,

Put business i' your face.   *Exit* VOLTORE.

  VOLPONE.   Excellent, Mosca!

Come hither, let me kiss thee.

  MOSCA.   Keep you still, sir.

Here is Corbaccio.

  VOLPONE.   Set the plate away.

The vulture's gone, and the old raven's come.

  MOSCA. Betake you to your silence, and your
   sleep.—

Stand there and multiply.—Now we shall see

A wretch who is indeed more impotent

Than this can feign to be, yet hopes to hop

Over his grave.

      Enter CORBACCIO.

    Signior Corbaccio!

You're very welcome, sir.

  CORBACCIO.   How does your patron?

  MOSCA. Troth, as he did, sir; no amends.

CORBACCIO. What! mends he?

MOSCA. No, sir, he is rather worse.

CORBACCIO. That's well. Where is he?

MOSCA. Upon his couch, sir, newly fall'n asleep.

CORBACCIO. Does he sleep well?

MOSCA. No wink, sir, all this night
Nor yesterday, but slumbers.

CORBACCIO. Good! he should take
Some counsel of physicians: I have brought him
An opiate here, from mine own doctor.

MOSCA. He will not hear of drugs.

CORBACCIO. Why? I myself
Stood by while't was made, saw all th' ingredients;
And know it cannot but most gently work.
My life for his, 'tis but to make him sleep.

VOLPONE. —Ay, his last sleep, if he would take it.

MOSCA. Sir,
He has no faith in physic.

CORBACCIO. Say you? say you?

MOSCA. He has no faith in physic; he does think
Most of your doctors are the greater danger,
And worse disease, t' escape. I often have
Heard him protest that your physician
Should never be his heir.

CORBACCIO. Not I his heir?

MOSCA. Not your physician, sir.

CORBACCIO. O no, no, no.
I do not mean it.

MOSCA. No, sir, nor their fees
He cannot brook; he says they flay a man
Before they kill him.

CORBACCIO. Right, I do conceive you.

MOSCA. And then, they do it by experiment;
For which the law not only doth absolve 'em,
But gives them great reward; and he is loath
To hire his death so.

CORBACCIO.   It is true, they kill
With as much licence as a judge.
    MOSCA.   Nay, more;
For he but kills, sir, where the law condemns,
And these can kill him too.
    CORBACCIO.   Ay, or me,
Or any man. How does his apoplex?
Is that strong on him still?
    MOSCA.   Most violent.
His speech is broken and his eyes are set,
His face drawn longer than 'twas wont——
    CORBACCIO.   How? how?
Stronger than he was wont?
    MOSCA.   No, sir; his face
Drawn longer than 'twas wont.
    CORBACCIO.   O, good!
    MOSCA.   His mouth
Is ever gaping, and his eyelids hang.
    CORBACCIO.   Good.
    MOSCA. A freezing numbness stiffens all his joints,
And makes the colour of his flesh like lead.
    CORBACCIO.   'Tis good.
    MOSCA. His pulse beats slow and dull.
    CORBACCIO.   Good symptoms still.
    MOSCA. And from his brain——
    CORBACCIO.   Ha! how? not from his brain?
    MOSCA. Yes, sir, and from his brain——
    CORBACCIO.   I conceive you; good.
    MOSCA. Flows a cold sweat, with a continual
    rheum,
Forth the resolvèd corners of his eyes.
    CORBACCIO. Is't possible? Yet I am better, ha!
How does he with the swimming of his head?
    MOSCA. O, sir, 'tis past the scotomy; he now
Hath lost his feeling, and hath left to snort.
You hardly can perceive him, that he breathes.

CORBACCIO. Excellent, excellent! sure I shall outlast him!
This makes me young again a score of years.

MOSCA. I was a-coming for you, sir.

CORBACCIO.   Has he made his will?
What has he giv'n me?

MOSCA.   No, sir.

CORBACCIO.   Nothing! ha?

MOSCA. He has not made his will, sir.

CORBACCIO.   Oh, oh, oh.
What then did Voltore, the lawyer, here?

MOSCA. He smelt a carcase, sir, when he but heard
My master was about his testament;
As I did urge him to it, for your good——

CORBACCIO. He came unto him, did he? I thought
so.

MOSCA. Yes, and presented him this piece of plate.

CORBACCIO. To be his heir?

MOSCA.   I do not know, sir.

CORBACCIO.   True,
I know it too.

MOSCA.   By your own scale, sir.

CORBACCIO.   Well,
I shall prevent him yet. See, Mosca, look,
Here I have brought a bag of bright sequines,
Will quite weigh down his plate.

MOSCA.   Yea, marry, sir,
This is true physic, this your sacred medicine!
No talk of opiates to this great elixir!

CORBACCIO. 'Tis aurum palpabile, if not potabile.

MOSCA. It shall be ministered to him in his bowl.

CORBACCIO. Ay, do, do, do.

MOSCA.   Most blessed cordial!
This will recover him.

CORBACCIO.   Yes, do, do, do.

MOSCA. I think it were not best, sir.

CORBACCIO. What?

MOSCA. To recover him.

CORBACCIO. O no, no, no, by no means.

MOSCA. Why, sir, this
Will work some strange effect, if he but feel it.

    CORBACCIO. 'Tis true, therefore forbear; I'll take
    my venture.
Give me 't again.

    MOSCA. At no hand, pardon me;
You shall not do yourself that wrong, sir. I
Will so advise you, you shall have it all.

    CORBACCIO. How?

    MOSCA. All, sir, 'tis your right, your own; no man
Can claim a part. 'Tis yours without a rival,
Decreed by destiny.

    CORBACCIO. How, how, good Mosca?

    MOSCA. I'll tell you, sir. This fit he shall recover—

    CORBACCIO. I do conceive you.

    MOSCA. And on first advantage
Of his gained sense, will I re-importune him
Unto the making of his testament;
And show him this.

    CORBACCIO. Good, good.

    MOSCA. 'Tis better yet,
If you will hear, sir.

    CORBACCIO. Yes, with all my heart.

    MOSCA. Now would I counsel you, make home
    with speed;
There, frame a will, whereto you shall inscribe
My master your sole heir.

    CORBACCIO. And disinherit
My son?

    MOSCA. O, sir, the better; for that colour
Shall make it much more taking.

    CORBACCIO. O, but colour?

    MOSCA. This will, sir, you shall send it unto me.

Now, when I come to enforce, as I will do,
Your cares, your watchings, and your many prayers,
Your more than many gifts, your this day's present;
And last, produce your will, where, without thought
Or least regard unto your proper issue,
A son so brave and highly meriting,
The stream of your diverted love hath thrown you
Upon my master, and made him your heir;
He cannot be so stupid, or stone-dead,
But out of conscience and mere gratitude——

CORBACCIO. He must pronounce me his?

MOSCA.   'Tis true.

CORBACCIO.   This plot
Did I think on before.

MOSCA.   I do believe it.

CORBACCIO. Do you not believe it?

MOSCA.   Yes, sir.

CORBACCIO.   Mine own project.

MOSCA. Which, when he hath done, sir——

CORBACCIO.   Published me his heir?

MOSCA. And you so certain to survive him——

CORBACCIO.   Ay.

MOSCA. Being so lusty a man——

CORBACCIO.   'Tis true.

MOSCA.   Yes, sir——

CORBACCIO. I thought on that, too. See, how he
    should be
The very organ to express my thoughts!

MOSCA. You have not only done yourself a good——

CORBACCIO. But multiplied it on my son!

MOSCA.   'Tis right, sir.

CORBACCIO. Still my invention.

MOSCA.   'Las, sir! Heaven knows,
It hath been all my study, all my care,—
I e'en grow gray withal—how to work things——

CORBACCIO. I do conceive, sweet Mosca.

MOSCA.   You are he
For whom I labour here.

CORBACCIO.   Ay, do, do, do!
I'll straight about it.

MOSCA.   Rook go with you, raven!

CORBACCIO. I know thee honest.

MOSCA.   You do lie, sir!

CORBACCIO.   And——

MOSCA. Your knowledge is no better than your
    ears, sir.

CORBACCIO. I do not doubt to be a father to thee.

MOSCA. Nor I to gull my brother of his blessing.

CORBACCIO. I may ha' my youth restored to me,
    why not?

MOSCA. Your worship is a precious ass!

CORBACCIO.   What sayest thou?

MOSCA. I do desire your worship to make haste,
    sir.

CORBACCIO. 'Tis done, 'tis done; I go.   *Exit.*

VOLPONE.   O, I shall burst!
Let out my sides, let out my sides——

MOSCA.   Contain
Your flux of laughter, sir. You know this hope
Is such a bait, it covers any hook.

VOLPONE. O, but thy working and thy placing it!
I cannot hold; good rascal, let me kiss thee!
I never knew thee in so rare a humour.

MOSCA. Alas, sir, I but do as I am taught;
Follow your grave instructions; give 'em words;
Pour oil into their ears, and send them hence.

VOLPONE. 'Tis true, 'tis true. What a rare punish-
    ment.
Is avarice to itself!

MOSCA.   Ay, with our help, sir.

VOLPONE. So many cares, so many maladies,
So many fears attending on old age,

Yea, death so often called on, as no wish
Can be more frequent with 'em, their limbs faint,
Their senses dull, their seeing, hearing, going,
All dead before them; yea, their very teeth,
Their instruments of eating, failing them;
Yet this is reckoned life! Nay, here was one,
Is now gone home, that wishes to live longer!
Feels not his gout, nor palsy; feigns himself
Younger by scores of years, flatters his age
With confident belying it, hopes he may
With charms, like Aeson, have his youth restored;
And with these thoughts so battens, as if fate
Would be as easily cheated on as he,
And all turns air! *Another knocks.* Who's that there,
    now? a third?
    MOSCA. Close, to your couch again. I hear his
      voice.
It is Corvino, our spruce merchant.
    VOLPONE.   Dead.
    MOSCA. Another bout, sir, with your eyes.—Who's
      there?

Enter CORVINO.

Signior Corvino! come most wished for! O,
How happy were you, if you know it, now!
    CORVINO. Why? what? wherein?
    MOSCA.   The tardy hour is come, sir.
    CORVINO. He is not dead?
    MOSCA.   Not dead, sir, but as good;
He knows no man.
    CORVINO.   How shall I do, then?
    MOSCA.   Why, sir?
    CORVINO. I have brought him here a pearl.
    MOSCA.   Perhaps he has
So much remembrance left as to know you, sir;

He still calls on you; nothing but your name
Is in his mouth. Is your pearl orient, sir?

 CORVINO. Venice was never owner of the like.

 VOLPONE. Signior Corvino!

 MOSCA.   Hark.

 VOLPONE.   Signior Corvino!

 MOSCA. He calls you; step and give it him.—He's
  here, sir,
And he has brought you a rich pearl.

 CORVINO.   How do you, sir?—
Tell him it doubles the twelfth carat.

 MOSCA.   Sir,
He cannot understand; his hearing's gone;
And yet it comforts him to see you——

 CORVINO.   Say
I have a diamond for him, too.

 MOSCA.   Best show't, sir,
Put it into his hand; 'tis only there
He apprehends. He has his feeling yet.
See how he grasps it!

 CORVINO.   'Las, good gentleman!
How pitiful the sight is!

 MOSCA.   Tut, forget, sir.
The weeping of an heir should still be laughter
Under a visor.

 CORVINO.   Why, am I his heir?

 MOSCA. Sir, I am sworn, I may not show the will
Till he be dead; but here has been Corbaccio,
Here has been Voltore, here were others too,
I cannot number 'em, they were so many,
All gaping here for legacies; but I,
Taking the vantage of his naming you,
'Signior Corvino,' 'Signior Corvino,' took
Paper and pen and ink, and there I asked him
Whom he would have his heir? 'Corvino!' Who
Should be executor? 'Corvino!' And

To any question he was silent to,
I still interpreted the nods he made,
Through weakness, for consent; and sent home th'
    others,
Nothing bequeathed them but to cry and curse.

    CORVINO. O my dear Mosca! *They embrace*. Does
      he not perceive us?

    MOSCA. No more than a blind harper. He knows
      no man,
No face of friend nor name of any servant,
Who 'twas that fed him last or gave him drink;
Not those he hath begotten or brought up
Can he remember.

    CORVINO.   Has he children?

    MOSCA.   Bastards,
Some dozen, or more, that he begot on beggars,
Gipsies, and Jews, and black-moors, when he was
    drunk.
Knew you not that, sir? 'Tis the common fable.
The dwarf, the fool, the eunuch, are all his;
He's the true father of his family,
In all save me—but he has giv'n 'em nothing.

    CORVINO. That's well, that's well! Art sure he does
      not hear us?

    MOSCA. Sure, sir? why, look you, credit your own
      sense.—
The pox approach, and add to your diseases,
If it would send you hence the sooner, sir!
For your incontinence it hath deserved it
Throughly and throughly, and the plague to boot!—
You may come near, sir.—Would you would once
    close
Those filthy eyes of yours, that flow with slime,
Like two frog-pits; and those same hanging cheeks,
Covered with hide instead of skin—nay, help, sir.——
That look like frozen dish-clouts set on end!

CORVINO. Or like an old smoked wall, on which
  the rain
Ran down in streaks!

MOSCA.   Excellent, sir! speak out;
You may be louder yet. A culverin
Discharged in his ear would hardly bore it.

CORVINO. His nose is like a common sewer, still
  running.

MOSCA. 'Tis good! And what his mouth!

CORVINO.   A very draught.

MOSCA. O, stop it up——

CORVINO.   By no means.

MOSCA.   Pray you let me.
Faith, I could stifle him rarely with a pillow,
As well as any woman that should keep him.

CORVINO. Do as you will, but I'll be gone.

MOSCA.   Be so;
It is your presence makes him last so long.

CORVINO. I pray you use no violence.

MOSCA.   No, sir! why?
Why should you be thus scrupulous, pray you, sir?

CORVINO. Nay, at your discretion.

MOSCA.   Well, good sir, begone.

CORVINO. I will not trouble him now to take my
  pearl.

MOSCA. Pooh! nor your diamond. What a needless
  care
Is this afflicts you? Is not all here yours?
Am not I here, whom you have made your creature,
That owe my being to you?

CORVINO.   Grateful Mosca!
Thou art my friend, my fellow, my companion,
My partner, and shalt share in all my fortunes.

MOSCA. Excepting one.

CORVINO.   What's that?

MOSCA.   Your gallant wife, sir.
                                        Exit CORVINO.

Now he is gone. We had no other means
To shoot him hence, but this.

    VOLPONE.   My divine Mosca!
Thou hast today outdone thyself. *Another knocks.*
    Who's there?
I will be troubled with no more. Prepare
Me music, dances, banquets, all delights;
The Turk is not more sensual in his pleasures
Than will Volpone. Let me see, a pearl!
A diamond! plate! sequines! Good morning's pur-
    chase.
Why, this is better than rob churches yet!
Or fat, by eating once a month a man——
Who is't?

    MOSCA. The beauteous Lady Wouldbe, sir,
Wife to the English knight, Sir Politic Wouldbe,—
This is the style, sir, is directed me—
Hath sent to know how you have slept tonight,
And if you would be visited?

    VOLPONE.   Not now.
Some three hours hence——

    MOSCA.   I told the squire so much.

    VOLPONE. When I am high with mirth and wine,
    then, then!
'Fore Heaven, I wonder at the desperate valour
Of the bold English, that they dare let loose
Their wives to all encounters!

    MOSCA.   Sir, this knight
Had not his name for nothing; he is politic,
And knows, howe'er his wife affect strange airs,
She hath not yet the face to be dishonest.
But had she Signior Corvino's wife's face——

    VOLPONE. Has she so rare a face?

    MOSCA.   O, sir, the wonder,
The blazing star of Italy! a wench
O' the first year! a beauty ripe as harvest!
Whose skin is whiter than a swan all over!

Than silver, snow, or lilies! a soft lip,
Would tempt you to eternity of kissing!
And flesh that melteth in the touch to blood!
Bright as your gold, and lovely as your gold!

VOLPONE. Why had not I known this before?

MOSCA.   Alas, sir,
Myself but yesterday discovered it.

VOLPONE. How might I see her?

MOSCA.   O, not possible.
She's kept as warily as is your gold;
Never does come abroad, never takes air
But at a window. All her looks are sweet
As the first grapes or cherries, and are watched
As near as they are.

VOLPONE.   I must see her!

MOSCA.   Sir,
There is a guard of ten spies thick upon her—
All his whole household—each of which is set
Upon his fellow, and have all their charge,
When he goes out, when he comes in, examined.

VOLPONE. I will go see her, though but at her
    window.

MOSCA. In some disguise, then.

VOLPONE.   That is true. I must
Maintain mine own shape still the same. We'll
    think.   *Exeunt.*

ACT TWO. SCENE ONE

Before Corvino's house, off the Piazza of Saint Mark

Enter SIR POLITIC WOULDBE *and* PEREGRINE.

SIR POLITIC. Sir, to a wise man, all the world's his
    soil.
It is not Italy, nor France, nor Europe,
That must bound me, if my fates call me forth.
Yet I protest, it is no salt desire
Of seeing countries, shifting a religion,
Nor any disaffection to the state
Where I was bred, and unto which I owe
My dearest plots, hath brought me out; much less
That idle, antique, stale, grey-headed project
Of knowing men's minds and manners, with Ulysses;
But a peculiar humour of my wife's,
Laid for this height of Venice, to observe,
To quote, to learn the language, and so forth——
I hope you travel, sir, with licence?
    PEREGRINE.   Yes.
    SIR POLITIC. I dare the safelier converse——How
    long, sir,
Since you left England?
    PEREGRINE.   Seven weeks.
    SIR POLITIC.   So lately!
You ha' not been with my Lord Ambassador?
    PEREGRINE. Not yet, sir.
    SIR POLITIC.   Pray you, what news, sir,
    vents our climate?
I heard last night a most strange thing reported

By some of my Lord's followers, and I long
To hear how 'twill be seconded!

    PEREGRINE.   What was 't, sir?

    SIR POLITIC. Marry, sir, of a raven that should build
In a ship royal of the King's.

    PEREGRINE.   —This fellow,
Does he gull me, trow, or is gulled?—Your name, sir?

    SIR POLITIC. My name is Politic Wouldbe.

    PEREGRINE.   —O, that speaks him.—
A knight, sir?

    SIR POLITIC. A poor knight, sir.

    PEREGRINE.   Your lady
Lies here in Venice, for intelligence
Of tires and fashions and behaviour
Among the courtesans? the fine Lady Wouldbe?

    SIR POLITIC. Yes, sir, the spider and the bee oft-
    times
Suck from one flower.

    PEREGRINE.   Good Sir Politic,
I cry you mercy! I have heard much of you.
'Tis true, sir, of your raven.

    SIR POLITIC.   On your knowledge?

    PEREGRINE. Yes, and your lion's whelping in the
    Tower.

    SIR POLITIC. Another whelp?

    PEREGRINE.   Another, sir.

    SIR POLITIC.   Now, Heaven!
What prodigies be these? The fires at Berwick!
And the new star! these things concurring, strange
And full of omen! Saw you those meteors?

    PEREGRINE. I did, sir.

    SIR POLITIC.   Fearful! Pray you, sir, con-
    firm me,
Were there three porpoises seen above the bridge,
As they give out?

PEREGRINE. Six, and a sturgeon, sir.

SIR POLITIC. I am astonished!

PEREGRINE. Nay, sir, be not so;
I'll tell you a greater prodigy than these——

SIR POLITIC. What should these things portend?

PEREGRINE. The very day—
Let me be sure—that I put forth from London,
There was a whale discovered in the river,
As high as Woolwich, that had waited there,
Few know how many months, for the subversion
Of the Stode fleet.

SIR POLITIC. Is't possible? Believe it,
'Twas either sent from Spain, or the Archduke's!
Spinola's whale, upon my life, my credit!
Will they not leave these projects? Worthy sir,
Some other news.

PEREGRINE. Faith, Stone the fool is dead,
And they do lack a tavern-fool extremely.

SIR POLITIC. Is Mas' Stone dead?

PEREGRINE. He's dead, sir; why, I hope
You thought him not immortal?—O, this knight,
Were he well known, would be a precious thing
To fit our English stage. He that should write
But such a fellow, should be thought to feign
Extremely, if not maliciously.

SIR POLITIC. Stone dead!

PEREGRINE. Dead. Lord, how deeply, sir, you apprehend it!
He was no kinsman to you?

SIR POLITIC. That I know of.
Well, that same fellow was an unknown fool.

PEREGRINE. And yet you knew him, it seems?

SIR POLITIC. I did so. Sir,
I knew him one of the most dangerous heads
Living within the state, and so I held him.

PEREGRINE. Indeed, sir?

SIR POLITIC.　　　　　　　While he lived, in action.
He has received weekly intelligence,
Upon my knowledge, out of the Low Countries,
For all parts of the world, in cabbages;
And those dispensed again t'ambassadors,
In oranges, muskmelons, apricots,
Lemons, pomecitrons, and suchlike; sometimes
In Colchester oysters, and your Selsey cockles.

PEREGRINE. You make me wonder!

SIR POLITIC.　　　　　　Sir, upon my knowledge.
Nay, I have observed him, at your public ordinary,
Take his advertisement from a traveller—
A concealed statesman—in a trencher of meat;
And instantly, before the meal was done,
Convey an answer in a toothpick.

PEREGRINE.　　　　　　　Strange!
How could this be, sir?

SIR POLITIC.　　　　　Why, the meat was cut
So like his character, and so laid, as he
Must easily read the cipher.

PEREGRINE.　　　　　　　I have heard
He could not read, sir.

SIR POLITIC.　　　　So 'twas given out,
In policy, by those that did employ him.
But he could read, and had your languages,
And to 't, as sound a noddle——

PEREGRINE.　　　　　　　　I have heard, sir,
That your baboons were spies, and that they were
A kind of subtle nation near to China.

SIR POLITIC. Ay, ay, your Mamaluchi. Faith, they
had
Their hand in a French plot or two; but they
Were so extremely given to women, as
They made discovery of all. Yet I

Had my advices here, on Wednesday last,
From one of their own coat, they were returned,
Made their relations, as the fashion is,
And now stand fair for fresh employment.

 PEREGRINE.   —Heart!
This Sir Poll will be ignorant of nothing.—
It seems, sir, you know all.

 SIR POLITIC.   Not all, sir, but
I have some general notions. I do love
To note and to observe. Though I live out,
Free from the active torrent, yet I'd mark
The currents and the passages of things,
For mine own private use; and know the ebbs
And flows of state.

 PEREGRINE.   Believe it, sir, I hold
Myself in no small tie unto my fortunes,
For casting me thus luckily upon you;
Whose knowledge, if your bounty equal it,
May do me great assistance, in instruction
For my behaviour and my bearing, which
Is yet so rude and raw——

 SIR POLITIC.   Why? came you forth
Empty of rules for travel?

 PEREGRINE.   Faith, I had
Some common ones, from out that vulgar grammar,
Which he that cried Italian to me, taught me.

 SIR POLITIC. Why, this it is that spoils all our brave
    bloods:
Trusting our hopeful gentry unto pedants,
Fellows of outside, and mere bark. You seem
To be a gentleman of ingenuous race——
I not profess it, but my fate hath been
To be where I have been consulted with,
In this high kind, touching some great men's sons,
Persons of blood and honour——

Enter MOSCA *and* NANO *disguised, followed by* GREGE.

PEREGRINE.   Who be these, sir?

MOSCA. Under that window, there 't must be. The
   same.

SIR POLITIC. Fellows to mount a bank! Did your
   instructor
In the dear tongues never discourse to you
Of the Italian mountebanks?

PEREGRINE.   Yes, sir.

SIR POLITIC.   Why,
Here you shall see one.

PEREGRINE.   They are quacksalvers,
Fellows that live by venting oils and drugs.

SIR POLITIC. Was that the character he gave you of
   them?

PEREGRINE. As I remember.

SIR POLITIC.   Pity his ignorance.
They are the only knowing men of Europe!
Great general scholars, excellent physicians,
Most admired statesmen, professed favourites,
And cabinet counsellors to the greatest princes!
The only languaged men of all the world!

PEREGRINE. And, I have heard they are most lewd
   impostors,
Made all of terms and shreds; no less beliers
Of great men's favours, than their own vile
   med'cines;
Which they will utter, upon monstrous oaths,
Selling that drug for twopence, ere they part,
Which they have valued at twelve crowns before.

SIR POLITIC. Sir, calumnies are answered best with
   silence.
Yourself shall judge.—Who is it mounts, my friends?

MOSCA. Scoto of Mantua, sir.

SIR POLITIC.   Is't he? Nay, then
I'll proudly promise, sir, you shall behold
Another man than has been fancied to you.
I wonder yet that he should mount his bank
Here in this nook, that has been wont t' appear
In face of the Piazza. Here he comes!

Enter VOLPONE *disguised as a mountebank.*

VOLPONE. Mount, zany.

GREGE.   Follow, follow, follow, follow, follow!

SIR POLITIC. See how the people follow him! he's
     a man
May write ten thousand crowns in bank here. Note,
Mark but his gesture. I do use to observe
The state he keeps in getting up.

PEREGRINE.   'Tis worth it, sir.

VOLPONE. 'Most noble gentlemen, and my worthy
patrons: It may seem strange that I, your Scoto
Mantuano, who was ever wont to fix my bank in
face of the public Piazza, near the shelter of the
portico to the Procuratia, should now, after eight
months' absence from this illustrious city of Venice,
humbly retire myself into an obscure nook of the
Piazza.'

SIR POLITIC. Did not I now object the same?

PEREGRINE.   Peace, sir.

VOLPONE. 'Let me tell you: I am not—as your
Lombard proverb saith—cold on my feet, or content
to part with my commodities at a cheaper rate than
I accustomed; look not for it. Nor that the calumnious reports of that impudent detractor and shame to
our profession—Alessandro Buttone, I mean—who
gave out in public, I was condemned a sforzato to
the galleys, for poisoning the Cardinal Bembo's—
cook, hath at all attached, much less dejected me.
No, no, worthy gentlemen, to tell you true, I cannot

endure to see the rabble of these ground ciarlatani, that spread their cloaks on the pavement as if they meant to do feats of activity, and then come in lamely, with their moudy tales out of Boccaccio, like stale Tabarine, the fabulist; some of them discoursing their travels, and of their tedious captivity in the Turk's galleys, when indeed—were the truth known—they were the Christian's galleys, where very temperately they eat bread and drunk water, as a wholesome penance, enjoined them by their confessors, for base pilferies.'

SIR POLITIC. Note but his bearing, and contempt of these.

VOLPONE. 'These turdy-facy-nasty-paty-lousy-fartical rogues, with one poor groatsworth of unprepared antimony, finely wrapped up in several scartoccios, are able very well to kill their twenty a week, and play. Yet these meagre, starved spirits, who have half stopped the organs of their minds with earthy oppilations, want not their favourers among your shrivelled, salad-eating artisans, who are overjoyed that they may have their half-pe'rth of physic; though it purge 'em into another world, 't makes no matter.'

SIR POLITIC. Excellent! ha' you heard better language, sir?

VOLPONE. 'Well, let 'em go. And, gentlemen, honourable gentlemen, know that for this time our bank, being thus removed from the clamours of the canaglia, shall be the scene of pleasure and delight; for I have nothing to sell, little or nothing to sell.'

SIR POLITIC. I told you, sir, his end.

PEREGRINE.   You did so, sir.

VOLPONE. 'I protest, I and my six servants are not able to make of this precious liquor, so fast as it is fetched away from my lodging by gentlemen of your

city, strangers of the Terra Firma, worshipful merchants, ay, and senators too; who, ever since my
arrival, have detained me to their uses, by their
splendidous liberalities. And worthily, for what
avails your rich man to have his magazines stuffed
with moscadelli, or of the purest grape, when his
physicians prescribe him, on pain of death, to drink
nothing but water cocted with aniseeds? O health,
health! the blessing of the rich! the riches of the
poor! who can buy thee at too dear a rate, since
there is no enjoying this world without thee? Be
not then so sparing of your purses, honourable
gentlemen, as to abridge the natural course of
life——'

PEREGRINE. You see his end?

SIR POLITIC.   Ay, is't not good?

VOLPONE. 'For when a humid flux, or catarrh, by
the mutability of air, falls from your head into an
arm, or shoulder, or any other part; take you a
ducat, or your sequine of gold, and apply to the
place affected; see what good effect it can work. No,
no, 'tis this blessed unguento, this rare extraction,
that hath only power to disperse all malignant humours, that proceed either of hot, cold, moist, or
windy causes——'

PEREGRINE. I would he had put in dry, too.

SIR POLITIC.   Pray you observe.

VOLPONE. 'To fortify the most indigest and crude
stomach, ay, were it of one that, through extreme
weakness, vomited blood, applying only a warm
napkin to the place, after the unction and fricace;
for the vertigine in the head, putting but a drop
into your nostrils, likewise behind the ears, a most
sovereign and approved remedy; the Mal Caduco,
cramps, convulsions, paralyses, epilepsies, Tremor
Cordia, retired nerves, ill vapours of the spleen,

stoppings of the liver, the stone, the strangury, Hernia Ventosa, Iliaca Passio; stops a Dysenteria immediately; easeth the torsion of the small guts; and cures Melancholia Hypocondriaca, being taken and applied, according to my printed receipt. *Pointing to his bill and his glass.* For this is the physician, this the medicine; this counsels, this cures; this gives the direction, this works the effect; and, in sum, both together may be termed an abstract of the theoric and practic in the Aesculapian art. 'Twill cost you eight crowns.—And, Zan Fritada, pray thee sing a verse extempore in honour of it.'

SIR POLITIC. How do you like him, sir?

PEREGRINE.   Most strangely, I!

SIR POLITIC. Is not his language rare?

PEREGRINE.   But alchemy, I never heard the like; or Broughton's books.

SONG.

'Had old Hippocrates or Galen,
That to their books put med'cines all in,
But known this secret, they had never—
Of which they will be guilty ever—
Been murderers of so much paper,
Or wasted many a hurtless taper.
No Indian drug had e'er been famèd,
Tobacco, sassafras not namèd;
Ne yet of guacum one small stick, sir,
Nor Raymund Lully's great elixir.
Ne had been known the Danish gonswart,
Or Paracelsus, with his long-sword.'

PEREGRINE. All this yet will not do; eight crowns is high.

VOLPONE. 'No more.—Gentlemen, if I had but time to discourse to you the miraculous effects of this my oil, surnamed Oglio del Scoto; with the

countless catalogue of those I have cured of th'
aforesaid and many more diseases; the patents and
privileges of all the princes and commonwealths of
Christendom; or but the depositions of those that
appeared on my part, before the signiory of the
Sanita and most learned college of physicians;
where I was authorized, upon notice taken of the
admirable virtues of my medicaments, and mine
own excellency in matter of rare and unknown
secrets, not only to disperse them publicly in this
famous city, but in all the territories that happily
joy under the government of the most pious and
magnificent states of Italy. But may some other
gallant fellow say, "O, there be divers that make
profession to have as good and as experimented
receipts as yours." Indeed, very many have assayed,
like apes, in imitation of that which is really and
essentially in me, to make of this oil; bestowed great
cost in furnaces, stills, alembics, continual fires, and
preparation of the ingredients,—as indeed there goes
to it six hundred several simples, besides some quantity of human fat, for the conglutination, which we
buy of the anatomists—but when these practitioners
come to the last decoction: blow, blow, puff, puff,
and all flies in fumo. Ha, ha, ha! Poor wretches! I
rather pity their folly and indiscretion, than their
loss of time and money; for those may be recovered
by industry, but to be a fool born is a disease incurable. For myself, I always from my youth have
endeavoured to get the rarest secrets, and book them,
either in exchange or for money. I spared nor cost
nor labour, where anything was worthy to be
learned. And gentlemen, honourable gentlemen, I
will undertake, by virtue of chemical art, out of the
honourable hat that covers your head, to extract
the four elements: that is to say, the fire, air, water,
and earth, and return you your felt without burn or

stain. For whilst others have been at the balloo, I
have been at my book; and am now past the craggy
paths of study, and come to the flowery plains of
honour and reputation.'

SIR POLITIC. I do assure you, sir, that is his aim.

VOLPONE. 'But to our price——'

PEREGRINE.   And that withal, Sir Poll.

VOLPONE. 'You all know, honourable gentlemen,
I never valued this ampulla, or vial, at less than
eight crowns; but for this time, I am content to be
deprived of it for six. Six crowns is the price, and
less, in courtesy, I know you cannot offer me. Take
it or leave it, howsoever, both it and I am at your
service. I ask you not as the value of the thing, for
then I should demand of you a thousand crowns; so
the Cardinals Montalto, Farnese, the Great Duke of
Tuscany, my gossip, with divers other princes, have
given me, but I despise money. Only to show my
affection to you, honourable gentlemen, and your
illustrious state here, I have neglected the messages
of these princes, mine own offices; framed my journey hither only to present you with the fruits of my
travels.—Tune your voices once more to the touch
of your instruments, and give the honourable assembly some delightful recreation.'

PEREGRINE. What monstrous and most painful
        circumstance
Is here, to get some three or four gazettes,
Some threepence i' the whole! for that 'twill come to.

SONG.

'You that would last long, list to my song,
Make no more coil, but buy of this oil.
Would you be ever fair and young?
Stout of teeth and strong of tongue?
Tart of palate? quick of ear?
Sharp of sight? of nostril clear?

Moist of hand and light of foot?
Or I will come nearer to't—
Would you live free from all diseases?
Do the act your mistress pleases,
Yet fright all aches from your bones?
Here's a med'cine for the nones.'

VOLPONE. 'Well, I am in a humour at this time to make a present of the small quantity my coffer contains; to the rich, in courtesy, and to the poor, for God's sake. Wherefore now mark: I asked you six crowns, and six crowns, at other times, you have paid me. You shall not give me six crowns, nor five, nor four, nor three, nor two, nor one; nor half a ducat; no, nor a moccenigo! Sixpence it will cost you, or six hundred pound—expect no lower price, for by the banner of my front, I will not bate a bagatine; that I will have, only, a pledge of your loves, to carry something from amongst you, to show I am not contemned by you. Therefore now, toss your handkerchiefs, cheerfully, cheerfully; and be advertised that the first heroic spirit that deigns to grace me with a handkerchief, I will give it a little remembrance of something beside, shall please it better than if I had presented it with a double pistolet.'

PEREGRINE. Will you be that heroic spark, Sir Poll?

CELIA, *at the window, throws down her hand-kerchief.*

O, see, the window has prevented you!

VOLPONE. 'Lady, I kiss your bounty; and for this timely grace you have done your poor Scoto of Mantua, I will return you, over and above my oil, a secret of that high and inestimable nature, shall make you forever enamoured on that minute wherein your eye first descended on so mean, yet not altogether to be despised, an object. Here is a powder concealed in this paper, of which, if I should speak to the worth, nine thousand volumes were but as one page, that page as a line, that line as a word; so short is this pilgrimage of man, which some call life, to the expressing of it. Would I reflect on the price? why, the whole world were but as an empire, that empire as a province, that province as a bank, that bank as a private purse, to the purchase of it. I will only tell you: it is the powder that made Venus a goddess,—given her by Apollo—that kept her perpetually young, cleared her wrinkles, firmed her gums, filled her skin, coloured her hair; from her derived to Helen, and at the sack of Troy unfortunately lost; till now, in this our age, it was as happily recovered, by a studious antiquary, out of some ruins of Asia; who sent a moiety of it to the court of France—but much sophisticated—wherewith the ladies there now colour their hair. The rest, at this present, remains with me; extracted to a quintessence, so that, wherever it but touches, in youth it perpetually preserves, in age restores the complexion; seats your teeth, did they dance like virginal jacks, firm as a wall; makes them white as ivory, that were black as——'

Enter CORVINO.

CORVINO. Spite o' the devil, and my shame! come down, here,
Come down! No house but mine to make your scene?
Signior Flaminio, will you down, sir? down?
What, is my wife your Franciscina, sir?
No windows on the whole Piazza here,
To make your properties, but mine? but mine?

He beats away VOLPONE, MOSCA, NANO, *and* GREGE.

Heart! ere tomorrow I shall be new christened,
And called the Pantalone di Bisognosi
About the town.

PEREGRINE.   What should this mean, Sir Poll?

SIR POLITIC. Some trick of state, believe it. I will
    home.

PEREGRINE. It may be some design on you.

SIR POLITIC.   I know not.
I'll stand upon my guard.

PEREGRINE.   It is your best, sir.

SIR POLITIC. This three weeks, all my advices, all
    my letters,
They have been intercepted.

PEREGRINE.   Indeed, sir?
Best have a care.

SIR POLITIC.   Nay, so I will.

PEREGRINE.   This knight,
I may not lose him, for my mirth, till night.

                            Exeunt.

ACT TWO. SCENE TWO

A street

Enter VOLPONE *and* MOSCA.

VOLPONE. O, I am wounded!

MOSCA.   Where, sir?

VOLPONE.   Not without;
Those blows were nothing. I could bear them ever.
But angry Cupid, bolting from her eyes,
Hath shot himself into me like a flame;
Where now he flings about his burning heat,

As in a furnace an ambitious fire,
Whose vent is stopped. The fight is all within me.
I cannot live, except thou help me, Mosca.
My liver melts, and I, without the hope
Of some soft air from her refreshing breath,
Am but a heap of cinders.

    MOSCA.   'Las, good sir,
Would you had never seen her!

    VOLPONE.   Nay, would thou
Hadst never told me of her!

    MOSCA.   Sir, 'tis true;
I do confess I was unfortunate,
And you unhappy; but I'm bound in conscience,
No less than duty, to effect my best
To your release of torment, and I will, sir.

    VOLPONE. Dear Mosca, shall I hope?

    MOSCA.   Sir, more than dear,
I will not bid you to despair of aught
Within a human compass.

    VOLPONE.   O, there spoke
My better angel. Mosca, take my keys,
Gold, plate, and jewels—all's at thy devotion.
Employ them how thou wilt; nay, coin me, too—
So thou in this but crown my longings, Mosca.

    MOSCA. Use but your patience.

    VOLPONE.   So I have.

    MOSCA.   I doubt not
To bring success to your desires.

    VOLPONE.   Nay, then,
I not repent me of my late disguise.

    MOSCA. If you can horn him, sir, you need not.

    VOLPONE.   True.
Besides, I never meant him for my heir.
Is not the colour o' my beard and eyebrows
To make me known?

    MOSCA.   No jot.

VOLPONE.   I did it well.

MOSCA. So well, would I could follow you in mine,
With half the happiness! and yet I would
Escape your epilogue.

VOLPONE.   But were they gulled
With a belief that I was Scoto?

MOSCA.   Sir,
Scoto himself could hardly have distinguished!
I have not time to flatter you now, we'll part;
And as I prosper, so applaud my art.   *Exeunt.*

ACT TWO. SCENE THREE

Corvino's house

Enter CORVINO *with* CELIA.

CORVINO. Death of mine honour, with the city's
    fool!
A juggling, tooth-drawing, prating mountebank!
And at a public window! where, whilst he,
With his strained action, and his dole of faces,
To his drug-lecture draws your itching ears,
A crew of old, unmarried, noted lechers
Stood leering up like satyrs; and you smile
Most graciously, and fan your favours forth,
To give your hot spectators satisfaction!
What, was your mountebank their call? their
    whistle?
Or were y' enamoured on his copper rings?
His saffron jewel with the toad-stone in't?
Or his embroidered suit, with the cope-stitch,
Made of a hearse-cloth? or his old tilt-feather?

Or his starched beard? Well, you shall have him,
    yes!
He shall come home, and minister unto you
The fricace for the mother. Or, let me see,
I think you'd rather mount; would you not mount?
Why, if you'll mount, you may; yes, truly, you may!
And so you may be seen, down to th' foot.
Get you a cittern, Lady Vanity,
And be a dealer with the virtuous man;
Make one. I'll but protest myself a cuckold,
And save your dowry. I'm a Dutchman, I!
For if you thought me an Italian,
You would be damned ere you did this, you whore!
Thou'dst tremble to imagine that the murder
Of father, mother, brother, all thy race,
Should follow, as the subject of my justice!

    CELIA. Good, sir, have patience.

    CORVINO.   What couldst thou propose
Less to thyself than, in this heat of wrath,
And stung with my dishonour, I should strike
This steel into thee, with as many stabs
As thou wert gazed upon with goatish eyes?

    CELIA. Alas, sir, be appeased! I could not think
My being at the window should more now
Move your impatience than at other times.

    CORVINO. No? not to seek and entertain a parley,
With a known knave, before a multitude!
You were an actor, with your handkerchief,
Which he most sweetly kissed in the receipt,
And might, no doubt, return it with a letter,
And 'point the place where you might meet—your
    sister's,
Your mother's, or your aunt's might serve the turn.

    CELIA. Why, dear sir, when do I make these ex-
    cuses,

Or ever stir abroad, but to the church?
And that so seldom——
    CORVINO.   Well, it shall be less;
And thy restraint before was liberty,
To what I now decree. And therefore mark me:
First, I will have this bawdy light dammed up;
And till't be done, some two or three yards off,
I'll chalk a line, o'er which if thou but chance
To set thy desp'rate foot, more hell, more horror,
More wild remorseless rage shall seize on thee,
Than on a conjuror that had heedless left
His circle's safety ere his devil was laid.
Then, here's a lock which I will hang upon thee;
And, now I think on't, I will keep thee backwards;
Thy lodging shall be backwards, thy walks back-
    wards,
Thy prospect all be backwards, and no pleasure,
That thou shalt know, but backwards. Nay, since
    you force
My honest nature, know it is your own
Being too open, makes me use you thus;
Since you will not contain your subtle nostrils
In a sweet room, but they must snuff the air
Of rank and sweaty passengers.   *Knock within.*
    One knocks.
Away, and be not seen, pain of thy life;
Nor look toward the window; if thou dost—
Nay, stay, hear this—let me not prosper, whore,
But I will make thee an anatomy,
Dissect thee mine own self, and read a lecture
Upon thee to the city, and in public.
Away!—   *Exit* CELIA.

      Enter SERVITORE.

    Who's there?
SERVITORE.   'Tis Signior Mosca, sir.

CORVINO. Let him come in. *Exit* SERVITORE. His
master's dead! There's yet
Some good to help the bad.

Enter MOSCA.

                          My Mosca, welcome!
I guess your news.
    MOSCA.   I fear you cannot, sir.
    CORVINO. Is't not his death?
    MOSCA.   Rather the contrary.
    CORVINO. Not his recovery?
    MOSCA.   Yes, sir.
    CORVINO.   I am cursed,
I am bewitched, my crosses meet to vex me!
How? how? how? how?
    MOSCA.   Why, sir, with Scoto's oil!
Corbaccio and Voltore brought of it,
Whilst I was busy in an inner room——
    CORVINO. Death! that damned mountebank! but
    for the law
Now, I could kill the rascal; 't cannot be
His oil should have that virtue. Ha' not I
Known him, a common rogue, come fiddling in
To th' ostería, with a tumbling whore,
And, when he has done all his forced tricks, been
    glad
Of a poor spoonful of dead wine, with flies in't?
It cannot be. All his ingredients
Are a sheep's gall, a roasted bitch's marrow,
Some few sod earwigs, pounded caterpillars,
A little capon's grease, and fasting spittle.
I know 'em to a dram.
    MOSCA.   I know not, sir,
But some on't there they poured into his ears,
Some in his nostrils, and recovered him,
Applying but the fricace!

CORVINO.   Pox o' that fricace!

MOSCA. And since, to seem the more officious,
And flatt'ring of his health, there they have had,
At extreme fees, the college of physicians
Consulting on him, how they might restore him;
Where one would have a cataplasm of spices,
Another a flayed ape clapped to his breast,
A third would ha' it a dog, a fourth an oil,
With wild cats' skins; at last, they all resolved
That, to preserve him, was no other means
But some young woman must be straight sought out,
Lusty and full of juice, to sleep by him.
And to this service, most unhappily,
And most unwillingly, am I now employed;
Which here I thought to pre-acquaint you with,
For your advice, since it concerns you most,
Because I would not do that thing might cross
Your ends, on whom I have my whole dependence,
    sir.
Yet, if I do it not, they may delate
My slackness to my patron, work me out
Of his opinion; and there all your hopes,
Ventures, or whatsoever, are all frustrate.
I do but tell you, sir. Besides, they are all
Now striving who shall first present him. There-
    fore—
I could entreat you, briefly, conclude somewhat;
Prevent 'em if you can!

CORVINO.   Death to my hopes,
This is my villainous fortune! Best to hire
Some common courtesan.

MOSCA.   Ay, I thought on that, sir;
But they are all so subtle, full of art;
And age again doting and flexible,
So as—I cannot tell—we may perchance
Light on a quean may cheat us all.

CORVINO.   'Tis true.

MOSCA. No, no. It must be one that has no tricks, sir,

Some simple thing, a creature made unto it;

Some wench you may command. Ha' you no kinswoman?

God's so'—Think, think, think, think, think, think, think, sir.

One o' the doctors offered there his daughter.

CORVINO. How!

MOSCA.   Yes, Signior Lupo, the physician.

CORVINO. His daughter!

MOSCA.   And a virgin, sir. Why, alas,

He knows the state of's body, what it is;

That nought căn warm his blood, sir, but a fever;

Nor any incantation raise his spirit—

A long forgetfulness hath seized that part.

Besides, sir, who shall know it? some one or two—

CORVINO. I pray thee give me leave. —If any man

But I had had this luck—The thing in'tself,

I know, is nothing—Wherefore should not I

As well command my blood and my affections

As this dull doctor? In the point of honour,

The cases are all one, of wife and daughter.

MOSCA. —I hear him coming.

CORVINO.   She shall do't. 'Tis done.

'Slight! if this doctor, who is not engaged,

Unless 't be for his counsel, which is nothing,

Offer his daughter, what should I, that am

So deeply in? I will prevent him. Wretch!

Covetous wretch!—Mosca, I have determined.

MOSCA. How, sir?

CORVINO.   We'll make all sure. The party you wot of

Shall be mine own wife, Mosca.

MOSCA.   Sir, the thing,

But that I would not seem to counsel you,
I should have motioned to you at the first;
And, make your count, you have cut all their
    throats.
Why, 'tis directly taking a possession!
And in his next fit, we may let him go.
'Tis but to pull the pillow from his head,
And he is throttled; 't had been done before,
But for your scrupulous doubts.

    CORVINO.   Ay, a plague on't,
My conscience fools my wit! Well, I'll be brief,
And so be thou, lest they should be before us.
Go home, prepare him, tell him with what zeal
And willingness I do it. Swear it was
On the first hearing—as thou mayst do, truly—
Mine own free motion.

    MOSCA.   Sir, I warrant you,
I'll so possess him with it, that the rest
Of his starved clients shall be banished all,
And only you received. But come not, sir,
Until I send, for I have something else
To ripen for your good; you must not know't.

    CORVINO. But do not you forget to send now.

    MOSCA.   Fear not.

                           Exit.

    CORVINO. Where are you, wife? my Celia! wife!

Re-enter CELIA.

                       What, blubbering?
Come, dry those tears. I think thou thought'st me
    in earnest!
Ha! by this light, I talked so but to try thee.
Methinks the lightness of the occasion
Should ha' confirmed thee. Come, I am not jealous.

    CELIA. No?

CORVINO.   Faith I am not, I, nor never was;
It is a poor, unprofitable humour.
Do not I know, if women have a will,
They'll do 'gainst all the watches o' the world?
And that the fiercest spies are tamed with gold?
Tut, I am confident in thee, thou shalt see't;
And see, I'll give thee cause, too, to believe it.
Come kiss me. Go, and make thee ready straight,
In all thy best attire, thy choicest jewels,
Put 'em all on, and, with 'em, thy best looks.
We are invited to a solemn feast
At old Volpone's, where it shall appear
How far I am free from jealousy or fear.   *Exeunt.*

ACT THREE. SCENE ONE

A street

Enter MOSCA.

MOSCA. I fear I shall begin to grow in love
With my dear self, and my most prosp'rous parts,
They do so spring and burgeon! I can feel
A whimsy i' my blood; I know not how,
Success hath made me wanton. I could skip
Out of my skin now, like a subtle snake,
I am so limber. O! your parasite
Is a most precious thing, dropped from above,
Not bred 'mongst clods and clodpoles here on earth.
I muse the mystery was not made a science,
It is so liberally professed! Almost
All the wise world is little else, in nature,
But parasites or sub-parasites. And yet

I mean not those that have your bare town-art,
To know who's fit to feed 'em; have no house,
No family, no care, and therefore mould
Tales for men's ears, to bait that sense; or get
Kitchen-invention, and some stale receipts
To please the belly and the groin; nor those,
With their court-dog tricks, that can fawn and fleer,
Make their revènue out of legs and faces,
Echo my lord, and lick away a moth;
But your fine, elegant rascal, that can rise
And stoop, almost together, like an arrow;
Shoot through the air as nimbly as a star;
Turn short as doth a swallow; and be here,
And there, and here, and yonder, all at once;
Present to any humour all occasion,
And change a visor swifter than a thought!
This is the creature had the art born with him;
Toils not to learn it, but doth practise it
Out of most excellent nature; and such sparks
Are the true parasites, others but their zanies.

Enter BONARIO.

Who's this? Bonario, old Corbaccio's son?
The person I was bound to seek.—Fair sir,
You are happ'ly met.

    BONARIO.   That cannot be by thee.

    MOSCA. Why, sir?

    BONARIO.   Nay, pray thee know thy way,
    and leave me.
I would be loath to interchange discourse
With such a mate as thou art.

    MOSCA.   Courteous sir,
Scorn not my poverty.

    BONARIO.   Not I, by Heaven!
But thou shalt give me leave to hate thy baseness.

    MOSCA. Baseness?

BONARIO.   Ay, answer me, is not thy sloth
Sufficient argument? thy flattery?
Thy means of feeding?
    MOSCA.   Heaven be good to me!
These imputations are too common, sir,
And eas'ly stuck on virtue when she's poor;
You are unequal to me, and howe'er
Your sentence may be righteous, yet you are not,
That, ere you know me, thus proceed in censure.
Saint Mark bear witness 'gainst you, 'tis inhuman!
    BONARIO. —What! does he weep? the sign is soft
        and good.
I do repent me that I was so harsh.
    MOSCA. 'Tis true that, swayed by strong necessity,
I am enforced to eat my careful bread
With too much obsequy. 'Tis true, beside,
That I am fain to spin mine own poor raiment
Out of my mere observance, being not born
To a free fortune. But that I have done
Base offices, in rending friends asunder,
Dividing families, betraying counsels,
Whispering false lies, or mining men with praises,
Trained their credulity with perjuries,
Corrupted chastity, or am in love
With mine own tender ease; but would not rather
Prove the most rugged and laborious course
That might redeem my present estimation,
Let me here perish, in all hope of goodness!
    BONARIO. This cannot be a personated passion.—
I was to blame, so to mistake thy nature
Pray thee forgive me, and speak out thy business.
    MOSCA. Sir, it concerns you; and though I may
        seem
At first to make a main offence in manners,
And in my gratitude unto my master,
Yet for the pure love which I bear all right,

And hatred of the wrong, I must reveal it.
This very hour your father is in purpose
To disinherit you——
    BONARIO.   How!
    MOSCA.   And thrust you forth,
As a mere stranger to his blood; 'tis true, sir!
The work no way engageth me, but as
I claim an interest in the general state
Of goodness and true virtue, which I hear
T' abound in you; and for which mere respect,
Without a second aim, sir, I have done it.
    BONARIO. This tale hath lost thee much of the late
       trust
Thou hadst with me; it is impossible.
I know not how to lend it any thought,
My father should be so unnatural.
    MOSCA. It is a confidence that well becomes
Your piety; and formed, no doubt, it is
From your own simple innocence; which makes
Your wrong more monstrous and abhorred. But,
      sir,
I now will tell you more: this very minute
It is, or will be, doing; and if you
Shall be but pleased to go with me, I'll bring you—
I dare not say where you shall see—but where
Your ear shall be a witness of the deed;
Hear yourself written bastard, and professed
The common issue of the earth.
    BONARIO.   I'm 'mazed!
    MOSCA. Sir, if I do it not, draw your just sword,
And score your vengeance on my front and face;
Mark me your villain. You have too much wrong,
And I do suffer for you, sir. My heart
Weeps blood in anguish——
    BONARIO.   Lead. I follow thee.
                     Exeunt.

ACT THREE. SCENE TWO

Volpone's house

Enter VOLPONE.

VOLPONE. Mosca stays long, methinks.—Bring forth your sports,
And help to make the wretched time more sweet.

Enter NANO, ANDROGYNO, *and* CASTRONE.

NANO. 'Dwarf, fool, and eunuch, well met here we be.
A question it were now, whether of us three,
Being all the known delicates of a rich man,
In pleasing him, claim the precedency can?'

CASTRONE. 'I claim for myself.'

ANDROGYNO.　　　　　　'And so doth the fool.'

NANO. ' 'Tis foolish indeed. Let me set you both to school:
First, for your dwarf, he's little and witty,
And everything, as it is little, is pretty;
Else why do men say to a creature of my shape,
So soon as they see him, "It's a pretty little ape?"
And why a pretty ape, but for pleasing imitation
Of greater men's actions, in a ridiculous fashion?
Beside, this feat body of mine doth not crave
Half the meat, drink, and cloth one of your bulks will have.
Admit your fool's face be the mother of laughter,
Yet, for his brain, it must always come after;
And though that do feed him, it's a pitiful case,
His body is beholden to such a bad face.'

One knocks.

VOLPONE. Who's there? my couch! Away! Look!
Nano, see! *Exeunt* ANDROGYNO *and* CASTRONE.
Give me my caps first—go, inquire. *Exit* NANO.
Now, Cupid
Send it be Mosca, and with fair return!
NANO. It is the beauteous Madam—
VOLPONE. Wouldbe—is it?
NANO. The same.
VOLPONE. Now torment on me! Squire her in;
For she will enter, or dwell here forever.
Nay, quickly, that my fit were past. I fear
A second hell, too, that my loathing this
Will quite expel my appetite to the other.
Would she were taking now her tedious leave.
Lord, how it threats me, what I am to suffer!

Re-enter NANO *with* LADY WOULDBE.

LADY WOULDBE. I thank you, good sir. Pray you
signify
Unto your patron I am here.—This band
Shows not my neck enough.—I trouble you, sir,
Let me request you bid one of my women
Come hither to me. In good faith, I am dressed
Most favourably today! It is no matter;
'Tis well enough.

Enter 1ST WOMAN.

Look, see these petulant things!
How they have done this!
VOLPONE. —I do feel the fever
Ent'ring in at mine ears. O for a charm
To fright it hence!
LADY WOULDBE. Come nearer. Is this curl
In his right place, or this? Why is this higher
Than all the rest? You ha' not washed your eyes
yet!

Or do they not stand even i' your head?
Where is your fellow? call her.   *Exit* 1ST WOMAN.
   NANO.   —Now, Saint Mark
Deliver us! anon she'll beat her women,
Because her nose is red.

     Re-enter 1ST WOMAN *with* 2ND WOMAN.

  LADY WOULDBE.   I pray you, view
This tire, forsooth; are all things apt, or no?
   1ST WOMAN. One hair a little here sticks out, for-
    sooth.
   LADY WOULDBE. Does't so, forsooth? and where was
    your dear sight,
When it did so, forsooth? What now! bird-eyed?
And you, too? Pray you both approach and mend it.
Now, by that light, I muse you're not ashamed!
I, that have preached these things so oft unto you,
Read you the principles, argued all the grounds,
Disputed every fitness, every grace,
Called you to counsel of so frequent dressings——
   NANO. —More carefully than of your fame or
    honour.
   LADY WOULDBE. Made you acquainted what an
    ample dowry
The knowledge of these things would be unto you,
Able alone to get you noble husbands
At your return; and you thus to neglect it!
Besides, you seeing what a curious nation
Th' Italians are, what will they say of me?
'The English lady cannot dress herself.'
Here's a fine imputation to our country!
Well, go your ways, and stay i' the next room.
This fucus was too coarse, too; it's no matter.—
Good sir, you'll give 'em entertainment?
               Exit NANO *with* WOMEN.
   VOLPONE. —The storm comes toward me.

LADY WOULDBE. How does my Volpone?

VOLPONE. Troubled with noise, I cannot sleep; I dreamt

That a strange fury entered now my house,

And, with the dreadful tempest of her breath,

Did cleave my roof asunder.

LADY WOULDBE. Believe me, and I

Had the most fearful dream, could I remember't——

VOLPONE. —Out on my fate! I ha' giv'n her the occasion

How to torment me: she will tell me hers.

LADY WOULDBE. Methought the golden mediocrity,

Polite and delicate——

VOLPONE. O, if you do love me,

No more! I sweat and suffer at the mention

Of any dream. Feel how I tremble yet.

LADY WOULDBE. Alas, good soul! the passion of the heart.

Seed-pearl were good now, boiled with syrup of apples,

Tincture of gold, and coral, citron pills,

Your elecampane root, myrobalanes——

VOLPONE. —Ay me, I have ta'en a grasshopper by the wing!

LADY WOULDBE. Burnt silk and amber; you have muscadel

Good i' the house——

VOLPONE. You will not drink, and part?

LADY WOULDBE. No, fear not that. I doubt we shall not get

Some English saffron,—half a dram would serve—

Your sixteen cloves, a little musk, dried mints,

Bugloss, and barley-meal——

VOLPONE. —She's in again!

Before, I feigned diseases; now I have one.

LADY WOULDBE. And these applied with a right
    scarlet cloth.

VOLPONE. —Another flood of words! a very torrent!

LADY WOULDBE. Shall I, sir, make you a poultice?

VOLPONE.   No, no, no!
I'm very well; you need prescribe no more.

LADY WOULDBE. I have a little studied physic; but
    now
I'm all for music, save, i' the forenoons,
An hour or two for painting. I would have
A lady, indeed, t' have all, letters and arts,
Be able to discourse, to write, to paint;
But principal—as Plato holds—your music—
And so does wise Pythagoras, I take it—
Is your true rapture; when there is consent
In face, in voice, and clothes; and is, indeed,
Our sex's chiefest ornament.

VOLPONE.   The poet
As old in time as Plato, and as knowing,
Says that your highest female grace is silence.

LADY WOULDBE. Which o' your poets? Petrarch, or
    Tasso, or Dante?
Guarini? Ariosto? Aretine?
Cieco di Hadria? I have read them all.

VOLPONE. —Is everything a cause to my destruc-
    tion?

LADY WOULDBE. I think I ha' two or three of 'em
    about me.

VOLPONE. —The sun, the sea, will sooner both
    stand still
Than her eternal tongue! nothing can 'scape it.

LADY WOULDBE. Here's 'Pastor Fido'——

VOLPONE.   —Profess obstinate silence,
That's now my safest.

LADY WOULDBE.   All our English writers,
I mean such as are happy in th' Italian,

Will deign to steal out of this author mainly,
Almost as much as from Montagnié.
He has so modern and facile a vein,
Fitting the time, and catching the court ear.
Your Petrarch is more passionate, yet he,
In days of sonnetting, trusted 'em with much.
Dante is hard, and few can understand him.
But, for a desperate wit, there's Aretine!
Only his pictures are a little obscene——
You mark me not.

   VOLPONE.   Alas, my mind's perturbed.

   LADY WOULDBE. Why, in such cases, we must cure
      ourselves.
Make use of our philosophy——

   VOLPONE.   O 'y me!

   LADY WOULDBE. And as we find our passions do
      rebel,
Encounter 'em with reason, or divert 'em,
By giving scope unto some other humour
Of lesser danger; as, in politic bodies,
There's nothing more doth overwhelm the judg-
    ment
And clouds the understanding, than too much
Settling and fixing and, as 'twere, subsiding
Upon one object. For the incorporating
Of these same outward things into that part
Which we call mental, leaves some certain faeces
That stop the organs, and, as Plato says,
Assassinates our knowledge.

   VOLPONE.   —Now, the spirit
Of patience help me!

   LADY WOULDBE.   Come, in faith, I must
Visit you more a-days, and make you well.
Laugh and be lusty!

   VOLPONE.   —My good angel save me!

LADY WOULDBE. There was but one sole man in all
    the world
With whom I e'er could sympathize; and he
Would lie you often three, four hours together,
To hear me speak; and be sometime so rapt,
As he would answer me quite from the purpose,
Like you, and you are like him, just. I'll discourse,
An't be but only, sir, to bring you asleep,
How we did spend our time and loves together,
For some six years.

    VOLPONE.   O, O, O, O, O, O!

    LADY WOULDBE. For we were coaetanei, and
      brought up——

    VOLPONE. Some power, some fate, some fortune
      rescue me!

Enter MOSCA.

MOSCA. God save you, madam!

    LADY WOULDBE.   Good sir.

    VOLPONE.   —Mosca! welcome,
Welcome to my redemption.

    MOSCA.   Why, sir?

    VOLPONE.   O,
Rid me of this my torture, quickly, there,
My madam with the everlasting voice!
The bells, in time of pestilence, ne'er made
Like noise, or were in that perpetual motion;
The cock-pit comes not near it. All my house,
But now, steamed like a bath with her thick breath;
A lawyer could not have been heard; nor scarce
Another woman, such a hail of words
She has let fall. For Hell's sake, rid her hence.

    MOSCA. Has she presented?

    VOLPONE.   O, I do not care!
I'll take her absence upon any price,
With any loss.

MOSCA.　　　Madam——

LADY WOULDBE.　　　I ha' brought your patron
A toy, a cap here, of mine own work—

MOSCA.　　　　　　'Tis well.
I had forgot to tell you I saw your knight,
Where you'd little think it——

LADY WOULDBE.　　　Where?

MOSCA.　　　　　　　Marry,
Where yet, if you make haste, you may apprehend
　　him;
Rowing upon the water in a gondole,
With the most cunning courtesan of Venice.

LADY WOULDBE. Is't true?

MOSCA.　　　Pursue 'em, and believe your eyes.
Leave me to make your gift.—I knew 'twould take.
For lightly, they that use themselves most licence,
Are still most jealous.

VOLPONE.　　　Mosca, hearty thanks
For thy quick fiction, and delivery of me.
Now to my hopes, what sayst thou?

LADY WOULDBE.　　　But do you hear, sir?——

VOLPONE. —Again! I fear a paroxysm.

LADY WOULDBE.　　　　Which way
Rowed they together?

MOSCA.　　　Toward the Rialto.

LADY WOULDBE. I pray you lend me your dwarf.

MOSCA.　　　　　I pray you take him.
　　　　　　　Exit LADY WOULDBE.
Your hopes, sir, are like happy blossoms fair,
And promise timely fruit, if you will stay
But the maturing. Keep you at your couch;
Corbaccio will arrive straight, with the will.
When he is gone, I'll tell you more.　　*Exit.*

VOLPONE.　　　　My blood,
My spirits are returned; I am alive!
And, like your wanton gamester at primero,

Whose thought had whispered to him, not go less,
Methinks I lie, and draw——for an encounter.

Enter MOSCA *with* BONARIO.

MOSCA. Sir, here concealed, you may hear all.
    But pray you
Have patience, sir. *One knocks.* The same's your
    father knocks.
I am compelled to leave you.
    BONARIO.   Do so.—Yet.
Cannot my thought imagine this a truth.

MOSCA *leaves* BONARIO, *and admits* CORVINO,
followed by CELIA.

MOSCA. Death on me! you are come too soon,
    what meant you?
Did not I say I would send?
    CORVINO.   Yes, but I feared
You might forget it, and then they prevent us.
    MOSCA. —Prevent! Did e'er man haste so for his
    horns?
A courtier would not ply it so for a place.—
Well, now there's no helping it, stay here;
I'll presently return.
    CORVINO.   Where are you, Celia?
You know not wherefore I have brought you hither?
    CELIA. Not well, except you told me.
    CORVINO.   Now I will:
Hark hither.   *Whispers to her.*
    MOSCA. *To* BONARIO. Sir, your father hath sent
    word,
It will be half an hour ere he come.
And therefore, if you please to walk the while
Into that gallery—at the upper end
There are some books to entertain the time—
And I'll take care no man shall come unto you, sir.

BONARIO. Yes, I will stay there.—I do doubt this
fellow.

MOSCA. There, he is far enough; he can hear
nothing;
And for his father, I can keep him off.
                    Withdraws to VOLPONE'S *couch.*

CORVINO. Nay, now there is no starting back, and
therefore
Resolve upon it; I have so decreed.
It must be done. Nor would I move't afore,
Because I would avoid all shifts and tricks
That might deny me.

CELIA.   Sir, let me beseech you,
Affect not these strange trials. If you doubt
My chastity, why, lock me up forever;
Make me the heir of darkness. Let me live
Where I may please your fears, if not your trust.

CORVINO. Believe it, I have no such humour, I.
All that I speak I mean; yet I'm not mad,
Not horn-mad, see you? Go to, show yourself
Obedient, and a wife.

CELIA.   O Heaven!

CORVINO.   I say it,
Do so.

CELIA. Was this the train?

CORVINO.   I've told you reasons:
What the physicians have set down, how much
It may concern me, what my engagements are,
My means, and the necessity of those means
For my recovery. Wherefore, if you be
Loyal, and mine, be won, respect my venture.

CELIA. Before your honour?

CORVINO.   Honour! tut, a breath;
There's no such thing in nature: a mere term
Invented to awe fools. What is my gold

The worse for touching? clothes for being looked
    on?
Why, this 's no more. An old, decrepit wretch,
That has no sense, no sinew; takes his meat
With others' fingers; only knows to gape
When you do scald his gums; a voice, a shadow;
And what can this man hurt you?

    CELIA.   Lord! what spirit
Is this hath entered him?

    CORVINO.   And for your fame,
That's such a jig; as if I would go tell it,
Cry it on the Piazza! Who shall know it
But he that cannot speak it, and this fellow,
Whose lips are i' my pocket? Save yourself—
If you'll proclaim't, you may. I know no other
Should come to know it.

    CELIA.   Are heaven and saints then nothing?
Will they be blind or stupid?

    CORVINO.   How?

    CELIA.   Good sir,
Be jealous still, emulate them; and think
What hate they burn with toward every sin.

    CORVINO. I grant you. If I thought it were a sin,
I would not urge you. Should I offer this
To some young Frenchman, or hot Tuscan blood,
That had read Aretine, conned all his prints,
Knew every quirk within lust's labyrinth,
And were professed critic in lechery;
And I would look upon him, and applaud him—
This were a sin. But here 'tis contrary:
A pious work, mere charity, for physic,
And honest policy, to assure mine own.

    CELIA. O Heaven! canst thou suffer such a change?

    VOLPONE. —Thou art mine honour, Mosca, and
    my pride,
My joy, my tickling, my delight! Go bring 'em.

MOSCA. Please you draw near, sir.

CORVINO.   Come on, what——
You will not be rebellious? by that light——

MOSCA. Sir, Signior Corvino, here, is come to see
  you.

VOLPONE. Oh!

MOSCA.   And hearing of the consultation had,
So lately, for your health, is come to offer,
Or rather, sir, to prostitute——

CORVINO.   Thanks, sweet Mosca.

MOSCA. Freely, unasked, or unentreated——

CORVINO.   Well!

MOSCA. As the true, fervent instance of his love,
His own most fair and proper wife, the beauty
Only of price in Venice——

CORVINO.   'Tis well urged.

MOSCA. To be your comfortress, and to preserve
  you.

VOLPONE. Alas, I'm past, already! Pray you thank
  'im
For his good care and promptness; but for that,
'Tis a vain labour e'en to fight 'gainst heaven,
Applying fire to stone,—uh, uh, uh, uh!—
Making a dead leaf grow again. I take
His wishes gently, though; and you may tell him
What I've done for him. Marry, my state is hopeless!
Will him to pray for me, and t' use his fortune
With reverence when he comes to 't.

MOSCA.   Do you hear, sir?
Go to him with your wife.

CORVINO.   Heart of my father!
Wilt thou persist thus? Come, I pray thee, come.
Thou seest 'tis nothing, Celia. By this hand,
I shall grow violent. Come, do't, I say.

CELIA. Sir, kill me, rather. I will take down poison,
Eat burning coals, do anything——

CORVINO.   Be damned!
Heart, I will drag thee hence home by the hair,
Cry thee a strumpet through the streets, rip up
Thy mouth unto thine ears, and slit thy nose
Like a raw rochet—Do not tempt me, come!
Yield, I am loath—Death! I will buy some slave,
Whom I will kill, and bind thee to him alive,
And at my window hang you forth; devising
Some monstrous crime, which I, in capital letters,
Will eat into thy flesh with aquafortis
And burning corsives, on this stubborn breast.
Now, by the blood thou hast incensed, I'll do it!

CELIA. Sir, what you please, you may; I am your
martyr.

CORVINO. Be not thus obstinate; I ha' not deserved
it.
Think who it is entreats you. Pray thee, sweet—
Good faith, thou shalt have jewels, gowns, attires,
What thou wilt think, and ask. Do but go kiss him.
Or touch him but. For my sake—At my suit—
This once—No? not? I shall remember this!
Will you disgrace me thus? D'you thirst my un-
doing?

MOSCA. Nay, gentle lady, be advised.

CORVINO.   No, no.
She has watched her time. God's precious, this is
scurvy,
'Tis very scurvy; and you are——

MOSCA.   Nay, good sir.

CORVINO. An arrant locust, by Heaven, a locust!
Whore,
Crocodile, that hast thy tears prepared,
Expecting how thou'lt bid 'em flow——

MOSCA.   Nay, pray you, sir,
She will consider.

CELIA.   Would my life would serve
To satisfy!

CORVINO. 'Sdeath! if she would but speak to him,
And save my reputation, it were somewhat;
But spitefully to affect my utter ruin!

MOSCA. Ay, now you've put your fortune in her
    hands.
Why, i'faith, it is her modesty; I must quit her.
If you were absent, she would be more coming;
I know it, and dare undertake for her.
What woman can before her husband? Pray you,
Let us depart, and leave her here.

CORVINO.   Sweet Celia,
Thou mayst redeem all yet; I'll say no more.
If not, esteem yourself as lost. Nay, stay there.
                 Exit with MOSCA.

CELIA. O God and his good angels! Whither,
    whither
Is shame fled human breasts, that with such ease,
Men dare put off your honours, and their own?
Is that which ever was a cause of life
Now placed beneath the basest circumstance,
And modesty an exile made, for money?

VOLPONE. *Leaps off from his couch.* Ay, in Corvino,
    and such earth-fed minds,
That never tasted the true heav'n of love.
Assure thee, Celia, he that would sell thee,
Only for hope of gain, and that uncertain,
He would have sold his part of paradise
For ready money, had he met a cope-man.
Why art thou 'mazed to see me thus revived?
Rather applaud thy beauty's miracle;
'Tis thy great work, that hath, not now alone,
But sundry times raised me in several shapes,
And, but this morning, like a mountebank,
To see thee at thy window. Ay, before

I would have left my practice for thy love,
In varying figures, I would have contended
With the blue Proteus, or the hornèd flood.
Now art thou welcome.

  CELIA.   Sir!

  VOLPONE.   Nay, fly me not.
Nor let thy false imagination
That I was bed-rid, make thee think I am so.
Thou shalt not find it. I am now as fresh,
As hot, as high, and in as jovial plight,
As when, in that so celebrated scene,
At recitation of our comedy
For entertainment of the great Valois,
I acted young Antinous; and attracted
The eyes and ears of all the ladies present,
T' admire each graceful gesture, note, and footing.

     SONG.

  'Come, my Celia, let us prove,
   While we can, the sports of love.
   Time will not be ours forever,
   He at length our good will sever;
   Spend not then his gifts in vain.
   Suns that set may rise again;
   But if once we lose this light,
   'Tis with us perpetual night.
   Why should we defer our joys?
   Fame and rumour are but toys.
   Cannot we delude the eyes
   Of a few poor household spies?
   Or his easier ears beguile,
   Thus removèd by our wile?
   'Tis no sin love's fruits to steal,
   But the sweet thefts to reveal:
   To be taken, to be seen,
   These have crimes accounted been.'

CELIA. Some sèrene blast me, or dire lightning
strike
This my offending face!
    VOLPONE.   Why droops my Celia?
Thou hast, in place of a base husband, found
A worthy lover; use thy fortune well,
With secrecy and pleasure. See, behold
What thou art queen of, not in expectation—
As I feed others—but possessed and crowned.
See, here, a rope of pearl, and each more orient
Than that the brave Egyptian queen caroused—
Dissolve and drink 'em. See, a carbuncle,
May put out both the eyes of our Saint Mark;
A diamond would have bought Lollia Paulina,
When she came in like starlight, hid with jewels
That were the spoils of provinces—take these
And wear, and lose 'em; yet remains an earring
To purchase them again, and this whole state.
A gem but worth a private patrimony,
Is nothing; we will eat such at a meal.
The heads of parrots, tongues of nightingales,
The brains of peacocks, and of estriches,
Shall be our food; and, could we get the phoenix,
Though nature lost her kind, she were our dish.
    CELIA. Good sir, these things might move a mind
affected
With such delights; but I, whose innocence
Is all I can think wealthy, or worth th' enjoying,
And which, once lost, I have nought to lose beyond
it,
Cannot be taken with these sensual baits.
If you have conscience——
    VOLPONE.   'Tis the beggar's virtue.
If thou hast wisdom, hear me, Celia.
Thy baths shall be the juice of gillyflowers,
Spirit of roses, and of violets,

The milk of unicorns, and panthers' breath
Gathered in bags, and mixed with Cretan wines.
Our drink shall be preparèd gold and amber,
Which we will take until my roof whirl round
With the vertigo; and my dwarf shall dance,
My eunuch sing, my fool make up the antic.
Whilst we, in changèd shapes, act Ovid's tales,
Thou like Europa now, and I like Jove,
Then I like Mars, and thou like Erycine;
So of the rest, till we have quite run through,
And wearied all the fables of the gods.
Then will I have thee in more modern forms,
Attirèd like some sprightly dame of France,
Brave Tuscan lady, or proud Spanish beauty;
Sometimes unto the Persian Sophy's wife,
Or the Grand Signior's mistress; and for change,
To one of our most artful courtesans,
Or some quick Negro, or cold Russian.
And I will meet thee in as many shapes;
Where we may so transfuse our wand'ring souls
Out at our lips, and score up sums of pleasures,
   'That the curious shall not know
   How to tell them as they flow;
   And the envious, when they find
   What their number is, be pined.'
 CELIA. If you have ears that will be pierced, or
  eyes
That can be opened, a heart may be touched,
Or any part that yet sounds man above you;
If you have touch of holy saints, or heaven,
Do me the grace to let me 'scape. If not,
Be bountiful and kill me. You do know
I am a creature hither ill betrayed,
By one whose shame I would forget it were.
If you will deign me neither of these graces,
Yet feed your wrath, sir, rather than your lust,—

It is a vice comes nearer manliness—
And punish that unhappy crime of nature
Which you miscall my beauty. Flay my face,
Or poison it with ointments, for seducing
Your blood to this rebellion. Rub these hands
With what may cause an eating leprosy,
E'en to my bones and marrow—anything
That may disfavour me, save in my honour.
And I will kneel to you, pray for you, pay down
A thousand hourly vows, sir, for your health;
Report and think you virtuous——

VOLPONE.   Think me cold,
Frozen, and impotent, and so report me?
That I had Nestor's hernia thou wouldst think.
I do degenerate, and abuse my nation,
To play with opportunity thus long.
I should have done the act, and then have parleyed.
Yield, or I'll force thee.

CELIA.   O! just God!

VOLPONE.   In vain——

BONARIO. *Leaps out from where* MOSCA *had placed
    him.* Forbear, foul ravisher! libidinous swine!
Free the forced lady or thou diest, impostor.
But that I am loath to snatch thy punishment
Out of the hand of justice, thou shouldst yet
Be made the timely sacrifice of vengeance,
Before this altar, and this dross, thy idol.—
Lady, let's quit the place; it is the den
Of villainy. Fear nought, you have a guard;
And he ere long shall meet his just reward.

                    Exeunt BONARIO *and* CELIA.

VOLPONE. Fall on me, roof, and bury me in ruin!
Become my grave, that wert my shelter! O!
I am unmasked, unspirited, undone,
Betrayed to beggary, to infamy——

Enter MOSCA.

MOSCA. Where shall I run, most wretched shame
of men,
To beat out my unlucky brains?
VOLPONE.　　　　　　　　　　Here, here.
What! dost thou bleed?
　　MOSCA.　　　　　　　　O that his well-driv'n sword
Had been so courteous to have cleft me down
Unto the navel, ere I lived to see
My life, my hopes, my spirits, my patron, all
Thus desperately engagèd by my error!
　　VOLPONE. Woe on thy fortune!
　　MOSCA.　　　　　　　　And my follies, sir.
VOLPONE. Th'ast made me miserable.
　　MOSCA.　　　　　　　　And myself, sir.
Who would have thought he would have hearkened
so?
　　VOLPONE. What shall we do?
　　MOSCA.　　　　　　　I know not; if my heart
Could expiate the mischance, I'd pluck it out.
Will you be pleased to hang me, or cut my throat?
And I'll requite you, sir. Let's die like Romans,
Since we have lived like Grecians.
　　　　　　　　　　　　　They knock without.
　　VOLPONE.　　　　　　　Hark! who's there?
I hear some footing; officers, the Saffi,
Come to apprehend us! I do feel the brand
Hissing already at my forehead; now
Mine ears are boring.
　　MOSCA.　　　　　　To your couch, sir; you
Make that place good, however. Guilty men
Suspect what they deserve still. Signior Corbaccio!

Enter CORBACCIO.

CORBACCIO. Why, how now, Mosca?
　　MOSCA.　　　　　　　O, undone, amazed, sir!

Your son,—I know not by what accident—
Acquainted with your purpose to my patron,
Touching your will, and making him your heir;
Entered our house with violence, his sword drawn,
Sought for you, called you wretch, unnatural,
Vowed he would kill you.

CORBACCIO.   Me?

MOSCA.   Yes, and my patron.

CORBACCIO. This act shall dishinherit him indeed!
Here is the will.

MOSCA.   'Tis well, sir.

CORBACCIO.   Right and well.
Be you as careful now for me.

Enter VOLTORE, *behind.*

MOSCA.   My life, sir,
Is not more tendered; I am only yours.

CORBACCIO. How does he? will he die shortly,
    think'st thou?

MOSCA.   I fear
He'll outlast May.

CORBACCIO.   Today?

MOSCA.   No, last out May, sir.

CORBACCIO. Couldst thou not gi' him a dram?

MOSCA.   O, by no means, sir.

CORBACCIO. Nay, I'll not bid you.

VOLTORE.   This is a knave, I see.

MOSCA. —How! Signior Voltore! did he hear me?

VOLTORE.   Parasite!

MOSCA. Who's that?—O sir, most timely welcome—

VOLTORE.   Scarce,
To the discovery of your tricks, I fear.
You are his only? And mine also, are you not?

MOSCA. Who? I, sir!

VOLTORE.   You, sir. What device is this
About a will?

MOSCA.   A plot for you, sir.

VOLTORE.   Come,
Put not your foists upon me; I shall scent 'em.
   MOSCA. Did you not hear it?
   VOLTORE.   Yes, I hear Corbaccio
Hath made your patron there his heir.
   MOSCA.   'Tis true;
By my device, drawn to it by my plot,
With hope——
   VOLTORE.   Your patron should reciprocate?
And you have promised?
   MOSCA.   For your good I did, sir.
Nay more, I told his son, brought, hid him here,
Where he might hear his father pass the deed;
Being persuaded to it by this thought, sir:
That the unnaturalness, first, of the act,
And then his father's oft disclaiming in him—
Which I did mean t'help on—would sure enrage him
To do some violence upon his parent;
On which the law should take sufficient hold,
And you be stated in a double hope.
Truth be my comfort, and my conscience,
My only aim was to dig you a fortune
Out of these two old, rotten sepulchres——
   VOLTORE. I cry thee mercy, Mosca.
   MOSCA.   Worth your patience,
And your great merit, sir. And see the change!
   VOLTORE. Why, what success?
   MOSCA.   Most hapless! you must help, sir.
Whilst we expected th' old raven, in comes
Corvino's wife, sent hither by her husband——
   VOLTORE. What, with a present?
   MOSCA.   No, sir, on visitation,—
I'll tell you how anon—and staying long,
The youth he grows impatient, rushes forth,
Seizeth the lady, wounds me, makes her swear—
Or he would murder her, that was his vow—

T' affirm my patron to have done her rape;
Which how unlike it is, you see! And hence
With that pretext he's gone, t' accuse his father,
Defame my patron, defeat you——
  VOLTORE.   Where's her husband?
Let him be sent for straight.
  MOSCA.   Sir, I'll go fetch him.
  VOLTORE. Bring him to the Scrutineo.
  MOSCA.   Sir, I will.
  VOLTORE. This must be stopped.
  MOSCA.   O, you do nobly, sir.
Alas, 'twas laboured all, sir, for your good;
Nor was there want of counsel in the plot.
But fortune can, at any time, o'erthrow
The projects of a hundred learned clerks, sir.
  CORBACCIO. What's that?
  VOLTORE.   Will't please you, sir, to go along?
                    Exit VOLTORE, *followed by* CORBACCIO.
  MOSCA. Patron, go in, and pray for our success.
  VOLPONE. Need makes devotion. Heaven your
    labour bless!   *Exeunt.*

ACT FOUR. SCENE ONE

A street

Enter SIR POLITIC WOULDBE *and* PEREGRINE.

  SIR POLITIC. I told you, sir, it was a plot. You see
What observation is. You mentioned me
For some instructions: I will tell you, sir,
Since we are met here in this height of Venice,
Some few particulars I have set down,

Only for this meridian, fit to be known
Of your crude traveller; and they are these.
I will not touch, sir, at your phrase, or clothes,
For they are old.

    PEREGRINE.   Sir, I have better.

    SIR POLITIC.   Pardon,
I meant, as they are themes.

    PEREGRINE.   O sir, proceed.
I'll slander you no more of wit, good sir.

    SIR POLITIC. First, for your garb, it must be grave
    and serious,
Very reserved and locked; not tell a secret
On any terms, not to your father; scarce
A fable, but with caution; make sure choice
Both of your company and discourse; beware
You never speak a truth——

    PEREGRINE.   How!

    SIR POLITIC.   Not to strangers,
For those be they you must converse with most;
Others I would not know, sir, but at distance,
So as I still might be a saver in 'em;
You shall have tricks else passed upon you hourly.
And then, for your religion, profess none,
But wonder at the diversity of all;
And, for your part, protest, were there no other
But simply the laws o' th' land, you could content
    you.
Nick Machiavel and Monsieur Bodin both
Were of this mind. Then must you learn the use
And handling of your silver fork at meals,
The metal of your glass,—these are main matters
With your Italian—and to know the hour
When you must eat your melons and your figs.

    PEREGRINE. Is that a point of state, too?

    SIR POLITIC.   Here it is.
For your Venetian, if he see a man

Preposterous in the least, he has him straight.
He has; he strips him. I ll acquaint you, sir,
I now have lived here 'tis some fourteen months;
Within the first week of my landing here,
And took me for a citizen of Venice.
I knew the forms so well——

    PEREGRINE.   —And nothing else.

    SIR POLITIC. I had read Contarene, took me a
      house,
Dealt with my Jews to furnish it with movables—
Well, if I could but find one man, one man
To mine own heart, whom I durst trust, I would——

    PEREGRINE. What, what, sir?

    SIR POLITIC.   Make him rich; make
      him a fortune.
He should not think again. I would command it.

    PEREGRINE. As how?

    SIR POLITIC.   With certain projects that I have,
Which I may not discover.

    PEREGRINE.   —If I had
But one to wager with, I would lay odds now,
He tells me instantly.

    SIR POLITIC.   One is—and that
I care not greatly who knows—to serve the state
Of Venice with red herrings for three years,
And at a certain rate, from Rotterdam,
Where I have correspondence. There's a letter,
Sent me from one o' th' States, and to that purpose.
He cannot write his name, but that's his mark.

    PEREGRINE. He is a chandler?

    SIR POLITIC.   No, a cheesemonger.
There are some other two with whom I treat
About the same negotiation;
And I will undertake it. For 'tis thus:
I'll do't with ease, I've cast it all. Your hoy
Carries but three men in her, and a boy,

And she shall make me three returns a year;
So if there come but one of three, I save;
If two, I can defalc. But this is now,
If my main project fail.

    PEREGRINE.   Then you have others?

    SIR POLITIC. I should be loath to draw the subtle
    air
Of such a place, without my thousand aims.
I'll not dissemble, sir, where'er I come,
I love to be considerative; and 'tis true
I have at my free hours thought upon
Some certain goods unto the state of Venice,
Which I do call my cautions; and, sir, which
I mean, in hope of pension, to propound
To the Great Council, then unto the Forty,
So to the Ten. My means are made already——

    PEREGRINE. By whom?

    SIR POLITIC.   Sir, one that though his
    place be obscure,
Yet he can sway, and they will hear him. He's
A commendatore.

    PEREGRINE.   What! a common sergeant?

    SIR POLITIC. Sir, such as they are, put it in their
    mouths,
What they should say, sometimes, as well as greater.
I think I have my notes to show you——

    PEREGRINE.   Good, sir.

    SIR POLITIC. But you shall swear unto me, on your
    gentry,
Not to anticipate——

    PEREGRINE.   I, sir?

    SIR POLITIC.   Nor reveal
A circumstance——My paper is not with me.

    PEREGRINE. O, but you can remember, sir.

    SIR POLITIC.   My first is
Concerning tinder-boxes. You must know,

No family is here without its box.
Now, sir, it being so portable a thing,
Put case that you or I were ill affected
Unto the state; sir, with it in our pockets,
Might not I go into the Arsenale?
Or you? come out again? and none the wiser?

  PEREGRINE. Except yourself, sir.

  SIR POLITIC.   Go to, then. I therefore
Advertise to the state, how fit it were
That none but such as were known patriots,
Sound lovers of their country, should be suffered
T' enjoy them in their houses; and even those
Sealed at some office, and at such a bigness
As might not lurk in pockets.

  PEREGRINE.   Admirable!

  SIR POLITIC. My next is, how t' inquire, and be
  resolved
By present demonstration, whether a ship,
Newly arrived from Syria, or from
Any suspected part of all the Levant,
Be guilty of the plague. And, where they use
To lie out forty, fifty days, sometimes,
About the Lazaretto, for their trial;
I'll save that charge and loss unto the merchant,
And in an hour clear the doubt.

  PEREGRINE.   Indeed, sir!

  SIR POLITIC. Or——I will lose my labour.

  PEREGRINE.   My faith, that's much.

  SIR POLITIC. Nay, sir, conceive me. 'Twill cost me,
  in onions,
Some thirty livres——

  PEREGRINE.   Which is one pound sterling.

  SIR POLITIC. Beside my waterworks. For this I do,
  sir:
First, I bring in your ship 'twixt two brick walls—
But those the state shall venture. On the one

I strain me a fair tarpaulin, and in that
I stick my onions, cut in halves; the other
Is full of loopholes, out at which I thrust
The noses of my bellows; and those bellows
I keep, with waterworks, in perpetual motion,
Which is the easiest matter of a hundred.
Now, sir, your onion, which doth naturally
Attract th' infection, and your bellows blowing
The air upon him, will show instantly,
By his changed colour, if there be contagion;
Or else remain as fair as at the first.
Now 'tis known, 'tis nothing.

> PEREGRINE. You are right, sir.
> SIR POLITIC. I would I had my note.
> PEREGRINE. Faith, so would I.—

But you ha' done well for once, sir.

> SIR POLITIC. Were I false,

Or would be made so, I could show you reasons
How I could sell this state now to the Turk,
Spite of their galleys, or their——

> PEREGRINE. Pray you, Sir Poll.
> SIR POLITIC. I have 'em not about me.
> PEREGRINE. That I feared.

They 're there, sir?

> SIR POLITIC. No, this is my diary,

Wherein I note my actions of the day.

> PEREGRINE. Pray you let's see, sir. What is here?—

'Notandum,
A rat had gnawn my spur-leathers; notwithstanding,
I put on new, and did go forth; but first
I threw three beans over the threshold. Item,
I went and bought two toothpicks, whereof one
I burst immediately, in a discourse
With a Dutch merchant, 'bout Ragion del Stato.
From him I went and paid a moccenigo

For piecing my silk stockings; by the way
I cheapened sprats; and at Saint Mark's I urined.'
Faith these are politic notes!

SIR POLITIC.   Sir, I do slip
No action of my life, thus, but I quote it.

  PEREGRINE. Believe me, it is wise!

  SIR POLITIC.   Nay, sir, read forth.

Enter LADY WOULDBE, NANO, *and two* WOMEN.

  LADY WOULDBE. Where should this loose knight be,
    trow? Sure, he's housed.

  NANO. Why, then he's fast.

  LADY WOULDBE.   Ay, he plays both with me!
I pray you stay.—This heat will do more harm
To my complexion than his heart is worth.
I do not care to hinder, but to take him.
How it comes off!

  1ST WOMAN.   My master's yonder.

  LADY WOULDBE.   Where?

  2ND WOMAN. With a young gentleman.

  LADY WOULDBE.   That same's the party,
In man's apparel!—Pray you, sir, jog my knight.
I will be tender to his reputation,
However he demerit.

  SIR POLITIC.   —My lady!

  PEREGRINE.   Where?

  SIR POLITIC. 'Tis she indeed, sir, you shall know
    her. She is,
Were she not mine, a lady of that merit,
For fashion and behaviour; and for beauty
I durst compare——

  PEREGRINE.   It seems you are not jealous,
That dare commend her.

  SIR POLITIC.   Nay, and for discourse——

  PEREGRINE. Being your wife, she cannot miss that.

SIR POLITIC. Madam,
Here is a gentleman, pray you, use him fairly;
He seems a youth, but he is——
    LADY WOULDBE. None.
    SIR POLITIC. Yes, one
Has put his face as soon into the world——
    LADY WOULDBE. You mean, as early? but today?
    SIR POLITIC. How's this?
    LADY WOULDBE. Why, in this habit, sir, you appre-
    hend me.
Well, Master Wouldbe, this doth not become you.
I had thought the odour, sir, of your good name
Had been more precious to you; that you would not
Have done this dire massacre on your honour;
One of your gravity, and rank besides!
But knights, I see, care little for the oath
They make to ladies, chiefly their own ladies.
    SIR POLITIC. Now, by my spurs, the symbol of my
      knighthood——
    PEREGRINE. —Lord, how his brain is humbled for
    an oath!
    SIR POLITIC. I reach you not.
    LADY WOULDBE. Right, sir, your policy
May bear it through thus.—Sir, a word with you.
I would be loath to contest publicly
With any gentlewoman, or to seem
Froward, or violent, as the courtier says—
It comes too near rusticity in a lady,
Which I would shun by all means. And, however
I may deserve from Master Wouldbe, yet
T' have one fair gentlewoman thus be made
Th' unkind instrument to wrong another,
And one she knows not, ay, and to persever;
In my poor judgment, is not warranted
From being a solecism in our sex,
If not in manners.

PEREGRINE.   How is this!

SIR POLITIC.   Sweet madam,
Come nearer to your aim.

LADY WOULDBE.   Marry, and will, sir.
Since you provoke me with your impudence,
And laughter of your light land-siren here,
Your Sporus, your hermaphrodite——

PEREGRINE.   What's here?
Poetic fury and historic storms!

SIR POLITIC. The gentleman, believe it, is of worth,
And of our nation.

LADY WOULDBE.   Ay, your Whitefriars nation!
Come, I blush for you, Master Wouldbe, I;
And am ashamed you should ha' no more forehead,
Than thus to be the patron, or Saint George,
To a lewd harlot, a base fricatrice,
A female devil in a male outside.

SIR POLITIC.   Nay,
An you be such a one, I must bid adieu
To your delights. The case appears too liquid.   *Exit.*

LADY WOULDBE. Ay, you may carry't clear, with you
    state-face!
But for your carnival concupiscence,
Who here is fled for liberty of conscience,
From furious persecution of the Marshal,
Her will I disc'ple.

PEREGRINE.   This is fine, i' faith!
And do you use this often? Is this part
Of your wit's exercise, 'gainst you have occasion?
Madam——

LADY WOULDBE. Go to, sir.

PEREGRINE.   Do you hear me, lady?
Why, if your knight have set you to beg shirts,
Or to invite me home, you might have done it
A nearer way by far.

LADY WOULDBE. This cannot work you
Out of my snare.

PEREGRINE. Why, am I in it, then?
Indeed your husband told me you were fair,
And so you are; only your nose inclines—
That side that's next the sun—to the queen-apple.

LADY WOULDBE. This cannot be endured by any
    patience.

Enter MOSCA.

MOSCA. What's the matter, madam?

LADY WOULDBE. If the Senate
Right not my quest in this, I will protest 'em
To all the world no aristocracy.

MOSCA. What is the injury, lady?

LADY WOULDBE. Why, the callet
You told me of, here I have ta'en disguised.

MOSCA. Who? this! what means your ladyship?
    The creature
I mentioned to you is apprehended now
Before the Senate, you shall see her——

LADY WOULDBE. Where?

MOSCA. I'll bring you to her. This young gentleman,
I saw him land this morning at the port.

LADY WOULDBE. Is't possible? how has my judg-
    ment wandered!
Sir, I must, blushing, say to you I have erred,
And plead your pardon.

PEREGRINE. What, more changes yet?

LADY WOULDBE. I hope y' ha' not the malice to
    remember
A gentlewoman's passion. If you stay
In Venice here, please you to use me, sir——

MOSCA. Will you go, madam?

LADY WOULDBE. Pray you, sir, use me. In faith,

The more you see me, the more I shall conceive
You have forgot our quarrel.

           Exeunt LADY WOULDBE, MOSCA, NANO, *and*
    WOMEN.

  PEREGRINE.   This is rare!
Sir Politic Wouldbe? no, Sir Politic Bawd,
To bring me thus acquainted with his wife!
Well, wise Sir Poll, since you have practised thus
Upon my freshmanship, I'll try your salt-head,
What proof it is against a counter-plot.   *Exit.*

ACT FOUR. SCENE TWO

The Scrutineo

Enter VOLTORE, CORBACCIO, CORVINO, *and* MOSCA.

  VOLTORE. Well, now you know the carriage of the
    business,
Your constancy is all that is required
Unto the safety of it.

  MOSCA.   Is the lie
Safely conveyed amongst us? is that sure?
Knows every man his burden?

  CORVINO.   Yes.

  MOSCA.   Then shrink not.

  CORVINO. —But knows the advocate the truth?

  MOSCA.   O sir,
By no means. I devised a formal tale,
That salved your reputation. But be valiant, sir.

  CORVINO. I fear no one but him, that this his
    pleading
Should make him stand for a co-heir——

MOSCA.   Co-halter!
Hang him, we will but use his tongue, his noise,
As we do Croaker's here.

CORVINO.   Ay, what shall he do?

MOSCA. When we have done, you mean?

CORVINO.   Yes.

MOSCA.   Why, we'll think:
Sell him for mummia; he's half dust already. *To*
    VOLTORE.
Do you not smile to see this buffalo,
How he doth sport it with his head?—I should,
If all were well and past. *To* CORBACCIO. Sir, only
    you
Are he that shall enjoy the crop of all,
And these not know for whom they toil.

CORBACCIO.   Ay, peace.

MOSCA. *To* CORVINO. But you shall eat it.—Much!—
    To VOLTORE. Worshipful sir,
Mercury sit upon your thund'ring tongue,
Or the French Hercules, and make your language
As conquering as his club, to beat along,
As with a tempest, flat, our adversaries;
But much more yours, sir.

VOLTORE.   Here they come, ha' done.

MOSCA. I have another witness, if you need, sir,
I can produce.

VOLTORE.   Who is it?

MOSCA.   Sir, I have her.

Enter four AVOCATORI, BONARIO, CELIA, NOTARIO,
            COMMENDATORI, &C.

1ST AVOCATORE. The like of this the Senate never
    heard of.

2ND AVOCATORE. 'Twill come most strange to them,
    when we report it.

4TH AVOCATORE. The gentlewoman has been ever
  held
Of unreprovèd name.

3RD AVOCATORE.   So the young man.

4TH AVOCATORE. The more unnatural part that of
  his father.

2ND AVOCATORE. More of the husband.

1ST AVOCATORE.   I not know to give
His act a name, it is so monstrous!

4TH AVOCATORE. But the impostor, he is a thing
  created
T' exceed example!

1ST AVOCATORE.   And all after-times!

2ND AVOCATORE. I never heard a true voluptuary
Described, but him.

3RD AVOCATORE.   Appear yet those were cited?

NOTARIO. All but the old magnifico, Volpone.

1ST AVOCATORE. Why is not he here?

MOSCA.   Please your fatherhoods,
Here is his advocate. Himself's so weak,
So feeble——

4TH AVOCATORE. Who are you?

BONARIO.   His parasite,
His knave, his pander! I beseech the court
He may be forced to come, that your grave eyes
May bear strong witness of his strange impostures.

VOLTORE. Upon my faith and credit with your
  virtues,
He is not able to endure the air.

2ND AVOCATORE. Bring him, however.

3RD AVOCATORE.   We will see him.

4TH AVOCATORE. Fetch him.   *Exeunt* OFFICERS.

VOLTORE. Your fatherhoods' fit pleasures be
  obeyed,
But sure the sight will rather move your pities
Than indignation. May it please the court,

In the meantime, he may be heard in me:
I know this place most void of prejudice,
And therefore crave it, since we have no reason
To fear our truth should hurt our cause.

    3RD AVOCATORE.   Speak free.

    VOLTORE. Then know, most honoured fathers, I
      must now

Discover to your strangely abusèd ears
The most prodigious and most frontless piece
Of solid impudence and treachery,
That ever vicious nature yet brought forth
To shame the state of Venice. This lewd woman,
That wants no artificial looks or tears
To help the visor she has now put on,
Hath long been known a close adulteress
To that lascivious youth there; not suspected,
I say, but known, and taken in the act
With him; and by this man, the easy husband,
Pardoned; whose timeless bounty makes him now
Stand here, the most unhappy, innocent person
That ever man's own goodness made accused.
For these, not knowing how to owe a gift
Of that dear grace, but with their shame; being
    placed
So above all powers of their gratitude,
Began to hate the benefit; and in place
Of thanks, devise t' extirp the memory
Of such an act. Wherein, I pray your fatherhoods
To observe the malice, yea, the rage of creatures
Discovered in their evils; and what heart
Such take, even from their crimes. But that anon
Will more appear. This gentleman, the father,
Hearing of this foul fact, with many others,
Which daily struck at his too tender ears,
And grieved in nothing more than that he could not
Preserve himself a parent,—his son's ills

Growing to that strange flood—at last decreed
To disinherit him.

    1ST AVOCATORE. These be strange turns!

    2ND AVOCATORE. The young man's fame was ever
        fair and honest.

    VOLTORE. So much more full of danger is his vice,
That can beguile so, under shade of virtue.
But, as I said, my honoured sires, his father
Having this settled purpose,—by what means
To him betrayed, we know not—and this day
Appointed for the deed; that parricide,
I cannot style him better, by confederacy
Preparing this his paramour to be there,
Entered Volpone's house,—who was the man,
Your fatherhoods must understand, designed
For the inheritance—there sought his father.
But with what purpose sought he him, my lords?
I tremble to pronounce it, that a son
Unto a father, and to such a father,
Should have so foul, felonious intent:
It was to murder him! When, being prevented
By his more happy absence, what then did he?
Not check his wicked thoughts; no, now new deeds,—
Mischief doth never end where it begins—
An act of horror, fathers! he dragged forth
The aged gentleman that had there lain bed-rid
Three years and more, out off his innocent couch,
Naked, upon the floor, there left him; wounded
His servant in the face; and with this strumpet,
The stale to his forged practice, who was glad
To be so active,—I shall here desire
Your fatherhoods to note but my collections,
As most remarkable—thought at once to stop
His father's ends, discredit his free choice
In the old gentleman, redeem themselves
By laying infamy upon this man,

To whom, with blushing, they should owe their
    lives.

    1ST AVOCATORE. What proofs have you of this?

    BONARIO.   Most honoured fathers,
I humbly crave there be no credit given
To this man's mercenary tongue.

    2ND AVOCATORE.   Forbear.

    BONARIO. His soul moves in his fee.

    3RD AVOCATORE.   O, sir!

    BONARIO.   This fellow,
For six sols more would plead against his Maker.

    1ST AVOCATORE. You do forget yourself.

    VOLTORE.   Nay, nay, grave fathers,
Let him have scope. Can any man imagine
That he will spare 's accuser, that would not
Have spared his parent?

    1ST AVOCATORE.   Well, produce your proofs.

    CELIA. —I would I could forget I were a creature!

    VOLTORE. Signior Corbaccio!

    4TH AVOCATORE.   What is he?

    VOLTORE.   The father.

    2ND AVOCATORE. Has he had an oath?

    NOTARIO.   Yes.

    CORBACCIO.   What must I do now?

    NOTARIO. Your testimony's craved.

    CORBACCIO.   Speak to the knave?
I'll ha' my mouth first stopped with earth. My heart
Abhors his knowledge. I disclaim in him.

    1ST AVOCATORE. But for what cause?

    CORBACCIO.   The mere portent of nature.
He is an utter stranger to my loins.

    BONARIO. Have they made you to this?

    CORBACCIO.   I will not hear thee,
Monster of men, swine, goat, wolf, parricide!
Speak not, thou viper.

BONARIO. Sir, I will sit down,
And rather wish my innocence should suffer,
Than I resist the authority of a father.

VOLTORE. Signior Corvino!

2ND AVOCATORE. This is strange.

1ST AVOCATORE. Who's this?

NOTARIO. The husband.

4TH AVOCATORE. Is he sworn?

NOTARIO. He is.

3RD AVOCATORE. Speak, then.

CORVINO. This woman, please your fatherhoods, is
   a whore
Of most hot exercise, more than a partridge,
Upon record——

1ST AVOCATORE. No more.

CORVINO. Neighs like a jennet.

NOTARIO. Preserve the honour of the court.

CORVINO. I shall,
And modesty of your most reverend ears.
And yet I hope that I may say these eyes
Have seen her glued unto that piece of cedar,
That fine, well-timbered gallant; and that here
The letters may be read, thorough the horn,
That make the story perfect.

MOSCA. —Excellent, sir!

CORVINO. —There is no shame in this now, is there?

MOSCA. None.

CORVINO. Or if I said, I hoped that she were on-
   ward
To her damnation, if there be a hell
Greater than whore and woman; a good Catholic
May make the doubt.

3RD AVOCATORE. His grief hath made him frantic.

1ST AVOCATORE. Remove him hence.

CELIA *swoons*.

2ND AVOCATORE.   Look to the woman.

CORVINO.   Rare!
Prettily feigned again!

4TH AVOCATORE.   Stand from about her.

1ST AVOCATORE. Give her the air.

3RD AVOCATORE.   What can you say?

MOSCA.   My wound,
May it please your wisdoms, speaks for me, received
In aid of my good patron, when he missed
His sought-for father, when that well-taught dame
Had her cue given her to cry out a rape.

BONARIO. O most laid impudence! Fathers—

3RD AVOCATORE.   Sir, be silent;
You had your hearing free, so must they theirs.

2ND AVOCATORE. I do begin to doubt th' imposture
    here.

4TH AVOCATORE. This woman has too many moods.

VOLTORE.   Grave fathers,
She is a creature of a most professed
And prostituted lewdness.

CORVINO.   Most impetuous,
Unsatisfied, grave fathers!

VOLTORE.   May her feignings
Not take your wisdoms; but this day she baited
A stranger, a grave knight, with her loose eyes
And more lascivious kisses. This man saw 'em
Together on the water in a gondola.

MOSCA. Here is the lady herself, that saw 'em
    too,
Without; who then had in the open streets
Pursued them, but for saving her knight's honour.

1ST AVOCATORE. Produce that lady.

2ND AVOCATORE.   Let her come. *Exit* MOSCA.

4TH AVOCATORE.   These things,
They strike with wonder!

3RD AVOCATORE.   I am turned a stone!

Re-enter MOSCA *with* LADY WOULDBE.

MOSCA. Be resolute, madam.

LADY WOULDBE.   Ay, this same is she.—
Out, thou chameleon harlot! now thine eyes
Vie tears with the hyena. Dar'st thou look
Upon my wrongèd face?—I cry your pardons.
I fear I have forgettingly transgressed
Against the dignity of the court——

2ND AVOCATORE.   No, madam,

LADY WOULDBE. And been exorbitant——

4TH AVOCATORE.   You have not, lady,
These proofs are strong.

LADY WOULDBE. Surely, I had no purpose
To scandalize your honours, or my sex's.

3RD AVOCATORE. We do believe it.

LADY WOULDBE.   Surely you may believe it.

2ND AVOCATORE. Madam, we do.

LADY WOULDBE. Indeed you may, my breeding
Is not so coarse——

4TH AVOCATORE. We know it.

LADY WOULDBE.   To offend
With pertinacy——

3RD AVOCATORE. Lady——

LADY WOULDBE.   Such a presence!
No surely.

1ST AVOCATORE. We well think it.

LADY WOULDBE.   You may think it.

1ST AVOCATORE. Let her o'ercome.—What witnesses
  have you,
To make good your report?

BONARIO.   Our consciences.

CELIA. And Heaven, that never fails the innocent.

4TH AVOCATORE. These are no testimonies.

BONARIO.   Not in your courts,
Where multitude and clamour overcomes.

1ST AVOCATORE. Nay, then you do wax insolent.

VOLPONE *is brought in, as impotent.*

VOLTORE. Here, here,
The testimony comes that will convince,
And put to utter dumbness their bold tongues!
See here, grave fathers, here's the ravisher,
The rider on men's wives, the great impostor,
The grand voluptuary! Do you not think
These limbs should affect venery? or these eyes
Covet a concubine? Pray you mark these hands;
Are they not fit to stroke a lady's breasts?
Perhaps he doth dissemble!

BONARIO. So he does.

VOLTORE. Would you ha' him tortured?

BONARIO. I would have him proved.

VOLTORE. Best try him then with goads, or burning
    irons;
Put him to the strappado. I have heard
The rack hath cured the gout—faith, give it him,
And help him of a malady; be courteous.
I'll undertake, before these honoured fathers,
He shall have yet as many left diseases,
As she has known adulterers, or thou strumpets.
O my most equal hearers, if these deeds,
Acts of this bold and most exorbitant strain,
May pass with sufferance, what one citizen
But owes the forfeit of his life, yea, fame,
To him that dares traduce him? Which of you
Are safe, my honoured fathers? I would ask,
With leave of your grave fatherhoods, if their plot
Have any face or colour like to truth?
Or if, unto the dullest nostril here,
It smell not rank, and most abhorrèd slander?
I crave your care of this good gentleman,
Whose life is much endangered by their fable;
And as for them, I will conclude with this:

That vicious persons, when they're hot, and fleshed
In impious acts, their constancy abounds.
Damned deeds are done with greatest confidence.

1ST AVOCATORE. Take 'em to custody, and sever
them.

2ND AVOCATORE. 'Tis pity two such prodigies
should live.

1ST AVOCATORE. Let the old gentleman be returned
with care.   *Exeunt* OFFICERS *with* VOLPONE.
I'm sorry our credulity hath wronged him.

4TH AVOCATORE. These are two creatures!

3RD AVOCATORE.   I have an earthquake in me!

2ND AVOCATORE. Their shame, even in their cradles, fled their faces.

4TH AVOCATORE. You've done a worthy service to
the state, sir,
In their discovery.

1ST AVOCATORE. You shall hear ere night
What punishment the court decrees upon 'em.
          Exeunt AVOCATORI, NOTARIO, *and* COMMENDATORI
               with BONARIO *and* CELIA.

VOLTORE. We thank your fatherhoods.—How like
you it?

MOSCA.   Rare.
I'd ha' your tongue, sir, tipped with gold for this;
I'd ha' you be the heir to the whole city;
The earth I'd have want men, ere you want living.
They're bound to erect your statue in Saint Mark's.—
Signior Corvino, I would have you go
And show yourself, that you have conquered.

CORVINO.   Yes.

MOSCA. It was much better that you should pro-
fess
Yourself a cuckold thus, than that the other
Should have been proved.

CORVINO.   Nay, I considered that.
Now it is her fault.

MOSCA.   Then it had been yours.

CORVINO. True. I do doubt this advocate still.

MOSCA.   I' faith,
You need not; I dare ease you of that care.

CORVINO. I trust thee, Mosca.   *Exit.*

MOSCA.   As your own soul, sir.

CORBACCIO.   Mosca!

MOSCA. Now for your business, sir.

CORBACCIO.   How! ha' you business?

MOSCA. Yes, yours, sir.

CORBACCIO.   O, none else.

MOSCA.   None else, not I.

CORBACCIO. Be careful, then.

MOSCA.   Rest you with both your eyes, sir.

CORBACCIO. Dispatch it.

MOSCA.   Instantly.

CORBACCIO.   And look that all
Whatever be put in, jewels, plate, moneys,
Household stuff, bedding, curtains.

MOSCA.   Curtain-rings, sir;
Only the advocate's fee must be deducted.

CORBACCIO. I'll pay him now; you'll be too prodigal.

MOSCA. Sir, I must tender it.

CORBACCIO.   Two sequines is well?

MOSCA. No, six, sir.

CORBACCIO.   'Tis too much.

MOSCA.   He talked a great while,
You must consider that, sir.

CORBACCIO.   Well, there's three——

MOSCA. I'll give it him.

CORBACCIO.   Do so, and there's for thee.
                                  Exit.

MOSCA. Bountiful bones! What horrid, strange offence

Did he commit 'gainst nature, in his youth,
Worthy this age?—You see, sir, how I work
Unto your ends; take you no notice.

    VOLTORE.   No,
I'll leave you.   *Exit.*

    MOSCA.   All is yours, the devil and all,
Good advocate!—Madam, I'll bring you home.

    LADY WOULDBE. No, I'll go see your patron.

    MOSCA.   That you shall not.
I'll tell you why: my purpose is to urge
My patron to reform his will, and for
The zeal you've shown today, whereas before
You were but third or fourth, you shall be now
Put in the first; which would appear as begged
If you were present. Therefore——

    LADY WOULDBE.   You shall sway me.
                                Exeunt.

ACT FIVE. SCENE ONE

Volpone's house

Enter VOLPONE.

    VOLPONE. Well, I am here, and all this brunt is
    past.
I ne'er was in dislike with my disguise
Till this fled moment. Here 'twas good, in private;
But in your public—Cavè, whilst I breathe.
'Fore God, my left leg 'gan to have the cramp,
And I apprehended straight some power had struck
    me
With a dead palsy. Well, I must be merry,

And shake it off. A many of these fears
Would put me into some villainous disease,
Should they come thick upon me. I'll prevent 'em.
Give me a bowl of lusty wine, to fright
This humour from my heart. *Drinks.* Hum, hum,
    hum!
'Tis almost gone already; I shall conquer.
Any device, now, of rare, ingenious knavery,
That would possess me with a violent laughter,
Would make me up again. *Drinks again.* So, so, so,
    so!
This heat is life; 'tis blood by this time!—Mosca!

Enter MOSCA.

  MOSCA. How now, sir! does the day look clear
    again?
Are we recovered, and wrought out of error,
Into our way, to see our path before us?
Is our trade free once more?
  VOLPONE.   Exquisite Mosca!
  MOSCA. Was it not carried learnedly?
  VOLPONE.   And stoutly.
Good wits are greatest in extremities.
  MOSCA. It were a folly beyond thought, to trust
Any grand act unto a cowardly spirit.
You are not taken with it enough, methinks.
  VOLPONE. O, more than if I had enjoyed the
    wench.
The pleasure of all womankind's not like it.
  MOSCA. Why, now you speak, sir! We must here
    be fixed;
Here we must rest. This is our masterpiece;
We cannot think to go beyond this.
  VOLPONE.   True,
Th'ast played thy prize, my precious Mosca.

MOSCA.   Nay, sir,
To gull the court——

VOLPONE.   And quite divert the torrent
Upon the innocent.

MOSCA.   Yes, and to make
So rare a music out of discords——

VOLPONE.   Right.
That yet to me's the strangest; how th'ast borne it!
That these, being so divided 'mongst themselves,
Should not scent somewhat, or in me or thee,
Or doubt their own side.

MOSCA.   True, they will not see't.
Too much light blinds 'em, I think. Each of 'em
Is so possessed and stuffed with his own hopes
That anything unto the contrary,
Never so true, or never so apparent,
Never so palpable, they will resist it——

VOLPONE. Like a temptation of the devil.

MOSCA.   Right, sir.
Merchants may talk of trade, and your great signiors
Of land that yields well; but if Italy
Have any glebe more fruitful than these fellows,
I am deceived. Did not your advocate rare?

VOLPONE. O—'My most honoured fathers, my grave
       fathers,
Under correction of your fatherhoods,
What face of truth is here? If these strange deeds
May pass, most honoured fathers'—I had much ado
To forbear laughing.

MOSCA.   'T seemed to me you sweat, sir.

VOLPONE. In troth, I did a little.

MOSCA.   But confess, sir,
Were you not daunted?

VOLPONE.   In good faith, I was
A little in a mist, but not dejected;
Never, but still myself.

MOSCA. I think it, sir.
Now, so truth help me, I must needs say this, sir,
And out of conscience for your advocate:
He 's taken pains, in faith, sir, and deserved,
In my poor judgment, I speak it under favour,
Not to contrary you, sir, very richly—
Well—to be cozened.

VOLPONE. Troth, and I think so too,
By that I heard him in the latter end.

MOSCA. O, but before, sir, had you heard him first
Draw it to certain heads, then aggravate,
Then use his vehement figures—I looked still
When he would shift a shirt; and doing this
Out of pure love, no hope of gain——

VOLPONE. 'Tis right.
I cannot answer him, Mosca, as I would,
Not yet; but for thy sake, at thy entreaty,
I will begin ev'n now—to vex 'em all,
This very instant.

MOSCA. Good, sir.

VOLPONE. Call the dwarf
And eunuch forth.

MOSCA. Castrone! Nano!

Enter CASTRONE *and* NANO.

NANO. Here.

VOLPONE. Shall we have a jig now?

MOSCA. What you please, sir.

VOLPONE. Go,
Straight give out about the streets, you two,
That I am dead; do it with constancy,
Sadly, do you hear? Impute it to the grief
Of this late slander. *Exeunt* CASTRONE *and* NANO.

MOSCA. What do you mean, sir?

VOLPONE. O,

I shall have instantly my vulture, crow,
Raven, come flying hither, on the news,
To peck for carrion, my she-wolf and all,
Greedy and full of expectation——
    MOSCA. And then to have it ravished from their
      mouths?
    VOLPONE. 'Tis true. I will ha' thee put on a gown,
And take upon thee as thou wert mine heir;
Show 'em a will. Open that chest, and reach
Forth one of those that has the blanks. I'll straight
Put in thy name.
    MOSCA.   It will be rare, sir.
    VOLPONE.   Ay,
When they e'en gape, and find themselves de-
    luded——
    MOSCA. Yes.
    VOLPONE. And thou use them scurvily! Dispatch,
Get on thy gown.
    MOSCA.   But what, sir, if they ask
After the body?
    VOLPONE.   Say it was corrupted.
    MOSCA. I'll say it stunk, sir; and was fain t' have it
Coffined up instantly, and sent away.
    VOLPONE. Anything, what thou wilt. Hold, here's
    my will.
Get thee a cap, a count-book, pen and ink,
Papers afore thee; sit as thou wert taking
An inventory of parcels. I'll get up
Behind the curtain, on a stool, and hearken;
Sometime peep over, see how they do look,
With what degrees their blood doth leave their
    faces.
O, 'twill afford me a rare meal of laughter!
    MOSCA. Your advocate will turn stark dull upon
    it.

VOLPONE. It will take off his oratory's edge.

MOSCA. But your clarissimo, old round-back, he
Will crump you like a hog-louse with the touch.

VOLPONE. And what Corvino?

MOSCA.   O sir, look for him
Tomorrow morning, with a rope and dagger,
To visit all the streets; he must run mad.
My lady too, that came into the court,
To bear false witness for your worship——

VOLPONE.   Yes,
And kissed me 'fore the fathers, when my face
Flowed all with oils——

MOSCA.   And sweat, sir. Why, your gold
Is such another med'cine, it dries up
All those offensive savours! It transforms
The most deformèd, and restores 'em lovely
As 'twere the strange poetical girdle. Jove
Could not invent t' himself a shroud more subtle
To pass Acrisius' guards. It is the thing
Makes all the world her grace, her youth, her
      beauty.

VOLPONE. I think she loves me.

MOSCA.   Who? the lady, sir?
She's jealous of you.

VOLPONE.   Dost thou say so?

MOSCA.   Hark,
There's some already.

VOLPONE.   Look.

MOSCA.   It is the vulture;
He has the quickest scent.

VOLPONE.   I'll to my place,
Thou to thy posture.

MOSCA.   I am set.

VOLPONE.   But, Mosca,
Play the artificer, now, torture 'em rarely.

Enter VOLTORE.

VOLTORE. How now, my Mosca?
MOSCA. *Writing.*   'Turkey carpets, nine——'
VOLTORE. Taking an inventory? that is well.
MOSCA. 'Two suits of bedding, tissue——'
VOLTORE.   Where's the will?
Let me read that the while.

Enter SERVITORI *with* CORBACCIO *in a chair.*

CORBACCIO.   So, set me down,
And get you home.   *Exeunt* SERVITORI.
VOLTORE.   Is he come now, to trouble us?
MOSCA. 'Of cloth of gold, two more——'
CORBACCIO.   Is it done, Mosca?
MOSCA. 'Of several velvets, eight——'
VOLTORE.   I like his care.
CORBACCIO. Dost thou not hear?

Enter CORVINO.

CORVINO.   Ha! is the hour come, Mosca?
VOLPONE. *Peeps from behind a traverse.* Ay, now
they muster.
CORVINO.   What does the advocate here,
Or this Corbaccio?
CORBACCIO.   What do these here?

Enter LADY WOULDBE.

LADY WOULDBE.   Mosca!
Is his thread spun?
MOSCA. 'Eight chests of linen——'
VOLPONE.   —O,
My fine Dame Wouldbe, too!
CORVINO.   Mosca, the will,
That I may show it these, and rid 'em hence.

MOSCA. 'Six chests of diaper, four of damask—'
There.

CORBACCIO. Is that the will?

MOSCA.   'Down-beds, and bolsters——'

VOLPONE.   —Rare!
Be busy still. Now they begin to flutter;
They never think of me. Look, see, see, see!
How their swift eyes run over the long deed,
Unto the name, and to the legacies,
What is bequeathed them there——

MOSCA.   'Ten suits of hangings——'

VOLPONE. —Ay, i' their garters, Mosca. Now their
hopes
Are at the gasp.

VOLTORE.   Mosca the heir!

CORBACCIO.   What's that?

VOLPONE. —My advocate is dumb; look to my mer-
chant,
He has heard of some strange storm, a ship is lost,
He faints; my lady will swoon. Old glazen-eyes
He hath not reached his despair yet.

CORBACCIO.   All these
Are out of hope; I'm sure the man.

CORVINO.   But, Mosca——

MOSCA. 'Two cabinets——'

CORVINO.   Is this in earnest?

MOSCA.   'One
Of ebony——'

CORVINO.   Or do you but delude me?

MOSCA. 'The other, mother of pearl'—I am very
busy.
Good faith, it is a fortune thrown upon me——
'Item, one salt of agate'—not my seeking.

LADY WOULDBE. Do you hear, sir?

MOSCA.   'A perfumed box'—Pray you forbear,
You see I'm troubled—'made of an onyx——'

LADY WOULDBE.   How!

MOSCA. Tomorrow or next day, I shall be at leisure
To talk with you all.

    CORVINO.   Is this my large hope's issue?

    LADY WOULDBE. Sir, I must have a fairer answer.

    MOSCA.   Madam!
Marry, and shall: pray you, fairly quit my house.
Nay, raise no tempest with your looks; but hark
    you,
Remember what your ladyship offered me
To put you in an heir; go to, think on 't;
And what you said e'en your best madams did
For maintenance, and why not you? Enough.
Go home, and use the poor Sir Poll, your knight,
    well,
For fear I tell some riddles. Go, be melancholic.
                        Exit LADY WOULDBE.

    VOLPONE. —O my fine devil!

    CORVINO.   Mosca, pray you a word.

    MOSCA. Lord! will not you take your dispatch
    hence yet?
Methinks of all you should have been th' example.
Why should you stay here? with what thought? what
    promise?
Hear you, do you not know I know you an ass,
And that you would most fain have been a wittol
If fortune would have let you? that you are
A declared cuckold, on good terms? This pearl,
You'll say, was yours? right. This diamond?
I'll not deny't, but thank you. Much here else?
It may be so. Why, think that these good works
May help to hide your bad. I'll not betray you,
Although you be but extraordinary,
And have it only in title, it sufficeth.
Go home, be melancholic too, or mad. *Exit* CORVINO.

VOLPONE. —Rare Mosca! how his villainy becomes
him!

VOLTORE. Certain, he doth delude all these for
me.

CORBACCIO. Mosca the heir?

VOLPONE. O, his four eyes have found it!

CORBACCIO. I am cozened, cheated, by a parasite
slave!
Harlot, th'ast gulled me.

MOSCA. Yes, sir. Stop your mouth,
Or I shall draw the only tooth is left.
Are not you he, that filthy, covetous wretch,
With the three legs, that here, in hope of prey,
Have, any time this three year, snuffed about,
With your most grov'ling nose; and would have
hired
Me to the pois'ning of my patron, sir?
Are not you he that have today in court
Professed the disinheriting of your son?
Perjured yourself? Go home, and die, and stink;
If you but croak a syllable, all comes out.
Away, and call your porters! *Exit* CORBACCIO. Go,
go, stink.

VOLPONE. —Excellent varlet!

VOLTORE. Now, my faithful Mosca,
I find thy constancy——

MOSCA. Sir!

VOLTORE. Sincere.

MOSCA. 'A table
Of porphyry'—I mar'l you'll be thus troublesome.

VOLTORE. Nay, leave off now, they are gone.

MOSCA. Why, who are you?
What! who did send for you? O, cry you mercy,
Reverend sir! Good faith, I am grieved for you,
That any chance of mine should thus defeat
Your—I must needs say—most deserving travails.

But I protest, sir, it was cast upon me,
And I could almost wish to be without it,
But that the will o' th' dead must be observed.
Marry, my joy is that you need it not;
You have a gift, sir,—thank your education—
Will never let you want, while there are men
And malice to breed causes. Would I had
But half the like, for all my fortune, sir!
If I have any suits,—as I do hope,
Things being so easy and direct, I shall not—
I will make bold with your obstreperous aid,
Conceive me, for your fee, sir. In meantime,
You that have so much law, I know ha' the con-
    science
Not to be covetous of what is mine.
Good sir, I thank you for my plate; 'twill help
To set up a young man. Good faith, you look
As you were costive; best go home and purge, sir.
                       Exit VOLTORE.

  VOLPONE. Bid him eat lettuce well! My witty mis-
    chief,
Let me embrace thee. O that I could now
Transform thee to a Venus—Mosca, go,
Straight take my habit of clarissimo,
And walk the streets; be seen, torment 'em more.
We must pursue, as well as plot. Who would
Have lost this feast?
  MOSCA.   I doubt it will lose them.
  VOLPONE. O, my recovery shall recover all.
That I could now but think on some disguise
To meet 'em in, and ask 'em questions;
How I would vex 'em still at every turn!
  MOSCA. Sir, I can fit you.
  VOLPONE.   Canst thou?
  MOSCA.   Yes, I know
One o' th' commendatori, sir, so like you,

Him will I straight make drunk, and bring you his
     habit.

VOLPONE. A rare disguise, and answering thy brain!
O, I will be a sharp disease unto 'em.

  MOSCA. Sir, you must look for curses——
     VOLPONE.   Till they burst;
The fox fares ever best when he is curst.   *Exeunt.*

ACT FIVE. SCENE TWO

Sir Politic's lodging

Enter PEREGRINE *disguised, and three* MERCATORI.

PEREGRINE. Am I enough disguised?
  1ST MERCATORE.   I warrant you.
  PEREGRINE. All my ambition is to fright him only.
  2ND MERCATORE. If you could ship him away,
     'twere excellent.
  3RD MERCATORE. To Zant, or to Aleppo!
     PEREGRINE.   Yes, and ha' his
Adventures put i' th' book of voyages,
And his gulled story registered for truth!
Well, gentlemen, when I am in a while,
And that you think us warm in our discourse,
Know your approaches.
  1ST MERCATORE.   Trust it to our care.
                              Exeunt MERCATORI.

Enter WOMAN.

PEREGRINE. Save you, fair lady! Is Sir Poll within?
WOMAN. I do not know, sir.

PEREGRINE.   Pray you say unto him,
Here is a merchant, upon urgent business,
Desires to speak with him.
    WOMAN.   I will see, sir.   *Exit.*
    PEREGRINE.   Pray you.
I see the family is all female here.

Re-enter WOMAN.

  WOMAN. He says, sir, he has weighty affairs of
    state,
That now require him whole; some other time
You may possess him.
    PEREGRINE.   Pray you say again,
If those require him whole, these will exact him,
Whereof I bring him tidings. *Exit* WOMAN. What
    might be
His grave affair of state now? how to make
Bolognian sausages here in Venice, sparing
One o' th' ingredients.

Re-enter WOMAN.

  WOMAN.   Sir, he says he knows
By your word 'tidings' that you are no statesman,
And therefore wills you stay.
    PEREGRINE.   Sweet, pray you return him,
I have not read so many proclamations,
And studied them for words, as he has done,
But—Here he deigns to come.

Enter SIR POLITIC.

  SIR POLITIC.   Sir, I must crave
Your courteous pardon. There hath chanced today
Unkind disaster 'twixt my lady and me,
And I was penning my apology,
To give her satisfaction, as you came now.

PEREGRINE. Sir, I am grieved I bring you worse
    disaster:
The gentleman you met at th' port today,
That told you he was newly arrived——

SIR POLITIC.   Ay, was
A fugitive punk?

PEREGRINE.   No, sir, a spy set on you;
And he has made relation to the Senate,
That you professed to him, to have a plot
To sell the state of Venice to the Turk.

SIR POLITIC. O me!

PEREGRINE.   For which warrants are signed
    by this time,
To apprehend you, and to search your study
For papers——

SIR POLITIC.   Alas, sir, I have none but notes
Drawn out of play-books——

PEREGRINE.   All the better, sir.

SIR POLITIC. And some essays. What shall I do?

PEREGRINE.   Sir, best
Convey yourself into a sugar-chest,
Or, if you could lie round, a frail were rare;
And I could send you aboard.

SIR POLITIC.   Sir, I but talked so,
For discourse sake merely.   *They knock without.*

PEREGRINE.   Hark! they are there.

SIR POLITIC. I am a wretch, a wretch!

PEREGRINE.   What will you do, sir?
Ha' you ne'er a currant-butt to leap into?
They'll put you to the rack; you must be sudden.

SIR POLITIC. Sir, I have an engine——

3RD MERCHANT.   Sir Politic Wouldbe!

2ND MERCHANT. Where is he?

SIR POLITIC. That I have thought upon before-
    time.

PEREGRINE. What is it?

SIR POLITIC.   I shall ne'er endure the torture!—
Marry, it is, sir, of a tortoise-shell,
Fitted for these extremities. Pray you, sir, help me.
Here I've a place, sir, to put back my legs;
Please you to lay it on, sir. With this cap,
And my black gloves, I'll lie, sir, like a tortoise,
Till they are gone.
    PEREGRINE.   And call you this an engine?
    SIR POLITIC. Mine own device——Good sir, bid my
        wife's women
To burn my papers.

Re-enter three MERCATORI.

    1ST MERCATORE.   Where's he hid?
    3RD MERCATORE.   We must.
And will sure find him.
    2ND MERCATORE.   Which is his study?
    1ST MERCATORE.   What
Are you, sir?
    PEREGRINE. I'm a merchant, that came here
To look upon this tortoise.
    3RD MERCATORE.   How!
    1ST MERCATORE.   Saint Mark!
What beast is this?
    PEREGRINE.   It is a fish.
    2ND MERCATORE.   Come out here!
    PEREGRINE. Nay, you may strike him, sir, and
        tread upon him.
He'll bear a cart.
    1ST MERCATORE. What, to run over him?
    PEREGRINE.   Yes.
    3RD MERCATORE. Let's jump upon him.
    2ND MERCATORE.   Can he not go?
    PEREGRINE.   He creeps, sir.
    1ST MERCATORE. Let's see him creep.
    PEREGRINE.   No, good sir, you will hurt him.

2ND MERCATORE. Heart, I'll see him creep, or prick
  his guts!

3RD MERCATORE. Come out here!

PEREGRINE.   Pray you, sir.—Creep a little.

1ST MERCATORE.   Forth.

2ND MERCATORE. Yet further.

PEREGRINE.   Good sir!—Creep

2ND MERCATORE.   We'll see his legs.
     They pull off the shell and discover SIR POLITIC.

3RD MERCATORE. God's so', he has garters!

1ST MERCATORE.   Ay, and gloves!

2ND MERCATORE.   Is this
Your fearful tortoise?

PEREGRINE.   Now, Sir Poll, we are even;
For your next project I shall be prepared.
I am sorry for the funeral of your notes, sir.

1ST MERCATORE. 'Twere a rare motion to be seen in
  Fleet Street.

2ND MERCATORE. Ay, i' the term.

1ST MERCATORE.   Or Smithfield, in the fair.

3RD MERCATORE. Methinks 'tis but a melancholic
  sight.

PEREGRINE. Farewell, most politic tortoise!
         Exeunt PEREGRINE *and* MERCATORI.

SIR POLITIC.   Where's my lady?
Knows she of this?

WOMAN.   I know not, sir.

SIR POLITIC.   Inquire.—
O, I shall be the fable of all feasts,
The freight of the gazetti, ship-boys' tale,
And, which is worst, even talk for ordinaries.

WOMAN. My lady's come most melancholic home,
And says, sir, she will straight to sea, for physic.

SIR POLITIC. And I, to shun this place and clime
  forever,

Creeping with house on back, and think it well
To shrink my poor head in my politic shell. *Exeunt.*

ACT FIVE. SCENE THREE

Volpone's house

Enter VOLPONE *in the habit of a commendatore, and*
MOSCA *in that of a clarissimo.*

VOLPONE. Am I then like him?

MOSCA.   O sir, you are he;
No man can sever you.

VOLPONE.   Good.

MOSCA.   But what am I?

VOLPONE. 'Fore Heav'n, a brave clarissimo, thou
  becom'st it!
Pity thou wert not born one.

MOSCA.   —If I hold
My made one, 'twill be well.

VOLPONE.   I'll go and see
What news first at the court.   *Exit.*

MOSCA.   Do so.—My fox
Is out on his hole, and ere he shall re-enter,
I'll make him languish in his borrowed case,
Except he come to composition with me.—
Androgyno, Castrone, Nano!

  Enter ANDROGYNO, CASTRONE, *and* NANO.

ALL.   Here.

MOSCA. Go, recreate yourselves abroad; go, sport.
                    Exeunt.
So, now I have the keys, and am possessed.

Since he will needs be dead afore his time,
I'll bury him or gain by him. I'm his heir,
And so will keep me, till he share at least.
To cozen him of all were but a cheat
Well placed; no man would construe it a sin.
Let his sport pay for 't. This is called the fox-trap.

Exit.

ACT FIVE. SCENE FOUR

A street

Enter CORBACCIO *and* CORVINO.

CORBACCIO. They say the court is set.

CORVINO.   We must maintain
Our first tale good, for both our reputations.

CORBACCIO. Why, mine's no tale! my son would
   there have killed me.

CORVINO. That's true, I had forgot.—Mine is, I'm
   sure.—
But for your will, sir.

CORBACCIO.   Ay, I'll come upon him
For that hereafter, now his patron's dead.

Enter VOLPONE.

VOLPONE. Signior Corvino! and Corbaccio! sir,
Much joy unto you.

CORVINO.   Of what?

VOLPONE.   The sudden good
Dropped down upon you——

CORBACCIO.   Where?

VOLPONE.   And none knows how,
From old Volpone, sir.

CORBACCIO.   Out, arrant knave!

VOLPONE. Let not your too much wealth, sir, make
   you furious.

CORBACCIO. Away, thou varlet.

VOLPONE.   Why, sir?

CORBACCIO.   Dost thou mock me?

VOLPONE. You mock the world, sir; did you not
   change wills?

CORBACCIO. Out, harlot!

VOLPONE.   O! belike you are the man,
Signior Corvino? Faith, you carry it well;
You grow not mad withal. I love your spirit.
You are not over-leavened with your fortune.
You should ha' some would swell now, like a wine-
   vat,
With such an autumn—Did he gi' you all, sir?

CORVINO. Avoid, you rascal.

VOLPONE.   Troth, your wife has shown
Herself a very woman! But you are well,
You need not care; you have a good estate,
To bear it out, sir, better by this chance—
Except Corbaccio have a share.

CORBACCIO.   Hence, varlet

VOLPONE. You will not be a'known, sir? Why, 'tis
   wise.
Thus do all gamesters, at all games, dissemble.
No man will seem to win. *Exeunt* CORVINO *and* COR-
   BACCIO. Here comes my vulture,
Heaving his beak up i' the air, and snuffing.

Enter VOLTORE.

VOLTORE. Outstripped thus, by a parasite! a slave,
Would run on errands, and make legs for crumbs!
Well, what I'll do——

VOLPONE.   The court stays for your worship.
I e'en rejoice, sir, at your worship's happiness,
And that it fell into so learnèd hands,
That understand the fingering——

VOLTORE.   What do you mean?

VOLPONE. I mean to be a suitor to your worship,
For the small tenement, out of reparations,
That, at the end of your long row of houses,
By the Pescheria—it was, in Volpone's time,
Your predecessor, ere he grew diseased,
A handsome, pretty, customed bawdy-house
As any was in Venice, none dispraised;
But fell with him. His body and that house
Decayed together.

VOLTORE.   Come, sir, leave your prating.

VOLPONE. Why, if your worship give me but your
          hand,
That I may ha' the refusal, I have done.
'Tis a mere toy to you, sir, candle-rents.
As your learnèd worship knows——

VOLTORE.   What do I know?

VOLPONE. Marry, no end o' your wealth, sir,
          God decrease it!

VOLTORE. Mistaking knave! what, mock'st thou
          my misfortune?   *Exit.*

VOLPONE. His blessing on your heart, sir; would
          'twere more!
Now to my first again, at the next corner.

Enter CORBACCIO *and* CORVINO, MOSCA *passing over
                    the stage.*

CORBACCIO. See, in our habit! see the impudent
          varlet!

CORVINO. That I could shoot mine eyes at him,
          like gun-stones!

VOLPONE. But is this true, sir, of the parasite?

CORBACCIO. Again, t' afflict us? monster!

VOLPONE. In good faith, sir,
I'm heartily grieved, a beard of your grave length
Should be so over-reached. I never brooked
That parasite's hair; methought his nose should
    cozen.
There still was somewhat in his look, did promise
The bane of a clarissimo.

CORBACCIO. Knave——

VOLPONE. Methinks
Yet you, that are so traded i' the world,
A witty merchant, the fine bird, Corvino,
That have such moral emblems on your name,
Should not have sung your shame; and dropped
    your cheese,
To let the fox laugh at your emptiness.

CORVINO. Sirrah, you think the privilege of the
    place,
And your red saucy cap, that seems to me
Nailed to your jolt-head with those two sequines,
Can warrant your abuses. Come you hither.
You shall perceive, sir, I dare beat you. Approach.

VOLPONE. No haste, sir, I do know your valour
    well,
Since you durst publish what you are, sir.

CORVINO. Tarry,
I'd speak with you.

VOLPONE. Sir, sir, another time——

CORVINO. Nay, now.

VOLPONE. O God, sir! I were a wise man,
Would stand the fury of a distracted cuckold.

                    MOSCA *walks by them.*

CORBACCIO. What, come again!

VOLPONE. —Upon 'em, Mosca; save me.

CORBACCIO. The air's infected where he breathes.

CORVINO.   Let's fly him.

           Exeunt CORVINO *and* CORBACCIO.

VOLPONE. Excellent basilisk! turn upon the vulture.

Enter VOLTORE.

VOLTORE. Well, flesh-fly, it is summer with you now;

Your winter will come on.

MOSCA.   Good advocate,

Prithee not rail, nor threaten out of place thus;

Thou'lt make a solecism, as Madam says.

Get you a biggen more; your brain breaks loose.

                       Exit.

VOLTORE. Well, sir.

VOLPONE.   Would you ha' me beat the insolent slave?

Throw dirt upon his first good clothes?

VOLTORE.   —This same

Is doubtless some familiar!

VOLPONE.   Sir, the court,

In troth, stays for you. I am mad, a mule

That never read Justinian, should get up,

And ride an advocate. Had you no quirk

To avoid gullage, sir, by such a creature?

I hope you do but jest; he has not done 't;

This's but confederacy to blind the rest.

You are the heir?

VOLTORE.   A strange, officious,

Troublesome knave! thou dost torment me.

VOLPONE.   I know——

It cannot be, sir, that you should be cozened;

'Tis not within the wit of man to do it.

You are so wise, so prudent; and 'tis fit

That wealth and wisdom still should go together.

                      Exeunt.

ACT FIVE. SCENE FIVE

The Scrutineo

Enter four AVOCATORI, NOTARIO, BONARIO, CELIA, CORBACCIO, CORVINO, COMMENDATORI, *&c.*

1ST AVOCATORE. Are all the parties here?
NOTARIO.   All but the advocate.
2ND AVOCATORE. And here he comes.

Enter VOLTORE *and* VOLPONE.

1ST AVOCATORE. Then bring 'em forth to sentence.
VOLTORE. O my most honoured fathers, let your mercy
Once win upon your justice, to forgive—
I am distracted——
VOLPONE.   —What will he do now?
VOLTORE.   O,
I know not which t' address myself to first;
Whether your fatherhoods, or these innocents——
CORVINO. —Will he betray himself?
VOLTORE   Whom equally
I have abused, out of most covetous ends——
CORVINO. The man is mad!
CORBACCIO.   What's that?
CORVINO.   He is possessed.
VOLTORE. For which, now struck in conscience, here I prostrate
Myself at your offended feet, for pardon.
1ST, 2ND AVOCATORI. Arise.
CELIA.   O Heaven, how just thou art!
VOLPONE.   —I'm caught
I' mine own noose——

CORVINO. —Be constant, sir; nought now
Can help but impudence.

1ST AVOCATORE. Speak forward.

COMMENDATORE. Silence!

VOLTORE. It is not passion in me, reverend fathers,
But only conscience, conscience, my good sires,
That makes me now tell truth. That parasite,
That knave, hath been the instrument of all.

1ST AVOCATORE. Where is that knave? fetch him.

VOLPONE. I go. _Exit._

CORVINO. Grave fathers,
This man's distracted; he confessed it now.
For, hoping to be old Volpone's heir,
Who now is dead——

3RD AVOCATORE. How!

2ND AVOCATORE. Is Volpone dead?

CORVINO. Dead since, grave fathers.—

BONARIO. O sure vengeance!

1ST AVOCATORE. Stay,
Then he was no deceiver.

VOLTORE. O, no, none;
The parasite, grave fathers. .

CORVINO. He does speak
Out of mere envy, 'cause the servant's made
The thing he gaped for. Please your fatherhoods,
This is the truth; though I'll not justify
The other, but he may be somewhere faulty.

VOLTORE. Ay, to your hopes, as well as mine, Cor-
vino.
But I'll use modesty. Pleaseth your wisdoms,
To view these certain notes, and but confer them;
As I hope favour, they shall speak clear truth.

CORVINO. The devil has entered him!

BONARIO. Or bides in you.

4TH AVOCATORE. We have done ill, by a public officer
To send for him, if he be heir.

2ND AVOCATORE. For whom?

4TH AVOCATORE. Him that they call the parasite.

3RD AVOCATORE. 'Tis true,
He is a man of great estate now left.

4TH AVOCATORE. —Go you, and learn his name, and say the court
Entreats his presence here, but to the clearing
Of some few doubts. *Exit* NOTARIO.

2ND AVOCATORE. This same's a labyrinth!

1ST AVOCATORE. Stand you unto your first report?

CORVINO. My state,
My life, my fame——

BONARIO. Where is't?

CORVINO. Are at the stake.

1ST AVOCATORE. Is yours so too?

CORBACCIO. The advocate's a knave,
And has a forkèd tongue——

2ND AVOCATORE. Speak to the point.

CORBACCIO. So is the parasite too.

1ST AVOCATORE. This is confusion.

VOLTORE. I do beseech your fatherhoods, read but those—

CORVINO. And credit nothing the false spirit hath writ.
It cannot be but he's possessed, grave fathers.

The scene closes.

ACT FIVE. SCENE SIX

A street

Enter VOLPONE.

VOLPONE. To make a snare for mine own neck! and run
My head into it wilfully, with laughter!
When I had newly 'scaped, was free and clear!
Out of mere wantonness! O, the dull devil
Was in this brain of mine when I devised it,
And Mosca gave it second; he must now
Help to sear up this vein, or we bleed dead.

Enter NANO, ANDROGYNO, *and* CASTRONE.

How now! who let you loose? whither go you now?
What, to buy gingerbread, or to drown kitlings?
　NANO. Sir, Master Mosca called us out of doors,
And bid us all go play, and took the keys.
　ANDROGYNO.　　　　　　　　　　　　Yes.
　VOLPONE. Did Master Mosca take the keys? Why, so!
I'm farther in. These are my fine conceits!
I must be merry, with a mischief to me!
What a vile wretch was I, that could not bear
My fortune soberly. I must ha' my crotchets
And my conundrums!—Well, go you and seek him.—
His meaning may be truer than my fear.—
Bid him, he straight come to me to the court;
Thither will I, and, if't be possible,
Unscrew my advocate, upon new hopes.
When I provoked him, then I lost myself.　*Exeunt.*

ACT FIVE. SCENE SEVEN

The Scrutineo

Four AVOCATORI, NOTARIO, VOLTORE, BONARIO, CELIA,
CORBACCIO, CORVINO, *&c., as before.*

1ST AVOCATORE. These things can ne'er be recon-
ciled. He here
Professeth that the gentleman was wronged,
And that the gentlewoman was brought thither,
Forced by her husband, and there left.

VOLTORE.   Most true.

CELIA. How ready is Heav'n to those that pray!

1ST AVOCATORE.   But that
Volpone would have ravished her, he holds
Utterly false, knowing his impotence.

CORVINO. Grave fathers, he is possessed; again,
I say,
Possessed. Nay, if there be possession and
Obsession, he has both.

3RD AVOCATORE.   Here comes our officer.

Enter VOLPONE.

VOLPONE. The parasite will straight be here, grave
fathers.

4TH AVOCATORE. You might invent some other
name, Sir Varlet.

3RD AVOCATORE. Did not the notary meet him?

VOLPONE.   Not that I know.

4TH AVOCATORE. His coming will clear all.

2ND AVOCATORE.   Yet it is misty.

VOLTORE. May't please your fatherhoods——

VOLPONE. *Whispers to* VOLTORE. Sir, the parasite

Willed me to tell you that his master lives;
That you are still the man; your hopes the same;
And this was only a jest——

VOLTORE.   How?

VOLPONE.   Sir, to try
If you were firm, and how you stood affected.

VOLTORE. Art sure he lives?

VOLPONE.   Do I live, sir?

VOLTORE.   O me!
I was too violent.

VOLPONE.   Sir, you may redeem it:
They said you were possessed; fall down, and seem
    so.
I'll help to make it good. VOLTORE *falls.* God bless
    the man!—
Stop your wind hard, and swell—See, see, see, see!
He vomits crooked pins! his eyes are set,
Like a dead hare's hung in a poulter's shop!
His mouth's running away! Do you see, signior?
Now 'tis in his belly.

CORVINO.   —Ay, the devil!

VOLPONE. Now in his throat.

CORVINO.   —Ay, I perceive it plain.

VOLTORE. 'Twill out, 'twill out! stand clear. See
    where it flies,
In shape of a blue toad, with a bat's wings!
Do you not see it, sir?

CORBACCIO.   What? I think I do.

CORVINO. —'Tis too manifest.

VOLPONE.   Look! he comes t' himself!

VOLTORE. Where am I?

VOLPONE. Take good heart, the worst is past, sir.
You are dispossessed.

1ST AVOCATORE.   What accident is this?

2ND AVOCATORE. Sudden, and full of wonder!

3RD AVOCATORE.   If he were
Possessed, as it appears, all this is nothing.

CORVINO. He has been often subject to these fits.

1ST AVOCATORE. Show him that writing.—Do you
    know it, sir?

VOLPONE. —Deny it, sir, forswear it, know it not.

VOLTORE. Yes, I do know it well, it is my hand;
But all that it contains is false.

BONARIO.   O practice!

2ND AVOCATORE. What maze is this!

1ST AVOCATORE.   Is he not guilty then,
Whom you there name the parasite?

VOLTORE.   Grave fathers,
No more than his good patron, old Volpone.

4TH AVOCATORE. Why, he is dead.

VOLTORE.   O, no, my honoured fathers,
He lives——

1ST AVOCATORE.   How! lives?

VOLTORE.   Lives.

2ND AVOCATORE.   This is subtler yet!

3RD AVOCATORE. You said he was dead.

VOLTORE.   Never.

3RD AVOCATORE.   You said so!

CORVINO.   I heard so.

4TH AVOCATORE. Here comes the gentleman; make
    him way.

3RD AVOCATORE. A stool!   *Enter* MOSCA.

4TH AVOCATORE. —A proper man and, were Vol-
    pone dead,
A fit match for my daughter.

3RD AVOCATORE.   Give him way.

VOLPONE. —Mosca, I was almost lost; the advocate
Had betrayed all; but now it is recovered.
All's o' the hinge again——Say I am living.

MOSCA. What busy knave is this?—Most reverend
    fathers,

I sooner had attended your grave pleasures,
But that my order for the funeral
Of my dear patron did require me——

VOLPONE.   —Mosca!

MOSCA. Whom I intend to bury like a gentleman.

VOLPONE. —Ay, quick, and cozen me of all.

2ND AVOCATORE.   Still stranger!
More intricate!

1ST AVOCATORE. And come about again!

4TH AVOCATORE. —It is a match, my daughter is bestowed.

MOSCA. —Will you gi' me half?

VOLPONE.   First I'll be hanged.

MOSCA.   I know
Your voice is good, cry not so loud.

1ST AVOCATORE.   Demand.
The advocate.—Sir, did not you affirm
Volpone was alive?

VOLPONE.   Yes, and he is;
This gent'man told me so.—Thou shalt have half.

MOSCA. Whose drunkard is this same? speak, some
that know him.
I never saw his face.—I cannot now
Afford it you so cheap.

VOLPONE.   No?

1ST AVOCATORE.   What say you?

VOLTORE. The officer told me.

VOLPONE.   I did, grave fathers,
And will maintain he lives, with mine own life,
And that this creature told me.—I was born
With all good stars my enemies!

MOSCA.   Most grave fathers,
If such an insolence as this must pass
Upon me, I am silent; 'twas not this
For which you sent, I hope.

2ND AVOCATORE.   Take him away.

VOLPONE. —Mosca!

3RD AVOCATORE.   Let him be whipped.

VOLPONE.   —Wilt thou betray me?
Cozen me?

3RD AVOCATORE. And taught to bear himself
Toward a person of his rank.

4TH AVOCATORE.   Away.

MOSCA. I humbly thank your fatherhoods.

VOLPONE.   —Soft, soft. Whipped!
And lose all that I have! If I confess,
It cannot be much more.

4TH AVOCATORE.   Sir, are you married?

VOLPONE. —They'll be allied anon; I must be
    resolute:
The fox shall here uncase.   *Puts off his disguise.*

MOSCA.   Patron!

VOLPONE.   Nay, now
My ruins shall not come alone; your match
I'll hinder sure: my substance shall not glue you
Nor screw you into a family.

MOSCA.   Why, patron!

VOLPONE. I am Volpone, and this is my knave;
This, his own knave; this, avarice's fool;
This, a chimera of wittol, fool, and knave.
And, reverend fathers, since we all can hope
Nought but a sentence, let's not now despair it.
You hear me brief.

CORVINO.   May it please your fatherhoods——

COMMENDATORE.   Silence!

1ST AVOCATORE. The knot is now undone by
    miracle.

2ND AVOCATORE. Nothing can be more clear.

3RD AVOCATORE.   Or can more prove
These innocent.

1ST AVOCATORE.   Give 'em their liberty.

BONARIO. Heaven could not long let such gross crimes be hid.

2ND AVOCATORE. If this be held the highway to get riches,

May I be poor!

3RD AVOCATORE. This's not the gain, but torment.

1ST AVOCATORE. These possess wealth, as sick men possess fevers,

Which trulier may be said to possess them.

2ND AVOCATORE. Disrobe that parasite.

CORVINO, MOSCA. Most honoured fathers——

1ST AVOCATORE. Can you plead aught to stay the course of justice?

If you can, speak.

CORVINO, VOLTORE. We beg favour.

CELIA. And mercy.

1ST AVOCATORE. You hurt your innocence, suing for the guilty.—

Stand forth; and first the parasite.—You appear
T'have been the chiefest minister, if not plotter,
In all these lewd impostures; and now, lastly,
Have with your impudence abused the court,
And habit of a gentleman of Venice,
Being a fellow of no birth or blood;
For which our sentence is, first thou be whipped;
Then live perpetual prisoner in our galleys.

VOLPONE. I thank you for him.

MOSCA. Bane to thy wolfish nature!

1ST AVOCATORE. Deliver him to the Saffi.—Thou, Volpone,

By blood and rank a gentleman, canst not fall
Under like censure; but our judgment on thee
Is that thy substance all be straight confiscate
To the hospital of the Incurabili.
And since the most was gotten by imposture,
By feigning lame, gout, palsy, and such diseases,

Thou art to lie in prison, cramped with irons,
Till thou be'st sick and lame indeed.—Remove him.

VOLPONE. This is called mortifying of a fox.

1ST AVOCATORE. Thou, Voltore, to take away the scandal,
Thou hast giv'n all worthy men of thy profession,
Art banished from their fellowship, and our state.—
Corbaccio, bring him near!—We here possess
Thy son of all thy state, and confine thee
To the monastery of San Spirito;
Where, since thou knew'st not how to live well here,
Thou shalt be learned to die well.

CORBACCIO.   Ha! what said he?

COMMENDATORE. You shall know anon, sir.

1ST AVOCATORE.   Thou, Corvino, shalt
Be straight embarked from thine own house, and rowed
Round about Venice, through the Grand Canale,
Wearing a cap, with fair, long ass's ears
Instead of horns; and so to mount, a paper
Pinned on thy breast, to the Berlina—

CORVINO.   Yes,
And have mine eyes beat out with stinking fish,
Bruised fruit, and rotten eggs—'Tis well. I'm glad
I shall not see my shame yet.

1ST AVOCATORE.   And to expiate
Thy wrongs done to thy wife, thou art to send her
Home to her father, with her dowry trebled.
And these are all your judgments——

ALL.   Honoured fathers!

1ST AVOCATORE. Which may not be revoked. Now you begin,
When crimes are done, and past, and to be punished,
To think what your crimes are.—Away with them!
Let all that see these vices thus rewarded,

Take heart, and love to study 'em. Mischiefs feed
Like beasts, till they be fat, and then they bleed.

Exeunt.

VOLPONE *comes forward.*

The seasoning of a play is the applause.
Now, though the fox be punished by the laws,
He yet doth hope there is no suffering due,
For any fact which he hath done 'gainst you.
If there be, censure him; here he doubtful stands.
If not, fare jovially, and clap your hands.   *Exit.*

Epicene,
or
The Silent Woman

———

THE PERSONS OF THE PLAY

MOROSE, *a gentleman that loves no noise*
SIR DAUPHINE EUGENIE, *his nephew*
NED CLERIMONT, *a gentleman, his friend*
TRUEWIT, *another friend*
EPICENE, *a young gentleman supposed the Silent Woman*
SIR JOHN DAW, *servant to* EPICENE
SIR AMOROUS LA FOOLE
THOMAS OTTER, *a land- and sea-captain*
CUTBEARD, *a barber*
MUTE, *one of* MOROSE'S *servants*
PARSON

LADY HAUGHTY
LADY CENTAUR   } *Ladies Collegiates*
MISTRESS DOLL MAVIS
MISTRESS OTTER, *the Captain's wife*
MISTRESS TRUSTY, *the* LADY HAUGHTY'S } *Pretenders*
  woman

Pages, Servants, &c.

The Scene: LONDON

PROLOGUE

Truth says, of old the art of making plays
    Was to content the people; and their praise
    Was to the poet money, wine, and bays.
But in this age a sect of writers are,
    That only for particular likings care,
    And will taste nothing that is popular.
With such we mingle neither brains nor breasts;
    Our wishes, like to those make public feasts,
    Are not to please the cooks' tastes, but the guests'.
Yet if those cunning palates hither come,
    They shall find guests' entreaty, and good room;
    And though all relish not, sure there will be some,
That when they leave their seats shall make 'em say,
    Who wrote that piece, could so have wrote a play;
    But that he knew this was the better way.
For, to present all custard or all tart,
    And have no other meats to bear a part,
    Or to want bread and salt, were but coarse art.
The poet prays you then, with better thought
    To sit; and when his cates are all in brought,
    Though there be none far-fet, there will dear-
        bought
Be, fit for ladies; some for lords, knights, squires;
    Some for your waiting-wench, and city-wires;
    Some for your men and daughters of Whitefriars.
Nor is it only while you keep your seat
    Here, that his feast will last; but you shall eat
    A week at ord'naries on his broken meat;
        If his muse be true,
        Who commends her to you.

ANOTHER

Occasioned by some person's impertinent exception

The ends of all, who for the scene do write,
Are, or should be, to profit and delight.
And still 't hath been the praise of all best times,
So persons were not touched, to tax the crimes.
Then in this play, which we present tonight,
And make the object of your ear and sight,
On forfeit of yourselves, think nothing true;
Lest so you make the maker to judge you.
For he knows poet never credit gained
By writing truths, but things like truths, well
    feigned.
If any yet will—with particular sleight
Of application—wrest what he doth write,
And that he meant or him or her, will say;
They make a libel, which he made a play.

SONNET

(Composed in reply to some impertinent question.)

The ends of all worlds the term do write,
... should be, by wrath and delight,—
Indeed I wish the whole type of all but stopped,
So persons were untouched, to tax the crime;
Then in the place which was predominating,
Suddenly the shout of sorrow and span,
The bottom of endless night, nothing real,
I ask you and taught the night to order you,
To-day those poet does understand,
Be writing frailty, but things like minds, well,
... stayed,
It above self, with particular shape,
Of sentiment—were where the doth say,
And that he count of man to save will say,
The nature's habit which he made a play.

EPICENE,

OR

THE SILENT WOMAN

ACT ONE

Clerimont's house

Enter CLERIMONT, *making himself ready, followed by*
BOY.

CLERIMONT. Ha' you got the song yet perfect I ga'
you, boy?

BOY. Yes, sir.

CLERIMONT. Let me hear it.

BOY. You shall, sir; but, i' faith, let nobody else.

CLERIMONT. Why, I pray?

BOY. It will get you the dangerous name of a poet
in town, sir, besides me a perfect deal of ill will at
the mansion you wot of, whose lady is the argument
of it; where now I am the welcom'st thing under a
man that comes there.

CLERIMONT. I think; and above a man, too, if the
truth were racked out of you.

BOY. No, faith, I'll confess before, sir. The gentlewomen play with me, and throw me o' the bed, and
carry me in to my Lady; and she kisses me with her
oiled face, and puts a peruke o' my head, and asks
me an I will wear her gown; and I say no. And then
she hits me a blow o' the ear, and calls me innocent,
and lets me go.

CLERIMONT. No marvel if the door be kept shut
against your master, when the entrance is so easy to

you—— Well, sir, you shall go there no more, lest I be fain to seek your voice in my lady's rushes a fortnight hence. Sing, sir.   BOY *sings*.

Enter TRUEWIT.

TRUEWIT. Why, here's the man that can melt away his time, and never feels it! What between his mistress abroad and his ingle at home, high fare, soft lodging, fine clothes, and his fiddle, he thinks the hours ha' no wings, or the day no post-horse. Well, Sir Gallant, were you struck with the plague this minute, or condemned to any capital punishment tomorrow, you would begin then to think, and value every article o' your time, esteem it at the true rate, and give all for't.

CLERIMONT. Why, what should a man do?

TRUEWIT. Why, nothing; or that which, when 'tis done, is as idle. Hearken after the next horse-race or hunting-match, lay wagers, praise Puppy, or Peppercorn, Whitefoot, Franklin; swear upon Whitemane's party; spend aloud, that my lords may hear you; visit my ladies at night, and be able to give 'em the character of every bowler or better o' the green. These be the things wherein your fashionable men exercise themselves, and I for company.

CLERIMONT. Nay, if I have thy authority, I'll not leave yet. Come, the other are considerations when we come to have grey heads and weak hams, moist eyes and shrunk members. We'll think on 'em then; then we'll pray and fast.

TRUEWIT. Ay, and destine only that time of age to goodness, which our want of ability will not let us employ in evil?

CLERIMONT. Why, then 'tis time enough.

TRUEWIT. Yes; as if a man should sleep all the term, and think to effect his business the last day. O,

Clerimont, this time, because it is an incorporeal thing, and not subject to sense, we mock ourselves the fineliest out of it, with vanity and misery indeed; not seeking an end of wretchedness, but only changing the matter still.

CLERIMONT. Nay, thou'lt not leave now——

TRUEWIT. See but our common disease! With what justice can we complain that great men will not look upon us, nor be at leisure to give our affairs such dispatch as we expect, when we will never do it to ourselves; nor hear, nor regard ourselves?

CLERIMONT. Foh! thou hast read Plutarch's 'Morals,' now, or some such tedious fellow, and it shows so vilely with thee, 'fore God, 'twill spoil thy wit utterly! Talk me of pins and feathers and ladies and rushes and such things, and leave this Stoicity alone till thou mak'st sermons.

TRUEWIT. Well, sir, if it will not take, I have learned to lose as little of my kindness as I can. I'll do good to no man against his will, certainly. When were you at the College?

CLERIMONT. What college?

TRUEWIT. As if you knew not!

CLERIMONT. No, faith, I came but from court yesterday.

TRUEWIT. Why, is it not arrived there yet, the news? A new foundation, sir, here i' the town, of ladies that call themselves the Collegiates, an order between courtiers and country madams, that live from their husbands and give entertainment to all the wits and braveries o' the time, as they call 'em; cry down, or up, what they like or dislike in a brain or a fashion, with most masculine, or rather, hermaphroditical authority; and every day gain to their college some new probationer.

CLERIMONT. Who is the president?

TRUEWIT. The grave and youthful matron, the Lady Haughty.

CLERIMONT. A pox of her autumnal face, her pieced beauty! There's no man can be admitted till she be ready nowadays, till she has painted, and perfumed, and washed, and scoured, but the boy here; and him she wipes her oiled lips upon, like a sponge. I have made a song—I pray thee hear it—o' the subject.

SONG.

'Still to be neat, still to be dressed
  As you were going to a feast,
  Still to be powdered, still perfumed;
  Lady, is it to be presumed,
  Though art's hid causes are not found,
  All is not sweet, all is not sound.

'Give me a look, give me a face,
  That makes simplicity a grace;
  Robes loosely flowing, hair as free—
  Such sweet neglect more taketh me,
  Than all th' adulteries of art.
  They strike mine eyes, but not my heart.'

TRUEWIT. And I am clearly o' the other side; I love a good dressing before any beauty o' the world. O, a woman is then like a delicate garden, nor is there one kind of it. She may vary every hour, take often counsel of her glass, and choose the best. If she have good ears, show 'em; good hair, lay it out; good legs, wear short clothes; a good hand, discover it often; practise any art to mend breath, cleanse teeth, repair eyebrows, paint, and profess it.

CLERIMONT. How! publicly?

TRUEWIT. The doing of it, not the manner; that must be private. Many things that seem foul i' the doing, do please done. A lady should, indeed, study her face, when we think she sleeps. Nor, when the doors are shut, should men be inquiring; all is sacred within, then. Is it for us to see their perukes put on, their false teeth, their complexion, their eyebrows, their nails? You see gilders will not work, but enclosed. They must not discover how little serves, with the help of art, to adorn a great deal. How long did the canvas hang afore Aldgate? Were the people suffered to see the City's Love and Charity, while they were rude stone, before they were painted and burnished? No. No more should servants approach their mistresses, but when they are complete and finished.

CLERIMONT. Well said, my Truewit.

TRUEWIT. And a wise lady will keep a guard always upon the place, that she may do things securely. I once followed a rude fellow into a chamber, where the poor madam, for haste, and troubled, snatched at her peruke to cover her baldness, and put it on the wrong way.

CLERIMONT. O prodigy!

TRUEWIT. And the unconscionable knave held her in compliment an hour with that reversed face, when I still looked when she should talk from the tother side.

CLERIMONT. Why, thou shouldst ha' relieved her.

TRUEWIT. No, faith, I let her alone, as we'll let this argument, if you please, and pass to another. When saw you Dauphine Eugenie?

CLERIMONT. Not these three days. Shall we go to him this morning? he is very melancholic, I hear.

TRUEWIT. Sick o' the uncle, is he? I met that stiff piece of formality, his uncle, yesterday, with a huge turban of nightcaps on his head, buckled over his ears.

CLERIMONT. O, that's his custom when he walks abroad. He can endure no noise, man.

TRUEWIT. So I have heard. But is the disease so ridiculous in him as it is made? They say he has been upon divers treaties with the fishwives and orange-women, and articles propounded between them. Marry, the chimney-sweepers will not be drawn in.

CLERIMONT. No, nor the broom-men; they stand out stiffly. He cannot endure a costermonger; he swoons if he hear one.

TRUEWIT. Methinks a smith should be ominous.

CLERIMONT. Or any hammer-man. A brazier is not suffered to dwell in the parish, nor an armourer. He would have hanged a pewterer's prentice once upon a Shrove Tuesday's riot, for being o' that trade, when the rest were quit.

TRUEWIT. A trumpet should fright him terribly, or the hautboys!

CLERIMONT. Out of his senses. The waits of the City have a pension of him, not to come near that ward. This youth practised on him one night, like the bellman, and never left till he had brought him down to the door with a long-sword, and there left him flourishing with the air.

BOY. Why, sir, he hath chosen a street to lie in, so narrow at both ends that it will receive no coaches, nor carts, nor any of these common noises. And therefore we that love him devise to bring him in such as we may, now and then, for his exercise, to breathe him. He would grow resty else, in his ease. His virtue would rust without action. I entreated a bear-ward one day to come down with the dogs of some four parishes that way, and I thank him, he did; and cried his games under Master Morose's window, till he was sent crying away with his head made a most bleeding spectacle to the multitude.

And another time, a fencer marching to his prize had his drum most tragically run through, for taking that street in his way, at my request.

TRUEWIT. A good wag! How does he for the bells?

CLERIMONT. O, i' the Queen's time, he was wont to go out of town every Saturday at ten o'clock, or on holiday eves. But now, by reason of the sickness, the perpetuity of ringing has made him devise a room with double walls and treble ceilings, the windows close shut and caulked, and there he lives by candle-light. He turned away a man last week, for having a pair of new shoes that creaked. And this fellow waits on him now in tennis-court socks, or slippers soled with wool; and they talk each to other in a trunk. See who comes here.

Enter SIR DAUPHINE EUGENIE.

DAUPHINE. How now! what ail you, sirs? dumb?

TRUEWIT. Struck into stone, almost, I am here, with tales o' thine uncle. There was never such a prodigy heard of.

DAUPHINE. I would you would once lose this subject, my masters, for my sake. They are such as you are, that have brought me into that predicament I am, with him.

TRUEWIT. How is that?

DAUPHINE. Marry, that he will disinherit me, no more. He thinks I and my company are authors of all the ridiculous acts and monuments are told of him.

TRUEWIT. 'Slid, I would be the author of more to vex him; that purpose deserves it; it gives thee law of plaguing him. I'll tell thee what I would do. I would make a false almanac, get it printed, and then ha' him drawn out on a coronation day to the Tower Wharf, and kill him with the noise of the ordnance.

Disinherit thee! he cannot, man. Art not thou next of blood, and his sister's son?

DAUPHINE. Ay, but he will thrust me out of it, he vows, and marry.

TRUEWIT. How! that's a more portent. Can he endure no noise, and will venture on a wife?

CLERIMONT. Yes. Why, thou art a stranger, it seems, to his best trick yet. He has employed a fellow this half-year all over England to hearken him out a dumb woman, be she of any form or any quality, so she be able to bear children; her silence is dowry enough, he says.

TRUEWIT. But I trust to God he has found none.

CLERIMONT. No, but he has heard of one that's lodged i' the next street to him, who is exceedingly soft-spoken, thrifty of her speech; that spends but six words a day. And her he's about now, and shall have her.

TRUEWIT. Is't possible! Who is his agent i' the business?

CLERIMONT. Marry, a barber, one Cutbeard; an honest fellow, one that tells Dauphine all here.

TRUEWIT. Why, you oppress me with wonder: a woman and a barber, and love no noise!

CLERIMONT. Yes, faith. The fellow trims him silently, and has not the knack with his shears or his fingers; and that continence in a barber he thinks so eminent a virtue, as it has made him chief of his counsel.

TRUEWIT. Is the barber to be seen, or the wench?

CLERIMONT. Yes, that they are.

TRUEWIT. I pray thee, Dauphine, let's go thither.

DAUPHINE. I have some business now; I cannot, i' faith.

TRUEWIT. You shall have no business shall make you neglect this, sir. We'll make her talk, believe it;

or, if she will not, we can give out at least so much as shall interrupt the treaty. We will break it. Thou art bound in conscience, when he suspects thee without cause, to torment him.

DAUPHINE. Not I, by any means. I'll give no suffrage to't. He shall never ha' that plea against me, that I opposed the least fancy of his. Let it lie upon my stars to be guilty, I'll be innocent.

TRUEWIT. Yes, and be poor, and beg; do, innocent; when some groom of his has got him an heir, or this barber, if he himself cannot. Innocent! I pray thee, Ned, where lies she? Let him be innocent still.

CLERIMONT. Why, right over against the barber's, in the house where Sir John Daw lies.

TRUEWIT. You do not mean to confound me!

CLERIMONT. Why?

TRUEWIT. Does he that would marry her know so much?

CLERIMONT. I cannot tell.

TRUEWIT. 'Twere enough of imputation to her, with him.

CLERIMONT. Why?

TRUEWIT. The only talking sir i' the town! Jack Daw! An he teach her not to speak—God b'w'you. I have some business too.

CLERIMONT. Will you not go thither, then?

TRUEWIT. Not with the danger to meet Daw, for mine ears.

CLERIMONT. Why? I thought you two had been upon very good terms.

TRUEWIT. Yes, of keeping distance.

CLERIMONT. They say he is a very good scholar.

TRUEWIT. Ay, and he says it first. A pox on him, a fellow that pretends only to learning, buys titles, and nothing else of books in him!

CLERIMONT. The world reports him to be very learned.

TRUEWIT. I am sorry the world should so conspire to belie him.

CLERIMONT. Good faith, I have heard very good things come from him.

TRUEWIT. You may. There's none so desperately ignorant to deny that; would they were his own! God b'w'you, gentlemen.   *Exit.*

CLERIMONT. This is very abrupt!

DAUPHINE. Come, you are a strange, open man, to tell everything thus.

CLERIMONT. Why, believe it, Dauphine, Truewit's a very honest fellow.

DAUPHINE. I think no other; but this frank nature of his is not for secrets.

CLERIMONT. Nay then, you are mistaken, Dauphine. I know where he has been well trusted, and discharged the trust very truly and heartily.

DAUPHINE. I contend not, Ned, but with the fewer a business is carried, it is ever the safer. Now we are alone, if you'll go thither, I am for you.

CLERIMONT. When were you there?

DAUPHINE. Last night; and such a Decameron of sport fallen out! Boccace never thought of the like. Daw does nothing but court her, and the wrong way. He would lie with her, and praises her modesty; desires that she would talk and be free, and commends her silence in verses, which he reads, and swears are the best that ever man made. Then rails at his fortunes, stamps, and mutines, why he is not made a councillor, and called to affairs of state.

CLERIMONT. I pray thee, let's go. I would fain partake this.—Some water, boy.   *Exit* BOY.

DAUPHINE. We are invited to dinner together, he and I, by one that came thither to him, Sir La Foole.

CLERIMONT. O, that's a precious mannikin!

DAUPHINE. Do you know him?

CLERIMONT. Ay, and he will know you too, if e'er he saw you but once, though you should meet him at church in the midst of prayers. He is one of the braveries, though he be none o' the wits. He will salute a judge upon the bench, and a bishop in the pulpit, a lawyer when he is pleading at the bar, and a lady when she is dancing in a masque, and put her out. He does give plays and suppers, and invites his guests to 'em aloud, out of his window, as they ride by in coaches. He has a lodging in the Strand for the purpose; or to watch when ladies are gone to the china-houses, or the Exchange, that he may meet 'em by chance, and give 'em presents, some two or three hundred pounds' worth of toys, to be laughed at. He is never without a spare banquet, or sweet-meats in his chamber, for their women to alight at, and come up to, for a bait.

DAUPHINE. Excellent! He was a fine youth last night, but now he is much finer! What is his Christian name? I ha' forgot.

Re-enter BOY.

CLERIMONT. Sir Amorous La Foole.

BOY. The gentleman is here below that owns that name.

CLERIMONT. Heart, he's come to invite me to dinner, I hold my life.

DAUPHINE. Like enough. Pray thee, let's ha' him up.

CLERIMONT. Boy, marshal him.

BOY. With a truncheon, sir?

CLERIMONT. Away, I beseech you. *Exit* BOY. I'll make him tell us his pedigree now, and what meat he has to dinner, and who are his guests, and the whole course of his fortunes, with a breath.

Enter SIR AMOROUS LA FOOLE.

LA FOOLE. Save, dear Sir Dauphine! honoured Master Clerimont!

CLERIMONT. Sir Amorous! you have very much honested my lodging with your presence.

LA FOOLE. Good faith, it is a fine lodging! almost as delicate a lodging as mine.

CLERIMONT. Not so, sir.

LA FOOLE. Excuse me, sir, if it were i' the Strand, I assure you. I am come, Master Clerimont, to entreat you wait upon two or three ladies, to dinner, today.

CLERIMONT. How, sir! wait upon 'em? Did you ever see me carry dishes!

LA FOOLE. No, sir, dispense with me; I meant, to bear 'em company.

CLERIMONT. O, that I will, sir. The doubtfulness o' your phrase, believe it, sir, would breed you a quarrel once an hour with the terrible boys, if you should but keep 'em fellowship a day.

LA FOOLE. It should be extremely against my will, sir, if I contested with any man.

CLERIMONT. I believe it, sir. Where hold you your feast?

LA FOOLE. At Tom Otter's, sir.

DAUPHINE. Tom Otter! What's he?

LA FOOLE. Captain Otter, sir; he is a kind of gamester, but he has had command both by sea and by land.

DAUPHINE. O, then he is animal amphibium?

LA FOOLE. Ay, sir. His wife was the rich chinawoman, that the courtiers visited so often; that gave the rare entertainment. She commands all at home.

CLERIMONT. Then she is Captain Otter.

LA FOOLE. You say very well, sir. She is my kins-woman, a La Foole by the mother side, and will in-vite any great ladies for my sake.

DAUPHINE. Not of the La Fooles of Essex?

LA FOOLE. No, sir, the La Fooles of London.

CLERIMONT. —Now he's in.

LA FOOLE. They all come out of our house, the La Fooles o' the north, the La Fooles of the west, the La Fooles of the east and south— We are as ancient a family as any is in Europe— But I myself am de-scended lineally of the French La Fooles— And we do bear for our coat yellow, or Or, checkered Azure, and Gules, and some three or four colours more, which is a very noted coat, and has sometimes been solemnly worn by divers nobility of our house— But let that go, antiquity is not respected now— I had a brace of fat does sent me, gentlemen, and half a dozen of pheasants, a dozen or two of godwits, and some other fowl, which I would have eaten while they are good, and in good company— There will be a great lady or two, my Lady Haughty, my Lady Centaur, Mistress Doll Mavis— And they come o' purpose to see the silent gentlewoman, Mistress Epicene, that honest Sir John Daw has promised to bring thither— And then, Mistress Trusty, my lady's woman, will be there, too, and this honourable knight, Sir Dauphine, with yourself, Master Cleri-mont— And we'll be very merry, and have fiddlers, and dance— I have been a mad wag in my time, and have spent some crowns since I was a page in court, to my Lord Lofty, and after, my Lady's gentleman-usher, who got me knighted in Ireland, since it pleased my elder brother to die— I had as fair a gold jerkin on that day as any was worn in the island voyage, or at Cadiz, none dispraised; and I came over in it hither, showed myself to my friends in court, and after went down to my tenants in the country, and surveyed my lands, let new leases, took their money, spent it in the eye o' the land here, upon ladies—and now I can take up at my pleasure.

DAUPHINE. Can you take up ladies, sir?

CLERIMONT. O, let him breathe, he has not recovered.

DAUPHINE. Would I were your half in that commodity——

LA FOOLE. No, sir, excuse me; I meant money, which can take up anything. I have another guest or two to invite, and say as much to, gentlemen. I'll take my leave abruptly, in hope you will not fail—— Your servant. *Exit.*

DAUPHINE. We will not fail you, Sir Precious La Foole; but she shall, that your ladies come to see, if I have credit afore Sir Daw.

CLERIMONT. Did you ever hear such a windfucker as this?

DAUPHINE. Or such a rook as the other, that will betray his mistress to be seen! Come, 'tis time we prevented it.

CLERIMONT. Go. *Exeunt.*

ACT TWO. SCENE ONE

Morose's house

Enter MOROSE *with a tube in his hand, followed by* MUTE.

MOROSE. Cannot I yet find out a more compendious method, than by this trunk, to save my servants the labour of speech, and mine ears the discord of

sounds? Let me see: all discourses but mine own afflict me; they seem harsh, impertinent, and irksome.
—Is it not possible that thou shouldst answer me by
signs, and I apprehend thee, fellow? Speak not,
though I question you. You have taken the ring off
from the street door, as I bade you? Answer me not
by speech, but by silence, unless it be otherwise.
MUTE *makes a leg.* Very good. And you have fas-
tened on a thick quilt, or flock-bed, on the outside of the door, that if they knock with their dag-
gers, or with brickbats, they can make no noise? But
with your leg, your answer, unless it be otherwise.
A leg. Very good.—This is not only fit modesty in a
servant, but good state and discretion in a master.—
And you have been with Cutbeard the barber, to
have him come to me? *A leg.* Good. And he will
come presently? Answer me not but with your leg,
unless it be otherwise; if it be otherwise, shake your
head, or shrug. *A leg.* So.—Your Italian and Spaniard
are wise in these, and it is a frugal and comely gravity!—How long will it be ere Cutbeard come? Stay,
if an hour, hold up your whole hand; if half an
hour, two fingers; if a quarter, one. *A sign.* Good,
half a quarter? 'tis well. And have you given him a
key, to come in without knocking? *A leg.* Good. And
is the lock oiled, and the hinges, today? *A leg.* Good.
And the quilting of the stairs nowhere worn out and
bare? *A leg.* Very good. I see, by much doctrine and
impulsion, it may be effected. Stand by.—The Turk,
in this divine discipline, is admirable, exceeding all
the potentates of the earth; still waited on by mutes,
and all his commands so executed; yea, even in the
war, as I have heard, and in his marches, most of his
charges and directions given by signs, and with silence—an exquisite art! And I am heartily ashamed,
and angry oftentimes, that the princes of Christendom should suffer a barbarian to transcend 'em in

so high a point of felicity. I will practise it hereafter. *One winds a horn without.* How now? O! O! what villain, what prodigy of mankind is that? Look. *Again. Exit* MUTE. O, cut his throat, cut his throat! What murderer, hell-hound, devil can this be?

Re-enter MUTE.

MUTE. It is a post from the court——

MOROSE. Out, rogue! and must thou blow thy horn, too?

MUTE. Alas, it is a post from the court, sir, that says he must speak with you, pain of death——

MOROSE. Pain of thy life, be silent!

Enter TRUEWIT.

TRUEWIT. By your leave, sir,—I am a stranger here —is your name Master Morose? is your name Master Morose? Fishes! Pythagoreans all! This is strange. What say you, sir? nothing! Has Harpocrates been here with his club, among you? Well, sir, I will believe you to be the man at this time; I will venture upon you, sir. Your friends at court commend 'em to you, sir——

MOROSE. O men! O manners! was there ever such an impudence?

TRUEWIT. And are extremely solicitous for you, sir.

MOROSE. Whose knave are you?

TRUEWIT. Mine own knave, and your compeer, sir.

MOROSE. Fetch me my sword——

TRUEWIT. You shall taste the one half of my dagger, if you do, groom; and you the other, if you stir, sir. Be patient, I charge you, in the King's name, and hear me without insurrection. They say you are to marry; to marry! do you mark, sir?

MOROSE. How then, rude companion!

TRUEWIT. Marry, your friends do wonder, sir, the

Thames being so near, wherein you may drown so handsomely; or London Bridge, at a low fall, with a fine leap, to hurry you down the stream; or such a delicate steeple i' the town, as Bow, to vault from; or a braver height, as Paul's; or, if you affected to do it nearer home, and a shorter way, an excellent garret-window into the street; or a beam in the said garret, with this halter—*Shows him a halter*—which they have sent, and desire that you would sooner commit your grave head to this knot, than to the wedlock noose; or take a little sublimate, and go out of the world like a rat, or a fly—as one said—with a straw i' your arse; any way rather than to follow this goblin, matrimony. Alas, sir, do you ever think to find a chaste wife in these times? now? when there are so many masques, plays, Puritan preachings, mad folks, and other strange sights to be seen daily, private and public? If you had lived in King Ethel-dred's time, sir, or Edward the Confessor's, you might perhaps have found in some cold country hamlet, then, a dull, frosty wench, would have been contented with one man. Now, they will as soon be pleased with one leg or one eye. I'll tell you, sir, the monstrous hazards you shall run with a wife.

MOROSE. Good sir, have I ever cozened any friends of yours of their land? bought their possessions? taken forfeit of their mortgage? begged a reversion from 'em? bastarded their issue? What have I done that may deserve this?

TRUEWIT. Nothing, sir, that I know, but your itch of marriage.

MOROSE. Why, if I had made an assassinate upon your father, vitiated your mother, ravished your sisters——

TRUEWIT. I would kill you, sir, I would kill you, if you had.

MOROSE. Why, you do more in this, sir. It were a vengeance centuple, for all facinorous acts that could be named, to do that you do——

TRUEWIT. Alas, sir, I am but a messenger. I but tell you what you must hear. It seems your friends are careful after your soul's health, sir, and would have you know the danger; but you may do your pleasure for all them, I persuade not, sir. If, after you are married, your wife do run away with a vaulter, or the Frenchman that walks upon ropes, or him that dances the jig, or a fencer for his skill at his weapon, why, it is not their fault; they have discharged their consciences, when you know what may happen. Nay, suffer valiantly, sir, for I must tell you all the perils that you are obnoxious to. If she be fair, young, and vegetous, no sweetmeats ever drew more flies; all the yellow doublets and great roses i' the town will be there. If foul and crooked, she'll be with them, and buy those doublets and roses, sir. If rich, and that you marry her dowry, not her, she'll reign in your house as imperious as a widow. If noble, all her kindred will be your tyrants. If fruitful, as proud as May and humorous as April; she must have her doctors, her midwives, her nurses, her longings every hour, though it be for the dearest morsel of man. If learned, there was never such a parrot; all your patrimony will be too little for the guests that must be invited to hear her speak Latin and Greek; and you must lie with her in those languages too, if you will please her. If precise, you must feast all the silenced brethren, once in three days; salute the sisters; entertain the whole family, or wood of 'em; and hear long-winded exercises, singings, and catechisings, which you are not given to, and yet must give for, to please the zealous matron your wife, who, for the holy cause, will cozen you over and above. You begin to sweat, sir? But this is not half, i' faith! You may do your pleasure, notwithstanding, as I said before; I come not to persuade you. MUTE *is stealing away.* Upon my faith, Master Serving-man, if you do stir, I will beat you.

MOROSE. O, what is my sin? what is my sin?

TRUEWIT. Then, if you love your wife, or rather, dote on her, sir, O how she'll torture you, and take pleasure i' your torments! You shall lie with her but when she lists; she will not hurt her beauty, her complexion; or it must be for that jewel, or that pearl, when she does. Every half-hour's pleasure must be bought anew, and with the same pain and charge you wooed her at first. Then you must keep what servants she please, what company she will; that friend must not visit you without her licence; and him she loves most, she will seem to hate eagerliest, to decline your jealousy; or feign to be jealous of you first, and for that cause go live with her she-friend, or cousin at the College, that can instruct her in all the mysteries of writing letters, corrupting servants, taming spies; where she must have that rich gown for such a great day, a new one for the next, a richer for the third; be served in silver; have the chamber filled with a succession of grooms, footmen, ushers, and other messengers, besides embroiderers, jewellers, tire-women, sempsters, feather-men, perfumers; while she feels not how the land drops away, nor the acres melt; nor foresees the change, when the mercer has your woods for her velvets; never weighs what her pride costs, sir, so she may kiss a page, or a smooth chin that has the despair of a beard; be a stateswoman, know all the news, what was done at Salisbury, what at the Bath, what at court, what in progress; or so she may censure poets and authors and styles, and compare 'em—Daniel with Spenser,

Jonson with the tother youth, and so forth; or be thought cunning in controversies or the very knots of divinity, and have often in her mouth the state of the question; and then skip to the mathematics and demonstration; and answer, in religion to one, in state to another, in bawdry to a third.

MOROSE. O! O!

TRUEWIT. All this is very true, sir. And then her going in disguise to that conjurer, and this cunning-woman, where the first question is how soon you shall die? next, if her present servant love her? next that, if she shall have a new servant? And how many? which of her family would make the best bawd, male or female? what precedence she shall have by her next match? and sets down the answers, and believes 'em above the scriptures. Nay, perhaps she'll study the art.

MOROSE. Gentle sir, ha' you done? ha' you had your pleasure o' me? I'll think of these things.

TRUEWIT. Yes, sir, and then comes reeking home of vapour and sweat, with going afoot, and lies in, a month, of a new face, all oil and birdlime; and rises in asses' milk, and is cleansed with a new fucus. God b'w'you, sir. One thing more, which I had almost forgot. This too, with whom you are to marry, may have made a conveyance of her virginity aforehand, as your wise widows do of their states, before they marry, in trust to some friend, sir. Who can tell? Or if she have not done it yet, she may do, upon the wedding day, or the night before, and antedate you cuckold. The like has been heard of in nature. 'Tis no devised, impossible thing, sir. God b'w'you. I'll be bold to leave this rope with you, sir, for a remembrance.—Farewell, Mute!   *Exit.*

MOROSE. Come, ha' me to my chamber; but first

shut the door. *The horn again.* O, shut the door, shut the door! Is he come again?

Enter CUTBEARD.

CUTBEARD. 'Tis I, sir, your barber.

MOROSE. O Cutbeard, Cutbeard, Cutbeard! here has been a cut-throat with me. Help me in to my bed, and give me physic with thy counsel.   *Exeunt.*

ACT TWO. SCENE TWO

Sir John Daw's house

Enter DAW, CLERIMONT, DAUPHINE, *and* EPICENE.

DAW. Nay, an she will, let her refuse at her own charges; 'tis nothing to me, gentlemen. But she will not be invited to the like feasts or guests every day.

CLERIMONT. O, by no means, she may not refuse—— to stay at home, if you love your reputation. 'Slight, you are invited thither o' purpose to be seen, and laughed at by the lady of the College and her shadows. This trumpeter hath proclaimed you. *They dissuade her privately.*

DAUPHINE. You shall not go. Let him be laughed at in your stead, for not bringing you; and put him to his extemporal faculty of fooling and talking loud to satisfy the company.

CLERIMONT. He will suspect us; talk aloud.—Pray, Mistress Epicene, let's see your verses; we have Sir John Daw's leave. Do not conceal your servant's merit, and your own glories.

EPICENE. They'll prove my servant's glories, if you have his leave so soon.

DAUPHINE. His vainglories, lady!

DAW. Show 'em, show 'em, mistress! I dare own 'em.

EPICENE. Judge you what glories.

DAW. Nay, I'll read 'em myself, too; an author must recite his own works. It is a madrigal of modesty:

'Modest and fair, for fair and good are near
          Neighbours, howe'er.'

DAUPHINE. Very good.

CLERIMONT. Ay, is't not?

DAW.

'No noble virtue ever was alone,
          But two in one.'

DAUPHINE. Excellent!

CLERIMONT. That again, I pray, Sir John.

DAUPHINE. It has something in't like rare wit and sense.

CLERIMONT. Peace.

DAW.

'No noble virtue ever was alone,
          But two in one.
Then, when I praise sweet modesty, I praise
          Bright beauty's rays;
And having praised both beauty and modesty,
          I have praised thee.'

DAUPHINE. Admirable!

CLERIMONT. How it chimes and cries tink i' the close divinely!

DAUPHINE. Ay, 'tis Seneca.

CLERIMONT. No, I think 'tis Plutarch.

DAW. The dor on Plutarch and Seneca, I hate it! They are mine own imaginations, by that light! I wonder those fellows have such credit with gentlemen.

CLERIMONT. They are very grave authors.

DAW. Grave asses! mere essayists! a few loose sentences, and that's all. A man would talk so his whole age. I do utter as good things every hour, if they were collected and observed, as either of 'em.

DAUPHINE. Indeed, Sir John!

CLERIMONT. He must needs, living among the wits, and braveries too.

DAUPHINE. Ay, and being president of 'em, as he is.

DAW. There's Aristotle, a mere commonplace fellow; Plato, a discourser; Thucydides and Livy, tedious and dry; Tacitus, an entire knot—sometimes worth the untying, very seldom.

CLERIMONT. What do you think of the poets, Sir John?

DAW. Not worthy to be named for authors. Homer, an old, tedious, prolix ass, talks of curriers and chines of beef; Virgil, of dunging of land, and bees; Horace, of I know not what.

CLERIMONT. —I think so.

DAW. And so Pindarus, Lycophron, Anacreon, Catullus, Seneca the tragedian, Lucan, Propertius, Tibullus, Martial, Juvenal, Ausonius, Statius, Politian, Valerius Flaccus, and the rest——

CLERIMONT. —What a sack-full of their names he has got!

DAUPHINE. And how he pours 'em out! Politian with Valerius Flaccus!

CLERIMONT. Was not the character right of him?

DAUPHINE. As could be made, i' faith.

DAW. And Persius, a crabbed coxcomb, not to be endured.

DAUPHINE. Why, whom do you account for authors, Sir John Daw?

DAW. Syntagma Juris Civilis, Corpus Juris Civilis, Corpus Juris Canonici, the King of Spain's Bible——

DAUPHINE. Is the King of Spain's Bible an author?

CLERIMONT. Yes, and Syntagma.

DAUPHINE. What was that Syntagma, sir?

DAW. A civil lawyer, a Spaniard.

DAUPHINE. Sure, Corpus was a Dutchman.

CLERIMONT. Ay, both the Corpuses, I knew 'em; they were very corpulent authors.

DAW. And then there's Vatablus, Pomponatius, Symancha; the other are not to be received within the thought of a scholar.

DAUPHINE. 'Fore God, you have a simple learned servant, lady,—in titles.

CLERIMONT. I wonder that he is not called to the helm, and made a councillor!

DAUPHINE. He is one extraordinary.

CLERIMONT. Nay, but in ordinary! to say truth, the state wants such.

DAUPHINE. Why, that will follow.

CLERIMONT. I muse a mistress can be so silent to the dotes of such a servant.

DAW. 'Tis her virtue, sir. I have written somewhat of her silence, too.

DAUPHINE. In verse, Sir John?

CLERIMONT. What else?

DAUPHINE. Why, how can you justify your own being of a poet, that so slight all the old poets?

DAW. Why, every man that writes in verse is not a poet; you have of the wits that write verses, and yet are no poets. They are poets that live by it, the poor fellows that live by it.

DAUPHINE. Why, would not you live by your verses, Sir John?

CLERIMONT. No, 'twere pity he should. A knight live by his verses? He did not make 'em to that end, I hope.

DAUPHINE. And yet the noble Sidney lives by his, and the noble family not ashamed.

CLERIMONT. Ay, he professed himself; but Sir John Daw has more caution. He'll not hinder his own rising i' the state so much! do you think he will? Your verses, good Sir John, and no poems.

DAW.
'Silence in woman is like speech in man,
     Deny 't who can.'

DAUPHINE. Not I, believe it; your reason, sir.

DAW.   'Nor is't a tale,
That female vice should be a virtue male,
Or masculine vice a female virtue be.
     You shall it see
     Proved with increase;
I know to speak, and she to hold her peace.'
Do you conceive me, gentlemen?

DAUPHINE. No, faith; how mean you 'with increase,' Sir John?

DAW. Why, 'with increase' is when I court her for the common cause of mankind, and she says nothing, but 'consentire videtur,' and in time is 'gravida.'

DAUPHINE. Then this is a ballad of procreation?

CLERIMONT. A madrigal of procreation, you mistake.

EPICENE. Pray give me my verses again, servant.

DAW. If you'll ask 'em aloud, you shall.

Enter TRUEWIT.

CLERIMONT. See, here's Truewit again! Where hast thou been, in the name of madness, thus accoutred with thy horn?

TRUEWIT. Where the sound of it might have pierced your senses with gladness, had you been in ear-reach of it. Dauphine, fall down and worship me; I have forbid the bans, lad. I have been with thy virtuous uncle, and have broke the match.

DAUPHINE. You ha' not, I hope.

TRUEWIT. Yes, faith, an thou shouldst hope otherwise, I should repent me. This horn got me entrance; kiss it. I had no other way to get in, but by feigning to be a post; but when I got in once, I proved none, but rather the contrary, turned him into a post, or a stone, or what is stiffer, with thundering into him the incommodities of a wife, and the miseries of marriage. If ever Gorgon were seen in the shape of a woman, he hath seen her in my description. I have put him off o' that scent forever. Why do you not applaud and adore me, sirs? Why stand you mute? Are you stupid? You are not worthy o' the benefit.

DAUPHINE. Did not I tell you? Mischief!

CLERIMONT. I would you had placed this benefit somewhere else.

TRUEWIT. Why so?

CLERIMONT. 'Slight, you have done the most inconsiderate, rash, weak thing, that ever man did to his friend.

DAUPHINE. Friend! if the most malicious enemy I have, had studied to inflict an injury upon me, it could not be a greater.

TRUEWIT. Wherein, for God's sake? Gentlemen, come to yourselves again.

DAUPHINE. But I presaged thus much afore to you.

CLERIMONT. Would my lips had been soldered when I spake on't! 'Slight, what moved you to be thus impertinent?

TRUEWIT. My masters, do not put on this strange face to pay my courtesy; off with this visor. Have good turns done you, and thank 'em this way!

DAUPHINE. 'Fore Heav'n, you have undone me.

That which I have plotted for, and been maturing
now these four months, you have blasted in a minute. Now I am lost I may speak. This gentlewoman
was lodged here by me o' purpose, and, to be put
upon my uncle, hath professed this obstinate silence
for my sake, being my entire friend, and one that for
the requital of such a fortune as to marry him,
would have made me very ample conditions;
where now all my hopes are utterly miscarried by
this unlucky accident.

CLERIMONT. Thus 'tis when a man will be ignorantly officious, do services and not know his why. I
wonder what courteous itch possessed you! You never
did absurder part i' your life, nor a greater trespass
to friendship, to humanity.

DAUPHINE. Faith, you may forgive it best; 'twas
your cause principally.

CLERIMONT. I know it, would it had not!

Enter CUTBEARD.

DAUPHINE. How now, Cutbeard! what news?

CUTBEARD. The best, the happiest that ever was,
sir. There has been a mad gentleman with your
uncle this morning—I think this be the gentleman—
that has almost talked him out of his wits, with
threatening him from marriage——

DAUPHINE. On, I pray thee.

CUTBEARD. And your uncle, sir, he thinks 'twas
done by your procurement. Therefore he will see the
party you wot of presently; and if he like her, he
says, and that she be so inclining to dumb as I have
told him, he swears he will marry her today, instantly, and not defer it a minute longer.

DAUPHINE. Excellent! beyond our expectation!

TRUEWIT. Beyond your expectation! by this light I
knew it would be thus.

DAUPHINE. Nay, sweet Truewit, forgive me.

TRUEWIT. No, I was ignorantly officious, impertinent; this was the absurd, weak part.

CLERIMONT. Wilt thou ascribe that to merit now, was mere fortune?

TRUEWIT. Fortune? mere providence! Fortune had not a finger in't. I saw it must necessarily in nature fall out so; my genius is never false to me in these things. Show me how it could be otherwise.

DAUPHINE. Nay, gentlemen, contend not; 'tis well now.

TRUEWIT. Alas, I let him go on with 'inconsiderate,' and 'rash,' and what he pleased.

CLERIMONT. Away, thou strange justifier of thyself, to be wiser than thou wert, by the event!

TRUEWIT. Event! by this light, thou shalt never persuade me but I foresaw it as well as the stars themselves.

DAUPHINE. Nay, gentlemen, 'tis well now. Do you two entertain Sir John Daw with discourse, while I send her away with instructions.

TRUEWIT. I'll be acquainted with her first, by your favour.

CLERIMONT. Master Truewit, lady, a friend of ours.

TRUEWIT. I am sorry I have not known you sooner, lady, to celebrate this rare virtue of your silence.

Exeunt DAUPHINE, EPICENE, *and* CUTBEARD.

CLERIMONT. Faith, an you had come sooner, you should ha' seen and heard her well celebrated in Sir John Daw's madrigals.

TRUEWIT. Jack Daw, God save you! when saw you La Foole?

DAW. Not since last night, Master Truewit.

TRUEWIT. That's a miracle! I thought you two had been inseparable.

DAW. He's gone to invite his guests.

TRUEWIT. God's so'! 'tis true! What a false memory have I towards that man! I am one. I met him e'en now upon that he calls his delicate, fine black horse, rid into foam with posting from place to place and person to person, to give 'em the cue——

CLERIMONT. Lest they should forget?

TRUEWIT. Yes. There was never poor captain took more pains at a muster to show men, than he at this meal to show friends.

DAW. It is his quarter-feast, sir.

CLERIMONT. What! do you say so, Sir John?

TRUEWIT. Nay, Jack Daw will not be out, at the best friends he has, to the talent of his wit. Where's his mistress, to hear and applaud him? is she gone?

DAW. Is Mistress Epicene gone?

CLERIMONT. Gone afore, with Sir Dauphine, I warrant, to the place.

TRUEWIT. Gone afore! That were a manifest injury, a disgrace and a half; to refuse him at such a festival time as this, being a bravery, and a wit too!

CLERIMONT. Tut, he'll swallow it like cream. He's better read in Jure Civili than to esteem anything a disgrace is offered him from a mistress.

DAW. Nay, let her e'en go; she shall sit alone and be dumb in her chamber a week together, for John Daw, I warrant her! Does she refuse me?

CLERIMONT. No, sir, do not take it so to heart; she does not refuse you, but a little neglect you. Good faith, Truewit, you were to blame, to put it into his head that she does refuse him.

TRUEWIT. She does refuse him, sir, palpably, however you mince it. An I were as he, I would swear to speak ne'er a word to her today for't.

DAW. By this light, no more I will not!

TRUEWIT. Nor to anybody else, sir.

DAW. Nay, I will not say so, gentlemen.

CLERIMONT. —It had been an excellent happy condition for the company, if you could have drawn him to it.

DAW. I'll be very melancholic, i' faith.

CLERIMONT. As a dog, if I were as you, Sir John.

TRUEWIT. Or a snail, or a hog-louse. I would roll myself up for this day; in troth, they should not unwind me.

DAW. By this picktooth, so I will.

CLERIMONT. —'Tis well done, he begins already to be angry with his teeth.

DAW. Will you go, gentlemen?

CLERIMONT. Nay, you must walk alone, if you be right melancholic, Sir John.

TRUEWIT. Yes, sir, we'll dog you; we'll follow you afar off. *Exit* DAW.

CLERIMONT. Was there ever such a two yards of knighthood measured out by Time to be sold to Laughter?

TRUEWIT. A mere talking mole, hang him! No mushroom was ever so fresh. A fellow so utterly nothing, as he knows not what he would be.

CLERIMONT. Let's follow him. But first let's go to Dauphine; he's hovering about the house to hear what news.

TRUEWIT. Content. *Exeunt.*

ACT TWO. SCENE THREE

Morose's house

Enter MOROSE *and* MUTE, *followed by* CUTBEARD *with*
EPICENE.

MOROSE. Welcome, Cutbeard! Draw near with
your fair charge, and in her ear softly entreat her to
unmask. So! Is the door shut? MUTE *makes a leg.*
Enough! Now, Cutbeard, with the same discipline I
use to my family, I will question you. As I conceive,
Cutbeard, this gentlewoman is she you have provided, and brought, in hope she will fit me in the
place and person of a wife? Answer me not but with
your leg, unless it be otherwise. CUTBEARD *makes a
leg.* Very well done, Cutbeard. I conceive besides,
Cutbeard, you have been preacquainted with her
birth, education, and qualities, or else you would
not prefer her to my acceptance, in the weighty consequence of marriage. This I conceive, Cutbeard.
Answer me not but with your leg, unless it be otherwise. *A leg.* Very well done, Cutbeard. Give aside
now a little, and leave me to examine her condition
and aptitude to my affection. *Goes about her and
views her.* She is exceeding fair, and of a special good
favour; a sweet composition, or harmony of limbs;
her temper of beauty has the true height of my
blood. The knave hath exceedingly well fitted me
without; I will now try her within.—Come near, fair
gentlewoman. Let not my behaviour seem rude,
though unto you, being rare, it may haply appear
strange. EPICENE *curtsies.* Nay, lady, you may speak,

though Cutbeard and my man might not; for of all
sounds, only the sweet voice of a fair lady has the
just length of mine ears. I beseech you, say, lady,—
out of the first fire of meeting eyes, they say, love is
stricken—do you feel any such emotion suddenly
shot into you, from any part you see in me? ha, lady?
Curtsy. Alas, lady, these answers by silent curtsies,
from you, are too courtless and simple. I have ever
had my breeding in court, and she that shall be my
wife must be accomplished with courtly and audacious ornaments. Can you speak, lady?

EPICENE. *Softly.* Judge you, forsooth.

MOROSE. What say you, lady? Speak out, I beseech
you.

EPICENE. Judge you, forsooth.

MOROSE. O' my judgment, a divine softness! But
can you naturally, lady, as I enjoin these by doctrine
and industry, refer yourself to the search of my judgment, and—not taking pleasure in your tongue,
which is a woman's chiefest pleasure—think it plausi-
ble to answer me by silent gestures, so long as my
speeches jump right with what you conceive? *Curtsy.*
Excellent! divine! if it were possible she should hold
out thus! Peace, Cutbeard, thou art made forever, as
thou hast made me, if this felicity have lasting; but
I will try her further. Dear lady, I am courtly, I tell
you, and I must have mine ears banqueted with
pleasant and witty conferences, pretty girds, scoffs,
and dalliance in her that I mean to choose for my
bed-fere. The ladies in court think it a most desperate impair to their quickness of wit, and good
carriage, if they cannot give occasion for a man to
court 'em; and when an amorous discourse is set on
foot, minister as good matter to continue it as himself. And do you alone so much differ from all them,
that what they, with so much circumstance, affect

and toil for—to seem learned, to seem judicious, to seem sharp and conceited—you can bury in yourself with silence? and rather trust your graces to the fair conscience of virtue, than to the world's or your own proclamation?

EPICENE. I should be sorry else.

MOROSE. What say you, lady? Good lady, speak out.

EPICENE. I should be sorry else.

MOROSE. That sorrow doth fill me with gladness! O Morose, thou art happy above mankind! pray that thou mayst contain thyself. I will only put her to it once more, and it shall be with the utmost touch and test of their sex.—But hear me, fair lady: I do also love to see her whom I shall choose for my heifer to be the first and principal in all fashions, precede all the dames at court by a fortnight, have her council of tailors, lineners, lace-women, embroiderers, and sit with 'em sometimes twice a day upon French intelligences; and then come forth varied like Nature, or oftener than she, and better by the help of Art, her emulous servant. This do I affect. And how will you be able, lady, with this frugality of speech, to give the manifold but necessary instructions, for that bodice, these sleeves, those skirts, this cut, that stitch, this embroidery, that lace, this wire, those knots, that ruff, those roses, this girdle, that fan, the tother scarf, these gloves, ha? What say you, lady?

EPICENE. I'll leave it to you, sir.

MOROSE. How, lady? Pray you rise a note.

EPICENE. I leave it to wisdom and you, sir.

MOROSE. Admirable creature! I will trouble you no more. I will not sin against so sweet a simplicity. Let me now be bold to print on those divine lips the seal of being mine. Cutbeard, I give thee the lease of thy house free; thank me not but with thy leg. I know what thou wouldst say: she's poor and her friends deceased. She has brought a wealthy dowry in her silence, Cutbeard; and in respect of her poverty, Cutbeard, I shall have her more loving and obedient, Cutbeard. Go thy ways, and get me a minister presently, with a soft, low voice, to marry us; and pray him he will not be impertinent, but brief as he can; away. Softly, Cutbeard. *Exit* CUTBEARD. Sirrah, conduct your mistress into the dining-room, your now mistress. *Exit* MUTE, *followed by* EPICENE. O my felicity! How I shall be revenged on my insolent kinsman, and his plots to fright me from marrying! This night I will get an heir, and thrust him out of my blood like a stranger. He would be knighted, forsooth, and thought by that means to reign over me; his title must do it. No, kinsman, I will now make you bring me the tenth lord's and the sixteenth lady's letter, kinsman; and it shall do you no good, kinsman. Your knighthood itself shall come on its knees, and it shall be rejected; it shall be sued for its fees to execution, and not be redeemed; it shall cheat at the twelvepenny ordinary, it knighthood, for its diet all the term time, and tell tales for it in the vacation to the hostess; or it knighthood shall do worse, take sanctuary in Cole Harbour, and fast. It shall fright all it friends with borrowing letters; and when one of the fourscore hath brought it knighthood ten shillings, it knighthood shall go to the Cranes, or the Bear at the Bridge-foot, and be drunk in fear. It shall not have money to discharge one tavern reckoning, to invite the old creditors to forbear it knighthood, or the new, that should be, to trust it knighthood. It shall be the tenth name in the bond to take up the commodity of pipkins and stone-jugs, and the part thereof shall not furnish it knighthood forth for the attempting of a baker's widow, a brown baker's widow. It shall give it knighthood's name for a stallion to all gamesome citizens' wives, and be refused, when the master of a dancing-school, or—how do you call him?—the worst reveller in the town, is taken. It shall want clothes, and by reason of that, wit, to fool lawyers. It shall not have hope to repair itself by Constantinople, Ireland, or Virginia; but the best and last fortune to it knighthood shall be to make Doll Tearsheet or Kate Common a lady; and so, it knighthood may eat.   *Exit.*

ACT TWO. SCENE FOUR

A lane near Morose's house

Enter TRUEWIT, DAUPHINE, *and* CLERIMONT.

TRUEWIT. Are you sure he has not gone by?

DAUPHINE. No, I stayed in the shop ever since.

CLERIMONT. But he may take the other end of the lane.

DAUPHINE. No, I told him I would be here at this end; I appointed him hither.

TRUEWIT. What a barbarian it is to stay then!

DAUPHINE. Yonder he comes.

CLERIMONT. And his charge left behind him, which is a very good sign, Dauphine.

Enter CUTBEARD.

DAUPHINE. How now, Cutbeard! succeeds it or no?

CUTBEARD. Past imagination, sir, omnia secunda;

you could not have prayed to have had it so well.
'Saltat senex,' as it is i' the proverb; he does triumph
in his felicity, admires the party! He has given me
the lease of my house, too! And I am now going for
a silent minister to marry 'em, and away.

TRUEWIT. 'Slight! get one o' the silenced ministers;
a zealous brother would torment him purely.

CUTBEARD. Cum privilegio, sir.

DAUPHINE. O, by no means; let's do nothing to
hinder it now. When 'tis done and finished, I am for
you, for any device of vexation.

CUTBEARD. And that shall be within this half hour,
upon my dexterity, gentlemen. Contrive what you
can in the mean time, bonis avibus.   *Exit.*

CLERIMONT. How the slave doth Latin it!

TRUEWIT. It would be made a jest to posterity, sirs,
this day's mirth, if ye will.

CLERIMONT. Beshrew his heart that will not, I pronounce.

DAUPHINE. And for my part. What is't?

TRUEWIT. To translate all La Foole's company and
his feast hither today, to celebrate this bridal.

DAUPHINE. Ay, marry, but how will't be done?

TRUEWIT. I'll undertake the directing of all the
lady-guests thither, and then the meat must follow.

CLERIMONT. For God's sake, let's effect it! It will be
an excellent comedy of affliction, so many several
noises.

DAUPHINE. But are they not at the other place already, think you?

TRUEWIT. I'll warrant you for the College Honours; one o' their faces has not the priming colour
laid on yet, nor the other her smock sleeked.

CLERIMONT. O, but they'll rise earlier than ordinary, to a feast.

TRUEWIT. Best go see, and assure ourselves.

CLERIMONT. Who knows the house?

TRUEWIT. I'll lead you. Were you never there yet?

DAUPHINE. Not I.

CLERIMONT. Nor I.

TRUEWIT. Where ha' you lived then? not know Tom Otter!

CLERIMONT. No. For God's sake, what is he?

TRUEWIT. An excellent animal, equal with your Daw or La Foole, if not transcendent, and does Latin it as much as your barber. He is his wife's subject; he calls her princess, and at such times as these follows her up and down the house like a page, with his hat off, partly for heat, partly for reverence. At this instant he is marshalling of his Bull, Bear, and Horse.

DAUPHINE. What be those, in the name of Sphinx?

TRUEWIT. Why, sir, he has been a great man at the bear-garden in his time, and from that subtle sport has ta'en the witty denomination of his chief carousing cups. One he calls his bull, another his bear, another his horse. And then he has his lesser glasses, that he calls his deer and his ape; and several degrees of 'em too; and never is well, nor thinks any entertainment perfect, till these be brought out and set o' the cupboard.

CLERIMONT. For God's love! we should miss this if we should not go.

TRUEWIT. Nay, he has a thousand things as good, that will speak him all day. He will rail on his wife, with certain commonplaces, behind her back; and to her face——

DAUPHINE. No more of him. Let's go see him, I petition you.   *Exeunt.*

ACT THREE. SCENE ONE

Mistress Otter's house

Enter CAPTAIN OTTER *and* MISTRESS OTTER.

OTTER. Nay, good Princess, hear me, *pauca verba.*

MISTRESS OTTER. By that light, I'll ha' you chained up, with your bulldogs and bear-dogs, if you be not civil the sooner. I'll send you to kennel, i' faith. You were best bait me with your Bull, Bear, and Horse! Never a time that the courtiers or Collegiates come to the house, but you make it a Shrove Tuesday! I would have you get your Whitsuntide velvet cap, and your staff i' your hand, to entertain 'em. Yes, in troth, do.

OTTER. Not so, Princess, neither, but under correction, sweet Princess, gi' me leave—these things I am known to the courtiers by. It is reported to them for my humour, and they receive it so, and do expect it. Tom Otter's Bull, Bear, and Horse is known all over England, *in rerum natura.*

MISTRESS OTTER. 'Fore me, I will na-ture 'em over to Paris Garden, and na-ture you thither too, if you pronounce 'em again. Is a bear a fit beast, or a bull, to mix in society with great ladies? Think i' your discretion, in any good policy.

OTTER. The horse then, good Princess.

MISTRESS OTTER. Well, I am contented for the horse; they love to be well horsed, I know. I love it myself.

OTTER. And it is a delicate fine horse this. *Po-etarum Pegasus.* Under correction, Princess, Jupiter

did turn himself into a—taurus, or bull, under correction, good Princess.

Enter TRUEWIT, CLERIMONT, *and* DAUPHINE *behind.*

MISTRESS OTTER. By my integrity, I'll send you over
to the Bankside, I'll commit you to the Master of the
Garden, if I hear but a syllable more. Must my house
or my roof be polluted with the scent of bears and
bulls, when it is perfumed for great ladies? Is this
according to the instrument, when I married you?
that I would be princess, and reign in mine own
house; and you would be my subject, and obey me?
What did you bring me, should make you thus
peremptory? Do I allow you your half-crown a day,
to spend where you will, among your gamesters, to
vex and torment me at such times as these? Who
gives you your maintenance, I pray you? Who allows
you your horse-meat and man's-meat? your three
suits of apparel a year? your four pair of stockings,
one silk, three worsted? your clean linen, your bands
and cuffs, when I can get you to wear 'em? 'Tis
mar'l you ha' 'em on now. Who graces you with
courtiers or great personages, to speak to you out of
their coaches and come home to your house? Were
you ever so much as looked upon by a lord or a lady
before I married you, but on the Easter or Whitsun-
holidays? and then out at the Banqueting House
window, when Ned Whiting or George Stone were
at the stake.

TRUEWIT. —For God's sake, let's go stave her off
him.

MISTRESS OTTER. Answer me to that. And did not I
take you up from thence, in an old, greasy buff
doublet, with points, and green velvet sleeves out at
the elbows? You forget this.

TRUEWIT. —She'll worry him, if we help not in time.

MISTRESS OTTER. O, here are some o' the gallants! Go to, behave yourself distinctly, and with good morality; or, I protest, I'll take away your exhibition.

TRUEWIT. By your leave, fair Mistress Otter, I'll be bold to enter these gentlemen in your acquaintance.

MISTRESS OTTER. It shall not be obnoxious or difficil, sir.

TRUEWIT. How does my noble Captain? Is the Bull, Bear, and Horse in rerum natura still?

OTTER. Sir, sic visum superis.

MISTRESS OTTER. I would you would but intimate 'em, do. Go your ways in, and get toasts and butter made for the woodcocks. That's a fit province for you.   *Exit* CAPTAIN OTTER.

CLERIMONT. —Alas, what a tyranny is this poor fellow married to.

TRUEWIT. O, but the sport will be anon, when we get him loose.

DAUPHINE. Dares he ever speak?

TRUEWIT. No Anabaptist ever railed with the like licence. But mark her language in the meantime, I beseech you.

MISTRESS OTTER. Gentlemen, you are very aptly come. My cousin, Sir Amorous, will be here briefly.

TRUEWIT. In good time, lady. Was not Sir John Daw here, to ask for him, and the company?

MISTRESS OTTER. I cannot assure you, Master Truewit. Here was a very melancholy knight in a ruff, that demanded my subject for somebody, a gentleman, I think.

CLERIMONT. Ay, that was he, lady.

MISTRESS OTTER. But he departed straight, I can resolve you.

DAUPHINE. What an excellent, choice phrase this lady expresses in!

TRUEWIT. O, sir, she is the only authentical courtier, that is not naturally bred one, in the City!

MISTRESS OTTER. You have taken that report upon trust, gentlemen.

TRUEWIT. No, I assure you, the court governs it so, lady, in your behalf.

MISTRESS OTTER. I am the servant of the court and courtiers, sir.

TRUEWIT. They are rather your idolaters.

MISTRESS OTTER. Not so, sir.

Enter CUTBEARD.

DAUPHINE. How now, Cutbeard! any cross?

CUTBEARD. O no, sir, omnia bene. 'Twas never better o' the hinges; all's sure. I have so pleased him with a curate, that he's gone to't almost with the delight he hopes for soon.

DAUPHINE. What is he for a vicar?

CUTBEARD. One that has catched a cold, sir, and can scarce be heard six inches off; as if he spoke out of a bulrush that were not picked, or his throat were full of pith; a fine, quick fellow, and an excellent barber of prayers. I came to tell you, sir, that you might 'omnem movere lapidem,' as they say, be ready with your vexation.

DAUPHINE. Gramercy, honest Cutbeard! be thereabouts with thy key to let us in.

CUTBEARD. I will not fail you, sir. Ad manum. *Exit.*

TRUEWIT. Well, I'll go watch my coaches.

CLERIMONT. Do; and we'll send Daw to you, if you meet him not. *Exit* TRUEWIT.

MISTRESS OTTER. Is Master Truewit gone?

DAUPHINE. Yes, lady, there is some unfortunate business fallen out.

MISTRESS OTTER. So I adjudged by the physiognomy of the fellow that came in; and I had a dream last night, too, of the new pageant, and my Lady Mayoress, which is always very ominous to me. I told it my Lady Haughty t'other day, when her honour came hither to see some China stuffs, and she expounded it out of Artemidorus, and I have found it since very true. It has done me many affronts.

CLERIMONT. Your dream, lady?

MISTRESS OTTER. Yes, sir, anything I do but dream o' the City. It stained me a damask tablecloth, cost me eighteen pound at one time, and burnt me a black satin gown, as I stood by the fire at my Lady Centaur's chamber in the College, another time. A third time, at the Lords' masque, it dropped all my wire and my ruff with wax candle, that I could not go up to the banquet. A fourth time, as I was taking coach to go to Ware, to meet a friend, it dashed me a new suit all over—a crimson satin doublet and black velvet skirts—with a brewer's horse, that I was fain to go in and shift me, and kept my chamber a leash of days for the anguish of it.

DAUPHINE. These were dire mischances, lady.

CLERIMONT. I would not dwell in the City an 'twere so fatal to me.

MISTRESS OTTER. Yes, sir, but I do take advice of my doctor to dream of it as little as I can.

DAUPHINE. You do well, Mistress Otter.

Enter SIR JOHN DAW, *and is taken aside by* CLERIMONT.

MISTRESS OTTER. Will it please you to enter the house farther, gentlemen?

DAUPHINE. And your favour, lady. But we stay to speak with a knight, Sir John Daw, who is here come. We shall follow you, lady.

MISTRESS OTTER. At your own time, sir. It is my cousin, Sir Amorous, his feast——

DAUPHINE. I know it, lady.

MISTRESS OTTER. And mine together. But it is for his honour, and therefore I take no name of it, more than of the place.

DAUPHINE. You are a bounteous kinswoman.

MISTRESS OTTER. Your servant, sir.   *Exit.*

CLERIMONT. Why, do not you know it, Sir John Daw?

DAW. No, I am a rook if I do.

CLERIMONT. I'll tell you then: she's married by this time. And whereas you were put i' the head, that she was gone with Sir Dauphine, I assure you Sir Dauphine has been the noblest, honestest friend to you, that ever gentleman of your quality could boast of. He has discovered the whole plot, and made your mistress so acknowledging, and indeed so ashamed of her injury to you, that she desires you to forgive her, and but grace her wedding with your presence today— She is to be married to a very good fortune, she says, his uncle, old Morose; and she willed me in private to tell you that she shall be able to do you more favours, and with more security, now, than before.

DAW. Did she say so, i' faith?

CLERIMONT. Why, what do you think of me, Sir John? Ask Sir Dauphine!

DAW. Nay, I believe you. Good Sir Dauphine, did she desire me to forgive her?

DAUPHINE. I assure you, Sir John, she did.

DAW. Nay, then, I do with all my heart, and I'll be jovial.

CLERIMONT. Yes, for look you, sir, this was the injury to you. La Foole intended this feast to honour her bridal day, and made you the property to invite the College ladies, and promise to bring her; and then at the time she should have appeared—as his friend—to have given you the dor. Whereas now Sir Dauphine has brought her to a feeling of it, with this kind of satisfaction, that you shall bring all the ladies to the place where she is, and be very jovial. And there she will have a dinner, which shall be in your name; and so disappoint La Foole, to make you good again, and, as it were, a saver i' the main.

DAW. As I am a knight, I honour her, and forgive her heartily.

CLERIMONT. About it then presently. Truewit is gone before to confront the coaches, and to acquaint you with so much, if he meet you. Join with him, and 'tis well. See, here comes your antagonist; but take you no notice, but be very jovial.

Enter SIR AMOROUS LA FOOLE.

LA FOOLE. Are the ladies come, Sir John Daw, and your mistress? *Exit* DAW. Sir Dauphine! you are exceeding welcome, and honest Master Clerimont. Where's my cousin? Did you see no Collegiates, gentlemen?

DAUPHINE. Collegiates! do you not hear, Sir Amorous, how you are abused?

LA FOOLE. How, sir!

CLERIMONT. Will you speak so kindly to Sir John Daw, that has done you such an affront?

LA FOOLE. Wherein, gentlemen? let me be a suitor to you to know, I beseech you!

CLERIMONT. Why, sir, his mistress is married today to Sir Dauphine's uncle, your cousin's neighbour, and he has diverted all the ladies, and all your company thither, to frustrate your provision, and stick a disgrace upon you. He was here now to have enticed us away from you too, but we told him his own, I think.

LA FOOLE. Has Sir John Daw wronged me so inhumanly?

DAUPHINE. He has done it, Sir Amorous, most maliciously and treacherously; but if you'll be ruled by us, you shall quit him, i' faith.

LA FOOLE. Good gentlemen, I'll make one, believe it. How, I pray?

DAUPHINE. Marry, sir, get me your pheasants, and your godwits, and your best meat, and dish it in silver dishes of your cousin's presently; and say nothing, but clap me a clean towel about you, like a sewer; and bareheaded, march afore it with a good confidence—'tis but over the way, hard by—and we'll second you, where you shall set it o' the board; and bid 'em welcome to 't, which shall show 'tis yours, and disgrace his preparation utterly. And for your cousin, whereas she should be troubled here at home with care of making and giving welcome, she shall transfer all that labour thither, and be a principal guest herself; sit ranked with the College Honours, and be honoured, and have her health drunk as often, as bare, and as loud as the best of 'em.

LA FOOLE. I'll go tell her presently. It shall be done, that's resolved. *Exit.*

CLERIMONT. I thought he would not hear it out but 'twould take him.

DAUPHINE. Well, there be guests and meat now; how shall we do for music?

CLERIMONT. The smell of the venison, going through the street, will invite one noise of fiddlers or other.

DAUPHINE. I would it would call the trumpeters thither!

CLERIMONT. Faith, there is hope; they have intelligence of all feasts. There's good correspondence betwixt them and the London cooks. 'Tis twenty to one but we have 'em.

DAUPHINE. 'Twill be a most solemn day for my uncle, and an excellent fit of mirth for us.

CLERIMONT. Ay, if we can hold up the emulation betwixt Foole and Daw, and never bring them to expostulate.

DAUPHINE. Tut, flatter 'em both, as Truewit says, and you may take their understandings in a purse-net. They'll believe themselves to be just such men as we make 'em, neither more nor less. They have nothing, not the use of their senses, but by tradition.

Re-enter LA FOOLE, *like a sewer.*

CLERIMONT. See! Sir Amorous has his towel on already. Have you persuaded your cousin?

LA FOOLE. Yes, 'tis very feasible. She'll do anything, she says, rather than the La Fooles shall be disgraced.

DAUPHINE. She is a noble kinswoman. It will be such a pestling device, Sir Amorous, it will pound all your enemy's practices to powder, and blow him up with his own mine, his own train!

LA FOOLE. Nay, we'll give fire, I warrant you.

CLERIMONT. But you must carry it privately, without any noise, and take no notice by any means——

Re-enter CAPTAIN OTTER.

OTTER. Gentlemen, my Princess says you shall have all her silver dishes, festinate; and she's gone to alter her tire a little, and go with you——

CLERIMONT. And yourself too, Captain Otter?

DAUPHINE. By any means, sir.

OTTER. Yes, sir, I do mean it; but I would entreat my cousin Sir Amorous, and you, gentlemen, to be suitors to my Princess, that I may carry my Bull and my Bear, as well as my Horse.

CLERIMONT. That you shall do, Captain Otter.

LA FOOLE. My cousin will never consent, gentle-men.

DAUPHINE. She must consent, Sir Amorous, to reason.

LA FOOLE. Why, she says they are no decorum among ladies.

OTTER. But they are decora, and that's better, sir.

CLERIMONT. Ay, she must hear argument. Did not Pasiphaë, who was a queen, love a bull? and was not Calisto, the mother of Arcas, turned into a bear, and made a star, Mistress Ursula, i' the heavens?

OTTER. O God! that I could ha' said as much! I will have these stories painted in the bear-garden, ex Ovidii Metamorphosi.

DAUPHINE. Where is your Princess, Captain? pray be our leader.

OTTER. That I shall, sir.

CLERIMONT. Make haste, good Sir Amorous.

Exeunt.

ACT THREE. SCENE TWO

Morose's house

Enter MOROSE, EPICENE, PARSON, *and* CUTBEARD.

MOROSE. Sir, there's an angel for yourself, and a brace of angels for your cold. Muse not at this manage of my bounty. It is fit we should thank for-tune, double to nature, for any benefit she confers upon us; besides, it is your imperfection, but my solace.

PARSON. *Speaks as having a cold.* I thank your worship; so is it mine now.

MOROSE. What says he, Cutbeard?

CUTBEARD. He says, presto, sir, whensoever your worship needs him, he can be ready with the like. He got this cold with sitting up late, and singing catches with cloth-workers.

MOROSE. No more. I thank him.

PARSON. God keep your worship, and give you much joy with your fair spouse! *Coughs.* Uh, uh!

MOROSE. O, O! Stay, Cutbeard! let him give me five shillings of my money back. As it is bounty to reward benefits, so it is equity to mulct injuries. I will have it. What says he?

CLERIMONT. He cannot change it, sir.

MOROSE. It must be changed.

CUTBEARD. —Cough again.

MOROSE. What says he?

CUTBEARD. He will cough out the rest, sir.

PARSON. *Coughs.* Uh, uh, uh!

MOROSE. Away, away with him! stop his mouth! away! I forgive it——   *Exit* CUTBEARD *with* PARSON.

EPICENE. Fie, Master Morose, that you will use this violence to a man of the church!

MOROSE. How!

EPICENE. It does not become your gravity or breeding, as you pretend, in court, to have offered this outrage on a waterman, or any more boisterous creature, much less on a man of his civil coat.

MOROSE. You can speak then!

EPICENE. Yes, sir.

MOROSE. Speak out, I mean.

EPICENE. Ay, sir. Why, did you think you had married a statue, or a motion only? one of the French puppets, with the eyes turned with a wire? or some innocent out of the hospital, that would stand with her hands thus, and a plaice-mouth, and look upon you?

MOROSE. O immodesty! a manifest woman! What, Cutbeard!

EPICENE. Nay, never quarrel with Cutbeard, sir; it is too late now. I confess it doth bate somewhat of the modesty I had, when I writ simply maid; but I hope I shall make it a stock still competent to the estate and dignity of your wife.

MOROSE. She can talk!

EPICENE. Yes indeed, sir.

Enter MUTE.

MOROSE. What, sirrah! None of my knaves there? Where is this impostor Cutbeard?

EPICENE. Speak to him, fellow, speak to him! I'll have none of this coacted, unnatural dumbness in my house, in a family where I govern. *Exit* MUTE.

MOROSE. She is my regent already! I have married a Penthesilea, a Semiramis! sold my liberty to a distaff!

Enter TRUEWIT.

TRUEWIT. Where's Master Morose?

MOROSE. Is he come again? Lord have mercy upon me!

TRUEWIT. I wish you all joy, Mistress Epicene, with your grave and honourable match.

EPICENE. I return you the thanks, Master Truewit, so friendly a wish deserves.

MOROSE. She has acquaintance, too!

TRUEWIT. God save you, sir, and give you all contentment in your fair choice here! Before, I was the bird of night to you, the owl; but now I am the messenger of peace, a dove, and bring you the glad wishes of many friends to the celebration of this good hour.

MOROSE. What hour, sir?

TRUEWIT. Your marriage hour, sir. I commend your resolution, that—notwithstanding all the dangers I laid afore you, in the voice of a night-crow—would yet go on, and be yourself. It shows you are a man constant to your own ends, and upright to your purposes, that would not be put off with left-handed cries.

MOROSE. How should you arrive at the knowledge of so much?

TRUEWIT. Why, did you ever hope, sir, committing the secrecy of it to a barber, that less than the whole town should know it? You might as well ha' told it the conduit, or the bakehouse, or the infantry that follow the court, and with more security. Could your gravity forget so old and noted a remnant as 'lippis et tonsoribus notum'? Well, sir, forgive it yourself now, the fault, and be communicable with your friends. Here will be three or four fashionable ladies from the College to visit you presently, and their train of minions and followers.

MOROSE. Bar my doors! bar my doors! Where are all my eaters, my mouths, now?——

Enter SERVANTS.

Bar up my doors, you varlets!

EPICENE. He is a varlet that stirs to such an office. Let 'em stand open. I would see him that dares move his eyes toward it. Shall I have a barricado made against my friends, to be barred of any pleasure they can bring in to me with honourable visitation?

Exeunt SERVANTS.

MOROSE. O Amazonian impudence!

TRUEWIT. Nay, faith, in this, sir, she speaks but reason; and, methinks, is more continent than you. Would you go to bed so presently, sir, afore noon? A man of your head and hair should owe more to that reverend ceremony, and not mount the marriage bed like a town-bull, or a mountain-goat; but stay the due season, and ascend it then with religion and fear. Those delights are to be steeped in the humour and silence of the night; and give the day to other open pleasures, and jollities of feast, of music, of revels, of discourse. We'll have all, sir, that may make your Hymen high and happy.

MOROSE. O my torment, my torment!

TRUEWIT. Nay, if you endure the first half hour, sir, so tediously, and with this irksomeness, what comfort or hope can this fair gentlewoman make to herself hereafter, in the consideration of so many years as are to come——

MOROSE. Of my affliction. Good sir, depart, and let her do it alone.

TRUEWIT. I have done, sir.

MOROSE. That cursed barber!

TRUEWIT. Yes, faith, a cursed wretch indeed, sir.

MOROSE. I have married his cittern, that's common to all men. Some plague above the plague——

TRUEWIT. All Egypt's ten plagues.

MOROSE. Revenge me on him!

TRUEWIT. 'Tis very well, sir. If you laid on a curse or two more, I'll assure you he'll bear 'em. As that he may get the pox with seeking to cure it, sir? Or that, while he is curling another man's hair, his own may drop off? Or, for burning some male bawd's lock, he may have his brain beat out with the curling-iron?

MOROSE. No, let the wretch live wretched. May he

get the itch, and his shop so lousy, as no man dare come at him, nor he come at no man!

TRUEWIT. Ay, and if he would swallow all his balls for pills, let not them purge him.

MOROSE. Let his warming-pan be ever cold!

TRUEWIT. A perpetual frost underneath it, sir.

MOROSE. Let him never hope to see fire again!

TRUEWIT. But in hell, sir.

MOROSE. His chairs be always empty, his scissors rust, and his combs mould in their cases!

TRUEWIT. Very dreadful that! And may he lose the invention, sir, of carving lanterns in paper.

MOROSE. Let there be no bawd carted that year, to employ a basin of his; but let him be glad to eat his sponge for bread!

TRUEWIT. And drink lotion to it, and much good do him!

MOROSE. Or, for want of bread——

TRUEWIT. Eat ear-wax, sir! I'll help you. Or draw his own teeth, and add them to the lute-string!

MOROSE. No, beat the old ones to powder, and make bread of them!

TRUEWIT. Yes, make meal o' the millstones.

MOROSE. May all the botches and burns that he has cured on others, break out upon him!

TRUEWIT. And he now forget the cure of 'em in himself, sir; or, if he do remember it, let him ha' scraped all his linen into lint for't, and have not a rag left him to set up with!

MOROSE. Let him never set up again, but have the gout in his hands forever! Now, no more, sir.

TRUEWIT. O, that last was too high set; you might go less with him, i' faith, and be revenged enough: as, that he be never able to new-paint his pole——

MOROSE. Good sir, no more. I forgot myself.

TRUEWIT. Or, want credit to take up with a comb-maker——

MOROSE. No more, sir.

TRUEWIT. Or, having broken his glass in a former despair, fall now into a much greater, of ever getting another——

MOROSE. I beeseech you, no more.

TRUEWIT. Or, that he never be trusted with trimming of any but chimney-sweepers——

MOROSE. Sir——

TRUEWIT. Or, may he cut a collier's throat with his razor, by chance-medley, and yet hang for't.

MOROSE. I will forgive him rather than hear any more. I beseech you, sir.

Enter DAW, *with* LADY HAUGHTY, LADY CENTAUR, MISTRESS MAVIS, *and* TRUSTY.

DAW. This way, madam.

MOROSE. O, the sea breaks in upon me! another flood! an inundation! I shall be o'erwhelmed with noise. It beats already at my shores. I feel an earthquake in myself for't.

DAW. Give you joy, mistress.

MOROSE. Has she servants too!

DAW. I have brought some ladies here to see and know you. My Lady Haughty—EPICENE *kisses them severally, as he presents them.*—this my Lady Centaur —Mistress Doll Mavis—Mistress Trusty, my Lady Haughty's woman. Where's your husband? let's see him. Can he endure no noise? let me come to him.

MOROSE. What nomenclator is this?

TRUEWIT. Sir John Daw, sir, your wife's servant, this.

MOROSE. A Daw, and her servant! O, 'tis decreed, 'tis decreed of me, an she have such servants.

TRUEWIT. Nay, sir, you must kiss the ladies; you

must not go away now. They come toward you to seek you out.

HAUGHTY. I' faith, Master Morose, would you steal a marriage thus, in the midst of so many friends, and not acquaint us? Well, I'll kiss you, notwithstanding the justice of my quarrel. You shall give me leave, mistress, to use a becoming familiarity with your husband.

EPICENE. Your ladyship does me an honour in it, to let me know he is so worthy your favour; as you have done both him and me grace to visit so unprepared a pair to entertain you.

MOROSE. Compliment! compliment!

EPICENE. But I must lay the burden of that upon my servant here.

HAUGHTY. It shall not need, Mistress Morose; we will all bear, rather than one shall be oppressed.

MOROSE. —I know it; and you will teach her the faculty, if she be to learn it.

HAUGHTY. Is this the Silent Woman?

CENTAUR. Nay, she has found her tongue since she was married, Master Truewit says.

HAUGHTY. O, Master Truewit, save you! What kind of creature is your bride here? She speaks, methinks!

TRUEWIT. Yes, madam, believe it, she is a gentlewoman of very absolute behaviour, and of a good race.

HAUGHTY. And Jack Daw told us she could not speak!

TRUEWIT. So it was carried in plot, madam, to put her upon this old fellow, by Sir Dauphine, his nephew, and one or two more of us. But she is a woman of an excellent assurance, and an extraordinary happy wit and tongue. You shall see her make rare sport with Daw ere night.

HAUGHTY. And he brought us to laugh at her!

TRUEWIT. That falls out often, madam, that he that thinks himself the master-wit, is the master-fool. I assure your ladyship, ye cannot laugh at her.

HAUGHTY. No, we'll have her to the College. An she have wit, she shall be one of us! Shall she not, Centaur? We'll make her a Collegiate.

CENTAUR. Yes, faith, madam, and Mavis and she will set up a side.

TRUEWIT. Believe it, madam, and Mistress Mavis, she will sustain her part.

MAVIS. I'll tell you that when I have talked with her, and tried her.

HAUGHTY. Use her very civilly, Mavis.

MAVIS. So I will, madam.

MOROSE. —Blessed minute! that they would whisper thus ever!

TRUEWIT. In the meantime, madam, would but your ladyship help to vex him a little. You know his disease; talk to him about the wedding ceremonies, or call for your gloves, or——

HAUGHTY. Let me alone. Centaur, help me. Master Bridegroom, where are you?

MOROSE. —O, it was too miraculously good to last!

HAUGHTY. We see no ensigns of a wedding here, no character of a bridal. Where be our scarfs and our gloves? I pray you, give 'em us. Let us know your bride's colours, and yours, at least.

CENTAUR. Alas, madam, he has provided none.

MOROSE. Had I known your ladyship's painter, I would.

HAUGHTY. He has given it you, Centaur, i' faith. But do you hear, Master Morose! a jest will not absolve you in this manner. You that have sucked the milk of the court, and from thence have been brought up to the very strong meats and wine of it;

been a courtier from the biggen to the nightcap, as we may say; and you to offend in such a high point of ceremony as this, and let your nuptials want all marks of solemnity! How much plate have you lost today,—if you had but regarded your profit—what gifts, what friends, through your mere rusticity!

MOROSE. Madam——

HAUGHTY. Pardon me, sir, I must insinuate your errors to you: no gloves? no garters? no scarfs? no epithalamium? no masque?

DAW. Yes, madam, I'll make an epithalamium, I promised my mistress. I have begun it already. Will your ladyship hear it?

HAUGHTY. Ay, good Jack Daw.

MOROSE. Will it please your ladyship command a chamber, and be private with your friend? You shall have your choice of rooms to retire to after. My whole house is yours. I know it hath been your ladyship's errand into the City at other times, however now you have been unhappily diverted upon me; but I shall be loath to break any honourable custom of your ladyship's. And therefore, good madam——

EPICENE. Come, you are a rude bridegroom, to entertain ladies of honour in this fashion.

CENTAUR. He is a rude groom indeed.

TRUEWIT. By that light, you deserve to be grafted, and have your horns reach from one side of the island to the other!—Do not mistake me, sir, I but speak this to give the ladies some heart again, not for any malice to you.

MOROSE. Is this your bravo, ladies?

TRUEWIT. As God help me, if you utter such another word, I'll take Mistress Bride in, and begin to you in a very sad cup, do you see? Go to, know your friends, and such as love you.

Enter CLERIMONT.

CLERIMONT. By your leave, ladies. Do you want any music? I have brought you variety of noises.— Play, sirs, all of you.   *Music of all sorts.*

MOROSE. O, a plot, a plot, a plot, a plot upon me! This day I shall be their anvil to work on; they will grate me asunder. 'Tis worse than the noise of a saw.

CLERIMONT. No, they are hair, rosin, and guts. I can give you the receipt.

TRUEWIT. Peace, boys!

CLERIMONT. Play, I say!

TRUEWIT. Peace, rascals! You see who's your friend now, sir? Take courage, put on a martyr's resolution. Mock down all their attemptings with patience. 'Tis but a day, and I would suffer heroically. Should an ass exceed me in fortitude? No. You betray your infirmity with your hanging, dull ears, and make them insult. Bear up bravely, and constantly. LA FOOLE *passes over, sewing the meat, followed by servants carrying dishes, and* MISTRESS OTTER. Look you here sir, what honour is done you unexpected, by your nephew; a wedding dinner come, and a knight-sewer before it, for the more reputation; and fine Mistress Otter, your neighbour, in the rump or tail of it.

MOROSE. Is that Gorgon, that Medusa come? Hide me, hide me!

TRUEWIT. I warrant you, sir, she will not transform you. Look upon her with a good courage. Pray you entertain her, and conduct your guests in. No? —Mistress Bride, will you entreat in the ladies? Your bridegroom is so shamefaced here——

EPICENE. Will it please your ladyship, madam?

HAUGHTY. With the benefit of your company, mistress.

EPICENE. Servant, pray you perform your duties.

DAW. And glad to be commanded, mistress.

CENTAUR. How like you her wit, Mavis?

MAVIS. Very prettily, absolutely well.

MISTRESS OTTER. 'Tis my place.

MAVIS. You shall pardon me, Mistress Otter.

MISTRESS OTTER. Why, I am a Collegiate.

MAVIS. But not in ordinary.

MISTRESS OTTER. But I am.

MAVIS. We'll dispute that within.   *Exeunt* LADIES.

CLERIMONT. Would this had lasted a little longer!

TRUEWIT. And that they had sent for the heralds!

Enter CAPTAIN OTTER

Captain Otter! what news?

OTTER. I have brought my Bull, Bear, and Horse, in private, and yonder are the trumpeters without, and the drum, gentlemen.

The drum and trumpets sound.

MOROSE. O, O, O!

OTTER. And we will have a rouse in each of 'em, anon, for bold Britons, i' faith!

MOROSE. O, O, O!

OMNES. Follow, follow, follow!   *Exeunt.*

ACT FOUR

Morose's house

Enter TRUEWIT *and* CLERIMONT.

TRUEWIT. Was there ever poor bridegroom so tormented? or man, indeed?

CLERIMONT. I have not read of the like in the chronicles of the land.

TRUEWIT. Sure, he cannot but go to a place of rest, after all this purgatory.

CLERIMONT. He may presume it, I think.

TRUEWIT. The spitting, the coughing, the laughter, the neezing, the farting, dancing, noise of the music, and her masculine and loud commanding, and urging the whole family, makes him think he has married a fury.

CLERIMONT. And she carries it up bravely.

TRUEWIT. Ay, she takes any occasion to speak; that's the height on't.

CLERIMONT. And how soberly Dauphine labours to satisfy him, that it was none of his plot!

TRUEWIT. And has almost brought him to the faith, i' the article. Here he comes.

Enter SIR DAUPHINE.

Where is he now? what's become of him, Dauphine?

DAUPHINE. O, hold me up a little, I shall go away i' the jest else. He has got on his whole nest of night-caps, and locked himself up i' the top o' the house, as high as ever he can climb from the noise. I peeped in at a cranny, and saw him sitting over a cross-beam o' the roof, like him o' the saddler's horse in Fleet Street, upright; and he will sleep there.

CLERIMONT. But where are your Collegiates?

DAUPHINE. Withdrawn with the bride in private.

TRUEWIT. O, they are instructing her i' the College grammar. If she have grace with them, she knows all their secrets instantly.

CLERIMONT. Methinks the Lady Haughty looks well today, for all my dispraise of her i' the morning. I think I shall come about to thee again, Truewit.

TRUEWIT. Believe it, I told you right. Women ought to repair the losses time and years have made i' their features, with dressings. And an intelligent woman, if she know by herself the least defect, will be most curious to hide it; and it becomes her. If she be short, let her sit much, lest, when she stands, she be thought to sit. If she have an ill foot, let her wear her gown the longer, and her shoe the thinner. If a fat hand and scald nails, let her carve the less, and act in gloves. If a sour breath, let her never discourse fasting, and always talk at her distance. If she have black and rugged teeth, let her offer the less at laughter, especially if she laugh wide and open.

CLERIMONT. O, you shall have some women, when they laugh you would think they brayed, it is so rude and——

TRUEWIT. Ay, and others that will stalk i' their gait like an estrich, and take huge strides. I cannot endure such a sight. I love measure i' the feet, and number i' the voice. They are gentlenesses that oft-times draw no less than the face.

DAUPHINE. How camest thou to study these creatures so exactly? I would thou wouldst make me a proficient.

TRUEWIT. Yes, but you must leave to live i' your chamber, then, a month together upon Amadis de Gaul, or Don Quixote, as you are wont; and come abroad where the matter is frequent, to court, to tiltings, public shows, and feasts, to plays, and church sometimes. Thither they come to show their new tires too, to see and to be seen. In these places a man shall find whom to love, whom to play with, whom to touch once, whom to hold ever. The variety arrests his judgment. A wench to please a man comes not down dropping from the ceiling, as he lies on his back droning a tobacco-pipe. He must go where she is.

DAUPHINE. Yes, and be never the nearer.

TRUEWIT. Out, heretic! That diffidence makes thee worthy it should be so.

CLERIMONT. He says true to you, Dauphine.

DAUPHINE. Why?

TRUEWIT. A man should not doubt to overcome any woman. Think he can vanquish 'em, and he shall; for though they deny, their desire is to be tempted. Penelope herself cannot hold out long. Ostend, you saw, was taken at last. You must persever and hold to your purpose. They would solicit us, but that they are afraid. Howsoever, they wish in their hearts we should solicit them. Praise 'em, flatter 'em, you shall never want eloquence or trust; even the chastest delight to feel themselves that way rubbed. With praises you must mix kisses too; if they take them, they'll take more. Though they strive, they would be overcome.

CLERIMONT. O, but a man must beware of force.

TRUEWIT. It is to them an acceptable violence, and has oft-times the place of the greatest courtesy. She that might have been forced, an you let her go free without touching, though she then seem to thank you, will ever hate you after; and, glad i' the face, is assuredly sad at the heart.

CLERIMONT. But all women are not to be taken all ways.

TRUEWIT. 'Tis true. No more than all birds, or all fishes. If you appear learned to an ignorant wench, or jocund to a sad, or witty to a foolish, why, she presently begins to mistrust herself. You must approach them i' their own height, their own line; for the contrary makes many that fear to commit themselves to noble and worthy fellows, run into the embraces of a rascal. If she love wit, give verses, though you borrow 'em of a friend, or buy 'em, to have good. If valour, talk of your sword, and be frequent in the mention of quarrels, though you be staunch in fighting. If activity, be seen o' your barbary often, or leaping over stools, for the credit of your back. If she love good clothes or dressing, have your learned council about you every morning, your French tailor, barber, linener, &c. Let your powder, your glass, and your comb be your dearest acquaintance. Take more care for the ornament of your head, than the safety; and wish the commonwealth rather troubled, than a hair about you. That will take her. Then, if she be covetous and craving, do you promise anything, and perform sparingly; so shall you keep her in appetite still. Seem as you would give, but be like a barren field that yields little, or unlucky dice to foolish and hoping gamesters. Let your gifts be slight and dainty, rather than precious. Let cunning be above cost. Give cherries at time of year, or apricots, and say they were sent you out o' the country, though you bought 'em in Cheapside. Admire her tires; like her in all fashions; compare her in every habit to some deity; invent excellent dreams to flatter her, and riddles; or, if she be a great one, perform always the second parts to her: like what she likes, praise whom she praises, and fail not to make the household and servants yours, yea, the whole family, and salute 'em by their names—'tis but light cost, if you can purchase 'em so—and make her physician your pensioner, and her chief woman. Nor will it be out of your gain to make love to her too, so she follow, not usher her lady's pleasure. All blabbing is taken away, when she comes to be a part of the crime.

DAUPHINE. On what courtly lap hast thou late slept, to come forth so sudden and absolute a courtling?

TRUEWIT. Good faith, I should rather question you,

that are so hearkening after these mysteries. I begin
to suspect your diligence, Dauphine. Speak, art thou
in love in earnest?

DAUPHINE. Yes, by my troth, am I! 'twere ill dissembling before thee.

TRUEWIT. With which of 'em, I pray thee?

DAUPHINE. With all the Collegiates.

CLERIMONT. Out on thee! We'll keep you at home,
believe it, i' the stable, an you be such a stallion.

TRUEWIT. No, I like him well. Men should love
wisely, and all women: some one for the face, and
let her please the eye; another for the skin, and let
her please the touch; a third for the voice, and let
her please the ear; and where the objects mix, let the
senses so, too. Thou wouldst think it strange if I
should make 'em all in love with thee afore night!

DAUPHINE. I would say thou hadst the best philtre
i' the world, and couldst do more than Madam
Medea, or Doctor Forman.

TRUEWIT. If I do not, let me play the mountebank
for my meat, while I live, and the bawd for my
drink.

DAUPHINE. So be it, I say.

Enter OTTER, DAW, *and* LA FOOLE.

OTTER. O Lord, gentlemen, how my knights and I
have missed you here!

CLERIMONT. Why, Captain, what service, what service?

OTTER. To see me bring up my Bull, Bear, and
Horse to fight.

DAW. Yes, faith, the Captain says we shall be his
dogs to bait 'em.

DAUPHINE. A good employment.

TRUEWIT. Come on, let's see a course, then.

LA FOOLE. I am afraid my cousin will be offended, if she come.

OTTER. Be afraid of nothing. Gentlemen, I have placed the drum and the trumpets, and one to give 'em the sign when you are ready. Here's my Bull for myself, and my Bear for Sir John Daw, and my Horse for Sir Amorous. Now set your foot to mine, and yours to his and——

LA FOOLE. Pray God my cousin come not.

OTTER. Saint George and Saint Andrew, fear no cousins.—Come, sound, sound!—'Et rauco strepuerunt cornua cantu.'   *Trumpets.*

TRUEWIT. Well said, Captain, i' faith! Well fought at the Bull.

CLERIMONT. Well held at the Bear.

TRUEWIT. Low, low, Captain!

DAUPHINE. O, the Horse has kicked off his dog already.

LA FOOLE. I cannot drink it, as I am a knight.

TRUEWIT. God's so', off with your spurs, somebody!

LA FOOLE. It goes against my conscience. My cousin will be angry with it.

DAW. I ha' done mine.

TRUEWIT. You fought high and fair, Sir John.

CLERIMONT. At the head.

DAUPHINE. Like an excellent bear-dog.

CLERIMONT. —You take no notice of the business, I hope?

DAW. Not a word, sir, you see we are jovial.

OTTER. Sir Amorous, you must not equivocate. It must be pulled down, for all my cousin.

CLERIMONT. —'Sfoot, if you take not your drink, they'll think you are discontented with something. You'll betray all, if you take the least notice.

LA FOOLE. Not I, I'll both drink and talk then.

OTTER. You must pull the horse on his knees, Sir Amorous; fear no cousins. Jacta est alea.

TRUEWIT. —O, now he's in his vein, and bold. The least hint given him of his wife now will make him rail desperately.

CLERIMONT. Speak to him of her.

TRUEWIT. Do you, and I'll fetch her to the hearing of it. *Exit.*

DAUPHINE. Captain he-Otter, your she-Otter is coming, your wife.

OTTER. Wife! buzz! Titivilitium! There's no such thing in nature. I confess, gentlemen, I have a cook, a laundress, a house-drudge, that serves my necessary turns, and goes under that title; but he's an ass that will be so uxorious to tie his affections to one circle. Come, the name dulls appetite. Here, replenish again; another bout. Wives are nasty, sluttish animals.

DAUPHINE. O, Captain.

OTTER. As ever the earth bare, tribus verbis. Where's Master Truewit?

DAW. He's slipped aside, sir.

CLERIMONT. But you must drink and be jovial.

DAW. Yes, give it me.

LA FOOLE. And me too.

DAW. Let's be jovial.

LA FOOLE. As jovial as you will.

OTTER. Agreed. Now you shall ha' the Bear, cousin, and Sir John Daw the Horse, and I'll ha' the Bull still.—Sound, Tritons o' the Thames!—'Nunc est bibendum, nunc pede libero——'

MOROSE. *Speaks from above, the trumpets sounding.* Villains, murderers, sons of the earth, and traitors, what do you there?

CLERIMONT. O, now the trumpets have waked him, we shall have his company.

OTTER. A wife is a scurvy clogdogdo, an unlucky thing, a very foresaid bear-whelp, without any good fashion or breeding, mala bestia.

Enter TRUEWIT *behind, with* MISTRESS OTTER.

DAUPHINE. Why did you marry one then, Captain?

OTTER. A pox! I married with six thousand pound, I. I was in love with that. I ha' not kissed my Fury these forty weeks.

CLERIMONT. The more to blame you, Captain.

TRUEWIT. —Nay, Mistress Otter, hear him a little first.

OTTER. She has a breath worse than my grandmother's, *profecto!*

MISTRESS OTTER. —O treacherous liar! Kiss me, sweet Master Truewit, and prove him a slandering knave.

TRUEWIT. I'll rather believe you, lady.

OTTER. And she has a peruke that's like a pound of hemp, made up in shoe-threads.

MISTRESS OTTER. —O viper, mandrake!

OTTER. A most vile face! and yet she spends me forty pound a year in mercury and hogs'-bones. All her teeth were made i' the Blackfriars, both her eyebrows i' the Strand, and her hair in Silver Street. Every part o' the town owns a piece of her.

MISTRESS OTTER. —I cannot hold.

OTTER. She takes herself asunder still when she goes to bed, into some twenty boxes; and about next day noon is put together again, like a great German clock; and so comes forth, and rings a tedious 'larum to the whole house, and then is quiet again for an hour, but for her quarters. Ha' you done me right, gentlemen?

MISTRESS OTTER. *Falls upon him and beats him.*

No, sir, I'll do you right with my quarters, with my quarters!

OTTER. O, hold, good Princess.

TRUEWIT. Sound, sound!

CLERIMONT. A battle, a battle! *Trumpets.*

MISTRESS OTTER. You notorious stinkardly bear-ward, does my breath smell?

OTTER. Under correction, dear Princess.—Look to my Bear and my Horse, gentlemen.

MISTRESS OTTER. Do I want teeth and eyebrows, thou bulldog?

TRUEWIT. Sound, sound still! *Trumpets.*

OTTER. No, I protest, under correction——

MISTRESS OTTER. Ay, now you are under correction, you protest; but you did not protest before correction, sir. Thou Judas, to offer to betray thy Princess! I'll make thee an example——

MOROSE descends with a long-sword.

MOROSE. I will have no such examples in my house, Lady Otter.

MISTRESS OTTER. Ah——

Exit MISTRESS OTTER, DAW, *and* LA FOOLE.

MOROSE. Mistress Mary Ambree, your examples are dangerous. Rogues, hellhounds, Stentors! out of my doors, you sons of noise and tumult, begot on an ill May-day, or when the galley-foist is afloat to Westminster! A trumpeter could not be conceived but then!

DAUPHINE. What ails you, sir?

MOROSE. They have rent my roof, walls, and all my windows asunder with their brazen throats. *Exit.*

TRUEWIT. Best follow him, Dauphine.

DAUPHINE. So I will.

CLERIMONT. Where's Daw and La Foole?

OTTER. They are both run away, sir. Good gentlemen, help to pacify my Princess, and speak to the great ladies for me. Now must I go lie with the bears this fortnight, and keep out o' the way, till my peace be made, for this scandal she has taken. Did you not see my bull-head, gentlemen?

CLERIMONT. Is't not on, Captain?

TRUEWIT. No; but he may make a new one, by that is on.

OTTER. O, here 'tis. An you come over, gentlemen, and ask for Tom Otter, we'll go down to Ratcliffe, and have a course, i' faith, for all these disasters. There's bona spes left.

TRUEWIT. Away, Captain, get off while you are well.　　　　　　　　　　　　　　　*Exit* OTTER.

CLERIMONT. I am glad we are rid of him.

TRUEWIT. You had never been, unless we had put his wife upon him. His humour is as tedious at last as it was ridiculous at first.

Enter LADY HAUGHTY, MISTRESS OTTER, LADY MAVIS, DAW, LA FOOLE, LADY CENTAUR, *and* EPICENE.

HAUGHTY. We wondered why you shrieked so, Mistress Otter.

MISTRESS OTTER. O God, madam, he came down with a huge, long, naked weapon in both his hands, and looked so dreadfully! Sure, he's beside himself.

MAVIS. Why, what made you there, Mistress Otter?

MISTRESS OTTER. Alas, Mistress Mavis, I was chastising my subject, and thought nothing of him.

DAW. Faith, mistress, you must do so, too. Learn to chastise. Mistress Otter corrects her husband so, he dares not speak but under correction.

LA FOOLE. And with his hat off to her. 'Twould do you good to see.

HAUGHTY. In sadness, 'tis good and mature coun-

sel. Practise it, Morose. I'll call you Morose still now,
as I call Centaur and Mavis; we four will be all one.

CENTAUR. And you'll come to the College, and live
with us?

HAUGHTY. Make him give milk and honey.

MAVIS. Look how you manage him at first, you
shall have him ever after.

CENTAUR. Let him allow you your coach and four
horses, your woman, your chambermaid, your page,
your gentleman-usher, your French cook, and four
grooms.

HAUGHTY. And go with us to Bedlam, to the china-
houses, and to the Exchange.

CENTAUR. It will open the gate to your fame.

HAUGHTY. Here's Centaur has immortalized herself with taming of her wild male.

MAVIS. Ay, she has done the miracle of the kingdom.

EPICENE. But, ladies, do you count it lawful to
have such plurality of servants, and do 'em all
graces?

HAUGHTY. Why not? Why should women deny
their favours to men? Are they the poorer, or the
worse?

DAW. Is the Thames the less for the dyers' water,
mistress?

LA FOOLE. Or a torch for lighting many torches?

TRUEWIT. Well said, La Foole.—What a new one he
has got!

CENTAUR. They are empty losses women fear in
this kind.

HAUGHTY. Besides, ladies should be mindful of the
approach of age, and let no time want his due use.
The best of our days pass first.

MAVIS. We are rivers that cannot be called back,

madam. She that now excludes her lovers may live to lie a forsaken beldam in a frozen bed.

CENTAUR. 'Tis true, Mavis; and who will wait on us to coach then? or write, or tell us the news then? make anagrams of our names, and invite us to the Cockpit, and kiss our hands all the play-time, and draw their weapons for our honours?

HAUGHTY. Not one.

DAW. Nay, my mistress is not altogether unintelligent of these things. Here be in presence have tasted of her favours.

CLERIMONT. —What a neighing hobby-horse is this!

EPICENE. But not with intent to boast 'em again, servant.—And have you those excellent receipts, madam, to keep yourselves from bearing of children?

HAUGHTY. O yes, Morose. How should we maintain our youth and beauty else? Many births of a woman make her old, as many crops make the earth barren.

Enter MOROSE *and* DAUPHINE.

MOROSE. O my cursed angel, that instructed me to this fate!

DAUPHINE. Why, sir?

MOROSE. That I should be seduced by so foolish a devil as a barber will make!

DAUPHINE. I would I had been worthy, sir, to have partaken your counsel; you should never have trusted it to such a minister.

MOROSE. Would I could redeem it with the loss of an eye, nephew, a hand, or any other member.

DAUPHINE. Marry, God forbid, sir, that you should geld yourself to anger your wife.

MOROSE. So it would rid me of her! and that I did supererogatory penance in a belfry, at Westminster Hall, i' the Cockpit, at the fall of a stag, the Tower

Wharf,—what place is there else?—London Bridge, Paris Garden, Billingsgate when the noises are at their height and loudest. Nay, I would sit out a play, that were nothing but fights at sea, drum, trumpet, and target!

DAUPHINE. I hope there shall be no such need, sir. Take patience, good uncle. This is but a day, and 'tis well worn, too, now.

MOROSE. O, 'twill be so forever, nephew, I foresee it, forever. Strife and tumult are the dowry that comes with a wife.

TRUEWIT. I told you so, sir, and you would not believe me.

MOROSE. Alas, do not rub those wounds, Master Truewit, to blood again. 'Twas my negligence. Add not affliction to affliction. I have perceived the effect of it too late in Madam Otter.

EPICENE. How do you, sir?

MOROSE. Did you ever hear a more unnecessary question? as if she did not see! Why, I do as you see, Empress, Empress.

EPICENE. You are not well, sir; you look very ill; something has distempered you.

MOROSE. O horrible, monstrous impertinencies! Would not one of these have served, do you think, sir? would not one of these have served?

TRUEWIT. Yes, sir, but these are but notes of female kindness, sir, certain tokens that she has a voice, sir.

MOROSE. O, is't so! Come, an't be no otherwise—— What say you?

EPICENE. How do you feel yourself, sir?

MOROSE. Again that!

TRUEWIT. Nay, look you, sir, you would be friends with your wife upon unconscionable terms—her silence.

EPICENE. They say you are run mad, sir.

MOROSE. Not for love, I assure you, of you, do you see?

EPICENE. O Lord, gentlemen, lay hold on him, for God's sake! What shall I do? Who's his physician—can you tell?—that knows the state of his body best, that I might send for him? Good sir, speak; I'll send for one of my doctors else.

MOROSE. What, to poison me, that I might die intestate, and leave you possessed of all!

EPICENE. Lord, how idly he talks, and how his eyes sparkle! He looks green about the temples! Do you see what blue spots he has!

CLERIMONT. Ay, it's melancholy.

EPICENE. Gentlemen, for Heaven's sake, counsel me. Ladies!—Servant, you have read Pliny and Paracelsus; ne'er a word now to comfort a poor gentlewoman? Ay me, what fortune had I to marry a distracted man!

DAW. I'll tell you, mistress——

TRUEWIT. —How rarely she holds it up!

MOROSE. What mean you, gentlemen?

EPICENE. What will you tell me, servant?

DAW. The disease in Greek is called μανία, in Latin 'insania, furor, vel ecstasis melancholica,' that is, 'egressio,' and a man 'ex melancholico evadit fanaticus.'

MOROSE. Shall I have a lecture read upon me alive?

DAW. But he may be but phreneticus yet, mistress; and phrenesis is only delirium, or so.

EPICENE. Ay, that is for the disease, servant; but what is this to the cure? We are sure enough of the disease.

MOROSE. Let me go.

TRUEWIT. Why, we'll entreat her to hold her peace, sir.

MOROSE. O no, labour not to stop her. She is like a conduit-pipe, that will gush out with more force when she opens again.

HAUGHTY. I'll tell you, Morose, you must talk divinity to him altogether, or moral philosophy.

LA FOOLE. Ay, and there's an excellent book of moral philosophy, madam, of Reynard the Fox and all the beasts, called 'Doni's Philosophy.'

CENTAUR. There is indeed, Sir Amorous La Foole.

MOROSE. O misery!

LA FOOLE. I have read it, my Lady Centaur, all over, to my cousin here.

MISTRESS OTTER. Ay, and 'tis a very good book as any is, of the moderns.

DAW. Tut, he must have Seneca read to him, and Plutarch, and the ancients. The moderns are not for this disease.

CLERIMONT. Why, you discommended them too, today, Sir John.

DAW. Ay, in some cases; but in these they are best, and Aristotle's 'Ethics.'

MAVIS. Say you so, Sir John? I think you are deceived; you took it upon trust.

HAUGHTY. Where's Trusty, my woman? I'll end this difference. I pr'y thee, Otter, call her. Her father and mother were both mad, when they put her to me.

MOROSE. I think so. Nay, gentlemen, I am tame. This is but an exercise, I know, a marriage ceremony, which I must endure.

HAUGHTY. And one of 'em, I know not which, was cured with 'The Sick Man's Salve,' and the other with 'Green's Groatsworth of Wit.'

TRUEWIT. A very cheap cure, madam.

HAUGHTY. Ay, it's very feasible.

Enter TRUSTY.

MISTRESS OTTER. My lady called for you, Mistress Trusty. You must decide a controversy.

HAUGHTY. O, Trusty, which was it you said, your father or your mother, that was cured with 'The Sick Man's Salve'?

TRUSTY. My mother, madam, with the 'Salve.'

TRUEWIT. Then it was the sick woman's salve!

TRUSTY. And my father with the 'Groatsworth of Wit.' But there was other means used: we had a preacher that would preach folk asleep still; and so they were prescribed to go to church, by an old woman that was their physician, thrice a week—

EPICENE. To sleep?

TRUSTY. Yes, forsooth, and every night they read themselves asleep on those books.

EPICENE. Good faith, it stands with great reason. I would I knew where to procure those books.

MOROSE. O!

LA FOOLE. I can help you with one of 'em, Mistress Morose, the 'Groatsworth of Wit.'

EPICENE. But I shall disfurnish you, Sir Amorous; can you spare it?

LA FOOLE. O yes, for a week or so; I'll read it myself to him.

EPICENE. No, I must do that, sir; that must be my office.

MOROSE. O, O!

EPICENE. Sure, he would do well enough if he could sleep.

MOROSE. No, I should do well enough if you could sleep. Have I no friend that will make her drunk? or give her a little laudanum, or opium?

TRUEWIT. Why, sir, she talks ten times worse in her sleep.

MOROSE. How!

CLERIMONT. Do you not know that, sir? Never ceases all night.

TRUEWIT. And snores like a porpoise.

MOROSE. O, redeem me, fate; redeem me, fate! For how many causes may a man be divorced, nephew?

DAUPHINE. I know not, truly, sir.

TRUEWIT. Some divine must resolve you in that, sir, or canon lawyer.

MOROSE. I will not rest, I will not think of any other hope or comfort, till I know.

Exit with DAUPHINE.

CLERIMONT. Alas, poor man!

TRUEWIT. You'll make him mad indeed, ladies, if you pursue this.

HAUGHTY. No, we'll let him breathe now, a quarter of an hour or so.

CLERIMONT. By my faith, a large truce!

HAUGHTY. Is that his keeper, that is gone with him?

DAW. It is his nephew, madam.

LA FOOLE. Sir Dauphine Eugenie.

CENTAUR. He looks like a very pitiful knight——

DAW. As can be. This marriage has put him out of all.

LA FOOLE. He has not a penny in his purse, madam——

DAW. He is ready to cry all this day.

LA FOOLE. A very shark; he set me i' the nick t'other night at primero.

TRUEWIT. —How these swabbers talk!

CLERIMONT. Ay, Otter's wine has swelled their humours above a spring-tide.

HAUGHTY. Good Morose, let's go in again. I like

your couches exceeding well; we'll go lie and talk there.

Exeunt LADY HAUGHTY, LADY CENTAUR, MISTRESS MAVIS, TRUSTY, LA FOOLE, *and* DAW.

EPICENE. I wait on you, madam.

TRUEWIT. 'Slight, I will have 'em as silent as signs, and their post too, ere I ha' done. Do you hear, Lady Bride? I pray thee now, as thou art a noble wench, continue this discourse of Dauphine within; but praise him exceedingly. Magnify him with all the height of affection thou canst—I have some purpose in't—and but beat off these two rooks, Jack Daw and his fellow, with any discontentment, hither, and I'll honour thee forever.

EPICENE. I was about it here. It angered me to the soul, to hear 'em begin to talk so malepert.

TRUEWIT. Pray thee perform it, and thou winn'st me an idolater to thee everlasting.

EPICENE. Will you go in and hear me do 't?

TRUEWIT. No, I'll stay here. Drive 'em out of your company, 'tis all I ask; which cannot be any way better done than by extolling Dauphine, whom they have so slighted.

EPICENE. I warrant you; you shall expect one of 'em presently. *Exit.*

CLERIMONT. What a cast of kastrils are these, to hawk after ladies thus!

TRUEWIT. Ay, and strike at such an eagle as Dauphine.

CLERIMONT. He will be mad when we tell him. Here he comes.

Re-enter DAUPHINE.

O, sir, you are welcome.

TRUEWIT. Where's thine uncle?

DAUPHINE. Run out o' doors in 's nightcap, to

talk with a casuist about his divorce. It works admirably.

TRUEWIT. Thou wouldst ha' said so, an thou hadst been here! The ladies have laughed at thee most comically, since thou went'st, Dauphine.

CLERIMONT. And asked if thou wert thine uncle's keeper.

TRUEWIT. And the brace of baboons answered yes; and said thou wert a pitiful, poor fellow, and didst live upon posts, and hadst nothing but three suits of apparel, and some few benevolences that lords ga' thee to fool to 'em and swagger.

DAUPHINE. Let me not live, I'll beat 'em! I'll bind 'em both to grand Madam's bed-posts, and have 'em baited with monkeys.

TRUEWIT. Thou shalt not need; they shall be beaten to thy hand, Dauphine. I have an execution to serve upon 'em, I warrant thee, shall serve; trust my plot.

DAUPHINE. Ay, you have many plots. So you had one to make all the wenches in love with me!

TRUEWIT. Why, if I do it not yet afore night, as near as 'tis, and that they do not every one invite thee, and be ready to scratch for thee, take the mortgage of my wit.

CLERIMONT. 'Fore God, I'll be his witness, thou shalt have it, Dauphine!—Thou shalt be his fool for ever, if thou dost not.

TRUEWIT. Agreed. Perhaps 'twill be the better estate. Do you observe this gallery, or rather lobby, indeed? Here are a couple of studies, at each end one: here will I act such a tragi-comedy between the Guelphs and the Ghibellines, Daw and La Foole——Which of 'em comes out first, will I seize on. You two shall be the chorus behind the arras, and whip out between the acts and speak. If I do not make 'em keep the peace for this remnant of the day, if not of the year, I have failed once——I hear Daw coming. Hide, and do not laugh, for God's sake!

Re-enter DAW.

DAW. Which is the way into the garden, trow?

TRUEWIT. O, Jack Daw! I am glad I have met with you. In good faith, I must have this matter go no further between you. I must ha' it taken up.

DAW. What matter, sir? Between whom?

TRUEWIT. Come, you disguise it—Sir Amorous and you. If you love me, Jack, you shall make use of your philosophy now, for this once, and deliver me your sword. This is not the wedding the Centaurs were at, though there be a she-one here. The bride has entreated me I will see no blood shed at her bridal; you saw her whisper me erewhile.

DAW. As I hope to finish Tacitus, I intend no murder.

TRUEWIT. Do you not wait for Sir Amorous?

DAW. Not I, by my knighthood.

TRUEWIT. And your scholarship too?

DAW. And my scholarship too.

TRUEWIT. Go to, then I return you your sword, and ask you mercy; but put it not up, for you will be assaulted. I understood that you had appre-hended it, and walked here to brave him; and that you had held your life contemptible, in regard of your honour.

DAW. No, no, no such thing, I assure you. He and I parted now as good friends as could be.

TRUEWIT. Trust not you to that visor. I saw him since dinner with another face. I have known many men in my time vexed with losses, with deaths, and with abuses, but so offended a wight as Sir Amorous did I never see or read of. For taking away his guests,

sir, today, that's the cause; and he declares it behind
your back with such threatenings and contempts——
He said to Dauphine you were the arrant'st ass——

DAW. Ay, he may say his pleasure.

TRUEWIT. And swears you are so protested a
coward, that he knows you will never do him any
manly or single right, and therefore he will take
his course.

DAW. I'll give him any satisfaction, sir,—but
fighting.

TRUEWIT. Ay, sir, but who knows what satisfaction he'll take? Blood he thirsts for, and blood he
will have; and whereabouts on you he will have it,
who knows but himself?

DAW. I pray you, Master Truewit, be you a
mediator.

TRUEWIT. Well, sir, conceal yourself then in this
study till I return. *Puts him up.* Nay, you must be
content to be locked in; for, for mine own reputation, I would not have you seen to receive a public
disgrace, while I have the matter in managing.
God's so', here he comes. Keep your breath close, that
he do not hear you sigh.—In good faith, Sir Amorous,
he is not this way. I pray you be merciful, do not
murder him; he is a Christian, as good as you. You
are armed as if you sought a revenge on all his race.
Good Dauphine, get him away from this place. I
never knew a man's choler so high, but he would
speak to his friends, he would hear reason.—Jack
Daw, Jack Daw! Asleep?

DAW. Is he gone, Master Truewit?

TRUEWIT. Ay, did you hear him?

DAW. O God, yes!

TRUEWIT. —What a quick ear fear has!

DAW. And is he so armed as you say?

TRUEWIT. Armed! did you ever see a fellow set out to take possession?

DAW. Ay, sir.

TRUEWIT. That may give you some light to conceive of him, but 'tis nothing to the principal. Some false brother i' the house has furnished him strangely; or, if it were out o' the house, it was Tom Otter.

DAW. Indeed, he's a captain, and his wife is his kinswoman.

TRUEWIT. He has got somebody's old two-hand sword, to mow you off at the knees; and that sword hath spawned such a dagger! But then he is so hung with pikes, halberds, petronels, calivers, and muskets, that he looks like a Justice of Peace's hall. A man of two thousand a year is not cessed at so many weapons as he has on. There was never fencer challenged at so many several foils. You would think he meant to murder all Saint 'Pulchre's parish. If he could but victual himself for half a year in his breeches, he is sufficiently armed to overrun a country.

DAW. Good Lord! what means he, sir? I pray you, Master Truewit, be you a mediator.

TRUEWIT. Well, I'll try if he will be appeased with a leg or an arm; if not, you must die once.

DAW. I would be loath to lose my right arm, for writing madrigals.

TRUEWIT. Why, if he will be satisfied with a thumb or a little finger, all's one to me. You must think, I'll do my best.

Puts him up again, and then comes forth.

DAW. Good sir, do.

CLERIMONT. What hast thou done?

TRUEWIT. He will let me do nothing, man, he does all afore me; he offers his left arm.

CLERIMONT. His left wing, for a jackdaw.

DAUPHINE. Take it, by all means.

TRUEWIT. How! maim a man forever, for a jest? What a conscience hast thou!

DAUPHINE. 'Tis no loss to him; he has no employment for his arms but to eat spoon-meat. Beside, as good maim his body as his reputation.

TRUEWIT. He is a scholar and a wit, and yet he does not think so. But he loses no reputation with us, for we all resolved him an ass before. To your places again.

CLERIMONT. I pray thee, let me be in it at the other a little.

TRUEWIT. Look, you'll spoil all; these be ever your tricks.

CLERIMONT. No, but I could hit off some things that thou wilt miss, and thou wilt say are good ones.

TRUEWIT. I warrant you. I pray, forbear, I'll leave it off else.

DAUPHINE. Come away, Clerimont.

Enter LA FOOLE.

TRUEWIT. Sir Amorous!

LA FOOLE. Master Truewit.

TRUEWIT. Whither were you going?

LA FOOLE. Down into the court to make water.

TRUEWIT. By no means, sir, you shall rather tempt your breeches.

LA FOOLE. Why, sir?

TRUEWIT. Enter here, if you love your life.

LA FOOLE. Why? why?

TRUEWIT. Question till your throat be cut, do! dally till the enraged soul find you.

LA FOOLE. Who's that?

TRUEWIT. Daw it is! Will you in?

LA FOOLE. Ay, ay, I'll in. What's the matter?

TRUEWIT. Nay, if he had been cool enough to tell us that, there had been some hope to atone you; but he seems so implacably enraged!

LA FOOLE. 'Slight, let him rage! I'll hide myself.

TRUEWIT. Do, good sir. But what have you done to him within, that should provoke him thus? You have broke some jest upon him afore the ladies——

LA FOOLE. Not I, never in my life broke jest upon any man. The bride was praising Sir Dauphine, and he went away in snuff, and I followed him—unless he took offence at me in his drink erewhile, that I would not pledge all the Horse full.

TRUEWIT. By my faith, and that may be; you remember well. But he walks the round up and down, through every room o' the house, with a towel in his hand, crying, 'Where's La Foole? Who saw La Foole?' And when Dauphine and I demanded the cause, we can force no answer from him but, 'O revenge, how sweet art thou! I will strangle him in this towel!' Which leads us to conjecture that the main cause of his fury is for bringing your meat today with a towel about you, to his discredit.

LA FOOLE. Like enough. Why, an he be angry for that, I'll stay here till his anger be blown over.

TRUEWIT. A good, becoming resolution, sir, if you can put it on o' the sudden.

LA FOOLE. Yes, I can put it on. Or, I'll away into the country presently.

TRUEWIT. How will you get out o' the house, sir? He knows you are i' the house, and he'll watch you this se'nnight, but he'll have you. He'll outwait a sergeant for you.

LA FOOLE. Why, then I'll stay here.

TRUEWIT. You must think how to victual yourself in time, then.

LA FOOLE. Why, sweet Master Truewit, will you

entreat my cousin Otter to send me a cold venison
pasty, a bottle or two of wine, and a chamber-pot.

TRUEWIT. A stool were better, sir, of Sir Ajax's invention.

LA FOOLE. Ay, that will be better indeed; and a
pallet to lie on.

TRUEWIT. O, I would not advise you to sleep, by
any means.

LA FOOLE. Would you not, sir? Why, then I will
not.

TRUEWIT. Yet there's another fear——

LA FOOLE. Is there! What is't?

TRUEWIT. No, he cannot break open this door
with his foot, sure.

LA FOOLE. I'll set my back against it, sir. I have a
good back.

TRUEWIT. But then if he should batter.

LA FOOLE. Batter! if he dare, I'll have an action
of batt'ry against him.

TRUEWIT. Cast you the worst. He has sent for
powder already, and what he will do with it no
man knows—perhaps blow up the corner o' the
house where he suspects you are. Here he comes; in
quickly. *He feigns as if one were present, to fright
the other, who is run in to hide himself.* I protest,
Sir John Daw, he is not this way. What will you do?
Before God, you shall hang no petard here! I'll die
rather. Will you not take my word? I never knew
one but would be satisfied.—Sir Amorous, there's
no standing out. He has made a petard of an old
brass pot, to force your door. Think upon some
satisfaction, or terms, to offer him.

LA FOOLE. Sir, I'll give him any satisfaction. I dare
give any terms.

TRUEWIT. You'll leave it to me then?

LA FOOLE. Ay, sir. I'll stand to any conditions.

TRUEWIT. *Calls forth* CLERIMONT *and* DAUPHINE. How now! what think you, sirs? Were't not a difficult thing to determine which of these two feared most?

CLERIMONT. Yes, but this fears the bravest; the other a whinneling, dastard jackdaw! But La Foole, a brave, heroic coward! and is afraid in a great look and a stout accent. I like him rarely.

TRUEWIT. Had it not been pity these two should ha' been concealed?

CLERIMONT. Shall I make a motion?

TRUEWIT. Briefly, for I must strike while 'tis hot.

CLERIMONT. Shall I go fetch the ladies to the catastrophe?

TRUEWIT. Umh? ay, by my troth.

DAUPHINE. By no mortal means. Let them continue in the state of ignorance, and err still; think 'em wits and fine fellows, as they have done. 'Twere sin to reform them.

TRUEWIT. Well, I will have 'em fetched, now I think on't, for a private purpose of mine. Do, Clerimont, fetch 'em, and discourse to 'em all that's passed, and bring 'em into the gallery here.

DAUPHINE. This is thy extreme vanity, now! Thou think'st thou wert undone if every jest thou mak'st were not published.

TRUEWIT. Thou shalt see how unjust thou art presently.—Clerimont, say it was Dauphine's plot. *Exit* CLERIMONT. Trust me not if the whole drift be not for thy good. There's a carpet i' the next room; put it on, with this scarf over thy face, and a cushion o' thy head, and be ready when I call Amorous. Away. *Exit* DAUPHINE. John Daw!

DAW. What good news, sir?

TRUEWIT. Faith, I have followed, and argued with him hard for you. I told him you were a knight and a scholar, and that you knew fortitude did consist 'magis patiendo quam faciendo, magis ferendo quam feriendo.'

DAW. It doth so indeed, sir.

TRUEWIT. And that you would suffer, I told him. So at first he demanded, by my troth, in my conceit too much.

DAW. What was it, sir?

TRUEWIT. Your upper lip and six o' your fore-teeth.

DAW. 'Twas unreasonable.

TRUEWIT. Nay, I told him plainly, you could not spare 'em all. So after long argument—pro et con, as you know—I brought him down to your two butter-teeth, and them he would have.

DAW. O, did you so? Why, he shall have 'em.

TRUEWIT. But he shall not, sir, by your leave. The conclusion is this, sir: because you shall be very good friends hereafter, and this never to be remembered or upbraided; besides, that he may not boast he has done any such thing to you in his own person; he is to come here in disguise, give you five kicks in private, sir, take your sword from you, and lock you up in that study during pleasure; which will be but a little while, we'll get it released presently.

DAW. Five kicks? he shall have six, sir, to be friends.

TRUEWIT. Believe me, you shall not overshoot your-self, to send him that word by me.

DAW. Deliver it, sir, he shall have it with all my heart, to be friends.

TRUEWIT. Friends! Nay, an he should not be so, and heartily too, upon these terms, he shall have me to enemy while I live. Come, sir, bear it bravely.

DAW. O God, sir, 'tis nothing!

TRUEWIT. True. What's six kicks to a man that reads Seneca?

DAW. I have had a hundred, sir.

TRUEWIT. Sir Amorous! No speaking one to another, or rehearsing old matters.

DAUPHINE *comes forth and kicks* DAW.

DAW. One, two, three, four, five. I protest, Sir Amorous, you shall have six.

TRUEWIT. Nay, I told you you should not talk. Come, give him six, an he will needs. Your sword. Now return to your safe custody. You shall presently meet afore the ladies, and be the dearest friends one to another.—Give me the scarf now, thou shalt beat the other barefaced. Stand by.—Sir Amorous!

LA FOOLE. What's here? A sword!

TRUEWIT. I cannot help it, without I should take the quarrel upon myself. Here he has sent you his sword——

LA FOOLE. I'll receive none on't.

TRUEWIT. And he wills you to fasten it against a wall, and break your head in some few several places against the hilts.

LA FOOLE. I will not; tell him roundly. I cannot endure to shed my own blood.

TRUEWIT. Will you not?

LA FOOLE. No. I'll beat it against a fair flat wall, if that will satisfy him. If not, he shall beat it himself, for Amorous.

TRUEWIT. Why, this is strange starting off, when a man undertakes for you! I offered him another condition; will you stand to that?

LA FOOLE. Ay, what is't?

TRUEWIT. That you will be beaten in private.

LA FOOLE. Yes, I am content, at the blunt.

TRUEWIT. Then you must submit yourself to be hoodwinked in this scarf and be led to him, where he will take your sword from you, and make you bear a blow over the mouth Gules, and tweaks by the nose, sans nombre.

LA FOOLE. I am content. But why must I be blinded?

TRUEWIT. That's for your good, sir; because if he should grow insolent upon this, and publish it hereafter to your disgrace,—which I hope he will not do—you might swear safely and protest he never beat you to your knowledge.

LA FOOLE. O, I conceive.

TRUEWIT. I do not doubt but you'll be perfect good friends upon't, and not dare to utter an ill thought, one of another, in future.

LA FOOLE. Not I, as God help me, of him.

TRUEWIT. Nor he of you, sir. If he should—Come, sir. All hid, Sir John!

DAUPHINE *enters to tweak him.*

LA FOOLE. Oh, Sir John, Sir John! Oh, o-o-o-o-o-oh—

TRUEWIT. Good Sir John, leave tweaking; you'll blow his nose off.—'Tis Sir John's pleasure you should retire into the study. Why, now you are friends. All bitterness between you, I hope, is buried; you shall come forth, by and by, Damon and Pythias upon 't, and embrace with all the rankness of friendship that can be.—I trust we shall have 'em tamer in their language hereafter. Dauphine, I worship thee. God's will, the ladies have surprised us!

Enter CLERIMONT, *with* LADY HAUGHTY, LADY CENTAUR, MISTRESS MAVIS, MISTRESS OTTER, EPICENE, *and* TRUSTY, *having discovered part of the past scene.*

HAUGHTY. Centaur, how our judgments were imposed on by these adulterate knights!

CENTAUR. Nay, madam, Mavis was more deceived

than we; 'twas her commendation uttered 'em in the College.

MAVIS. I commended but their wits, madam, and their braveries. I never looked toward their valours.

HAUGHTY. Sir Dauphine is valiant, and a wit too, it seems.

MAVIS. And a bravery too.

HAUGHTY. Was this his project?

MISTRESS OTTER. So Master Clerimont intimates, madam.

HAUGHTY. Good Morose, when you come to the College, will you bring him with you? He seems a very perfect gentleman.

EPICENE. He is so, madam, believe it.

CENTAUR. But when will you come, Morose?

EPICENE. Three or four days hence, madam, when I have got me a coach and horses.

HAUGHTY. No, tomorrow, good Morose; Centaur shall send you her coach.

MAVIS. Yes, faith, do, and bring Sir Dauphine with you.

HAUGHTY. She has promised that, Mavis.

MAVIS. He is a very worthy gentleman in his exteriors, madam.

HAUGHTY. Ay, he shows he is judicial in his clothes.

CENTAUR. And yet not so superlatively neat as some, madam, that have their faces set in a brake.

HAUGHTY. Ay, and have every hair in form.

MAVIS. That wear purer linen than ourselves, and profess more neatness than the French hermaphrodite.

EPICENE. Ay, ladies, they, what they tell one of us, have told a thousand; and are the only thieves of our fame, that think to take us with that perfume, or with that lace, and laugh at us unconscionably when they have done.

HAUGHTY. But Sir Dauphine's carelessness becomes him.

CENTAUR. I could love a man for such a nose!

MAVIS. Or such a leg!

CENTAUR. He has an exceeding good eye, madam!

MAVIS. And a very good lock!

CENTAUR. Good Morose, bring him to my chamber first.

MISTRESS OTTER. Please your honours to meet at my house, madam.

TRUEWIT. —See how they eye thee, man! they are taken, I warrant thee.

HAUGHTY. You have unbraced our brace of knights here, Master Truewit.

TRUEWIT. Not I, madam, it was Sir Dauphine's engine; who, if he have disfurnished your ladyship of any guard or service by it, is able to make the place good again in himself.

HAUGHTY. There's no suspicion of that, sir.

CENTAUR. —God's so', Mavis, Haughty is kissing.

MAVIS. Let us go, too, and take part.

HAUGHTY. But I am glad of the fortune—beside the discovery of two such empty caskets—to gain the knowledge of so rich a mine of virtue as Sir Dauphine.

CENTAUR. We would be all glad to style him of our friendship, and see him at the College.

MAVIS. He cannot mix with a sweeter society, I'll prophesy, and I hope he himself will think so.

DAUPHINE. I should be rude to imagine otherwise, lady.

TRUEWIT. —Did not I tell thee, Dauphine? Why, all their actions are governed by crude opinion, without reason or cause. They know not why they do anything; but as they are informed, believe, judge, praise, condemn, love, hate, and in emulation one of another, do all these things alike. Only they have a natural inclination sways 'em generally to the worst, when they are left to themselves. But pursue it, now thou hast 'em.

HAUGHTY. Shall we go in again, Morose?

EPICENE. Yes, madam.

CENTAUR. We'll entreat Sir Dauphine's company.

TRUEWIT. Stay, good madam, the interview of the two friends, Pylades and Orestes. I'll fetch 'em out to you straight.

HAUGHTY. Will you, Master Truewit?

DAUPHINE. Ay, but, noble ladies, do not confess in your countenance, or outward bearing to 'em, any discovery of their follies, that we may see how they will bear up again, with what assurance and erection.

HAUGHTY. We will not, Sir Dauphine.

CENTAUR, MAVIS. Upon our honours, Sir Dauphine.

TRUEWIT. Sir Amorous! Sir Amorous! The ladies are here.

LA FOOLE. Are they?

TRUEWIT. Yes, but slip out by and by, as their backs are turned, and meet Sir John here, as by chance, when I call you.—Jack Daw!

DAW. What say you, sir?

TRUEWIT. Whip out behind me suddenly; and no anger i' your looks to your adversary. Now, now!

LA FOOLE. Noble Sir John Daw! where ha' you been?

DAW. To seek you, Sir Amorous.

LA FOOLE. Me! I honour you.

DAW. I prevent you, sir.

CLERIMONT. They have forgot their rapiers!

TRUEWIT. O, they meet in peace, man.

DAUPHINE. Where's your sword, Sir John?

CLERIMONT. And yours, Sir Amorous?

DAW. Mine? my boy had it forth to mend the handle, e'en now.

LA FOOLE. And my gold handle was broke, too, and my boy had it forth.

DAUPHINE. Indeed, sir!—How their excuses meet!

CLERIMONT. What a consent there is, i' the handles!

TRUEWIT. Nay, there is so i' the points too, I warrant you.

Enter MOROSE, *having found the two swords drawn within.*

MISTRESS OTTER. O me! madam, he comes again, the madman! Away!

Exit LADIES, DAW, *and* LA FOOLE.

MOROSE. What make these naked weapons here, gentlemen?

TRUEWIT. O sir! here hath like to been murder since you went—a couple of knights fallen out about the bride's favours! We were fain to take away their weapons; your house had been begged by this time else.

MOROSE. For what?

CLERIMONT. For manslaughter, sir, as being accessory.

MOROSE. And for her favours?

TRUEWIT. Ay, sir, heretofore, not present. Clerimont, carry 'em their swords now. They have done all the hurt they will do.

Exit CLERIMONT.

DAUPHINE. Ha' you spoke with a lawyer, sir?

MOROSE. O no! there is such a noise i' the court that they have frighted me home with more violence than I went! Such speaking and counterspeaking, with their several voices of citations, appellatons, allegations, certificates, attachments, interrogatories, references, convictions, and afflictions indeed, among the doctors and proctors, that the noise here is silence to't, a kind of calm midnight!

TRUEWIT. Why, sir, if you would be resolved indeed, I can bring you hither a very sufficient lawyer, and a learned divine, that shall inquire into every least scruple for you.

MOROSE. Can you, Master Truewit?

TRUEWIT. Yes, and are very sober, grave persons, that will dispatch it in a chamber, with a whisper or two.

MOROSE. Good sir, shall I hope this benefit from you, and trust myself into your hands?

TRUEWIT. Alas, sir! your nephew and I have been ashamed and oft-times mad, since you went, to think how you are abused. Go in, good sir, and lock yourself up till we call you; we'll tell you more anon, sir.

MOROSE. Do your pleasure with me, gentlemen. I believe in you, and that deserves no delusion— *Exit.*

TRUEWIT. You shall find none, sir,—but heaped, heaped plenty of vexation.

DAUPHINE. What wilt thou do now, Wit?

TRUEWIT. Recover me hither Otter and the barber, if you can, by any means, presently.

DAUPHINE. Why? to what purpose?

TRUEWIT. O, I'll make the deepest divine and gravest lawyer out o' them two, for him——

DAUPHINE. Thou canst not, man; these are waking dreams.

TRUEWIT. Do not fear me. Clap but a civil gown with a welt o' the one, and a canonical cloak with sleeves o' the other, and give 'em a few terms i' their mouths; if there come not forth as able a doctor and complete a parson, for this turn, as may be wished, trust not my election. And I hope, without wronging the dignity of either profession, since they are

but persons put on, and for mirth's sake, to torment
him. The barber smatters Latin, I remember.

DAUPHINE. Yes, and Otter, too.

TRUEWIT. Well then, if I make 'em not wrangle out
this case to his no-comfort, let me be thought a jackdaw, or La Foole, or anything worse. Go you to your
ladies, but first send for them.

DAUPHINE. I will. *Exeunt.*

ACT FIVE

Morose's house

Enter LA FOOLE, CLERIMONT, *and* DAW.

LA FOOLE. Where had you our swords, Master
Clerimont?

CLERIMONT. Why, Dauphine took 'em from the
madman.

LA FOOLE. And he took 'em from our boys, I warrant you!

CLERIMONT. Very like, sir.

LA FOOLE. Thank you, good Master Clerimont.
Sir John Daw and I are both beholden to you.

CLERIMONT. Would I knew how to make you so,
gentlemen.

DAW. Sir Amorous and I are your servants, sir.

Enter MISTRESS MAVIS.

MAVIS. Gentlemen, have any of you a pen and ink?
I would fain write out a riddle in Italian, for Sir
Dauphine to translate.

CLERIMONT. Not I, in troth, lady, I am no scrivener.

DAW. I can furnish you, I think, lady.

Exeunt DAW *and* MAVIS.

CLERIMONT. He has it in the haft of a knife, I believe.

LA FOOLE. No, he has his box of instruments.

CLERIMONT. Like a surgeon!

LA FOOLE. For the mathematics—his square, his compasses, his brass pens, and black-lead, to draw maps of every place and person where he comes.

CLERIMONT. How, maps of persons!

LA FOOLE. Yes, sir, of Nomentack, when he was here, and of the Prince of Moldavia, and of his mistress, Mistress Epicene.

Re-enter DAW.

CLERIMONT. Away! he has not found out her latitude, I hope.

LA FOOLE. You are a pleasant gentleman, sir. ·

CLERIMONT. Faith, now we are in private, let's wanton it a little, and talk waggishly.—Sir John, I am telling Sir Amorous here, that you two govern the ladies; where'er you come, you carry the feminine gender afore you.

DAW. They shall rather carry us afore them, if they will, sir.

CLERIMONT. Nay, I believe that they do withal—But that you are the prime men in their affections, and direct all their actions——

DAW. Not I; Sir Amorous is.

LA FOOLE. I protest, Sir John is.

DAW. As I hope to rise i' the state, Sir Amorous, you ha' the person.

LA FOOLE. Sir John, you ha' the person, and the discourse too.

DAW. Not I, sir. I have no discourse—and then you have activity beside.

LA FOOLE. I protest, Sir John, you come as high from Tripoli as I do, every whit; and lift as many joint-stools, and leap over 'em, if you would use it—

CLERIMONT. Well, agree on't together, knights, for between you, you divide the kingdom or commonwealth of ladies' affections. I see it, and can perceive a little how they observe you, and fear you indeed. You could tell strange stories, my masters, if you would, I know.

DAW. Faith, we have seen somewhat, sir.

LA FOOLE. That we have—velvet petticoats, and wrought smocks, or so.

DAW. Ay, and——

CLERIMONT. Nay, out with it, Sir John! Do not envy your friend the pleasure of hearing, when you have had the delight of tasting.

DAW. Why—a—do you speak, Sir Amorous.

LA FOOLE. No, do you, Sir John Daw.

DAW. I' faith, you shall.

LA FOOLE. I' faith, you shall.

DAW. Why, we have been——

LA FOOLE. In the great bed at Ware together in our time. On, Sir John.

DAW. Nay, do you, Sir Amorous.

CLERIMONT. And these ladies with you, knights?

LA FOOLE. No, excuse us, sir.

DAW. We must not wound reputation.

LA FOOLE. No matter—they were these, or others. Our bath cost us fifteen pound when we came home.

CLERIMONT. Do you hear, Sir John? You shall tell me but one thing truly, as you love me.

DAW. If I can, I will, sir.

CLERIMONT. You lay in the same house with the bride here?

DAW. Yes, and conversed with her hourly, sir.

CLERIMONT. And what humour is she of? Is she coming and open, free?

DAW. O, exceeding open, sir. I was her servant, and Sir Amorous was to be.

CLERIMONT. Come, you have both had favours from her? I know, and have heard so much.

DAW. O no, sir.

LA FOOLE. You shall excuse us, sir; we must not wound reputation.

CLERIMONT. Tut, she is married now, and you cannot hurt her with any report, and therefore speak plainly: how many times, i' faith? which of you led first? ha?

LA FOOLE. Sir John had her maidenhead, indeed.

DAW. O, it pleases him to say so, sir, but Sir Amorous knows what's what as well.

CLERIMONT. Dost thou, i' faith, Amorous?

LA FOOLE. In a manner, sir.

DAW. Why, I commend you, lads. Little knows Don Bridegroom of this; nor shall he, for me.

DAW. Hang him, mad ox!

CLERIMONT. Speak softly, here comes his nephew, with the Lady Haughty. He'll get the ladies from you, sirs, if you look not to him in time.

LA FOOLE. Why, if he do, we'll fetch 'em home again, I warrant you. *Exit with* DAW.

Enter DAUPHINE *and* LADY HAUGHTY.

HAUGHTY. I assure you, Sir Dauphine, it is the price and estimation of your virtue only, that hath embarked me to this adventure, and I could not but make out to tell you so. Nor can I repent me of the act, since it is always an argument of some virtue in ourselves, that we love and affect it so in others.

DAUPHINE. Your ladyship sets too high a price on my weakness.

HAUGHTY. Sir, I can distinguish gems from pebbles——

DAUPHINE. —Are you so skilful in stones?

HAUGHTY. And howsoever I may suffer in such a judgment as yours, by admitting equality of rank or society with Centaur or Mavis——

DAUPHINE. You do not, madam; I perceive they are your mere foils.

HAUGHTY. Then are you a friend to truth, sir. It makes me love you the more. It is not the outward but the inward man that I affect. They are not apprehensive of an eminent perfection, but love flat and dully.

CENTAUR. Where are you, my Lady Haughty?

HAUGHTY. I come presently, Centaur.—My chamber, sir, my page shall show you; and Trusty, my woman, shall be ever awake for you. You need not fear to communicate anything with her, for she is a Fidelia. I pray you wear this jewel for my sake, Sir Dauphine.

Enter LADY CENTAUR.

Where's Mavis, Centaur?

CENTAUR. Within, madam, a-writing. I'll follow you presently. *Exit* HAUGHTY. I'll but speak a word with Sir Dauphine.

DAUPHINE. With me, madam?

CENTAUR. Good Sir Dauphine, do not trust Haughty, nor make any credit to her, whatever you do besides. Sir Dauphine, I give you this caution: she is a perfect courtier, and loves nobody

but for her uses; and for her uses, she loves all.
Besides, her physicians give her out to be none o'
the clearest; whether she pay 'em or no, Heaven
knows! And she's above fifty, too, and pargets!
See her in a forenoon. Here comes Mavis, a worse
face than she! you would not like this, by candle-
light.

Re-enter MISTRESS MAVIS.

If you'll come to my chamber one o' these mornings early, or late in an evening, I'll tell you more.
—Where's Haughty, Mavis?

MAVIS. Within, Centaur.

CENTAUR. What ha' you there?

MAVIS. An Italian riddle for Sir Dauphine. You
shall not see it, i' faith, Centaur. *Exit* CENTAUR.
Good Sir Dauphine, solve it for me. I'll call for
it anon.   *Exit.*

CLERIMONT. How now, Dauphine! how dost thou
quit thyself of these females?

DAUPHINE. 'Slight, they haunt me like fairies, and
give me jewels here; I cannot be rid of 'em.

CLERIMONT. O, you must not tell though.

DAUPHINE. Mass, I forgot that! I was never so
assaulted. One loves for virtue, and bribes me with
this. Another loves me with caution, and so would
possess me. A third brings me a riddle here; and
all are jealous, and rail each at other.

CLERIMONT. A riddle! pray le'me see't.

Reads the paper.

'Sir Dauphine: I chose this way of intimation
for privacy. The ladies here, I know, have both
hope and purpose to make a Collegiate and servant
of you. If I might be so honoured as to appear at
any end of so noble a work, I would enter into

a fame of taking physic tomorrow, and continue it four or five days, or longer, for your visitation.

Mavis.'

By my faith, a subtle one! Call you this a riddle? What's their plain-dealing, trow?

DAUPHINE. We lack Truewit, to tell us that.

CLERIMONT. We lack him for somewhat else, too: his knights reformados are wound up as high and insolent as ever they were.

DAUPHINE. You jest.

CLERIMONT. No drunkards, either with wine or vanity, ever confessed such stories of themselves. I would not give a fly's leg in balance against all the women's reputations here, if they could be but thought to speak truth; and for the bride, they have made their affidavit against her directly——

DAUPHINE. What, that they have lain with her?

CLERIMONT. Yes, and tell times and circumstances, with the cause why, and the place where. I had almost brought 'em to affirm that they had done it today.

DAUPHINE. Not both of 'em?

CLERIMONT. Yes, faith, with a sooth or two more I had effected it. They would ha' set it down under their hands.

DAUPHINE. Why, they will be our sport, I see, still, whether we will or no.

Enter TRUEWIT.

TRUEWIT. O, are you here? Come, Dauphine, go call your uncle presently. I have fitted my divine and my canonist, dyed their beards and all. The knaves do not know themselves, they are so exalted and altered. Preferment changes any man. Thou shalt keep one door and I another, and then Clerimont in the midst, that he may have no means of escape from their cavilling, when they grow hot once. And then the women—as I have given the bride her instructions—to break in upon him i' the l'envoy. O, 'twill be full and twanging! Away, fetch him! *Exit* DAUPHINE.

Enter OTTER, *disguised as a divine, and* CUTBEARD *as a canon lawyer.*

Come, Master Doctor, and Master Parson, look to your parts now, and discharge 'em bravely. You are well set forth, perform it as well. If you chance to be out, do not confess it with standing still or humming or gaping one at another; but go on, and talk aloud, and eagerly; use vehement action, and only remember your terms, and you are safe. Let the matter go where it will; you have many will do so. But at first be very solemn and grave, like your garments, though you loose yourselves after, and skip out like a brace of jugglers on a table. Here he comes! Set your faces, and look superciliously, while I present you.

Re-enter DAUPHINE *with* MOROSE.

MOROSE. Are these the two learned men?

TRUEWIT. Yes, sir, please you salute 'em.

MOROSE. Salute 'em! I had rather do anything than wear out time so unfruitfully, sir. I wonder how these common forms, as 'God save you,' and 'You are welcome,' are come to be a habit in our lives; or 'I am glad to see you'—when I cannot see what the profit can be of these words, so long as it is no whit better with him whose affairs are sad and grievous, that he hears this salutation.

TRUEWIT. 'Tis true, sir; we'll go to the matter then.—Gentlemen, Master Doctor and Master Parson, I have acquainted you sufficiently with the business for which you are come hither, and you are not now to inform yourselves in the state of the question, I know. This is the gentleman who expects your resolution, and therefore, when you please, begin.

OTTER. Please you, Master Doctor.

CUTBEARD. Please you, good Master Parson.

OTTER. I would hear the canon law speak first.

CUTBEARD. It must give place to positive divinity, sir.

MOROSE. Nay, good gentlemen, do not throw me into circumstances. Let your comforts arrive quickly at me, those that are. Be swift in affording me my peace, if so I shall hope any. I love not your disputations or your court tumults. And that it be not strange to you, I will tell you: my father, in my education, was wont to advise me that I should always collect and contain my mind, not suffering it to flow loosely; that I should look to what things were necessary to the carriage of my life, and what not, embracing the one and eschewing the other; in short, that I should endear myself to rest, and avoid turmoil; which now is grown to be another nature to me. So that I come not to your public pleadings, or your places of noise; not that I neglect those things that make for the dignity of the commonwealth; but for the mere avoiding of clamours, and impertinences of orators that know not how to be silent. And for the cause of noise am I now a suitor to you. You do not know in what a misery I have been exercised this day, what a torrent of evil! My very house turns round with the tumult! I dwell in a windmill! The perpetual motion is here, and not at Eltham.

TRUEWIT. Well, good Master Doctor, will you break the ice? Master Parson will wade after.

CUTBEARD. Sir, though unworthy, and the weaker, I will presume.

OTTER. 'Tis no presumption, Domine Doctor.

MOROSE. Yet again!

CUTBEARD. Your question is, for how many causes a man may have divortium legitimum, a lawful divorce? First you must understand the nature of the word 'divorce,' à divertendo——

MOROSE. No excursions upon words, good Doctor, to the question briefly.

CUTBEARD. I answer then, the canon law affords divorce but in few cases; and the principal is in the common case, the adulterous case. But there are duodecim impedimenta, twelve impediments as we call 'em, all which do not 'dirimere contractum,' but 'irritum reddere matrimonium,' as we say in the canon law, not take away the bond, but cause a nullity therein.

MOROSE. I understood you before, good sir, avoid your impertinency of translation.

OTTER. He cannot open this too much, sir, by your favour.

MOROSE. Yet more!

TRUEWIT. O, you must give the learned men leave, sir.—To your impediments, Master Doctor.

CUTBEARD. The first is impedimentum erroris.

OTTER. Of which there are several species.

CUTBEARD. Ay, as error personae.

OTTER. If you contract yourself to one person, thinking her another.

CUTBEARD. Then, error fortunae.

OTTER. If she be a beggar, and you thought her rich.

CUTBEARD. Then, error qualitatis.

OTTER. If she prove stubborn or headstrong, that you thought obedient.

MOROSE. How! is that, sir, a lawful impediment? One at once, I pray you, gentlemen.

OTTER. Ay, ante copulam, but not post copulam, sir.

CUTBEARD. Master Parson says right. 'Nec post nuptiarum benedictionem.' It doth indeed but 'irrita reddere sponsalia,' annul the contract; after marriage it is of no obstancy.

TRUEWIT. Alas, sir, what a hope are we fallen from by this time!

CUTBEARD. The next is conditio: if you thought her free-born and she prove a bondwoman, there is impediment of estate and condition.

OTTER. Ay, but, Master Doctor, those servitudes are sublatae now, among us Christians.

CUTBEARD. By your favour, Master Parson——

OTTER. You shall give me leave, Master Doctor.

MOROSE. Nay, gentlemen, quarrel not in that question; it concerns not my case. Pass to the third.

CUTBEARD. Well, then, the third is votum: if either party have made a vow of chastity. But that practice, as Master Parson said of the other, is taken away among us, thanks be to discipline. The fourth is cognatio: if the persons be of kin within the degrees.

OTTER. Ay; do you know what the degrees are, sir?

MOROSE. No, nor I care not, sir. They offer me no comfort in the question, I am sure.

CUTBEARD. But there is a branch of this impediment may, which is cognatio spiritualis. If you were her godfather, sir, then the marriage is incestuous.

OTTER. That comment is absurd and superstitious, Master Doctor. I cannot endure it. Are we not all brothers and sisters, and as much akin in that as godfathers and god-daughters?

MOROSE. O me! to end the controversy, I never was

a godfather, I never was a godfather in my life, sir. Pass to the next.

CUTBEARD. The fifth is crimen adulterii, the known case. The sixth, cultus disparitas, difference of religion; have you ever examined her, what religion she is of?

MOROSE. No, I would rather she were of none, than be put to the trouble of it!

OTTER. You may have it done for you, sir.

MOROSE. By no means, good sir; on to the rest. Shall you ever come to an end, think you?

TRUEWIT. Yes, he has done half, sir.—On to the rest.—Be patient, and expect, sir.

CUTBEARD. The seventh is vis: if it were upon compulsion or force.

MOROSE. O no, it was too voluntary, mine, too voluntary.

CUTBEARD. The eighth is ordo: if ever she have taken holy orders.

OTTER. That's superstitious too.

MOROSE. No matter, Master Parson; would she would go into a nunnery yet!

CUTBEARD. The ninth is ligamen: if you were bound, sir, to any other before.

MOROSE. I thrust myself too soon into these fetters.

CUTBEARD. The tenth is publica honestas: which is inchoata quaedam affinitas.

OTTER. Ay, or affinitas orta ex sponsalibus; and is but leve impedimentum.

MOROSE. I feel no air of comfort blowing to me in all this.

CUTBEARD. The eleventh is affinitas ex fornicatione.

OTTER. Which is no less vera affinitas than the other, Master Doctor.

CUTBEARD. True, 'quae oritur ex legitimo matrimonio.'

OTTER. You say right, venerable Doctor; and, 'nascitur ex eo, quod per conjugium duae personae efficiuntur una caro——'

TRUEWIT. Hey-day, now they begin!

CUTBEARD. I conceive you, Master Parson. 'Ita per fornicationem aeque est verus pater, qui sic generat——'

OTTER. 'Et vere filius qui sic generatur——'

MOROSE. What's all this to me?

CLERIMONT. Now it grows warm.

CUTBEARD. The twelfth and last is, si forte coire nequibis.

OTTER. Ay, that is impedimentum gravissimum. It doth utterly annul and annihilate, that. If you have manifestam frigiditatem, you are well, sir.

TRUEWIT. Why, there is comfort come at length, sir. Confess yourself but a man unable, and she will sue to be divorced first.

OTTER. Ay, or if there be morbus perpetuus et insanabilis, as paralysis, elephantiasis, or so——

DAUPHINE. O, but frigiditas is the fairer way, gentlemen.

OTTER. You say troth, sir, and as it is in the canon, Master Doctor——

CUTBEARD. I conceive you, sir.

CLERIMONT. —Before he speaks!

OTTER. That a boy, or child under years, is not fit for marriage, because he cannot reddere debitum. So your omnipotentes——

TRUEWIT. —Your impotentes, you whoreson lobster!

OTTER. Your impotentes, I should say, are minime apti ad contrahenda matrimonium.

TRUEWIT. —'Matrimonium?' we shall have most unmatrimonial Latin with you. 'Matrimonia,' and be hanged!

DAUPHINE. You put 'em out, man.

CUTBEARD. But then there will arise a doubt, Master Parson, in our case, post matrimonium: that frigiditate praeditus—do you conceive me, sir?

OTTER. Very well, sir.

CUTBEARD. Who cannot uti uxore pro uxore, may habere eam pro sorore.

OTTER. Absurd, absurd, absurd, and merely apostatical!

CUTBEARD. You shall pardon me, Master Parson, I can prove it.

OTTER. You can prove a will, Master Doctor, you can prove nothing else. Does not the verse of your own canon say:

'Haec socianda vetant connubia, facta retractant?'

CUTBEARD. I grant you; but how do they retractare, Master Parson?

MOROSE. —O, this was it I feared.

OTTER. In aeternum, sir.

CUTBEARD. That's false in divinity, by your favour.

OTTER. 'Tis false in humanity to say so. Is he not prorsus inutilis ad thorum? Can be praestare fidem datam? I would fain know.

CUTBEARD. Yes; how if he do convalere?

OTTER. He cannot convalere, it is impossible.

TRUEWIT. Nay, good sir, attend the learned men; they'll think you neglect 'em else.

CUTBEARD. Or if he do simulare himself frigidum, odio uxoris, or so?

OTTER. I say he is adulter manifestus, then.

DAUPHINE. —They dispute it very learnedly, i' faith.

OTTER. And prostitutor uxoris, and this is positive.

MOROSE. Good sir, let me escape.

TRUEWIT. You will not do me that wrong, sir?

OTTER. And, therefore, if he be *manifeste frigidus,* sir——

CUTBEARD. Ay, if he be *manifeste frigidus,* I grant you——

OTTER. Why, that was my conclusion.

CUTBEARD. And mine too.

TRUEWIT. Nay, hear the conclusion, sir.

OTTER. Then, *frigiditatis causa*——

CUTBEARD. Yes, *causa frigiditatis*——

MOROSE. O mine ears!

OTTER. She may have *libellum divortii* against you.

CUTBEARD. Ay, *divortii libellum* she will sure have.

MOROSE. Good echoes, forbear.

OTTER. If you confess it——

CUTBEARD. Which I would do, sir——

MOROSE. I will do anything.

OTTER. And clear myself, *in foro conscientiae*——

CUTBEARD. Because you want indeed——

MOROSE. Yet more?

OTTER. *Exercendi potestate.*

Enter EPICENE, *followed by* LADY HAUGHTY, LADY CENTAUR, MISTRESS MAVIS, MISTRESS OTTER, DAW, *and* LA FOOLE.

EPICENE. I will not endure it any longer. Ladies, I beseech you help me. This is such a wrong as never was offered to poor bride before. Upon her marriage day to have her husband conspire against her, and a couple of mercenary companions to be brought in, for form's sake, to persuade a separation! If you had bloor or virtue in you, gentlemen, you would not suffer such earwigs about a husband, or scorpions to creep between man and wife——

MOROSE. O, the variety and changes of my torment!

HAUGHTY. Let 'em be cudgelled out of doors by our grooms.

CENTAUR. I'll lend you my footman.

MAVIS. We'll have our men blanket 'em i' the hall.

MISTRESS OTTER. As there was one at our house, madam, for peeping in at the door.

DAW. Content, i' faith.

TRUEWIT. Stay, ladies and gentlemen, you'll hear before you proceed?

MAVIS. I'd have the bridegroom blanketed, too.

CENTAUR. Begin with him first.

HAUGHTY. Yes, by my troth.

MOROSE. O mankind generation!

DAUPHINE. Ladies, for my sake forbear.

HAUGHTY. Yes, for Sir Dauphine's sake.

CENTAUR. He shall command us.

LA FOOLE. He is as fine a gentleman of his inches, madam, as any is about the town, and wears as good colours when he list.

TRUEWIT. Be brief, sir, and confess your infirmity. She'll be afire to be quit of you, if she but hear that named once. You shall not entreat her to stay; she'll fly you like one that had the marks upon him.

MOROSE. Ladies, I must crave all your pardons——

TRUEWIT. Silence, ladies.

MOROSE. For a wrong I have done to your whole sex, in marrying this fair and virtuous gentlewoman——

CLERIMONT. Hear him, good ladies.

MOROSE. Being guilty of an infirmity which, before I conferred with these learned men, I thought I might have concealed——

TRUEWIT. But now being better informed in his

conscience by them, he is to declare it, and give satisfaction by asking your public forgiveness.

MOROSE. I am no man, ladies.

ALL. How!

MOROSE. Utterly unabled in nature, by reason of frigidity, to perform the duties or any the least office of a husband.

MAVIS. Now out upon him, prodigious creature!

CENTAUR. Bridegroom uncarnate!

HAUGHTY. And would you offer it to a young gentlewoman?

MISTRESS OTTER. A lady of her longings?

EPICENE. Tut, a device, a device, this! it smells rankly, ladies. A mere comment of his own.

TRUEWIT. Why, if you suspect that, ladies, you may have him searched.

DAW. As the custom is, by a jury of physicians.

LA FOOLE. Yes, faith, 'twill be brave.

MOROSE. O me, must I undergo that?

MISTRESS OTTER. No, let women search him, madam. We can do it ourselves.

MOROSE. Out on me, worse!

EPICENE. No, ladies, you shall not need; I'll take him with all his faults.

MOROSE. Worst of all!

CLERIMONT. Why then, 'tis no divorce, Doctor, if she consent not?

CUTBEARD. No, if the man be frigidus, it is de parte uxoris, that we grant libellum divortii in the law.

OTTER. Ay, it is the same in theology.

MOROSE. Worse, worse than worst!

TRUEWIT. Nay, sir, be not utterly disheartened; we have yet a small relic of hope left, as near as our comfort is blown out.—Clerimont, produce your brace of knights.—What was that, Master Parson, you told me, in errore qualitatis, e'en now?—Dauphine, whisper the bride, that she carry it as if she were guilty and ashamed.

OTTER. Marry, sir, in errore qualitatis,—which Master Doctor did forbear to urge—if she be found corrupta, that is, vitiated or broken up, that was pro virgine desponsa, espoused for a maid——

MOROSE. What then, sir?

OTTER. It doth dirimere contractum, and irritum reddere, too.

TRUEWIT. If this be true, we are happy again, sir, once more. Here are an honourable brace of knights that shall affirm so much.

DAW. Pardon us, good Master Clerimont.

LA FOOLE. You shall excuse us, Master Clerimont.

CLERIMONT. Nay, you must make it good now, knights, there is no remedy. I'll eat no words for you, nor no men; you know you spoke it to me.

DAW. Is this gentlemanlike, sir?

TRUEWIT. Jack Daw, he's worse than Sir Amorous, fiercer a great deal.—Sir Amorous, beware, there be ten Daws in this Clerimont.

LA FOOLE. I'll confess it, sir.

DAW. Will you, Sir Amorous? will you wound reputation?

LA FOOLE. I am resolved.

TRUEWIT. So should you be too, Jack Daw. What should keep you off? She's but a woman, and in disgrace. He'll be glad on't.

DAW. Will he? I thought he would ha' been angry.

CLERIMONT. You will despatch, knights, it must be done, i' faith.

TRUEWIT. Why, an it must, it shall, sir, they say. They'll ne'er go back.—Do not tempt his patience.

DAW. It is true indeed, sir.

LA FOOLE. Yes, I assure you, sir.

MOROSE. What is true, gentlemen? what do you assure me?

DAW. That we have known your bride, sir——

LA FOOLE. In good fashion. She was our mistress, or so——

CLERIMONT. You must be plain, knights, as you were to me.

OTTER. Ay, the question is, if you have carnaliter, or no?

LA FOOLE. Carnaliter! what else, sir?

OTTER. It is enough; a plain nullity.

EPICENE. I am undone, I am undone!

MOROSE. O, let me worship and adore you, gentlemen!

EPICENE. I am undone!

MOROSE. Yes, to my hand, I thank these knights. Master Parson, let me thank you otherwise.

CENTAUR. And ha' they confessed?

MAVIS. Now, out upon 'em, informers!

TRUEWIT. You see what creatures you may bestow your favours on, madams.

HAUGHTY. I would except against 'em as beaten knights, wench, and not good witnesses in law.

MISTRESS OTTER. Poor gentlewoman, how she takes it!

HAUGHTY. Be comforted, Morose, I love you the better for 't.

CENTAUR. So do I, I protest.

CUTBEARD. But, gentlemen, you have not known her since matrimonium?

DAW. Not today, Master Doctor.

LA FOOLE. No, sir, not today.

CUTBEARD. Why, then I say, for any act before, the matrimonium is good and perfect; unless the worshipful bridegroom did precisely, before witness, demand if she were virgo ante nuptias.

EPICENE. No, that he did not, I assure you, Master Doctor.

CUTBEARD. If he cannot prove that, it is ratum conjugium, notwithstanding the premises; and they do no way impedire. And this is my sentence, this I pronounce.

OTTER. I am of Master Doctor's resolution, too, sir, if you made not that demand ante nuptias.

MOROSE. O my heart! wilt thou break? wilt thou break? This is worst of all worst worsts that Hell could have devised! Marry a whore, and so much noise!

DAUPHINE. Come, I see now plain confederacy in this doctor and this parson, to abuse a gentleman. You study his affliction. I pray begone, companions. —And, gentlemen, I begin to suspect you for having parts with 'em.—Sir, will it please you, hear me?

MOROSE. O do not talk to me; take not from me the pleasure of dying in silence, nephew.

DAUPHINE. Sir, I must speak to you. I have been long your poor, despised kinsman, and many a hard thought has strengthened you against me; but now it shall appear if either I love you or your peace, and prefer them to all the world beside. I will not be long or grievous to you, sir. If I free you of this un-happy match absolutely and instantly, after all this trouble, and almost in your despair, now——

MOROSE. It cannot be.

DAUPHINE. Sir, that you be never troubled with a murmur of it more, what shall I hope for, or de-serve of you?

MOROSE. O, what thou wilt, nephew! thou shalt deserve me, and have me.

DAUPHINE. Shall I have your favour perfect to me, and love hereafter?

MOROSE. That, and anything beside. Make thine

own conditions. My whole estate is thine. Manage it; I will become thy ward.

DAUPHINE. Nay, sir, I will not be so unreasonable.

EPICENE. Will Sir Dauphine be mine enemy, too?

DAUPHINE. You know I have been long a suitor to you, uncle, that out of your estate, which is fifteen hundred a year, you would allow me but five hundred during life, and assure the rest upon me after; to which I have often, by myself and friends, tendered you a writing to sign, which you would never consent or incline to. If you please but to effect it now——

MOROSE. Thou shalt have it, nephew. I will do it, and more.

DAUPHINE. If I quit you not, presently and forever, of this cumber, you shall have power instantly, afore all these, to revoke your act, and I will become whose slave you will give me to, forever.

MOROSE. Where is the writing? I will seal to it, that, or to a blank, and write thine own conditions.

EPICENE. O me, most unfortunate, wretched gentlewoman!

HAUGHTY. Will Sir Dauphine do this?

EPICENE. Good sir, have some compassion on me.

MOROSE. O, my nephew knows you, belike; away, crocodile!

CENTAUR. He does it not, sure, without good ground.

DAUPHINE. Here, sir.

MOROSE. Come, nephew, give me the pen. I will subscribe to anything, and seal to what thou wilt, for my deliverance. Thou art my restorer. Here I deliver it thee as my deed. If there be a word in it lacking, or writ with false orthography, I protest before God I will not take the advantage.

DAUPHINE. Then here is your release, sir. *Takes off*

EPICENE's *peruke*. You have married a boy, a gentleman's son that I have brought up this half year at
my great charges, and for this composition which I
have now made with you. What say you, Master
Doctor? This is justum impedimentum, I hope,
error personae?

OTTER. Yes, sir, in primo gradu.

CUTBEARD. In primo gradu.

DAUPHINE. I thank you, good Doctor Cutbeard,
and Parson Otter. *Pulls off their beards and disguise.*
You are beholden to 'em, sir, that have taken this
pains for you; and my friend, Master Truewit, who
enabled 'em for the business. Now you may go in
and rest; be as private as you will, sir. *Exit* MOROSE.
I'll not trouble you till you trouble me with your
funeral, which I care not how soon it come.—Cutbeard, I'll make your lease good. Thank me not, but
with your leg, Cutbeard. And Tom Otter, your Princess shall be reconciled to you.—How now, gentlemen, do you look at me?

CLERIMONT. A boy!

DAUPHINE. Yes, Mistress Epicene.

TRUEWIT. Well, Dauphine, you have lurched your
friends of the better half of the garland, by concealing this part of the plot; but much good do it thee,
thou deserv'st it, lad! And, Clerimont, for thy unexpected bringing in these two to confession, wear
my part of it freely. Nay, Sir Daw and Sir La Foole,
you see the gentlewoman that has done you the favours! We are all thankful to you, and so should the
womankind here, specially for lying on her, though
not with her! You meant so, I am sure. But that we
have stuck it upon you today, in your own imagined
persons, and so lately, this Amazon, the champion of
the sex, should beat you now thriftily, for the common slanders which ladies receive from such cuckoos

as you are. You are they that, when no merit or fortune can make you hope to enjoy their bodies, will yet lie with their reputations, and make their fame suffer. Away, you common moths of these and all ladies' honours. Go travel, to make legs and faces, and come home with some new matter to be laughed at. You deserve to live in an air as corrupted as that wherewith you feed rumour. *Exeunt* DAW *and* LA FOOLE. Madams, you are mute upon this new metamorphosis! But here stands she that has vindicated your fames. Take heed of such insectae hereafter. And let it not trouble you that you have discovered any mysteries to this young gentleman. He is almost of years, and will make a good visitant within this twelvemonth. In the meantime, we'll all undertake for his secrecy, that can speak so well of his silence.— Spectators, if you like this comedy, rise cheerfully, and now Morose is gone in, clap your hands. It may be that noise will cure him, at least please him.

Exeunt.

The Alchemist

THE PERSONS OF THE PLAY

SUBTLE, *the alchemist*
FACE, *the housekeeper*
DOLL COMMON, *their colleague*
DAPPER, *a clerk*
DRUGGER, *a tobacco-man*
SIR EPICURE MAMMON, *a knight*
PERTINAX SURLY, *a gamester*
TRIBULATION WHOLESOME, *a pastor of Amsterdam*
ANANIAS, *a deacon there*
KASTRIL, *the angry boy*
DAME PLIANT, *his sister, a widow*
LOVEWIT, *master of the house*
PARSON

Neighbours, Officers, Mutes, &c.

The Scene: LONDON

THE ARGUMENT

T he sickness hot, a master quit, for fear,
H is house in town, and left one servant there.
E ase him corrupted, and gave means to know

A cheater and his punk; who, now brought low,
L eaving their narrow practice, were become
C oz'ners at large; and, only wanting some
H ouse to set up, with him they here contract,
E ach for a share, and all begin to act.
M uch company they draw, and much abuse,
I n casting figures, telling fortunes, news,
S elling of flies, flat bawdry, with the Stone—
T ill it, and they, and all in fume are gone.

PROLOGUE

Fortune, that favours fools, these two short hours
We wish away, both for your sakes and ours,
Judging spectators; and desire, in place,
To th' author justice, to ourselves but grace.
Our scene is London, 'cause we would make known,
No country's mirth is better than our own.
No clime breeds better matter for your whore,
Bawd, squire, impostor, many persons more,
Whose manners, now called humours, feed the stage;
And which have still been subject for the rage
Or spleen of comic writers. Though this pen
Did never aim to grieve, but better men;
Howe'er the age he lives in doth endure
The vices that she breeds, above their cure.
But when the wholesome remedies are sweet,
And in their working gain and profit meet,
He hopes to find no spirit so much diseased,
But will with such fair correctives be pleased.
For here he doth not fear who can apply.
If there be any that will sit so nigh
Unto the stream, to look what it doth run,
They shall find things they'd think or wish were
    done;
They are so natural follies, but so shown,
As even the doers may see, and yet not own.

THE ALCHEMIST

ACT ONE

Lovewit's house

Enter FACE, SUBTLE, *and* DOLL.

FACE. Believe 't, I will.

SUBTLE.   Thy worst. I fart at thee.

DOLL. Ha' you your wits? Why, gentlemen! for
love——

FACE. Sirrah, I'll strip you——

SUBTLE.   What to do? lick figs
Out at my—

FACE.   Rogue, rogue!—out of all your sleights.

DOLL. Nay, look ye! Sovereign, General, are you
madmen?

SUBTLE. O, let the wild sheep loose. I'll gum your
silks.
With good strong water, an you come.

DOLL.   Will you have
The neighbours hear you? will you betray all?
Hark! I hear somebody.

FACE.   Sirrah——

SUBTLE.   I shall mar
All that the tailor has made, if you approach.

FACE. You most notorious whelp, you insolent
slave,
Dare you do this?

SUBTLE.   Yes, faith; yes, faith.

FACE.   Why, who
Am I, my mongrel, who am I?

SUBTLE.   I'll tell you,
Since you know not yourself—

FACE. Speak lower, rogue.

SUBTLE. Yes, you were once—time's not long past—the good,
Honest, plain livery-three-pound-thrum, that kept
Your master's worship's house, here in the Friars,
For the vacations——

FACE. Will you be so loud?

SUBTLE. Since, by my means, translated suburb-captain.

FACE. By your means, Doctor Dog!

SUBTLE. Within man's memory,
All this I speak of.

FACE. Why, I pray you, have I
Been countenanced by you? or you by me?
Do but collect, sir, where I met you first.

SUBTLE. I do not hear well.

FACE. Not of this, I think it.
But I shall put you in mind, sir,—at Pie Corner,
Taking your meal of steam in, from cooks' stalls,
Where, like the father of hunger, you did walk
Piteously costive, with your pinched horn-nose,
And your complexion of the Roman wash
Stuck full of black and melancholic worms,
Like powder-corns shot at th' artillery-yard.

SUBTLE. I wish you could advance your voice a little.

FACE. When you went pinned up in the several rags
You'd raked and picked from dunghills before day,
Your feet in mouldy slippers for your kibes,
A felt of rug, and a thin threaden cloak,
That scarce would cover your no-buttocks——

SUBTLE. So, sir!

FACE. When all your alchemy, and your algebra,
Your minerals, vegetals, and animals,
Your conjuring, coz'ning, and your dozen of trades,

Could not relieve your corpse with so much linen
Would make you tinder, but to see a fire;
I ga' you count'nance, credit for your coals,
Your stills, your glasses, your materials;
Built you a furnace, drew you customers,
Advanced all your black arts; lent you, beside,
A house to practise in——

    SUBTLE.   Your master's house!

    FACE. Where you have studied the more thriving
      skill
Of bawdry, since.

    SUBTLE.   Yes, in your master's house;
You and the rats here kept possession.
Make it not strange. I know y' were one could keep
The butt'ry-hatch still locked, and save the chip-
      pings,
Sell the dole-beer to aqua-vitae men,
The which, together with your Christmas vails
At post-and-pair, your letting out of counters,
Made you a pretty stock, some twenty marks,
And gave you credit to converse with cobwebs
Here, since your mistress' death hath broke up
      house.

    FACE. You might talk softlier, rascal.

    SUBTLE.   No, you scarab,
I'll thunder you in pieces. I will teach you
How to beware to tempt a fury again
That carries tempest in his hand and voice.

    FACE. The place has made you valiant.

    SUBTLE.   No, your clothes.
Thou vermin, have I ta'en thee out of dung,
So poor, so wretched, when no living thing
Would keep thee company, but a spider, or worse?
Raised thee from brooms and dust and wat'ring-
      pots?
Sublimed thee, and exalted thee, and fixed thee

I' the third region, called our state of grace?
Wrought thee to spirit, to quintessence, with pains
Would twice have won me the Philosophers' Work?
Put thee in words and fashion, made thee fit
For more than ordinary fellowships?
Giv'n thee thy oaths, thy quarrelling dimensions,
Thy rules to cheat at horse-race, cockpit, cards,
Dice, or whatever gallant tincture else?
Made thee a second in mine own great art?
And have I this for thanks! Do you rebel,
Do you fly out i' the projection?
Would you be gone now?

DOLL.   Gentlemen, what mean you?
Will you mar all?

SUBTLE.   Slave, thou hadst had no name——

DOLL. Will you undo yourselves with civil war?

SUBTLE. Never been known, past Equi Clibanum,
The heat of horse-dung, underground in cellars,
Or an ale-house darker than Deaf John's; been lost
To all mankind, but laundresses and tapsters,
Had not I been.

DOLL. D'you know who hears you, Sovereign?

FACE. Sirrah——

DOLL. Nay, General, I thought you were civil.

FACE. I shall turn desperate, if you grow thus loud.

SUBTLE. And hang thyself, I care not.

FACE.   Hang thee, collier,
And all thy pots and pans, in picture, I will,
Since thou hast moved me——

DOLL.   O, this'll o'erthrow all.

FACE. Write thee up bawd in Paul's, have all thy
     tricks
Of coz'ning with a hollow coal, dust, scrapings,
Searching for things lost, with a sieve and shears,
Erecting figures in your rows of houses,
And taking in of shadows with a glass,

Told in red letters; and a face cut for thee,
Worse than Gamaliel Ratsey's.

DOLL.   Are you sound?
Ha' you your senses, masters?

FACE.   I will have
A book but barely reckoning thy impostures,
Shall prove a true Philosophers' Stone to printers.

SUBTLE. Away, you trencher-rascal!

FACE.   Out, you dog-leech!
The vomit of all prisons——

DOLL.   Will you be
Your own destructions, gentlemen?

FACE.   Still spewed out
For lying too heavy o' the basket.

SUBTLE.   Cheater!

FACE. Bawd!

SUBTLE.   Cowherd!

FACE.   Conjurer!

SUBTLE.   Cutpurse!

FACE.   Witch!

DOLL.   O me,
We are ruined! lost! Ha' you no more regard
To your reputations? Where's your judgment?
    'Slight,
Have yet some care of me, o' your republic——

FACE. Away, this brach! I'll bring thee, rogue,
    within
The statute of sorcery, Tricesimo Tertio
Of Harry the Eighth; ay, and perhaps thy neck
Within a noose, for laund'ring gold and barbing it.

DOLL. You'll bring your head within a coxcomb,
    will you? *Catches out* FACE's *sword and breaks*
    SUBTLE's *glass.*
And you, sir, with your menstrue—gather it up.
'Sdeath, you abominable pair of stinkards,

Leave off your barking, and grow one again,
Or, by the light that shines, I'll cut your throats.
I'll not be made a prey unto the Marshal
For ne'er a snarling dog-bolt o' you both.
Ha' you together cozened all this while,
And all the world, and shall it now be said,
You've made most courteous shift to cozen your-
        selves?—
You will accuse him! You will bring him in
Within the statute! Who shall take your word?
A whoreson, upstart, apocryphal captain,
Whom not a Puritan in Blackfriars will trust
So much as for a feather!—And you, too,
Will give the cause, forsooth! You will insult,
And claim a primacy in the divisions!
You must be chief! as if you only, had
The powder to project with? and the work
Were not begun out of equality?
The venture tripartite? all things in common?
Without priority? 'Sdeath! you perpetual curs,
Fall to your couples again, and cozen kindly,
And heartily, and lovingly, as you should;
And loose not the beginning of a term,
Or, by this hand, I shall grow factious, too,
And take my part, and quit you.

    FACE.   'Tis his fault;
He ever murmurs, and objects his pains,
And says, the weight of all lies upon him.

    SUBTLE. Why, so it does.

    DOLL.   How does it? do not we
Sustain our parts?

    SUBTLE.   Yes, but they are not equal.

    DOLL. Why, if your part exceed today, I hope
Ours may tomorrow match it.

    SUBTLE.   Ay, they may.

DOLL. May, murmuring mastiff! Ay, and do. God's
     will!
Help me to throttle him.

    SUBTLE.   Dorothy! Mistress Dorothy!
'Ods precious, I'll do anything. What do you mean?

    DOLL. Because o' your fermentation and cibation!

    SUBTLE. Not I, by Heaven——

    DOLL.   Your Sol and Luna—Help me.

    SUBTLE. Would I were hanged then! I'll conform
     myself.

    DOLL. Will you, sir? Do so then, and quickly!
     Swear.

    SUBTLE. What should I swear?

    DOLL.   To leave your faction, sir,
And labour kindly in the common work.

    SUBTLE. Let me not breathe if I meant aught be-
     side.
I only used those speeches as a spur
To him.

    DOLL. I hope we need no spurs, sir. Do we?

    FACE. 'Slid, prove today who shall shark best.

    SUBTLE.   Agreed.

    DOLL. Yes, and work close and friendly.

    SUBTLE.   'Slight, the knot
Shall grow the stronger, for this breach, with me.

    DOLL. Why, so, my good baboons! Shall we go
     make
A sort of sober, scurvy, precise neighbours,
That scarce have smiled twice since the King came
     in,
A feast of laughter at our follies? rascals,
Would run themselves from breath, to see me ride,
Or you t' have but a hole to thrust your heads in,
For which you should pay ear-rent! No, agree.
And may Don Provost ride a-feasting long,
In his old velvet jerkin and stained scarfs,

My noble Sovereign, and worthy General,
Ere we contribute a new crewel garter
To his most worsted worship.

    SUBTLE.   Royal Doll!
Spoken like Claridiana, and thyself.

    FACE. For which at supper, thou shalt sit in tri-
      umph,
And not be styled Doll Common, but Doll Proper,
Doll Singular; the longest cut at night,
Shall draw thee for his Doll Particular.

                       Bell rings without.

    SUBTLE. Who's that? one rings. To the window,
      Doll.—Pray Heaven,
The Master do not trouble us this quarter.

    FACE. O, fear not him. While there dies one a
      week
O' the plague, he's safe from thinking toward
      London;
Beside, he's busy at his hop-yards now—
I had a letter from him. If he do,
He'll send such word, for airing o' the house,
As you shall have sufficient time to quit it;
Though we break up a fortnight, 'tis no matter.

    SUBTLE. Who is it, Doll?

    DOLL.   A fine young quodling.

    FACE.   O,
My lawyer's clerk I lighted on last night,
In Holborn, at the Dagger. He would have—
I told you of him—a familiar,
To rifle with, at horses, and win cups.

    DOLL. O, let him in.

    SUBTLE.   Stay. Who shall do't?

    FACE.   Get you
Your robes on. I will meet him, as going out.

    DOLL. And what shall I do?

FACE.   Not be seen; away!

                                             Exit DOLL.

Seem you very reserved.

SUBTLE.   Enough.   *Exit.*

FACE.   God b'w'you, sir!
I pray you let him know that I was here.
His name is Dapper. I would gladly have stayed,
    but——

Enter DAPPER.

DAPPER. Captain, I am here.

FACE.   Who's that? He's come, I think, Doctor.—
Good faith, sir, I was going away.

DAPPER.   In truth,
I'm very sorry, Captain.

FACE.   But I thought
Sure I should meet you.

DAPPER.   Ay, I'm very glad.
I had a scurvy writ or two to make,
And I had lent my watch last night to one
That dines today at the Sheriff's, and so was robbed
Of my pass-time.

Re-enter SUBTLE *in his robes.*

                    Is this the cunning-man?

FACE. This is his worship.

DAPPER.   Is he a doctor?

FACE.   Yes.

DAPPER. And ha' you broke with him, Captain?

FACE.   Ay.

DAPPER.   And how?

FACE. Faith, he does make the matter, sir, so
    dainty,
I know not what to say.

DAPPER.   Not so, good Captain.

FACE. Would I were fairly rid on't, believe me.

DAPPER. Nay, now you grieve me, sir. Why should
 you wish so?
I dare assure you I'll not be ungrateful.

FACE. I cannot think you will, sir. But the law
Is such a thing—— And then he says, Read's matter
Falling so lately——

DAPPER.   Read! he was an ass,
And dealt, sir, with a fool.

FACE.   It was a clerk, sir.

DAPPER. A clerk!

FACE.   Nay, hear me, sir, you know the law
Better, I think——

DAPPER.   I should, sir, and the danger.
You know I showed the statute to you.

FACE.   You did so.

DAPPER. And will I tell, then? By this hand of flesh,
Would it might never write good court-hand more,
If I discover. What do you think of me,
That I am a chouse?

FACE.   What's that?

DAPPER.   The Turk was, here——
As one would say, do you think I am a Turk?

FACE. I'll tell the Doctor so.

DAPPER.   Do, good sweet Captain.

FACE. Come, noble Doctor, pray thee let's prevail;
This is the gentleman, and he is no chouse.

SUBTLE. Captain, I have returned you all my an-
 swer.
I would do much, sir, for your love—— But this
I neither may, nor can.

FACE.   Tut, do not say so.
You deal now with a noble fellow, Doctor,
One that will thank you richly; and he's no chouse.
Let that, sir, move you.

SUBTLE.   Pray you, forbear——

FACE.   He has
Four angels here——

    SUBTLE.   You do me wrong, good sir.

    FACE. Doctor, wherein? To tempt you with these
        spirits?

    SUBTLE. To tempt my art and love, sir, to my peril.
'Fore Heav'n, I scarce can think you are my friend,
That so would draw me to apparent danger.

    FACE. I draw you? A horse draw you, and a halter,
You and your flies together——

    DAPPER.   Nay, good Captain.

    FACE. That knows no difference of men!

    SUBTLE.   Good words, sir.

    FACE. Good deeds, sir, Doctor Dogs'-meat. 'Slight,
        I bring you
No cheating Clim-o'-the-Cloughs, or Claribels,
That look as big as five-and-fifty, and flush,
And spit out secrets like hot custard——

    DAPPER.   Captain!

    FACE. Nor any melancholic under-scribe,
Shall tell the Vicar; but a special gentle,
That is the heir to forty marks a year,
Consorts with the small poets of the time,
Is the sole hope of his old grandmother;
That knows the law, and writes you six fair hands,
Is a fine clerk, and has his ciph'ring perfect,
Will take his oath o' the Greek Testament,
If need be, in his pocket; and can court
His mistress out of Ovid.

    DAPPER.   Nay, dear Captain——

    FACE. Did you not tell me so?

    DAPPER.   Yes, but I'd ha' you
Use Master Doctor with some more respect.

    FACE. Hang him, proud stag, with his broad velvet
        head!
But for your sake, I'd choke ere I would change

An article of breath with such a puckfist!
Come, let's be gone.

SUBTLE. Pray you le' me speak with you.

DAPPER. His worship calls you, Captain.

FACE. I am sorry
I e'er embarked myself in such a business.

DAPPER. Nay, good sir, he did call you.

FACE. Will he take, then?

SUBTLE. First, hear me——

FACE. Not a syllable, 'less you take.

SUBTLE. Pray ye, sir——

FACE. Upon no terms but an assumpsit.

SUBTLE. Your humour must be law.

Takes the money.

FACE. Why now, sir, talk;
Now I dare hear you with mine honour. Speak;
So may this gentleman too.

SUBTLE. Why, sir——

FACE. No whisp'ring.

SUBTLE. 'For Heav'n, you do not apprehend the loss
You do yourself in this.

FACE. Wherein? For what?

SUBTLE. Marry, to be so importunate for one
That, when he has it, will undo you all.
He'll win up all the money i' the town.

FACE. How?

SUBTLE. Yes, and blow up gamester after gamester,
As they do crackers in a puppet-play.
If I do give him a familiar,
Give you him all you play for; never set him;
For he will have it.

FACE. You're mistaken, Doctor.
Why, he does ask one but for cups and horses,
A rifling fly—none o' your great familiars.

DAPPER. Yes, Captain, I would have it for all
    games.

SUBTLE. I told you so.

FACE.   'Slight, that's a new business!—
I understood you, a tame bird, to fly
Twice in a term, or so, on Friday nights,
When you had left the office, for a nag
Of forty or fifty shillings.

DAPPER.   Ay, 'tis true, sir,
But I do think now I shall leave the law,
And therefore——

FACE.   Why, this changes quite the case.
D'you think that I dare move him?

DAPPER.   If you please, sir,
All's one to him, I see.

FACE.   What! for that money?
I cannot, with my conscience; nor should you
Make the request, methinks.

DAPPER.   No, sir, I mean
To add consideration.

FACE.   Why then, sir,
I'll try.— Say that it were for all games, Doctor?

SUBTLE. I say then, not a mouth shall eat for him
At any ordinary, but o' the score,
That is a gaming mouth, conceive me.

FACE.   Indeed!

SUBTLE. He'll draw you all the treasure of the
    realm,
If it be set him.

FACE.   Speak you this from art?

SUBTLE. Ay, sir, and reason too, the ground of art.
He's o' the only best complexion,
The Queen of Faery loves.

FACE.   What! is he?

SUBTLE.   Peace,
He'll overhear you. Sir, should she but see him——

FACE. What?

SUBTLE.   Do not you tell him.

FACE.   Will he win at cards too?

SUBTLE. The spirits of dead Holland, living Isaac,
You'd swear were in him; such a vigorous luck
As cannot be resisted. 'Slight, he'll put
Six o' your gallants to a cloak, indeed.

    FACE. A strange success, that some man shall be
      born to!

    SUBTLE. He hears you, man——

    DAPPER.   Sir, I'll not be ungrateful.

    FACE. Faith, I have confidence in his good nature.
You hear, he says he will not be ungrateful.

    SUBTLE. Why, as you please, my venture follows
      yours.

    FACE. Troth, do it, Doctor. Think him trusty, and
      make him.
He may make us both happy in an hour;
Win some five thousand pound, and send us two
    on't.

    DAPPER. Believe it, and I will, sir.

    FACE.   And you shall, sir.
                        Takes him aside.
You have heard all?

    DAPPER.   No, what was't? Nothing, I, sir.

    FACE. Nothing!

    DAPPER.   A little, sir.

    FACE.   Well, a rare star
Reigned at your birth.

    DAPPER.   At mine, sir! No.

    FACE.   The Doctor
Swears that you are——

    SUBTLE.   Nay, Captain, you'll tell all now.

    FACE. Allied to the Queen of Faery.

    DAPPER.   Who? that I am?
Believe it, no such matter——

FACE.   Yes, and that
Y' were born with a caul o' your head.

DAPPER.   Who says so?

FACE.   Come,
You know it well enough, though you dissemble it.

DAPPER. I' fac, I do not. You are mistaken.

FACE.   How!
Swear by your fac, and in a thing so known
Unto the Doctor? How shall we, sir, trust you
I' the other matter? Can we ever think,
When you have won five or six thousand pound,
You'll send us shares in't, by this rate?

DAPPER.   By Gad, sir,
I'll win ten thousand pound, and send you half.
I' fac's no oath.

SUBTLE.   No, no, he did but jest.

FACE. Go to. Go thank the Doctor. He's your friend
To take it so.

DAPPER.   I thank his worship.

FACE.   So!—
Another angel.

DAPPER.   Must I?

FACE.   Must you! 'Slight,
What else is thanks? Will you be trivial?—Doctor,
When must he come for his familiar?

DAPPER. Shall I not ha' it with me?

SUBTLE.   O, good sir!
There must a world of ceremonies pass;
You must be bathed and fumigated first.
Besides, the Queen of Faëry does not rise
Till it be noon.

FACE.   Not if she danced tonight.

SUBTLE. And she must bless it.

FACE.   Did you never see
Her royal Grace yet?

DAPPER. Whom?

FACE. Your aunt of Faery?

SUBTLE. Not since she kissed him in the cradle,
Captain;
I can resolve you that.

FACE. Well, see her Grace,
Whate'er it cost you, for a thing that I know!
It will be somewhat hard to compass, but
However, see her. You are made, believe it,
If you can see her. Her Grace is a lone woman,
And very rich; and if she take a fancy,
She will do strange things. See her, at any hand.
'Slid, she may hap to leave you all she has!
It is the Doctor's fear.

DAPPER. How will't be done, then?

FACE. Let me alone, take you no thought. Do you
But say to me, 'Captain, I'll see her Grace.'

DAPPER. Captain, I'll see her Grace.

FACE. Enough.
One knocks without.

SUBTLE. Who's there?
Anon.—Conduct him forth by the back way.—
Sir, against one o'clock prepare yourself;
Till when, you must be fasting; only take
Three drops of vinegar in at your nose,
Two at your mouth, and one at either ear;
Then bathe your fingers' ends and wash your eyes,
To sharpen your five senses; and cry 'hum'
Thrice, and then 'buzz' as often; and then, come.

FACE. Can you remember this?

DAPPER. I warrant you.

FACE. Well then, away. 'T is but your bestowing
Some twenty nobles 'mong her Grace's servants;
And put on a clean shirt. You do not know
What grace her Grace may do you in clean linen.
Exeunt FACE and DAPPER.

SUBTLE. Come in!—Goodwives, I pray you forbear
me now.
Troth, I can do you no good till afternoon——

Enter DRUGGER.

What is your name, say you, Abel Drugger?
  DRUGGER.   Yes, sir.
  SUBTLE. A seller of tobacco?
  DRUGGER.   Yes, sir.
  SUBTLE.   Hmh!
Free of the grocers?
  DRUGGER.   Ay, an't please you.
  SUBTLE.   Well——
Your business, Abel?
  DRUGGER.   This, an't please your worship:
I am a young beginner, and am building
Of a new shop, an't like your worship, just
At corner of a street,—here's the plot on't——
And I would know by art, sir, of your worship,
Which way I should make my door, by necromancy;
And where my shelves; and which should be for
   boxes,
And which for pots. I would be glad to thrive, sir.
And I was wished to your worship by a gentleman,
One Captain Face, that says you know men's planets,
And their good angels and their bad.
  SUBTLE.   I do,
If I do see 'em——

Re-enter FACE.

  FACE.   What! my honest Abel?
Thou art well met here.
  DRUGGER.   Troth, sir, I was speaking,
Just as your worship came here, of your worship.
I pray you speak for me to Master Doctor.

FACE. He shall do anything. Doctor, do you hear?
This is my friend Abel, an honest fellow;
He lets me have good tobacco, and he does not
Sophisticate it with sack-lees or oil,
Nor washes it in muscadel and grains,
Nor buries it in gravel underground,
Wrapped up in greasy leather, or pissed clouts;
But keeps it in fine lily-pots that, opened,
Smell like conserve of roses, or French beans.
He has his maple block, his silver tongs,
Winchester pipes, and fire of juniper—
A neat, spruce, honest fellow, and no goldsmith.

SUBTLE. He's a fortunate fellow, that I am sure
    on,—

FACE. Already, sir, ha' you found it? Lo thee, Abel!

SUBTLE. And in right way toward riches.

FACE.   Sir!

SUBTLE.   This summer
He will be of the clothing of his company,
And next spring called to the scarlet; spend what he
    can.

FACE. What, and so little beard?

SUBTLE.   Sir, you must think,
He may have a receipt to make hair come.
But he'll be wise—preserve his youth—and fine for 't;
His fortune looks for him another way.

FACE. 'Slid, Doctor, how canst thou know this so
    soon?
I am amused at that!

SUBTLE.   By a rule, Captain,
In metoposcopy, which I do work by;
A certain star i' the forehead, which you see not.
Your chestnut or your olive-coloured face
Does never fail, and your long ear doth promise.
I knew 't, by certain spots, too, in his teeth,
And on the nail of his mercurial finger.

FACE. Which finger's that?

SUBTLE.   His little finger. Look.—
Y' were born upon a Wednesday?

DRUGGER.   Yes indeed, sir.

SUBTLE. The thumb, in chiromancy, we give Venus,
The forefinger to Jove, the midst to Saturn,
The ring to Sol, the least to Mercury,
Who was the lord, sir, of his horoscope,
His house of life being Libra; which foreshowed
He should be a merchant, and should trade with
  balance.

FACE. Why, this is strange! Is it not, honest Nab?

SUBTLE. There is a ship now coming from Ormus,
That shall yield him such a commodity
Of drugs——This is the west, and this the south?

DRUGGER. Yes, sir.

SUBTLE.   And those are your two sides?

DRUGGER.   Ay, sir.

SUBTLE. Make me your door then south, your
  broad side west;
And on the east side of your shop, aloft,
Write Mathlai, Tarmiel, and Baraborat;
Upon the north part, Rael, Velel, Thiel.
They are the names of those mercurial spirits
That do fright flies from boxes.

DRUGGER.   Yes, sir.

SUBTLE.   And
Beneath your threshold, bury me a loadstone
To draw in gallants that wear spurs. The rest,
They'll seem to follow.

FACE.   That's a secret, Nab!

SUBTLE. And, on your stall, a puppet, with a vice,
And a court-fucus to call City dames.
You shall deal much with minerals.

DRUGGER.   Sir, I have,
At home, already——

SUBTLE.   Ay, I know you've ars'nic,
Vitriol, sal-tartar, argol, alkali,
Cinoper; I know all. This fellow, Captain,
Will come, in time, to be a great distiller,
And give a say—I will not say directly,
But very fair—at the Philosophers' Stone.
   FACE. Why, how now, Abel! Is this true?
   DRUGGER.   —Good Captain,
What must I give?
   FACE.   Nay, I'll not counsel thee.
Thou hear'st what wealth he says—spend what thou
    canst—
Thou'rt like to come to.
   DRUGGER.   I would gi' him a crown.
   FACE. A crown! and toward such a fortune? Heart,
Thou shalt rather gi' him thy shop. No gold about
    thee?
   DRUGGER. Yes, I have a portague, I ha' kept this
    half-year.
   FACE. Out on thee, Nab! 'Slight, there was such an
    offer—
Shalt keep't no longer, I'll gi'it him for thee.—
    Doctor,
Nab prays your worship to drink this, and swears
He will appear more grateful, as your skill
Does raise him in the world.
   DRUGGER.   I would entreat
Another favour of his worship.
   FACE.   What is't, Nab?
   DRUGGER. But to look over, sir, my almanac,
And cross out my ill days, that I may neither
Bargain nor trust upon them.
   FACE.   That he shall, Nab.
Leave it, it shall be done, 'gainst afternoon.
   SUBTLE. And a direction for his shelves.

FACE.   Now, Nab,
Art thou well pleased, Nab?
   DRUGGER.   Thank, sir, both your worships.
   FACE.   Away.
                          Exit DRUGGER.
Why, now, you smoky persecutor of nature!
Now do you see that something's to be done,
Beside your beech-coal, and your corsive waters,
Your crosslets, crucibles, and cucurbites?
You must have stuff, brought home to you, to work
    on!
And yet you think I am at no expense
In searching out these veins, then following 'em,
Then trying 'em out. 'Fore God, my intelligence
Costs me more money than my share oft comes to,
In these rare works.
   SUBTLE.   You're pleasant, sir.

              Re-enter DOLL.

                        How now!
What says my dainty Dolkin?
   DOLL.   Yonder fishwife
Will not away. And there's your giantess,
The bawd of Lambeth.
   SUBTLE.   Heart, I cannot speak with 'em.
   DOLL. Not afore night, I have told 'em, in a voice,
Thorough the trunk, like one of your familiars.
But I have spied Sir Epicure Mammon——
   SUBTLE.   Where?
   DOLL. Coming along, at far end of the lane,
Slow of his feet, but earnest of his tongue
To one that's with him.
   SUBTLE.   Face, go you and shift.
                        Exit FACE.
Doll, you must presently make ready too.
   DOLL. Why, what's the matter?

SUBTLE.   O, I did look for him
With the sun's rising; marvel he could sleep!
This is the day I am to perfect for him
The magisterium, our great work, the Stone;
And yield it, made, into his hands; of which
He has, this month, talked as he were possessed.
And now he's dealing pieces on't away.
Methinks I see him ent'ring ordinaries,
Dispensing for the pox; and plaguy houses,
Reaching his dose; walking Moorfields for lepers;
And off'ring citizen's wives pomander bracelets,
As his preservative, made of the elixir;
Searching the Spittle, to make old bawds young;
And the highways, for beggars, to make rich.
I see no end of his labours. He will make
Nature ashamed of her long sleep; when Art,
Who's but a step-dame, shall do more than she,
In her best love to mankind, ever could.
If his dream last, he'll turn the age to gold. *Exeunt.*

ACT TWO

Lovewit's house

Enter SIR EPICURE MAMMON *and* SURLY.

MAMMON. Come on, sir. Now you set your foot on
    shore
In Novo Orbe; here's the rich Peru,
And there within, sir, are the golden mines,
Great Solomon's Ophir! He was sailing to't
Three years, but we have reached it in ten months.
This is the day wherein, to all my friends,

I will pronounce the happy word, 'Be rich!'
This day you shall be spectatissimi.
You shall no more deal with the hollow die
Or the frail card. No more be at charge of keeping
The livery-punk for the young heir, that must
Seal, at all hours, in his shirt; no more,
If he deny, ha' him beaten to't, as he is
That brings him the commodity. No more
Shall thirst of satin, or the covetous hunger
Of velvet entrails for a rude-spun cloak,
To be displayed at Madam Augusta's, make
The sons of sword and hazard fall before
The golden calf, and on their knees, whole nights,
Commit idolatry with wine and trumpets;
Or go a-feasting after drum and ensign.
No more of this. You shall start up young viceroys,
And have your punks and punketees, my Surly.
And unto thee I speak it first: 'Be rich!'
Where is my Subtle, there? Within, ho!

    FACE. *Within.*   Sir,
He'll come to you by and by.

    MAMMON.   That's his fire-drake,
His lungs, his Zephyrus, he that puffs his coals
Till he firk nature up, in her own centre.
You are not faithful, sir. This night I'll change
All that is metal in my house to gold.
And early in the morning will I send
To all the plumbers and the pewterers,
And buy their tin and lead up; and to Lothbury,
For all the copper.

    SURLY.   What, and turn that, too?

    MAMMON. Yes, and I'll purchase Devonshire and
        Cornwall,
And make them perfect Indies! You admire now?

    SURLY. No, faith.

MAMMON.   But when you see th' effects of
    the great med'cine,
Of which one part, projected on a hundred
Of Mercury, or Venus, or the moon,
Shall turn it to as many of the sun—
Nay, to a thousand—so, ad infinitum;
You will believe me.
    SURLY.   Yes, when I see't, I will.
But if my eyes do cozen me so, and I
Giving 'em no occasion, sure I'll have
'A whore, shall piss 'em out next day.
    MAMMON.   Ha! Why?
Do you think I fable with you? I assure you,
He that has once the flower of the sun,
The perfect ruby, which we call elixir,
Not only can do that, but by its virtue,
Can confer honour, love, respect, long life;
Give safety, valour, yea, and victory,
To whom he will. In eight and twenty days,
I'll make an old man of fourscore a child.
    SURLY. No doubt, he's that already.
    MAMMON.   Nay, I mean,
Restore his years; renew him, like an eagle,
To the fifth age; make him get sons and daughters,
Young giants, as our philosophers have done,—
The ancient patriarchs afore the flood—
But taking, once a week, on a knife's point,
The quantity of a grain of mustard of it;
Becomes stout Marses, and beget young Cupids.
    SURLY. The decayed vestals of Picthatch would
    thank you,
That keep the fire alive there.
    MAMMON.   'Tis the secret
Of nature, naturized 'gainst all infections;
Cures all diseases coming of all causes,
A month's grief in a day, a year's in twelve,

And, of what age soever, in a month;
Past all the doses of your drugging doctors.
I'll undertake, withal, to fright the plague
Out o' the kingdom in three months.

    SURLY.   And I'll
Be bound, the players shall sing your praises then,
Without their poets.

    MAMMON.   Sir, I'll do't. Meantime,
I'll give away so much, unto my man,
Shall serve th' whole city with preservative
Weekly, each house his dose, and at the rate——

    SURLY. As he that built the waterwork does with
       water?

    MAMMON. You are incredulous.

    SURLY.   Faith, I have a humour,
I would not willingly be gulled. Your Stone
Cannot transmute me.

    MAMMON.   Pertinax, my Surly,
Will you believe antiquity? records?
I'll show you a book where Moses, and his sister,
And Solomon have written of the art;
Ay, and a treatise penned by Adam——

    SURLY.   How!

    MAMMON. O' the Philosophers' Stone, and in High
       Dutch.

    SURLY. Did Adam write, sir, in High Dutch?

    MAMMON.   He did;
Which proves it was the primitive tongue

    SURLY.   What paper?

    MAMMON. On cedar board.

    SURLY.   O, that indeed, they say,
Will last 'gainst worms.

    MAMMON.   'Tis like your Irish wood,
'Gainst cobwebs. I have a piece of Jason's fleece too,
Which was no other than a book of alchemy,
Writ in large sheepskin, a good fat ram-vellum.

Such was Pythagoras' thigh, Pandora's tub,
And all that fable of Medea's charms,
The manner of our work: the bulls, our furnace,
Still breathing fire; our argent-vive, the dragon;
The dragon's teeth, mercury sublimate,
That keeps the whiteness, hardness, and the biting;
And they are gathered into Jason's helm,
Th' alembic, and then sowed in Mars's field,
And thence sublimed so often, till they are fixed.
Both this, th' Hesperian garden, Cadmus' story,
Jove's shower, the boon of Midas, Argus' eyes,
Boccace's Demogorgon, thousands more,
All abstract riddles of our Stone.

Enter FACE *as a servant.*

                                        How now!
Do we succeed? Is our day come? and holds it?
    FACE. The evening will set red upon you, sir;
You have colour for it, crimson; the red ferment
Has done his office. Three hours hence prepare you
To see projection.
    MAMMON.   Pertinax, my Surly,
Again I say to thee aloud, 'Be rich!'
This day thou shalt have ingots, and tomorrow
Give lords th' affront.—Is it, my Zephyrus, right?
Blushes the bolt's-head?
    FACE.   Like a wench with child, sir,
That were but now discovered to her master.
    MAMMON. Excellent, witty Lungs! My only care is
Where to get stuff enough now, to project on;
This town will not half serve me.
    FACE.   No, sir? Buy
The covering off o' churches.
    MAMMON.   That's true.
    FACE.   Yes.
Let 'em stand bare, as do their auditory;
Or cap 'em new with shingles.

MAMMON. No, good thatch—
Thatch will lie light upo' the rafters, Lungs.
Lungs, I will manumit thee from the furnace;
I will restore thee thy complexion, Puff,
Lost in the embers; and repair this brain,
Hurt wi' the fume o' the metals.

FACE. I have blown, sir,
Hard, for your worship; thrown by many a coal,
When 'twas not beech; weighed those I put in just,
To keep your heat still even. These bleared eyes
Have waked to read your several colours, sir,
Of the Pale Citron, the Green Lion, the Crow,
The Peacock's Tail, the Plumèd Swan.

MAMMON. And lastly,
Thou hast descried the flower, the Sanguis Agni?

FACE. Yes, sir.

MAMMON. Where's Master?

FACE. At's prayers, sir, he;
Good man, he's doing his devotions
For the success.

MAMMON. Lungs, I will set a period
To all thy labours: thou shalt be the master
Of my seraglio.

FACE. Good, sir.

MAMMON. But do you hear?
I'll geld you, Lungs.

FACE. Yes, sir.

MAMMON. For I do mean
To have a list of wives and concubines
Equal with Solomon, who had the Stone
Alike with me; and I will make me a back,
With the elixir, that shall be as tough
As Hercules, to encounter fifty a night.
Th' art sure thou saw'st it blood?

FACE. Both blood and spirit, sir.

MAMMON. I will have all my beds blown up, not
stuffed—

Down is too hard. And then, mine oval room
Filled with such pictures as Tiberius took
From Elephantis, and dull Aretine
But coldly imitated. Then, my glasses
Cut in more subtle angles, to disperse
And multiply the figures, as I walk
Naked between my succubae. My mists
I'll have of perfume, vapoured 'bout the room,
To lose ourselves in; and my baths, like pits
To fall into, from whence we will come forth,
And roll us dry in gossamer and roses.—
Is it arrived at ruby?——Where I spy
A wealthy citizen, or rich lawyer,
Have a sublimed, pure wife, unto that fellow
I'll send a thousand pound to be my cuckold.

   FACE. And I shall carry it?

   MAMMON.   No. I'll ha' no bawds
But fathers and mothers—they will do it best,
Best of all others. And my flatterers
Shall be the pure and gravest of divines
That I can get for money. My mere fools
Eloquent burgesses, and then my poets
The same that writ so subtly of the fart,
Whom I will entertain still for that subject.
The few that would give out themselves to be
Court- and town-stallions, and eachwhere bely
Ladies who are known most innocent for them,
Those will I beg, to make me eunuchs of;
And they shall fan me with ten estrich tails
Apiece, made in a plume to gather wind.
We will be brave, Puff, now we ha' the med'cine.
My meat shall all come in, in Indian shells,
Dishes of agate, set in gold, and studded
With emeralds, sapphires, hyacinths, and rubies.
The tongues of carps, dormice, and camels' heels,

Boiled i' the spirit of Sol, and dissolved pearl,—
Apicius' diet, 'gainst the epilepsy—
And I will eat these broths with spoons of amber,
Headed with diamond and carbuncle.
My footboy shall eat pheasants, calvered salmons,
Knots, godwits, lampreys; I myself will have
The beards of barbels served, instead of salads;
Oiled mushrooms; and the swelling, unctuous paps
Of a fat, pregnant sow, newly cut off,
Dressed with an exquisite and poignant sauce,
For which I'll say unto my cook, 'There's gold;
Go forth, and be a knight!'

    FACE.   Sir, I'll go look
A little, how it heightens.   *Exit.*

    MAMMON.   Do.—My shirts
I'll have of taffeta-sarsnet, soft and light
As cobwebs; and for all my other raiment,
It shall be such as might provoke the Persian,
Were he to teach the world riot anew.
My gloves of fishes' and birds' skins, perfumed
With gums of paradise, and eastern air——

    SURLY. And do you think to have the Stone with
      this?

    MAMMON. No, I do think t' have all this with the
      Stone.

    SURLY. Why, I have heard he must be homo frugi,
A pious, holy, and religious man,
One free from mortal sin, a very virgin.

    MAMMON. That makes it, sir, he is so. But I buy it;
My venture brings it me. He, honest wretch,
A notable, superstitious, good soul,
Has worn his knees bare, and his slippers bald,
With prayer and fasting for it. And, sir, let him
Do it alone, for me, still. Here he comes.
Not a profane word afore him; 'tis poison.

Enter SUBTLE.

Good morrow, father.

SUBTLE.   Gentle son, good morrow,
And to your friend there. What is he, is with you?

MAMMON. An heretic, that I did bring along,
In hope, sir, to convert him.

SUBTLE.   Son, I doubt
You're covetous, that thus you meet your time
I' the just point; prevent your day at morning.
This argues something worthy of a fear
Of importune and carnal appetite.
Take heed you do not cause the blessing leave you,
With your ungoverned haste. I should be sorry
To see my labours, now e'en at perfection,
Got by long watching and large patience,
Not prosper where my love and zeal hath placed 'em.
Which—Heaven I call to witness, with yourself,
To whom I have poured my thoughts—in all my
        ends,
Have looked no way, but unto public good,
To pious uses, and dear charity,
Now grown a prodigy with men. Wherein
If you, my son, should now prevaricate,
And to your own particular lusts employ
So great and catholic a bliss, be sure
A curse will follow, yea, and overtake
Your subtle and most secret ways.

MAMMON.   I know, sir,
You shall not need to fear me. I but come
To ha' you confute this gentleman.

SURLY.   Who is,
Indeed, sir, somewhat costive of belief
Toward your Stone; would not be gulled.

SUBTLE.   Well, son,
All that I can convince him in, is this:

The work is done; bright Sol is in his robe.
We have a med'cine of the triple soul,
The glorifièd spirit. Thanks be to Heaven,
And make us worthy of it!—Eulenspiegel!

FACE. Anon, sir.

SUBTLE.   Look well to the register.
And let your heat still lessen by degrees,
To the aludels.

FACE.   Yes, sir.

SUBTLE.   Did you look
O' the bolt's-head yet?

FACE.   Which? on D., sir?

SUBTLE.   Ay,
What's the complexion?

FACE.   Whitish.

SUBTLE.   Infuse vinegar,
To draw his volatile substance and his tincture;
And let the water in glass E. be filtered,
And put into the Gripe's Egg. Lute him well,
And leave him closed in balneo.

FACE.   I will, sir.

SURLY. What a brave language here is! next to
    canting!

SUBTLE. I have another work you never saw, son,
That, three days since, passed the Philosophers'
    Wheel,
In the lent heat of Athanor, and's become
Sulphur o' Nature.

MAMMON.   But 'tis for me?

SUBTLE.   What need you?
You have enough in that is perfect.

MAMMON.   O, but——

SUBTLE. Why, this is covetise!

MAMMON.   No, I assure you,
I shall employ it all in pious uses,
Founding of colleges and grammar-schools,

Marrying young virgins, building hospitals,
And now and then a church.

Re-enter FACE.

SUBTLE. How now!

FACE. Sir, please you,
Shall I not change the filter?

SUBTLE. Marry, yes,
And bring me the complexion of glass B. *Exit* FACE.

MAMMON. Ha' you another?

SUBTLE. Yes, son, were I assured
Your piety were firm, we would not want
The means to glorify it. But I hope the best.
I mean to tinct C. in sand-heat tomorrow,
And give him imbibition.

MAMMON. Of white oil?

SUBTLE. No, sir, of red. F. is come over the helm,
   too,—
I thank my Maker—in Saint Mary's bath,
And shows Lac Virginis. Blessèd be Heaven!
I sent you of his faeces there calcined.
Out of that calx, I ha' won the salt of mercury.

MAMMON. By pouring on your rectifièd water?

SUBTLE. Yes, and reverberating in Athanor.

Re-enter FACE.

How now! what colour says it?

FACE. The ground black, sir.

MAMMON. That's your crow's-head.

SURLY. —Your coxcomb's, is it not?

SUBTLE. No, 'tis not perfect. Would it were the
   Crow!
That work wants something.

SURLY. —O, I looked for this.
The hay is a-pitching.

SUBTLE.   Are you sure you loosed 'em
I' their own menstrue?

FACE.   Yes, sir, and then married 'em;
And put 'em in a bolt's-head, nipped to digestion,
According as you bade me, when I set
The liquor of Mars to circulation
In the same heat.

SUBTLE.   The process then was right.

FACE. Yes, by the token, sir, the retort brake,
And what was saved was put into the Pelican,
And signed with Hermes' seal.

SUBTLE.   I think 'twas so.
We should have a new amalgama.

SURLY.   —O, this ferret
Is rank as any polecat.

SUBTLE.   But I care not.
Let him e'en die; we have enough beside,
In embryon. H. has his white shirt on?

FACE.   Yes, sir,
He's ripe for inceration; he stands warm,
In his ash-fire. I would not you should let
Any die now, if I might counsel, sir,
For luck's sake to the rest. It is not good.

MAMMON. He says right.

SURLY.   —Ay, are you bolted?

FACE.   Nay, I know't, sir,
I've seen th' ill fortune. What is some three ounces
Of fresh materials?

MAMMON.   Is't no more?

FACE.   No more, sir,
Of gold, t' amalgam with some six of mercury.

MAMMON. Away, here's money. What will serve?

FACE.   Ask him, sir.

MAMMON. How much?

SUBTLE.   Give him nine pound—you may gi'
    him ten.

SURLY. Yes, twenty, and be cozened, do.

MAMMON.   There 'tis.

SUBTLE. This needs not, but that you will have it so,
To see conclusions of all; for two
Of our inferior works are at fixation,
A third is in ascension.—Go your ways.
Ha' you set the oil of Luna in chymia?

FACE. Yes, sir.

SUBTLE.   And the Philosophers' Vinegar?

FACE.   Ay. *Exit.*

SURLY. We shall have a salad!

MAMMON.   When do you make projection?

SUBTLE. Son, be not hasty. I exalt our med'cine,
By hanging him in balneo vaporoso,
And giving him solution; then congeal him;
And then dissolve him; then again congeal him.
For look, how oft I iterate the work,
So many times I add unto his virtue.
As, if at first, one ounce convert a hundred,
After his second loose, he'll turn a thousand;
His third solution, ten; his fourth, a hundred;
After his fifth, a thousand thousand ounces
Of any imperfect metal, into pure
Silver or gold, in all examinations,
As good as any of the natural mine.
Get you your stuff here, against afternoon,
Your brass, your pewter, and your andirons.

MAMMON. Not those of iron?

SUBTLE.   Yes, you may bring them too;
We'll change all metals.

SURLY.   I believe you in that.

MAMMON. Then I may send my spits?

SUBTLE.   Yes, and your racks.

SURLY. And dripping-pans, and pot-hangers, and
    hooks?
Shall he not?

SUBTLE. If he please.

SURLY. To be an ass.

SUBTLE. How, sir!

MAMMON. This gent'man you must bear withal.
I told you he had no faith.

SURLY. And little hope, sir,
But much less charity, should I gull myself.

SUBTLE. Why, what have you observed, sir, in our
   art,
Seems so impossible?

SURLY. But your whole work, no more:
That you should hatch gold in a furnace, sir,
As they do eggs in Egypt!

SUBTLE. Sir, do you
Believe that eggs are hatched so?

SURLY. If I should?

SUBTLE. Why, I think that the greater miracle.
No egg but differs from a chicken more
Than metals in themselves.

SURLY. That cannot be.
The egg's ordained by nature to that end,
And is a chicken in potentia.

SUBTLE. The same we say of lead, and other metals,
Which would be gold if they had time.

MAMMON. And that
Our art doth further.

SUBTLE. Ay, for 'twere absurd
To think that nature, in the earth, bred gold
Perfect, i' the instant. Something went before.
There must be remote matter.

SURLY. Ay, what is that?

SUBTLE. Marry, we say——

MAMMON. Ay, now it heats! Stand, father,
Pound him to dust.

SUBTLE. It is, of the one part,
A humid exhalation, which we call
Materia liquida, or the unctuous water;

On th' other part, a certain crass and viscous
Portion of earth; both which, concorporate,
Do make the elementary matter of gold;
Which is not yet propria materia,
But common to all metals and all stones.
For, where it is forsaken of that moisture,
And hath more dryness, it becomes a stone;
Where it retains more of the humid fatness,
If turns to sulphur, or to quicksilver,
Who are the parents of all other metals.
Nor can this remote matter suddenly
Progress so from extreme unto extreme,
As to grow gold, and leap o'er all the means.
Nature doth first beget th' imperfect, then
Proceeds she to the perfect. Of that airy
And oily water, mercury is engendered;
Sulphur o' the fat and earthy part—the one
Which is the last, supplying the place of male;
The other, of the female, in all metals.
Some do believe hermaphrodeity,
That both do act and suffer. But these two
Make the rest ductile, malleable, extensive.
And even in gold they are, for we do find
Seeds of them by our fire, and gold in them;
And can produce the species of each metal
More perfect thence, than nature doth in earth.
Beside, who doth not see, in daily practice,
Art can beget bees, hornets, beetles, wasps,
Out of the carcases and dung of creatures;
Yea, scorpions of an herb, being rightly placed?
And these are living creatures, far more perfect
And excellent than metals.

    MAMMON.   Well said, father!—
Nay, if he take you in hand, sir, with an argument.
He'll bray you in a mortar.

SURLY.   Pray you, sir, stay.
Rather than I'll be brayed, sir, I'll believe
That alchemy is a pretty kind of game,
Somewhat like tricks o' the cards, to cheat a man
With charming.
    SUBTLE.   Sir?
    SURLY.   What else are all your terms,
Whereon no one o' your writers 'grees with other?
Of your elixir, your Lac Virginis,
Your Stone, your med'cine, and your chrysosperm,
Your sal, your sulphur, and your mercury,
Your oil of height, your Tree of Life, your blood,
Your marcasite, your tutie, your magnesia,
Your Toad, your Crow, your Dragon, and your
     Panther,
Your sun, your moon, your firmament, your adrop,
Your lato, azoch, zarnich, kibrit, heautarit,
And then your Red Man, and your White Woman,
With all your broths, your menstrues, and materials
Of piss and egg-shells, women's terms, man's blood,
Hair o' the head, burnt clouts, chalk, merds, and
     clay,
Powder of bones, scalings of iron, glass,
And worlds of other strange ingredients,
Would burst a man to name?
    SUBTLE.   And all these named,
Intending but one thing; which art our writers
Used to obscure their art.
    MAMMON.   Sir, so I told him—
Because the simple idiot should not learn it,
And make it vulgar.
    SUBTLE.   Was not all the knowledge
Of the Egyptians writ in mystic symbols?
Speak not the scriptures oft in parables?
Are not the choicest fables of the poets,

That were the fountains and first springs of wisdom,
Wrapped in perplexèd allegories?

MAMMON.   I urged that,
And cleared to him, that Sisyphus was damned
To roll the ceaseless stone, only because
He would have made ours common. DOLL *is seen.*
    Who is this?

    SUBTLE. God's precious! What do you mean? Go
    in, good lady,
Let me entreat you.—Where's this varlet?

Re-enter FACE.

    FACE.   Sir.
    SUBTLE. You very knave! do you use me thus?
    FACE.   Wherein, sir?
    SUBTLE. Go in and see, you traitor. Go!   *Exit* FACE.
    MAMMON.   Who is it, sir?
    SUBTLE. Nothing, sir; nothing.
    MAMMON.   What's the matter, good sir?
I have not seen you thus distempered. Who is't?

    SUBTLE. All arts have still had, sir, their adver-
        saries,
But ours the most ignorant.

Re-enter FACE.

                            What now?
    FACE. 'Twas not my fault, sir, she would speak
    with you.
    SUBTLE. Would she, sir? Follow me.   *Exit.*
    MAMMON.   Stay, Lungs.
    FACE.   I dare not, sir.
    MAMMON. Stay, man; what is she?
    FACE.   A lord's sister, sir.
    MAMMON. How! pray thee, stay.
    FACE.   She's mad, sir, and sent hither—
He'll be mad, too.

MAMMON.   I warrant thee. Why sent hither?

FACE. Sir, to be cured.

SUBTLE.   Why, rascal!

FACE.   Lo you—Here, sir!

Exit.

MAMMON. 'Fore God, a Bradamante, a brave piece!

SURLY. Heart, this is a bawdy-house! I'll be burnt
else.

MAMMON. O, by this light, no. Do not wrong him.
He's
Too scrupulous that way. It is his vice.
No, he's a rare physician, do him right,
An excellent Paracelsian; and has done
Strange cures with mineral physic. He deals all
With spirits, he. He will not hear a word
Of Galen, or his tedious recipes.

Re-enter FACE.

How now, Lungs!

FACE.   Softly, sir, speak softly. I meant
To ha' told your worship all.—This must not hear.

MAMMON. No, he will not be gulled; let him alone.

FACE. You're very right, sir, she is a most rare
scholar,
And is gone mad with studying Broughton's works.
If you but name a word touching the Hebrew,
She falls into her fit, and will discourse
So learnedly of genealogies,
As you would run mad, too, to hear her, sir.

MAMMON. How might one do t' have conference
with her, Lungs?

FACE. O, divers have run mad upon the confer-
ence;
I do not know, sir. I am sent in haste
To fetch a vial.

SURLY.   Be not gulled, Sir Mammon.

MAMMON. Wherein? Pray ye, be patient.

SURLY.   Yes, as you are;
And trust confederate knaves and bawds and whores.

MAMMON. You are too foul, believe it.—Come here,
    Eulen,
One word.

FACE.   I dare not, in good faith.

MAMMON.   Stay, knave.

FACE. He's extreme angry that you saw her, sir.

MAMMON. Drink that. *Gives him money.* What is
    she when she's out of her fit?

FACE. O, the most affablest creature, sir! so merry!
So pleasant! She'll mount you up, like quicksilver
Over the helm, and circulate like oil,
A very vegetal; discourse of state,
Of mathematics, bawdry, anything——

MAMMON. Is she no way accessible? no means,
No trick to give a man a taste of her——
Wit——or so?

SUBTLE.   Eulen!

FACE.   I'll come to you again, sir. *Exit.*

MAMMON. Surly, I did not think one o' your breed-
    ing
Would traduce personages of worth.

SURLY.   Sir Epicure,
Your friend to use; yet still loath to be gulled.
I do not like your philosophical bawds.
Their Stone is lechery enough to pay for,
Without this bait.

MAMMON.   Heart, you abuse yourself.
I know the lady, and her friends, and means,
The original of this disaster. Her brother
Has told me all.

SURLY.   And yet you ne'er saw her
Till now?

MAMMON. O yes, but I forgot. I have—believe it—
One o' the treacherous't memories, I do think,
Of all mankind.

    SURLY.   What call you her—brother?

    MAMMON.   My Lord——
He wi' not have his name known, now I think on't.

    SURLY. A very treacherous memory!

    MAMMON.   O' my faith——

    SURLY. Tut, if you have it not about you, pass it,
Till we meet next.

    MAMMON.   Nay, by this hand, 'tis true.
He's one I honour, and my noble friend,
And I respect his house.

    SURLY.   Heart! can it be
That a grave sir, a rich, that has no need,
A wise sir, too, at other times, should thus,
With his own oaths and arguments, make hard
    mean
To gull himself? An this be your elixir,
Your lapis mineralis, and your lunary,
Give me your honest trick yet at primero,
Or gleek; and take your lutum sapientis,
Your menstruum simplex! I'll have gold before you,
And with less danger of the quicksilver,
Or the hot sulphur.

Re-enter FACE.

    FACE. *To* SURLY. Here's one from Captain Face, sir.
Desires you meet him i' the Temple Church,
Some half-hour hence, and upon earnest business.

                      Whispers MAMMON.
Sir, if you please to quit us now, and come
Again within two hours, you shall have
My master busy examining o' the works;
And I will steal you in, unto the party,

That you may see her converse.—Sir, shall I say
You'll meet the Captain's worship?

SURLY.　　　　　　　　　　Sir, I will.—
But, by attorney, and to a second purpose.
Now I am sure it is a bawdy-house;
I'll swear it, were the Marshal here to thank me!
The naming this commander doth confirm it.
Don Face! Why, he's the most authentic dealer
I' these commodities, the superintendent
To all the quainter traffickers in town!
He is their visitor, and does appoint
Who lies with whom, and at what hour, what price,
Which gown, and in what smock, what fall, what
　　　tire.
Him will I prove, by a third person, to find
The subtleties of this dark labyrinth;
Which if I do discover, dear Sir Mammon,
You'll give your poor friend leave, though no phi-
　　　losopher,
To laugh; for you that are, 'tis thought, shall weep.
　FACE. Sir, he does pray you'll not forget.
SURLY.　　　　　　　　　　I will not, sir.
Sir Epicure, I shall leave you.　　　　　　*Exit.*
　MAMMON.　　　　　　I follow you straight.
　FACE. But do so, good sir, to avoid suspicion.
This gent'man has a parlous head.
　MAMMON.　　　　　　　But wilt thou, Eulen,
Be constant to thy promise?
　FACE.　　　　　　　As my life, sir.
　MAMMON. And wilt thou insinuate what I am, and
　　　praise me,
And say I am a noble fellow?
　FACE.　　　　　　　O, what else, sir?
And that you'll make her royal with the Stone,
An empress; and yourself King of Bantam.
　MAMMON. Wilt thou do this?

FACE.   Will I, sir?

MAMMON.   Lungs, my Lungs!
I love thee.

FACE.   Send your stuff, sir, that my master
May busy himself about projection.

MAMMON. Th' ast witched me, rogue, Take, go.

FACE.   Your jack, and all, sir.

MAMMON. Thou art a villain—I will send my jack,
And the weights too. Slave, I could bite thine ear.
Away, thou dost not care for me.

FACE.   Not I, sir?

MAMMON. Come, I was born to make thee, my
    good weasel;
Set thee on a bench, and ha' thee twirl a chain
With the best lord's vermin of 'em all.

FACE.   Away, sir.

MAMMON. A count, nay, a count palatine——

FACE.   Good sir, go.

MAMMON. Shall not advance thee better; no, nor
    faster.   *Exit.*

Re-enter SUBTLE *and* DOLL.

SUBTLE. Has he bit? has he bit?

FACE.   And swallowed, too, my Subtle.
I ha' giv'n him line, and now he plays, i' faith.

SUBTLE. And shall we twitch him?

FACE.   Thorough both the gills.
A wench is a rare bait, with which a man
No sooner's taken, but he straight firks mad.

SUBTLE. Doll, my Lord Whatchum's sister, you
    must now
Bear yourself statelich.

DOLL.   O, let me alone.
I'll not forget my race, I warrant you.
I'll keep my distance, laugh and talk aloud;

Have all the tricks of a proud, scurvy lady,
And be as rude's her woman.

  FACE.   Well said, Sanguine!

  SUBTLE. But will he send his andirons?

  FACE.   His jack, too,
And's iron shoeing-horn. I ha' spoke to him. Well,
I must not lose my wary gamester yonder.

  SUBTLE. O, Monsieur Caution, that will not be
  gulled?

  FACE. Ay, if I can strike a fine hook into him now,
The Temple Church, there I have cast mine angle.
Well, pray for me. I'll about it.   *One knocks.*

  SUBTLE.   What, more gudgeons!
Doll, scout, scout!—Stay, Face, you must go to the
  door.
Pray God it be my Anabaptist—Who is't, Doll?

  DOLL. I know him not. He looks like a gold-end
  man.

  SUBTLE. God's so'! 'tis he; he said he would send.
  What call you him,
The sanctifièd elder, that should deal
For Mammon's jack and andirons? Let him in.
Stay, help me off, first, with my gown. *Exit* FACE.
  Away,
Madam, to your withdrawing chamber. *Exit* DOLL.
  Now,
In a new tune, new gesture, but old language.
This fellow is sent from one negotiates with me
About the Stone, too, for the holy Brethren
Of Amsterdam, the exiled Saints, that hope
To raise their discipline by it. I must use him
In some strange fashion now, to make him admire
  me.

Enter ANANIAS.

Where is my drudge?

Re-enter FACE.

FACE. Sir!

SUBTLE. Take away the recipient,
And rectify your menstrue from the phlegma.
Then pour it o' the Sol, in the cucurbite,
And let 'em macerate together.

FACE. Yes, sir.
And save the ground?

SUBTLE. No. Terra damnata
Must not have entrance in the work.—Who are you?

ANANIAS. A faithful Brother, if it please you.

SUBTLE. What's that?
A Lullianist? a Ripley? Filius artis?
Can you sublime and dulcify? calcine?
Know you the sapor pontic? sapor styptic?
Or what is homogene or heterogene?

ANANIAS. I understand no heathen language, truly.

SUBTLE. Heathen? you Knipperdoling! is Ars Sacra,
Or chrysopoeia, or spagyrica,
Or the pamphysic, or panarchic knowledge,
A heathen language?

ANANIAS. Heathen Greek, I take it.

SUBTLE. How! heathen Greek?

ANANIAS. All's heathen but the Hebrew.

SUBTLE. Sirrah my varlet, stand you forth and
speak to him
Like a philosopher. Answer i' the language.
Name the vexations and the martyrizations
Of metals in the work.

FACE. Sir, putrefaction,
Solution, ablution, sublimation,
Cohobation, calcination, ceration, and
Fixation.

SUBTLE. This is heathen Greek to you now?—
And when comes vivification?

FACE. After mortification.

SUBTLE. What's cohobation?

FACE. 'Tis the pouring on
Your Aqua Regis, and then drawing him off,
To the trine circle of the Seven Spheres.

SUBTLE. What's the proper passion of metals?

FACE. Malleation.

SUBTLE. What's your ultimum supplicium auri?

FACE. Antimonium.

SUBTLE. This's heathen Greek to you?—And what's
your mercury?

FACE. A very fugitive, he will be gone, sir.

SUBTLE. How know you him?

FACE. By his viscosity,
His oleosity, and his suscitability.

SUBTLE. How do you sublime him?

FACE. With the calx of egg-shells,
White marble, talc.

SUBTLE. Your magisterium now,
What's that?

FACE. Shifting, sir, your elements,
Dry into cold, cold into moist, moist in-
To hot, hot into dry.

SUBTLE. This's heathen Greek to you still?—
Your Lapis Philosophicus?

FACE. 'Tis a stone
And not a stone, a spirit, a soul, and a body;
Which if you do dissolve, it is dissolved;
If you coagulate, it is coagulated;
If you make it to fly, it flieth.

SUBTLE. Enough. *Exit* FACE.
This's heathen Greek to you? What are you, sir?

ANANIAS. Please you, a servant of the exiled
Brethren,
That deal with widows' and with orphans' goods,

And make a just account unto the Saints—
A deacon.

    SUBTLE. O, you are sent from Master Wholesome,
Your teacher?

    ANANIAS. From Tribulation Wholesome,
Our very zealous pastor.

    SUBTLE. Good! I have
Some orphans' goods to come here.

    ANANIAS. Of what kind, sir?

    SUBTLE. Pewter and brass, andirons and kitchen-
    ware,
Metals that we must use our med'cine on;
Wherein the Brethren may have a penn'orth
For ready money.

    ANANIAS. Were the orphans' parents
Sincere professors?

    SUBTLE. Why do you ask?

    ANANIAS. Because
We then are to deal justly, and give, in truth,
Their utmost value.

    SUBTLE. 'Slid, you'd cozen else,
And if their parents were not of the faithful!
I will not trust you, now I think on it,
Till I ha' talked with your pastor. Ha' you brought
    money
To buy more coals?

    ANANIAS. No, surely.

    SUBTLE. No! How so?

    ANANIAS. The Brethren bid me say unto you, sir,
Surely, they will not venture any more
Till they may see projection.

    SUBTLE. How!

    ANANIAS. You've had,
For the instruments, as bricks and loam and glasses,
Already thirty pound; and for materials,

They say, some ninety more; and they have heard
    since,
That one at Heidelberg made it of an egg
And a small paper of pin-dust.

    SUBTLE.   What's your name?

    ANANIAS. My name is Ananias.

    SUBTLE.   Out, the varlet
That cozened the Apostles! Hence, away!
Flee, mischief! Had your holy consistory
No name to send me of another sound,
Than wicked Ananias? Send your elders
Hither, to make atonement for you, quickly,
And gi' me satisfaction; or out goes
The fire, and down th' alembics and the furnace,
Piger Henricus, or what not. Thou wretch!
Both sericon and bufo shall be lost,
Tell 'em. All hope of rooting out the bishops
Or th' Antichristian hierarchy, shall perish,
If they stay threescore minutes. The aqueity,
Terreity, and sulphureity
Shall run together again, and all be annulled,
Thou wicked Ananias! *Exit* ANANIAS. This will fetch
    'em,
And make 'em haste towards their gulling more.
A man must deal like a rough nurse, and fright
Those that are froward, to an appetite.

Re-enter FACE *in his uniform, followed by* DRUGGER.

    FACE. He's busy with his spirits, but we'll upon
      him.

    SUBTLE. How now! what mates, what Bayards ha'
      we here?

    FACE. I told you he would be furious.—Sir, here's
      Nab
Has brought y' another piece of gold to look on.—

We must appease him. Give it me.—And prays you,
You would devise—what is it, Nab?

    DRUGGER.   A sign, sir.

    FACE. Ay, a good lucky one, a thriving sign,
      Doctor.

    SUBTLE. I was devising now.

    FACE.   —'Slight, do not say so,
He will repent he ga' you any more.—
What say you to his constellation, Doctor,
The Balance?

    SUBTLE.   No, that way is stale and common.
A townsman, born in Taurus, gives the bull,
Or the bull's head; in Aries, the ram.
A poor device! No, I will have his name
Formed in some mystic character, whose radii,
Striking the senses of the passers-by,
Shall, by a virtual influence, breed affections
That may result upon the party owns it;
As thus——

    FACE.   Nab!

    SUBTLE.   He shall have a bell, that's 'Abel';
And by it standing one whose name is Dee,
In a rug gown, there's D. and rug, that's 'Drug';
And right anenst him a dog snarling 'Er';
There's 'Drugger,' 'Abel Drugger.' That's his sign;
And here's now mystery and hieroglyphic!

    FACE. Abel, thou art made.

    DRUGGER.   Sir, I do thank his worship.

    FACE. Six o' thy legs more will not do it, Nab.—
He has brought you a pipe of tobacco, Doctor.

    DRUGGER.   Yes, sir.
I have another thing I would impart——

    FACE. Out with it, Nab.

    DRUGGER.   Sir, there is lodged, hard by me,
A rich young widow——

    FACE.   Good! a bona roba?

DRUGGER. But nineteen, at the most.

FACE.   Very good, Abel.

DRUGGER. Marry, she's not in fashion yet; she wears
A hood, but't stands a-cop.

FACE.   No matter, Abel.

DRUGGER. And I do now and then give her a
    fucus——

FACE. What! dost thou deal, Nab?

SUBTLE.   I did tell you, Captain.

DRUGGER. And physic too, sometime, sir; for which
    she trusts me
With all her mind. She's come up here of purpose
To learn the fashion.

FACE.   Good—his match too!—On, Nab.

DRUGGER. And she does strangely long to know her
    fortune.

FACE. God's lid, Nab! send her to the Doctor,
    hither.

DRUGGER. Yes, I have spoke to her of his worship
    already;
But she's afraid it will be blown abroad,
And hurt her marriage.

FACE.   Hurt it! 'tis the way
To heal it, if 'twere hurt; to make it more
Followed and sought. Nab, thou shalt tell her this:
She'll be more known, more talked of; and your
    widows
Are ne'er of any price till they be famous.
Their honour is their multitude of suitors.
Send her, it may be thy good fortune. What!
Thou dost not know?

DRUGGER.   No, sir, she'll never marry
Under a knight. Her brother has made a vow.

FACE. What! and dost thou despair, my little Nab,
Knowing what the Doctor has set down for thee,
And seeing so many o' the City dubbed?

One glass o' thy water, with a madam I know,
Will have it done, Nab. What's her brother, a
    knight?

  DRUGGER. No, sir, a gentleman, newly warm in's
    land, sir,
Scarce cold in his one-and-twenty, that does govern
His sister here; and is a man himself
Of some three thousand a year, and is come up
To learn to quarrel, and to live by his wits,
And will go down again, and die i' the country.

  FACE. How! to quarrel?

  DRUGGER.   Yes, sir, to carry quarrels
As gallants do, and manage 'em by line.

  FACE. 'Slid, Nab, the Doctor is the only man
In Christendom for him! He has made a table,
With mathematical demonstrations,
Touching the art of quarrels. He will give him
An instrument to quarrel by. Go, bring 'em both,
Him and his sister. And, for thee, with her
The Doctor haply may persuade. Go to.
Shalt give his worship a new damask suit
Upon the premises.

  SUBTLE.   O, good Captain!

  FACE.   He shall,
He is the honestest fellow, Doctor.—Stay not,
No offers; bring the damask, and the parties.

  DRUGGER. I'll try my power, sir.

  FACE.   And thy will too, Nab.

  SUBTLE. 'Tis good tobacco, this! What is't an
    ounce?

  FACE. He'll send you a pound, Doctor.

  SUBTLE.   O, no.

  FACE.   He will do't.
It is the goodest soul.—Abel, about it.
Thou shalt know more anon. Away, be gone.

                            Exit DRUGGER.

A miserable rogue, and lives with cheese,
And has the worms. That was the cause, indeed,
Why he came now. He dealt with me in private,
To get a med'cine for 'em.

SUBTLE.   And shall, sir. This works.

FACE. A wife, a wife for one of us, my dear Subtle!
We'll e'en draw lots, and he that fails shall have
The more in goods, the other has in tail.

SUBTLE. Rather the less, for she may be so light
She may want grains.

FACE.   Ay, or be such a burden,
A man would scarce endure her for the whole.

SUBTLE. Faith, best let's see her first, and then determine.

FACE. Content. But Doll must ha' no breath on't.

SUBTLE.   Mum.
Away! you to your Surly yonder, catch him.

FACE. Pray God, I ha' not stayed too long.

SUBTLE.   I fear it.

Exeunt.

ACT THREE. SCENE ONE

Before Lovewit's house

Enter TRIBULATION WHOLESOME *and* ANANIAS.

TRIBULATION. These chastisements are common to
the Saints,
And such rebukes we of the Separation
Must bear with willing shoulders, as the trials
Sent forth to tempt our frailties.

ANANIAS. In pure zeal,
I do not like the man. He is a heathen,
And speaks the language of Canaan, truly.

TRIBULATION. I think him a profane person indeed.

ANANIAS. He bears
The visible mark of the Beast in his forehead.
And for his Stone, it is a work of darkness,
And with philosophy blinds the eyes of man.

TRIBULATION. Good Brother, we must bend unto
all means
That may give furtherance to the Holy Cause.

ANANIAS. Which his cannot. The sanctified Cause
Should have a sanctified course.

TRIBULATION. Not always necessary.
The children of perdition are oft-times
Made instruments even of the greatest works.
Beside, we should give somewhat to man's nature,
The place he lives in, still about the fire
And fume of metals, that intoxicate
The brain of man, and make him prone to passion.
Where have you greater atheists than your cooks?
Or more profane, or choleric, than your glass-men?
More Antichristian than your bell-founders?
What makes the devil so devilish, I would ask you,
Satan, our common enemy, but his being
Perpetually about the fire, and boiling
Brimstone and ars'nic? We must give, I say,
Unto the motives, and the stirrers up
Of humours in the blood. It may be so,
Whenas the work is done, the Stone is made,
This heat of his may turn into a zeal,
And stand up for the beauteous discipline,
Against the menstruous cloth and rag of Rome.
We must await his calling, and the coming
Of the good spirit. You did fault, t' upbraid him

With the Brethren's blessing of Heidelberg, weigh-
ing
What need we have to hasten on the work
For the restoring of the silenced Saints,
Which ne'er will be, but by the Philosophers' Stone.
And so a learnèd elder, one of Scotland,
Assured me; aurum potabile being
The only med'cine for the civil magistrate,
T' incline him to a feeling of the Cause;
And must be daily used in the disease.

    ANANIAS. I have not edified more, truly, by man,
Not since the beautiful light first shone on me;
And I am sad my zeal hath so offended.

    TRIBULATION. Let us call on him then.

    ANANIAS.   The motion's good,
And of the spirit; I will knock first.—Peace be
    within!   *They enter.*

ACT THREE. SCENE TWO

Within Lovewit's house

Enter SUBTLE, *followed by* TRIBULATION *and* ANANIAS.

    SUBTLE. O, are you come? 'Twas time. Your three-
score minutes
Were at last thread, you see; and down had gone
Furnus acediae, turris circulatorius;
'Lembic, bolt's-head, retort, and Pelican
Had all been cinders. Wicked Ananias!
Art thou returned? Nay, then it goes down yet.

    TRIBULATION. Sir, be appeasèd; he is come to hum-
ble

Himself in spirit, and to ask your patience,
If too much zeal hath carried him aside
From the due path.

 SUBTLE.   Why, this doth qualify!

 TRIBULATION. The Brethren had no purpose,
  verily,
To give you the least grievance, but are ready
To lend their willing hands to any project
The spirit and you direct.

 SUBTLE.   This qualifies more!

 TRIBULATION. And for the orphans' goods, let them
  be valued,
Or what is needful else; to the holy work
It shall be numbered. Here, by me, the Saints
Throw down their purse before you.

 SUBTLE.   This qualifies most!
Why, thus it should be, now you understand.
Have I discoursed so unto you of our Stone,
And of the good that it shall bring your cause?
Showed you—beside the main of hiring forces
Abroad, drawing the Hollanders, your friends,
From th' Indies, to serve you, with all their fleet—
That even the med'cinal use shall make you a faction
And party in the realm? As, put the case,
That some great man in state, he have the gout;
Why, you but send three drops of your elixir,
You help him straight. There you have made a
 friend.
Another has the palsy, or the dropsy;
He takes of your incombustible stuff,
He's young again. There you have made a friend.
A lady that is past the feat of body,
Though not of mind, and hath her face decayed
Beyond all cure of paintings, you restore,
With the oil of talc. There you have made a friend,
And all her friends. A lord that is a leper,

A knight that has the bone-ache, or a squire
That hath both these, you make 'em smooth and
    sound,
With a bare fricace of your med'cine. Still
You increase your friends.

    TRIBULATION.   Ay, 'tis very pregnant.

    SUBTLE. And then the turning of this lawyer's
    pewter
To plate at Christmas——

    ANANIAS.   Christ-tide, I pray you.

    SUBTLE. Yet, Ananias?

    ANANIAS.   I have done.

    SUBTLE.   Or changing
His parcel gilt to massy gold. You cannot
But raise you friends. Withal, to be of power
To pay an army in the field, to buy
The King of France out of his realms, or Spain
Out of his Indies—what can you not do
Against lords spiritual or temporal,
That shall oppone you?

    TRIBULATION.   Verily, 'tis true.
We may be temporal lords ourselves, I take it.

    SUBTLE. You may be anything, and leave off to
    make
Long-winded exercises, or suck up
Your 'ha' and 'hum' in a tune. I not deny
But such as are not gracèd in a state,
May, for their ends, be adverse in religion,
And get a tune to call the flock together.
For, to say sooth, a tune does much with women,
And other phlegmatic people; it is your bell.

    ANANIAS. Bells are profane; a tune may be reli-
    gious.

    SUBTLE. No warning with you? Then farewell my
    patience.
'Slight, it shall down! I will not be thus tortured.

TRIBULATION. I pray you, sir.

SUBTLE. All shall perish. I have spoke it.

TRIBULATION. Let me find grace, sir, in your eyes.
    The man
He stands corrected. Neither did his zeal,
But as yourself, allow a tune somewhere;
Which now, being toward the Stone, we shall not
    need.

SUBTLE. No, nor your holy vizard, to win widows
To give you legacies, or make zealous wives
To rob their husbands for the common cause;
Nor take the start of bonds, broke but one day,
And say they were forfeited by providence.
Nor shall you need o'ernight to eat huge meals,
To celebrate your next day's fast the better;
The whilst the Brethren and the Sisters, humbled,
Abate the stiffness of the flesh. Nor cast
Before your hungry hearers scrupulous bones:
As whether a Christian may hawk or hunt,
Or whether matrons of the holy assembly
May lay their hair out, or wear doublets,
Or have that idol, Starch, about their linen.

ANANIAS. It is indeed an idol.

TRIBULATION. Mind him not, sir.—
I do command thee, spirit of zeal, but trouble,
To peace within him!—Pray you, sir, go on.

SUBTLE. Nor shall you need to libel 'gainst the prel-
    ates,
And shorten so your ears, against the hearing
Of the next wire-drawn grace. Nor of necessity
Rail against plays, to please the alderman
Whose daily custard you devour; nor lie
With zealous rage till you are hoarse; not one
Of these so singular arts. Nor call yourselves
By names of Tribulation, Persecution,
Restraint, Long Patience, and suchlike, affected

By the whole family or wood of you,
Only for glory, and to catch the ear
Of the disciple.

 TRIBULATION. Truly, sir, they are
Ways that the godly Brethren have invented,
For propagation of the glorious Cause,
As very notable means, and whereby, also,
Themselves grow soon and profitably famous.

 SUBTLE. O, but the Stone, all's idle to it! nothing!
The art of angels, nature's miracle,
The divine secret that doth fly in clouds
From east to west, and whose tradition
Is not from men, but spirits!

 ANANIAS.   I hate traditions!
I do not trust them——

 TRIBULATION.   Peace!

 ANANIAS.   They are popish all.
I will not peace. I will not——

 TRIBULATION.   Ananias!

 ANANIAS. Please the profane to grieve the godly, I
  may not.

 SUBTLE. Well, Ananias, thou shalt overcome.

 TRIBULATION. It is an ignorant zeal that haunts
  him, sir;
But truly else, a very faithful Brother,
A botcher, and a man, by revelation,
That hath a competent knowledge of the truth.

 SUBTLE. Has he a competent sum there, i' the bag,
To buy the goods within? I am made guardian,
And must, for charity and conscience' sake,
Now see the most be made for my poor orphan;
Though I desire the Brethren, too, good gainers.
There they are, within. When you have viewed and
  bought 'em,
And ta'en the inventory of what they are,
They are ready for projection; there's no more

To do. Cast on the med'cine so much silver
As there is tin there, so much gold as brass,
I'll gi'it you in, by weight.

    TRIBULATION.   But how long time,
Sir, must the Saints expect yet?

    SUBTLE.   Let me see,
How's the moon now? Eight, nine, ten days hence,
He will be silver potate; then, three days,
Before he citronize. Some fifteen days,
The magisterium will be perfected.

    ANANIAS. About the second day of the third week,
In the ninth month?

    SUBTLE.   Yes, my good Ananias.

    TRIBULATION. What will the orphans' goods arise
    to, think you?

    SUBTLE. Some hundred marks, as much as filled
        three cars
Unladed now. You'll make six millions of 'em.
But I must ha' more coals laid in.

    TRIBULATION.   How!

    SUBTLE.   Another load,
And then we ha' finished. We must now increase
Our fire to ignis ardens; we are past
Fimus equinus, balnei, cineris,
And all those lenter heats. If the holy purse
Should with this draught fall low, and that the
        Saints
Do need a present sum, I have a trick
To melt the pewter you shall buy now, instantly,
And with a tincture make you as good Dutch dollars
As any are in Holland.

    TRIBULATION.   Can you so?

    SUBTLE. Ay, and shall bide the third examination.

    ANANIAS. It will be joyful tidings to the Brethren.

    SUBTLE. But you must carry it secret.

TRIBULATION.　　　　　　　　　　　Ay, but stay,
This act of coining, is it lawful?

ANANIAS.　　　　　　　　　Lawful!
We know no magistrate; or, if we did,
This's foreign coin.

SUBTLE.　　　　　It is no coining, sir,
It is but casting.

TRIBULATION.　Ha! you distinguish well.
Casting of money may be lawful.

ANANIAS.　　　　　　　　　'Tis, sir.

TRIBULATION. Truly, I take it so.

SUBTLE.　　　　　　　　　There is no scruple,
Sir, to be made of it, believe Ananias.
This case of conscience he is studied in.

TRIBULATION. I'll make a question of it to the
　　Brethren.

ANANIAS. The Brethren shall approve it lawful,
　　doubt not.
Where shall it be done?　　　　*Knock without.*

SUBTLE.　　　　　For that we'll talk anon.
There's some to speak with me. Go in, I pray you,
And view the parcels. That's the inventory.
I'll come to you straight.

　　　　　　　Exeunt TRIBULATION *and* ANANIAS.
　　　　　　　　Who is it? Face! appear.

　　　　　Enter FACE *in his uniform.*

How now! Good prize?

FACE.　　　　　　Good pox! Yon costive cheater
Never came on.

SUBTLE.　　　How then?

FACE.　　　　　　　　I ha' walked the round
Till now, and no such thing.

SUBTLE.　　　　　　And have you quit him?

FACE. Quit him! an Hell would quit him, too, he
　　were happy.

'Slight! would you have me stalk like a mill-jade
All day, for one that will not yield us grains?
I know him of old.

    SUBTLE.   O, but to ha' gulled him
Had been a mast'ry.

    FACE.   Let him go, black boy,
And turn thee, that some fresh news may possess
    thee:
A noble count, a Don of Spain,—my dear,
Delicious compeer, and my party-bawd—
Who is come hither private, for his conscience,
And brought munition with him, six great slops,
Bigger than three Dutch hoys, beside round trunks,
Furnished with pistolets, and pieces of eight,
Will straight be here, my rogue, to have thy bath—
That is the colour—and to make his batt'ry
Upon our Doll, our castle, our Cinque Port,
Our Dover Pier, our what thou wilt. Where is she?
She must prepare perfumes, delicate linen,
The bath in chief, a banquet, and her wit,
For she must milk his epididymis.
Where is the doxy?

    SUBTLE.   I'll send her to thee;
And but dispatch my brace of little John Leydens,
And come again myself.

    FACE.   Are they within, then?

    SUBTLE. Numb'ring the sum.

    FACE.   How much?

    SUBTLE.   A hundred marks, boy.
                       Exit.

    FACE. Why, this's a lucky day. Ten pounds of
    Mammon!
Three o' my clerk! a portague o' my grocer!
This o' the Brethren! beside reversions
And states to come i' the widow, and my count!
My share today will not be bought for forty——

Enter DOLL.

DOLL. What?

FACE. Pounds, dainty Dorothy! art thou so near?

DOLL. Yes. Say, Lord General, how fares our camp?

FACE. As with the few that had entrenched themselves

Safe, by their discipline, against a world, Doll;
And laughed within those trenches, and grew fat
With thinking on the booties, Doll, brought in
Daily by their small parties. This dear hour,
A doughty Don is taken with my Doll;
And thou mayst make his ransom what thou wilt,
My Dousabel. He shall be brought here, fettered
With thy fair looks, before he sees thee; and thrown
In a down-bed, as dark as any dungeon;
Where thou shalt keep him waking with thy drum—
Thy drum, my Doll, thy drum—till he be tame
As the poor blackbirds were i' the great frost,
Or bees are with a basin; and so hive him
I' the swan-skin coverlet and cambric sheets,
Till he work honey and wax, my little God's-Gift.

DOLL. What is he, General?

FACE. An Adelantado,

A grandee, girl. Was not my Dapper here yet?

DOLL. No.

FACE. Nor my Drugger?

DOLL. Neither.

FACE. A pox on 'em,

They are so long a-furnishing! Such stinkards
Would not be seen upon these festival days.

Re-enter SUBTLE.

How now! ha' you done?

SUBTLE. Done. They are gone. The sum

Is here in bank, my Face. I would we knew
Another chapman now, would buy 'em outright.

    FACE. 'Slid, Nab shall do't, against he have the
      widow,
To furnish household.

    SUBTLE.   Excellent, well thought on!
Pray God he come!

    FACE.   I pray he keep away
Till our new business be o'erpassed.

    SUBTLE.   But, Face,
How cam'st thou by this secret Don?

    FACE.   A spirit
Brought me th' intelligence, in a paper here,
As I was conjuring yonder in my circle
For Surly. I ha' my flies abroad. Your bath
Is famous, Subtle, by my means. Sweet Doll,
You must go tune your virginal, no losing
O' the least time. And, do you hear? good action.
Firk like a flounder; kiss like a scallop, close;
And tickle him with thy mother-tongue. His great
Verdugoship has not a jot of language—
So much the easier to be cozened, my Dolly.
He will come here in a hired coach, obscure,
And our own coachman, whom I have sent as guide,
No creature else. *One knocks.* Who's that?

    SUBTLE.   It i' not he?
                         Exit DOLL.

    FACE. O no, not yet this hour.

Re-enter DOLL.

    SUBTLE.   Who is't?

    DOLL.   Dapper,
Your clerk.

    FACE.   God's will then, Queen of Faëry,
On with your tire. *Exit* DOLL. And, Doctor, with
    your robes.

Let's dispatch him, for God's sake.

SUBTLE. 'Twill be long.

FACE. I warrant you, take but the cues I give you,
It shall be brief enough.—'Slight, here are more!
Abel, and I think the angry boy, the heir,
That fain would quarrel.

SUBTLE. And the widow?

FACE. No,
Not that I see. Away! *Exit* SUBTLE.

Enter DAPPER.

O sir, you are welcome.
The Doctor is within, a-moving for you;
I have had the most ado to win him to it.
He swears you'll be the darling o' the dice;
He never heard her Highness dote till now.
Your aunt has giv'n you the most gracious words
That can be thought on.

DAPPER. Shall I see her Grace?

FACE. See her, and kiss her too.

Enter DRUGGER, *followed by* KASTRIL.

What! honest Nab?
Hast brought the damask?

NAB. No, sir, here's tobacco.

FACE. 'Tis well done, Nab. Thou'lt bring the
damask too?

DRUGGER. Yes. Here's the gentleman, Captain, Master Kastril,
I have brought to see the Doctor.

FACE. Where's the widow?

DRUGGER. Sir, as he likes, his sister—he says—shall
come.

FACE. O, is it so? Good time. Is your name Kastril,
sir?

KASTRIL. Ay, and the best o' the Kastrils, I'd be
  sorry else,
By fifteen hundred a year. Where is this doctor?
My mad tobacco-boy here tells me of one
That can do things. Has he any skill?

FACE.   Wherein, sir?

KASTRIL. To carry a business, manage a quarrel
  fairly,
Upon fit terms.

FACE.   It seems, sir, you're but young
About the town, that can make that a question!

KASTRIL. Sir, not so young but I have heard some
  speech
Of the angry boys, and seen 'em take tobacco,
And in his shop; and I can take it, too.
And I would fain be one of 'em, and go down
And practise i' the country.

FACE.   Sir, for the duello,
The Doctor, I assure you, shall inform you,
To the least shadow of a hair; and show you
An instrument he has, of his own making,
Wherewith no sooner shall you make report
Of any quarrel, but he will take the height on't
Most instantly, and tell in what degree
Of safety it lies in, or mortality;
And how it may be borne, whether in a right line
Or a half-circle; or may else be cast
Into an angle blunt, if not acute;
And this he will demonstrate. And then, rules
To give and take the lie by.

KASTRIL.   How! to take it?

FACE. Yes, in oblique, he'll show you, or in circle;
But never in diameter. The whole town
Study his theorems, and dispute them ordinarily
At the eating academies.

KASTRIL. But does he teach
Living by the wits, too?

FACE. Anything whatever.
You cannot think that subtlety, but he reads it.
He made me a captain. I was a stark pimp,
Just o' your standing, 'fore I met with him;
It i' not two months since. I'll tell you his method:
First, he will enter you at some ordinary.

KASTRIL. No, I'll not come there. You shall pardon
me.

FACE. For why, sir?

KASTRIL. There's gaming there, and tricks

FACE. Why, would you be
A gallant, and not game?

KASTRIL. Ay, 'twill spend a man.

FACE. Spend you! it will repair you when you are
spent.
How do they live by their wits there, that have
vented
Six times your fortunes?

KASTRIL. What, three thousand a year!

FACE. Ay, forty thousand.

KASTRIL. Are there such?

FACE. Ay, sir,
And gallants yet. Here's a young gentleman
Is born to nothing—forty marks a year,
Which I count nothing. He's to be initiated,
And have a fly o' the Doctor. He will win you
By unresistible luck, within this fortnight,
Enough to buy a barony. They will set him
Upmost, at the groom-porter's, all the Christmas!
And, for the whole year through, at every place
Where there is play, present him with the chair;
The best attendance, the best drink, sometimes
Two glasses of Canary, and pay nothing;
The purest linen and the sharpest knife,

The partridge next his trencher; and somewhere
The dainty bed, in private, with the dainty.
You shall ha' your ordinaries bid for him,
As playhouses for a poet; and the master
Pray him aloud to name what dish he affects,
Which must be buttered shrimps; and those that
    drink
To no mouth else, will drink to his, as being
The goodly president-mouth of all the board.

    KASTRIL. Do you not gull one?

    FACE.   God's my life! do you think it?
You shall have a cast commander—can but get
In credit with a glover, or a spurrier,
For some two pair of either's ware aforehand—
Will, by most swift posts, dealing with him,
Arrive at competent means to keep himself,
His punk, and naked boy, in excellent fashion;
And be admired for't.

    KASTRIL.   Will the Doctor teach this?

    FACE. He will do more, sir: when your land is
    gone,—
As men of spirit hate to keep earth long—
In a vacation, when small money is stirring,
And ordinaries suspended till the term,
He'll show a perspective, where on one side
You shall behold the faces and the persons
Of all sufficient young heirs in town,
Whose bonds are current for commodity;
On th' other side, the merchants' forms, and others
That, without help of any second broker,—
Who would expect a share—will trust such parcels;
In the third square, the very street and sign
Where the commodity dwells, and does but wait
To be delivered, be it pepper, soap,
Hops, or tobacco, oatmeal, wood, or cheeses.

All which you may so handle, to enjoy
To your own use, and never stand obliged.

    KASTRIL. I' faith! is he such a fellow?

    FACE.   Why, Nab here knows him.
And then for making matches for rich widows,
Young gentlewomen, heirs, the fortunat'st man!
He's sent to, far and near, all over England,
To have his counsel, and to know their fortunes.

    KASTRIL. God's will, my suster shall see him!

    FACE.   I'll tell you, sir,
What he did tell me of Nab. It's a strange thing!—
By the way, you must eat no cheese, Nab; it breeds
    melancholy,
And that same melancholy breeds worms. But pass
    it.—
He told me honest Nab here was ne'er at tavern
But once in 's life.

    DRUGGER.   Truth, and no more I was not.

    FACE. And then he was so sick——

    DRUGGER.   Could he tell you that too?

    FACE. How should I know it?

    DRUGGER.   In troth, we had been a-shooting,
And had a piece of fat ram-mutton to supper,
That lay so heavy o' my stomach——

    FACE.   And he has no head
To bear any wine; for, what with the noise o' the
    fiddlers,
And care of his shop, for he dares keep no serv-
    ants——

    DRUGGER. My head did so ache——

    FACE.   As he was fain to be brought home,
The Doctor told me. And then a good old woman——

    DRUGGER. Yes, faith, she dwells in Seacoal Lane—
    did cure me,
With sodden ale, and pellitory o' the wall—

Cost me but twopence. I had another sickness
Was worse than that.

FACE.   Ay, that was with the grief
Thou took'st for being cessed at eighteenpence,
For the waterwork.

DRUGGER.   In truth, and it was like
T' have cost me almost my life.

FACE.   Thy hair went off?

DRUGGER. Yes, sir, 'twas done for spite.

FACE.   Nay, so says the Doctor.

KASTRIL. Pray thee, tobacco-boy, go fetch my
    suster.
I'll see this learnèd boy before I go,
And so shall she.

FACE.   Sir, he is busy now.
But, if you have a sister to fetch hither,
Perhaps your own pains may command her sooner;
And he by that time will be free.

KASTRIL.   I go.   *Exit.*

FACE. Drugger, she's thine! The damask. *Exit*
    ABEL. Subtle and I
Must wrestle for her.—Come on, Master Dapper,
You see how I turn clients here away,
To give your cause dispatch. Ha' you performed
The ceremonies were enjoined you?

DAPPER.   Yes, o' the vinegar,
And the clean shirt.

FACE.   'Tis well, that shirt may do you
More worship than you think. Your aunt's afire,
But that she will not show it, t' have a sight on you.
Ha' you provided for her Grace's servants?

DAPPER. Yes, here are six score Edward shillings.

FACE.   Good.

DAPPER. And an old Harry's sovereign.

FACE.   Very good.

DAPPER. And three James shillings, and an Elizabeth groat;
Just twenty nobles.

FACE.   O, you are too just.
I would you had had the other noble in Maries.

DAPPER. I have some Philip and Maries.

FACE.   Ay, those same
Are best of all. Where are they? Hark, the Doctor.

Enter SUBTLE, *disguised like a priest of Faery.*

SUBTLE. Is yet her Grace's cousin come?

FACE.   He is come.

SUBTLE. And is he fasting?

FACE.   Yes.

SUBTLE.   And hath cried 'hum'?

FACE. —Thrice, you must answer.

DAPPER.   Thrice.

SUBTLE.   And as oft 'buzz'?

FACE. —If you have, say.

DAPPER.   I have,

SUBTLE.   Then, to her coz,
Hoping that he hath vinegared his senses,
As he was bid, the Faery Queen dispenses,
By me, this robe, the petticoat of Fortune;
Which that he straight put on, she doth importune.
And though to Fortune near be her petticoat,
Yet nearer is her smock, the Queen doth note.
And therefore, even of that a piece she hath sent,
Which, being a child, to wrap him in, was rent;
And prays him for a scarf he now will wear it,
With as much love as then her Grace did tear it,
About his eyes, to show he is fortunate. *They blind*
   DAPPER *with a rag.*
And, trusting unto her to make his state,
He'll throw away all worldly pelf about him;

Which that he will perform, she doth not doubt
    him.
FACE. She need not doubt him, sir. Alas, he has
    nothing
But what he will part withal as willingly,
Upon her Grace's word,—Throw away your purse—
As she would ask it.—Handkerchiefs and all—
She cannot bid that thing but he'll obey.—
If you have a ring about you, cast it off,
Or a silver seal at your wrist. Her Grace will send
Her fairies here to search you, therefore deal
Directly with her Highness. If they find
That you conceal a mite, you are undone.
                    DAPPER *throws away, as they bid him.*
DAPPER. Truly, there's all.
FACE.   All what?
DAPPER.   My money, truly.
FACE. Keep nothing that is transitory about you.—
Bid Doll play music. DOLL *plays on a cittern.* Look,
    the elves are come.
To pinch you, if you tell not truth. Advise you.
                            They pinch him.
DAPPER. O! I have a paper with a spur-royal in't.
FACE.   'Ti, ti.'
They knew't, they say.
SUBTLE.   'Ti-ti-ti-ti.' He has more yet.
FACE. 'Ti-ti-ti-ti.' I' the tother pocket?
SUBTLE.   'Titi-titi-titi-titi.'
They must pinch him or he will never confess, they
    say.
DAPPER. O, O!
FACE.   Nay, pray you hold. He is her
    Grace's nephew.—
'Ti, ti, ti?'—What care you? Good faith, you shall
    care.—

Deal plainly, sir, and shame the fairies. Show
You are an innocent.

    DAPPER.   By this good light, I ha' nothing.

    SUBTLE. 'Ti-ti-ti-ti-to-ta.' He does equivocate, she
      says—

'Ti-ti-do-ti, ti-ti-do-ti, da'—and swears by the light,
    when he is blinded.

    DAPPER. By this good dark, I ha' nothing but a
    half-crown

Of gold, about my wrist, that my love gave me;
And a leaden heart I wore sin' she forsook me.

    FACE. I thought 'twas something. And would you
    incur

Your aunt's displeasure for these trifles? Come,
I had rather you had thrown away twenty half-
    crowns.

You may wear your leaden heart still.

Enter DOLL.

                    How now!

    SUBTLE. What news, Doll?

    DOLL.   Yonder's your knight,
    Sir Mammon.

    FACE. God's lid, we never thought of him till now!
Where is he?

    DOLL. Here hard by, he's at the door.

    SUBTLE. And you are not ready now! Doll, get his
    suit.   *Exit* DOLL.

He must not be sent back.

    FACE.   O, by no means.

What shall we do with this same puffin here,
Now he's o' the spit?

    SUBTLE.   Why, lay him back awhile,

With some device.—'Ti, ti-ti, ti-ti-ti.' Would her
    Grace speak with me?

I come.—Help, Doll!   *Re-enter* DOLL.

FACE. *Speaks through the keyhole,* MAMMON
knocking. Who's there? Sir Epicure,
My master's i' the way. Please you to walk
Three or four turns, but till his back be turned,
And I am for you.—Quickly, Doll!

SUBTLE.   Her Grace
Commends her kindly to you, Master Dapper.

DAPPER. I long to see her Grace.

SUBTLE.   She now is set
At dinner in her bed; and she has sent you,
From her own private trencher, a dead mouse,
And a piece of gingerbread, to be merry withal,
And stay your stomach, lest you faint with fasting.
Yet if you could hold out till she saw you, she says,
It would be better for you.

FACE.   Sir, he shall
Hold out, an 'twere this two hours, for her High-
    ness;
I can assure you that. We will not lose
All we ha' done.

SUBTLE.   He must not see, nor speak
To anybody, till then.

FACE.   For that we'll put, sir,
A stay in's mouth.

SUBTLE.   Of what?

FACE.   Of gingerbread.
Make you it fit. He that hath pleased her Grace
Thus far, shall not now crinkle for a little.——
Gape, sir, and let him fit you.

SUBTLE.   Where shall we now
Bestow him?

DOLL. I' the privy.

SUBTLE.   Come along, sir,
I now must show you Fortune's privy lodgings.

FACE. Are they perfumed, and his bath ready?

SUBTLE.   All.
Only the fumigation's somewhat strong.

FACE. Sir Epicure, I am yours, sir, by and by.

Exeunt with DAPPER.

ACT FOUR. SCENE ONE

Lovewit's house

Enter FACE *and* MAMMON.

FACE. O, sir, you 're come i' the only finest time——

MAMMON. Where's Master?

FACE.   Now preparing for projection, sir.
Your stuff will be all changed shortly.

MAMMON.   Into gold?

FACE. To gold and silver, sir.

MAMMON.   Silver I care not for.

FACE. Yes, sir, a little to give beggars.

MAMMON.   Where's the lady?

FACE. At hand here. I ha' told her such brave
    things of you,
Touching your bounty and your noble spirit——

MAMMON.   Hast thou?

FACE. As she is almost in her fit to see you.
But, good sir, no divinity i' your conference,
For fear of putting her in rage.

MAMMON.   I warrant thee.

FACE. Six men will not hold her down. And then,
If the old man should hear or see you——

MAMMON.   Fear not.

FACE. The very house, sir, would run mad. You
    know it,

How scrupulous he is, and violent,
'Gainst the least act of sin. Physic or mathematics,
Poetry, state, or bawdry, as I told you,
She will endure, and never startle; but
No word of controversy.

    MAMMON.   I am schooled, good Eulen.

    FACE. And you must praise her house, remember
      that,
And her nobility.

    MAMMON.   Let me alone.
No herald, no, nor antiquary, Lungs,
Shall do it better. Go.

    FACE.   —Why, this is yet
A kind of modern happiness, to have
Doll Common for a great lady.   *Exit.*

    MAMMON.   Now, Epicure,
Heighten thyself, talk to her all in gold;
Rain her as many showers as Jove did drops
Unto his Danaë; show the god a miser,
Compared with Mammon. What! the Stone will
    do't.
She shall feel gold, taste gold, hear gold, sleep
    gold—
Nay, we will concumberè gold. I will be puissant
And mighty in my talk to her!   ·

    Re-enter FACE *with* DOLL *richly dressed.*

                    Here she comes.

    FACE. To him, Doll, suckle him.—This is the noble
      knight
I told your ladyship——

    MAMMON   Madam, with your pardon,
I kiss your vesture.

    DOLL.   Sir, I were uncivil
If I would suffer that; my lip to you, sir.

MAMMON. I hope my Lord your brother be in
  health, lady?

DOLL. My Lord my brother is, though I no lady,
  sir.

FACE. —Well said, my guinea-bird.

MAMMON.   Right noble madam——

FACE. —O, we shall have most fierce idolatry.

MAMMON. 'Tis your prerogative.

DOLL.   Rather your courtesy.

MAMMON. Were there nought else t' enlarge your
  virtues to me,
These answers speak your breeding and your blood.

DOLL. Blood we boast none, sir, a poor baron's
  daughter.

MAMMON. Poor! and gat you? Profane not. Had
  your father
Slept all the happy remnant of his life
After that act, lain but there still, and panted,
He'd done enough to make himself, his issue,
And his posterity noble.

DOLL.   Sir, although
We may be said to want the gilt and trappings,
The dress of honour, yet we strive to keep
The seeds and the materials.

MAMMON.   I do see
The old ingredient, virtue, was not lost,
Nor the drug, money, used to make your compound.
There is a strange nobility i' your eye,
This lip, that chin! Methinks you do resemble
One o' the Austriac princes.

FACE.   —Very like!
Her father was an Irish costermonger.

MAMMON. The house of Valois just had such a
  nose,
And such a forehead yet the Medici
Of Florence boast.

DOLL.   Troth, and I have been likened
To all these princes.

FACE.   —I'll be sworn, I heard it.

MAMMON. I know not how; it is not any one,
But e'en the very choice of all their features.

FACE. —I'll in, and laugh.   *Exit.*

MAMMON.   A certain touch, or air,
That sparkles a divinity beyond
An earthly beauty!

DOLL.   O, you play the courtier.

MAMMON. Good lady, gi' me leave——

DOLL.   In faith, I may not,
To mock me, sir.

MAMMON.   To burn i' this sweet flame.
The phoenix never knew a nobler death.

DOLL. Nay, now you court the courtier, and de-
    stroy
What you would build. This art, sir, i' your words,
Calls your whole faith in question.

MAMMON.   By my soul——

DOLL. Nay, oaths are made o' the same air, sir.

MAMMON.   Nature
Never bestowed upon mortality
A more unblamed, a more harmonious feature.
She played the step-dame in all faces else.
Sweet madam, le' me be particular——

DOLL. Particular, sir! I pray you know your dis-
    tance.

MAMMON. In no ill sense, sweet lady, but to ask
How your fair graces pass the hours? I see
You're lodged here i' the house of a rare man,
An excellent artist; but what's that to you?

DOLL. Yes, sir. I study here the mathematics,
And distillation.

MAMMON.   O, I cry your pardon.
He's a divine instructor! can extract

The souls of all things by his art; call all
The virtues, and the miracles of the sun,
Into a temperate furnace; teach dull nature
What her own forces are. A man the Emp'ror
Has courted above Kelly; sent his medals
And chains, t' invite him.

  DOLL.   Ay, and for his physic, sir——
  MAMMON. Above the art of Aesculapius,
That drew the envy of the Thunderer!
I know all this, and more.

  DOLL.   Troth, I am taken, sir,
Whole with these studies, that contemplate nature.

  MAMMON. It is a noble humour. But this form
Was not intended to so dark a use.
Had you been crooked, foul, of some coarse mould,
A cloister had done well; but such a feature,
That might stand up the glory of a kingdom,
To live recluse, is a mere solecism,
Though in a nunnery. It must not be!
I muse my Lord your brother will permit it!
You should spend half my land first, were I he.
Does not this diamond better on my finger
Than i' the quarry?

  DOLL.   Yes.
  MAMMON.   Why, you are like it.
You were created, lady, for the light.
Here, you shall wear it; take it, the first pledge
Of what I speak, to bind you to believe me.

  DOLL. In chains of adamant?
  MAMMON.   Yes, the strongest bands.
And take a secret, too: here, by your side,
Doth stand this hour the happiest man in Europe.

  DOLL. You are contented, sir?
  MAMMON.   Nay, in true being,
The envy of princes and the fear of states.

  DOLL. Say you so, Sir Epicure?

MAMMON.   Yes, and thou shalt prove it,
Daughter of honour. I have cast mine eye
Upon thy form, and I will rear this beauty
Above all styles.

DOLL.   You mean no treason, sir?

MAMMON. No, I will take away that jealousy.
I am the lord of the Philosophers' Stone,
And thou the lady.

DOLL.   How, sir! ha' you that?

MAMMON. I am the master of the mastery.
This day the good old wretch here o' the house
Has made it for us. Now he's at projection.
Think therefore thy first wish now, let me hear it;
And it shall rain into thy lap no shower,
But floods of gold, whole cataracts, a deluge,
To get a nation on thee!

DOLL.   You are pleased, sir,
To work on the ambition of our sex.

MAMMON. I'm pleased the glory of her sex should
    know
This nook, here, of the Friars, is no climate
For her to live obscurely in, to learn
Physic and surgery, for the constable's wife
Of some odd hundred in Essex; but come forth,
And taste the air of palaces; eat, drink
The toils of emp'rics, and their boasted practice;
Tincture of pearl and coral, gold and amber;
Be seen at feasts and triumphs; have it asked
What miracle she is? set all the eyes
Of court afire, like a burning-glass,
And work 'em into cinders, when the jewels
Of twenty states adorn thee, and the light
Strikes out the stars; that, when thy name is men-
    tioned,
Queens may look pale; and, we but showing our
    love,

Nero's Poppaea may be lost in story!
Thus will we have it.

    DOLL.   I could well consent, sir.
But in a monarchy, how will this be?
The Prince will soon take notice, and both seize
You and your Stone, it being a wealth unfit
For any private subject.

    MAMMON.   If he knew it.

    DOLL. Yourself do boast it, sir.

    MAMMON.   To thee, my life.

    DOLL. O, but beware, sir! You may come to end
The remnant of your days in a loathed prison,
By speaking of it.

    MAMMON.   'Tis no idle fear!
We'll therefore go withal, my girl, and live
In a free state, where we will eat our mullets
Soused in High Country wines, sup pheasants' eggs,
And have our cockles boiled in silver shells;
Our shrimps to swim again, as when they lived,
In a rare butter made of dolphins' milk,
Whose cream does look like opals; and with these
Delicate meats, set ourselves high for pleasure,
And take us down again, and then renew
Our youth and strength with drinking the elixir,
And so enjoy a perpetuity
Of life and lust. And thou shalt ha' thy wardrobe
Richer than Nature's, still to change thyself,
And vary oftener, for thy pride, than she,
Or Art, her wise and almost equal servant.

Re-enter FACE.

    FACE. Sir, you are too loud. I hear you, every
        word,
Into the laboratory. Some fitter place:
The garden, or great chamber above. How like you
        her?

MAMMON. Excellent, Lungs! There's for thee.

FACE. But do you hear?
Good sir, beware, no mention of the rabbins.

MAMMON. We think not on 'em.

Exeunt MAMMON *and* DOLL.

FACE. O, it is well, sir. Subtle!

Enter SUBTLE.

Dost thou not laugh?

SUBTLE. Yes. Are they gone?

FACE. All's clear.

SUBTLE. The widow is come.

FACE. And your quarrelling disciple?

SUBTLE. Ay.

FACE. I must to my captainship again then.

SUBTLE. Stay, bring 'em in first.

FACE. So I meant. What is she,
A bonnibel?

SUBTLE. I know not.

FACE. We'll draw lots,
You'll stand to that?

SUBTLE. What else?

FACE. O, for a suit
To fall now, like a curtain, flap!

SUBTLE. To th' door, man.

FACE. You'll ha' the first kiss, 'cause I am not
ready.

SUBTLE. Yes, and perhaps hit you through both
the nostrils.

Enter KASTRIL, *followed by* DAME PLIANT.

FACE. Who would you speak with?

KASTRIL. Where's the Captain?

FACE. Gone, sir,
About some business.

KASTRIL. Gone?

FACE. He'll return straight.
But, Master Doctor, his lieutenant, is here. *Exit.*

SUBTLE. Come near, my worshipful boy, my terrae
  fili,
That is, my boy of land; make thy approaches.
Welcome, I know thy lusts and thy desires,
And I will serve and satisfy 'em. Begin,
Charge me from thence, or thence, or in this line.
Here is my centre; ground thy quarrel.

KASTRIL. You lie.

SUBTLE. How, child of wrath and anger! the loud
  lie?
For what, my sudden boy?

KASTRIL. Nay, that look you to,
I am aforehand.

SUBTLE. O, this 's no true grammar,
And as ill logic! You must render causes, child,
Your first and second intentions; know your canons
And your divisions, moods, degrees, and differences;
Your predicaments, substance and accident,
Series extern and intern, with their causes,
Efficient, material, formal, final;
And have your elements perfect——

KASTRIL. What is this!
The angry tongue he talks in?

SUBTLE. That false precept
Of being aforehand, has deceived a number,
And made 'em enter quarrels oftentimes
Before they were aware; and afterward,
Against their wills.

KASTRIL. How must I do then, sir?

SUBTLE. I cry this lady mercy. She should first
Have been saluted. *Kisses her.* I do call you lady,
Because you are to be one ere t' be long,
My soft and buxom widow.

KASTRIL. Is she, i' faith?

SUBTLE. Yes, or my art is an egregious liar.

KASTRIL. How know you?

SUBTLE.   By inspection on her forehead,
And subtlety of her lip, which must be tasted
Often to make a judgment. *Kisses her again.* 'Slight,
    she melts
Like a myrobalan!—Here is yet a line,
In rivo frontis, tells me he is no knight.

DAME PLIANT. What is he then, sir?

SUBTLE.   Let me see your hand.
O, your linea Fortunae makes it plain;
And stella, here, in monte Veneris;
But, most of all, junctura annularis.
He is a soldier, or a man of art, lady,
But shall have some great honour shortly.

DAME PLIANT.   Brother,
He's a rare man, believe me!

    Re-enter FACE, *in his uniform.*

KASTRIL.   Hold your peace.
Here comes the tother rare man.—Save you, Cap-
    tain.

FACE. Good Master Kastril! Is this your sister?

KASTRIL.   Ay, sir.
Please you to kuss her, and be proud to know her?

FACE. I shall be proud to know you, lady.

                        Kisses her.

DAME PLIANT.   Brother,
He calls me lady too.

KASTRIL.   Ay, peace. I heard it.

FACE. —The Count is come.

SUBTLE.   Where is he?

FACE.   At the door.

SUBTLE. Why, you must entertain him.

FACE.   What 'll you do
With these the while?

SUBTLE. Why, have 'em up, and show 'em
Some fustian book, or the dark glass.

FACE. 'Fore God,
She is a delicate dabchick! I must have her. *Exit.*

SUBTLE. Must you! ay, if your fortune will, you
must.—
Come, sir, the Captain will come to us presently.
I'll ha' you to my chamber of demonstrations,
Where I'll show you both the grammar and logic
And rhetoric of quarrelling, my whole method
Drawn out in tables; and my instrument,
That hath the several scale upon't, shall make you
Able to quarrel, at a straw's breadth, by moonlight.
And, lady, I'll have you look in a glass,
Some half an hour, but to clear your eyesight,
Against you see your fortune; which is greater
Than I may judge upon the sudden, trust me.

Exit, followed by KASTRIL *and* DAME PLIANT.

Re-enter FACE.

FACE. Where are you, Doctor?

SUBTLE. I'll come to you presently.

FACE. I will ha' this same widow, now I ha' seen
her,
On any composition.

Re-enter SUBTLE.

SUBTLE. What do you say?

FACE. Ha' you disposed of them?

SUBTLE. I ha' sent 'em up.

FACE. Subtle, in troth, I needs must have this
widow.

SUBTLE. Is that the matter?

FACE. Nay, but hear me.

SUBTLE. Go to,

If you rebel once, Doll shall know it all.
Therefore be quiet, and obey your chance.
   FACE. Nay, thou art so violent now. Do but con-
     ceive,
Thou art old, and canst not serve——
   SUBTLE.   Who? cannot I?
'Slight, I will serve her with thee, for a——
   FACE.   Nay,
But understand: I'll gi' you composition.
   SUBTLE. I will not treat with thee. What! sell my
     fortune?
'Tis better than my birthright. Do not murmur;
Win her, and carry her. If you grumble, Doll
Knows it directly.
   FACE.   Well, sir, I am silent.
Will you go help to fetch in Don, in state?   *Exit.*
   SUBTLE. I follow you, sir. We must keep Face in
     awe,
Or he will overlook us like a tyrant.

    Re-enter FACE, *with* SURLY *like a Spaniard.*

Brain of a tailor! Who comes here? Don John!
   SURLY. Señores, beso las manos a vuestras mer-
     cedes.
   SUBTLE. Would you had stooped a little, and
     kissed our anos!
   FACE. Peace, Subtle.
   SUBTLE.   Stab me, I shall never hold, man!
He looks, in that deep ruff, like a head in a platter,
Served in by a short cloak upon two trestles.
   FACE. Or what do you say to a collar of brawn,
     cut down
Beneath the souse, and wriggled with a knife?
   SUBTLE. 'Slud, he does look too fat to be a Span-
     iard.

FACE. Perhaps some Fleming or some Hollander
got him
In D'Alva's time; Count Egmont's bastard.

SUBTLE.   Don,
Your scurvy, yellow, Madrid face is welcome.

SURLY. Gratia.

SUBTLE.   He speaks out of a fortification.
Pray God he has no squibs in those deep sets.

SURLY. Por Dios, señores, muy linda casa!

SUBTLE. What says he?

FACE.   Praises the house, I think;
I know no more but 's action.

SUBTLE.   Yes, the casa,
My precious Diego, will prove fair enough
To cozen you in. Do you mark? You shall
Be cozened, Diego.

FACE.   Cozened, do you see?
My worthy Donzel, cozened.

SURLY.   Entiendo.

SUBTLE. Do you intend it? So do we, dear Don.
Have you brought pistolets, or portagues,
My solemn Don?—Dost thou feel any?

FACE. *Feels his pockets.*   Full.

SUBTLE. You shall be emptied, Don, pumpèd and
drawn
Dry, as they say.

FACE.   Milkèd, in troth, sweet Don.

SUBTLE. See, all the monsters, the great lion of all,
Don.

SURLY. Con licencia, se puede ver a esta señora?

SUBTLE. What talks he now?

FACE.   O' the señora.

SUBTLE.   O, Don,
This is the lioness, which you shall see
Also, my Don.

FACE.   'Slid, Subtle, how shall we do?

SUBTLE. For what?

FACE. Why, Doll's employed, you know.

SUBTLE. That's true!
'Fore Heav'n, I know not. He must stay, that's all.

FACE. Stay! that he must not, by no means.

SUBTLE. No! why?

FACE. Unless you'll mar all. 'Slight, he'll suspect
it;
And then he will not pay, not half so well.
This is a travelled punk-master, and does know
All the delays; a notable hot rascal,
And looks already rampant.

SUBTLE. 'Sdeath, and Mammon
Must not be troubled.

FACE. Mammon? in no case!

SUBTLE. What shall we do then?

FACE. Think; you must be sudden.

SURLY. Entiendo que la señora es tan hermosa,
que codicio tan a verla, como la bien aventuranza
de mi vida.

FACE. Mi vida? 'Slid, Subtle, he puts me in mind
o' the widow.
What dost thou say to draw her to it, ha?
And tell her 'tis her fortune? All our venture
Now lies upon't. It is but one man more,
Which on 's chance to have her; and beside,
There is no maidenhead to be feared or lost.
What dost thou think on't, Subtle?

SUBTLE. Who, I? Why——

FACE. The credit of our house, too, is engaged.

SUBTLE. You make me an offer for my share erewhile.
What wilt thou gi' me, i' faith?

FACE. O, by that light,
I'll not buy now. You know your doom to me.

E'en take your lot, obey your chance, sir; win her,
And wear her out for me.

    SUBTLE.   'Slight, I'll not work her then.

    FACE. It is the common cause; therefore bethink
       you.

Doll else must know it, as you said.

    SUBTLE.   I care not.

    SURLY. Señores, por qué se tarda tanto?

    SUBTLE. Faith, I am not fit, I am old.

    FACE.   That's now no reason, sir.

    SURLY. Puede ser de hacer burla de mi amor?

    FACE. You hear the Don, too? By this air I call,
And loose the hinges. Doll!

    SUBTLE.   A plague of Hell——

    FACE. Will you then do?

    SUBTLE.   You're a terrible rogue!
I'll think of this. Will you, sir, call the widow?

    FACE. Yes, and I'll take her, too, with all her
      faults,

Now I do think on't better.

    SUBTLE.   With all my heart, sir.
Am I discharged o' the lot?

    FACE.   As you please.

    SUBTLE.   Hands.

    FACE. Remember now, that upon any change,
You never claim her.

    SUBTLE.   Much good joy and health to you, sir.
Marry a whore! Fate, let me wed a witch first.

    SURLY. Por estas honradas barbas——

    SUBTLE.   He swears by his beard.
Dispatch, and call the brother too.   *Exit* FACE.

    SURLY.   Tengo duda, señores,
Que no me hagan alguna traición.

    SUBTLE. How, issue on? Yes, presto, señor. Please
      you

Enthratha the chambratha, worthy Don;
Where if it please the fates, in your bathada,
You shall be soaked and stroked, and tubbed and
     rubbed,
And scrubbed and fubbed, dear Don, before you go.
You shall, in faith, my scurvy baboon Don,
Be curried, clawed, and flawed, and tawed, indeed.
I will the heartlier go about it now,
And make the widow a punk so much the sooner,
To be revenged on this impetuous Face.
The quickly doing of it is the grace.

Exit SUBTLE *with* SURLY.

ACT FOUR. SCENE TWO

Subtle's chamber

Enter FACE, KASTRIL, *and* DAME PLIANT.

FACE. Come, lady, I knew the Doctor would not
     leave
Till he had found the very nick of her fortune.

KASTRIL. To be a countess, say you, a Spanish
     countess, sir?

DAME PLIANT. Why, is that better than an English
     countess?

FACE. Better! 'Slight, make you that a question,
     lady?

KASTRIL. Nay, she is a fool, Captain; you must
     pardon her.

FACE. Ask from your courtier to your inns-of-
     court man,
To your mere milliner. They will tell you all,

Your Spanish jennet is the best horse; your Spanish
Stoop is the best garb; your Spanish beard
Is the best cut; your Spanish ruffs are the best
Wear; your Spanish pavan the best dance;
Your Spanish titillation in a glove
The best perfume. And for your Spanish pike
And Spanish blade, let your poor Captain speak.
Here comes the Doctor.

Enter SUBTLE

SUBTLE. My most honoured lady,—
For so I am now to style you, having found,
By this my scheme, you are to undergo
An honourable fortune very shortly—
What will you say now, if some——

FACE. I ha' told her all, sir,
And her right worshipful brother here, that she
    shall be
A countess,—do not delay 'em, sir—a Spanish coun-
    tess.

SUBTLE. Still, my scarce worshipful Captain, you
    can keep
No secret! Well, since he has told you, madam,
Do you forgive him, and I do.

KASTRIL. She shall do that, sir;
I'll look to't, 'tis my charge.

SUBTLE. Well then, naught rests
But that she fit her love now to her fortune.

DAME PLIANT. Truly, I shall never brook a
    Spaniard.

SUBTLE. No?

DAME PLIANT. Never sin' 'eighty-eight, could I
    abide 'em,
And that was some three year afore I was born, in
    truth.

SUBTLE. Come, you must love him, or be miserable;
Choose which you will.

FACE. By this good rush, persuade her,
She will cry strawberries else, within this twelvemonth.

SUBTLE. Nay, shads and mackerel, which is worse.

FACE. Indeed, sir?

KASTRIL. God's lid, you shall love him, or I'll kick
you!

DAME PLIANT. Why,
I'll do as you will ha' me, brother.

KASTRIL. Do,
Or by this hand I'll maul you.

FACE. Nay, good sir,
Be not so fierce.

SUBTLE. No, my enragèd child;
She will be ruled. What, when she comes to taste
The pleasures of a countess! to be courted——

FACE. And kissed, and ruffled!

SUBTLE. Ay, behind the hangings.

FACE. And then come forth in pomp!

SUBTLE. And know her state!

FACE. Of keeping all th' idolaters o' the chamber
Barer to her, than at their prayers!

SUBTLE. Is served
Upon the knee!

FACE. And has her pages, ushers,
Footmen, and coaches——

SUBTLE. Her six mares——

FACE. Nay, eight!

SUBTLE. To hurry her through London to th' Exchange,
Bedlam, the china-houses——

FACE. Yes, and have
The citizens gape at her, and praise her tires,
And my Lord's goose-turd bands, that ride with her!

KASTRIL. Most brave! By this hand, you are not
 my suster
If you refuse.

DAME PLIANT.   I will not refuse, brother.

Enter SURLY.

SURLY. Qué es esto, señores, que no se venga?
Esta tardanza me mata!

FACE.   It is the Count come!
The Doctor knew he would be here, by his art.

SUBTLE. En gallanta madama, Don! gallantissima!

SURLY. Por todos los dioses, la más acabada
Hermosura, que he visto en mi vida!

FACE. Is't not a gallant language that they speak?

KASTRIL. An admirable language! Is't not French?

FACE. No, Spanish, sir.

KASTRIL.   It goes like law-French,
And that, they say, is the court-liest language.

FACE.   List, sir.

SURLY. El sol ha perdido su lumbre, con el
Resplandor que trae esta dama. Válgame Dios!

FACE. H' admires your sister.

KASTRIL.   Must not she make curtsy?

SUBTLE. God's will, she must go to him, man, and
 kiss him!
It is the Spanish fashion, for the women
To make first court.

FACE.   'Tis true he tells you, sir,
His art knows all.

SURLY.   Por qué no se acude?

KASTRIL. He speaks to her, I think.

FACE.   That he does, sir.

SURLY. Por el amor de Dios, qué es esto, qué se
 tarda?

KASTRIL. Nay, see, she will not understand him!
 Gull,
Noddy.

DAME PLIANT. What say you, brother?

KASTRIL. Ass, my suster,
Go kuss him, as the cunning-man would have you,
I'll thrust a pin i' your buttocks else.

FACE. O no, sir.

SURLY. Señora mía, mi persona muy indigna está
Allegar a tanta hermosura.

FACE. Does he not use her bravely?

KASTRIL. Bravely, i' faith!

FACE. Nay, he will use her better.

KASTRIL. Do you think so?

SURLY. Señora, si será servida, entremos.

Exit with DAME PLIANT.

KASTRIL. Where does he carry her?

FACE. Into the garden, sir;
Take you no thought. I must interpret for her.

SUBTLE. Give Doll the word. *Exit* FACE. Come, my
fierce child, advance,
We'll to our quarrelling lesson again.

KASTRIL. Agreed.
I love a Spanish boy, with all my heart.

SUBTLE. Nay, and by this means, sir, you shall be
brother
To a great count.

KASTRIL. Ay, I knew that at first.
This match will advance the house of the Kastrils.

SUBTLE. Pray God your sister prove but pliant!

KASTRIL. Why,
Her name is so, by her other husband.

SUBTLE. How!

KASTRIL. The Widow Pliant. Knew you not that?

SUBTLE. No, faith, sir,
Yet, by erection of her figure, I guessed it.
Come, let's go practise.

KASTRIL. Yes, but do you think, Doctor,
I e'er shall quarrel well?

SUBTLE. I warrant you. *Exeunt.*

ACT FOUR. SCENE THREE

The chamber above

Enter DOLL *in her fit of talking, followed by*
MAMMON.

DOLL. For after Alexander's death——
MAMMON.   Good lady——
DOLL. That Perdiccas and Antigonus were slain,
The two that stood, Seleuc' and Ptolemy——
MAMMON. Madam——
DOLL.   Made up the two legs, and
    the fourth beast.
That was Gog-North and Egypt-South; which after
Was called Gog-Iron-Leg and South-Iron-Leg——
MAMMON.   Lady——
DOLL. And then Gog-Hornèd. So was Egypt, too.
Then Egypt-Clay-Leg, and Gog-Clay-Leg——
MAMMON.   Sweet madam——
DOLL. And last Gog-Dust, and Egypt-Dust, which
    fall
In the last link of the fourth chain. And these
Be stars in story, which none see or look at——
MAMMON. What shall I do?
DOLL.   For, as he says, except
We call the rabbins, and the heathen Greeks——
MAMMON. Dear lady——
DOLL.   To come from Salem,
    and from Athens,
And teach the people of Great Britain——

Enter FACE, *in his servant's dress.*

FACE.   What's the matter, sir?
DOLL. To speak the tongue of Eber and Javan——

MAMMON.   O,
She's in her fit.
    DOLL.   We shall know nothing——
    FACE.   Death, sir,
We are undone!
    DOLL.   Where then a learned linguist
Shall see the ancient used communion
Of vowels and consonants——
    FACE.   My master will hear!
    DOLL. A wisdom, which Pythagoras held most
      high——
    MAMMON. Sweet honourable lady!
    DOLL.   To comprise
All sounds of voices, in few marks of letters——
    FACE. Nay, you must never hope to lay her now.
                    They speak together.

    DOLL. And so we may arrive, by Talmud skill
And profane Greek, to raise the building up
Of Helen's house against the Ishmaelite,
King of Togarmah, and his habergeons
Brimstony, blue, and fiery; and the force
Of king Abaddon, and the beast of Cittim,
Which Rabbi David Kimchi, Onkelos,
And Aben Ezra do interpret Rome.

    FACE. How did you put her into't?
    MAMMON. Alas, I talked
Of a Fifth Monarchy I would erect
With the Philosophers' Stone, by chance, and she
Falls on the other four straight.
    FACE.   Out of Broughton!
I told you so. 'Slid, stop her mouth.
    MAMMON.   Is't best?
    FACE. She'll never leave else.
If the old man hear her,
We are but faeces, ashes.
    SUBTLE. What's to do there?
    FACE. O, we are lost! Now she hears him, she is quiet.
                 Exit with DOLL.

Enter SUBTLE.

MAMMON. Where shall I hide me!

SUBTLE. How! what sight is here?
Close deeds of darkness, and that shun the light!
Bring him again. Who is he? What, my son!
O, I have lived too long.

MAMMON. Nay, good, dear Father,
There was no unchaste purpose.

SUBTLE. Not! and flee me,
When I come in?

MAMMON. That was my error.

SUBTLE. Error!
Guilt, guilt, my son. Give it the right name. No
    marvel,
If I found check in our great work within,
When such affairs as these were managing!

MAMMON. Why, have you so?

SUBTLE. It has stood still this half hour;
And all the rest of our less works gone back.
Where is the instrument of wickedness,
My lewd, false drudge?

MAMMON. Nay, good sir, blame not him;
Believe me, 'twas against his will or knowledge——
I saw her by chance.

SUBTLE. Will you commit more sin,
T'excuse a varlet?

MAMMON. By my hope, 'tis true, sir.

SUBTLE. Nay, then I wonder less, if you, for whom
The blessing was prepared, would so tempt Heaven,
And lose your fortunes.

MAMMON. Why, sir?

SUBTLE. This'll retard
The work a month at least.

MAMMON. Why, if it do,
What remedy? But think it not, good Father:

Our purposes were honest.

SUBTLE.   As they were,
So the reward will prove.

A great crack and noise within.

How now! Ay me,
God and all saints be good to us.

Re-enter FACE.

What's that?

FACE. O sir, we are defeated! All the works
Are flown in fumo, every glass is burst;
Furnace and all rent down, as if a bolt
Of thunder had been driven through the house!
Retorts, receivers, Pelicans, bolt-heads,
All struck in shivers!

SUBTLE *falls down, as in a swoon.*

Help, good sir! Alas,
Coldness and death invades him. Nay, Sir Mammon,
Do the fair offices of a man! You stand
As you were readier to depart than he.

One knocks.

Who's there? My Lord her brother is come.

MAMMON.   Ha, Lungs?

FACE. His coach is at the door. Avoid his sight,
For he's as furious as his sister's mad.

MAMMON. Alas!

FACE.   My brain is quite undone with
    the fume, sir,
I ne'er must hope to be mine own man again.

MAMMON. Is all lost, Lungs? Will nothing be pre-
    served
Of all our cost?

FACE.   Faith, very little, sir,
A peck of coals or so, which is cold comfort, sir.

MAMMON. O my voluptuous mind! I am justly
    punished.

FACE. And so am I, sir.

MAMMON.   Cast from all my hopes——

FACE. Nay, certainties, sir.

MAMMON.   By mine own base affections.

SUBTLE. *Seeming to come to himself.* O, the curst
     fruits of vice and lust!

MAMMON.   Good father,
It was my sin. Forgive it.

SUBTLE.   Hangs my roof
Over us still, and will not fall, O Justice,
Upon us, for this wicked man!

FACE.   Nay, look, sir,
You grieve him now with staying in his sight.
Good sir, the nobleman will come too, and take you,
And that may breed a tragedy.

MAMMON.   I'll go.

FACE. Ay, and repent at home, sir. It may be,
For some good penance you may ha' it yet;
A hundred pound to the box at Bedlam——

MAMMON.   Yes.

FACE. For the restoring such as ha' their wits.

MAMMON.   I'll do't.

FACE. I'll send one to you to receive it.

MAMMON.   Do.
Is no projection left?

FACE.   All flown, or stinks, sir.

MAMMON. Will nought be saved that's good for
     med'cine, think'st thou?

FACE. I cannot tell, sir. There will be perhaps
Something, about the scraping of the shards,
Will cure the itch—though not your itch of mind,
     sir.
It shall be saved for you, and sent home. Good sir,
This way for fear the Lord should meet you.

                                   Exit MAMMON.

SUBTLE.   Face!

FACE. Ay.

SUBTLE.   Is he gone?

FACE.   Yes, and as heavily
As all the gold he hoped for were in his blood.
Let us be light though.

SUBTLE.   Ay, as balls, and bound,
And hit our heads against the roof for joy!
There's so much of our care now cast away.

FACE. Now to our Don.

SUBTLE.   Yes, your young widow by this time
Is made a countess, Face. She's been in travail
Of a young heir for you.

FACE.   Good, sir.

SUBTLE.   Off with your case,
And greet her kindly, as a bridegroom should,
After these common hazards.

FACE.   Very well, sir.
Will you go fetch Don Diego off the while?

SUBTLE. And fetch him over, too, if you'll be
    pleased, sir.
Would Doll were in her place, to pick his pockets
    now!

FACE. Why, you can do't as well, if you would set
    to't.
I pray you prove your virtue.

SUBTLE.   For your sake, sir.

                    Exeunt.

ACT FOUR. SCENE FOUR

The garden

Enter SURLY *and* DAME PLIANT.

SURLY. Lady, you see into what hands you are
    fall'n;
'Mongst what a nest of villains! and how near
Your honour was t'have catched a certain clap,
Through your credulity, had I but been
So punctually forward, as place, time,
And other circumstance would ha' made a man—
For you're a handsome woman; would y' were wise,
    too!
I am a gentleman, come here disguised,
Only to find the knaveries of this citadel;
And where I might have wronged your honour, and
    have not,
I claim some interest in your love. You are,
They say, a widow rich, and I'm a bachelor
Worth nought. Your fortunes may make me a man,
As mine ha' preserved you a woman. Think upon it,
And whether I have deserved you or no.

DAME PLIANT.   I will, sir.

SURLY. And for these household-rogues, let me
    alone
To treat with them.

Enter SUBTLE.

SUBTLE.   How doth my noble Diego,
And my dear madam Countess? Hath the Count
Been courteous, lady, liberal and open?

Donzel, methinks you look melancholic,
After your coitum, and scurvy! Truly,
I do not like the dulness of your eye;
It hath a heavy cast, 'tis upsea Dutch,
And says you are a lumpish whoremaster.
Be lighter; I will make your pockets so.

Falls to picking SURLY'S *pockets.*

SURLY. Will you, Don Bawd and Pickpurse? How
  now! reel you?
Stand up, sir, you shall find, since I am so heavy,
I'll gi' you equal weight.
  SUBTLE.   Help! murder!
  SURLY.   No, sir,
There's no such thing intended. A good cart
And a clean whip shall ease you of that fear.
I am the Spanish Don, that should be cozened,
Do you see? cozened! Where's your Captain Face,
That parcel-broker and whole-bawd, all rascal?

Enter FACE *in his uniform.*

FACE. How, Surly!
  SURLY.   O, make your approach, good Captain.
I've found from whence your copper rings and
  spoons
Come, now, wherewith you cheat abroad in taverns.
'Twas here you learned t'anoint your boot with
  brimstone,
Then rub men's gold on't, for a kind of touch,
And say 'twas naught, when you had changed the
  colour,
That you might ha't for nothing. And this doctor,
Your sooty, smoky-bearded compeer, he
Will close you so much gold, in a bolt's-head,
And, on a turn, convey i' the stead another
With sublimed mercury, that shall burst i' the heat,
And fly out all in fumo! Then weeps Mammon;

Then swoons his worship. Or, he is the Faustus,
That casteth figures and can conjure, cures
Plagues, piles, and pox, by the Ephemerides,
And holds intelligence with all the bawds
And midwives of three shires; while you send in——

                                  Exit FACE.

Captain!—What! is he gone?—damsels with child,
Wives that are barren, or the waiting-maid
With the greensickness.—Nay, sir, you must tarry,
Though he be 'scaped; and answer by the ears, sir.

           Re-enter FACE *with* KASTRIL.

  FACE. Why, now's the time, if ever you will
    quarrel
Well, as they say, and be a true-born child.
The Doctor and your sister both are abused.

  KASTRIL. Where is he? Which is he? He is a slave,
Whate'er he is, and the son of a whore.—Are you
The man, sir, I would know?

  SURLY.   I should be loath, sir,
To confess so much.

  KASTRIL.   Then you lie i' your throat.

  SURLY.   How!

  FACE. —A very arrant rogue, sir, and a cheater,
Employed here by another conjurer
That does not love the Doctor, and would cross him
If he knew how—

  SURLY.   Sir, you are abused.

  KASTRIL.   You lie,
And 'tis no matter.

  FACE.   Well said, sir! He is
The impudent'st rascal——

  SURLY.   You are, indeed.—Will you hear me, sir?

  FACE. By no means; bid him be gone.

  KASTRIL.   Begone, sir, quickly.

SURLY. This's strange!—Lady, do you inform your
    brother.

FACE. There is not such a foist in all the town,
The Doctor had him presently; and finds yet
The Spanish Count will come here.—Bear up, Subtle.

SUBTLE. Yes, sir, he must appear within this hour.

FACE. And yet this rogue would come in a dis-
    guise,
By the temptation of another spirit,
To trouble our art, though he could not hurt it!

KASTRIL.   Ay,
I know.—Away, you talk like a foolish mauther.

SURLY. Sir, all is truth she says.

FACE.   Do not believe him, sir,
He is the lying'st swabber! Come your ways, sir.

SURLY. You are valiant out of company!

KASTRIL.   Yes, how then, sir?

Enter DRUGGER.

FACE. Nay, here's an honest fellow, too, that knows
    him,
And all his tricks.—Make good what I say, Abel.
This cheater would ha' cozened thee o' the widow.—
He owes this honest Drugger here seven pound,
He has had on him in twopenny'orths of tobacco.

DRUGGER. Yes, sir. And he's damned himself three
    terms to pay me.

FACE. And what does he owe for lotion?

DRUGGER.   Thirty shillings, sir,
And for six syringes.

SURLY.   Hydra of villainy!

FACE. —Nay, sir, you must quarrel him out o' the
    house.

KASTRIL.   I will.
—Sir, if you get not out o' doors, you lie;
And you are a pimp.

SURLY.   Why, this is madness, sir,
Not valour in you. I must laugh at this.

KASTRIL. It is my humour: you are a pimp and a
    trig,
And an Amadis de Gaul, or a Don Quixote.

DRUGGER. Or a knight o' the curious coxcomb, do
    you see?

Enter ANANIAS.

ANANIAS. Peace to the household!

KASTRIL.   I'll keep peace for no man.

ANANIAS. Casting of dollars is concluded lawful.

KASTRIL. Is he the Constable?

SUBTLE.   Peace, Ananias.

FACE. No, sir.

KASTRIL.   Then you are an otter, and a shad,
    a whit,
A very tim.

SURLY.   You'll hear me, sir?

KASTRIL.   I will not.

ANANIAS. What is the motive?

SUBTLE.   Zeal in the young gentleman,
Against his Spanish slops.

ANANIAS.   They are profane,
Lewd, superstitious, and idolatrous breeches.

SURLY. New rascals!

KASTRIL.   Will you be gone, sir?

ANANIAS.   Avoid, Satan!
Thou art not of the light. That ruff of pride,
About thy neck, betrays thee; and is the same
With that which the unclean birds, in 'seventy-seven,
Were seen to prank it with, on divers coasts.
Thou look'st like Antichrist in that lewd hat.

SURLY. I must give way.

KASTRIL.   Begone, sir.

SURLY.   But I'll take
A course with you,——

ANANIAS. Depart, proud Spanish fiend!

SURLY. Captain, and Doctor,——

ANANIAS. Child of perdition!

KASTRIL. Hence, sir!

Exit SURLY.

Did I not quarrel bravely?

FACE. Yes, indeed, sir.

KASTRIL. Nay, an I give my mind to't, I shall do't.

FACE. O, you must follow, sir, and threaten him
tame.

He'll turn again else.

KASTRIL. I'll re-turn him then. *Exit.*

FACE. —Drugger, this rogue prevented us, for thee.
We had determined that thou should'st ha' come
In a Spanish suit, and ha' carried her so; and he
A brokerly slave, goes, puts it on himself!
Hast brought the damask?

DRUGGER. Yes, sir.

FACE. Thou must borrow

A Spanish suit. Hast thou no credit with the players?

DRUGGER. Yes, sir, did you never see me play the
fool?

FACE. I know not, Nab.—Thou shalt, if I can help
it.—

Hieronimo's old cloak, ruff, and hat will serve;

Exit DRUGGER.

I'll tell thee more when thou bring'st 'em.

ANANIAS. *Having whispered with* SUBTLE *this
while.* Sir, I know
The Spaniard hates the Brethren, and hath spies
Upon their actions; and that this was one
I make no scruple. But the Holy Synod
Have been in prayer and meditation for it;
And 'tis revealed no less to them than me,
That casting of money is most lawful.

SUBTLE. True.

But here I cannot do it; if the house
Should chance to be suspected, all would out,
And we be locked up in the Tower forever,
To make gold there for th' state, never come out;
And then are you defeated.

ANANIAS.   I will tell
This to the elders and the weaker Brethren,
That the whole company of the Separation
May join in humble prayer again.

SUBTLE.   —And fasting.

ANANIAS. Yea, for some fitter place. The peace of
    mind
Rest with these walls!   *Exit.*

SUBTLE.   Thanks, courteous Ananias.

FACE. What did he come for?

SUBTLE.   About casting dollars
Presently, out of hand. And so I told him
A Spanish minister came here to spy
Against the faithful——

FACE.   I conceive. Come, Subtle,
Thou art so down upon the least disaster!
How wouldst th' ha' done, if I had not helped thee
    out?

SUBTLE. I thank thee, Face, for the angry boy, i'
    faith.

FACE. Who would ha' looked it should ha' been
    that rascal
Surly? He had dyed his beard and all. Well, sir,
Here's damask come, to make you a suit.

SUBTLE.   Where's Drugger?

FACE. He is gone to borrow me a Spanish habit;
I'll be the Count now.

SUBTLE.   But where's the widow?

FACE. Within, with my Lord's sister; Madam Doll
Is entertaining her.

SUBTLE. By your favour, Face,
Now she is honest, I will stand again.

FACE. You will not offer it?

SUBTLE. Why?

FACE. Stand to your word,
Or—here comes Doll—she knows——

SUBTLE. You're tyrannous still.

Enter DOLL.

FACE. Strict for my right.—How now, Doll! Hast told her
The Spanish Count will come?

DOLL. Yes, but another is come,
You little looked for!

FACE. Who is that?

DOLL. Your master,
The master of the house.

SUBTLE. How, Doll!

FACE. She lies,
This is some trick. Come, leave your quibblings, Dorothy.

DOLL. Look out and see.

SUBTLE. Art thou in earnest?

DOLL. 'Slight,
Forty o' the neighbours are about him, talking.

FACE. 'Tis he, by this good day!

DOLL. 'Twill prove ill day
For some on us.

FACE. We are undone, and taken!

DOLL. Lost, I'm afraid.

SUBTLE. You said he would not come,
While there died one a week within the liberties.

FACE. No, 'twas within the walls.

SUBTLE. Was't so! Cry you mercy,
I thought the liberties. What shall we do now, Face?

FACE. Be silent; not a word, if he call or knock.

I'll into mine old shape again, and meet him,
Of Jeremy, the butler. I' the meantime,
Do you two pack up all the goods and purchase,
That we can carry i' the two trunks. I'll keep him
Off for today, if I cannot longer; and then
At night, I'll ship you both away to Ratcliffe,
Where we will meet tomorrow; and there we'll share.
Let Mammon's brass and pewter keep the cellar;
We'll have another time for that. But, Doll,
Prithee go heat a little water quickly;
Subtle must shave me. All my captain's beard
Must off, to make me appear smooth Jeremy.
You'll do't?

    SUBTLE.   Yes, I'll shave you, as well as I can.
    FACE. And not cut my throat, but trim me?
    SUBTLE.   You shall see, sir.
                                          Exeunt.

ACT FIVE. SCENE ONE

Before Lovewit's door

Enter LOVEWIT, *with* NEIGHBOURS.

    LOVEWIT. Has there been such resort, say you?
    1ST NEIGHBOUR.   Daily, sir.
    2ND NEIGHBOUR. And nightly, too.
    3RD NEIGHBOUR.   Ay, some as brave as lords.
    4TH NEIGHBOUR. Ladies and gentlewomen.
    5TH NEIGHBOUR.   Citizens' wives.
    1ST NEIGHBOUR. And knights.
    6TH NEIGHBOUR.   In coaches.
    2ND NEIGHBOUR.   Yes, and oyster-women.

1ST NEIGHBOUR. Beside other gallants.

3RD NEIGHBOUR.   Sailors' wives.

4TH NEIGHBOUR.   Tobacco-men.

5TH NEIGHBOUR. Another Pimlico!

LOVEWIT.   What should my knave advance,
To draw this company? He hung out no banners
Of a strange calf with five legs, to be seen,
Or a huge lobster with six claws?

6TH NEIGHBOUR.   No, sir.

3RD NEIGHBOUR. We had gone in then, sir.

LOVEWIT.   He has no gift
Of teaching i' the nose, that e'er I knew of.
You saw no bills set up that promised cure
Of agues, or the toothache?

2ND NEIGHBOUR.   No such thing, sir!

LOVEWIT. Nor heard a drum struck, for baboons or
    puppets?

5TH NEIGHBOUR. Neither, sir.

LOVEWIT.   What device should he
    bring forth now?
I love a teeming wit as I love my nourishment.
Pray God he ha' not kept such open house,
That he hath sold my hangings and my bedding!
I left him nothing else. If he have eat 'em,
A plague o' the moth, say I! Sure he has got
Some bawdy pictures to call all this ging;
The Friar and the Nun, or the new motion
Of the knight's courser covering the parson's mare;
The boy of six year old with the great thing.
Or 't may be, he has the fleas that run at tilt
Upon a table, or some dog to dance.
When saw you him?

1ST NEIGHBOUR.   Who, sir, Jeremy?

2ND NEIGHBOUR.   Jeremy butler?
We saw him not this month.

LOVEWIT.   How!

4TH NEIGHBOUR.   Not these five weeks, sir.

1ST NEIGHBOUR. These six weeks at the least.

LOVEWIT.   Y'amaze me, neighbours!

5TH NEIGHBOUR. Sure, if your worship know not
    where he is,

He's slipped away.

6TH NEIGHBOUR.   Pray God he be not made away!

LOVEWIT. Ha! it's no time to question, then.

                                 Knocks.

6TH NEIGHBOUR.   About

Some three weeks since, I heard a doleful cry,

As I sat up a-mending my wife's stockings.

LOVEWIT. 'Tis strange that none will answer! Did'st
    thou hear

A cry, sayst thou?

6TH NEIGHBOUR. Yes, sir, like unto a man

That had been strangled an hour, and could not
    speak.

2ND NEIGHBOUR. I heard it too, just this day three
    weeks, at two o'clock

Next morning.

LOVEWIT.   These be miracles, or you make 'em
    so!

A man an hour strangled, and could not speak,

And both you heard him cry?

3RD NEIGHBOUR.   Yes, downward, sir.

LOVEWIT. Thou art a wise fellow. Give me thy
    hand, I pray thee.

What trade art thou on?

3RD NEIGHBOUR.   A smith, an't please your
    worship.

LOVEWIT. A smith! then lend me thy help to get
    this door open.

3RD NEIGHBOUR. That I will presently, sir, but
    fetch my tools——   *Exit.*

1ST NEIGHBOUR. Sir, best to knock again, afore
you break it.

LOVEWIT. I will.

Enter FACE *in his butler's livery.*

FACE.   What mean you, sir?

1ST, 2ND, 4TH NEIGHBOURS.   O, here's Jeremy!

FACE. Good sir, come from the door.

LOVEWIT.   Why, what's the matter?

FACE. Yet farther, you are too near yet.

LOVEWIT.   I' the name of wonder,
What means the fellow?

FACE.   The house, sir, has been visited.

LOVEWIT. What, with the plague? Stand thou then
farther.

FACE.   No, sir,
I had it not.

LOVEWIT.   Who had it then? I left
None else but thee i' the house.

FACE.   Yes, sir. My fellow,
The cat that kept the butt'ry, had it on her
A week, before I spied it; but I got her
Conveyed away i' the night. And so I shut
The house up for a month——

LOVEWIT.   How!

FACE.   Purposing then, sir,
T' have burnt rose-vinegar, treacle, and tar,
And ha' made it sweet, that you should ne'er ha'
known it;
Because I knew the news would but afflict you, sir.

LOVEWIT. Breathe less, and farther off! Why this is
stranger!
The neighbours tell me all, here, that the doors
Have still been open——

FACE.   How, sir!

LOVEWIT.   Gallants, men and women,
And of all sorts, tag-rag, been seen to flock here
In threaves, these ten weeks, as to a second Hogs-
    den,
In days of Pimlico and Eyebright.

FACE.   Sir,
Their wisdoms will not say so!

LOVEWIT.   Today they speak
Of coaches and gallants. One in a French hood
Went in, they tell me; and another was seen
In a velvet gown at the window. Divers more
Pass in and out.

FACE.   They did pass through the doors then,
Or walls, I assure their eyesights and their spectacles.
For here, sir, are the keys, and here have been,
In this my pocket, now above twenty days;
And for before, I kept the fort alone there.
But that 'tis yet not deep i' the afternoon,
I should believe my neighbours had seen double
Through the black pot, and made these apparitions!
For, on my faith to your worship, for these three
    weeks
And upwards, the door has not been opened.

LOVEWIT.   Strange!

1ST NEIGHBOUR. Good faith, I think I saw a coach.

2ND NEIGHBOUR.   And I, too,
I'd ha' been sworn.

LOVEWIT.   Do you but think it now?
And but one coach?

4TH NEIGHBOUR.   We cannot tell, sir. Jeremy
Is a very honest fellow.

FACE.   Did you see me at all?

1ST NEIGHBOUR. No, that we are sure on.

2ND NEIGHBOUR.   I'll be sworn o' that.

LOVEWIT. Fine rogues to have your testimonies
    built on!

Re-enter 3RD NEIGHBOUR.

3RD NEIGHBOUR. Is Jeremy come?

1ST NEIGHBOUR.   O yes, you may leave your tools.
We were deceived, he says.

2ND NEIGHBOUR.   He's had the keys,
And the door has been shut these three weeks

3RD NEIGHBOUR.   Like enough.

LOVEWIT. Peace, and get hence, you changelings.

Enter SURLY *and* MAMMON.

FACE.   —Surly come!
And Mammon made acquainted! They'll tell all.
How shall I beat them off? What shall I do?
Nothing's more wretched than a guilty conscience.

SURLY. No, sir, he was a great physician. This,
It was no bawdy-house, but a mere chancel!
You knew the Lord and his sister.

MAMMON.   Nay, good Surly,——

SURLY. The happy word, 'Be rich,'——

MAMMON.   Play not the tyrant—

SURLY. Should be today pronounced to all your
    friends.
And where be your andirons now, and your brass
    pots,
That should ha' been golden flagons, and great
    wedges?

MAMMON. Let me but breathe. *They knock.* What?
    They ha' shut their doors,
Methinks!

SURLY.   Ay, now 'tis holiday with them.

MAMMON.   Rogues,
Cozeners, impostors, bawds!

FACE.   What mean you, sir?

MAMMON. To enter if we can.

FACE.   Another man's house!
Here is the owner, sir. Turn you to him,
And speak your business.

MAMMON.   Are you, sir, the owner?

LOVEWIT. Yes, sir.

MAMMON.   And are those knaves, within, your
    cheaters?

LOVEWIT. What knaves? What cheaters?

MAMMON.   Subtle and his Lungs.

FACE. The gentleman is distracted, sir! No lungs
Nor lights ha' been seen here these three weeks,
    sir,
Within these doors, upon my word!

SURLY.   Your word,
Groom arrogant!

FACE.   Yes, sir, I am the housekeeper,
And know the keys ha' not been out o' my hands.

SURLY. This's a new Face.

FACE.   You do mistake the house, sir.
What sign was't at?

SURLY.   You rascal! This is one
O' the confederacy. Come, let's get officers,
And force the door.

LOVEWIT.   Pray you stay, gentlemen.

SURLY. No, sir, we'll come with warrant.

MAMMON.   Ay, and then
We shall ha' your doors open.

                   Exeunt MAMMON *and* SURLY.

LOVEWIT.   What means this?

FACE. I cannot tell, sir.

1ST NEIGHBOUR.   These are two o' the gallants
That we do think we saw.

FACE.   Two o' the fools!
You talk as idly as they. Good faith, sir,
I think the moon has crazed 'em all.

Enter KASTRIL.

—O me,
The angry boy come too! He'll make a noise,
And ne'er away till he have betrayed us all.

KASTRIL. *Knocks.* What, rogues, bawds, slaves,
you'll open the door, anon!
Punk, cockatrice, my suster! By this light,
I'll fetch the Marshal to you. You are a whore,
To keep your castle——

FACE.   Who would you speak with, sir?

KASTRIL. The bawdy Doctor, and the cozening
Captain,
And Puss, my suster.

LOVEWIT.   This is something, sure.

FACE. Upon my trust, the doors were never open,
sir.

KASTRIL. I have heard all their tricks told me
twice over,
By the fat knight and the lean gentleman.

LOVEWIT. Here comes another.

Enter ANANIAS *and* TRIBULATION.

FACE.   Ananias, too!
And his pastor!

TRIBULATION. *Beating at the door.* The doors are
shut against us.

ANANIAS. Come forth, you seed of sulphur, sons of
fire!
Your stench it is broke forth; abomination
Is in the house.

KASTRIL.   Ay, my suster's there.

ANANIAS.   The place,
It is become a cage of unclean birds.

KASTRIL. Yes, I will fetch the Scavenger, and the
Constable.

TRIBULATION. You shall do well.

ANANIAS.   We'll join, to weed them out.

KASTRIL. You will not come then, punk-device, my suster?

ANANIAS. Call her not sister. She is a harlot verily.

KASTRIL. I'll raise the street.

LOVEWIT.   Good gentlemen, a word.

ANANIAS. Satan, avoid, and hinder not our zeal!

Exeunt ANANIAS, TRIBULATION, *and* KASTRIL.

LOVEWIT. The world's turned Bedlam.

FACE.   These are all broke loose,
Out of Saint Katherine's, where they use to keep
The better sort of mad-folks.

1ST NEIGHBOUR.   All these persons
We saw go in and out here.

2ND NEIGHBOUR.   Yes, indeed, sir.

3RD NEIGHBOUR. These were the parties.

FACE.   Peace, you drunkards! Sir,
I wonder at it! Please you to give me leave
To touch the door, I'll try an the lock be changed.

LOVEWIT. It amazes me!

FACE.   Good faith, sir, I believe
There's no such thing. 'Tis all deceptio visus.—
Would I could get him away!

DAPPER. *Cries out within.* Master Captain! Master Doctor!

LOVEWIT. Who's that?

FACE.   —Our clerk within, that I
forgot!—I know not, sir.

DAPPER. For God's sake, when will her Grace be at leisure?

FACE.   Ha!
Illusions, some spirit 'o the air!—His gag is melted,
And now he sets out the throat.

DAPPER.   I am almost stifled——

FACE. —Would you were altogether.

LOVEWIT.   'Tis in the house.
Ha, list!

FACE. Believe it, sir, i' the air.

LOVEWIT.   Peace, you——

DAPPER. Mine aunt's Grace does not use me well.

SUBTLE.   You fool,
Peace, you'll mar all.

FACE.   —Or you will else, you rogue.

LOVEWIT. O, is it so? Then you converse with
    spirits!
Come, sir. No more o' your tricks, good Jeremy;
The truth, the shortest way.

FACE.   Dismiss this rabble, sir.—
What shall I do? I am catched.

LOVEWIT.   Good neighbours,
I thank you all. You may depart. *Exeunt* NEIGH-
    BOURS. Come, sir,
You know that I am an indulgent master;
And therefore conceal nothing. What's your med'-
    cine,
To draw so many several sorts of wildfowl?

FACE. Sir, you were wont to affect mirth and
    wit——
But here's no place to talk on't i' the street.
Give me but leave to make the best of my fortune,
And only pardon me th' abuse of your house.
It's all I beg. I'll help you to a widow,
In recompense, that you shall gi' me thanks for,
Will make you seven years younger, and a rich one.
'Tis but your putting on a Spanish cloak;
I have her within. You need not fear the house,
It was not visited.

LOVEWIT.   But by me, who came
Sooner than you expected.

FACE.   It is true, sir.
Pray you forgive me.

LOVEWIT.   Well—let's see your widow.

Exeunt.

ACT FIVE. SCENE TWO

Lovewit's house

Enter SUBTLE *with* DAPPER.

SUBTLE. How! ha' you eaten your gag?

DAPPER.   Yes, faith, it crumbled
Away i' my mouth.

SUBTLE.   You ha' spoiled all then.

DAPPER.   No!
I hope my aunt of Faery will forgive me.

SUBTLE. Your aunt's a gracious lady, but in troth
You were to blame.

DAPPER.   The fume did overcome me,
And I did do't to stay my stomach. Pray you
So satisfy her Grace. Here comes the Captain.

Enter FACE *in his uniform.*

FACE. How now! is his mouth down?

SUBTLE.   Ay, he has spoken!

FACE. A pox, I heard him, and you too!—He's
    undone then.—
I have been fain to say the house is haunted
With spirits, to keep churl back.

SUBTLE.   And hast thou done it?

FACE. Sure, for this night.

SUBTLE.   Why, then triumph and sing
Of Face so famous, the precious king
Of present wits.

FACE.   Did you not hear the coil
About the door?

SUBTLE.   Yes, and I dwindled with it.

FACE. Show him his aunt, and let him be dis-
    patched.
I'll send her to you.   *Exit* FACE.

SUBTLE.   Well, sir, your aunt, her Grace,
Will give you audience presently, on my suit,
And the Captain's word that you did not eat your
    gag
In any contempt of her Highness.

DAPPER.   Not I, in troth, sir.

Enter DOLL *like the Queen of Faery.*

SUBTLE. Here she is come. Down o' your knees and
    wriggle.
She has a stately presence.—Good! Yet nearer,
And bid, 'God save you!'

DAPPER.   Madam!

SUBTLE.   And your aunt.

DAPPER. And my most gracious aunt, God save
    your Grace.

DOLL. Nephew, we thought to have been angry
    with you;
But that sweet face of yours hath turned the tide,
And made it flow with joy, that ebbed of love.
Arise, and touch our velvet gown.

SUBTLE.   —The skirts,
And kiss 'em. So!

DOLL.   Let me now stroke that head:
'Much, nephew, shalt thou win, much shalt thou
    spend,
Much shalt thou give away, much shalt thou lend.'

SUBTLE. Ay, much, indeed!—Why do you not
    thank her Grace?

DAPPER. I cannot speak for joy.

SUBTLE.   See, the kind wretch!
Your Grace's kinsman right.

DOLL.   Give me the bird.
Here is your fly in a purse, about your neck, cousin;
Wear it, and feed it about this day sev'night
On your right wrist——

SUBTLE.   Open a vein with a pin,
And let it suck but once a week. Till then,
You must not look on't.

DOLL.   No; and, kinsman,
Bear yourself worthy of the blood you come on.

SUBTLE. Her Grace would ha' you eat no more
    Woolsack pies,
No Dagger frumenty.

DOLL.   Nor break his fast
In Heaven and Hell.

SUBTLE.   She's with you everywhere!
Nor play with costermongers, at mumchance, tray-
    trip,
God-make-you-rich,—whenas your aunt has done it—
    but keep
The gallant'st company, and the best games——

DAPPER.   Yes, sir.

SUBTLE. Gleek and primero; and what you get, be
    true to us.

DAPPER. By this hand, I will.

SUBTLE.   You may bring 's a thousand pound
Before tomorrow night, if but three thousand
Be stirring, an you will.

DAPPER.   I swear I will then.

SUBTLE. Your fly will learn you all games.

FACE.   Ha' you done there?

SUBTLE. Your Grace will command him no more
    duties?

DOLL.   No,
But come and see me often. I may chance
To leave him three or four hundred chests of
    treasure,
And some twelve thousand acres of Fairyland,
If he game well and comely with good gamesters,

SUBTLE. There's a kind aunt! Kiss her departing
    part.
But you must sell your forty mark a year now.

DAPPER. Ay, sir, I mean.

SUBTLE.   Or gi't away, pox on't!

DAPPER. I'll gi't mine aunt. I'll go and fetch the
    writings.   *Exit.*

SUBTLE. 'Tis well, away!

Re-enter FACE.

FACE.   Where's Subtle?

SUBTLE.   Here. What news?

FACE. Drugger is at the door; go take his suit,
And bid him fetch a parson presently;
Say he shall marry the widow. Thou shalt spend
A hundred pound by the service!   *Exit* SUBTLE.
                  Now, Queen Doll,
Ha' you packed up all?

DOLL.   Yes.

FACE.   And how do you like
The Lady Pliant?

DOLL.   A good, dull innocent.

Re-enter SUBTLE.

SUBTLE. Here's your Hieronimo's cloak and hat.

FACE.   Give me 'em.

SUBTLE. And the ruff too?

FACE.   Yes; I'll come to you presently.

                                        Exit.

SUBTLE. Now he is gone about his project, Doll,
I told you of, for the widow.

DOLL.   'Tis direct
Against our articles.

SUBTLE.   Well, we'll fit him, wench.
Hast thou gulled her of her jewels or her bracelets?

DOLL. No, but I will do 't.

SUBTLE.   Soon at night, my Dolly,
When we are shipped, and all our goods aboard,
Eastward for Ratcliffe; we will turn our course
To Brainford, westward, if thou sayst the word,
And take our leaves of this o'erweening rascal,
This peremptory Face.

DOLL.   Content, I'm weary of him.

SUBTLE. Th'ast cause, when the slave will run a-
    wiving, Doll,
Against the instrument that was drawn between us.

DOLL. I'll pluck his bird as bare as I can.

SUBTLE.   Yes, tell her
She must, by any means, address some present
To th' cunning-man; make him amends for wrong-
    ing
His art with her suspicion; send a ring,
Or chain of pearl. She will be tortured else
Extremely in her sleep, say; and ha' strange things
Come to her. Wilt thou?

DOLL.   Yes.

SUBTLE.   My fine flittermouse,
My bird o' the night! we'll tickle it at the Pigeons,
When we have all, and may unlock the trunks,
And say, this 's mine, and thine; and thine, and
    mine——   *They kiss.*

Re-enter FACE.

FACE. What now! a-billing?

SUBTLE. Yes, a little exalted
In the good passage of our stock-affairs.

FACE. Drugger has brought his parson; take him in, Subtle,
And send Nab back again to wash his face.

SUBTLE. I will; and shave himself? *Exit.*

FACE. If you can get him.

DOLL. You are hot upon it, Face, whate'er it is!

FACE. A trick that Doll shall spend ten pound a month by.

Re-enter SUBTLE.

Is he gone?

SUBTLE. The chaplain waits you in the hall, sir.

FACE. I'll go bestow him. *Exit.*

DOLL. He'll now marry her instantly.

SUBTLE. He cannot yet; he is not ready. Dear Doll,
Cozen her of all thou canst. To deceive him
Is no deceit, but justice, that would break
Such an inextricable tie as ours was.

DOLL. Let me alone to fit him.

Re-enter FACE.

FACE. Come, my venturers,
You ha' packed up all? Where be the trunks? Bring forth.

SUBTLE. Here.

FACE. Let's see 'em. Where's the money?

SUBTLE. Here,
In this.

FACE. Mammon's ten pound; eight score before;

The Brethren's money this; Drugger's, and Dap-
    per's—
What paper's that?

    DOLL.   The jewel of the waiting-maid's,
That stole it from her lady, to know certain——

    FACE. If she should have precedence of her mis-
    tress?

    DOLL. Yes.

    FACE. What box is that?

    SUBTLE.   The fishwife's rings, I think,
And th' alewife's single money. Is't not, Doll?

    DOLL. Yes, and the whistle that the sailor's wife
Brought you, to know an her husband were with
    Ward.

    FACE. We'll wet it tomorrow; and our silver
    beakers
And tavern cups. Where be the French petticoats,
And girdles and hangers?

    SUBTLE.   Here, i' the trunk,
And the bolts of lawn.

    FACE.   Is Drugger's damask there,
And the tobacco?

    SUBTLE.   Yes.

    FACE.   Give me the keys.

    DOLL. Why you the keys?

    SUBTLE.   No matter, Doll, because
We shall not open 'em before he comes.

    FACE. 'Tis true, you shall not open them, indeed;
Nor have 'em forth, do you see? not forth, Doll.

    DOLL.   No!

    FACE. No, my smock-rampant. The right is, my
    master
Knows all, has pardoned me, and he will keep 'em.
Doctor, 'tis true,—you look—for all your figures!
I sent for him, indeed. Wherefore, good partners,
Both he and she, be satisfied; for here

Determines the indenture tripartite
'Twixt Subtle, Doll, and Face. All I can do
Is to help you over the wall, o' the back-side,
Or lend you a sheet to save your velvet gown, Doll.
Here will be officers presently. Bethink you
Of some course suddenly to 'scape the dock,
For thither you will come else. Hark you, thunder.

Some knock.

SUBTLE. You are a precious fiend!

OFFICERS. Open the door.

FACE. Doll, I am sorry for thee i' faith. But hear'st
thou?
It shall go hard, but I will place thee somewhere;
Thou shalt ha' my letter to Mistress Amo——

DOLL. Hang you—

FACE. Or Madam Caesarean.

DOLL. Pox upon you, rogue,
Would I had but time to beat thee!

FACE. Subtle,
Let's know where you set up next; I'll send you
A customer, now and then, for old acquaintance.
What new course have you?

SUBTLE. Rogue, I'll hang myself;
That I may walk a greater devil than thou,
And haunt thee i' the flock-bed and the buttery.

Exit with DOLL.

ACT FIVE. SCENE THREE

Within Lovewit's door

Enter LOVEWIT *in the Spanish dress, with a* PARSON.

LOVEWIT. What do you mean, my masters?

MAMMON. *Knocking without.*   Open your door,
Cheaters, bawds, conjurers.

OFFICER.   Or we'll break it open.

LOVEWIT. What warrant have you?

OFFICER.   Warrant enough, sir, doubt not,
If you'll not open it.

LOVEWIT.   Is there an officer there?

OFFICER. Yes, two or three for failing.

LOVEWIT.   Have but patience,
And I will open it straight.

Enter FACE *as butler.*

FACE.   Sir, ha' you done?
Is it a marriage? perfect?

LOVEWIT.   Yes, my brain.

FACE. Off with your ruff and cloak then; be yourself, sir.

SURLY. Down with the door!

KASTRIL.   'Slight, ding it open!

LOVEWIT.   Hold,
Hold, gentlemen, what means this violence?

Enter MAMMON, SURLY, KASTRIL, ANANIAS, TRIBULA-
TION, *and* OFFICERS.

MAMMON. Where is this collier?

SURLY.   And my Captain Face?

MAMMON. These day-owls.

SURLY. That are birding in men's purses.

MAMMON. Madam Suppository.

KASTRIL. Doxy, my suster.

ANANIAS. Locusts
Of the foul pit.

TRIBULATION. Profane as Bel and the Dragon.

ANANIAS. Worse than the grasshoppers, or the lice
of Egypt.

LOVEWIT. Good gentlemen, hear me.—Are you officers,
And cannot stay this violence?

1ST OFFICER. Keep the peace!

LOVEWIT. Gentlemen, what is the matter? Whom
do you seek?

MAMMON. The chemical cozener.

SURLY. And the captain pander.

KASTRIL. The nun, my suster.

MAMMON. Madam Rabbi.

ANANIAS. Scorpions
And caterpillars.

LOVEWIT. Fewer at once, I pray you.

1ST OFFICER. One after another, gentlemen, I
charge you,
By virtue of my staff——

ANANIAS. They are the vessels
Of pride, lust, and the cart.

LOVEWIT. Good zeal, lie still
A little while.

TRIBULATION. Peace, Deacon Ananias.

LOVEWIT. The house is mine here, and the doors
are open.
If there be any such persons as you seek for,
Use your authority, search on, o' God's name.
I am but newly come to town, and finding

This tumult 'bout my door, to tell you true,
It somewhat 'mazed me; till my man here, fearing
My more displeasure, told me he had done
Somewhat an insolent part, let out my house—
Belike presuming on my known aversion
From any air o' the town, while there was sickness—
To a doctor and a captain. Who, what they are,
Or where they be, he knows not.

    MAMMON.   Are they gone?

    LOVEWIT. You may go in and search, sir. *Exeunt*
MAMMON, ANANIAS, *and* TRIBULATION. Here, I find
The empty walls, worse than I left 'em, smoked;
A few cracked pots and glasses, and a furnace;
The ceiling filled with poesies of the candle;
And madam with a dildo writ o' the walls.
Only one gentlewoman I met here,
That is within, that said she was a widow——

    KASTRIL. Ay, that's my suster. I'll go thump her.
    Where is she?   *Exit.*

    LOVEWIT. And should ha' married a Spanish count,
    but he,
When he came to't, neglected her so grossly,
That I, a widower, am gone through with her.

    SURLY. How! have I lost her then?

    LOVEWIT.   Were you the Don, sir?
Good faith, now she does blame y' extremely, and
    says
You swore, and told her you had ta'en the pains
To dye your beard, and umber o'er your face;
Borrowed a suit and ruff, all for her love;
And then did nothing. What an oversight,
And want of putting forward, sir, was this!
Well fare an old harquebusier yet,
Could prime his powder, and give fire, and hit,
All in a twinkling!

Re-enter MAMMON.

MAMMON.   The whole nest are fled!

LOVEWIT. What sort of birds were they?

MAMMON.   A kind of choughs,
Or thievish daws, sir, that have picked my purse
Of eight score and ten pounds within these five
    weeks,
Beside my first materials; and my goods,
That lie i' the cellar, which I am glad they ha' left,
I may have home yet.

LOVEWIT.   Think you so, sir?

MAMMON.   Ay.

LOVEWIT. By order of law, sir, but not otherwise.

MAMMON. Not mine own stuff!

LOVEWIT.   Sir, I can take no knowledge
That they are yours, but by public means.
If you can bring certificate that you were gulled
    of 'em,
Or any formal writ, out of a court,
That you did cozen yourself, I will not hold them.

MAMMON. I'll rather lose 'em.

LOVEWIT.   That you shall not, sir,
By me, in troth. Upon these terms, they 're yours.
What should they ha' been, sir? turned into gold
    all?

MAMMON. No.
I cannot tell—it may be they should. What then?

LOVEWIT. What a great loss in hope have you
    sustained!

MAMMON. Not I, the commonwealth has.

FACE.   Ay, he would ha' built
The city new; and made a ditch about it
Of silver, should have run with cream from Hogs-
    den;

That every Sunday, in Moorfields, the younkers,
And tits, and tom-boys should have fed on, gratis.
   MAMMON. I will go mount a turnip-cart, and
     preach
The end o' the world within these two months.
     Surly,
What! in a dream?
   SURLY.   Must I needs cheat myself
With that same foolish vice of honesty!
Come, let us go and hearken out the rogues.
That Face I'll mark for mine, if e'er I meet him.
   FACE. If I can hear of him, sir, I'll bring you word
Unto your lodging. For in troth, they were strangers
To me; I thought 'em honest as myself, sir.
                Exeunt MAMMON *and* SURLY.

       Re-enter ANANIAS *and* TRIBULATION.

   TRIBULATION. 'Tis well, the Saints shall not lose all
     yet. Go
And get some carts——
   LOVEWIT.   For what, my zealous friends?
   ANANIAS. To bear away the portion of the right-
     eous
Out of this den of thieves.
   LOVEWIT.   What is that portion?
   ANANIAS. The goods, sometimes the orphans', that
     the Brethren
Bought with their silver pence.
   LOVEWIT.   What, those i' the cellar,
The knight Sir Mammon claims?
   ANANIAS.   I do defy
The wicked Mammon; so do all the Brethren,
Thou profane man! I ask thee with what conscience
Thou canst advance that idol, against us

That have the seal? Were not the shillings num-
    bered
That made the pounds? Were not the pounds told
    out
Upon the second day of the fourth week,
In the eighth month, upon the table dormant,
The year of the last patience of the Saints,
Six hundred and ten?

  LOVEWIT.   Mine earnest, vehement botcher,
And deacon also, I cannot dispute with you;
But if you get you not away the sooner,
I shall confute you with a cudgel.

  ANANIAS.   Sir!

  TRIBULATION. Be patient, Ananias.

  ANANIAS.   I am strong,
And will stand up, well girt, against an host
That threaten Gad in exile.

  LOVEWIT.   I shall send you
To Amsterdam, to your cellar.

  ANANIAS.   I will pray there,
Against thy house: may dogs defile thy walls,
And wasps and hornets breed beneath thy roof,
This seat of falsehood, and this cave of cozenage!

                Exeunt ANANIAS *and* TRIBULATION.

                  Enter DRUGGER

  LOVEWIT. Another, too?

  DRUGGER.   Not I, sir, I am no Brother.

  LOVEWIT. *Beats* DRUGGER *away.* Away, you Harry
    Nicholas! do you talk?

  FACE. No, this was Abel Drugger. *To the* PARSON.
    Good sir, go,
And satisfy him; tell him all is done.
He strayed too long a-washing of his face.
The Doctor, he shall hear of him at Westchester;

And of the Captain, tell him, at Yarmouth, or
Some good port-town else, lying for a wind.

Exit PARSON.

If you can get off the angry child now, sir——

Enter KASTRIL *with* DAME PLIANT.

KASTRIL. Come on, you ewe, you have matched
most sweetly, ha' you not?
Did not I say, I would never ha' you tupped
But by a dubbed boy, to make you a lady-tom?
'Slight, you are a mammet! O, I could touse you
now.
Death, mun you marry with a pox?

LOVEWIT.   You lie, boy!
As sound as you; and I am aforehand with you.

KASTRIL.   Anon?

LOVEWIT. Come, will you quarrel? I will feeze
you, sirrah.
Why do you not buckle to your tools?

KASTRIL.   God's light,
This is a fine old boy as e'er I saw!

LOVEWIT. What, do you change your copy now?
Proceed,
Here stands my dove; stoop at her if you dare.

KASTRIL. 'Slight, I must love him! I cannot choose,
i' faith,
An I should be hanged for't! Suster, I protest,
I honour thee for this match.

LOVEWIT.   O, do you so, sir?

KASTRIL. Yes, an thou canst take tobacco and
drink, old boy,
I'll give her five hundred pound more to her marriage,
Than her own state.

LOVEWIT.   Fill a pipe-full, Jeremy.

FACE. Yes, but go in and take it, sir.

LOVEWIT.   We will.
I will be ruled by thee in anything, Jeremy.
    KASTRIL. 'Slight, thou art not hide-bound! thou
      art a jovy boy!
Come, let's in, I pray thee, and take our whiffs.
    LOVEWIT. Whiff in with your sister, brother boy.
    Exeunt KASTRIL *and* DAME PLIANT. That master
That had received such happiness by a servant,
In such a widow, and with so much wealth,
Were very ungrateful, if he would not be
A little indulgent to that servant's wit,
And help his fortune, though with some small strain
Of his own candour. Therefore, gentlemen,
And kind spectators, if I have outstripped
An old man's gravity, or strict canon, think
What a young wife and a good brain may do:
Stretch age's truth sometimes, and crack it too.—
Speak for thyself, knave.
    FACE.   So I will, sir.—Gentlemen,
My part a little fell in this last scene,
Yet 'twas decorum. And though I am clean
Got off from Subtle, Surly, Mammon, Doll,
Hot Ananias, Dapper, Drugger, all
With whom I traded; yet I put myself
On you, that are my country; and this pelf,
Which I have got, if you do quit me, rests
To feast you often, and invite new guests.   *Exeunt.*

Every Man
in His Humour

THE PERSONS OF THE PLAY

KNOWELL, *an old gentleman*

EDWARD KNOWELL, *his son*

BRAINWORM, *the father's man*

MASTER STEPHEN, *a country gull*

MASTER MATTHEW, *a town gull*

CAPTAIN BOBADILL, *a Paul's man*

GEORGE DOWNRIGHT, *a plain squire*

WELLBRED, *his half-brother*

KITELY, *a merchant, their brother-in-law*

THOMAS CASH, *his cashier*

OLIVER COB, *a water-bearer*

JUSTICE CLEMENT, *an old merry magistrate*

ROGER FORMAL, *his clerk*

DAME KITELY, KITELY'S *wife*

MISTRESS BRIDGET, *his sister*

TIB, COB'S *wife*

Servants, &c.

The Scene: LONDON

PROLOGUE

Though need make many poets, and some such
As art and nature have not bettered much;
Yet ours, for want, hath not so loved the stage,
As he dare serve th' ill customs of the age,
Or purchase your delight at such a rate,
As, for it, he himself must justly hate:
To make a child, now swaddled, to proceed
Man, and then shoot up, in one beard and weed,
Past threescore years; or, with three rusty swords,
And help of some few foot-and-half-foot words,
Fight over York and Lancaster's long jars,
And in the tiring-house bring wounds to scars.
He rather prays you will be pleased to see
One such, today, as other plays should be;
Where neither chorus wafts you o'er the seas,
Nor creaking throne comes down the boys to please,
Nor nimble squib is seen to make afeard
The gentlewomen, nor rolled bullet heard
To say it thunders, nor tempestuous drum
Rumbles to tell you when the storm doth come;
But deeds and language such as men do use,
And persons such as Comedy would choose,
When she would show an image of the times,
And sport with human follies, not with crimes;
Except we make 'em such, by loving still
Our popular errors, when we know they're ill.
I mean such errors, as you'll all confess,
By laughing at them, they deserve no less;
Which when you heartily do, there's hope left then,
You, that have so graced monsters, may like men.

EVERY MAN
IN HIS HUMOUR

ACT ONE. SCENE ONE

Before Knowell's house

Enter KNOWELL.

KNOWELL. A goodly day toward, and a fresh morning!—Brainworm,

Enter BRAINWORM.

Call up your young master; bid him rise, sir.
Tell him I have some business to employ him.

BRAINWORM. I will, sir, presently.

KNOWELL. But hear you, sirrah,
If he be 't his book, disturb him not.

BRAINWORM. Well, sir.

Exit.

KNOWELL. How happy yet should I esteem myself,
Could I, by any practice, wean the boy
From one vain course of study he affects.
He is a scholar, if a man may trust
The liberal voice of fame in her report,
Of good account in both our Universities,
Either of which hath favoured him with graces;
But their indulgence must not spring in me
A fond opinion that he cannot err.
Myself was once a student, and indeed,
Fed with the self-same humour he is now,
Dreaming on nought but idle poetry,
That fruitless and unprofitable art,

Good unto none, but least to the professors,
Which then I thought the mistress of all knowl-
 edge;
But since, time and the truth have waked my judg-
 ment,
And reason taught me better to distinguish
The vain from th' useful learnings.

Enter STEPHEN.

        Cousin Stephen,
What news with you, that you are here so early?

 STEPHEN. Nothing, but e'en come to see how you
do, uncle.

 KNOWELL. That's kindly done; you are welcome,
coz.

 STEPHEN. Ay, I know that, sir, I would not ha'
come else.
How does my cousin Edward, uncle?

 KNOWELL. O well, coz, go in and see; I doubt he
be scarce stirring yet.

 STEPHEN. Uncle, afore I go in, can you tell me an
he have e'er a book of the sciences of hawking and
hunting? I would fain borrow it.

 KNOWELL. Why, I hope you will not a-hawking
now, will you?

 STEPHEN. No, wuss; but I'll practise against next
year, uncle; I have bought me a hawk, and a hood,
and bells, and all; I lack nothing but a book to keep
it by.

 KNOWELL. O, most ridiculous!

 STEPHEN. Nay, look you now, you are angry, uncle;
why you know, an a man have not skill in the hawking and hunting languages nowadays, I'll not give a
rush for him. They are more studied than the Greek
or the Latin. He is for no gallants' company without 'em. And by gadslid I scorn it, I, so I do, to be

a consort for every humdrum; hang 'em, scroyles,
there's nothing in 'em i' the world. What do you
talk on it? Because I dwell at Hogsden, I shall keep
company with none but the archers of Finsbury, or
the citizens that come a-ducking to Islington ponds?
A fine jest, i' faith! 'Slid, a gentleman mun show
himself like a gentleman. Uncle, I pray you be not
angry; I know what I have to do, I trow, I am no
novice.

    KNOWELL. You are a prodigal, absurd coxcomb.
       Go to!
Nay, never look at me; it's I that speak.
Take't as you will sir, I'll not flatter you.
Ha' you not yet found means enow to waste
That which your friends have left you, but you must
Go cast away your money on a kite,
And know not how to keep it, when you ha' done?
O, it's comely! this will make you a gentleman!
Well, cousin, well! I see you are e'en past hope
Of all reclaim.—Ay, so, now you're told on it,
You look another way.

    STEPHEN.   What would you ha' me do?
    KNOWELL. What would I have you do? I'll tell
       you, kinsman,
Learn to be wise and practise how to thrive,
That would I have you do; and not to spend
Your coin on every bauble that you fancy,
Or every foolish brain that humours you.
I would not have you to invade each place,
Nor thrust yourself on all societies,
Till men's affections or your own desert
Should worthily invite you to your rank.
He that is so respectless in his courses
Oft sells his reputation at cheap market.
Nor would I, you should melt away yourself
In flashing bravery, lest, while you affect

To make a blaze of gentry to the world,
A little puff of scorn extinguish it,
And you be left like an unsav'ry snuff
Whose property is only to offend.
I'd ha' you sober, and contain yourself,
Not that your sail be bigger than your boat;
But moderate your expenses now, at first,
As you may keep the same proportion still;
Nor stand so much on your gentility,
Which is an airy and mere borrowed thing
From dead men's dust and bones, and none of yours,
Except you make or hold it.—Who comes here?

Enter a SERVANT.

SERVANT. Save you, gentlemen!

STEPHEN. Nay, we don't stand much on our gentility, friend, yet you are welcome; and I assure you, mine uncle here is a man of a thousand a year, Middlesex land; he has but one son in all the world, I am his next heir at the common law, Master Stephen, as simple as I stand here, if my cousin die, as there's hope he will. I have a pretty living o' mine own, too, beside, hard by here.

SERVANT. In good time, sir.

STEPHEN. In good time, sir? Why, and in very good time, sir! You do not flout, friend, do you?

SERVANT. Not I, sir.

STEPHEN. Not you, sir? you were not best, sir; an you should, here be them can perceive it, and that quickly, too; go to. And they can give it again soundly, too, an need be.

SERVANT. Why, sir, let this satisfy you: good faith, I had no such intent.

STEPHEN. Sir, an I thought you had, I would talk with you, and that presently.

SERVANT. Good Master Stephen, so you may, sir,
at your pleasure.

STEPHEN. And so I would, sir, good my saucy companion! an you were out o' mine uncle's ground,
I can tell you; though I do not stand upon my
gentility, neither, in't.

KNOWELL. Cousin, cousin! will this ne'er be left?

STEPHEN. Whoreson base fellow! a mechanical
serving-man! By this cudgel, an 'twere not for shame,
I would——

KNOWELL. What would you do, you peremptory
  gull?
If you cannot be quiet, get you hence.
You see the honest man demeans himself
Modestly towards you, giving no reply
To your unseasoned, quarrelling, rude fashion;
And still you huff it, with a kind of carriage
As void of wit as of humanity.
Go, get you in; 'fore Heaven, I am ashamed
Thou hast a kinsman's interest in me.

        Exit STEPHEN.

SERVANT. I pray you, sir, is this Master Knowell's
house?

KNOWELL. Yes, marry, is it, sir.

SERVANT. I should inquire for a gentleman here,
one Master Edward Knowell. Do you know any such,
sir, I pray you?

KNOWELL. I should forget myself else, sir.

SERVANT. Are you the gentleman? Cry you mercy,
sir. I was required by a gentleman i' the City, as I
rode out at this end o' the town, to deliver you this
letter, sir.

KNOWELL. To me, sir! What do you mean? Pray
you remember your court'sy. 'To his most selected
friend, Master Edward Knowell.' What might the

gentleman's name be, sir, that sent it? Nay, pray you be covered.

SERVANT. One Master Wellbred, sir.

KNOWELL. Master Wellbred! a young gentleman, is he not?

SERVANT. The same, sir; Master Kitely married his sister—the rich merchant i' the Old Jewry.

KNOWELL. You say very true.—Brainworm!

Re-enter BRAINWORM.

BRAINWORM. Sir.

KNOWELL. Make this honest friend drink here.— Pray you, go in. *Exeunt* BRAINWORM *and* SERVANT.
This letter is directed to my son;
Yet I am Edward Knowell, too, and may,
With the safe conscience of good manners, use
The fellow's error to my satisfaction.
Well, I will break it ope—old men are curious—
Be it but for the style's sake and the phrase,
To see if both do answer my son's praises,
Who is almost grown the idolater
Of this young Wellbred. What have we here? What's this?
Reads. 'Why, Ned, I beseech thee, hast thou forsworn all thy friends i' the Old Jewry? or dost thou think us all Jews that inhabit there yet? If thou dost, come over and but see our frippery; change an old shirt for a whole smock with us. Do not conceive that antipathy between us and Hogsden, as was between Jews and hogs'-flesh. Leave thy vigilant father alone to number over his green apricots, evening and morning, o' the north-west wall. An I had been his son, I had saved him the labour long since, if taking in all the young wenches that pass by at the backdoor, and codling every kernel of the fruit for 'em, would ha' served. But, pr'ythee, come over to me quickly this morning; I have such a present for thee

—our Turkey Company never sent the like to the
Grand Signior. One is a rhymer, sir, o' your own
batch, your own leaven; but doth think him himself poet-major o' the town, willing to be shown and
worthy to be seen. The other—I will not venture his
description with you till you come, because I would
ha' you make hither with an appetite. If the worst
of 'em be not worth your journey, draw your bill of
charges, as unconscionable as any Guildhall verdict
will give it you, and you shall be allowed your
viaticum.   From the Windmill.'
From the Bordello it might come as well,
The Spittle, or Picthatch. Is this the man
My son hath sung so, for the happiest wit,
The choicest brain, the times hath sent us forth?
I know not what he may be in the arts,
Nor what in schools, but surely, for his manners,
I judge him a profane and dissolute wretch,
Worse by possession of such great good gifts,
Being the master of so loose a spirit.
Why, what unhallowed ruffian would have writ
In such a scurrilous manner to a friend!
Why should he think I tell my apricots,
Or play th' Hesperian dragon with my fruit,
To watch it? Well, my son, I'd thought
You'd had more judgment t' have made election
Of your companions, than t' have ta'en on trust
Such petulant, jeering gamesters, that can spare
No argument or subject from their jest.
But I perceive affection makes a fool
Of any man too much the father—Brainworm!

Re-enter BRAINWORM.

BRAINWORM. Sir.
KNOWELL.   Is the fellow gone that brought
this letter?

BRAINWORM. Yes, sir, a pretty while since.

KNOWELL. And where's your young master?

BRAINWORM. In his chamber, sir.

KNOWELL. He spake not with the fellow, did he?

BRAINWORM. No, sir, he saw him not.

KNOWELL. Take you this letter, and deliver it my son,
But with no notice that I have opened it, on your life.

BRAINWORM. O Lord, sir, that were a jest indeed!
Exit.

KNOWELL. I am resolved I will not stop his journey,
Nor practise any violent mean to stay
The unbridled course of youth in him; for that,
Restrain'd, grows more impatient, and in kind
Like to the eager but the generous greyhound,
Who ne'er so little from his game withheld,
Turns head and leaps up at his holder's throat.
There is a way of winning more by love
And urging of the modesty, than fear;
Force works on servile natures, not the free.
He that's compelled to goodness may be good,
But 'tis but for that fit; where others, drawn
By softness and example, get a habit.
Then, if they stray, but warn 'em, and the same
They should for virtue've done, they'll do for
shame. *Exit.*

ACT ONE. SCENE TWO

Within Knowell's house

Enter EDWARD *followed by* BRAINWORM.

EDWARD. Did he open it, sayest thou?

BRAINWORM. Yes, o' my word, sir, and read the contents.

EDWARD. That scarce contents me. What countenance, pr'ythee, made he i' the reading of it? Was he angry or pleased?

BRAINWORM. Nay, sir, I saw him not read it nor open it, I assure your worship.

EDWARD. No? how know'st thou, then, that he did either?

BRAINWORM. Marry, sir, because he charged me, on my life, to tell nobody that he opened it; which, unless he had done, he would never fear to have it revealed.

EDWARD. That's true. Well, I thank thee, Brainworm.

Enter STEPHEN.

STEPHEN. O, Brainworm, didst thou not see a fellow here in a what-sha-call-him doublet? He brought mine uncle a letter e'en now.

BRAINWORM. Yes, Master Stephen, what of him?

STEPHEN. O, I ha' such a mind to beat him. Where is he, canst thou tell?

BRAINWORM. Faith, he is not of that mind; he is gone, Master Stephen.

STEPHEN. Gone! which way? when went he? how long since?

BRAINWORM. He is rid hence. He took horse at the street door.

STEPHEN. And I stayed i' the fields! Whoreson Scanderbeg rogue! O that I had but a horse to fetch him back again!

BRAINWORM. Why, you may ha' my master's gelding, to save your longing, sir.

STEPHEN. But I ha' no boots, that's the spite on't.

BRAINWORM. Why, a fine wisp of hay, rolled hard, Master Stephen.

STEPHEN. No, faith, it's no boot to follow him now; let him e'en go and hang. Pray thee, help to truss me a little. He does so vex me——

BRAINWORM. You'll be worse vexed when you are trussed, Master Stephen. Best keep unbraced, and walk yourself till you be cold; your choler may founder you else.

STEPHEN. By my faith, and so I will, now thou tell'st me on't.—How dost thou like my leg, Brainworm?

BRAINWORM. A very good leg, Master Stephen! but the woollen stocking does not commend it so well.

STEPHEN. Foh! the stockings be good enough, now summer is coming on, for the dust; I'll have a pair of silk again' winter, that I go to dwell i' the town. I think my leg would show in a silk hose.

BRAINWORM. Believe me, Master Stephen, rarely well.

STEPHEN. In sadness, I think it would; I have a reasonable good leg.

BRAINWORM. You have an excellent good leg, Master Stephen, but I cannot stay to praise it longer now, and I am very sorry for't.   *Exit.*

STEPHEN. Another time will serve, Brainworm. Gramercy for this.

EDWARD. *Laughs, having read the letter.* Ha, ha, ha!

STEPHEN. Slid, I hope he laughs not at me; an he do——

EDWARD. Here was a letter indeed, to be intercepted by a man's father and do him good with him! He cannot but think most virtuously, both of me and the sender, sure, that make the careful costermonger of him in our familiar epistles. Well, if he read this with patience, I'll be gelt, and troll ballads for Master John Trundle yonder, the rest of my mortality. It is true and likely my father may have as much patience as another man, for he takes much physic, and oft taking physic makes a man very patient. But would your packet, Master Wellbred, had arrived at him in such a minute of his patience! Then we had known the end of it, which now is doubtful, and threatens—What, my wise cousin! Nay then, I'll furnish our feast with one gull more toward the mess. He writes to me of a brace, and here's one—that's three. O for a fourth! Fortune, if ever thou'lt use thine eyes, I entreat thee——

STEPHEN. O, now I see who he laughed at. He laughed at somebody in that letter. By this good light, an he had laughed at me——

EDWARD. How now, cousin Stephen, melancholy?

STEPHEN. Yes, a little. I thought you had laughed at me, cousin.

EDWARD. Why, what an I had, coz? what would you ha' done?

STEPHEN. By this light, I would ha' told mine uncle.

EDWARD. Nay, if you would ha' told your uncle, I did laugh at you, coz.

STEPHEN. Did you, indeed?

EDWARD. Yes, indeed.

STEPHEN. Why, then——

EDWARD. What then?

STEPHEN. I am satisfied; it is sufficient.

EDWARD. Why, be so, gentle coz, and I pray you let me entreat a courtesy of you. I am sent for, this morning, by a friend i' the Old Jewry, to come to him. It's but crossing over the fields to Moorgate. Will you bear me company? I protest, it is not to draw you into bond, or any plot against the state, coz.

STEPHEN. Sir, that's all one an 'twere; you shall command me twice so far as Moorgate, to do you good in such a matter. Do you think I would leave you? I protest——

EDWARD. No, no, you shall not protest, coz.

STEPHEN. By my fackins, but I will, by your leave; I'll protest more to my friend than I'll speak of at this time.

EDWARD. You speak very well, coz.

STEPHEN. Nay, not so neither, you shall pardon me, but I speak to serve my turn.

EDWARD. Your turn, coz? do you know what you say? A gentleman of your sort, parts, carriage, and estimation, to talk o' your turn i' this company, and to me alone, like a tankard-bearer at a conduit! Fie! A wight that, hitherto, his every step hath left the stamp of a great foot behind him, as every word the savour of a strong spirit! And he, this man, so graced, gilded, or—to use a more fit metaphor—so tin-foiled by nature, as not ten housewives' pewter, again' a good time, shows more bright to the world than he! And he,—as I said last, so I say again, and still shall say it—this man, to conceal such real ornaments as these, and shadow their glory as a milliner's wife does her wrought stomacher, with a smoky lawn or a black cypress! O, coz, it cannot be answered; go not about it. Drake's old ship at Deptford may sooner circle the world again. Come, wrong not the quality of your desert with looking downward, coz, but hold up your head, so; and let the idea of what you are be portrayed i' your face that men may read i' your phys'nomy, 'Here within this place is to be seen the true, rare, and accomplished monster, or miracle of nature,' which is all one. What think you of this, coz?

STEPHEN. Why, I do think of it; and I will be more proud and melancholy and gentlemanlike than I have been, I'll insure you.

EDWARD. Why, that's resolute, Master Stephen!— Now, if I can but hold him up to his height, as it is happily begun, it will do well for a suburb humour; we may hap have a match with the City, and play him for forty pound.—Come, coz.

STEPHEN. I'll follow you.

EDWARD. Follow me! you must go before.

STEPHEN. Nay, an I must, I will. Pray you, show me, good cousin.   *Exeunt.*

ACT ONE. SCENE THREE

Before Cob's house

Enter MATTHEW.

MATTHEW. I think this be the house.—What, ho!

Enter COB.

COB. Who's there? O, Master Matthew! gi' your worship good morrow.

MATTHEW. What, Cob! how dost thou, good Cob? dost thou inhabit here, Cob?

COB. Ay, sir, I and my lineage ha' kept a poor house here, in our days.

MATTHEW. Thy lineage, Monsieur Cob! what lineage, what lineage?

COB. Why, sir, an ancient lineage, and a princely. Mine ance'try came from a king's belly, no worse man; and yet no man neither—by your worship's leave, I did lie in that—but Herring, the king of fish, from his belly I proceed, one o' the monarchs o' the world, I assure you. The first red herring that was broiled in Adam and Eve's kitchen, do I fetch my pedigree from, by the harrot's books. His cob was my great-great-mighty-great-grandfather.

MATTHEW. Why mighty? why mighty, I pray thee?

COB. O, it was a mighty while ago, sir, and a mighty great cob.

MATTHEW. How know'st thou that?

COB. How know I? Why, I smell his ghost ever and anon.

MATTHEW. Smell a ghost? O unsavoury jest! and the ghost of a herring cob?

COB. Ay, sir, with favour of your worship's nose, Master Matthew, why not the ghost of a herring-cob, as well as the ghost of rasher-bacon?

MATTHEW. Roger Bacon, thou wouldst say?

COB. I say rasher-bacon. They were both broiled o' the coals, and a man may smell broiled meat, I hope? You are a scholar, upsolve me that, now.

MATTHEW. O raw ignorance!—Cob, canst thou show me of a gentlemen, one Captain Bobadill, where his lodging is?

COB. O, my guest, sir, you mean.

MATTHEW. Thy guest! Alas! ha, ha!

COB. Why do you laugh, sir? Do you not mean Captain Bobadill?

MATTHEW. Cob, pray thee advise thyself well: do

not wrong the gentleman, and thyself too. I dare be
sworn he scorns thy house, he! He lodge in such a
base, obscure place as thy house! Tut, I know his
disposition so well, he would not lie in thy bed if
thou'dst gi' it him.

COB. I will not give it him though, sir. Mass, I
thought somewhat was in't, we could not get him to
bed all night! Well, sir, though he lie not o' my
bed, he lies o' my bench; an't please you to go up,
sir, you shall find him with two cushions under his
head, and his cloak wrapped about him, as though
he had neither won nor lost, and yet, I warrant, he
ne'er cast better in his life than he has done tonight.

MATTHEW. Why, was he drunk?

COB. Drunk, sir? you hear not me say so. Perhaps
he swallowed a tavern-token or some such device,
sir; I have nothing to do withal. I deal with water
and not with wine.—Gi' me my tankard there, ho!
—God b' wi' you, sir. It's six o'clock; I should ha'
carried two turns by this.—What ho! my stopple!
come.

Enter TIB *with tankard.*

MATTHEW. Lie in a water-bearer's house! A gentleman of his havings? Well, I'll tell him my mind.

COB. What, Tib! show this gentleman up to the
Captain. *Exit* MATTHEW *with* TIB. O, an my house
were the Brazen Head now, faith it would e'en speak
'Mo fools yet.' You should ha' some now would
take this Master Matthew to be a gentleman at the
least. His father's an honest man, a worshipful
fishmonger, and so forth; and now does he creep and
wriggle into acquaintance with all the brave gallants
about the town, such as my guest is,—O, my guest is
a fine man!—and they flout him invincibly. He useth
every day to a merchant's house where I serve water,

one Master Kitely's, i' the Old Jewry; and here's the
jest: he is in love with my master's sister, Mistress
Bridget, and calls her mistress, and there he will sit
you a whole afternoon sometimes, reading o' these
same abominable, vile,—a pox on 'em, I cannot
abide them!—rascally verses, poyetry, poyetry, and
speaking of interludes; 'twill make a man burst to
hear him. And the wenches, they do so jeer and
tee-hee at him—Well, should they do so much to
me, I'd forswear them all, by the foot of Pharaoh!
There's an oath! How many water-bearers shall you
hear swear such an oath? O, I have a guest—he
teaches me—he does swear the legiblest of any man
christened: 'By Saint George! the foot of Pharaoh!
the body of me! as I am a gentleman and a soldier!'
such dainty oaths! And withal he does take this same
filthy roguish tobacco, the finest and cleanliest; it
would do a man good to see the fume come forth
at 's tunnels! Well, he owes me forty shillings—my
wife lent him out of her purse, by sixpence at a
time—besides his lodging; I would I had it! I shall
ha' it, he says, the next action. Helter-skelter, hang
sorrow, care'll kill a cat, up-tails all, and a louse
for the hangman!   *Exit.*

ACT ONE. SCENE FOUR

The upper chamber in Cob's house

BOBADILL *is discovered lying on his bench.*

BOBADILL. Hostess, hostess!

Enter TIB.

TIB. What say you, sir?

BOBADILL. A cup o' thy small beer, sweet hostess.

TIB. Sir, there's a gentleman below would speak with you.

BOBADILL. A gentleman! 'odso, I am not within.

TIB. My husband told him you were, sir.

BOBADILL. What a plague—what meant he?

MATTHEW. Captain Bobadill!

BOBADILL. Who's there?—Take away the basin, good hostess.—Come up, sir.

TIB. —He would desire you to come up, sir. You come into a cleanly house, here!

Enter MATTHEW.

MATTHEW. Save you, sir; save you, Captain!

BOBADILL. Gentle Master Matthew! Is it you, sir? Please you sit down.

MATTHEW. Thank you, good Captain; you may see I am somewhat audacious.

BOBADILL. Not so, sir. I was requested to supper last night by a sort of gallants, where you were wished for and drunk to, I assure you.

MATTHEW. Vouchsafe me, by whom, good Captain?

BOBADILL. Marry, by young Wellbred, and others. —Why, hostess, a stool here, for this gentleman.

MATTHEW. No haste, sir, 'tis very well.

BOBADILL. Body of me! it was so late ere we parted last night, I can scarce open my eyes yet; I was but new risen, as you came. How passes the day abroad, sir? you can tell.

MATTHEW. Faith, some half hour to seven. Now trust me, you have an exceeding fine lodging here, very neat and private!   *Exit* TIB.

BOBADILL. Ay, sir, sit down, I pray you. Master Matthew, in any case, possess no gentlemen of our acquaintance with notice of my lodging.

MATTHEW. Who? I, sir? no.

BOBADILL. Not that I need to care who know it, for the cabin is convenient, but in regard I would not be too popular and generally visited, as some are.

MATTHEW. True, Captain, I conceive you.

BOBADILL. For, do you see, sir, by the heart of valour in me, except it be to some peculiar and choice spirits, to whom I am extraordinarily engaged, as yourself, or so, I could not extend thus far.

MATTHEW. O Lord, sir, I resolve so.

BOBADILL. I confess I love a cleanly and quiet privacy above all the tumult and roar of fortune. What new book ha' you there? What? 'Go by, Hieronymo'?

MATTHEW. Ay, did you ever see it acted? Is't not well penned?

BOBADILL. Well penned? I would fain see all the poets of these times pen such another play as that was! They'll prate and swagger and keep a stir of art and devices, when—as I am a gentleman—read 'em, they are the most shallow, pitiful, barren fellows that live upon the face of the earth again.

MATTHEW. Indeed, here are a number of fine speeches in this book. 'O eyes, no eyes, but fountains fraught with tears!' There's a conceit: 'fountains fraught with tears!' 'O life, no life, but lively form of death!' another! 'O world, no world, but mass of public wrongs!' a third! 'Confused and filled with murder and misdeeds!' a fourth! O the muses! Is't not excellent? Is't not simply the best that ever you heard, Captain, ha? How do you like it?

BOBADILL. 'Tis good.

MATTHEW. 'To thee, the purest object to my sense,
The most refinèd essence heaven covers,
Send I these lines, wherein I do commence
The happy state of turtle-billing lovers.
If they prove rough, unpolished, harsh, and rude,
Haste made the waste. Thus, mildly, I conclude.'

BOBADILL. *Making him ready all this while.* Nay, proceed, proceed. Where's this?

MATTHEW. This, sir? a toy o' mine own, in my nonage; the infancy of my muses. But when will you come and see my study? good faith, I can show you some very good things I have done of late— That boot becomes your leg passing well, Captain, methinks.

BOBADILL. So, so. It's the fashion gentlemen now use.

MATTHEW. Troth, Captain, and now you speak o' the fashion, Master Wellbred's elder brother and I are fallen out exceedingly. This other day I happened to enter into some discourse of a hanger, which, I assure you, both for fashion and workmanship, was most peremptory, beautiful and gentlemanlike; yet he condemned and cried it down for the most pied and ridiculous that ever he saw.

BOBADILL. Squire Downright, the half-brother, was't not?

MATTHEW. Ay, sir, he.

BOBADILL. Hang him, rook, he! why, he has no

more judgment than a malt-horse. By Saint George, I wonder you'd lose a thought upon such an animal: the most peremptory, absurd clown of Christendom this day, he is holden. I protest to you, as I am a gentleman and a soldier, I ne'er changed words with his like. By his discourse, he should eat nothing but hay. He was born for the manger, pannier, or pack-saddle! He has not so much as a good phrase in his belly, but all old iron and rusty proverbs; a good commodity for some smith to make hob-nails of!

MATTHEW. Ay, and he thinks to carry it away with his manhood still, where he comes. He brags he will gi' me the bastinado, as I hear.

BOBADILL. How! he the bastinado! How came he by that word, trow?

MATTHEW. Nay, indeed, he said cudgel me; I termed it so, for my more grace.

BOBADILL. That may be, for I was sure it was none of his word. But when, when said he so?

MATTHEW. Faith, yesterday, they say; a young gallant, a friend of mine, told me so.

BOBADILL. By the foot of Pharaoh, an 'twere my case now, I should send him a chartel presently. The bastinado! a most proper and sufficient dependence, warranted by the great Carranza. Come hither. You shall chartel him. I'll show you a trick or two you shall kill him with, at pleasure; the first stoccata, if you will, by this air.

MATTHEW. Indeed, you have absolute knowledge i' the mystery, I have heard, sir.

BOBADILL. Of whom? of whom, ha' you heard it, I beseech you?

MATTHEW. Troth, I have heard it spoken of divers, that you have very rare and un-in-one-breath-utter-able skill, sir.

BOBADILL. By Heaven, no, not I; no skill i' the

earth; some small rudiments i' the science, as to know my time, distance, or so. I have professed it more for noblemen and gentlemen's use than mine own practice, I assure you.—Hostess, accommodate us with another bed-staff here quickly. Lend us another bed-staff.—The woman does not understand the words of action. Look you, sir! Exalt not your point above this state, at any hand, and let your poniard maintain your defence, thus.—Give it the gentleman, and leave us.—So, sir. Come on! O, twine your body more about, that you may fall to a more sweet, comely, gentlemanlike guard. So, indifferent. Hollow your body more, sir, thus. Now, stand fast o' your left leg, note your distance, keep your due proportion of time—O, you disorder your point most irregularly.

MATTHEW. How is the bearing of it now, sir?

BOBADILL. O, out of measure ill! a well-experienced hand would pass upon you at pleasure.

MATTHEW. How mean you, sir, pass upon me?

BOBADILL. Why, thus, sir—make a thrust at me. Come in upon the answer, control your point, and make a full career at the body. The best-practised gallants of the time name it the passada—a most desperate thrust, believe it.

MATTHEW. Well, come, sir.

BOBADILL. Why, you do not manage your weapon with any facility or grace to invite me; I have no spirit to play with you. Your dearth of judgment renders you tedious.

MATTHEW. But one venue, sir.

BOBADILL. Venue! fie! most gross denomination as ever I heard. O, the stoccata while you live, sir. Note that. Come, put on your cloak, and we'll go to some private place where you are acquainted, some tavern, or so—and have a bit. I'll send for one of these fencers, and he shall breathe you by my direction, and then I will teach you your trick. You shall kill him with it at the first, if you please. Why, I will learn you, by the true judgment of the eye, hand, and foot, to control any enemy's point i' the world. Should your adversary confront you with a pistol, 'twere nothing, by this hand; you should, by the same rule, control his bullet in a line—except it were hail-shot, and spread. What money ha' you about you, Master Matthew?

MATTHEW. Faith, I ha' not past a two shillings or so.

BOBADILL. 'Tis somewhat with the least; but come. We will have a bunch of radish, and salt, to taste our wine; and a pipe of tobacco to close the orifice of the stomach; and then we'll call upon young Wellbred. Perhaps we shall meet the Corydon his brother there, and put him to the question. *Exeunt.*

ACT TWO. SCENE ONE

Kitely's house

Enter KITELY, CASH, *and* DOWNRIGHT.

KITELY. Thomas, come hither.
There lies a note within upon my desk;
Here, take my key—It is no matter, neither.
Where is the boy?

CASH.   Within, sir, i' the warehouse.

KITELY. Let him tell over straight that Spanish gold,
And weigh it, with th' pieces of eight. Do you

See the delivery of those silver stuffs
To Master Lucar. Tell him, if he will,
He shall ha' the grograms at the rate I told him,
And I will meet him on the Exchange anon.

    CASH. Good, sir. *Exit.*

    KITELY. Do you see that fellow, brother
      Downright?

    DOWNRIGHT. Ay, what of him?

    KITELY. He is a jewel, brother.
I took him of a child up at my door,
And christened him, gave him mine own name,
    Thomas;
Since bred him at the Hospital, where proving
A toward imp, I called him home, and taught him
So much, as I have made him my cashier,
And giv'n him, who had none, a surname, Cash;
And find him, in his place, so full of faith
That I durst trust my life into his hands.

    DOWNRIGHT. So would not I in any bastard's,
      brother,
As it is like he is, although I knew
Myself his father. But you said you'd somewhat
To tell me, gentle brother; what is't? what is't?

    KITELY. Faith, I am very loath to utter it,
As fearing it may hurt your patience;
But that I know your judgment is of strength,
Against the nearness of affection——

    DOWNRIGHT. What need this circumstance? Pray
      you be direct.

    KITELY. I will not say how much I do ascribe
Unto your friendship, nor in what regard
I hold your love; but let my past behaviour,
And usage of your sister, but confirm
How well I've been affected to your——

    DOWNRIGHT. You are too tedious; come to the mat-
      ter, the matter.

KITELY. Then, without further ceremony, thus:
My brother Wellbred, sir, I know not how,
Of late is much declined in what he was,
And greatly altered in his disposition.
When he came first to lodge here in my house,
Ne'er trust me if I were not proud of him;
Methought he bare himself in such a fashion,
So full of man and sweetness in his carriage,
And—what was chief—it showed not borrowed in
    him,
But all he did became him as his own,
And seemed as perfect, proper, and possessed,
As breath with life, or colour with the blood.
But now his course is so irregular,
So loose, affected, and deprived of grace,
And he himself withal so far fall'n off
From that first place, as scarce no note remains
To tell men's judgments where he lately stood.
He's grown a stranger to all due respect,
Forgetful of his friends; and not content
To stale himself in all societies,
He makes my house here common as a mart,
A theatre, a public receptacle
For giddy humour and diseasèd riot;
And here, as in a tavern or a stews,
He and his wild associates spend their hours
In repetition of lascivious jests,
Swear, leap, drink, dance, and revel night by night,
Control my servants; and, indeed, what not?

DOWNRIGHT. 'Sdeins, I know not what I should
say to him, i' the whole world! He values me at a
cracked three-farthings, for aught I see. It will never
out o' the flesh that's bred i' the bone. I have told
him enough, one would think, if that would serve;
but counsel to him is as good as a shoulder of mutton to a sick horse. Well, he knows what to trust

to, 'fore George! Let him spend and spend, and
domineer till his heart ache; an he think to be relieved by me, when he is got into one o' your city-
pounds, the Counters, he has the wrong sow by
the ear, i' faith, and claps his dish at the wrong
man's door. I'll lay my hand o' my halfpenny ere
I part with 't to fetch him out, I'll assure him.

KITELY. Nay, good brother, let it not trouble you
thus.

DOWNRIGHT. 'Sdeath, he mads me! I could eat my
very spur-leathers for anger! But why are you so
tame? Why do not you speak to him, and tell him
how he disquiets your house?

KITELY. O, there are divers reasons to dissuade,
          brother.
But, would yourself vouchsafe to travail in it,—
Though but with plain and easy circumstance—
It would both come much better to his sense,
And savour less of stomach or of passion.
You are his elder brother, and that title
Both gives and warrants you authority,
Which, by your presence seconded, must breed
A kind of duty in him, and regard;
Whereas, if I should intimate the least,
It would but add contempt to his neglect,
Heap worse on ill, make up a pile of hatred
That, in the rearing, would come tott'ring down,
And in the ruin bury all our love.
Nay, more than this, brother, if I should speak,
He would be ready, from his heat of humour
And overflowing of the vapour in him,
To blow the ears of his familiars
With the false breath of telling what disgraces
And low disparagements I had put upon him.
Whilst they, sir, to relieve him in the fable,
Make their loose comments upon every word,

Gesture, or look I use; mock me all over,
From my flat cap unto my shining shoes;
And, out of their impetuous rioting fancies,
Beget some slander that shall dwell with me.
And what would that be, think you? Marry, this:
They would give out—because my wife is fair,
Myself but lately married, and my sister
Here sojourning a virgin in my house—
That I were jealous! Nay, as sure as death,
That they would say; and how that I had quarrelled
My brother purposely, thereby to find
An apt pretext to banish them my house.

    DOWNRIGHT. Mass, perhaps so. They're like enough
    to do it.

    KITELY. Brother, they would, believe it; so should
    I,
Like one of these penurious quacksalvers,
But set the bills up to mine own disgrace,
And try experiments upon myself;
Lend scorn and envy opportunity
To stab my reputation and good name——

        Enter MATTHEW *with* BOBADILL.

    MATTHEW. I will speak to him——

    BOBADILL. Speak to him? Away; by the foot of
Pharaoh, you shall not, you shall not do him that
grace!—The time of day to you, gentleman o' the
house. Is Master Wellbred stirring?

    DOWNRIGHT. How then? what should he do?

    BOBADILL. Gentleman of the house, it is to you:
is he within, sir?

    KITELY. He came not to his lodging tonight, sir,
I assure you.

    DOWNRIGHT. Why, do you hear, you?

    BOBADILL. The gentleman-citizen hath satisfied
me; I'll talk to no scavenger.

        Exeunt BOBADILL *and* MATTHEW.

DOWNRIGHT. How! scavenger? stay, sir, stay!

KITELY. Nay, brother Downright.

DOWNRIGHT. Heart! stand you away, an you love me.

KITELY. You shall not follow him now, I pray
    you, brother;
Good faith, you shall not; I will overrule you.

DOWNRIGHT. Ha! scavenger? Well, go to, I say little; but, by this good day—God forgive me I should
swear!—if I put it up so, say I am the rankest cow
that ever pissed. 'Sdeins, an I swallow this, I'll
ne'er draw my sword in the sight of Fleet Street
again, while I live; I'll sit in a barn with Madge
Howlet and catch mice, first. Scavenger? Heart!
and I'll go near to fill that huge tumbrel-slop of
yours with somewhat, an I have good luck; your
Gargantua breech cannot carry it away so.

KITELY. O, do not fret yourself thus, never think
    on't.

DOWNRIGHT. These are my brother's consorts,
these! these are his comrades, his walking mates!
He's a gallant, a cavaliero, too, right hangman cut!
Let me not live, an I could not find in my heart
to swinge the whole ging of 'em, one after another,
and begin with him first. I am grieved it should be
said he is my brother, and take these courses. Well,
as he brews, so shall he drink, 'fore George again.
Yet he shall hear on't, and that tightly too, an
I live, i' faith.

KITELY. But, brother, let your reprehension, then,
Run in an easy current, not o'er-high
Carried, with rashness or devouring choler;
But rather use the soft, persuading way,
Whose powers will work more gently, and compose
Th' imperfect thoughts you labour to reclaim,
More winning than enforcing the consent.

DOWNRIGHT. Ay, ay, let me alone for that, I warrant you. *Bell rings.*

KITELY. How now! Oh, the bell rings to breakfast.
Brother, I pray you go in and bear my wife
Company till I come. I'll but give order
For some dispatch of business to my servants.

Exit DOWNRIGHT.

COB *passes by with his tankard.*

KITELY. What, Cob! our maids will have you by the back, i' faith, for coming so late this morning.

COB. Perhaps so, sir; take heed somebody have not them by the belly, for walking so late in the evening. *Exit.*

KITELY. Well, yet my troubled spirit's somewhat eased,
Though not reposed in that security
As I could wish; but I must be content.
Howe'er I set a face on't to the world,
Would I had lost this finger at a venture,
So Wellbred had ne'er lodged within my house.
Why't cannot be, where there is such resort
Of wanton gallants and young revellers,
That any woman should be honest long.
Is't like, that factious beauty will preserve
The public-weal of chastity unshaken,
When such strong motives muster and make head
Against her single peace? No, no. Beware,
When mutual appetite doth meet to treat,
And spirits of one kind and quality
Come once to parley in the pride of blood;
It is no slow conspiracy that follows.
Well, to be plain, if I but thought the time
Had answered their affections, all the world
Should not persuade me but I were a cuckold.

Marry, I hope they ha' not got that start;
For opportunity hath balked 'em yet,
And shall do still, while I have eyes and ears
To attend the impositions of my heart.
My presence shall be as an iron bar
'Twixt the conspiring motions of desire;
Yea, every look or glance mine eye ejects,
Shall check occasion, as one doth his slave,
When he forgets the limits of prescription.

Enter DAME KITELY *and* BRIDGET.

DAME KITELY. Sister Bridget, pray you fetch down the rose-water above in the closet.　　*Exit* BRIDGET.
Sweetheart, will you come in to breakfast?

KITELY. —An she have overheard me now!

DAME KITELY. I pray thee, good Muss, we stay for you.

KITELY. —By Heaven, I would not for a thousand
　　angels!

DAME KITELY. What ail you, sweetheart? Are you not well? Speak, good Muss.

KITELY. Troth, my head aches extremely on a
　　sudden.

DAME KITELY. O, the Lord!

KITELY. How now? What?

DAME KITELY. Alas, how it burns! Muss, keep you warm; good truth, it is this new disease, there's a number are troubled withal! For love's sake, sweetheart, come in out of the air.

KITELY. —How simple and how subtle are her an-
　　swers!
A new disease, and many troubled with it?
Why, true. She heard me, all the world to nothing.

DAME KITELY. I pray thee, good sweetheart, come in. The air will do you harm, in troth.

KITELY. —The air! she has me i' the wind.—Sweet-
    heart,
I'll come to you presently. 'Twill away, I hope.
    DAME KITELY. Pray Heaven it do.   *Exit.*
    KITELY. A new disease? I know not, new or old,
But it may well be called poor mortals' plague;
For, like a pestilence, it doth infect
The houses of the brain. First, it begins
Solely to work upon the phantasy,
Filling her seat with such pestiferous air,
As soon corrupts the judgment; and from thence,
Sends like contagion to the memory,
Still each to other giving the infection;
Which, as a subtle vapour, spreads itself
Confusedly through every sensive part,
Till not a thought or motion in the mind
Be free from the black poison of suspect.
Ah, but what misery is it to know this?
Or, knowing it, to want the mind's erection,
In such extremes? Well, I will once more strive,
In spite of this black cloud, myself to be,
And shake the fever off that thus shakes me.   *Exit.*

ACT TWO. SCENE TWO

Moorfields

Enter BRAINWORM *disguised as a maimed soldier.*

BRAINWORM. 'Slid, I cannot choose but laugh, to
see myself translated thus, from a poor creature to a
creator; for now must I create an intolerable sort
of lies, or my present profession loses the grace;

and yet the lie, to a man of my coat, is as ominous
a fruit as the fico. O sir, it holds for good policy
ever, to have that outwardly in vilest estimation,
that inwardly is most dear to us. So much for my
borrowed shape. Well, the troth is, my old master
intends to follow my young, dry-foot, over Moorfields to London this morning; now I, knowing
of this hunting-match, or rather conspiracy, and
to insinuate with my young master,—for so must we
that are blue waiters, and men of hope and service
do, or perhaps we may wear motley at the year's
end, and who wears motley, you know—have got
me afore, in this disguise, determining here to lie
in ambuscado, and intercept him in the mid-way.
If I can but get his cloak, his purse, his hat, nay,
anything to cut him off, that is, to stay his journey,
'Veni, vidi, vici,' I may say with Captain Caesar;
I am made for ever, i' faith. Well, now must I practise to get the true garb of one of these lance-
knights, my arm here, and my—young master! and
his cousin, Master Stephen, as I am a true counterfeit man of war, and no soldier!

Enter EDWARD KNOWELL *and* STEPHEN.

EDWARD. So, sir, and how then, coz?

STEPHEN. 'Sfoot, I have lost my purse, I think.

EDWARD. How! lost your purse? Where? When
had you it?

STEPHEN. I cannot tell; stay.

BRAINWORM. —'Slid, I am afeard they will know
me; would I could get by them!

EDWARD. What? ha' you it?

STEPHEN. No, I think I was bewitched, I——

EDWARD. Nay, do not weep the loss; hang it, let
it go.

STEPHEN. Oh, it's here. No, an it had been lost,

I had not cared, but for a jet ring Mistress Mary sent me.

EDWARD. A jet ring! O, the poesy, the poesy?

STEPHEN. Fine, i' faith.

> 'Though fancy sleep,
> My love is deep.'

Meaning that though I did not fancy her, yet she loved me dearly.

EDWARD. Most excellent!

STEPHEN. And then I sent her another, and my poesy was:

> 'The deeper the sweeter,
> I'll be judged by Saint Peter.'

EDWARD. How, by Saint Peter? I do not conceive that.

STEPHEN. Marry, Saint Peter, to make up the metre.

EDWARD. Well, there the saint was your good patron, he help'd you at your need; thank him, thank him.

BRAINWORM. I cannot take leave on 'em so; I will venture, come what will. *He is come back.* Gentlemen, please you change a few crowns for a very excellent good blade here? I am a poor gentleman, a soldier; one that, in the better state of my fortunes, scorned so mean a refuge; but now it is the humour of necessity to have it so. You seem to be gentlemen well affected to martial men, else should I rather die with silence than live with shame; however, vouchsafe to remember, it is my want speaks, not myself. This condition agrees not with my spirit——

EDWARD. Where hast thou served?

BRAINWORM. May it please you, sir, in all the late wars of Bohemia, Hungaria, Dalmatia, Poland, where not, sir? I have been a poor servitor, by sea and land, any time this fourteen years, and followed the fortunes of the best commanders in Christendom. I was twice shot at the taking of Aleppo, once at the relief of Vienna; I have been at Marseilles, Naples, and the Adriatic Gulf, a gentleman-slave in the galleys thrice, where I was most dangerously shot in the head, through both the thighs, and yet, being thus maimed, I am void of maintenance, nothing left me but my scars, the noted marks of my resolution.

STEPHEN. How will you sell this rapier, friend?

BRAINWORM. Generous sir, I refer it to your own judgment; you are a gentleman, give me what you please.

STEPHEN. True, I am a gentleman, I know that, friend; but what though? I pray you say, what would you ask?

BRAINWORM. I assure you, the blade may become the side or thigh of the best prince in Europe.

EDWARD. Ay, with a velvet scabbard, I think.

STEPHEN. Nay, an't be mine, it shall have a velvet scabbard, coz, that's flat. I'd not wear it as 'tis, an you would give me an angel.

BRAINWORM. At your worship's pleasure, sir. Nay, 'tis a most pure Toledo.

STEPHEN. I had rather it were a Spaniard! But tell me, what shall I give you for it? An it had a silver hilt——

EDWARD. Come, come, you shall not buy it.—Hold, there's a shilling, fellow; take thy rapier.

STEPHEN. Why, but I will buy it now, because you say so, and there's another shilling, fellow. I scorn to be outbidden. What, shall I walk with a cudgel, like Higginbottom, and may have a rapier for money?

EDWARD. You may buy one in the City.

STEPHEN. Tut! I'll buy this i' the field, so I will; I have a mind to't, because 'tis a field rapier.—Tell me your lowest price.

EDWARD. You shall not buy it, I say.

STEPHEN. By this money, but I will, though I give more than 'tis worth.

EDWARD. Come away, you are a fool.

STEPHEN. Friend, I am a fool, that's granted; but I'll have it, for that word's sake. Follow me, for your money.

BRAINWORM. At your service, sir.　　　　*Exeunt.*

Enter KNOWELL.

KNOWELL. I cannot lose the thought yet of this
　　letter
Sent to my son, nor leave t' admire the change
Of manners, and the breeding of our youth
Within the kingdom, since myself was one.
When I was young, he lived not in the stews,
Durst have conceived a scorn, and uttered it
On a gray head; age was authority
Against a buffoon; and a man had then
A certain reverence paid unto his years,
That had none due unto his life. So much
The sanctity of some prevailed for others.
But now, we all are fall'n: youth, from their fear;
And age from that which bred it, good example.
Nay, would ourselves were not the first, even
　　parents,
That did destroy the hopes in our own children;
Or they not learned our vices in their cradles,
And sucked in our ill customs with their milk.
Ere all their teeth be born, or they can speak,
We make their palates cunning! The first words
We form their tongues with, are licentious jests!
Can it call whore, cry bastard? O, then kiss it!

A witty child! Can't swear? The father's darling!
Give it two plums. Nay, rather than't shall learn
No bawdy song, the mother herself will teach it!
But this is in the infancy, the days
Of the long coat; when it puts on the breeches,
It will put off all this. Ay, it is like,
When it is gone into the bone already!
No, no, this dye goes deeper than the coat,
Or shirt, or skin. It stains unto the liver
And heart, in some; and, rather than it should not,
Note what we fathers do! Look how we live!
What mistresses we keep at what expense!
In our sons' eyes, where they may handle our gifts,
Hear our lascivious courtships, see our dalliance,
Taste of the same provoking meats with us,
To ruin of our states! Nay, when our own
Portion is fled, to prey on their remainder,
We call them into fellowship of vice!
Bait 'em with the young chambermaid, to seal!
And teach 'em all bad ways to buy affliction.
This is one path, but there are millions more,
In which we spoil our own with leading them.
Well, I thank Heaven, I never yet was he
That travelled with my son, before sixteen,
To show him the Venetian courtesans;
Nor read the grammar of cheating I had made,
To my sharp boy, at twelve, repeating still
The rule, 'Get money,' still, 'Get money, boy,
No matter by what means; money will do
More, boy, than my lord's letter.' Neither have I
Dressed snails or mushrooms curiously before him,
Perfumed my sauces, and taught him to make 'em;
Preceding still, with my gray gluttony,
At all the ordinaries, and only feared
His palate should degenerate, not his manners.
These are the trade of fathers, now; however,

My son, I hope, hath met within my threshold
None of these household precedents, which are
    strong,
And swift to rape youth to their precipice.
But let the house at home be ne'er so clean-
Swept, or kept sweet from filth, nay, dust and cob-
    webs,
If he will live abroad with his companions,
In dung and leystals, it is worth a fear;
Nor is the danger of conversing less
Than all that I have mentioned of example.

Enter BRAINWORM *disguised as a soldier.*

BRAINWORM. —My master! Nay, faith, have at you;
I am fleshed now, I have sped so well.——Worshipful
sir, I beseech you, respect the estate of a poor soldier. I am ashamed of this base course of life—
God's my comfort—but extremity provokes me to't;
what remedy?

KNOWELL. I have not for you, now.

BRAINWORM. By the faith I bear unto truth, gentleman, it is no ordinary custom in me, but only
to preserve manhood. I protest to you, a man I
have been, a man I may be, by your sweet bounty.

KNOWELL. Pray thee, good friend, be satisfied.

BRAINWORM. Good sir, by that hand, you may do
the part of a kind gentleman, in lending a poor
soldier the price of two cans of beer, a matter of
small value; the King of Heaven shall pay you,
and I shall rest thankful. Sweet worship——

KNOWELL. Nay, an you be so importunate——

BRAINWORM. O, tender sir, need will have his
course; I was not made to this vile use! Well, the
edge of the enemy could not have abated me so
much. It's hard when a man hath served in his
prince's cause, and be thus—*Weeps.* Honourable

worship, let me derive a small piece of silver from you; it shall not be given in the course of time. By this good ground, I was fain to pawn my rapier last night for a poor supper; I had sucked the hilts long before, I am a pagan else. Sweet honour——

KNOWELL. Believe me, I am taken with some wonder,
To think a fellow of thy outward presence
Should, in the frame and fashion of his mind,
Be so degenerate and sordid-base!
Art thou a man, and sham'st thou not to beg?
To practise such a servile kind of life?
Why, were thy education ne'er so mean,
Having thy limbs, a thousand fairer courses
Offer themselves to thy election.
Either the wars might still supply thy wants,
Or service of some virtuous gentleman,
Or honest labour; nay, what can I name,
But would become thee better than to beg?
But men of thy condition feed on sloth,
As doth the beetle on the dung she breeds in,
Not caring how the metal of your minds
Is eaten with the rust of idleness.
Now, afore me, whate'er he be, that should
Relieve a person of thy quality,
While thou insist'st in this loose, desperate course,
I would esteem the sin not thine, but his.

BRAINWORM. Faith, sir, I would gladly find some other course, if so——

KNOWELL. Ay, you'd gladly find it, but you will not seek it.

BRAINWORM. Alas, sir, where should a man seek? In the wars, there's no ascent by desert in these days, but——and for service, would it were as soon purchased as wished for, the air's my comfort! I know what I would say——

KNOWELL. What's thy name?

BRAINWORM. Please you, FitzSword, sir.

KNOWELL. FitzSword!
Say that a man should entertain thee now,
Wouldst thou be honest, humble, just, and true?

BRAINWORM. Sir, by the place and honour of a
soldier——

KNOWELL. Nay, nay, I like not those affected oaths;
Speak plainly, man: what think'st thou of my
words?

BRAINWORM. Nothing, sir, but wish my fortunes
were as happy as my service should be honest.

KNOWELL. Well, follow me; I'll prove thee, if thy
deeds
Will carry a proportion to thy words. *Exit*.

BRAINWORM. Yes, sir, straight, I'll but garter my
hose. O that my belly were hooped now, for I am
ready to burst with laughing! Never was bottle or
bagpipe fuller. 'Slid, was there ever seen a fox in
years to betray himself thus! Now shall I be possessed of all his counsels, and, by that conduit, my
young master. Well, he is resolved to prove my
honesty; faith, and I am resolved to prove his patience. O, I shall abuse him intolerably. This small
piece of service will bring him clean out of love
with the soldier forever. He will never come within
the sign of it, the sight of a cassock or a musket-
rest again. He will hate the musters at Mile End
for it, to his dying day. It's no matter, let the world
think me a bad counterfeit, if I cannot give him
the slip at an instant; why, this is better than to
have stayed his journey! Well, I'll follow him. O,
how I long to be employed! *Exit*.

ACT THREE. SCENE ONE

The Windmill Tavern

Enter MATTHEW, WELLBRED, *and* BOBADILL.

MATTHEW. Yes, faith, sir, we were at your lodging to seek you, too.

WELLBRED. O, I came not there tonight.

BOBADILL. Your brother delivered us as much.

WELLBRED. Who, my brother Downright?

BOBADILL. He. Master Wellbred, I know not in what kind you hold me, but let me say to you this: as sure as honour, I esteem it so much out of the sunshine of reputation, to throw the least beam of regard upon such a——

WELLBRED. Sir, I must hear no ill words of my brother.

BOBADILL. I protest to you, as I have a thing to be saved about me, I never saw any gentlemanlike part——

WELLBRED. Good Captain, faces about to some other discourse.

BOBADILL. With your leave, sir, an there were no more men living upon the face of the earth, I should not fancy him, by Saint George!

MATTHEW. Troth, nor I. He is a rustical cut, I know not how; he doth not carry himself like a gentleman of fashion.

WELLBRED. O, Master Matthew, that's a grace peculiar but to a few, 'quos aequus amavit Jupiter.'

MATTHEW. I understand you, sir.

WELLBRED. No question you do—or you do not, sir.

Enter EDWARD *with* STEPHEN.

Ned Knowell! by my soul, welcome; how dost thou, sweet spirit, my genius? 'Slid, I shall love Apollo and the mad Thespian girls the better, while I live, for this, my dear fury, now I see there's some love in thee. Sirrah, these be the two I writ to thee of. Nay, what a drowsy humour is this now! why dost thou not speak?

EDWARD. O, you are a fine gallant, you sent me a rare letter!

WELLBRED. Why, was't not rare?

EDWARD. Yes, I'll be sworn, I was ne'er guilty of reading the like; match it in all Pliny, or Symmachus' epistles, and I'll have my judgment burned in the ear for a rogue; make much of thy vein, for it is inimitable. But I mar'l what camel it was that had the carriage of it; for doubtless he was no ordinary beast that brought it!

WELLBRED. Why?

EDWARD. Why, sayest thou? Why, dost thou think that any reasonable creature, especially in the morning—the sober time of the day, too—could have mista'en my father for me?

WELLBRED. 'Slid, you jest, I hope?

EDWARD. Indeed the best use we can turn it to, is to make a jest on't, now; but I'll assure you, my father had the full view o' your flourishing style some hour before I saw it.

WELLBRED. What a dull slave was this! But, sirrah, what said he to it, i'faith?

EDWARD. Nay, I know not what he said, but I have a shrewd guess what he thought.

WELLBRED. What, what?

EDWARD. Marry, that thou art some strange, dissolute young fellow, and I a grain or two better, for keeping thee company.

WELLBRED. Tut, that thought is like the moon in her last quarter; 'twill change shortly. But, sirrah, I pray thee be acquainted with my two hang-by's here; thou wilt take exceeding pleasure in 'em, if thou hear'st 'em once go: my wind-instruments. I'll wind 'em up——But what strange piece of silence is this? The sign of the Dumb Man?

EDWARD. O, sir, a kinsman of mine, one that may make your music the fuller, an he please; he has his humour, sir.

WELLBRED. O, what is't, what is't?

EDWARD. Nay, I'll neither do your judgment nor his folly that wrong, as to prepare your apprehension. I'll leave him to the mercy o' your search; if you can take him, so!

WELLBRED. Well, Captain Bobadill, Master Matthew, pray you know this gentleman here; he is a friend of mine, and one that will deserve your affection. *To* STEPHEN. I know not your name, sir, but I shall be glad of any occasion to render me more familiar to you.

STEPHEN. My name is Master Stephen, sir; I am this gentleman's own cousin, sir; his father is mine uncle, sir; I am somewhat melancholy, but you shall command me, sir, in whatsoever is incident to a gentleman.

BOBADILL. *To* EDWARD. Sir, I must tell you this: I am no general man, but for Master Wellbred's sake,—you may embrace it at what height of favour you please—I do communicate with you, and conceive you to be a gentleman of some parts; I love few words.

EDWARD. And I fewer, sir. I have scarce enow to thank you.

MATTHEW. *To* STEPHEN. But are you, indeed, sir, so given to it?

STEPHEN. Ay, truly, sir, I am mightily given to melancholy.

MATTHEW. O, it's your only fine humour, sir! your true melancholy breeds your perfect fine wit, sir. I am melancholy myself divers times, sir, and then do I no more but take pen and paper presently, and overflow you half a score or a dozen of sonnets at a sitting.

EDWARD. —Sure he utters them then by the gross.

STEPHEN. Truly, sir, and I love such things out of measure.

EDWARD. —I'faith, better than in measure, I'll undertake.

MATTHEW. Why, I pray you, sir, make use of my study, it's at your service.

STEPHEN. I thank you, sir, I shall be bold, I warrant you. Have you a stool there to be melancholy upon?

MATTHEW. That I have, sir, and some papers there of mine own doing, at idle hours, that you'll say there's some sparks of wit in 'em, when you see them.

WELLBRED. —Would the sparks would kindle once, and become a fire amongst 'em! I might see self-love burnt for her heresy.

STEPHEN. Cousin, is it well? am I melancholy enough?

EDWARD. O ay, excellent.

WELLBRED. Captain Bobadill, why muse you so?

EDWARD. He is melancholy too.

BOBADILL. Faith, sir, I was thinking of a most honourable piece of service, was performed tomorrow, being Saint Mark's day, shall be some ten years now.

EDWARD. In what place, Captain?

BOBADILL. Why, at the beleaguering of Strigonium, where, in less than two hours, seven hundred
resolute gentlemen, as any were in Europe, lost their
lives upon the breach. I'll tell you, gentlemen, it
was the first, but the best leaguer that ever I beheld
with these eyes, except the taking in of—what do
you call it, last year, by the Genoways? but that,
of all other, was the most fatal and dangerous exploit that ever I was ranged in, since I first bore
arms before the face of the enemy, as I am a gentleman and soldier.

STEPHEN. 'So! I had as lief as an angel I could
swear as well as that gentleman!

EDWARD. Then you were a servitor at both, it
seems! at Strigonium and What-do-you-call't?

BOBADILL. O Lord, sir! By Saint George, I was
the first man that entered the breach; and had I
not effected it with resolution, I had been slain,
if I had had a million of lives.

EDWARD. 'Twas pity you had not ten—a cat's and
your own, i'faith.—But was it possible?

MATTHEW. —Pray you mark this discourse, sir.

STEPHEN. So I do.

BOBADILL. I assure you, upon my reputation, 'tis
true, and yourself shall confess.

EDWARD. —You must bring me to the rack, first.

BOBADILL. Observe me, judicially, sweet sir: they
had planted me three demi-culverins just in the
mouth of the breach; now, sir, as we were to give
on, their master-gunner—a man of no mean skill
and mark, you must think—confronts me with his
linstock, ready to give fire; I, spying his intendment,
discharged my petronel in his bosom, and with
these single arms, my poor rapier, ran violently

upon the Moors that guarded the ordnance, and put 'em pell-mell to the sword.

WELLBRED. To the sword? to the rapier, Captain!

EDWARD. O, it was a good figure observed, sir.— But did you all this, Captain, without hurting your blade?

BOBADILL. Without any impeach o' the earth; you shall perceive, sir. It is the most fortunate weapon that ever rid on poor gentleman's thigh. Shall I tell you, sir? You talk of Morglay, Excalibur, Durindana or so? Tut! I lend no credit to that is fabled of 'em, I know the virtue of mine own, and therefore I dare the boldlier maintain it.

STEPHEN. I mar'l whether it be a Toledo or no.

BOBADILL. A most perfect Toledo, I assure you, sir.

STEPHEN. I have a countryman of his, here.

MATTHEW. Pray you, let's see, sir. Yes, faith, it is.

BOBADILL. This a Toledo? Pish!

STEPHEN. Why do you pish, Captain?

BOBADILL. A Fleming, by Heaven! I'll buy them for a guilder apiece, an I would have a thousand of them.

EDWARD. How say you, cousin? I told you thus much.

WELLBRED. Where bought you it, Master Stephen?

STEPHEN. Of a scurvy rogue soldier—a hundred of lice go with him—he swore it was a Toledo.

BOBADILL. A poor provant rapier, no better.

MATTHEW. Mass, I think it be indeed, now I look on't better.

EDWARD. Nay, the longer you look on't, the worse. Put it up, put it up.

STEPHEN. Well, I will put it up; but by—I ha' forgot the Captain's oath, I thought to ha' sworn by it—an e'er I meet him——

WELLBRED. O, it is past help now, sir, you must have patience.

STEPHEN. Whoreson, coney-catching rascal! I could eat the very hilts for anger.

EDWARD. A sign of good digestion! you have an ostrich stomach, cousin.

STEPHEN. A stomach? would I had him here, you should see an I had a stomach.

WELLBRED. It's better as 'tis. Come, gentlemen, shall we go?

Enter BRAINWORM *as a soldier.*

EDWARD. A miracle, cousin; look here, look here!

STEPHEN. O, God's lid! By your leave, do you know me, sir?

BRAINWORM. Ay, sir, I know you by sight.

STEPHEN. You sold me a rapier, did you not?

BRAINWORM. Yes, marry did I, sir.

STEPHEN. You said it was a Toledo, ha?

BRAINWORM. True, I did so.

STEPHEN. But it is none?

BRAINWORM. No, sir, I confess it, it is none.

STEPHEN. Do you confess it?—Gentlemen, bear witness, he has confessed it.—By God's will, an you had not confessed it——

EDWARD. O, cousin, forbear, forbear!

STEPHEN. Nay, I have done, cousin.

WELLBRED. Why, you have done like a gentleman; he has confessed it, what would you more?

STEPHEN. Yet, by his leave, he is a rascal, under his favour, do you see?

EDWARD. —Ay, by his leave, he is, and under favour; a pretty piece of civility! Sirrah, how dost thou like him?

WELLBRED. O, it's a most precious fool, make much

on him! I can compare him to nothing more happily than a drum, for everyone may play upon him.

EDWARD. No, no, a child's whistle were far the fitter.

BRAINWORM. —Sir, shall I entreat a word with you?

EDWARD. With me, sir? you have not another Toledo to sell, ha' you?

BRAINWORM. You are conceited, sir; your name is Master Knowell as I take it?

EDWARD. You are i' the right; you mean not to proceed in the catechism, do you?

BRAINWORM. No, sir; I am none of that coat.

EDWARD. Of as bare a coat, though. Well, say, sir,

BRAINWORM. Faith, sir, I am but servant to the drum extraordinary, and indeed—this smoky varnish being washed off, and three or four patches removed—I appear your worship's in reversion, after the decease of your good father, Brainworm.

EDWARD. Brainworm! 'Slight, what breath of a conjurer hath blown thee hither in this shape?

BRAINWORM. The breath o' your letter, sir, this morning; the same that blew you to the Windmill and your father after you.

EDWARD. My father?

BRAINWORM. Nay, never start, 'tis true: he has followed you over the fields by the foot, as you would do a hare i' the snow.

EDWARD. Sirrah Wellbred, what shall we do, sirrah? My father is come over after me.

WELLBRED. Thy father! Where is he?

BRAINWORM. At Justice Clement's house here in Coleman Street, where he but stays my return; and then——

WELLBRED. Who's this? Brainworm!

BRAINWORM. The same, sir.

WELLBRED. Why, how, i' the name of wit, com'st thou transmuted thus?

BRAINWORM. Faith, a device, a device. Nay, for the love of reason, gentleman, and avoiding the danger, stand not here; withdraw, and I'll tell you all.

WELLBRED. But art thou sure he will stay thy return?

BRAINWORM. Do I live, sir? what a question is that!

WELLBRED. We'll prorogue his expectation, then, a little. Brainworm, thou shalt go with us.——Come on, gentlemen.——Nay, I pray thee, sweet Ned, droop not. Heart, an our wits be so wretchedly dull, that one old plodding brain can outstrip us all, would we were e'en pressed to make porters of, and serve out the remnant of our days in Thames Street, or at Custom House Quay, in a civil war against the carmen!

BRAINWORM. Amen, Amen, Amen, say I. *Exeunt.*

ACT THREE. SCENE TWO

Kitely's warehouse

Enter KITELY *and* CASH.

KITELY. What says he, Thomas? Did you speak with him?

CASH. He will expect you, sir, within this half-hour.

KITELY. Has he the money ready, can you tell?

CASH. Yes, sir, the money was brought in last night.

KITELY. O, that's well. Fetch me my cloak, my
  cloak!   *Exit* CASH.
Stay, let me see, an hour to go and come;
Ay, that will be the least; and then 'twill be
An hour before I can dispatch with him,
Or very near; well, I will say two hours.
Two hours? ha! things never dreamt of yet
May be contrived, ay, and effected too,
In two hours' absence; well, I will not go.
Two hours! No, fleering Opportunity,
I will not give your subtlety that scope.
Who will not judge him worthy to be robbed,
That sets his doors wide open to a thief,
And shows the felon where his treasure lies?
Again, what earthy spirit but will attempt
To taste the fruit of beauty's golden tree,
When leaden sleep seals up the dragon's eyes?
I will not go. Business, go by, for once.
No, beauty, no; you are of too good carat,
To be left so, without a guard, or open!
Your lustre, too, 'll inflame, at any distance,
Draw courtship to you, as a jet doth straws,
Put motion in a stone, strike fire from ice,
Nay, make a porter leap you, with his burden!
You must be then kept up, close, and well watched,
For, give you opportunity, no quicksand
Devours or swallows swifter! He that lends
His wife—if she be fair—or time or place,
Compels her to be false. I will not go.
The dangers are too many. And then, the dressing
Is a most main attractive! Our great heads,
Within the City, never were in safety,
Since our wives wore these little caps. I'll change
  'em,
I'll change 'em straight, in mine; mine shall no more

Wear three-piled acorns, to make my horns ache.
Nor will I go. I am resolved for that.—

Re-enter CASH *with a cloak.*

Carry in my cloak again.—Yet stay.—Yet do, too;
I will defer going, on all occasions.

    CASH. Sir, Snare, your scrivener, will be there with
th' bonds.

    KITELY. That's true! fool on me! I had clean forgot
      it;
I must go. What's o'clock?

    CASH.   Exchange time, sir.

    KITELY. Heart, then will Wellbred presently be
      here, too,
With one or other of his loose consorts.
I am a knave, if I know what to say,
What course to take, or which way to resolve.
My brain, methinks, is like an hour-glass,
Wherein my imaginations run like sands,
Filling up time; but then are turned, and turned,
So that I know not what to stay upon,
And less to put in act. It shall be so.
Nay, I dare build upon his secrecy,
He knows not to deceive me.—Thomas!

    CASH.   Sir.

    KITELY. Yet now I have bethought me too, I will
      not.—
Thomas, is Cob within?

    CASH.   I think he be, sir.

    KITELY. But he'll prate, too, there is no speech of
      him.
No, there were no man o' the earth to Thomas,
If I durst trust him; there is all the doubt.
But, should he have a chink in him, I were gone,
Lost i' my fame forever, talk for th' Exchange!
The manner he hath stood with, till this present,

Doth promise no such change; what should I fear
  then?
Well, come what will, I'll tempt my fortune, once.—
Thomas—you may deceive me, but, I hope—
Your love to me is more——
    CASH.   Sir, if a servant's
Duty, with faith, may be called love, you are
More than in hope, you are possessed of it.
    KITELY. I thank you, heartily, Thomas, gi' me your
  hand;
With all my heart, good Thomas. I have, Thomas,
A secret to impart unto you—but,
When once you have it, I must seal your lips up:——
So far I tell you, Thomas.
    CASH.   Sir, for that——
    KITELY. Nay, hear me out. Think I esteem you,
  Thomas,
When I will let you in, thus, to my private.
It is a thing sits nearer to my crest
Than thou art 'ware of, Thomas. If thou shouldst
Reveal it, but——
    CASH.   How! I reveal it?
    KITELY.   Nay,
I do not think thou would'st; but if thou shouldst,
'Twere a great weakness.
    CASH.   A great treachery;
Give it no other name.
    KITELY.   Thou wilt not do't, then?
    CASH. Sir, if I do, mankind disclaim me ever!
    KITELY. —He will not swear, he has some reserva-
  tion,
Some concealed purpose and close meaning, sure;
Else being urged so much, how should he choose
But lend an oath to all this protestation?
He's no precisian, that I am certain of,

Nor rigid Roman Catholic. He'll play
At fayles and tick-tack; I have heard him swear.
What should I think of it? urge him again,
And by some other way? I will do so.—
Well, Thomas, thou hast sworn not to disclose;
Yes, you did swear?

    CASH.   Not yet, sir, but I will,
Please you——

    KITELY.   No, Thomas, I dare take thy word,
But, if thou wilt swear, do as thou think'st good;
I am resolved without it; at thy pleasure.

    CASH. By my soul's safety then, sir, I protest,
My tongue shall ne'er take knowledge of a word
Delivered me in nature of your trust.

    KITELY. It is too much; these ceremonies need not;
I know thy faith to be as firm as rock.
Thomas, come hither, near; we cannot be
Too private in this business. So it is,—
Now he has sworn, I dare the safelier venture——
I have of late, by divers observations——
But, whether his oath can bind him, yea, or no,
Being not taken lawfully, ha?—say you?—
I will ask counsel, ere I do proceed——
Thomas, it will be now too long to stay,
I'll spy some fitter time soon, or tomorrow.

    CASH. Sir, at your pleasure.

    KITELY.   I will think. And, Thomas,
I pray you search the books 'gainst my return,
For the receipts 'twixt me and Traps.

    CASH.   I will, sir.

    KITELY. And hear you, if your mistress' brother,
      Wellbred,
Chance to bring hither any gentlemen,
Ere I come back, let one straight bring me word.

    CASH. Very well, sir.

KITELY.   To the Exchange, do you hear?
Or here in Coleman Street, to Justice Clement's.
Forget it not, nor be not out of the way.

CASH. I will not, sir.

KITELY.   I pray you have a care on't.
Or, whether he come or no, if any other,
Stranger or else, fail not to send me word.

CASH. I shall not, sir.

KITELY.   Be't your special business
Now to remember it.

CASH.   Sir, I warrant you.

KITELY. But, Thomas, this is not the secret,
    Thomas,
I told you of.

CASH.   No, sir, I do suppose it.

KITELY. Believe me, it is not.

CASH.   Sir, I do believe you.

KITELY. By Heaven, it is not, that's enough. But,
    Thomas,
I would not you should utter it, do you see,
To any creature living, yet I care not.
Well, I must hence. Thomas, conceive thus much:
It was a trial of you, when I meant
So deep a secret to you, I mean not this,
But that I have to tell you; this is nothing, this.
But, Thomas, keep this from my wife, I charge you,
Lock'd up in silence, midnight, buried here.—
No greater hell than to be slave to fear.   *Exit.*

CASH. 'Locked up in silence, midnight, buried
    here!'
Whence should this flood of passion, trow, take
    head? ha?
Best dream no longer of this running humour,
For fear I sink! The violence of the stream
Already hath transported me so far,

That I can feel no ground at all! But soft—
O, 'tis our water-bearer; somewhat has crossed him
    now.

Enter COB.

COB. Fasting-days! what tell you me of fasting-days? 'Slid, would they were all on a light fire for me! They say the whole world shall be consumed with fire one day, but would I had these Ember Weeks and villanous Fridays burnt in the mean time, and then——

CASH. Why, how now, Cob? what moves thee to this choler, ha?

COB. Collar, Master Thomas? I scorn your collar, I, sir, I am none o' your cart-horse, though I carry and draw water. An you offer to ride me, with your collar, or halter either, I may hap show you a jade's trick, sir.

CASH. O, you'll slip your head out of the collar? why, Goodman Cob, you mistake me.

COB. Nay, I have my rheum, and I can be angry as well as another, sir.

CASH. Thy rheum, Cob? thy humour, thy humour —thou mistak'st.

COB. Humour! mack, I think it be so indeed. What is that humour? Some rare thing, I warrant.

CASH. Marry, I'll tell thee, Cob: it is a gentleman-like monster, bred in the special gallantry of our time by affectation, and fed by folly.

COB. How! must it be fed?

CASH. O ày, humour is nothing if it be not fed. Did'st thou never hear that? It's a common phrase, 'Feed my humour.'

COB. I'll none on it. Humour, avaunt! I know you not, begone! Let who will make hungry meals for your monstership, it shall not be I. Feed you, quoth

he! 'Slid, I ha' much ado to feed myself, especially
on these lean rascally days, too; an't had been any
other day but a fasting-day—a plague on them all
for me—by this light, one might have done the
commonwealth good service and have drowned them
all i' the flood, two or three hundred thousand years
ago. O, I do stomach them hugely! I have a maw
now, an 'twere for Sir Bevis's horse, against 'em.

CASH. I pray thee, good Cob, what makes thee so
out of love with fasting-days?

COB. Marry, that which will make any man out of
love with 'em, I think: their bad conditions, an you
will needs know. First, they are of a Flemish breed,
I am sure on't, for they raven up more butter than
all the days of the week beside; next, they stink of
fish and leek-porridge miserably; thirdly, they'll keep
a man devoutly hungry all day, and at night send
him supperless to bed.

CASH. Indeed, these are faults, Cob.

COB. Nay, an this were all, 'twere something, but
they are the only known enemies to my generation.
A fasting-day no sooner comes, but my lineage goes
to wrack. Poor cobs, they smoke for it, they are made
martyrs o' the gridiron, they melt in passion! And
your maids, too, know this, and yet would have me
turn Hannibal and eat my own fish and blood. *Pulls
out a red herring.* My princely coz, fear nothing; I
have not the heart to devour you, an I might be
made as rich as King Cophetua. O, that I had room
for my tears, I could weep salt-water enough now
to preserve the lives of ten thousand of my kin! But
I may curse none but these filthy almanacs; for an't
were not for them, these days of persecution would
ne'er be known. I'll be hanged, an some fishmonger's
son do not make of 'em, and puts in more fasting-

days than he should do, because he would utter his father's dried stockfish and stinking conger.

CASH. 'Slight, peace! thou'lt be beaten like a stock-fish else; here's Master Matthew.—Now must I look out for a messenger to my master. *Exit with* COB.

Enter WELLBRED, EDWARD, BRAINWORM, MATTHEW, BOBADILL, *and* STEPHEN.

WELLBRED. Beshrew me, but it was an absolute good jest, and exceedingly well carried!

EDWARD. Ay, and our ignorance maintained it as well, did it not?

WELLBRED. Yes, faith, but was 't possible thou shouldst not know him? I forgive Master Stephen, for he is stupidity itself.

EDWARD. 'Fore God, not I, an I might have been joined patent with one of the Seven Wise Masters for knowing him. He had so writhen himself into the habit of one of your poor infantry, your decayed, ruinous, worm-eaten gentlemen of the round; such as have vowed to sit on the skirts of the City, let your Provost and his half-dozen of halberdiers do what they can; and have translated begging out of the old hackney pace to a fine easy amble, and made it run as smooth off the tongue as a shove-groat shilling. Into the likeness of one of these reformados had he moulded himself so perfectly, observing every trick of their action, as varying the accent, swearing with an emphasis, indeed all, with so special and exquisite a grace, that hadst thou seen him, thou wouldst have sworn he might have been sergeant-major, if not lieutenant-colonel to the regiment.

WELLBRED. Why, Brainworm, who would have thought thou hadst been such an artificer?

EDWARD. An artificer? an architect! Except a man

had studied begging all his lifetime, and been a weaver of language from his infancy, for the clothing of it, I never saw his rival!

WELLBRED. Where got'st thou this coat, I mar'l?

BRAINWORM. Of a Houndsditch man, sir, one of the devil's near kinsmen, a broker.

WELLBRED. That cannot be, if the proverb hold: for a crafty knave needs no broker.

BRAINWORM. True, sir; but I did need a broker, ergo——

WELLBRED. Well put off; no crafty knave, you'll say.

EDWARD. Tut, he has more of these shifts.

BRAINWORM. And yet, where I have one, the broker has ten, sir.

Re-enter CASH.

CASH. Francis! Martin! Ne'er a one to be found, now? What a spite's this!

WELLBRED. How now, Thomas! is my brother Kitely within?

CASH. No, sir, my master went forth e'en now, but Master Downright is within.—Cob! what, Cob! Is he gone, too?

WELLBRED. Whither went your master, Thomas, canst thou tell?

CASH. I know not; to Justice Clement's, I think, sir.—Cob! *Exit.*

EDWARD. Justice Clement! what's he?

WELLBRED. Why, dost thou not know him? He is a city magistrate, a justice here, an excellent good lawyer, and a great scholar; but the only mad, merry old fellow in Europe. I showed him you the other day.

EDWARD. O, is that he? I remember him now. Good faith, and he has a very strange presence, methinks;

it shows as if he stood out of the rank from other men. I have heard many of his jests i' the University. They say he will commit a man for taking the wall of his horse.

WELLBRED. Ay, or wearing his cloak of one shoulder, or serving of God; anything, indeed, if it come in the way of his humour.

CASH *goes in and out calling.*

CASH. Gasper! Martin! Cob! Heart, where should they be, trow?

BOBADILL. Master Kitely's man, pray thee vouchsafe us the lighting of this match.

CASH. Fire on your match! no time but now to vouchsafe?—Francis! Cob!   *Exit.*

BOBADILL. Body o' me! here's the remainder of seven pound, since yesterday was seven-night. 'Tis your right Trinidado! Did you never take any, Master Stephen?

STEPHEN. No truly, sir, but I'll learn to take it now, since you commend it so.

BOBADILL. Sir, believe me, upon my relation, for what I tell you the world shall not reprove. I have been in the Indies, where this herb grows, where neither myself nor a dozen gentlemen more, of my knowledge, have received the taste of any other nutriment in the world, for the space of one and twenty weeks, but the fume of this simple only. Therefore, it cannot be but 'tis most divine! Further, take it in the nature, in the true kind, so, it makes an antidote that, had you taken the most deadly poisonous plant in all Italy, it should expel it and clarify you, with as much ease as I speak. And for your green wound, your balsamum and your Saint John's wort are all mere gulleries and trash to it, especially your Trinidado; your Nicotian is good, too. I could say what I know of the virtue of it for the expulsion of rheums, raw humours, crudities, obstructions, with a thousand of this kind; but I profess myself no quacksalver. Only thus much, by Hercules, I do hold it, and will affirm it before any prince in Europe, to be the most sovereign and precious weed that ever the earth tendered to the use of man.

EDWARD. This speech would ha' done decently in a tobacco-trader's mouth.

Re-enter CASH *with* COB.

CASH. At Justice Clement's he is, in the middle of Coleman Street.

COB. Oh, oh!

BOBADILL. Where's the match I gave thee, Master Kitely's man?

CASH. —Would his match, and he, and pipe, and all, were at Santo Domingo! I had forgot it. *Exit.*

COB. By God's me, I mar'l what pleasure or felicity they have in taking this roguish tobacco! It's good for nothing but to choke a man, and fill him full of smoke and embers. There were four died out of one house, last week, with taking of it; and two more the bell went for, yesternight. One of them, they say, will ne'er 'scape it; he voided a bushel of soot yesterday, upward and downward. By the stocks, an there were no wiser men than I, I'd have it present whipping, man or woman, that should but deal with a tobacco-pipe. Why, it will stifle them all in the end, as many as use it; it's little better than ratsbane or rosaker. BOBADILL *beats him with a cudgel.*

ALL. O, good Captain, hold, hold!

BOBADILL. You base cullion, you!

Re-enter CASH.

CASH. Sir, here's your match.—Come, thou must needs be talking, too, thou'rt well enough served.

COB. Nay, he will not meddle with his match, I warrant you. Well, it shall be a dear beating, an I live.

BOBADILL. Do you prate? Do you murmur?

EDWARD. Nay, good Captain, will you regard the humour of a fool?—Away, knave.

WELLBRED. Thomas, get him away.

Exit CASH *with* COB.

BOBADILL. A whoreson filthy slave, a dung-worm, an excrement! Body o' Caesar, but that I scorn to let forth so mean a spirit, I'd ha' stabbed him to the earth.

WELLBRED. Marry, the law forbid, sir.

BOBADILL. By Pharaoh's foot, I would have done it!

STEPHEN. O, he swears admirably! By Pharaoh's foot! Body of Caesar! I shall never do it, sure— Upon mine honour, and by Saint George!—No, I ha' not the right grace.

MATTHEW. Master Stephen, will you any? By this air, the most divine tobacco that ever I drunk!

STEPHEN. None, I thank you, sir.—O, this gentleman does it rarely, too, but nothing like the other! *Practising to the post.* By this air! As I am a gentleman! By——

BRAINWORM. Master, glance, glance!—Master Wellbred! *Exeunt* BOBADILL *and* MATTHEW.

STEPHEN. As I have somewhat to be saved, I protest——

WELLBRED. —You are a fool; it needs no affidavit.

EDWARD. Cousin, will you any tobacco?

STEPHEN. I, sir! Upon my reputation——

EDWARD. How now, cousin!

STEPHEN. I protest, as I am a gentleman, but no soldier, indeed——

WELLBRED. No, Master Stephen? As I remember, your name is entered in the artillery-garden.

STEPHEN. Ay, sir, that's true. Cousin, may I swear as I am a soldier, by that?

EDWARD. O yes, that you may. It's all you have for your money.

STEPHEN. Then, as I am a gentleman and a soldier, it is divine tobacco!

WELLBRED. But soft, where's Master Matthew? Gone?

BRAINWORM. No, sir, they went in here.

WELLBRED. O, let's follow them; Master Matthew is gone to salute his mistress in verse. We shall ha' the happiness to hear some of his poetry now. He never comes unfurnished.—Brainworm!

STEPHEN. Brainworm? Where? Is this Brainworm?

EDWARD. Ay, cousin, no words of it, upon your gentility.

STEPHEN. Not I, body o' me! By this air, Saint George, and the foot of Pharaoh!

WELLBRED. Rare! your cousin's discourse is simply drawn out with oaths.

EDWARD. 'Tis larded with 'em; a kind of French dressing, if you love it.   *Exeunt.*

ACT THREE. SCENE THREE

Justice Clement's house

Enter KITELY *and* COB.

KITELY. Ha! how many are there, sayest thou?

COB. Marry, sir, your brother, Master Wellbred——

KITELY. Tut, beside him; what strangers are there, man?

COB. Strangers? let me see, one, two—mass, I know not well, there are so many.

KITELY. How! so many?

COB. Ay, there's some five or six of them, at the most.

KITELY. —A swarm, a swarm!
Spite of the devil, how they sting my head
With forkèd stings, thus wide and large!——But, Cob,
How long hast thou been coming hither, Cob?

COB. A little while, sir.

KITELY. Didst thou come running?

COB.   No, sir,

KITELY. —Nay, then I am familiar with thy haste!
Bane to my fortunes, what meant I to marry?
I, that before was ranked in such content,
My mind at rest too, in so soft a peace,
Being free master of mine own free thoughts,
And now become a slave? What? never sigh,
Be of good cheer, man; for thou art a cuckold,
'Tis done, 'tis done! nay, when such flowering store,
Plenty itself, falls in my wife's lap,
The cornucopiae will be mine, I know.—But, Cob,

What entertainment had they? I am sure
My sister and my wife would bid them welcome, ha?

COB. Like enough, sir, yet I heard not a word of it.

KITELY. No, their lips were sealed with kisses, and
the voice
Drowned in a flood of joy at their arrival,
Had lost her motion, state, and faculty.—
Cob, which of them was't that first kissed my wife?
My sister, I should say; my wife, alas,
I fear not her, ha? who was it, say'st thou?

COB. By my troth, sir, will you have the truth
of it?

KITELY. O ay, good Cob, I pray thee, heartily.

COB. Then I am a vagabond, and fitter for Bridewell than your worship's company, if I saw anybody
to be kissed, unless they would have kissed the post
in the middle of the warehouse; for there I left them
all at their tobacco, with a pox!

KITELY. How? were they not gone in, then, ere
thou cam'st?

COB. O no, sir.

KITELY. Spite of the devil! what do I stay here
then? Cob, follow me.   *Exit.*

COB. Nay, soft and fair; I have eggs on the spit; I
cannot go yet, sir. Now am I, for some five and fifty
reasons, hammering, hammering revenge. O, for
three or four gallons of vinegar, to sharpen my wits!
Revenge, vinegar revenge, vinegar and mustard revenge! Nay, an he had not lain in my house, 'twould
never have grieved me, but being my guest, one that
I'll be sworn my wife has lent him her smock off
her back, while his one shirt has been at washing;
pawned her neckerchers for clean bands for him;
sold almost all my platters to buy him tobacco; and
he to turn monster of ingratitude, and strike his

lawful host! Well, I hope to raise up an host of fury for't; here comes Justice Clement.

Enter CLEMENT, KNOWELL, *and* FORMAL.

CLEMENT. What's Master Kitely gone? Roger!

FORMAL. Ay, sir.

CLEMENT. Heart of me! what made him leave us so abruptly?—How now, sirrah? what make you here? what would you have, ha?

COB. An't please your worship, I am a poor neighbour of your worship's——

CLEMENT. A poor neighbour of mine! why, speak, poor neighbour.

COB. I dwell, sir, at the sign of the Water Tankard, hard by the Green Lattice; I have paid scot and lot there any time this eighteen years.

CLEMENT. To the Green Lattice?

COB. No, sir, to the parish; marry, I have seldom scaped scot-free at the Lattice.

CLEMENT. O, well! what business has my poor neighbour with me?

COB. An't like your worship, I am come to crave the peace of your worship.

CLEMENT. Of me, knave? Peace of me, knave! Did I ever hurt thee, or threaten thee, or wrong thee, ha?

COB. No, sir, but your worship's warrant for one that has wronged me, sir; his arms are at too much liberty; I would fain have them bound to a treaty of peace, an my credit could compass it with your worship.

CLEMENT. Thou goest far enough about for't, I'm sure.

KNOWELL. Why, dost thou go in danger of thy life for him, friend?

COB. No, sir, but I go in danger of my death every hour, by his means; an I die within a twelvemonth and a day, I may swear by the law of the land that he killed me.

CLEMENT. How, how, knave? swear he killed thee, and by the law? What pretence, what colour hast thou for that?

COB. Marry, an't please your worship, both black and blue; colour enough, I warrant you. I have it here to show your worship.

CLEMENT. What is he that gave you this, sirrah?

COB. A gentleman and a soldier, he says he is, o' the City here.

CLEMENT. A soldier o' the City! What call you him?

COB. Captain Bobadill.

CLEMENT. Bobadill! and why did he bob and beat you, sirrah? How began the quarrel betwixt you, ha? Speak truly, knave, I advise you.

COB. Marry, indeed, an't please your worship, only because I spake against their vagrant tobacco, as I came by 'em when they were taking on't; for nothing else.

CLEMENT. Ha! you speak against tobacco? Formal, his name.

FORMAL. What's your name, sirrah?

COB. Oliver, sir, Oliver Cob, sir.

CLEMENT. Tell Oliver Cob he shall go to the jail, Formal.

FORMAL. Oliver Cob, my master, Justice Clement, says you shall go to the jail.

COB. O, I beseech your worship, for God's sake, dear Master Justice!

CLEMENT. Nay God's precious! an such drunkards and tankards as you are, come to dispute of tobacco once, I have done. Away with him!

COB. O good Master Justice!—Sweet old gentleman!

KNOWELL. Sweet Oliver, would I could do thee any good!—Justice Clement, let me entreat you, sir.

CLEMENT. What? a thread-bare rascal! a beggar! a slave that never drunk out of better than piss-pot metal in his life! and he to deprave and abuse the virtue of an herb so generally received in the courts of princes, the chambers of nobles, the bowers of sweet ladies, the cabins of soldiers!—Roger, away with him! By God's precious—I say, go to!

COB. Dear Master Justice, let me be beaten again, I have deserved it; but not the prison, I beseech you.

KNOWELL. Alas, poor Oliver!

CLEMENT. Roger, make him a warrant.—He shall not go, I but fear the knave.

FORMAL. Do not stink, sweet Oliver, you shall not go; my master will give you a warrant.

COB. O, the Lord maintain his worship, his worthy worship!

CLEMENT. Away, dispatch him. *Exit* FORMAL *with* COB. How now, Master Knowell! In dumps, in dumps? Come, this becomes not.

KNOWELL. Sir, would I could not feel my cares——

CLEMENT. Your cares are nothing; they are like my cap, soon put on and as soon put off. What! your son is old enough to govern himself; let him run his course, it's the only way to make him a staid man. If he were an unthrift, a ruffian, a drunkard, or a licentious liver, then you had reason, you had reason to take care; but being none of these, mirth's my witness, an I had twice so many cares as you have, I'd drown them all in a cup of sack. Come, come, let's try it! I muse your parcel of a soldier returns not all this while. *Exeunt.*

ACT FOUR. SCENE ONE

Kitely's house

Enter DOWNRIGHT *and* DAME KITELY.

DOWNRIGHT. Well, sister, I tell you true; and you'll find it so in the end.

DAME KITELY. Alas, brother, what would you have me to do? I cannot help it. You see my brother brings 'em in here; they are his friends.

DOWNRIGHT. His friends? his fiends. 'Slud! they do nothing but haunt him up and down like a sort of unlucky sprites, and tempt him to all manner of villainy that can be thought of. Well, by this light, a little thing would make me play the devil with some of 'em; an 'twere not more for your husband's sake than anything else, I'd make the house too hot for the best on 'em; they should say and swear hell were broken loose, ere they went hence. But, by God's will, 'tis nobody's fault but yours; for an you had done as you might have done, they should have been parboiled, and baked too, every mother's son, ere they should ha' come in, e'er a one of 'em.

DAME KITELY. God's my life! did you ever hear the like? What a strange man is this! Could I keep out all them, think you? I should put myself against half a dozen men, should I? Good faith, you'd mad the patient'st body in the world, to hear you talk so, without any sense or reason!

Enter BRIDGET *with* MATTHEW *and* BOBADILL, *followed by* WELLBRED, EDWARD, STEPHEN, *and* BRAINWORM.

BRIDGET. Servant, in troth, you are too prodigal
Of your wit's treasure, thus to pour it forth
Upon so mean a subject as my worth!

MATTHEW. You say well, mistress, and I mean as well.

DOWNRIGHT. Hoy-day, here is stuff!

WELLBRED. —O, now stand close; pray Heaven, she can get him to read! He should do it, of his own natural impudency.

BRIDGET. Servant, what is this same, I pray you?

MATTHEW. Marry, an elegy, an elegy, an odd toy——

DOWNRIGHT. —To mock an ape withal! O, I could sew up his mouth, now.

DAME KITELY. Sister, I pray you let's hear it.

DOWNRIGHT. Are you rhyme-given too?

MATTHEW. Mistress, I'll read it, if you please.

BRIDGET. Pray you do, servant.

DOWNRIGHT. —O, here's no foppery! Death! I can endure the stocks better. *Exit.*

EDWARD. What ails thy brother? can he not hold his water at reading of a ballad?

WELLBRED. Oh, no; a rhyme to him is worse than cheese, or a bagpipe. But mark, you lose the protestation.

MATTHEW. Faith, I did it in an humour; I know not how it is. But please you come near, sir. This gentleman has judgment, he knows how to censure of a—pray you, sir, you can judge.

STEPHEN. Not I, sir, upon my reputation, and by the foot of Pharaoh!

WELLBRED. O, chide your cousin for swearing.

EDWARD. Not I, so long as he does not forswear himself.

BOBADILL. Master Matthew, you abuse the expectation of your dear mistress and her fair sister. Fie! while you live, avoid this prolixity.

MATTHEW. I shall, sir; well, 'incipere dulce.'

EDWARD. How! 'insipere dulce?' a sweet thing to be a fool, indeed!

WELLBRED. What, do you take 'incipere' in that sense?

EDWARD. You do not, you? This was your villainy, to gull him with a motte.

WELLBRED. O, the benchers' phrase: 'pauca verba, pauca verba!'

MATTHEW. 'Rare creature, let me speak without
        offence:
Would God my rude words had the influence
To rule thy thoughts, as thy fair looks do mine;
Then shouldst thou be his prisoner, who is thine.'

EDWARD. —This is in 'Hero and Leander.'

WELLBRED. O ay! peace, we shall have more of this.

MATTHEW. 'Be not unkind and fair; misshapen
        stuff
Is of behaviour boisterous and rough.'

WELLBRED. How like you that, sir?

                STEPHEN *answers with shaking his head.*

EDWARD. 'Slight, he shakes his head like a bottle, to feel an there be any brain in it.

MATTHEW. But observe the catastrophe now:
'And I in duty will exceed all other,
As you in beauty do excel Love's mother.'

EDWARD. Well, I'll have him free of the wit-brokers, for he utters nothing but stolen remnants.

WELLBRED. O, forgive it him.

EDWARD. A filching rogue, hang him! And from the dead! it's worse than sacrilege.

WELLBRED, EDWARD, *and* STEPHEN *come forward.*

WELLBRED. Sister, what ha' you here? verses? pray you, let's see. Who made these verses? they are excellent good.

MATTHEW. O, Master Wellbred, 'tis your disposition to say so, sir. They were good i' the morning; I made 'em extempore this morning.

WELLBRED. How? extempore?

MATTHEW. Ay, would I might be hanged else; ask Captain Bobadill. He saw me write them, at the— pox on it!—the Star, yonder.

BRAINWORM. —Can he find in his heart to curse the stars so?

EDWARD. Faith, his are even with him; they ha' cursed him enough already.

STEPHEN. Cousin, how do you like this gentleman's verses?

EDWARD. O, admirable; the best that ever I heard, coz.

STEPHEN. Body o' Caesar, they are admirable! The best that ever I heard, as I am a soldier!

R-enter DOWNRIGHT.

DOWNRIGHT. —I am vexed, I can hold ne'er a bone of me still! Heart, I think they mean to build and breed here.

WELLBRED. Sister, you have a simple servant here, that crowns your beauty with such encomiums and devices; you may see what it is, to be the mistress of a wit that can make your perfections so transparent, that every blear eye may look through them, and see him drowned, over head and ears, in the deep well of desire. Sister Kitely, I marvel you get you not a servant that can rhyme and do tricks, too.

DOWNRIGHT. —O monster! impudence itself! tricks!

DAME KITELY. Tricks, brother? what tricks?

BRIDGET. Nay, speak, I pray you, what tricks?

DAME KITELY. Ay, never spare anybody here, but say what tricks.

BRIDGET. Passion of my heart! do tricks?

WELLBRED. 'Slight, here's a trick vied and revied! Why, you monkeys, you, what a caterwauling do you keep! has he not given you rhymes and verses and tricks?

DOWNRIGHT. —O, the fiend!

WELLBRED. Nay, you lamp of virginity, that take it in snuff so, come and cherish this tame poetical fury in your servant, you'll be begged else shortly for a concealment; go to, reward his muse. You cannot give him less than a shilling, in conscience, for the book he had it out of cost him a teston at least. How now, gallants? Master Matthew? Captain? What, all sons of silence, no spirit?

DOWNRIGHT. Come, you might practise your ruffian tricks somewhere else, and not here, I wuss; this is no tavern, nor drinking-school, to vent your exploits in.

WELLBRED. How now! whose cow has calved?

DOWNRIGHT. Marry, that has mine, sir. Nay, boy, never look askance at me for the matter; I'll tell you of it, I, sir; you and your companions, mend yourselves when I ha' done.

WELLBRED. My companions?

DOWNRIGHT. Yes, sir, your companions, so I say; I am not afraid of you, nor them neither, your hang-bys here. You must have your poets and your pot-lings, your soldados and foolados to follow you up and down the City, and here they must come to domineer and swagger.—Sirrah, you ballad-singer, and Slops your fellow there, get you out, get you

home; or, by this steel, I'll cut off your ears, and
that presently.

WELLBRED. 'Slight, stay, let's see what he dare do:
cut off his ears? cut a whetstone! You are an ass, do
you see? touch any man here, and, by this hand, I'll
run my rapier to the hilts in you.

DOWNRIGHT. Yea, that would I fain see, boy.

They all draw.

DAME KITELY. O Jesu! murder! Thomas! Gasper!

BRIDGET. Help, help! Thomas!

EDWARD. Gentlemen, forbear, I pray you!

Enter CASH *and some of the house to part them.*

BOBADILL. Well, sirrah, you Holofernes, by my
hand, I will pink your flesh full of holes with my
rapier for this; I will, by this good Heaven!—Nay,
let him come, let him come, gentlemen; by the body
of Saint George, I'll not kill him.

They offer to fight again, and are parted.

CASH. Hold, hold, good gentlemen.

DOWNRIGHT. You whoreson bragging coystril!

Enter KITELY.

KITELY. Why, how now? what's the matter? what's
the stir here?
Whence springs the quarrel? Thomas! Where is he?
Put up your weapons, and put off this rage.
My wife and sister, they are cause of this.—
What, Thomas? Where is this knave?

CASH. Here, sir.

WELLBRED. Come, let's go; this is one of my brother's ancient humours, this.

STEPHEN. I am glad nobody was hurt by his ancient
humour.

Exeunt WELLBRED, EDWARD, MATTHEW, STEPHEN,
BOBADILL, *and* BRAINWORM.

KITELY. Why, how now, brother, who enforced this brawl?

DOWNRIGHT. A sort of lewd rakehells that care neither for God nor the devil! And they must come here, to read ballads, and roguery, and trash! I'll mar the knot of 'em ere I sleep, perhaps; especially Bob there, he that's all manner of shapes; and Songs and Sonnets, his fellow.

BRIDGET. Brother, indeed you are too violent,
Too sudden, in your humour; and you know
My brother Wellbred's temper will not bear
Any reproof, chiefly in such a presence,
Where every slight disgrace he should receive
Might wound him in opinion and respect.

DOWNRIGHT. Respect! what talk you of respect, 'mong such
As ha' no spark of manhood nor good manners?
'Sdeins, I am ashamed to hear you! respect! *Exit.*

BRIDGET. Yes, there was one a civil gentleman,
And very worthily demeaned himself.

KITELY. O, that was some love of yours, sister.

BRIDGET. A love of mine? I would it were no worse, brother!
You'd pay my portion sooner than you think for.

DAME KITELY. Indeed he seemed to be a gentleman of an exceeding fair disposition, and of very excellent good parts.

Exeunt DAME KITELY *and* BRIDGET.

KITELY. Her love, by Heaven! my wife's minion!
Fair disposition? excellent good parts?
Death, these phrases are intolerable!
Good parts? how should she know his parts?
His parts! Well, well, well, well, well, well!
It is too plain, too clear.—Thomas, come hither.
What, are they gone?

CASH. Ay, sir, they went in.
My mistress and your sister——

KITELY. Are any of the gallants within?

CASH. No, sir, they are all gone.

KITELY. Art thou sure of it?

CASH. I can assure you, sir.

KITELY. What gentleman was that they praised so, Thomas?

CASH. One, they call him Master Knowell, a handsome young gentleman, sir.

KITELY. Ay, I thought so; my mind gave me as
    much.
I'll die, but they have hid him i' the house
Somewhere; I'll go and search. Go with me, Thomas.
Be true to me, and thou shalt find me a master.

Exeunt.

ACT FOUR. SCENE TWO

Before Cob's house

Enter COB.

COB. What, Tib! Tib, I say!

TIB. How now, what cuckold is that knocks so hard?—O, husband, is't you? What's the news.

COB. Nay, you have stunned me, i'faith! you ha' given me a knock o' the forehead will stick by me. Cuckold! 'Slid, cuckold!

TIB. Away, you fool! did I know it was you that knocked? Come, come, you may call me as bad, when you list.

COB. May I? Tib, you are a whore.

TIB. You lie in your throat, husband.

COB. How, the lie? and in my throat, too! Do you long to be stabbed, ha?

TIB. Why, you are no soldier, I hope.

COB. O, must you be stabbed by a soldier? Mass, that's true! When was Bobadill here, your Captain? that rogue, that foist, that fencing Burgullion? I'll tickle him, i'faith.

TIB. Why, what's the matter, trow?

COB. O, he has basted me rarely, sumptuously! but I have it here in black and white, for his black and blue, shall pay him. *Pulls out the warrant.* O, the Justice! the honestest old brave Trojan in London! I do honour the very flea of his dog. A plague on him though, he put me once in a villainous filthy fear; marry, it vanished away like the smoke of tobacco, but I was smoked soundly first. I thank the devil, and his good angel, my guest. Well, wife, or Tib, which you will, get you in and lock the door; I charge you, let nobody in to you, wife, nobody in to you; those are my words. Not Captain Bob himself, nor the fiend in his likeness; you are a woman, you have flesh and blood enough in you to be tempted; therefore, keep the door shut upon all comers.

TIB. I warrant you, there shall nobody enter here without my consent.

COB. Nor with your consent, sweet Tib, and so I leave you.

TIB. It's more than you know, whether you leave me so.

COB. How?

TIB. Why, sweet.

COB. Tut, sweet or sour, thou art a flower.
Keep close thy door, I ask no more. *Exeunt.*

ACT FOUR. SCENE THREE

The Windmill Tavern

Enter EDWARD, WELLBRED, STEPHEN, *and* BRAINWORM
as a soldier.

EDWARD. Well, Brainworm, perform this business happily, and thou makest a purchase of my love forever.

WELLBRED. I'faith, now let thy spirits use their best faculties. But, at any hand, remember the message to my brother; for there's no other means to start him.

BRAINWORM. I warrant you, sir, fear nothing. I have a nimble soul has waked all forces of my fancy by this time, and put 'em in true motion. What you have possessed me withal, I'll discharge it amply, sir. Make it no question. *Exit.*

WELLBRED. Forth, and prosper, Brainworm. Faith, Ned, how dost thou approve of my abilities in this device?

EDWARD. Troth, well, howsoever; but it will come excellent, if it take.

WELLBRED. Take, man? why it cannot choose but take, if the circumstances miscarry not. But tell me, ingenuously, dost thou affect my sister Bridget as thou pretend'st?

EDWARD. Friend, am I worth belief?

WELLBRED. Come, do not protest. In faith, she is a maid of good ornament and much modesty; and, except I conceived very worthily of her, thou shouldest not have her.

EDWARD. Nay, that, I am afraid, will be a question yet, whether I shall have her or no?

WELLBRED. 'Slid, thou shalt have her; by this light, thou shalt.

EDWARD. Nay, do not swear.

WELLBRED. By this hand, thou shalt have her; I'll go fetch her presently. 'Point but where to meet, and as I am an honest man, I'll bring her.

EDWARD. Hold, hold, be temperate.

WELLBRED. Why, by—what shall I swear by? thou shalt have her, as I am——

EDWARD. Pray thee, be at peace, I am satisfied; and do believe thou wilt omit no offered occasion to make my desires complete.

WELLBRED. Thou shalt see and know, I will not.

Exeunt.

ACT FOUR. SCENE FOUR

The Old Jewry

Enter FORMAL *and* KNOWELL.

FORMAL. Was your man a soldier, sir?

KNOWELL.   Ay,
A knave; I took him begging o' the way,
This morning, as I came over Moorfields.

Enter BRAINWORM *as a soldier.*

O, here he is!—You've made fair speed, believe me.
Where i' the name of sloth could you be thus——

BRAINWORM. Marry, peace be my comfort, where

I thought I should have had little comfort of your worship's service.

KNOWELL. How so?

BRAINWORM. O, sir! your coming to the City, your entertainment of me, and your sending me to watch —indeed all the circumstances either of your charge or my employment, are as open to your son as to yourself!

KNOWELL. How should that be! unless that villain, Brainworm,
Have told him of the letter, and discovered
All that I strictly charged him to conceal? 'Tis so.

BRAINWORM. I am partly o' the faith 'tis so, indeed.

KNOWELL. But how should he know thee to be my man?

BRAINWORM. Nay, sir, I cannot tell, unless it be by the black art! Is not your son a scholar, sir?

KNOWELL. Yes, but I hope his soul is not allied
Unto such hellish practice; if it were,
I had just cause to weep my part in him,
And curse the time of his creation.
But, where did'st thou find them, FitzSword?

BRAINWORM. You should rather ask where they found me, sir; for I'll be sworn, I was going along in the street, thinking nothing, when, of a sudden, a voice calls, 'Master Knowell's man!' another cries 'Soldier!' and thus half a dozen of 'em, till they had called me within a house, where I no sooner came, but they seemed men, and out flew all their rapiers at my bosom, with some three or fourscore oaths to accompany 'em; and all to tell me I was but a dead man, if I did not confess where you were, and how I was employed, and about what; which when they could not get out of me—as, I protest, they must ha' dissected and made an anatomy o' me first, and so I told 'em—they locked me up into a room i' the top of a high house; whence, by great miracle, having a light heart, I slid down by a bottom of packthread into the street, and so 'scaped. But, sir, thus much I can assure you, for I heard it while I was locked up: there were a great many rich merchants and brave citizens' wives with 'em at a feast, and your son, Master Edward, withdrew with one of 'em, and has 'pointed to meet her anon at one Cob's house, a water-bearer that dwells by the Wall. Now, there your worship shall be sure to take him, for there he preys, and fail he will not.

KNOWELL. Nor, will I fail to break his match, I doubt not.
Go thou along with Justice Clement's man,
And stay there for me. At one Cob's house, say'st thou?

BRAINWORM. Ay, sir, there you shall have him. *Exit*
KNOWELL. Yes—invisible! Much wench or much son! 'Slight, when he has stayed there three or four hours, travailing with the expectation of wonders, and at length be delivered of air! O, the sport that I should then take to look on him, if I durst! But now I mean to appear no more afore him in this shape. I have another trick to act yet. O that I were so happy as to light on a nupson, now, of this justice's novice! —Sir, I make you stay somewhat long.

FORMAL. Not a whit, sir. Pray you, what do you mean, sir?

BRAINWORM. I was putting up some papers——

FORMAL. You ha' been lately in the wars, sir, it seems.

BRAINWORM. Marry have I, sir, to my loss; and expense of all, almost——

FORMAL. Troth, sir, I would be glad to bestow a pottle of wine o' you, if it please you to accept it——

BRAINWORM. O sir——

FORMAL. But, to hear the manner of your services and your devices in the wars; they say they be very strange, and not like those a man reads in the Roman histories, or sees at Mile End.

BRAINWORM. No, I assure you, sir. Why, at any time when it please you, I shall be ready to discourse to you all I know—and more too, somewhat.

FORMAL. No better time than now, sir; we'll go to the Windmill; there we shall have a cup of neat grist, we call it. I pray you, sir, let me request you to the Windmill.

BRAINWORM. I'll follow you, sir,—and make grist o' you, if I have good luck.   *Exeunt.*

ACT FOUR. SCENE FIVE

Moorfields

Enter MATTHEW, EDWARD, BOBADILL, *and* STEPHEN.

MATTHEW. Sir, did your eyes ever taste like clown of him where we were today, Master Wellbred's half-brother? I think the whole earth cannot show his parallel, by this daylight.

EDWARD. We were now speaking of him: Captain Bobadill tells me he is fallen foul o' you too.

MATTHEW. O ay, sir, he threatened me with the bastinado.

BOBADILL. Ay, but I think I taught you prevention, this morning, for that—You shall kill him, beyond question, if you be so generously minded.

MATTHEW. Indeed, it is a most excellent trick!
                    Practises at a post.

BOBADILL. O, you do not give spirit enough to your motion, you are too tardy, too heavy! O, it must be done like lightning, hey?

MATTHEW. Rare Captain!

BOBADILL. Tut! 'tis nothing, an't be not done in a—punto!

EDWARD. Captain, did you ever prove yourself upon any of our masters of defence here?

MATTHEW. O, good sir! Yes, I hope, he has.

BOBADILL. I will tell you, sir. Upon my first coming to the City, after my long travail for knowledge in that mystery only, there came three or four of 'em to me, at a gentleman's house where it was my chance to be resident at that time, to entreat my presence at their schools, and withal so much importuned me, that—I protest to you, as I am a gentleman—I was ashamed of their rude demeanour, out of all measure. Well, I told 'em that to come to a public school, they should pardon me, it was opposite in diameter to my humour; but, if so be they would give their attendance at my lodging, I protested to do them what right or favour I could, as I was a gentleman, and so forth.

EDWARD. So, sir, then you tried their skill?

BOBADILL. Alas, soon tried! you shall hear, sir. Within two or three days after, they came; and, by honesty, fair sir, believe me, I graced them exceedingly, showed them some two or three tricks of prevention, have purchased 'em since a credit, to admiration! They cannot deny this; and yet now, they hate me, and why? because I am excellent, and for no other vile reason on the earth!

EDWARD. This is strange and barbarous, as ever I heard!

BOBADILL. Nay, for a more instance of their preposterous natures, but note, sir. They have assaulted

me some three, four, five, six of them together, as I
have walked alone in divers skirts i' the town, as
Turnbull, Whitechapel, Shoreditch, which were
then my quarters; and since, upon the Exchange,
at my lodging, and at my ordinary, where I have
driven them afore me the whole length of a street,
in the open view of all our gallants, pitying to hurt
them, believe me. Yet all this lenity will not o'ercome their spleen; they will be doing with a
pismire, raising a hill a man may spurn abroad with
his foot, at pleasure. By myself, I could have slain
them all, but I delight not in murder. I am loath to
bear any other than this bastinado for 'em; yet I
hold it good policy not to go disarmed, for though
I be skilful, I may be oppressed with multitudes.

EDWARD. Ay, believe me, may you, sir; and, in my
conceit, our whole nation should sustain the loss by
it, if it were so.

BOBADILL. Alas, no! what's a peculiar man to a
nation? not seen.

EDWARD. O, but your skill, sir.

BOBADILL. Indeed, that might be some loss; but
who respects it? I will tell you, sir, by the way of
private, and under seal: I am a gentleman, and live
here obscure and to myself. But, were I known to
her Majesty and the Lords,—observe me—I would
undertake, upon this poor head and life, for the
public benefit of the state, not only to spare the
entire lives of her subjects in general; but to save
the one half, nay, three parts of her yearly charge
in holding war, and against what enemy soever. And
how would I do it, think you?

EDWARD. Nay, I know not, nor can I conceive.

BOBADILL. Why thus, sir. I would select nineteen
more, to myself, throughout the land; gentlemen
they should be of good spirit, strong and able con-

stitution; I would choose them by an instinct, a character that I have; and I would teach these nineteen the special rules, as your punto, your reverso, your stoccata, your imbroccata, your passada, your montanto, till they could all play very near or altogether as well as myself. This done, say the enemy were forty thousand strong; we twenty would come into the field the tenth of March, or thereabouts, and we would challenge twenty of the enemy; they could not, in their honour, refuse us; well, we would kill them; challenge twenty more, kill them; twenty more, kill them; twenty more, kill them, too; and thus would we kill, every man his twenty a day, that's twenty score; twenty score, that's two hundred; two hundred a day, five days, a thousand; forty thousand; forty times five, five times forty, two hundred days kills them all up, by computation. And this will I venture my poor gentlemanlike carcase to perform—provided there be no treason practised upon us—by fair and discreet manhood, that is, civilly by the sword.

EDWARD. Why, are you so sure of your hand, Captain, at all times?

BOBADILL. Tut! never miss thrust, upon my reputation with you.

EDWARD. I would not stand in Downright's state then, an you meet him, for the wealth' of any one street in London.

BOBADILL. Why, sir, you mistake me! if he were here now, by this welkin, I would not draw my weapon on him! Let this gentleman do his mind; but I will bastinado him, by the bright sun, wherever I meet him.

MATTHEW. Faith, and I'll have a fling at him, at my distance.

EDWARD. God's so', look where he is! yonder he goes.

DOWNRIGHT walks over the stage.

DOWNRIGHT. What peevish luck have I, I cannot meet with these bragging rascals?

BOBADILL. It's not he, is it?

EDWARD. Yes, faith, it is he.

MATTHEW. I'll be hanged, then, if that were he.

EDWARD. Sir, keep your hanging good for some greater matter, for I assure you that was he.

STEPHEN. Upon my reputation, it was he.

BOBADILL. Had I thought it had been he, he must not have gone so; but I can hardly be induced to believe it was he, yet.

EDWARD. That I think, sir.

Re-enter DOWNRIGHT.

But see, he is come again.

DOWNRIGHT. O, Pharaoh's foot, have I found you? Come, draw, to your tools! Draw, gipsy, or I'll thrash you!

BOBADILL. Gentleman of valour, I do believe in thee, hear me——

DOWNRIGHT. Draw your weapon then.

BOBADILL. Tall man, I never thought on it till now—Body of me! I had a warrant of the peace served on me, even now as I came along, by a water-bearer; this gentleman saw it, Master Matthew.

DOWNRIGHT. 'Sdeath! you will not draw then?

Beats BOBADILL and disarms him; MATTHEW runs away.

BOBADILL. Hold, hold, under thy favour, forbear!

DOWNRIGHT. Prate again, as you like this, you whoreson foist you! You'll control the point, you! Your consort is gone? had he stayed, he had shared with you, sir. *Exit.*

BOBADILL. Well, gentlemen, bear witness, I was bound to the peace, by this good day.

EDWARD. No, faith, it's an ill day. Captain, never

reckon it other. But, say you were bound to the peace, the law allows you to defend yourself; that'll prove but a poor excuse.

BOBADILL. I cannot tell, sir. I desire good construction, in fair sort. I never sustained the like disgrace, by Heaven! Sure I was struck with a planet thence, for I had no power to touch my weapon.

EDWARD. Ay, like enough, I have heard of many that have been beaten under a planet. Go, get you to a surgeon. 'Slid! an these be your tricks, your passadas and your montantos, I'll none of them. *Exit* BOBADILL. O manners! that this age should bring forth such creatures! that nature should be at leisure to make 'em! Come, coz.

STEPHEN. Mass, I'll ha' this cloak.

EDWARD. God's will, 'tis Downright's.

STEPHEN. Nay, it's mine now, another might have ta'en't up as well as I. I'll wear it, so I will.

EDWARD. How, an he see it? he'll challenge it, assure yourself.

STEPHEN. Ay, but he shall not ha' it; I'll say I bought it.

EDWARD. Take heed you buy it not too dear, coz.
Exeunt.

ACT FOUR. SCENE SIX

Kitely's house

Enter KITELY, WELLBRED, DAME KITELY, *and* BRIDGET.

KITELY. Now, trust me, brother, you were much
    to blame,
T'incense his anger, and disturb the peace

Of my poor house, where there are sentinels,
That every minute watch, to give alarms
Of civil war, without adjection
Of your assistance, or occasion.

WELLBRED. No harm done, brother, I warrant you, since there is no harm done. Anger costs a man nothing, and a tall man is never his own man till he be angry. To keep his valour in obscurity is to keep himself, as it were, in a cloak-bag. What's a musician, unless he play? What's a tall man, unless he fight? For indeed, all this my wise brother stands upon absolutely; and that made me fall in with him so resolutely.

DAME KITELY. Ay, but what harm might have come of it, brother!

WELLBRED. Might, sister? so might the good warm clothes your husband wears, be poisoned, for anything he knows; or the wholesome wine he drunk even now at the table——

KITELY. Now, God forbid!—O me! Now I remember
My wife drunk to me last; and changed the cup;
And bade me wear this cursèd suit today.
See, if Heav'n suffer murder undiscovered!—
I feel me ill; give me some mithridate,
Some mithridate and oil, good sister, fetch me;
O, I am sick at heart! I burn, I burn.
If you will save my life, go fetch it me.

WELLBRED. O strange humour! my very breath has poisoned him.

BRIDGET. Good brother, be content, what do you mean?
The strength of these extreme conceits will kill you.

DAME KITELY. Beshrew your heart-blood, brother Wellbred, now,
For putting such a toy into his head!

WELLBRED. Is a fit simile a toy? will he be poisoned with a simile? Brother Kitely, what a strange and idle imagination is this! For shame, be wiser. O' my soul, there's no such matter.

KITELY. Am I not sick? how am I, then, not poisoned?
Am I not poisoned? how am I, then, so sick?

DAME KITELY. If you be sick, your own thoughts make you sick.

WELLBRED. His jealousy is the poison he has taken.

Enter BRAINWORM *disguised as* FORMAL.

BRAINWORM. Master Kitely, my master, Justice Clement, salutes you, and desires to speak with you with all possible speed.

KITELY. No time but now? when I think I am sick? very sick! Well, I will wait upon his worship. —Thomas! Cob!—I must seek them out and set 'em sentinels till I return.—Thomas! Cob! Thomas!
Exit.

WELLBRED. —This is perfectly rare, Brainworm! but how got'st thou this apparel of the Justice's man?

BRAINWORM. Marry, sir, my proper fine penman would needs bestow the grist o' me, at the Windmill, to hear some martial discourse; where so I marshalled him that I made him drunk—with admiration—and, because too much heat was the cause of his distemper, I stripped him stark naked, as he lay along asleep, and borrowed his suit to deliver this counterfeit message in, leaving a rusty armour and an old brown bill, to watch him till my return; which shall be when I ha' pawned his apparel, and spent the better part o' the money, perhaps.

WELLBRED. Well, thou art a successful merry knave, Brainworm; his absence will be a good sub-

ject for more mirth. I pray thee, return to thy
young master, and will him to meet me and my
sister Bridget at the Tower instantly; for here, tell
him, the house is so stored with jealousy, there is
no room for love to stand upright in. We must get
our fortunes committed to some larger prison, say;
and than the Tower I know no better air, nor
where the liberty of the house may do us more
present service. Away.   *Exit* BRAINWORM.

Re-enter KITELY *with* CASH.

KITELY. Come hither, Thomas. Now, my secret's
      ripe,
And thou shalt have it: lay to both thine ears.
Hark what I say to thee. I must go forth, Thomas.
Be careful of thy promise, keep good watch,
Note every gallant, and observe him well,
That enters in my absence to thy mistress.
If she would show him rooms,—the jest is stale—
Follow 'em, Thomas, or else hang on him,
And let him not go after; mark their looks;
Note if she offer but to see his band
Or any other amorous toy about him,
But praise his leg, or foot, or if she say
The day is hot, and bid him feel her hand,
How hot it is—O, that's a monstrous thing!
Note me all this, good Thomas, mark their sighs,
And, if they do but whisper, break 'em off;
I'll bear thee out in it. Wilt thou do this?
Wilt thou be true, my Thomas?
CASH.   As truth's self, sir.
      KITELY. Why, I believe thee. Where is Cob, now?
      Cob!   *Exit*.
      DAME KITELY. He's ever calling for Cob! I wonder
how he employs Cob so!
      WELLBRED. Indeed, sister, to ask how he employs

Cob is a necessary question, for you that are his
wife, and a thing not very easy for you to be satisfied. But this I'll assure you: Cob's wife is an
excellent bawd, sister, and oftentimes, your husband
haunts her house; marry, to what end? I cannot
altogether accuse him; imagine you what you think
convenient. But I have known fair hides have foul
hearts ere now, sister.

DAME KITELY. Never said you truer than that,
brother, so much I can tell you for your learning.
—Thomas, fetch your cloak and go with me. *Exit*
CASH. I'll after him presently. I would to fortune
I could take him there, i'faith. I'd return him his
own, I warrant him! *Exit.*

WELLBRED. So, let 'em go; this may make sport
anon.—Now, my fair sister-in-law, that you knew
but how happy a thing it were, to be fair and
beautiful.

BRIDGET. That touches not me, brother.

WELLBRED. That's true; that's even the fault of
it; for indeed, beauty stands a woman in no stead,
unless it procure her touching. But sister, whether
it touch you or no, it touches your beauties, and
I am sure they will abide the touch; an they do
not, a plague of all ceruse, say I! and it touches
me, too, in part, though not in the—— Well, there's
a dear and respected friend of mine, sister, stands
very strongly and worthily affected toward you, and
hath vowed to inflame whole bonfires of zeal at his
heart, in honour of your perfections. I have already
engaged my promise to bring you where you shall
hear him confirm much more. Ned Knowell is the
man, sister. There's no exception against the party.
You are ripe for a husband, and a minute's loss
to such an occasion is a great trespass in a wise

beauty. What say you, sister? On my soul, he loves you. Will you give him the meeting?

BRIDGET. Faith, I had very little confidence in mine own constancy, brother, if I durst not meet a man; but this motion of yours savours of an old knight-adventurer's servant a little too much, methinks.

WELLBRED. What's that, sister?

BRIDGET. Marry, of the squire.

WELLBRED. No matter if it did; I would be such an one for my friend. But see who is returned to hinder us!

Re-enter KITELY.

KITELY. What villainy is this? called out on a
    false message?
This was some plot! I was not sent for.—Bridget,
Where's your sister?

BRIDGET.   I think she be gone forth, sir.

KITELY. How! is my wife gone forth? whither, for
    God's sake?

BRIDGET. She's gone abroad with Thomas.

KITELY. Abroad with Thomas!—O, that villain
    dors me.
He hath discovered all unto my wife!
Beast that I was, to trust him!—Whither, I pray you,
Went she?

BRIDGET. I know not, sir.

WELLBRED.   I'll tell you, brother,
Whither I suspect she's gone.

KITELY.   Whither, good brother?

WELLBRED. To Cob's house, I believe; but, keep
    my counsel.

KITELY. I will, I will.—To Cob's house? doth she
    haunt Cob's?
She's gone o' purpose now to cuckold me,

With that lewd rascal, who to win her favour
Hath told her all.　　　　　　　　　　*Exit.*

WELLBRED.　　　　　Come, he's once more gone.
Sister, let's lose no time; the affair is worth it.

　　　　　　　　　　　　　　　　Exeunt.

ACT FOUR. SCENE SEVEN

A street

Enter MATTHEW *and* BOBADILL.

MATTHEW. I wonder, Captain, what they will say
of my going away, ha?

BOBADILL. Why, what should they say, but as of
a discreet gentleman? quick, wary, respectful of nature's fair lineaments; and that's all.

MATTHEW. Why, so! but what can they say of your
beating?

BOBADILL. A rude part, a touch with soft wood,
a kind of gross battery used, laid on strongly, borne
most patiently; and that's all.

MATTHEW. Ay, but would any man have offered it
in Venice, as you say?

BOBADILL. Tut, I assure you, no! you shall have
there your nobilis, your gentilezza, come in bravely
upon your reverse, stand you close, stand you firm,
stand you fair, save your retricato with his left leg,
come to the assalto with the right, thrust with brave
steel, defy your base wood! But wherefore do I
awake this remembrance? I was fascinated, by Jupiter, fascinated! but I will be unwitched and revenged by law.

MATTHEW. Do you hear? is't not best to get a warrant, and have him arrested and brought before Justice Clement?

BOBADILL. It were not amiss; would we had it.

Enter BRAINWORM *disguised as* FORMAL.

MATTHEW. Why, here comes his man, let's speak to him.

BOBADILL. Agreed, do you speak.

MATTHEW. Save you, sir!

BRAINWORM. With all my heart, sir.

MATTHEW. Sir, there is one Downright hath abused this gentleman and myself, and we determine to make our amends by law; now, if you would do us the favour to procure a warrant to bring him afore your master, you shall be well considered, I assure you, sir.

BRAINWORM. Sir, you know my service is my living; such favours as these, gotten of my master, is his only preferment; and therefore you must consider me, as I may make benefit of my place.

MATTHEW. How is that, sir?

BRAINWORM. Faith, sir, the thing is extraordinary, and the gentleman may be of great account; yet, be what he will, if you will lay me down a brace of angels in my hand, you shall have it; otherwise not.

MATTHEW. How shall we do, Captain? he asks a brace of angels, you have no money?

BOBADILL. Not a cross, by fortune.

MATTHEW. Nor I, as I am a gentleman, but two-pence, left of my two shillings in the morning for wine and radish. Let's find him some pawn.

BOBADILL. Pawn? we have none to the value of his demand.

MATTHEW. O yes. I'll pawn this jewel in my ear,

and you may pawn your silk stockings, and pull up your boots; they will ne'er be missed. It must be done now.

BOBADILL. Well, an there be no remedy, I'll step aside and pull 'em off.

MATTHEW. Do you hear, sir? we have no store of money at this time, but you shall have good pawns—look you, sir, this jewel, and that gentleman's silk stockings—because we would have it dispatched ere we went to our chambers.

BRAINWORM. I am content, sir, I will get you the warrant presently. What's his name, say you? Downright?

MATTHEW. Ay, ay, George Downright.

BRAINWORM. What manner of man is he?

MATTHEW. A tall, big man, sir; he goes in a cloak most commonly, of silk-russet laid about with russet lace.

BRAINWORM. 'Tis very good, sir.

MATTHEW. Here, sir, here's my jewel.

BOBADILL. And here are stockings.

BRAINWORM. Well, gentlemen, I'll procure you this warrant presently; but who will you have to serve it?

MATTHEW. That's true, Captain; that must be considered.

BOBADILL. Body o' me, I know not! 'tis service of danger!

BRAINWORM. Why, you were best get one o' the varlets o' the City, a sergeant. I'll appoint you one, if you please.

MATTHEW. Will you, sir? why, we can wish no better.

BOBADILL. We'll leave it to you, sir.

Exeunt BOBADILL *and* MATTHEW.

BRAINWORM. This is rare! Now will I go pawn this

cloak of the Justice's man's at the broker's, for a
varlet's suit, and be the varlet myself; and get either
more pawns or more money of Downright, for the
arrest.   *Exit.*

ACT FOUR. SCENE EIGHT

Before Cob's house

Enter KNOWELL.

KNOWELL. O, here it is; I am glad I have found
  it now.
Ho! who is within here?

TIB. I am within, sir; what's your pleasure?

KNOWELL. To know who is within besides yourself.

TIB. *Opening door.* Why, sir, you are no constable, I hope?

KNOWELL. O! fear you the Constable? then I
  doubt not,
You have some guests within, deserve that fear.
I'll fetch him straight.

TIB.   O' God's name, sir!

KNOWELL. Go to. Come, tell me, is not young
  Knowell here?

TIB. Young Knowell? I know none such, sir,
o' mine honesty.

KNOWELL. Your honesty? dame, it flies too lightly
  from you.
There is no way but fetch the Constable.

TIB. The Constable? the man is mad, I think.
                                      Closes door.

Enter DAME KITELY *and* CASH.

CASH. Ho! who keeps house, here?

KNOWELL. —O, this is the female copesmate of my
son.

Now shall I meet him straight.

DAME KITELY.   Knock, Thomas, hard.

CASH. Ho, goodwife?

TIB. *Re-opening door.* Why, what's the matter
with you?

DAME KITELY. Why, woman, grieves it you to ope
your door?

Belike you get something to keep it shut.

TIB. What mean these questions, pray ye?

DAME KITELY. So strange you make it! Is not my
husband here?

KNOWELL. —Her husband!

DAME KITELY. My trièd husband, Master Kitely?

TIB. I hope he needs not to be trièd here.

DAME KITELY. No, dame; he does it not for need,
but pleasure.

TIB. Neither for need nor pleasure is he here.

KNOWELL. —This is but a device to balk me withal.

Soft, who is this? 'Tis not my son, disguised?

DAME KITELY *spies* KITELY *come, and runs to him.*

DAME KITELY. O, sir, have I forestalled your honest market?

Found your close walks? you stand amazed now, do
you?

I'faith, I am glad I have smoked you yet at last!

What is your jewel, trow? In, come, let's see her.—

Fetch forth your housewife, dame.—If she be fairer,

In any honest judgment, than myself,

I'll be content with it. But she is change,

She feeds you fat, she soothes your appetite,

And you are well; your wife, an honest woman,
Is meat twice sod to you, sir! O you treacher!

KNOWELL. —She cannot counterfeit thus palpably.

KITELY. Out on thy more than strumpet's impudence!

Steal'st thou thus to thy haunts? and have I taken
Thy bawd, and thee, and thy companion,
This hoary-headed lecher, this old goat,
Close at your villainy, and wouldst thou 'scuse it
With this stale harlot's jest, accusing me? *Pointing*
to old Knowell.

O old incontinent, dost not thou shame,
When all thy powers in chastity is spent,
To have a mind so hot? and to entice,
And feed th' enticements of a lustful woman?

DAME KITELY. Out, I defy thee, I, dissembling
wretch!

KITELY. Defy me, strumpet? Ask thy pander here,
Can he deny it, or that wicked elder?

KNOWELL. Why, hear you, sir.

KITELY.   Tut, tut, tut, never speak.
Thy guilty conscience will discover thee.

KNOWELL. What lunacy is this that haunts this
man?

KITELY. Well, Goodwife B. A. 'D., Cob's wife,—
and you

That make your husband such a hoddy-doddy,—
And you, young apple-squire,—and old cuckold-
maker,—
I'll ha' you every one before a justice.
Nay, you shall answer it, I charge you go.   ·

KNOWELL. Marry, with all my heart, sir. I go willingly.—

Though I do taste this as a trick, put on me
To punish my impertinent search, and justly;
And half forgive my son for the device.

KITELY. Come, will you go?

DAME KITELY. Go? to thy shame, believe it.

Enter COB.

COB. Why, what's the matter here, what's here to do?

KITELY. O, Cob, art thou come? I have been abused,

And i' thy house. Never was man so wronged!

COB. 'Slid, in my house? My Master Kitely? Who wrongs you in my house?

KITELY. Marry, young lust in old, and old in young, here.

Thy wife's their bawd; here have I taken 'em.

COB. How, bawd? Is my house come to that? Am I preferred thither? Did I charge you to keep your doors shut, Is'bel, and do you let 'em lie open for all comers? *Falls upon his wife and beats her.*

KNOWELL. Friend, know some cause, before thou beat'st thy wife,

This's madness in thee.

COB. Why, is there no cause?

KITELY. Yes, I'll show cause before the Justice, Cob.

Come, let her go with me.

COB. Nay, she shall go.

TIB. Nay, I will go. I'll see an you may be allowed to make a bundle o' hemp o' your right and lawful wife thus, at every cuckoldly knave's pleasure. Why do you not go?

KITELY. A bitter quean! Come, we'll ha' you tamed. *Exeunt.*

ACT FOUR. SCENE NINE

A street

Enter BRAINWORM *disguised as a sergeant.*

BRAINWORM. Well, of all my disguises yet, now am I most like myself, being in this sergeant's gown. A man of my present profession never counterfeits, till he lays hold upon a debtor, and says he 'rests him; for then he brings him to all manner of unrest. A kind of little kings we are, bearing the diminutive of a mace, made like a young artichoke, that always carries pepper and salt in itself. Well, I know not what danger I undergo by this exploit, pray Heaven I come well off!

Enter MATTHEW *and* BOBADILL.

MATTHEW. See, I think yonder is the varlet, by his gown.

BOBADILL. Let's go in quest of him.

MATTHEW. Save you, friend! are not you here by appointment of Justice Clement's man?

BRAINWORM. Yes, an't please you, sir; he told me two gentlemen had willed him to procure a warrant from his master, which I have about me, to be served on one Downright.

MATTHEW. It is honestly done of you both; and see where the party comes you must arrest. Serve it upon him quickly, afore he be aware——

BOBADILL. Bear back, Master Matthew.

Enter STEPHEN *in* DOWNRIGHT'S *cloak.*

BRAINWORM. Master Downright, I arrest you i' the Queen's name, and must carry you afore a justice, by virtue of this warrant.

STEPHEN. Me, friend? I am no Downright, I. I am Master Stephen, you do not well to arrest me, I tell you truly. I am in nobody's bonds nor books, I, would you should know it! A plague on you heartily, for making me thus afraid afore my time!

BRAINWORM. Why, now are you deceived, gentlemen!

BOBADILL. He wears such a cloak, and that deceived us. But see, here 'a comes indeed! This is he, Officer.

Enter DOWNRIGHT.

DOWNRIGHT. Why, how now, Signior Gull! are you turned filcher of late? come, deliver my cloak.

STEPHEN. Your cloak, sir? I bought it even now, in open market.

BRAINWORM. Master Downright, I have a warrant I must serve upon you, procured by these two gentlemen.

DOWNRIGHT. These gentlemen? these rascals!

BRAINWORM. Keep the peace, I charge you, in her Majesty's name.

DOWNRIGHT. I obey thee. What must I do, Officer?

BRAINWORM. Go before Master Justice Clement, to answer what they can object against you, sir. I will use you kindly, sir.

MATTHEW. Come, let's before, and make the Justice, Captain.

BOBADILL. The varlet's a tall man, afore Heaven!
                    Exeunt BOBADILL *and* MATTHEW.
DOWNRIGHT. Gull, you'll gi' me my cloak.

STEPHEN. Sir, I bought it, and I'll keep it.

DOWNRIGHT. You will?

STEPHEN. Ay, that I will.

DOWNRIGHT. Officer, there's thy fee, arrest him.

BRAINWORM. Master Stephen, I must arrest you.

STEPHEN. Arrest me! I scorn it. There, take your cloak, I'll none on't.

DOWNRIGHT. Nay, that shall not serve your turn now, sir. Officer, I'll go with thee to the Justice's; bring him along.

STEPHEN. Why, is not here your cloak? what would you have?

DOWNRIGHT. I'll ha' you answer it, sir.

BRAINWORM. Sir, I'll take your word; and this gentleman's too, for his appearance.

DOWNRIGHT. I'll ha' no words taken. Bring him along.

BRAINWORM. Sir, I may choose to do that. I may take bail.

DOWNRIGHT. 'Tis true, you may take bail and choose, at another time. But you shall not now, varlet. Bring him along or I'll swinge you.

BRAINWORM. Sir, I pity the gentleman's case. Here's your money again.

DOWNRIGHT. 'Sdeins, tell not me of my money; bring him away, I say.

BRAINWORM. I warrant you he will go with you of himself, sir.

DOWNRIGHT. Yet more ado?

BRAINWORM. —I have made a fair mash on't.

STEPHEN. Must I go?

BRAINWORM. I know no remedy, Master Stephen.

DOWNRIGHT. Come along afore me, here. I do not love your hanging look behind.

STEPHEN. Why, sir, I hope you cannot hang me for it.—Can he, fellow?

BRAINWORM. I think not, sir. It is but a whipping matter, sure.

STEPHEN. Why, then, let him do his worst, I am resolute. *Exeunt.*

ACT FIVE

Justice Clement's house

Enter CLEMENT, KNOWELL, KITELY, DAME KITELY, TIB, CASH, COB, *and Servants.*

CLEMENT. Nay, but stay, stay, give me leave.—My chair, sirrah.—You, Master Knowell, say you went thither to meet your son?

KNOWELL. Ay, sir.

CLEMENT. But who directed you thither?

KNOWELL. That did mine own man, sir.

CLEMENT. Where is he?

KNOWELL. Nay, I know not, now; I left him with your clerk, and appointed him to stay here for me.

CLEMENT. My clerk? about what time was this?

KNOWELL. Marry, between one and two, as I take it.

CLEMENT. And what time came my man with the false message to you, Master Kitely?

KITELY. After two, sir.

CLEMENT. Very good. But, Mistress Kitely, how chance that you were at Cob's, ha?

DAME KITELY. An please you, sir, I'll tell you: my brother Wellbred told me that Cob's house was a suspected place——

CLEMENT. So it appears, methinks; but on.

DAME KITELY. And that my husband used thither daily.

CLEMENT. No matter, so he used himself well, mistress.

DAME KITELY. True, sir, but you know what grows by such haunts oftentimes.

CLEMENT. I see rank fruits of a jealous brain, Mistress Kitely. But did you find your husband there, in that case, as you suspected?

KITELY. I found her there, sir.

CLEMENT. Did you so? that alters the case. Who gave you knowledge of your wife's being there?

KITELY. Marry, that did my brother Wellbred.

CLEMENT. How? Wellbred first tell her, then tell you after? Where is Wellbred?

KITELY. Gone with my sister, sir, I know not whither.

CLEMENT. Why, this is a mere trick, a device; you are gulled in this most grossly, all!—Alas, poor wench, wert thou beaten for this?

TIB. Yes, most pitifully, an't please you.

COB. And worthily, I hope, if it shall prove so.

CLEMENT. Ay, that's like, and a piece of a sentence.—

Enter a SERVANT.

How now, sir? what's the matter?

SERVANT. Sir, there's a gentleman i' the court without, desires to speak with your worship.

CLEMENT. A gentleman! what's he?

SERVANT. A soldier, sir, he says.

CLEMENT. A soldier? Take down my armour, my sword, quickly. A soldier speak with me! Why, when, knaves? Come on, come on, hold my cap there, so; give me my gorget, my sword. *Arms him-*

self. —Stand by, I will end your matters anon.—Let the soldier enter. *Exit* SERVANT.

Enter BOBADILL, *followed by* MATTHEW.

Now sir, what ha' you to say to me?

BOBADILL. By your worship's favour——

CLEMENT. Nay, keep out, sir, I know not your pretence; you send me word, sir, you are a soldier. Why, sir, you shall be answered here; here be them have been amongst soldiers. Sir, your pleasure.

BOBADILL. Faith, sir, so it is, this gentleman and myself have been most uncivilly wronged and beaten by one Downright, a coarse fellow about the town here; and for mine own part, I protest, being a man in no sort given to this filthy humour of quarrelling, he hath assaulted me in the way of my peace, despoiled me of mine honour, disarmed me of my weapons, and rudely laid me along in the open streets; when I not so much as once offered to resist him.

CLEMENT. O God's precious! is this the soldier? Here, take my armour off quickly, 'twill make him swoon, I fear; he is not fit to look on't, that will put up a blow.

MATTHEW. An't please your worship, he was bound to the peace.

CLEMENT. Why, an he were, sir, his hands were not bound, were they?

Re-enter SERVANT.

SERVANT. There's one of the varlets of the City, sir, has brought two gentlemen here, one upon your worship's warrant.

CLEMENT. My warrant?

SERVANT. Yes, sir, the officer says, procured by these two.

CLEMENT. Bid him come in. *Exit* SERVANT. Set by this picture.

Enter DOWNRIGHT, STEPHEN, *with* BRAINWORM *disguised as a sergeant.*

What, Master Downright! are you brought at Master Freshwater's suit here?

DOWNRIGHT. I'faith, sir. And here's another brought at my suit.

CLEMENT. What are you, sir?

STEPHEN. A gentleman, sir.—O, uncle!

CLEMENT. Uncle? who? Master Knowell?

KNOWELL. Ay, sir, this is a wise kinsman of mine.

STEPHEN. God's my witness, uncle, I am wronged here monstrously; he charges me with stealing of his cloak, and would I might never stir, if I did not find it in the street by chance!

DOWNRIGHT. O, did you find it now? You said you bought it, erewhile.

STEPHEN. And you said I stole it; nay, now my uncle is here, I'll do well enough with you.

CLEMENT. Well, let this breathe awhile.—You that have cause to complain there, stand forth. Had you my warrant for this gentleman's apprehension?

BOBADILL. Ay, an't please your worship.

CLEMENT. Nay, do not speak in passion so. Where had you it?

BOBADILL. Of your clerk, sir.

CLEMENT. That's well! an my clerk can make warrants and my hand not at 'em! Where is the warrant?—Officer, have you it?

BRAINWORM. No, sir, your worship's man, Master Formal, bid me do it for these gentlemen, and he would be my discharge.

CLEMENT. Why, Master Downright, are you such a novice, to be served and never see the warrant?

DOWNRIGHT. Sir—he did not serve it on me.

CLEMENT. No? how then?

DOWNRIGHT. Marry, sir, he came to me, and said he must serve it, and he would use me kindly, and so——

CLEMENT. O, God's pity, was it so, sir? He must serve it? Give me my long-sword there, and help me off; so. Come on, Sir Varlet, I must cut off your legs, sirrah. Nay, stand up, I'll use you kindly. I must cut off your legs, I say.

Flourishes over BRAINWORM *with his long-sword.*

BRAINWORM. O, good sir, I beseech you; nay, good Master Justice!

CLEMENT. I must do it; there is no remedy. I must cut off your legs, sirrah; I must cut off your ears, you rascal, I must do it; I must cut off your nose; I must cut off your head.

BRAINWORM. O, good your worship!

CLEMENT. Well, rise. How dost thou do now? dost thou feel thyself well? hast thou no harm?

BRAINWORM. No, I thank your good worship, sir.

CLEMENT. Why, so! I said, 'I must cut off thy legs, and I must cut off thy arms, and I must cut off thy head;' but I did not do it. So you said you must serve this gentleman with my warrant, but you did not serve him. You knave, you slave, you rogue, do you say you must?—Sirrah, away with him to the jail; I'll teach you a trick for your must, sir.

BRAINWORM. Good sir, I beseech you, be good to me.

CLEMENT. Tell him he shall to the jail; away with him, I say.

BRAINWORM. Nay, sir, if you will commit me, it shall be for committing more than this. I will not lose, by my travail, any grain of my fame, certain.

Throws off his sergeant's gown.

CLEMENT. How is this!

KNOWELL. My man Brainworm!

STEPHEN. O, yes, uncle. Brainworm has been with my cousin Edward and I all this day.

CLEMENT. I told you all there was some device.

BRAINWORM. Nay, excellent Justice, since I have laid myself thus open to you, now stand strong for me, both with your sword and your balance.

CLEMENT. Body o' me, a merry knave!—Give me a bowl of sack.—If he belong to you, Master Knowell, I bespeak your patience.

BRAINWORM. That is it I have most need of. Sir, if you'll pardon me only, I'll glory in all the rest of my exploits.

KNOWELL. Sir, you know I love not to have my favours come hard from me.—You have your pardon, though I suspect you shrewdly for being of counsel with my son against me.

BRAINWORM. Yes, faith, I have, sir, though you retained me doubly this morning for yourself: first, as Brainworm; after, as FitzSword. I was your reformed soldier, sir. 'Twas I sent you to Cob's, upon the errand without end.

KNOWELL. Is it possible! or that thou shouldst disguise thy language so as I should not know thee?

BRAINWORM. O, sir, this has been the day of my metamorphosis. It is not that shape alone that I have run through today. I brought this gentleman, Master Kitely, a message too, in the form of Master Justice's man here, to draw him out o' the way, as well as your worship; while Master Wellbred might make a conveyance of Mistress Bridget to my young master.

KITELY. How! my sister stolen away?

KNOWELL. My son is not married, I hope!

BRAINWORM. Faith, sir, they are both as sure as

love, a priest, and three thousand pound—which is her portion—can make 'em; and by this time are ready to bespeak their wedding supper at the Windmill, except some friend here prevent 'em, and invite 'em home.

CLEMENT. Marry, that will I; I thank thee for putting me in mind on't.—Sirrah, go you and fetch 'em hither, upon my warrant. *Exit* SERVANT. Neither's friends have cause to be sorry, if I know the young couple aright.—Here, I drink to thee for thy good news. But I pray thee, what hast thou done with my man, Formal?

BRAINWORM. Faith, sir, after some ceremony past, as making him drunk, first with story and then with wine,—but all in kindness—and stripping him to his shirt, I left him in that cool vein, departed, sold your worship's warrant to these two, pawned his livery for that varlet's gown, to serve it in; and thus have brought myself, by my activity, to your worship's consideration.

CLEMENT. And I will consider thee in another cup of sack. Here's to thee; which having drunk off, this is my sentence: pledge me. Thou hast done or assisted to nothing, in my judgment, but deserves to be pardoned for the wit o' the offence. If thy master, or any man here, be angry with thee, I shall suspect his engine, while I know him, for't.—How now, what noise is that?

Enter SERVANT.

SERVANT. Sir, it is Roger is come home.
CLEMENT. Bring him in, bring him in.

Enter FORMAL *in a suit of armour.*

What! drunk, in arms against me? Your reason, your reason for this?

FORMAL. I beseech your worship to pardon me; I happened into ill company by chance, that cast me into a sleep and stripped me of all my clothes——

CLEMENT. Well, tell him I am Justice Clement, and do pardon him.—But what is this to your armour? what may that signify?

FORMAL. An't please you, sir, it hung up i' the room where I was stripped; and I borrowed it of one o' the drawers to come home in, because I was loath to do penance through the street i' my shirt.

CLEMENT. Well, stand by a while.

Enter EDWARD, WELLBRED, *and* BRIDGET.

Who be these? O, the young company—welcome, welcome! Gi' you joy. Nay, Mistress Bridget, blush not; you are not so fresh a bride, but the news of it is come hither afore you. Master Bridegroom, I ha' made your peace, give me your hand; so will I for all the rest, ere you foresake my roof.

EDWARD. We are the more bound to your humanity, sir.

CLEMENT. Only these two have so little of man in 'em, they are no part of my care.

WELLBRED. Yes, sir, let me pray you for this gentleman; he belongs to my sister, the bride.

CLEMENT. In what place, sir?

WELLBRED. Of her delight, sir, below the stairs and in public: her poet, sir.

CLEMENT. A poet? I will challenge him myself presently at extempore.

'Mount up thy Phlegon, Muse, and testify
    How Saturn, sitting in an ebon cloud,
Disrobed his podex, white as ivory,
    And through the welkin thundered all aloud.'

WELLBRED. He is not for extempore, sir. He is all

for the pocket-muse; please you command a sight of it.

CLEMENT. Yes, yes, search him for a taste of his vein.

WELLBRED. You must not deny the Queen's Justice, sir, under a writ o' rebellion.

CLEMENT. What! all this verse? Body o' me, he carries a whole realm, a commonwealth of paper, in 's hose! Let's see some of his subjects:
'Unto the boundless ocean of thy face,
 Runs this poor river, charged with streams of eyes.'
How? this is stolen.

EDWARD. A parody! a parody! with a kind of miraculous gift to make it absurder than it was.

CLEMENT. Is all the rest of this batch?—Bring me a torch; lay it together, and give fire. Cleanse the air.—Here was enough to have infected the whole City, if it had not been taken in time. See, see, how our poet's glory shines! brighter and brighter! still it increases! O, now it's at the highest, and now it declines as fast. You may see. 'Sic transit gloria mundi!'

KNOWELL. There's an emblem for you, son, and your studies!

CLEMENT. Nay, no speech or act of mine be drawn against such as profess it worthily. They are not born every year, as an alderman. There goes more to the making of a good poet than a sheriff, Master Kitely. You look upon me! though I live i' the City here, amongst you, I will do more reverence to him, when I meet him, than I will to the Mayor, out of his year. But these paper-pedlars! these ink-dabblers! they cannot expect reprehension or reproach. They have it with the fact.

EDWARD. Sir, you have saved me the labour of a defence.

CLEMENT. It shall be discourse for supper, between your father and me, if he dare undertake me. But, to dispatch away these,—you sign o' the Soldier, and picture o' the Poet, but both so false I will not ha' you hanged out at my door till midnight. While we are at supper, you two shall penitently fast it out in my court without; and, if you will, you may pray there that we may be so merry within, as to forgive or forget you when we come out. Here's a third, because we tender your safety, shall watch you; he is provided for the purpose. *To* FORMAL. Look to your charge, sir.

STEPHEN. And what shall I do?

CLEMENT. Oh! I had lost a sheep, an he had not bleated! Why, sir, you shall give Master Downright his cloak; and I will entreat him to take it. A trencher and a napkin you shall have, i' the buttery, and keep Cob and his wife company, here; whom I will entreat first to be reconciled, and you to endeavour with your wit to keep 'em so.

STEPHEN. I'll do my best.

COB. Why, now I see thou art honest, Tib, I receive thee as my dear and mortal wife again.

TIB. And I you, as my loving and obedient husband.

CLEMENT. Good compliment! It will be their bridal night, too. They are married anew. Come, I conjure the rest to put off all discontent. You, Master Downright, your anger; you Master Knowell, your cares; Master Kitely and his wife, their jealousy. For, I must tell you both, while that is fed, Horns i' the mind are worse than o' the head.

KITELY. Sir, thus they go from me.—Kiss me, sweetheart.
See what a drove of horns fly in the air,
Winged with my cleansèd and my credulous breath!

Watch 'em, suspicious eyes, watch where they fall.
See, see! on heads that think they've none at all!
O, what a plenteous world of this will come!
When air rains horns, all may be sure of some.
I ha' learned so much verse out of a jealous man's
part in a play.

CLEMENT. 'Tis well, 'tis well! This night we'll
dedicate to friendship, love, and laughter. Master
Bridegroom, take your bride, and lead; everyone, a
fellow. Here is my mistress, Brainworm! to whom
all my addresses of courtship shall have their refer-
ence; whose adventures this day, when our grand-
children shall hear to be made a fable, I doubt not
but it shall find both spectators and applause.

Exeunt.

Bartholomew Fair

___

THE PERSONS OF THE PLAY

JOHN LITTLEWIT, *a proctor*

ZEAL-OF-THE-LAND BUSY, *suitor to* DAME PURECRAFT, *a Banbury man*

WINWIFE, *his rival, a gentleman*

TOM QUARLOUS, *companion to* WINWIFE, *a gamester*

BARTHOLOMEW COKES, *an esquire of Harrow*

HUMPHREY WASP, *his man*

ADAM OVERDO, *a Justice of Peace*

LANTERN LEATHERHEAD, *a hobby-horse seller*

EZEKIEL EDGWORTH, *a cutpurse*

NIGHTINGALE, *a ballad-singer*

MOONCALF, *tapster to* URSULA

DAN 'JORDAN' KNOCKEM, *a horse-courser and ranger o' Turnbull*

VAL CUTTING, *a roarer*

CAPTAIN WHIT, *a bawd*

TROUBLEALL, *a madman*

NORTHERN, *a clothier (a Northern man)*

PUPPY, *a wrestler (a Western man)*

BRISTLE,
HAGGIS, *watchmen*

POACHER, *a beadle*

FILCHER,
SHARKWELL, *door-keepers to the puppet-show*

SOLOMON, LITTLEWIT'S *man*

WIN-THE-FIGHT LITTLEWIT
DAME PURECRAFT, *her mother, and a widow*
DAME OVERDO
GRACE WELLBORN, *ward to* JUSTICE OVERDO
JOAN TRASH, *a gingerbread-woman*
URSULA, *a pig-woman*
PUNK ALICE, *mistress o' the game*

Costermonger, Tinder-box-man, Corn-cutter, Watch,
Porters, Puppets, Passengers, Mob, Boys, &c.

THE PROLOGUE

To the King's Majesty

Your Majesty is welcome to a fair:
Such place, such men, such language, and such ware
You must expect; with these, the zealous noise
Of your land's faction, scandalized at toys,
As babies, hobby-horses, puppet-plays;
And suchlike rage, whereof the petulant ways
Yourself have known, and have been vexed with
    long.
These for your sport, without particular wrong,
Or just complaint of any private man,
Who of himself or shall think well or can,
The maker doth present, and hopes tonight
To give you, for a fairing, true delight.

BARTHOLOMEW FAIR

THE INDUCTION

On the Stage

Enter STAGE-KEEPER.

STAGE-KEEPER. Gentlemen, have a little patience, they are e'en upon coming instantly. He that should begin the play, Master Littlewit, the proctor, has a stitch new fall'n in his black silk stocking; 'twill be drawn up ere you can tell twenty. He plays one o' the Arches, that dwells about the Hospital, and he has a very pretty part. But for the whole play, will you ha' the truth on't?—I am looking, lest the poet hear me, or his man, Master Brome, behind the arras—it is like to be a very conceited, scurvy one, in plain English. When 't comes to the Fair once, you were e'en as good go to Virginia, for anything there is of Smithfield. He has not hit the humours, he does not know 'em; he has not conversed with the Bartholomew birds, as they say. He has ne'er a sword-and-buckler man in his Fair; nor a Little Davy, to take toll o' the bawds there, as in my time; nor a Kindheart, if anybody's teeth should chance to ache, in his play; nor a juggler with a well-educated ape, to come over the chain for the King of England, and back again for the Prince, and sit still on his arse for the Pope and the King of Spain. None o' these fine sights! Nor has he the canvas cut i' the night, for a hobby-horse man to creep in to his she-neighbour, and take his leap there. Nothing! No, an some writer that I know had had but the penning o' this matter, he would ha' made you such a jig-a-jog i' the booths, you should ha' thought an earthquake had been i' the Fair! But these master-poets, they will ha' their own absurd courses; they will be informed of nothing! He has—sir reverence—kicked me three or four times about the tiring-house, I thank him, for but offering to put in with my experience. I'll be judged by you, gentlemen, now, but for one conceit of mine: would not a fine pump upon the stage ha' done well for a property now? and a punk set under upon her head, with her stern upward, and ha' been soused by my witty young masters o' the Inns o' Court? What think you o' this for a show, now? he will not hear o' this! I am an ass, I, and yet I kept the stage in Master Tarleton's time, I thank my stars! Ho! an that man had lived to have played in 'Bartholomew Fair,' you should ha' seen him ha' come in, and ha' been cozened i' the Cloth Quarter, so finely! And Adams, the rogue, ha' leaped and capered upon him, and ha' dealt his vermin about, as though they had cost him nothing! And then a substantial watch to ha' stol'n in upon 'em, and taken 'em away, with mistaking words, as the fashion is, in the stage practice.

Enter the BOOKHOLDER *with a* SCRIVENER.

BOOKHOLDER. How now! what rare discourse are you fall'n upon, ha? Ha' you found any familiars here, that you are so free? What's the business?

STAGE-KEEPER. Nothing, but the understanding gentlemen o' the ground here asked my judgment.

BOOKHOLDER. Your judgment, rascal! for what? sweeping the stage, or gathering up the broken apples for the bears within? Away, rogue, it's come to a fine degree in these spectacles, when such a youth as you pretend to a judgment. *Exit* STAGE-KEEPER. And yet he may, i' the most of this matter,

i' faith; for the author hath writ it just to his
meridian, and the scale of the grounded judgments
here, his playfellows in wit.—Gentlemen, not for
want of a prologue, but by way of a new one, I am
sent out to you here, with a scrivener, and certain
articles drawn out in haste between our author and
you; which if you please to hear, and as they appear
reasonable, to approve of, the play will follow presently.—Read, scribe; gi' me the counterpane.

SCRIVENER. 'Articles of agreement indented between the spectators or hearers, at the Hope on the
Bankside in the county of Surrey, on the one party;
and the author of "Bartholomew Fair," in the said
place and county, on the other party; the one and
thirtieth day of October, 1614, and in the twelfth
year of the reign of our sovereign lord, James, by
the grace of God, King of England, France, and
Ireland, Defender of the Faith, and of Scotland the
seven and fortieth.

'Imprimis, it is covenanted and agreed, by and
between the parties abovesaid and the said spectators and hearers, as well the curious and envious as
the favouring and judicious, as also the grounded
judgments and understandings, do for themselves
severally covenant and agree to remain in the places
their money or friends have put them in, with patience, for the space of two hours and an half, and
somewhat more. In which time the author promiseth
to present them by us, with a new, sufficient play
called "Bartholomew Fair," merry, and as full of
noise as sport, made to delight all and to offend
none; provided they have either the wit or the
honesty to think well of themselves.

'It is further agreed that every person here have
his or their free-will of censure, to like or dislike at
their own charge, the author having now departed

with his right. It shall be lawful for any man to judge his sixpenn'orth, his twelvepenn'orth, so to his eighteen-pence, two shillings, half a crown, to the value of his place; provided always his place get not about his wit. And if he pay for half a dozen, he may censure for all them too, so that he will undertake that they shall be silent. He shall put in for censures here, as they do for lots at the lottery; marry, if he drop but sixpence at the door, and will censure a crown's worth, it is thought there is no conscience or justice in that.

'It is also agreed that every man here exercise his own judgment, and not censure by contagion, or upon trust, from another's voice or face, that sits by him, be he never so first in the commission of wit; as also, that he be fixed and settled in his censure, that what he approves or not approves today, he will do the same tomorrow; and if tomorrow, the next day, and so the next week, if need be; and not to be brought about by any that sits on the bench with him, though they indict and arraign plays daily. He that will swear "Jeronimo" or "Andronicus" are the best plays yet, shall pass unexcepted at here, as a man whose judgment shows it is constant, and hath stood still these five and twenty or thirty years. Though it be an ignorance, it is a virtuous and staid ignorance; and next to truth, a confirmed error does well; such a one the author knows where to find him.

'It is further covenanted, concluded, and agreed, that how great soever the expectation be, no person here is to expect more than he knows, or better ware than a fair will afford; neither to look back to the sword-and-buckler age of Smithfield, but content himself with the present. Instead of a Little Davy, to take toll o' the bawds, the author doth promise a strutting horse-courser, with a leer drunkard, two or three to attend him, in as good equipage as you would wish. And then for Kindheart, the tooth-drawer, a fine, oily pig-woman, with her tapster, to bid you welcome, and a consort of roarers for music; a wise Justice of Peace meditant, instead of a juggler with an ape; a civil cutpurse searchant; a sweet singer of new ballads, allurant; and as fresh an hypocrite as ever was broached, rampant. If there be never a servant monster i' the Fair, who can help it, he says, nor a nest of antics? He is loath to make nature afraid in his plays, like those that beget tales, tempests, and suchlike drolleries, to mix his head with other men's heels; let the concupiscence of jigs and dances reign as strong as it will amongst you. Yet if the puppets will please anybody, they shall be entreated to come in.

'In consideration of which, it is finally agreed, by the foresaid hearers and spectators, that they neither in themselves conceal, nor suffer by them to be concealed, any state-decipherer, or politic picklock of the scene, so solemnly ridiculous as to search out who was meant by the gingerbread-woman, who by the hobby-horse man, who by the costermonger, nay, who by their wares. Or that will pretend to affirm, on his own inspired ignorance, what mirror of magistrates is meant by the Justice, what great lady by the pig-woman, what concealed statesman by the seller of mouse-traps, and so of the rest. But that such person, or persons, so found, be left discovered to the mercy of the author, as a forfeiture to the stage, and your laughter aforesaid. As also, such as shall so desperately or ambitiously play the fool by his place aforesaid, to challenge the author of scurrility, because the language somewhere savours of Smithfield, the booth, and the pig-broth; or of profaneness, because a madman cries, "God quit you," or "Bless you." In witness whereof, as you have preposterously put to your seals already, which is your money, you will now add the other part of suffrage, your hands. The play shall presently begin. And though the Fair be not kept in the same region that some here perhaps would have it, yet think that therein the author hath observed a special decorum, the place being as dirty as Smithfield, and as stinking, every whit.

'Howsoever, he prays you to believe his ware is still the same; else you will make him justly suspect that he that is so loath to look on a baby or an hobby-horse here, would be glad to take up a commodity of them, at any laughter or loss, in another place.' *Exeunt.*

ACT ONE

Littlewit's house

Enter LITTLEWIT.

LITTLEWIT. A pretty conceit, and worth the finding! I ha' such luck to spin out these fine things still, and, like a silk-worm, out of myself. Here's Master Bartholomew Cokes, of Harrow o' th' Hill, i' th' county of Middlesex, Esquire, takes forth his licence to marry Mistress Grace Wellborn, of the said place and county—and when does he take it forth? Today, the four and twentieth of August, Bartholomew Day! Bartholomew upon Bartholomew, there's the device! Who would have marked such a leap-frog chance now? A very less than amesace, on two dice! Well, go thy ways, John Littlewit, Proctor John Littlewit; one o' the pretty wits of Paul's, the Littlewit of London, so thou art called, and something beside. When a quirk or a quibbling does 'scape thee, and thou dost not watch and apprehend it, and bring it afore the constable of conceit,— there now, I speak quib, too—let 'em carry thee out o' the Archdeacon's Court into his kitchen, and make a jack of thee, instead of a John. There I am again, la!

Enter MISTRESS LITTLEWIT.

Win, good morrow, Win. Ay marry, Win, now you look finely indeed, Win! This cap does convince! You'd not ha' worn it, Win, nor ha' had it velvet, but a rough country beaver, with a copper band, like the coney-skin woman of Budge Row. Sweet Win, let me kiss it! And her fine high shoes, like the Spanish lady! Good Win, go a little, I would fain see thee pace, pretty Win! By this fine cap, I could never leave kissing on't.

MISTRESS LITTLEWIT. Come indeed, la, you are such a fool still!

LITTLEWIT. No, but half a one, Win, you are the tother half; man and wife make one fool, Win. Good! Is there the proctor, or doctor indeed, i' the diocese, that ever had the fortune to win him such a Win! There I am again! I do feel conceits coming upon me, more than I am able to turn tongue to. A pox o' these pretenders to wit, your Three Cranes, Mitre, and Mermaid men! Not a corn of true salt, not a grain of right mustard amongst them all. They may stand for places or so, again' the next wit-fall, and pay twopence in a quart more for their canary than other men. But gi' me the man can start up a justice of wit out of six-shillings beer, and give the law to all the poets and poet-suckers i' town, because they are the players' gossips! 'Slid, other men have wives as fine as the players, and as well dressed. Come hither, Win.

Enter WINWIFE.

WINWIFE. Why, how now, Master Littlewit! measuring of lips or moulding of kisses, which is it?

LITTLEWIT. Troth, I am a little taken with my Win's dressing here. Does't not fine, Master Winwife? How do you apprehend, sir? She would not ha' worn this habit. I challenge all Cheapside to show such another; Moorfields, Pimlico Path, or the Exchange, in a summer evening, with a lace to boot, as this has. Dear Win, let Master Winwife kiss you. He comes a-wooing to our mother, Win, and may be our father perhaps, Win. There's no harm in him, Win.

WINWIFE. None i' the earth, Master Littlewit.

LITTLEWIT. I envy no man my delicates, sir.

WINWIFE. Alas, you ha' the garden where they grow still! A wife here with a strawberry breath, cherry lips, apricot cheeks, and a soft velvet head, like a melicotton.

LITTLEWIT. Good, i' faith! Now dulness upon me, that I had not that before him, that I should not light on't as well as he! Velvet head!

WINWIFE. But my taste, Master Littlewit, tends to fruit of a later kind: the sober matron, your wife's mother.

LITTLEWIT. Ay, we know you are a suitor, sir. Win and I both wish you well. By this licence here, would you had her, that your two names were as fast in it, as here are a couple! Win would fain have a fine young father-i'-law with a feather, that her mother might hood it and chain it with Mistress

OVERDO. But you do not take the right course, Master Winwife.

WINWIFE. No, Master Littlewit, why?

LITTLEWIT. You are not mad enough.

WINWIFE. How! is madness a right course?

LITTLEWIT. I say nothing, but I wink upon Win. You have a friend, one Master Quarlous, comes here sometimes.

WINWIFE. Why, he makes no love to her, does he?

LITTLEWIT. Not a tokenworth that ever I saw, I assure you. But——

WINWIFE. What?

LITTLEWIT. He is the more madcap o' the two. You do not apprehend me.

MISTRESS LITTLEWIT. You have a hot coal i' your mouth now, you cannot hold.

LITTLEWIT. Let me out with it, dear Win.

MISTRESS LITTLEWIT. I'll tell him myself.

LITTLEWIT. Do, and take all the thanks, and much do good thy pretty heart, Win.

MISTRESS LITTLEWIT. Sir, my mother has had her nativity-water cast lately by the cunning-men in Cow Lane; and they ha' told her her fortune, and do ensure her she shall never have happy hour, unless she marry within this se'nnight; and when it is, it must be a madman, they say.

LITTLEWIT. Ay, but it must be a gentleman mad-man.

MISTRESS LITTLEWIT. Yes, so the tother man of Moorfields says.

WINWIFE. But does she believe 'em?

LITTLEWIT. Yes, and has been at Bedlam twice since, every day, to inquire if any gentleman be there, or to come there, mad.

WINWIFE. Why, this is a confederacy, a mere piece of practice upon her, by these impostors.

LITTLEWIT. I tell her so; or else, say I, that they mean some young madcap gentleman—for the devil can equivocate as well as a shopkeeper—and therefore would I advise you to be a little madder than Master Quarlous, hereafter.

WINWIFE. Where is she, stirring yet?

LITTLEWIT. Stirring! Yes, and studying an old elder come from Banbury, a suitor that puts in here at meal-tide, to praise the painful Brethren, or pray that the sweet singers may be restored; says a grace as long as his breath lasts him! Sometime the spirit is so strong with him, it gets quite out of him, and then my mother or Win are fain to fetch it again with malmsey or aqua-caelestis.

MISTRESS LITTLEWIT. Yes, indeed, we have such a tedious life with him for his diet, and his clothes too; he breaks his buttons, and cracks seams at every saying he sobs out.

LITTLEWIT. He cannot abide my vocation, he says.

MISTRESS LITTLEWIT. No, he told my mother, a proctor was a claw of the beast, and that she had little less than committed abomination in marrying me so as she has done.

LITTLEWIT. Every line, he says, that a proctor writes, when it comes to be read in the Bishop's Court, is a long, black hair, kembed out of the tail of Antichrist.

WINWIFE. When came this proselyte?

LITTLEWIT. Some three days since.

Enter QUARLOUS.

QUARLOUS. O sir, ha' you ta'en soil here? It's well, a man may reach you after three hours running yet! What an unmerciful companion art thou, to quit thy lodging at such ungentlemanly hours! None but a scattered covey of fiddlers, or one of these rag-rakers in dunghills, or some marrow-bone man at most, would have been up when thou wert gone abroad, by all description. I pray thee what ailest thou, thou canst not sleep? Hast thou thorns i' thy eyelids, or thistles i' thy bed?

WINWIFE. I cannot tell. It seems you had neither i' your feet, that took this pain to find me.

QUARLOUS. No, an I had, all the lime-hounds o' the City should have drawn after you by the scent rather. —Master John Littlewit! God save you, sir. 'Twas a hot night with some of us, last night, John; shall we pluck a hair o' the same wolf today, Proctor John?

LITTLEWIT. Do you remember, Master Quarlous, what we discoursed on last night?

QUARLOUS. Not I, John, nothing that I either discourse or do; at those times I forfeit all to forgetfulness.

LITTLEWIT. No? not concerning Win? Look you, there she is, and dressed as I told you she should be. Hark you, sir, had you forgot?

QUARLOUS. By this head, I'll beware how I keep you company, John, when I am drunk, an you have this dangerous memory, that's certain!

LITTLEWIT. Why, sir?

QUARLOUS. Why! we were all a little stained last night, sprinkled with a cup or two, and I agreed with Proctor John here, to come and do somewhat with Win—I know not what 'twas—today; and he puts me in mind on't now; he says he was coming to fetch me. Before truth, if you have that fearful quality, John, to remember when you are sober, John, what you promise drunk, John, I shall take heed of you, John. For this once I am content to wink at you. Where's your wife? Come hither, Win.

Kisses her.

MISTRESS LITTLEWIT. Why, John! do you see this, John? Look you, help me, John!

LITTLEWIT. O Win, fie, what do you mean, Win? Be womanly, Win; make an outcry to your mother, Win? Master Quarlous is an honest gentleman, and our worshipful good friend, Win; and he is Master Winwife's friends, too. And Master Winwife comes a suitor to your mother, Win, as I told you before, Win, and may perhaps be our father, Win. They'll do you no harm, Win, they are both our worshipful good friends. Master Quarlous! you must know Master Quarlous, Win; you must not quarrel with Master Quarlous, Win.

QUARLOUS. No, we'll kiss again, and fall in.

LITTLEWIT. Yes, do, good Win.

MISTRESS LITTLEWIT. I' faith, you are a fool, John.

LITTLEWIT. A fool-john, she calls me, do you mark that, gentlemen? Pretty Littlewit of velvet, a fool-john!

QUARLOUS. —She may call you an apple-john, if you use this.

WINWIFE. Pray thee forbear, for my respect, somewhat.

QUARLOUS. Hoy-day! how respective you are become o' the sudden! I fear this family will turn you reformed, too; pray you come about again. Because she is in possibility to be your daughter-in-law, and may ask you blessing hereafter, when she courts it to Tottenham to eat cream! Well, I will forbear, sir, but, i' faith, would thou wouldst leave thy exercise of widow-hunting once—this drawing after an old, reverend smock by the splay-foot! There cannot be an ancient tripe or trillibub i' the town, but thou art straight nosing it, and 'tis a fine occupation thou'lt confine thyself to when thou hast got one: scrubbing a piece of buff, as if thou hadst the per-

petuity of Pannier Alley to stink in; or perhaps
worse, currying a carcass that thou hast bound thyself to alive. I'll be sworn, some of them that thou
art, or hast been, a suitor to, are so old as no chaste
or married pleasure can ever become 'em. The
honest instrument of procreation has, forty years
since, left to belong to 'em. Thou must visit 'em as
thou wouldst do a tomb, with a torch or three hand-
fuls of link, flaming hot; and so thou mayst hap
to make 'em feel thee, and after, come to inherit
according to thy inches. A sweet course for a man
to waste the brand of life for, to be still raking
himself a fortune in an old woman's embers! We
shall ha' thee, after thou hast been but a month
married to one of 'em, look like the quartan ague
and the black jaundice met in a face, and walk as if
thou hadst borrowed legs of a spinner and voice of
a cricket. I would endure to hear fifteen sermons a
week for her, and such coarse and loud ones as some
of 'em must be! I would e'en desire of fate, I might
dwell in a drum, and take in my sustenance with
an old, broken tobacco-pipe and a straw. Dost thou
ever think to bring thine ears or stomach to the
patience of a dry grace, as long as thy table-cloth;
and droned out by thy son here, that might be thy
father, till all the meat o' thy board has forgot it
was that day i' the kitchen? Or to brook the noise
made in a question of predestination by the good
labourers and painful eaters assembled together, put
to 'em by the matron your spouse, who moderates
with a cup of wine ever and anon, and a sentence
out of Knox between? Or the perpetual spitting
before and after a sober-drawn exhortation of six
hours, whose better part was the hum-ha-hum? Or to
hear prayers groaned out over thy iron chests, as if
they were charms to break 'em? And all this for

the hope of two apostle-spoons to suffer, and a cup to eat a caudle in! For that will be thy legacy. She'll ha' conveyed her state safe enough from thee, an she be a right widow.

WINWIFE. Alas, I am quite off that scent now.

QUARLOUS. How so?

WINWIFE. Put off by a Brother of Banbury, one that, they say, is come here, and governs all already.

QUARLOUS. What do you call him? I knew divers of those Banburians when I was in Oxford.

WINWIFE. Master Littlewit can tell us.

LITTLEWIT. Sir!—Good Win, go in, and if Master Bartholomew Cokes's man come for the licence,— the little old fellow—let him speak with me. *Exit* MISTRESS LITTLEWIT. What say you, gentlemen?

WINWIFE. What call you the reverend elder you told me of, your Banbury man?

LITTLEWIT. Rabbi Busy, sir. He is more than an elder, he is a prophet, sir.

QUARLOUS. O, I know him! A baker, is he not?

LITTLEWIT. He was a baker, sir, but he does dream now and see visions; he has given over his trade.

QUARLOUS. I remember that, too—out of a scruple he took that, in spiced conscience, those cakes he made, were served to bridals, may-poles, morrises, and such profane feasts and meetings. His Christian name is Zeal-of-the-Land.

LITTLEWIT. Yes, sir, Zeal-of-the-Land Busy.

WINWIFE. How! what a name's there!

LITTLEWIT. O, they have all such names, sir. He was witness for Win here—they will not be called godfathers—and named her Win-the-Fight. You thought her name had been Winifred, did you not?

WINWIFE. I did indeed.

LITTLEWIT. He would ha' thought himself a stark reprobate if it had.

QUARLOUS. Ay, for there was a blue-starch woman o' the name, at the same time. A notable, hypocritical vermin it is, I know him; one that stands upon his face more than his faith at all times; ever in seditious motion, and reproving for vainglory; of a most lunatic conscience and spleen; and affects the violence of singularity in all he does. He has undone a grocer here in Newgate Market, that broke with him, trusted him with currants, as arrant a zeal as he—that's by the way. By his profession he will ever be i' the state of innocence, though, and childhood; derides all antiquity, defies any other learning than inspiration; and what discretion soever years should afford him, it is all prevented in his original ignorance. Ha' not to do with him, for he is a fellow of a most arrogant and invincible dulness, I assure you. Who is this?

Re-enter MISTRESS LITTLEWIT *with* WASP.

WASP. By your leave, gentlemen, with all my heart to you, and God you good morrow! Master Littlewit, my business is to you. Is this licence ready?

LITTLEWIT. Here, I ha' it for you in my hand, Master Humphrey.

WASP. That's well. Nay, never open or read it to me, it's labour in vain, you know. I am no clerk, I scorn to be saved by my book, i' faith, I'll hang first. Fold it up o' your word, and gi' it me. What must you ha' for't?

LITTLEWIT. We'll talk of that anon, Master Humphrey.

WASP. Now, or not at all, good Master Proctor, I am for no anons, I assure you.

LITTLEWIT. Sweet Win, bid Solomon send me the little black box within, in my study.

WASP. Ay, quickly, good mistress, I pray you, for

I have both eggs o' the spit and iron i' the fire. *Exit* MISTRESS LITTLEWIT. Say what you must have, good Master Littlewit.

LITTLEWIT. Why, you know the price, Master Numps.

WASP. I know! I know nothing, I, what tell you me of knowing? Now I am in haste, sir, I do not know, and I will not know, and I scorn to know; and yet, now I think on't, I will, and do know as well as another. You must have a mark for your thing here, and eightpence for the box. I could ha' saved twopence i' that, an I had bought it myself; but here's fourteen shillings for you. Good Lord, how long your little wife stays! Pray God, Solomon, your clerk, be not looking i' the wrong box, Master Proctor.

LITTLEWIT. Good, i' faith! No, I warrant you, Solomon is wiser than so, sir.

WASP. Fie, fie, fie, by your leave, Master Littlewit, this is scurvy, idle, foolish, and abominable, with all my heart; I do not like it.

WINWIFE. —Do you hear? Jack Littlewit, what business does thy pretty head think this fellow may have, that he keeps such a coil with?

QUARLOUS. More than buying of gingerbread i' the cloister here—for that we allow him—or a gilt pouch i' the Fair?

LITTLEWIT. Master Quarlous, do not mistake him. He is his master's both-hands, I assure you.

QUARLOUS. What! to pull on his boots o' mornings, or his stockings, does he?

LITTLEWIT. Sir, if you have a mind to mock him, mock him softly, and look t'other way; for if he apprehend you flout him once, he will fly at you presently. A terrible testy old fellow, and his name is Wasp, too.

QUARLOUS. Pretty insect! make much on him.

WASP. A plague o' this box, and the pox too, and on him that made it, and her that went for't, and all that should ha' sought it, sent it, or brought it, do you see, sir?

LITTLEWIT. Nay, good Master Wasp.

WASP. Good Master Hornet, turd i' your teeth, hold you your tongue! Do not I know you? your father was a 'pothecary, and sold clysters, more than he gave, I wuss. And turd i' your little wife's teeth, too—here she comes—'twill make her spit, as fine as she is, for all her velvet custard on her head, sir.

Re-enter MISTRESS LITTLEWIT.

LITTLEWIT. O, be civil, Master Numps.

WASP. Why, say I have a humour not to be civil, how then? who shall compel me, you?

LITTLEWIT. Here is the box now.

WASP. Why, a pox o' your box once again! Let your little wife stale in it, an she will. Sir, I would have you to understand, and these gentlemen too, if they please——

WINWIFE. With all our hearts, sir.

WASP. That I have a charge, gentlemen.

LITTLEWIT. They do apprehend, sir.

WASP. Pardon me, sir, neither they nor you can apprehend me yet. You are an ass. I have a young master, he is now upon his making and marring; the whole care of his well-doing is now mine. His foolish schoolmasters have done nothing but run up and down the country with him, to beg pud-dings and cake-bread of his tenants, and almost spoiled him. He has learned nothing but to sing catches, and repeat 'Rattle, bladder, rattle' and 'O, Madge.' I dare not let him walk alone, for fear of learning of vile tunes, which he will sing at supper, and in the sermon-times! If he meet but a carman i' the street, and I find him not talk to keep him off on him, he will whistle him and all his tunes over, at night in his sleep! He has a head full of bees! I am fain now, for this little time I am absent, to leave him in charge with a gentlewoman. 'Tis true, she is a Justice of Peace's wife, and a gentle-woman o' the hood, and his natural sister; but what may happen under a woman's government, there's the doubt. Gentlemen, you do not know him; he is another manner of piece than you think for: but nineteen year old, and yet he is taller than either of you, by the head, God bless him!

QUARLOUS. Well, methinks this is a fine fellow.

WINWIFE. He has made his master a finer by this description, I should think.

QUARLOUS. 'Faith, much about one, it's cross-and-pile, whither for a new farthing.

WASP. I'll tell you, gentlemen——

LITTLEWIT. Will't please you drink, Master Wasp?

WASP. Why, I ha' not talked so long to be dry, sir. You see no dust or cobwebs come out o' my mouth, do you? You'd ha' me gone, would you?

LITTLEWIT. No, but you were in haste e'en now, Master Numps.

WASP. What an I were! so I am still, and yet I will stay, too. Meddle you with your match, your Win there; she has as little wit as her husband, it seems. I have others to talk to.

LITTLEWIT. She's my match, indeed, and as little wit as I, good!

WASP. We ha' been but a day and a half in town, gentlemen, 'tis true; and yesterday i' the afternoon we walked London, to show the City to the gentle-woman he shall marry, Mistress Grace; but afore I

will endure such another half-day with him, I'll be
drawn with a good gib-cat through the great pond
at home, as his uncle Hodge was! Why, we could
not meet that heathen thing all day, but stayed him.
He would name you all the signs over, as he went,
aloud; and where he spied a parrot or a monkey,
there he was pitched, with all the little long-coats
about him, male and female; no getting him away!
I thought he would ha' run mad o' the black boy in
Bucklersbury, that takes the scurvy, roguy tobacco
there.

LITTLEWIT. You say true, Master Numps, there's
such a one indeed.

WASP. It's no matter whether there be or no,
what's that to you?

QUARLOUS. —He will not allow of John's reading
at any hand.

Enter COKES, MISTRESS OVERDO, *and* GRACE.

COKES. O Numps! are you here, Numps? Look
where I am, Numps, and Mistress Grace too! Nay,
do not look angerly, Numps, my sister is here, and
all; I do not come without her.

WASP. What the mischief do you come with her?
or she with you?

COKES. We came all to seek you, Numps.

WASP. To seek me! why, did you all think I was
lost? or run away with your fourteen shillings worth
of small ware here? or that I had changed it i' the
Fair for hobby-horses? 'Sprecious, to seek me!

MISTRESS OVERDO. Nay, good Master Numps, do
you show discretion, though he be exorbitant, as
Master Overdo says, an't be but for conservation o'
the peace.

WASP. Marry gip, Goody She-Justice, Mistress

French-Hood! turd i' your teeth, and turd i' your French hood's teeth, too, to do you service, do you see? Must you quote your Adam to me! You think you are Madam Regent still, Mistress Overdo, when I am in place? No such matter, I assure you, your reign is out when I am in, dame.

MISTRESS OVERDO. I am content to be in abeyance, sir, and be governed by you; so should he too, if he did well; but 'twill be expected you should also govern your passions.

WASP. Will't so, forsooth? Good Lord, how sharp you are, with being at Bedlam yesterday! Whetstone has set an edge upon you, has he?

MISTRESS OVERDO. Nay, if you know not what belongs to your dignity, I do yet to mine.

WASP. Very well, then.

COKES. Is this the licence, Numps? for love's sake let me see't. I never saw a licence.

WASP. Did you not so? Why, you shall not see't, then.

COKES. An you love me, good Numps.

WASP. Sir, I love you, and yet I do not love you i' these fooleries, set your heart at rest. There's nothing in't but hard words, and what would you see't for?

COKES. I would see the length and the breadth on't, that's all; and I will see't now, so I will.

WASP. You shan't see it here.

COKES. Then I'll see it at home, and I'll look upo' the case here.

WASP. Why, do so. A man must give way to him a little in trifles, gentlemen. These are errors, diseases of youth, which he will mend when he comes to judgment and knowledge of matters. I pray you conceive so, and I thank you; and I pray you pardon him, and I thank you again.

QUARLOUS. —Well, this dry-nurse, I say still, is a delicate man.

WINWIFE. And I am for the cosset, his charge. Did you ever see a fellow's face more accuse him for an ass?

QUARLOUS. Accuse him! it confesses him one without accusing. What pity 'tis yonder wench should marry such a cokes!

WINWIFE. 'Tis true.

QUARLOUS. She seems to be discreet, and as sober as she is handsome.

WINWIFE. Ay, and if you mark her, what a restrained scorn she casts upon all his behaviour and speeches!

COKES. Well, Numps, I am now for another piece of business more, the Fair, Numps, and then——

WASP. Bless me! deliver me! help, hold me! the Fair!

COKES. Nay, never fidge up and down, Numps, and vex itself. I am resolute Bartholomew in this; I'll make no suit on't to you. 'Twas all the end of my journey indeed, to show Mistress Grace my Fair. I call it my Fair, because of Bartholomew: you know my name is Bartholomew, and Bartholomew Fair.

LITTLEWIT. That was mine afore, gentlemen, this morning. I had that, i' faith, upon his licence, believe me, there he comes after me.

QUARLOUS. Come, John, this ambitious wit of yours, I am afraid, will do you no good i' the end.

LITTLEWIT. No? why, sir?

QUARLOUS. You grow so insolent with it, and overdoing, John, that if you look not to it, and tie it up, it will bring you to some obscure place in time, and there 'twill leave you.

WINWIFE. Do not trust it too much, John, be more

sparing, and use it but now and then. A wit is a dangerous thing in this age; do not over-buy it.

LITTLEWIT. Think you so, gentlemen? I'll take heed on't hereafter.

MISTRESS LITTLEWIT. Yes, do, John.

COKES. A pretty little soul, this same Mistress Littlewit, would I might marry her!

GRACE. —So would I; or anybody else, so I might 'scape you.

COKES. Numps, I will see it, Numps, 'tis decreed; never be melancholy for the matter.

WASP. Why, see it, sir, see it, do see it! Who hinders you? Why do you not go see it? 'Slid, see it.

COKES. The Fair, Numps, the Fair.

WASP. Would the Fair, and all the drums and rattles in't, were i' your belly for me! They are already i' your brain. He that had the means to travel your head now, should meet finer sights than any are i' the Fair, and make a finer voyage on't; to see it all hung with cockleshells, pebbles, fine wheat-straws, and here and there a chicken's feather, and a cobweb.

QUARLOUS. —Good faith, he looks, methinks, an you mark him, like one that were made to catch flies, with his Sir Cranion legs.

WINWIFE. And his Numps, to flap 'em away.

WASP. God be w' you, sir, there's your bee in a box, and much good do't you.

COKES. Why, your friend and Bartholomew, an you be so contumacious.

QUARLOUS. What mean you, Numps?

WASP. I'll not be guilty, I, gentlemen.

MISTRESS OVERDO. You will not let him go, brother, and lose him?

COKES. Who can hold that will away? I had rather lose him than the Fair, I wuss.

WASP. You do not know the inconvenience, gentlemen, you persuade to, nor what trouble I have with him in these humours. If he go to the Fair, he will buy of everything, to a baby, there; and household stuff for that, too. If a leg or an arm on him did not grow on, he would lose it i' the press. Pray Heaven I bring him off with one stone! And then he is such a ravener after fruit! you will not believe what a coil I had t'other day to compound a business between a Cather'ne-pear-woman and him, about snatching! 'Tis intolerable, gentlemen.

WINWIFE. O, but you must not leave him now to these hazards, Numps.

WASP. Nay, he knows too well I will not leave him, and that makes him presume.—Well, sir, will you go now? If you have such an itch i' your feet to foot it to the Fair, why do you stop, am I your tarriers? Go, will you go, sir? why do you not go?

COKES. O Numps, have I brought you about? Come, Mistress Grace, and sister, I am resolute Bat, i' faith, still.

GRACE. Truly, I have no such fancy to the Fair, nor ambition to see it. There's none goes thither of any quality or fashion.

COKES. O Lord, sir! you shall pardon me, Mistress Grace, we are enow of ourselves to make it a fashion; and for qualities, let Numps alone, he'll find qualities.

Exit with GRACE, MISTRESS OVERDO *and* WASP.

QUARLOUS. What a rogue in apprehension is this, to understand her language no better!

WINWIFE. Ay, and offer to marry to her! Well, I will leave the chase of my widow for today, and directly to the Fair. These flies cannot, this hot season, but engender us excellent creeping sport.

QUARLOUS. A man that has but a spoonful of brain would think so.—Farewell, John.

Exeunt QUARLOUS *and* WINWIFE.

LITTLEWIT. Win, you see 'tis in fashion to go to the Fair, Win. We must to the Fair, too, you and I, Win. I have an affair i' the Fair, Win, a puppet-play of mine own making—say nothing—that I writ for the motion-man, which you must see, Win.

MISTRESS LITTLEWIT. I would I might, John, but my mother will never consent to such a—profane motion, she will call it.

LITTLEWIT. Tut, we'll have a device, a dainty one. Now, Wit, help at a pinch, good Wit come, come, good Wit, an't be thy will! I have it, Win, I have it, 'i faith, and 'tis a fine one. Win, long to eat of a pig, sweet Win, i' the Fair, do you see, i' the heart o' the Fair, not at Pie Corner. Your mother will do anything, Win, to satisfy your longing, you know. Pray thee long presently, and be sick o' the sudden, good Win. I'll go in and tell her. Cut thy lace i' the meantime, and play the hypocrite, sweet Win.

MISTRESS LITTLEWIT. No, I'll not make me unready for it. I can be hypocrite enough, though I were never so strait-laced.

LITTLEWIT. You say true, you have been bred i' the family, and brought up to't. Our mother is a most elect hypocrite, and has maintained us all this seven year with it, like gentlefolks.

MISTRESS LITTLEWIT. Ay, let her alone, John, she is not a wise, wilful widow for nothing, nor a sanctified sister for a song. And let me alone, too; I ha' somewhat o' the mother in me, you shall see. Fetch her, fetch her. *Exit* LITTLEWIT. Ah! ah!

Re-enter LITTLEWIT *with* DAME PURECRAFT.

PURECRAFT. Now the blaze of the beauteous discipline fright away this evil from our house! How now, Win-the-Fight, child! how do you? Sweet child, speak to me.

MISTRESS LITTLEWIT. Yes, forsooth.

DAME PURECRAFT. Look up, sweet Win-the-Fight, and suffer not the enemy to enter you at this door; remember that your education has been with the purest. What polluted one was it, that named first the unclean beast, pig, to you, child?

MISTRESS LITTLEWIT. Uh! uh!

LITTLEWIT. Not I, o' my sincerity, mother. She longed above three hours ere she would let me know it.—Who was it, Win?

MISTRESS LITTLEWIT. A profane black thing with a beard, John.

DAME PURECRAFT. O, resist it, Win-the-Fight, it is the Tempter, the wicked Tempter; you may know it by the fleshly motion of pig. Be strong against it, and its foul temptations, in these assaults, whereby it broacheth flesh and blood, as it were on the weaker side; and pray against its carnal provocations, good child, sweet child, pray.

LITTLEWIT. Good mother, I pray you that she may eat some pig, and her bellyful, too; and do not you cast away your own child, and perhaps one of mine, with your tale of the Tempter. How do you, Win? Are you not sick?

MISTRESS LITTLEWIT. Yes, a great deal, John. Uh! uh!

DAME PURECRAFT. What shall we do? Call our zealous brother Busy hither, for his faithful fortification in this charge of the adversary. *Exit* LITTLEWIT. Child, my dear child, you shall eat pig; be comforted, my sweet child.

MISTRESS LITTLEWIT. Ay, but i' the Fair, mother.

DAME PURECRAFT. I mean i' the Fair, if it can be any way made or found lawful.

Re-enter LITTLEWIT.

Where is our Brother Busy? Will he not come?—
Look up, child.

LITTLEWIT. Presently, mother, as soon as he has
cleansed his beard. I found him fast by the teeth i'
the cold turkey-pie i' the cupboard, with a great
white loaf on his left hand, and a glass of malmsey
on his right.

DAME PURECRAFT. Slander not the Brethren, wicked
one.

LITTLEWIT. Here he is now, purified, mother.

Enter ZEAL-OF-THE-LAND BUSY.

DAME PURECRAFT. O Brother Busy! your help here,
to edify and raise us up in a scruple: my daughter
Win-the-Fight is visited with a natural disease of
women, called a longing to eat pig.

LITTLEWIT. Ay, sir, a Bartholomew-pig, and in the
Fair.

DAME PURECRAFT. And I would be satisfied from
you, religiously wise, whether a widow of the Sanctified Assembly, or a widow's daughter, may commit
the act without offence to the weaker Sisters.

BUSY. Verily, for the disease of longing, it is a
disease, a carnal disease, or appetite, incident to
women; and as it is carnal and incident, it is natural, very natural. Now pig, it is a meat, and a meat
that is nourishing, and may be longed for, and so
consequently eaten. It may be eaten, very exceeding well eaten. But in the Fair, and as a Bartholomew-pig, it cannot be eaten; for the very calling it a
Bartholomew-pig, and to eat it so, is a spice of idolatry, and you make the Fair no better than one of the
High Places. This, I take it, is the state of the question: a High Place.

LITTLEWIT. Ay, but in state of necessity, place should give place, Master Busy.—I have a conceit left yet.

DAME PURECRAFT. Good brother Zeal-of-the-Land, think to make it as lawful as you can.

LITTLEWIT. Yes, sir, and as soon as you can, for it must be, sir; you see the danger my little wife is in, sir.

DAME PURECRAFT. Truly, I do love my child dearly, and I would not have her miscarry, or hazard her first-fruits, if it might be otherwise.

BUSY. Surely, it may be otherwise, but it is subject to construction; subject, and hath a face of offence with the weak, a great face, a foul face. But that face may have a veil put over it, and be shadowed, as it were. It may be eaten, and in the Fair, I take it, in a booth, the tents of the wicked. The place is not much, not very much; we may be religious in midst of the profane, so it be eaten with a reformed mouth, with sobriety and humbleness; not gorged in with gluttony or greediness—there's the fear. For, should she go there as taking pride in the place, or delight in the unclean dressing, to feed the vanity of the eye or lust of the palate, it were not well, it were not fit, it were abominable, and not good.

LITTLEWIT. Nay, I knew that afore, and told her on't. But courage, Win, we'll be humble enough. We'll seek out the homeliest booth i' the Fair, that's certain; rather than fail, we'll eat it o' the ground.

DAME PURECRAFT. Ay, and I'll go with you myself, Win-the-Fight, and my brother Zeal-of-the-Land shall go with us, too, for our better consolation.

MISTRESS LITTLEWIT. Uh! uh!

LITTLEWIT. Ay, and Solomon too, Win, the more

the merrier, Win.—We'll leave Rabbi Busy in a booth.—Solomon, my cloak!

Enter SOLOMON.

SOLOMON. Here, sir.

BUSY. In the way of comfort to the weak, I will go and eat. I will eat exceedingly, and prophesy. There may be a good use made of it, too, now I think on't: by the public eating of swine's flesh, to profess our hate and loathing of Judaism, whereof the Brethren stand taxed. I will therefore eat, yea, I will eat exceedingly.

LITTLEWIT. Good, i' faith, I will eat heartily, too, because I will be no Jew; I could never away with that stiff-necked generation. And truly, I hope my little one will be like me, that cries for pig so, i' the mother's belly.

BUSY. Very likely, exceeding likely, very exceeding likely.   *Exeunt.*

ACT TWO

The Fair

Enter JUSTICE OVERDO *in disguise.*

OVERDO. Well, in justice' name and the King's, and for the commonwealth! defy all the world, Adam Overdo, for a disguise, and all story; for thou hast fitted thyself, I swear. Fain would I meet the Lynceus now, that eagle's eye, that piercing Epidaurian serpent,—as my Quintus Horace calls him—that could discover a Justice of Peace, and lately of the

Quorum, under this covering. They may have seen
many a fool in the habit of a justice, but never till
now a justice in the habit of a fool. Thus must we
do, though, that wake for the public good; and thus
hath the wise magistrate done in all ages. There is
a doing of right out of wrong, if the way be found.
Never shall I enough commend a worthy, worshipful man, sometime a capital member of this City,
for his high wisdom in this point, who would take
you now the habit of a porter, now of a carman;
now of the dog-killer, in this month of August; and
in the winter, of a seller of tinder-boxes. And what
would he do in all these shapes? Marry, go you into
every alehouse, and down into every cellar; measure
the length of puddings, take the gauge of black pots
and cans, ay, and custards, with a stick; and their
circumference with a thread; weigh the loaves of
bread on his middle finger; then would he send for
'em home; give the puddings to the poor, the bread
to the hungry, the custards to his children; break
the pots and burn the cans himself—he would not
trust his corrupt officers, he would do't himself.
Would all men in authority would follow this
worthy precedent! For alas, as we are public persons, what do we know? nay, what can we know?
We hear with other men's ears, we see with other
men's eyes. A foolish constable or a sleepy watchman is all our information; he slanders a gentleman by the virtue of his place, as he calls it, and
we, by the vice of ours, must believe him. As, a
while agone, they made me—yea, me—to mistake
an honest, zealous pursuivant for a Seminary, and
a proper young bachelor of music for a bawd. This
we are subject to, that live in high place: all our
intelligence is idle, and most of our intelligencers
knaves; and, by your leave, ourselves thought little

better, if not arrant fools, for believing 'em. I, Adam Overdo, am resolved therefore to spare spy-money hereafter, and make mine own discoveries. Many are the yearly enormities of this Fair, in whose Courts of Pie-powders I have had the honour, during the three days sometimes, to sit as judge. But this is the special day for detection of those foresaid enormities. Here is my black book for the purpose; this the cloud that hides me; under this covert I shall see and not be seen. On, Junius Brutus. And as I began, so I'll end: in justice' name and the King's, and for the commonwealth!

URSULA'S *booth is revealed, with* LEATHERHEAD, TRASH, *and others, sitting at their stalls.*

LEATHERHEAD. The Fair's pestilence-dead, methinks; people come not abroad today, whatever the matter is. Do you hear, sister Trash, Lady o' the Basket? Sit farther with your gingerbread progeny there, and hinder not the prospect of my shop, or I'll ha' it proclaimed i' the Fair, what stuff they are made on.

TRASH. Why, what stuff are they made on, brother Leatherhead? Nothing but what's wholesome, I assure you.

LEATHERHEAD. Yes, stale bread, rotten eggs, musty ginger, and dead honey, you know.

OVERDO. —Ay! Have I met with enormity so soon?

LEATHERHEAD. I shall mar your market, old Joan.

TRASH. Mar my market, thou too proud pedlar! Do thy worst, I defy thee, I, and thy stable of hobby-horses. I pay for my ground as well as thou dost. An thou wrong'st me, for all thou art parcel-poet and an engineer, I'll find a friend shall right me, and make a ballad of thee and thy cattle all over. Are you puffed up with the pride of your wares, your arsedine?

LEATHERHEAD. Go to, old Joan, I'll talk with you anon, and take you down, too, afore Justice Overdo; he is the man must charm you. I'll ha' you i' the Pie-powders.

TRASH. Charm me! I'll meet thee face to face, afore his Worship, when thou dar'st. And though I be a little crooked o' my body, I shall be found as upright in my dealing as any woman in Smithfield, I. Charm me!

OVERDO. —I am glad to hear my name is their terror yet. This is doing of justice.

A number of people pass over the stage.

LEATHERHEAD. What do you lack? What is't you buy? What do you lack? Rattles, drums, halberds, horses, babies o' the best, fiddles o' the finest?

Enter COSTERMONGER, *followed by* NIGHTINGALE.

COSTERMONGER. Buy any pears, pears, fine, very fine pears?

TRASH. Buy any gingerbread, gilt gingerbread?

NIGHTINGALE. Hey,

'Now the Fair's a-filling!
O for a tune to startle
The birds o' the booths here billing,
Yearly with old Saint Bartle!
The drunkards they are wading,
The punks and chapmen trading;
Who'd see the Fair without his lading?'

Buy any ballads, new ballads?

Enter URSULA.

URSULA. Fie upon't, who would wear out their youth and prime thus, in roasting of pigs, that had any cooler vocation? Hell's a kind of cold cellar to't, a very fine vault, o' my conscience!—What, Mooncalf!

MOONCALF. Here, mistress.

NIGHTINGALE. How now, Ursula! in a heat, in a heat?

URSULA. My chair, you false faucet, you; and my morning's draught, quickly, a bottle of ale, to quench me, rascal.—I am all fire and fat, Nightingale, I shall e'en melt away to the first woman, a rib again, I am afraid. I do water the ground in knots, as I go, like a great garden-pot; you may follow me by the S's I make.

NIGHTINGALE. Alas, good Urse! Was 'Zekiel here this morning?

URSULA. 'Zekiel? What 'Zekiel?

NIGHTINGALE. 'Zekiel Edgworth, the civil cutpurse, you know him well enough; he that talks bawdy to you still. I call him my secretary.

URSULA. He promised to be here this morning, I remember.

NIGHTINGALE. When he comes, bid him stay. I'll be back again presently.

URSULA. Best take your morning's dew in your belly, Nightingale.

Enter MOONCALF *with the chair.*

Come, sir, set it here. Did not I bid you should get this chair let out o' the sides for me, that my hips might play? You'll never think of anything till your dame be rump-galled. 'Tis well, changeling! Because it can take in your grasshopper's thighs, you care for no more. Now you look as you had been i' the corner o' the booth, fleaing your breech with a candle's end, and set fire o' the Fair. Fill, stote, fill.

OVERDO. —This pig-woman do I know, and I will

put her in, for my second enormity. She hath been before me, punk, pinnace, and bawd, any time these two and twenty years, upon record i' the Pie-powders.

URSULA. Fill again, you unlucky vermin!

MOONCALF. Pray you be not angry, mistress, I'll ha' it widened anon.

URSULA. No, no, I shall e'en dwindle away to't, ere the Fair be done, you think, now you ha' heated me? A poor, vexed thing I am; I feel myself dropping already as fast as I can. Two stone o' suet a day is my proportion. I can but hold life and soul together with this—here's to you, Nightingale—and a whiff of tobacco, at most. Where's my pipe now? not filled? thou arrant incubee!

NIGHTINGALE. Nay, Ursula, thou'lt gall between the tongue and the teeth, with fretting, now.

URSULA. How can I hope that ever he'll discharge his place of trust, tapster, a man of reckoning under me, that remembers nothing I say to him? *Exit* NIGHTINGALE. But look to't, sirrah, you were best: threepence a pipe-full, I will ha' made, of all my whole half-pound of tobacco, and a quarter of a pound of colts-foot mixed with it, too, to itch it out. I that have dealt so long in the fire, will not be to seek in smoke now. Then six and twenty shillings a barrel I will advance o' my beer, and fifty shillings a hundred o' my bottle-ale; I ha' told you the ways how to raise it. Froth your cans well i' the filling, at length, rogue, and jog your bottles o' the buttock, sirrah, then skink out the first glass ever, and drink with all companies, though you be sure to be drunk; you'll misreckon the better, and be less ashamed on't. But your true trick, rascal, must be to be ever busy, and mistake away the bottles and cans, in haste, before they be half drunk off, and never hear anybody call—if they should chance to mark you—till you ha' brought fresh, and be able to forswear 'em. Give me a drink of ale.

OVERDO. —This is the very womb and bed of enormity, gross as herself! This must all down for enormity, all, every whit on't.

One knocks.

URSULA. Look who's there, sirrah! Five shillings a pig is my price, at least; if it be a sow-pig, sixpence more; if she be a great-bellied wife, and long for't, sixpence more for that.

OVERDO. —O tempora! O mores! I would not ha' lost my discovery of this one grievance, for my place and worship o' the bench. How is the poor subject abused here! Well, I will fall in with her, and with her Mooncalf, and win out wonders of enormity! —By thy leave, goodly woman, and the fatness of the Fair, oily as the King's Constable's lamp, and shining as his shoeing-horn: hath thy ale virtue, or thy beer strength, that the tongue of man may be tickled, and his palate pleased in the morning? Let thy pretty nephew here go search and see.

URSULA. What new roarer is this?

MOONCALF. O Lord, do you not know him, mistress? 'Tis mad Arthur of Bradley, that makes the orations.—Brave master, old Arthur of Bradley, how do you? Welcome to the Fair! When shall we hear you again, to handle your matters, with your back again' a booth, ha? I ha' been one o' your little disciples, i' my days.

OVERDO. Let me drink, boy, with my love, thy aunt here, that I may be eloquent; but of thy best, lest it be bitter in my mouth, and my words fall foul on the Fair.

URSULA. Why dost thou not fetch him drink, and offer him to sit?

MOONCALF. Is it ale or beer, Master Arthur?

OVERDO. Thy best, pretty stripling, thy best; the same thy dove drinketh, and thou drawest on holidays.

URSULA. Bring him a sixpenny bottle of ale; they say a fool's handsel is lucky.

OVERDO. Bring both, child. Ale for Arthur, and beer for Bradley. Ale for thine aunt, boy. *Exit* MOONCALF. —My disguise takes to the very wish and reach of it. I shall, by the benefit of this, discover enough and more; and yet get off with the reputation of what I would be: a certain middling thing, between a fool and a madman.

Enter KNOCKEM.

KNOCKEM. What! my little lean Ursula! my she-bear! art thou alive yet, with thy litter of pigs, to grunt out another Bartholomew Fair, ha?

URSULA. Yes, and to amble afoot, when the Fair is done, to hear you groan out of a cart, up the heavy hill.

KNOCKEM. Of Holborn, Ursula, mean'st thou so? For what, for what, pretty Urse?

URSULA. For cutting halfpenny purses, or stealing little penny dogs out o' the Fair.

KNOCKEM. Oh! good words, good words, Urse.

OVERDO. —Another special enormity! a cutpurse of the sword, the boot, and the feather—those are his marks!

Re-enter MOONCALF.

URSULA. You are one of those horse-leeches that gave out I was dead, in Turnbull Street, of a surfeit of bottle-ale and tripes?

KNOCKEM. No, 'twas better meat, Urse: cows' udders, cows' udders!

URSULA. Well, I shall be meet with your mumbling mouth one day.

KNOCKEM. What, thou'lt poison me with a newt in a bottle of ale, wilt thou? or a spider in a tobacco-pipe, Urse? Come, there's no malice in these fat folks; I never fear thee, an I can 'scape thy lean Mooncalf here. Let's drink it out, good Urse, and no vapours!   *Exit* URSULA.

OVERDO. Dost thou hear, boy? There's for thy ale, and the remnant for thee. Speak in thy faith of a faucet now; is this goodly person before us here, this vapours, a knight of the knife?

MOONCALF. What mean you by that, Master Arthur?

OVERDO. I mean a child of the horn-thumb, a babe of booty, boy, a cutpurse.

MOONCALF. O Lord, sir! far from it. This is Master Daniel Knockem, Jordan, the ranger of Turnbull. He is a horse-courser, sir.

OVERDO. Thy dainty dame, though, called him cutpurse.

MOONCALF. Like enough, sir, she'll do forty such things in an hour, an you listen to her, for her recreation, if the toy take her i' the greasy kerchief. It makes her fat, you see. She battens with it.

OVERDO. —Here I might ha' been deceived now, and ha' put a fool's blot upon myself, if I had not played an after-game o' discretion!

Re-enter URSULA, *dropping.*

KNOCKEM. Alas, poor Urse! this 's an ill season for thee.

URSULA. Hang yourself, hackney-man!

KNOCKEM. How, how, Urse! vapours? motion breed vapours?

URSULA. Vapours! Never tusk, nor twirl your dibble, good Jordan, I know what you'll take to a very drop. Though you be captain o' the roarers, and fight well at the case of piss-pots, you shall not fright me with your lion-chap, sir, nor your tusks. You angry! you are hungry. Come, a pig's head will stop your mouth and stay your stomach at all times.

KNOCKEM. Thou art such another mad, merry Urse, still! Troth, I do make conscience of vexing thee, now i' the dog-days, this hot weather, for fear of foundering thee i' the body, and melting down a pillar of the Fair. Pray thee take thy chair again, and keep state; and let's have a fresh bottle of ale, and a pipe of tobacco; and no vapours. I'll ha' this belly o' thine taken up, and thy grass scoured, wench.

Enter EDGWORTH.

Look, here's Ezekiel Edgworth, a fine boy of his inches as any is i' the Fair! has still money in his purse, and will pay all, with a kind heart, and good vapours.

EDGWORTH. That I will indeed, willingly, Master Knockem.—Fetch some ale and tobacco.

Exit MOONCALF

LEATHERHEAD. What do you lack, gentlemen? Maid, see a fine hobby-horse for your young master; cost you but a token a week his provender.

Enter CORN-CUTTER, TINDER-BOX-MAN, *and divers passengers.*

CORN-CUTTER. Ha' you any corns i' your feet and toes?

TINDER-BOX-MAN. Buy a mousetrap, a mousetrap, or a tormentor for a flea?

TRASH. Buy some gingerbread?

Re-enter NIGHTINGALE.

NIGHTINGALE. Ballads, ballads, fine new ballads:

'Hear for your love, and buy for your money,
A delicate ballad o' the Ferret and the Coney;
A preservative again' the Punk's Evil,
Another of Goose-Green Starch and the Devil,
A dozen of divine points, and the Godly Garters;
The Fairing of Good Counsel, of an ell and three
quarters.'

What is't you buy?

'The Windmill blown down by the Witch's Fart,
Or Saint George, that, O! did break the Dragon's
heart.'

Re-enter MOONCALF.

EDGWORTH. Master Nightingale, come hither, leave
your mart a little.

NIGHTINGALE. O my secretary! what says my secretary?

OVERDO. —Child o' the bottles, what's he, what's
he?

MOONCALF. A civil young gentleman, Master
Arthur, that keeps company with the roarers, and
disburses all, still. He has ever money in his purse.
He pays for them, and they roar for him. One does
good offices for another. They call him the secretary, but he serves nobody. A great friend of the
ballad-man's, they are never asunder.

OVERDO. What pity 'tis, so civil a young man
should haunt this debauched company! Here's the
bane of the youth of our time apparent. A proper
penman, I see't in his countenance; he has a good
clerk's look with him, and I warrant him a quick
hand.

MOONCALF. A very quick hand, sir.   *Exit.*

EDGWORTH. *Whispering with* NIGHTINGALE *and* URSULA. All the purses and purchases I give you today by conveyance, bring hither to Ursula's presently. Here we will meet at night in her lodge, and share. Look you choose good places for your standing i' the Fair, when you sing, Nightingale.

URSULA. Ay, near the fullest passages; and shift 'em often.

EDGWORTH. And i' your singing, you must use your hawk's eye nimbly, and fly the purse to a mark still, where 'tis worn, and o' which side; that you may gi' me the sign with your beak, or hang your head that way i' the tune.

URSULA. Enough, talk no more on't. Your friendship, masters, is not now to begin. Drink your draught of indenture, your sup of covenant, and away. The Fair fills apace, company begins to come in, and I ha' ne'er a pig ready yet.

KNOCKEM. Well said! Fill the cups, and light the tobacco! Let's give fire i' th' works, and noble vapours.

EDGWORTH. And shall we ha' smocks, Ursula, and good whimsies, ha?

URSULA. Come, you are i' your bawdy vein! The best the Fair will afford, 'Zekiel, if Bawd Whit keep his word.

Re-enter MOONCALF.

How do the pigs, Mooncalf?

MOONCALF. Very passionate, mistress, one on 'em has wept out an eye. Master Arthur o' Bradley is melancholy here, nobody talks to him. Will you any tobacco, Master Arthur?

OVERDO. No, boy, let my meditations alone.

MOONCALF. He's studying for an oration now.

OVERDO. —If I can, with this day's travail and all

my policy, but rescue this youth here out of the hands of the lewd man and the strange woman, I will sit down at night, and say with my friend Ovid, 'Iamque opus exegi, quod nec Jovis ira, nec ignis, &c.'　　　　　　　　　　　　　　　*Exit* URSULA.

KNOCKEM. Here, 'Zekiel, here's a health to Ursula, and a kind vapour! Thou hast money i' thy purse still, and store; how dost thou come by it? Pray thee vapour thy friends some in a courteous vapour.

EDGWORTH. Half I have, Master Dan Knockem, is always at your service.

OVERDO. —Ha, sweet nature! what goshawk would prey upon such a lamb?

KNOCKEM. Let's see what 'tis, 'Zekiel, count it. Come, fill him to pledge me!

Enter WINWIFE *and* QUARLOUS.

WINWIFE. We are here before 'em, methinks.

QUARLOUS. All the better, we shall see 'em come in now.

LEATHERHEAD. What do you lack, gentlemen, what is't you lack? A fine horse, a lion, a bull, a bear, a dog, or a cat? an excellent fine Bartholomew-bird, or an instrument? What is't you lack?

QUARLOUS. 'Slid! here's Orpheus among the beasts, with his fiddle and all!

TRASH. Will you buy any comfortable bread, gentlemen?

QUARLOUS. And Ceres selling her daughter's picture in ginger-work.

WINWIFE. That these people should be so ignorant to think us chapmen for 'em! Do we look as if we would buy gingerbread or hobby-horses?

QUARLOUS. Why, they know no better ware than they have, nor better customers than come; and our very being here makes us fit to be demanded, as well as others. Would Cokes would come! there were a true customer for 'em.

KNOCKEM. How much is't? thirty shillings? Who's yonder? Ned Winwife and Tom Quarlous, I think! Yes. Gi' me it all, gi' me it all.—Master Winwife! Master Quarlous! will you take a pipe of tobacco with us?—Do not discredit me now, 'Zekiel.

WINWIFE. —Do not see him. He is the roaring horse-courser, pray thee let's avoid him. Turn down this way.

QUARLOUS. 'Slud, I'll see him, and roar with him, too, an he roared as loud as Neptune. Pray thee go with me.

WINWIFE. You may draw me to as likely an inconvenience, when you please, as this.

QUARLOUS. Go to then, come along. We ha' nothing to do, man, but to see sights now.

KNOCKEM. Welcome, Master Quarlous, and Master Winwife! will you take any froth and smoke with us?

QUARLOUS. Yes, sir, but you'll pardon us if we knew not of so much familiarity between us afore.

KNOCKEM. As what, sir?

QUARLOUS. To be so lightly invited to smoke and froth.

KNOCKEM. A good vapour! Will you sit down, sir? This is old Ursula's mansion; how like you her bower? Here you may ha' your punk and your pig in state, sir, both piping hot.

QUARLOUS. I had rather ha' my punk cold, sir.

OVERDO. —There's for me: punk! and pig!

URSULA. *Within.* What, Mooncalf, you rogue!

MOONCALF. By and by, the bottle is almost off, mistress. Here, Master Arthur.

URSULA. I'll part you and your play-fellow there, i' the guarded coat, an you sunder not the sooner.

KNOCKEM. Master Winwife, you are proud, me-thinks; you do not talk, nor drink. Are you proud?

WINWIFE. Not of the company I am in, sir, nor the place, I assure you.

KNOCKEM. You do not except at the company, do you? Are you in vapours, sir?

MOONCALF. Nay, good Master Daniel Knockem, respect my mistress' bower, as you call it. For the honour of our booth, none o' your vapours here.

Enter URSULA *with a firebrand.*

URSULA. —Why, you thin, lean polecat you, an they have a mind to be i' their vapours, must you hinder 'em? What did you know, vermin, if they would ha' lost a cloak, or such trifle? Must you be drawing the air of pacification here, while I am tormented within i' the fire, you weasel?

MOONCALF. Good mistress, 'twas in behalf of your booth's credit that I spoke.

URSULA. Why? would my booth ha' broke if they had fall'n out in't, sir? or would their heat ha' fired it? In, you rogue, and wipe the pigs, and mend the fire that they fall not, or I'll both baste and roast you till your eyes drop out like 'em. Leave the bottle behind you, and be curst awhile!

Exit MOONCALF.

QUARLOUS. Body o' the Fair! what's this? mother o' the bawds?

KNOCKEM. No, she mother o' the pigs, sir, mother o' the pigs.

WINWIFE. Mother o' the Furies I think, by her firebrand.

QUARLOUS. Nay, she is too fat to be a Fury, sure, some walking sow of tallow!

WINWIFE. An inspired vessel of kitchen-stuff!

QUARLOUS. She'll make excellent gear for the

coachmakers here in Smithfield to anoint wheels and axletrees with.

URSULA. *Having drunk this while.* Ay, ay, gamesters, mock a plain, plump, soft wench o' the suburbs, do, because she's juicy and wholesome. You must ha' your thin pinched ware, pent up i' the compass of a dog-collar, or 'twill not do; that looks like a long-laced conger set upright, and a green feather, like fennel i' the joll on't.

KNOCKEM. Well said, Urse, my good Urse! to 'em, Urse!

QUARLOUS. Is she your quagmire, Daniel Knockem? is this your bog?

NIGHTINGALE. We shall have a quarrel presently.

KNOCKEM. How! bog? quagmire? foul vapours! humph!

QUARLOUS. Yes, he that would venture for't, I assure him, might sink into her and be drowned a week, ere any friend he had could find where he were.

WINWIFE. And then he would be a fortnight weighing up again.

QUARLOUS. 'Twere like falling into a whole shire of butter; they had need be a team of Dutchmen, should draw him out.

KNOCKEM. Answer 'em, Urse. Where's thy Bartholomew wit now, Urse, thy Bartholomew wit?

URSULA. Hang 'em, rotten, roguy cheaters, I hope to see 'em plagued one day—poxed they are already, I am sure—with lean playhouse poultry, that has the bony rump sticking out like the ace of spades or the point of a partizan, that every rib of 'em is like the tooth of a saw; and will so grate 'em with their hips and shoulders as—take 'em altogether—they were as good lie with a hurdle.

QUARLOUS. Out upon her, how she drips! She's able

to give a man the sweating sickness with looking on her.

URSULA. Marry look off, with a patch o' your face and a dozen i' your breech, though they be o' scarlet, sir! I have seen as fine outsides as either o' yours, bring lousy linings to the brokers, ere now, twice a week.

QUARLOUS. Do you think there may be a fine new cucking-stool i' the Fair, to be purchased? one large enough, I mean? I know there is a pond of capacity for her.

URSULA. For your mother, you rascal! Out you rogue, you hedge-bird, you pimp, you pannier-man's bastard, you!

QUARLOUS. Ha, ha, ha!

URSULA. Do you sneer, you dog's-head, you trendle-tail? You look as you were begotten atop of a cart in harvest time, when the whelp was hot and eager. Go, snuff after your brother's bitch, Mistress Commodity, that's the livery you wear; 'twill be out at the elbows shortly. It's time you went to't for the tother remnant.

KNOCKEM. Peace, Urse, peace, Urse.—They'll kill the poor whale and make oil of her.—Pray thee go in.

URSULA. I'll see 'em poxed first, and piled and double piled.

WINWIFE. Let's away, her language grows greasier than her pigs.

URSULA. Does 't so, snotty-nose? Good Lord! are you snivelling? You were engendered on a she-beggar in a barn, when the bald thrasher, your sire, was scarce warm.

WINWIFE. Pray thee, let's go.

QUARLOUS. No, faith, I'll stay the end of her now. I know she cannot last long; I find by her similes she wanes apace.

URSULA. Does she so? I'll set you gone. Gi' me my pig-pan hither a little. I'll scald you hence, an you will not go.   *Exit.*

KNOCKEM. Gentlemen, these are very strange vapours, and very idle vapours, I assure you.

QUARLOUS. You are a very serious ass, we assure you.

KNOCKEM. Humph! ass? and serious? Nay, then pardon me my vapour. I have a foolish vapour, gentlemen: any man that does vapour me the ass, Master Quarlous——

QUARLOUS. What then, Master Jordan?

KNOCKEM. I do vapour him the lie.

QUARLOUS. Faith, and to any man that vapours me the lie, I do vapour that!

KNOCKEM. Nay then, vapours upon vapours!

They fight.

Re-enter URSULA *with the scalding-pan.*

EDGWORTH, NIGHTINGALE. 'Ware the pan, the pan, the pan! She comes with the pan, gentlemen! URSULA *falls with the pan.* God bless the woman!

URSULA. Oh!   *Exeunt* QUARLOUS *and* WINWIFE.

TRASH. What's the matter?

OVERDO. Goodly woman!

MOONCALF. Mistress!

URSULA. Curse of Hell, that ever I saw these fiends! Oh! I ha' scalded my leg, my leg, my leg, my leg! I ha' lost a limb in the service! Run for some cream and salad oil, quickly. Are you under-peering, you baboon! Rip off my hose, an you be men, men, men!

MOONCALF. Run you for some cream, good Mother Joan. I'll look to your basket.   *Exit* TRASH.

LEATHERHEAD. Best sit up i' your chair, Ursula. Help, gentlemen.

KNOCKEM. Be of good cheer, Urse, thou hast hindered me the currying of a couple of stallions here, that abused the good race-bawd o' Smithfield. 'Twas time for 'em to go.

NIGHTINGALE. I' faith, when the pan came;—they had made you run else.—This had been a fine time for purchase, if you had ventured.

EDGWORTH. Not a whit, these fellows were too fine to carry money.

KNOCKEM. Nightingale, get some help to carry her leg out o' the air; take off her shoes. Body o' me! she has the mallanders, the scratches, the crown scab, and the quitter bone i' the tother leg.

URSULA. Oh, the pox! why do you put me in mind o' my leg thus, to make it prick and shoot? Would you ha' me i' the Hospital afore my time?

KNOCKEM. Patience, Urse, take a good heart, 'tis but a blister as big as a windgall. I'll take it away with the white of an egg, a little honey, and hog's grease. Ha' thy pasterns well rolled, and thou shalt pace again by tomorrow. I'll tend thy booth and look to thy affairs the while. Thou shalt sit i' thy chair, and give directions, and shine Ursa Major.

Exeunt KNOCKEM *and* MOONCALF *with* URSULA *in her chair.*

OVERDO. These are the fruits of bottle-ale and tobacco! the foam of the one, and the fumes of the other! Stay, young man, and despise not the wisdom of these few hairs, that are grown grey in care of thee.

EDGWORTH. Nightingale, stay a little. Indeed I'll hear some o' this!

Enter COKES, WASP, MISTRESS OVERDO, *and* GRACE.

COKES. Come, Numps, come, where are you? Welcome into the Fair, Mistress Grace.

EDGWORTH. —'Slight, he will call company, you shall see, and put us into doings presently.

OVERDO. Thirst not after that frothy liquor, ale; for who knows, when he openeth the stopple, what may be in the bottle? Hath not a snail, a spider, yea, a newt been found there? Thirst not after it, youth, thirst not after it.

COKES. This is a brave fellow, Numps, let's hear him.

WASP. 'Sblood! how brave is he? in a guarded coat? You were best truck with him; e'en strip, and truck presently, it will become you. Why will you hear him? because he is an ass, and may be akin to the Cokeses?

COKES. O, good Numps!

OVERDO. Neither do thou lust after that tawny weed, tobacco.

COKES. Brave words!

OVERDO. Whose complexion is like the Indian's that vents it.

COKES. Are they not brave words, sister?

OVERDO. And who can tell, if, before the gathering and making up thereof, the alligarta hath not pissed thereon?

WASP. 'Heart, let 'em be brave words, as brave as they will! An they were all the brave words in a country, how then? Will you away yet, ha' you enough on him? Mistress Grace, come you away, I pray you, be not you accessory. If you do lose your licence, or somewhat else, sir, with listening to his fables, say Numps is a witch, with all my heart, do, say so.

COKES. Avoid i' your satin doublet, Numps.

OVERDO. The creeping venom of which subtle serpent, as some late writers affirm, neither the cutting of the perilous plant, nor the drying of it, nor the lighting or burning, can any way persway or assuage.

COKES. Good, i' faith! is't not, sister?

OVERDO. Hence it is that the lungs of the tobacconist are rotted, the liver spotted, the brain smoked like the backside of the pig-woman's booth here, and the whole body within, black as her pan you saw e'en now without.

COKES. A fine similitude that, sir! Did you see the pan?

EDGWORTH. Yes, sir.

OVERDO. Nay, the hole in the nose here of some tobacco-takers, or the third nostril—if I may so call it—which makes that they can vent the tobacco out, like the ace of clubs, or rather the flower-de-lice, is caused from the tobacco, the mere tobacco! When the poor innocent pox, having nothing to do there, is miserably and most unconscionably slandered.

COKES. Who would ha' missed this, sister?

MISTRESS OVERDO. Not anybody but Numps.

COKES. He does not understand.

EDGWORTH. *Picks* COKES' *purse.*—Nor you feel.

COKES. What would you have, sister, of a fellow that knows nothing but a basket-hilt, and an old fox in't? The best music i' the Fair will not move a log.

EDGWORTH. —In, to Ursula, Nightingale, and carry her comfort; see it told. This fellow was sent to us by fortune, for our first fairing. *Exit* NIGHTINGALE.

OVERDO. But what speak I of the diseases of the body, children of the Fair?

COKES. That's to us, sister. Brave, i' faith!

OVERDO. Hark, O you sons and daughters of Smithfield! and hear what malady it doth the mind: it causeth swearing, it causeth swaggering, it causeth snuffling and snarling, and now and then a hurt.

MISTRESS OVERDO. He hath something of Master Overdo, methinks, brother.

COKES. So methought, sister, very much of my brother Overdo; and 'tis when he speaks.

OVERDO. Look into any angle o' the town—the Straights, or the Bermudas—where the quarrelling lesson is read, and how do they entertain the time, but with bottle-ale and tobacco? The lecturer is o' one side, and his pupils o' the other; but the seconds are still bottle-ale and tobacco, for which the lecturer reads, and the novices pay. Thirty pound a week in bottle-ale! forty in tobacco! and ten more in ale again. Then, for a suit to drink in, so much; and, that being slavered, so much for another suit; and then a third suit, and a fourth suit! And still the bottle-ale slavereth, and the tobacco stinketh.

WASP. Heart of a madman! are you rooted here? will you never away? What can any man find out in this bawling fellow, to grow here for? He is a full handful higher sin' he heard him. Will you fix here, and set up a booth, sir?

OVERDO. I will conclude briefly——

WASP. Hold your peace, you roaring rascal, I'll run my head i' your chaps else.—You were best build a booth, and entertain him; make your will, an you say the word, and him your heir! Heart, I never knew one taken with a mouth of a peck afore. By this light, I'll carry you away o' my back, an you will not come. *He gets* COKES *up on pick-back.*

COKES. Stay, Numps, stay, set me down! I ha' lost my purse, Numps. O my purse! One o' my fine purses is gone!

MISTRESS OVERDO. Is't indeed, brother?

COKES. Ay, as I am an honest man, would I were an arrant rogue else! A plague of all roguy, damned cutpurses for me.

WASP. Bless 'em with all my heart, with all my heart, do you see? Now, as I am no infidel, that I know of, I am glad on't. Ay, I am,—here's my witness—do you see, sir? I did not tell you of his fables, I! No, no, I am a dull malt-horse, I, I know nothing. Are you not justly served, i' your conscience now? speak i' your conscience. Much good do you with all my heart, and his good heart that has it, with all my heart again!

EDGWORTH. —This fellow is very charitable, would he had a purse, too! But I must not be too bold all at a time.

COKES. Nay, Numps, it is not my best purse.

WASP. Not your best! Death! why should it be your worst? Why should it be any, indeed, at all? answer me to that, gi' me a reason from you, why it should be any?

COKES. Nor my gold, Numps, I ha' that yet. Look here else, sister.

WASP. Why so, there's all the feeling he has!

MISTRESS OVERDO. I pray you have a better care of that, brother.

COKES. Nay, so I will, I warrant you; let him catch this, that catch can. I would fain see him get this, look you here.

WASP. So, so, so, so, so, so, so, so! Very good.

COKES. I would ha' him come again now, and but offer at it. Sister, will you take notice of a good jest? I will put it just where th' other was, and if we ha' good luck, you shall see a delicate fine trap to catch the cutpurse nibbling.

EDGWORTH. —Faith, and he'll try, ere you be out o' the Fair.

COKES. Come, Mistress Grace, pr'ythee be not melancholy for my mischance; sorrow wi' not keep it, sweetheart.

GRACE. I do not think on't, sir.

COKES. 'Twas but a little scurvy white money, hang it! it may hang the cutpurse one day. I ha' gold left to gi' thee a fairing yet, as hard as the world goes. Nothing angers me but that nobody here looked like a cutpurse, unless 'twere Numps.

WASP. How! I? I look like a cutpurse? Death! your sister's a cutpurse! and your mother and father and all your kin were cutpurses! And here is a rogue is the bawd o' the cutpurses, whom I will beat to begin with.

They speak all together, and WASP *beats* OVERDO.

COKES. Numps! Numps!

MISTRESS OVERDO. Good Master Humphrey!

WASP. You are the Patrico, are you? the patriarch of the cutpurses? You share, sir, they say; let them share this with you. Are you i' your hot fit of preaching again? I'll cool you.

OVERDO. Hold thy hand, child of wrath and heir of anger, make it not Childermass Day in thy fury, or the feast of the French Bartholomew, parent of the massacre. Murder, murder, murder!

Exeunt.

ACT THREE

The Fair

LEATHERHEAD, TRASH, *and others, sitting at their stalls before* URSULA's *booth.*

Enter WHIT, HAGGIS, *and* BRISTLE.

WHIT. Nay, tish all gone, now! dish tish, phen tou vilt not be phitin call, Mashter Offisher. Phat ish a man te better to lishen out noishes for tee, and tou art in an oder 'orld, being very shuffishient noishes, and gallantsh too? One o' their brabblesh vould have fed ush all dish fortnight, but tou art so bushy about beggersh still, tou hast no leshure to intend shentlemen, an 't be.

HAGGIS. Why, I told you, Davy Bristle.

BRISTLE. Come, come, you told me a pudding, Toby Haggis, a matter of nothing; I am sure it came to nothing. You said let's go to Ursula's, indeed; but then you met the man with the monsters, and I could not get you from him. An old fool, not leave seeing yet!

HAGGIS. Why, who would ha' thought anybody would ha' quarrelled so early, or that the ale o' the Fair would ha' been up so soon?

WHIT. Phy, phat o' clock tost tou tink it ish, man?

HAGGIS. I cannot tell.

WHIT. Tou art a vishe vatchman, i' te meanteem.

HAGGIS. Why, should the watch go by the clock, or the clock by the watch, I pray?

BRISTLE. One should go by another, if they did well.

WHIT. Tou art right now! Phen didst tou ever know or hear of a shuffishient vatchman, but he did tell te clock, phat bushiness soever he had?

BRISTLE. Nay, that's most true, a sufficient watchman knows what o'clock it is.

WHIT. Shleeping or vaking, ash well as te clock himshelf, or te jack dat shtrikes him!

BRISTLE. Let's inquire of Master Leatherhead, or Joan Trash here.—Master Leatherhead, do you hear, Master Leatherhead?

WHIT. If it be a Ledderhead, tish a very tick Ledderhead, tat sho mush noish vill not piersh him.

LEATHERHEAD. I have a little business now, good friends, do not trouble me.

WHIT. Phat, because o' ty wrought neetcap and ty phelvet sherkin, man? Phy, I have sheen tee in ty ledder sherkin ere now, mashter o' de hobby-horses, as bushy and as shtately as tou sheem'st to be.

TRASH. Why, what an you have, Captain Whit? He has his choice of jerkins, you may see by that, and his caps too, I assure you, when he pleases to be either sick or employed.

LEATHERHEAD. God-a-mercy, Joan, answer for me.

WHIT. Away, be not sheen i' my company; here be shentlemen, and men of vorship.

Exeunt HAGGIS *and* BRISTLE.

Enter QUARLOUS *and* WINWIFE.

QUARLOUS. We had wonderful ill luck, to miss this prologue o' the purse; but the best is, we shall have five acts of him ere night. He'll be spectacle enough, I'll answer for't.

WHIT. O Creesh! Duke Quarlous, how dosht tou? Tou dosht not know me, I fear? I am te vishesht man, but Justish Overdo, in all Bartholomew Fair now. Gi' me twelvepence from tee, I vill help tee to a vife vorth forty marks for't, an't be.

QUARLOUS. Away, rogue; pimp, away.

WHIT. And she shall show tee as fine cut'ork for't in her shmock, too, as tou cansht vish, i' faith. Vilt tou have her, vorshipful Vinvife? I vill help tee to her here, be an't be, in te Pig Quarter, gi' me ty twelvepence from tee.

WINWIFE. Why, there's twelvepence, pray thee wilt thou begone?

WHIT. Tou art a vorthy man, and a vorshipful man still.

QUARLOUS. Get you gone, rascal.

WHIT. I do mean it, man. Prinsh Quarlous, if tou hasht need on me, tou shalt find me here at Ursula's; I vill see phat ale and punk ish i' te pigshty for tee, bless ty good vorship. *Exit.*

QUARLOUS. Look who comes here! John Littlewit!

WINWIFE. And his wife, and my widow, her mother—the whole family.

QUARLOUS. 'Slight, you must gi' 'em all fairings now.

WINWIFE. Not I, I'll not see 'em.

QUARLOUS. They are going a-feasting. What school-master's that, is with 'em?

WINWIFE. That's my rival, I believe, the baker!

Enter BUSY, DAME PURECRAFT, LITTLEWIT, *and*
MISTRESS LITTLEWIT.

BUSY. So, walk on in the middle way, fore-right, turn neither to the right hand nor to the left. Let not your eyes be drawn aside with vanity, nor your ear with noises.

QUARLOUS. O, I know him by that start!

LEATHERHEAD. What do you lack? What do you buy, pretty mistress? a fine hobby-horse, to make your son a tilter? a drum, to make him a soldier? a fiddle, to make him a reveller? What is't you lack? little dogs for your daughters? or babies, male or female?

BUSY. Look not toward them, hearken not. The place is Smithfield, or the field of smiths, the grove of hobby-horses and trinkets; the wares are the wares of devils, and the whole Fair is the shop of Satan! They are hooks and baits, very baits, that are hung out on every side to catch you, and to hold you, as it were, by the gills and by the nostrils, as the fisher doth; therefore you must not look nor turn toward them. The heathen man could top his ears with wax against the harlot o' the sea; do you the like with your fingers against the bells of the Beast.

WINWIFE. What flashes come from him!

QUARLOUS. O, he has those of his oven; a notable hot baker 'twas when he plied the peel. He is leading his flock into the Fair now.

WINWIFE. Rather driving 'em to the pens, for he will let 'em look upon nothing.

Enter KNOCKEM *and* WHIT.

KNOCKEM. Gentlewomen, the weather's hot! whither walk you? Have a care o' your fine velvet caps, the Fair is dusty. Take a sweet, delicate booth, with boughs, here i' the way, and cool yourselves i' the shade, you and your friends. The best pig and bottle-ale i' the Fair, sir. Old Ursula is cook, there you may read it; the pig's head speaks it. Poor soul, she has had a stringhalt, the maryhinchco; but she's prettily amended. LITTLEWIT *is gazing at the sign, which is the Pig's Head, with a large writing under it.*

WHIT. A delicate show-pig, little mistress, with shweet sauce, and crackling, like de bay-leaf i' de fire, la! Tou shalt ha' de clean side o' de table-cloth, and dy glass vashed with phatersh of Dame Annesh Clear.

LITTLEWIT. This 's fine verily. 'Here be the best pigs, and she does roast 'em as well as ever she did,' the Pig's Head says.

KNOCKEM. Excellent, excellent, mistress! with fire o' juniper and rosemary branches! The oracle of the Pig's Head, that, sir.

DAME PURECRAFT. Son, were you not warned of the vanity of the eye? Have you forgot the wholesome admonition so soon?

LITTLEWIT. Good mother, how shall we find a pig, if we do not look about for't! Will it run off o' the spit into our mouths, think you, as in Lubberland, and cry 'wee, wee'?

BUSY. No, but your mother, religiously wise, conceiveth it may offer itself by other means to the sense, as by way of steam, which I think it doth here in this place—huh, huh—yes, it doth. *Scents after it like a hound.* And it were a sin of obstinacy, great obstinacy, high and horrible obstinacy, to decline or resist the good titillation of the famelic sense, which is the smell. Therefore be bold—huh, huh, huh—follow the scent. Enter the tents of the unclean, for once, and satisfy your wife's frailty. Let your frail wife be satisfied; your zealous mother, and my suffering self, will also be satisfied.

LITTLEWIT. Come, Win, as good winny here as go farther and see nothing.

BUSY. We 'scape so much of the other vanities, by our early entering.

DAME PURECRAFT. It is an edifying consideration.

MISTRESS LITTLEWIT. This is scurvy, that we must come into the Fair, and not look on't.

LITTLEWIT. Win, have patience, Win, I'll tell you more anon.

Exeunt LITTLEWIT, MISTRESS LITTLEWIT, DAME PURECRAFT, *and* BUSY.

KNOCKEM. Mooncalf, entertain within there, the best pig i' the booth, a pork-like pig. These are Banbury bloods, o' the sincere stud, come a-pig-hunting. Whit, wait, Whit, look to your charge.

Exit WHIT.

BUSY. *Within.* A pig prepare presently, let a pig be prepared to us.

Enter MOONCALF *and* URSULA.

MOONCALF. 'Slight, who be these?

URSULA. Is this the good service, Jordan, you'd do me?

KNOCKEM. Why, Urse, why, Urse? thou'lt have vapours i' thy leg again presently; pray thee go in, 't may turn to the scratches else.

URSULA. Hang your vapours, they are stale, and stink like you! Are these the guests o' the game you promised to fill my pit withal today?

KNOCKEM. Ay, what ail they, Urse?

URSULA. Ail they! They are all sippers, sippers o' the City; they look as they would not drink off two penn'orth of bottle-ale amongst 'em.

MOONCALF. A body may read that i' their small printed ruffs.

KNOCKEM. Away, thou art a fool, Urse, and thy Mooncalf, too, i' your ignorant vapours now! Hence! good guests, I say, right hypocrites, good gluttons. In, and set a couple o' pigs o' the board, and half a dozen of the biggest bottles afore 'em, and call Whit.

Exit MOONCALF. I do not love to hear innocents abused: fine ambling hypocrites, and a stone-puritan with a sorrel head and beard! good mouthed gluttons, two to a pig, away!

URSULA. Are you sure they are such?

KNOCKEM. O' the right breed, thou shalt try 'em by the teeth, Urse. Where's this Whit?

Re-enter WHIT.

WHIT.
     'Behold, man, and see
     What a worthy man am ee!
     With the fury of my sword,
     And the shaking of my beard,
     I will make ten thousand men afeard.'

KNOCKEM. Well said, brave Whit! In, and fear the ale out o' the bottles into the bellies of the Brethren and the Sisters; drink to the Cause, and pure vapours.   *Exeunt* KNOCKEM, WHIT, *and* URSULA.

QUARLOUS. My roarer is turned tapster, methinks. Now were a fine time for thee, Winwife, to lay aboard thy widow; thou'lt never be master of a better season or place. She that will venture herself into the Fair, and a pig-box, will admit any assault, be assured of that.

WINWIFE. I love not enterprises of that suddenness, though.

QUARLOUS. I'll warrant thee, then, no wife out o' the Widows' Hundred. If I had but as much title to her, as to have breathed once on that straight stomacher of hers, I would now assure myself to carry her yet, ere she went out of Smithfield; or she should carry me, which were the fitter sight, I confess. But you are a modest undertaker, by circumstances and degrees. Come, 'tis disease in thee, not judgment; I should offer at all together.

Enter OVERDO.

Look, here's the poor fool again, that was stung by the Wasp erewhile.

OVERDO. I will make no more orations, shall draw on these tragical conclusions. And I begin now to think that, by a spice of collateral justice, Adam Overdo deserved this beating; for I, the said Adam, was one cause—a by-cause—why the purse was lost; and my wife's brother's purse, too, which they know not of yet. But I shall make very good mirth with it at supper—that will be the sport—and put my little friend Master Humphrey Wasp's choler quite out of countenance; when, sitting at the upper end o' my table, as I use, and drinking to my brother Cokes, and Mistress Alice Overdo, as I will, my wife, for their good affection to old Bradley, I deliver to 'em it was I that was cudgelled, and show 'em the marks. To see what bad events may peep out o' the tail of good purposes! The care I had of that civil young man I took fancy to this morning, and have not left it yet, drew me to that exhortation; which drew the company, indeed; which drew the cut-purse; which drew the money; which drew my brother Cokes's loss; which drew on Wasp's anger; which drew on my beating—a pretty gradation! And they shall ha' it i' their dish, i' faith, at night for fruit; I love to be merry at my table. I had thought once, at one special blow he ga' me, to have revealed myself; but then—I thank thee, fortitude—I remembered that a wise man, and who is ever so great a part o' the commonwealth in himself, for no particular disaster ought to abandon a public good design. The husbandman ought not, for one unthankful year, to forsake the plough; the shepherd ought not, for one scabbed sheep, to throw by his tar-box; the pilot ought not, for one leak i' the poop, to quit the helm; nor the alderman ought not, for one custard more at a meal, to give up his cloak; the constable ought not to break his staff and forswear the watch, for one roaring night; nor the piper o' the parish—'ut parvis componere magna solebam' —to put up his pipes, for one rainy Sunday. These are certain knocking conclusions; out of which I am resolved, come what come can, come beating, come imprisonment, come infamy, come banishment, nay, come the rack, come the hurdle,—welcome all—I will not discover who I am, till my due time; and yet still, all shall be, as I said ever, in justice' name and the King's, and for the commonwealth.

WINWIFE. What does he talk to himself, and act so seriously, poor fool?

QUARLOUS. No matter what. Here's fresher argument, intend that.

Enter COKES, MISTRESS OVERDO, *and* GRACE WELLBORN, *followed by* WASP, *loaded with toys.*

COKES. Come, Mistress Grace, come, sister, here's more fine sights yet, i' faith. God's lid, where's Numps?

LEATHERHEAD. What do you lack, gentlemen? What is't you buy? Fine rattles, drums, babies, little dogs, and birds for ladies? What do you lack?

COKES. Good honest Numps, keep afore; I am so afraid thou'lt lose somewhat. My heart was at my mouth when I missed thee.

WASP. You were best buy a whip i' your hand to drive me.

COKES. Nay, do not mistake, Numps, thou art so apt to mistake. I would but watch the goods. Look you now, the treble fiddle was e'en almost like to be lost.

WASP. Pray you take heed you lose not yourself;
your best way were e'en get up and ride for more
surety. Buy a token's worth of great pins, to fasten
yourself to my shoulder.

LEATHERHEAD. What do you lack, gentlemen? fine
purses, pouches, pin-cases, pipes? What is't you lack?
a pair o' smiths to wake you i' the morning? or a
fine whistling bird?

COKES. Numps, here be finer things than any we
ha' bought, by odds! and more delicate horses, a
great deal! Good Numps, stay, and come hither.

WASP. Will you scourse with him? You are in
Smithfield, you may fit yourself with a fine, easy-
going street-nag for your saddle, again' Michaelmas
term, do. Has he ne'er a little odd cart for you to
make a caroch on i' the country, with four pied
hobby-horses? Why the measles should you stand
here, with your train, cheaping of dogs, birds, and
babies? You ha' no children to bestow 'em on, ha'
you?

COKES. No, but again' I ha' children, Numps,
that's all one.

WASP. Do, do, do, do; how many shall you have,
think you? An I were as you, I'd buy for all my
tenants, too; they are a kind o' civil savages, that
will part with their children for rattles, pipes, and
knives. You were best buy a hatchet or two, and
truck with 'em.

COKES. Good Numps, hold that little tongue o'
thine, and save it a labour. I am resolute Bat, thou
know'st.

WASP. A resolute fool you are, I know, and a very
sufficient coxcomb, with all my heart! Nay, you
have it, sir, an you be angry: turd i' your teeth,
twice, if I said it not once afore, and much good do
you.

WINWIFE. —Was there ever such a self-affliction, and so impertinent?

QUARLOUS. Alas, his care will go near to crack him; let's in and comfort him.

WASP. Would I had been set i' the ground, all but the head on me, and had my brains bowled at, or threshed out, when first I underwent this plague of a charge!

QUARLOUS. How now, Numps! almost tired i' your protectorship? overparted, overparted?

WASP. Why, I cannot tell, sir, it may be I am; does't grieve you?

QUARLOUS. No, I swear does't not, Numps, to satisfy you.

WASP. Numps! 'Sblood, you are fine and familiar! How long ha' we been acquainted, I pray you!

QUARLOUS. I think it may be remembered, Numps, that: 'twas since morning, sure.

WASP. Why, I hope I know't well enough, sir, I did not ask to be told.

QUARLOUS. No! why, then?

WASP. It's no matter why, you see with your eyes now what I said to you today? you'll believe me another time?

QUARLOUS. Are you removing the Fair, Numps?

WASP. A pretty question, and a very civil one! Yes, faith, I ha' my lading, you see, or shall have anon; you may know whose beast I am, by my burden. If the pannier-man's jack were ever better known by his loins of mutton, I'll be flayed, and feed dogs for him when his time comes.

WINWIFE. How melancholy Mistress Grace is yonder! Pray thee let's go enter ourselves in grace with her.

COKES. Those six horses, friend, I'll have——

WASP. How!

COKES. And the three Jew's-trumps; and half a dozen o' birds, and that drum—I have one drum already—and your smiths; I like that device o' your smiths, very pretty well; and four halberds——and, le' me see, that fine painted great lady, and her three women for state, I'll have.

WASP. No, the shop; buy the whole shop, it will be best, the shop, the shop!

LEATHERHEAD. If his worship please.

WASP. Yes, and keep it during the Fair, Bobchin.

COKES. Peace, Numps.—Friend, do not meddle with him, an you be wise, and would show your head above board; he will sting thorough your wrought nightcap, believe me. A set of these violins I would buy, too, for a delicate young noise I have i' the country, that are every one a size less than another, just like your fiddles. I would fain have a fine young masque at my marriage, now I think on't. But I do want such a number o' things! And Numps will not help me now, and I dare not speak to him.

TRASH. Will your worship buy any gingerbread, very good bread, comfortable bread?

COKES. Gingerbread! yes, let's see.

Runs to her shop.

WASP. There's the tother springe.

LEATHERHEAD. Is this well, Goody Joan, to interrupt my market in the midst, and call away my customers? Can you answer this at the Pie-powders?

TRASH. Why, if his Mastership has a mind to buy, I hope my ware lies as open as another's. I may show my ware, as well as you yours.

COKES. Hold your peace, I'll content you both: I'll buy up his shop, and thy basket.

WASP. Will you, i' faith?

LEATHERHEAD. Why should you put him from it, friend?

WASP. Cry you mercy! you'd be sold, too, would you? What's the price on you, jerkin and all, as you stand? Ha' you any qualities?

TRASH. Yes, Goodman Angry-Man, you shall find he has qualities, if you cheapen him.

WASP. God's so', you ha' the selling of him! What are they? will they be bought for love or money?

TRASH. No indeed, sir.

WASP. For what then, victuals?

TRASH. He scorns victuals, sir, he has bread and butter at home, thanks be to God! and yet he will do more for a good meal, if the toy take him i' the belly. Marry, then they must not set him at lower end; if they do, he'll go away, though he fast. But put him atop o' the table, where his place is, and he'll do you forty fine things. He has not been sent for and sought out for nothing, at your great City suppers, to put down Coryat and Cokely; and been laughed at for his labour. He'll play you all the puppets i' the town over, and the players, every company, and his own company too; he spares nobody!

COKES. I' faith?

TRASH. He was the first, sir, that ever baited the fellow i' the bear's skin, an't like your worship. No dog ever came near him since. And for fine motions!

COKES. Is he good at those, too? Can he set out a masque, trow?

TRASH. O Lord, master! sought to, far and near, for his inventions; and he engrosses all, he makes all the puppets i' the Fair.

COKES. Dost thou, in troth, old velvet jerkin? Give me thy hand.

TRASH. Nay, sir, you shall see him in his velvet jerkin, and a scarf too, at night, when you hear him interpret Master Littlewit's motion.

COKES. Speak no more, but shut up shop presently,

friend. I'll buy both it and thee too, to carry down
with me, and her hamper beside. Thy shop shall
furnish out the masque, and hers the banquet. I cannot go less, to set out anything with credit. What's
the price, at a word, o' thy whole shop, case and all
as it stands?

LEATHERHEAD. Sir, it stands me in six-and-twenty
shillings sevenpence halfpenny, besides three shillings for my ground.

COKES. Well, thirty shillings will do all then!—
And what comes yours to?

TRASH. Four shillings and elevenpence, sir, ground
and all, an't like your worship.

COKES. Yes, it does like my worship very well, poor
woman; that's five shillings more. What a masque
shall I furnish out, for forty shillings—twenty pound
Scotch! And a banquet of gingerbread, there's a
stately thing! Numps! Sister! And my wedding
gloves too—that I never thought on afore. All my
wedding gloves gingerbread? O me, what a device
will there be, to make 'em eat their fingers' ends!
And delicate brooches for the bride-men and all!
And then I'll ha' this poesy put to 'em: 'For the best
grace,' meaning Mistress Grace, my wedding poesy.

GRACE. I am beholden to you, sir, and to your
Bartholomew wit.

WASP. You do not mean this, do you? Is this your
first purchase?

COKES. Yes, faith, and I do not think, Numps, but
thou'lt say it was the wisest act that ever I did in
my wardship.

WASP. Like enough! I shall say anything, I!

Enter EDGWORTH, NIGHTINGALE, *and others, followed
by* OVERDO.

OVERDO. —I cannot beget a project, with all my
political brain yet: my project is how to fetch off

this proper young man from his debauched company. I have followed him all the Fair over, and still I find him with this songster; and I begin shrewdly to suspect their familiarity, and the young man of a terrible taint, poetry! with which idle disease if he be infected, there's no hope of him, in a state course. 'Actum est' of him for a commonwealth's-man, if he go to't in rhyme once.

EDGWORTH. —Yonder he is buying o' gingerbread; set in quickly, before he part with too much on his money.

NIGHTINGALE. 'My masters and friends and good people, draw near——'

COKES. Ballads! hark! hark! Pray thee, fellow, stay a little! Good Numps, look to the goods. *Runs to* NIGHTINGALE. What ballads hast thou? Let me see, let me see, myself.

WASP. Why so! he's flown to another lime-bush; there he will flutter as long more, till he ha' ne'er a feather left. Is there a vexation like this, gentlemen? Will you believe me now, hereafter, shall I have credit with you?

QUARLOUS. Yes, faith, shalt thou, Numps, and thou art worthy on't, for thou sweatest for't. I never saw a young pimp-errant and his squire better matched.

WINWIFE. Faith, the sister comes after 'em well, too.

GRACE. Nay, if you saw the Justice her husband, my guardian, you were fitted for the mess, he is such a wise one his way——

WINWIFE. I wonder we see him not here.

GRACE. O, he is too serious for this place; and yet better sport than the other three, I assure you, gentlemen, where'er he is, though 't be o' the bench.

COKES. How dost thou call it? 'A Caveat against Cutpurses'! A good jest, i' faith! I would fain see that demon, your cutpurse you talk of, that delicate-handed devil. They say he walks hereabout; I would see him walk now. Look you, sister, here, here—*Shows his purse boastingly*—let him come, sister, and welcome. Ballad-man, does any cutpurse haunt hereabout? Pray thee raise me one or two; begin, and show me one.

NIGHTINGALE. Sir, this is a spell against 'em, spick and span new; and 'tis made as 'twere in mine own person, and I sing it in mine own defence. But 'twill cost a penny alone, if you buy it.

COKES. No matter for the price; thou dost not know me, I see; I am an odd Bartholomew.

MISTRESS OVERDO. Has't a fine picture, brother?

COKES. O, sister, do you remember the ballads over the nursery chimney at home, o' my own pasting up? There be brave pictures, other manner of pictures than these, friend.

WASP. Yet these will serve to pick the pictures out o' your pockets, you shall see.

COKES. So I heard 'em say. Pray thee mind him not, fellow; he'll have an oar in everything.

NIGHTINGALE. It was intended, sir, as if a purse should chance to be cut in my presence, now, I may be blameless though; as by the sequel will more plainly appear.

COKES. We shall find that i' the matter. Pray thee begin.

NIGHTINGALE. To the tune of 'Packington's Pound,' sir.

COKES. 'Fa, la la la, la la la, fa la la la!' Nay, I'll put thee in tune and all! Mine own country dance! Pray thee begin.

NIGHTINGALE. It is a gentle admonition, you must know, sir, both to the purse-cutter and the purse-bearer.

COKES. Not a word more out o' the tune, an thou lov'st me: 'Fa, la la la, la la la, fa la la la.' Come, when?

NIGHTINGALE. 'My masters and friends and good
    people, draw near,
And look to your purses, for that I do say—'

COKES. Ha, ha, this chimes! Good counsel at first dash.

NIGHTINGALE. 'And though little money in them
    you do bear,
It cost more to get, than to lose in a day.'

COKES. Good!

NIGHTINGALE.
               'You oft have been told,
                 Both the young and the old,
And bidden beware of the cutpurse so bold.'

COKES. Well said! he were to blame that would not, i' faith.

NIGHTINGALE. 'Then if you take heed not, free me
    from the curse,
Who both give you warning, for and the cutpurse.
Youth, youth, thou hadst better been starved by thy
    nurse,
Than live to be hangèd for cutting a purse.'

COKES. Good, i' faith! How say you, Numps, is there any harm i' this?

NIGHTINGALE. 'It hath been upbraided to men of
    my trade,
That oftentimes we are the cause of this crime—'

COKES. The more coxcombs they that did it, I wuss.

NIGHTINGALE. 'Alack and for pity, why should it
    be said?
As if they regarded or places or time!
                 Examples have been
                 Of some that were seen
In Westminster Hall, yea, the pleaders between;

Then why should the judges be free from this curse,
More than my poor self, for cutting the purse?'

COKES. God-a-mercy for that! Why should they be
more free, indeed?

NIGHTINGALE. 'Youth, youth, thou hadst better
    been starved by thy nurse,
Than live to be hangèd for cutting a purse.'

COKES. That again, good ballad-man, that again.
Sings the burden with NIGHTINGALE. O rare!—I
would fain rub mine elbow now, but I dare not
pull out my hand.—On, I pray thee; he that made
this ballad shall be poet to my masque.

NIGHTINGALE. 'At Worcester, 'tis known well, and
    even i' the jail,
A knight of good worship did there show his face,
Against the foul sinners, in zeal for to rail,
And lost, ipso facto, his purse in the place.'

COKES. Is it possible?

NIGHTINGALE.

        'Nay, once from the seat
        Of judgment so great,
A judge there did lose a fair pouch of velvete.'

COKES. I' faith?

NIGHTINGALE. 'O Lord, for thy mercy, how wicked
    or worse
Are those that so venture their necks for a purse!
Youth, youth, thou hadst better been starved by thy
    nurse,
Than live to be hangèd for cutting a purse.'

COKES. 'Youth, youth, &c.' Pray thee stay a little,
friend.—Yet o' thy conscience, Numps, speak, is there
any harm i' this?

WASP. To tell you true, 'tis too good for you, 'less
you had grace to follow it.

OVERDO. —It doth discover enormity, I'll mark it

more. I ha' not liked a paltry piece of poetry so well a good while.

COKES. 'Youth, youth, &c.' Where's this youth now? A man must call upon him for his own good, and yet he will not appear. Look here, here's for him! *Shows his purse.* Handy-dandy, which hand will he have? On, I pray thee, with the rest; I do hear of him, but I cannot see him, this Master Youth the cutpurse.

NIGHTINGALE. 'At plays, and at sermons, and at the
    sessions,
'Tis daily their practice such booty to make;
Yea, under the gallows at executions,
They stick not the stare-abouts' purses to take;
        Nay, one without grace,
        At a better place,
At court, and in Christmas, before the King's face.'

COKES. That was a fine fellow! I would have him now.

NIGHTINGALE. 'Alack, then, for pity, must I bear
    the curse
That only belongs to the cunning cutpurse?'

COKES. But where's their cunning now, when they should use it? they are all chained now, I warrant you. 'Youth, youth, thou hadst better, &c.'—The rat-catchers' charms are all fools and asses to this! A pox on 'em, that they will not come! That a man should have such a desire to a thing, and want it!

QUARLOUS. —'Fore God, I'd give half the Fair, an 'twere mine, for a cutpurse for him, to save his longing.

COKES. Look you, sister! *Shows his purse again.* Here, here, where is't now? which pocket is't in, for a wager?

WASP. I beseech you leave your wagers, and let him end his matter, an't may be.

COKES. O, are you edified, Numps?

OVERDO. —Indeed he does interrupt him too much. There Numps spoke to purpose.

NIGHTINGALE. 'Youth, youth, thou hadst better been starved by thy nurse,
Than live to be hangèd for cutting a purse.'

COKES. Sister, I am an ass, I cannot keep my purse! *Shows it again.* On, on, I pray thee, friend.

EDGWORTH *gets up to* COKES *and tickles him in the ear with a straw twice to draw his hand out of his pocket.*

NIGHTINGALE. 'But O, you vile nation of cutpurses all,
Relent and repent, and amend and be sound,
And know that you ought not, by honest men's fall,
Advance your own fortunes, to die above ground.'

WINWIFE. —Will you see sport? Look, there's a fellow gathers up to him, mark.

QUARLOUS. Good, i' faith! O, he has lighted on the wrong pocket.

WINWIFE. He has it! 'Fore God, he is a brave fellow; pity he should be detected.

NIGHTINGALE. 'And though you go gay,
　　　　　In silks, as you may,
It is not the highway to Heaven, as they say.
Repent then, repent you, for better, for worse,
And kiss not the gallows for cutting a purse.
Youth, youth, thou hadst better been starved by thy nurse,
Than live to be hangèd for cutting a purse.'

ALL. An excellent ballad! an excellent ballad!

EDGWORTH. Friend, let me ha' the first, let me ha' the first, I pray you.

COKES. Pardon me, sir, first come first served; and I'll buy the whole bundle too.

WINWIFE. —That conveyance was better than all,

did you see't? He has given the purse to the ballad-singer.

QUARLOUS. Has he?

EDGWORTH. Sir, I cry you mercy, I'll not hinder the poor man's profit. Pray you, mistake me not.

COKES. Sir, I take you for an honest gentleman, if that be mistaking; I met you today afore. Ha! humph! O God! my purse is gone, my purse, my purse, &c.!

WASP. Come, do not make a stir, and cry yourself an ass thorough the Fair afore your time.

COKES. Why, has thou it, Numps? Good Numps, how came you by it, I mar'l?

WASP. I pray you seek some other gamester to play the fool with. You may lose it time enough, for all your Fair wit.

COKES. By this good hand, glove and all, I ha' lost it already, if thou hast it not; feel else, and Mistress Grace's handkercher too, out o' the tother pocket.

WASP. Why, 'tis well, very well, exceeding pretty and well.

EDGWORTH. Are you sure you ha' lost it, sir?

COKES. O God, yes! As I am an honest man, I had it but e'en now, at 'Youth, youth.'

NIGHTINGALE. I hope you suspect not me, sir?

EDGWORTH. Thee? that were a jest indeed! Dost thou think the gentleman is foolish? Where hadst thou hands, I pray thee?—Away, ass, away!

Exit NIGHTINGALE.

OVERDO. —I shall be beaten again if I be spied.

EDGWORTH. Sir, I suspect an odd fellow, yonder, is stealing away.

MISTRESS OVERDO. Brother, it is the preaching fellow! you shall suspect him. He was at your tother purse, you know!—Nay, stay, sir, and view the work you ha' done; an you be beneficed at the gallows, and preach there, thank your own handiwork.

COKES. Sir, you shall take no pride in your preferment; you shall be silenced quickly.

OVERDO. What do you mean, sweet buds of gentility?

COKES. To ha' my pennyworths out on you, bud. No less than two purses a day serve you? I thought you a simple fellow, when my man Numps beat you, i' the morning, and pitied you—

MISTRESS OVERDO. So did I, I'll be sworn, brother; but now I see he is a lewd and pernicious enormity, as Master Overdo calls him.

OVERDO. —Mine own words turned upon me, like swords.

COKES. Cannot a man's purse be at quiet for you, i' the master's pocket, but you must entice it forth and debauch it? _OVERDO is carried off._

WASP. Sir, sir, keep your debauch and your fine Bartholomew terms to yourself, and make as much on 'em as you please. But gi' me this from you i' the meantime, I beseech you, see if I can look to this.

COKES. Why, Numps?

WASP. Why? because you are an ass, sir, there's a reason the shortest way, an you will needs ha' it. Now you ha' got the trick of losing, you'd lose your breech an 'twere loose. I know you, sir, come, deliver. _Takes the licence from_ COKES. You'll go and crack the vermin you breed now, will you? 'tis very fine! Will you ha' the truth on't? they are such retchless flies as you are, that blow cutpurses abroad in every corner; your foolish having of money makes 'em. An there were no wiser than I, sir, the trade should lie open for you, sir, it should, i' faith, sir. I would teach your wit to come to your head, sir, as well as your land to come into your hand, I assure you, sir.

WINWIFE. Alack, good Numps!

WASP. Nay, gentlemen, never pity me, I am not worth it. Lord send me at home once to Harrow o' the Hill again; if I travel any more, call me Coryat, with all my heart.

Exeunt WASP, COKES, *and* MISTRESS OVERDO, *followed by* EDGWORTH.

QUARLOUS. Stay, sir, I must have a word with you in private. Do you hear?

EDGWORTH. With me, sir! What's your pleasure, good sir?

QUARLOUS. Do not deny it, you are a cutpurse, sir. This gentleman here and I saw you. Nor do we mean to detect you, though we can sufficiently inform ourselves toward the danger of concealing you; but you must do us a piece of service.

EDGWORTH. Good gentlemen, do not undo me; I am a civil young man, and but a beginner indeed.

QUARLOUS. Sir, your beginning shall bring on your ending for us. We are no catchpoles nor constables. That you are to undertake is this: you saw the old fellow with the black box here?

EDGWORTH. The little old governor, sir?

QUARLOUS. That same, I see you have flown him to a mark already. I would ha' you get away that box from him, and bring it us.

EDGWORTH. Would you ha' the box and all, sir, or only that that is in't? I'll get you that, and leave him the box to play with still—which will be the harder o' the two—because I would gain your worship's good opinion of me.

WINWIFE. He says well, 'tis the greater mastery, and 'twill make the more sport when 'tis missed.

EDGWORTH. Ay, and 'twill be the longer a-missing, to draw on the sport.

QUARLOUS. But look you do it, now, sirrah, and keep your word, or——

EDGWORTH. Sir, if ever I break my word with a gentleman, may I never read word at my need. Where shall I find you?

QUARLOUS. Some where i' the Fair, hereabouts. Dispatch it quickly. *Exit* EDGEWORTH. I would fain see the careful fool deluded! Of all beasts, I love the serious ass: he that takes pains to be one, and plays the fool with the greatest diligence that can be.

GRACE. Then you would not choose, sir, but love my guardian, Justice Overdo, who is answerable to that description in every hair of him.

QUARLOUS. So I have heard. But how came you, Mistress Wellborn, to be his ward, or have relation to him at first?

GRACE. Faith, through a common calamity: he bought me, sir. And now he will marry me to his wife's brother, this wise gentleman that you see, or else I must pay value o' my land.

QUARLOUS. 'Slid, is there no device of disparagement, or so? Talk with some crafty fellow, some picklock o' the law. Would I had studied a year longer i' the Inns of Court, an 't had been but i' your case!

WINWIFE. —Ay, Master Quarlous, are you proffering?

GRACE. You'd bring but little aid, sir.

WINWIFE. I'll look to you, i' faith, gamester.—An unfortunate foolish tribe you are fall'n into, lady, I wonder you can endure 'em.

GRACE. Sir, they that cannot work their fetters off, must wear 'em.

WINWIFE. You see what care they have on you, to leave you thus.

GRACE. Faith, the same they have of themselves,

sir. I cannot greatly complain if this were all the plea I had against 'em.

WINWIFE. 'Tis true. But will you please to withdraw with us a little, and make them think they have lost you. I hope our manners ha' been such, hitherto, and our language, as will give you no cause to doubt yourself in our company.

GRACE. Sir, I will give myself no cause. I am so secure of mine own manners, as I suspect not yours.

QUARLOUS. Look where John Littlewit comes.

WINWIFE. Away, I'll not be seen by him.

QUARLOUS. No, you were not best; he'd tell his mother, the widow.

WINWIFE. Heart, what do you mean?

QUARLOUS. Cry you mercy, is the wind there? must not the widow be named?　　　　　*Exeunt.*

Enter LITTLEWIT *followed by* MISTRESS LITTLEWIT.

LITTLEWIT. Do you hear, Win, Win?

MISTRESS LITTLEWIT. What say you, John?

LITTLEWIT. While they are paying the reckoning, Win, I'll tell you a thing, Win: we shall never see any sights i' the Fair, Win, except you long still, Win. Good Win, sweet Win, long to see some hobby-horses, and some drums, and rattles, and dogs, and fine devices, Win. The bull with the five legs, Win, and the great hog. Now you ha' begun with pig, you may long for anything, Win, and so for my motion, Win.

MISTRESS LITTLEWIT. But we sha'nt eat o' the bull and the hog, John; how shall I long, then?

LITTLEWIT. O yes, Win! you may long to see as well as to taste, Win. How did the 'pothecary's wife, Win, that longed to see the anatomy, Win? or the lady, Win, that desired to spit i' the great lawyer's

mouth, after an eloquent pleading? I assure you,
they longed, Win; good Win, go in and long.

   Exeunt LITTLEWIT *and* MISTRESS LITTLEWIT.

TRASH. I think we are rid of our new customer,
brother Leatherhead, we shall hear no more of him.

LEATHERHEAD. All the better, let's pack up all and
be gone, before he find us. *They plot to be gone.*

TRASH. Stay a little, yonder comes a company. It
may be we may take some more money.

Enter KNOCKEM *and* BUSY.

KNOCKEM. Sir, I will take your counsel, and cut
my hair, and leave vapours. I see that tobacco, and
bottle-ale, and pig, and Whit, and very Ursula herself, is all vanity.

BUSY. Only pig was not comprehended in my
admonition; the rest were. For long hair, it is an
ensign of pride, a banner; and the world is full of
those banners, very full of banners. And bottle-ale
is the drink of Satan's, a diet-drink of Satan's, devised to puff us up, and make us swell in this later
stage of vanity; as the smoke of tobacco, to keep us
in mist and error. But the fleshly woman, which you
call Ursula, is above all to be avoided, having the
marks upon her of the three enemies of man: the
world, as being in the Fair; the devil, as being in
the fire; and the flesh, as being herself.

Enter DAME PURECRAFT.

DAME PURECRAFT. Brother Zeal-of-the-Land! what
shall we do? My daughter Win-the-Fight is fall'n into
her fit of longing again.

BUSY. For more pig? There is no more, is there?

DAME PURECRAFT. To see some sights i' the Fair.

BUSY. Sister, let her fly the impurity of the place

swiftly, lest she partake of the pitch thereof. Thou art the seat of the beast, O Smithfield, and I will leave thee! Idolatry peepeth out on every side of thee.

KNOCKEM. —An excellent right hypocrite! now his belly is full, he falls a-railing and kicking, the jade. A very good vapour! I'll in, and joy Ursula with telling how her pig works; two and a half he eat to his share, and he has drunk a pailful. He eats with his eyes, as well as his teeth.   *Exit.*

LEATHERHEAD. What do you lack, gentlemen? What is't you buy? Rattles, drums, babies——

BUSY. Peace, with thy apocryphal wares, thou profane publican; thy bells, thy dragons, and thy Toby's dogs. Thy hobby-horse is an idol, a very idol, a fierce and rank idol; and thou the Nebuchadnezzar, the proud Nebuchadnezzar of the Fair, that sett'st it up, for children to fall down to, and worship.

LEATHERHEAD. Cry you mercy, sir, will you buy a fiddle to fill up your noise?

Re-enter LITTLEWIT *and* MISTRESS LITTLEWIT.

LITTLEWIT. Look, Win, do, look o' God's name, and save your longing. Here be fine sights.

DAME PURECRAFT. Ay, child, so you hate 'em, as our brother Zeal does, you may look on 'em.

LEATHERHEAD. Or what do you say to a drum, sir?

BUSY. It is the broken belly of the Beast, and thy bellows there are his lungs, and these pipes are his throat, those feathers are of his tail, and thy rattles the gnashing of his teeth.

TRASH. And what's my gingerbread, I pray you?

BUSY. The provender that pricks him up. Hence with thy basket of popery, thy nest of images, and whole legend of ginger-work.

LEATHERHEAD. Sir, if you be not quiet the quicklier, I'll ha' you clapped fairly by the heels, for disturbing the Fair.

BUSY. The sin of the Fair provokes me; I cannot be silent.

DAME PURECRAFT. Good brother Zeal!

LEATHERHEAD. Sir, I'll make you silent, believe it.

LITTLEWIT. —I'd give a shilling you could, i' faith, friend.

LEATHERHEAD. Sir, give me your shilling; I'll give you my shop, if I do not, and I'll leave it in pawn with you i' the meantime.

LITTLEWIT. A match, i' faith, but do it quickly then.   *Exit* LEATHERHEAD.

BUSY. *To* DAME PURECRAFT. Hinder me not, woman. I was moved in spirit, to be here this day, in this Fair, this wicked and foul Fair—and fitter may it be called a Foul than a Fair—to protest against the abuses of it, the foul abuses of it, in regard of the afflicted Saints, that are troubled, very much troubled, exceedingly troubled, with the opening of the merchandise of Babylon again, and the peeping of popery upon the stalls here, here, in the high places. See you not Goldylocks, the purple strumpet there, in her yellow gown and green sleeves? the profane pipes, the tinkling timbrels? A shop of relics!

LITTLEWIT. Pray you forbear, I am put in trust with 'em.

BUSY. And this idolatrous grove of images, this flasket of idols, which I will pull down——

                              Overthrows the gingerbread.

TRASH. O my ware, my ware! God bless it!

BUSY. In my zeal, and glory to be thus exercised.

Re-enter LEATHERHEAD *with Officers.*

LEATHERHEAD. Here he is, pray you lay hold on his zeal. We cannot sell a whistle, for him, in tune. Stop his noise first.

BUSY. Thou canst not, 'tis a sanctified noise. I will make a loud and most strong noise, till I have daunted the profane enemy. And for this cause——

LEATHERHEAD. Sir, here's no man afraid of you, or your cause. You shall swear it i' the stocks, sir.

BUSY. I will thrust myself into the stocks, upon the pikes of the land.

LEATHERHEAD. Carry him away.

DAME PURECRAFT. What do you mean, wicked men?

BUSY. Let them alone, I fear them not.

Exeunt Officers with BUSY, *followed by* DAME PURECRAFT.

LITTLEWIT. Was not this shilling well ventured, Win, for our liberty? Now we may go play, and see over the Fair, where we list ourselves. My mother is gone after him, and let her e'en go, and lose us.

MISTRESS LITTLEWIT. Yes, John, but I know not what to do.

LITTLEWIT. For what, Win?

MISTRESS LITTLEWIT. For a thing I am ashamed to tell you, i' faith; and 'tis too far to go home.

LITTLEWIT. I pray thee be not ashamed, Win. Come, i' faith, thou shalt not be ashamed. Is it any-thing about the hobby-horse man? an't be, speak freely.

MISTRESS LITTLEWIT. Hang him, base Bobchin, I scorn him. No, I have very great what-sha-call-um, John.

LITTLEWIT. O, is that all, Win? We'll go back to Captain Jordan, to the pig-woman's, Win. He'll help us, or she, with a dripping-pan, or an old kettle, or something. The poor greasy soul loves you, Win. And after, we'll visit the Fair all over, Win, and see my puppet-play, Win, you know it's a fine matter, Win. *Exeunt* LITTLEWIT *and* MISTRESS LITTLEWIT.

LEATHERHEAD. Let's away, I counselled you to pack up afore, Joan.

TRASH. A pox of his Bedlam purity, he has spoiled half my ware! But the best is, we lose nothing if we miss our first merchant.

LEATHERHEAD. It shall be hard for him to find or know us, when we are translated, Joan. *Exeunt.*

ACT FOUR. SCENE ONE

The stocks in the Fair

Enter BRISTLE *and* HAGGIS, *with* OVERDO, *followed by* COKES *and* TROUBLEALL.

TROUBLEALL. My masters, I do make no doubt but you are officers.

BRISTLE. What then, sir?

TROUBLEALL. And the King's loving and obedient subjects.

BRISTLE. Obedient, friend? take heed what you speak, I advise you; Oliver Bristle advises you. His loving subjects, we grant you, but not his obedient, at this time, by your leave. We know ourselves a little better than so. We are to command, sir, and such as you are to be obedient. Here's one of his obedient subjects going to the stocks; and we'll make you such another, if you talk.

TROUBLEALL. You are all wise enough i' your places, I know.

BRISTLE. If you know it, sir, why do you bring it in question?

TROUBLEALL. I question nothing, pardon me. I do only hope you have warrant for what you do, and so quit you, and so multiply you.   *Exit.*

HAGGIS. What's he?—Bring him up to the stocks there. Why bring you him not up?

Re-enter TROUBLEALL.

TROUBLEALL. If you have Justice Overdo's warrant, 'tis well; you are safe. That is the warrant of warrants. I'll not give this button for any man's warrant else.

BRISTLE. Like enough, sir, but let me tell you, an you play away your buttons thus, you will want 'em ere night, for any store I see about you. You might keep 'em, and save pins, I wuss.   *Exit* TROUBLEALL.

OVERDO. —What should he be, that doth so esteem and advance my warrant? He seems a sober and discreet person! It is a comfort to a good conscience to be followed with a good fame in his sufferings. The world will have a pretty taste by this, how I can bear adversity; and it will beget a kind of reverence toward me hereafter, even from mine enemies, when they shall see I carry my calamity nobly, and that it doth neither break me nor bend me.

HAGGIS. Come, sir, here's a place for you to preach in. Will you put in your leg?

OVERDO. That I will, cheerfully.

They put him in the stocks.

BRISTLE. O' my conscience, a Seminary! he kisses the stocks.

COKES. Well, my masters, I'll leave him with you. Now I see him bestowed, I'll go look for my goods, and Numps.

HAGGIS. You may, sir, I warrant you. Where's the t'other bawler? Fetch him too, you shall find 'em both fast enough. *Exit* COKES.

OVERDO. —In the midst of this tumult, I will yet be the author of mine own rest; and, not minding their fury, sit in the stocks in that calm as shall be able to trouble a triumph.

Re-enter TROUBLEALL.

TROUBLEALL. Do you assure me upon your words? May I undertake for you, if I be asked the question, that you have this warrant?

HAGGIS. What's this fellow, for God's sake?

TROUBLEALL. Do but show me Adam Overdo, and I am satisfied. *Exit.*

BRISTLE. He is a fellow that is distracted, they say, one Troubleall. He was an officer in the Court of Pie-powders here last year, and put out on his place by Justice Overdo.

OVERDO. —Ha!

BRISTLE. Upon which he took an idle conceit, and's run mad upon't, so that ever since he will do nothing but by Justice Overdo's warrant. He will not eat a crust, nor drink a little, nor make him in his apparel ready. His wife—sir reverence—cannot get him make his water, or shift his shirt, without his warrant.

OVERDO. —If this be true, this is my greatest disaster! How am I bound to satisfy this poor man, that is of so good a nature to me, out of his wits, where there is no room left for dissembling!

Re-enter TROUBLEALL.

TROUBLEALL. If you cannot show me Adam Overdo, I am in doubt of you. I am afraid you cannot answer it. *Exit.*

HAGGIS. Before me, neighbour Bristle, and now I think on't better, Justice Overdo is a very parantory person.

BRISTLE. O, are you advised of that? and a severe justicer, by your leave.

OVERDO. Do I hear ill o' that side too?

BRISTLE. He will sit as upright o' the bench, an you mark him, as a candle i' the socket, and give light to the whole court in every business.

HAGGIS. But he will burn blue, and swell like a boil,—God bless us—an he be angry.

BRISTLE. Ay, and he will be angry too, when him list, that's more; and when he is angry, be it right or wrong, he has the law on's side ever. I mark that too.

OVERDO. —I will be more tender hereafter. I see compassion may become a justice, though it be a weakness, I confess, and nearer a vice than a virtue.

HAGGIS. Well, take him out o' the stocks again. We'll go a sure way to work; we'll ha' the ace of hearts of our side, if we can. *They take* OVERDO *out.*

Enter POACHER *and Officers, with* BUSY, *followed by*
DAME PURECRAFT.

POACHER. Come, bring him away to his fellow there.—Master Busy, we shall rule your legs, I hope, though we cannot rule your tongue.

BUSY. No, minister of darkness, no, thou canst not rule my tongue. My tongue it is mine own, and with it I will both knock and mock down your Bartholomew abominations, till you be made a hissing to the neighbour parishes round about.

HAGGIS. Let him alone, we have devised better upon't.

DAME PURECRAFT. And shall he not into the stocks then?

BRISTLE. No, mistress, we'll have 'em both to Justice Overdo, and let him do over 'em as is fitting. Then I, and my gossip Haggis, and my beadle Poacher are discharged.

DAME PURECRAFT. O, I thank you, blessed, honest men!

BRISTLE. Nay, never thank us, but thank this madman that comes here; he put it in our heads.

Re-enter TROUBLEALL.

DAME PURECRAFT. Is he mad? Now Heaven increase his madness, and bless it, and thank it.—Sir, your poor handmaid thanks you.

TROUBLEALL. Have you a warrant? An you have a warrant, show it.

DAME PURECRAFT. Yes, I have a warrant out of the word, to give thanks for removing any scorn intended to the Brethren.

Exeunt all but TROUBLEALL.

TROUBLEALL. It is Justice Overdo's warrant that I look for. If you have not that, keep your word; I'll keep mine. Quit ye, and multiply ye.

Enter EDGWORTH *and* NIGHTINGALE.

EDGWORTH. Come away, Nightingale, I pray thee.

TROUBLEALL. Whither go you? where's your warrant?

EDGWORTH. Warrant for what, sir?

TROUBLEALL. For what you go about, you know how fit it is. An you have no warrant, bless you, I'll pray for you; that's all I can do. *Exit.*

EDGWORTH. What means he?

NIGHTINGALE. A madman that haunts the Fair, do you not know him? It's marvel he has not more followers after his ragged heels.

EDGWORTH. Beshrew him, he startled me: I thought he had known of our plot. Guilt's a terrible thing. Ha' you prepared the costermonger?

NIGHTINGALE. Yes, and agreed for his basket of pears; he is at the corner here, ready. And your prize, he comes down sailing that way all alone, without his protector; he is rid of him, it seems.

EDGWORTH. Ay, I know. I should ha' followed his Protectorship, for a feat I am to do upon him; but this offered itself so i' the way, I could not let it 'scape. Here he comes, whistle. Be this sport called 'Doring the Dotterel.'

Enter COKES.

NIGHTINGALE. *Whistles.* Wh, wh, wh, wh, &c.

COKES. By this light, I cannot find my gingerbread-wife nor my hobby-horse-man in all the Fair now, to ha' my money again; and I do not know the way out on't, to go home for more. Do you hear, friend, you that whistle? What tune is that you whistle?

NIGHTINGALE. A new tune I am practising, sir.

COKES. Dost thou know where I dwell, I pray thee? Nay, on with thy tune, I ha' no such haste for an answer. I'll practise with thee.

Enter COSTERMONGER.

COSTERMONGER. Buy any pears, very fine pears, pears fine!

NIGHTINGALE *sets his foot afore* COSTERMONGER, *who falls with his basket.*

COKES. God's so'! a muss, a muss, a muss, a muss!

COSTERMONGER. Good gentlemen, my ware, my ware! I am a poor man. Good sir, my ware.

NIGHTINGALE. —Let me hold your sword, sir, it troubles you.

COKES. Do, and my cloak an thou wilt, and my hat too.   *Falls a-scrambling.*

EDGWORTH. —A delicate great boy! methinks he outscrambles 'em all. I cannot persuade myself but he goes to grammar-school yet, and plays the truant today.

NIGHTINGALE. Would he had another purse to cut, 'Zekiel.

EDGWORTH. Purse! a man might cut out his kidneys, I think, and he never feel 'em, he is so earnest at the sport.

NIGHTINGALE. His soul is half-way out on's body at the game.

EDGWORTH. Away, Nightingale, that way.

          NIGHTINGALE *runs away with* COKES' *things.*

COKES. I think I am furnished for Cather'ne pears for one under-meal. Gi' me my cloak.

COSTERMONGER. Good gentleman, give me my ware.

COKES. Where's the fellow I ga' my cloak to? my cloak and my hat? Ha! God's lid, is he gone? Thieves, thieves! Help me to cry, gentlemen.

          Runs out.

EDGWORTH. Away, costermonger, come to us to Ursula's. *Exit* COSTERMONGER. Talk of him to have a soul! Heart, if he have any more than a thing given him instead of salt, only to keep him from stinking, I'll be hanged afore my time, presently. Where should it be, trow? in his blood? He has not so much toward it in his whole body as will maintain a good flea. And if he take this course, he will not ha' so much land left as to rear a calf, within this twelvemonth. Was there ever green plover so pulled! That his little overseer had been here now, and been but tall enough to see him steal pears, in exchange for his beaver hat and his cloak thus! I must go find him out next, for his black box, and his patent—it seems—he has of his place; which I think the gentleman would have a reversion of, that spoke to me for it so earnestly. *Exit.*

Re-enter COKES.

COKES. Would I might lose my doublet, and hose too, as I am an honest man, and never stir, if I think there be anything but thieving and cozening i' this whole Fair. Bartholomew Fair, quoth he! An ever any Bartholomew had that luck in't that I have had, I'll be martyred for him, and in Smithfield, too. I ha' paid for my pears, a rot on 'em! I'll keep 'em no longer. *Throws away his pears.* You were choke-pears to me. I had been better ha' gone to mumchance for you, I wuss. Methinks the Fair should not have used me thus, an 'twere but for my name's sake, I would not ha' used a dog o' the name so. O, Numps will triumph now!

Enter TROUBLEALL.

Friend, do you know who I am, or where I lie? I do not myself, I'll be sworn. Do but carry me home, and I'll please thee; I ha' money enough there. I ha' lost myself, and my cloak, and my hat, and my fine sword, and my sister, and Numps, and Mistress Grace, a gentlewoman that I should ha' married, and a cut-work handkerchief she ga' me, and two purses, today; and my bargain o' hobby-horses and gingerbread, which grieves me worst of all.

TROUBLEALL. By whose warrant, sir, have you done all this?

COKES. Warrant! thou art a wise fellow indeed; as if a man need a warrant to lose anything with.

TROUBLEALL. Yes, Justice Overdo's warrant, a man may get and lose with, I'll stand to't.

COKES. Justice Overdo! dost thou know him? I lie there; he is my brother-in-law; he married my sister. Pray thee show me the way; dost thou know the house?

TROUBLEALL. Sir, show me your warrant; I know nothing without a warrant, pardon me.

COKES. Why, I warrant thee, come along. Thou shalt see I have wrought pillows there, and cambric sheets, and sweet bags too. Pray thee guide me to the house.

TROUBLEALL. Sir, I'll tell you: go you thither yourself first alone, tell your worshipful brother your mind, and but bring me three lines of his hand, or his clerk's, with Adam Overdo underneath; here I'll stay you, I'll obey you, and I'll guide you presently.

COKES. 'Slid, this is an ass, I ha' found him. Pox upon me, what do I talking to such a dull fool! Farewell, you are a very coxcomb, do you hear?

TROUBLEALL. I think I am; if Justice Overdo sign to it, I am, and so we are all. He'll quit us all, multiply us all.   *Exeunt.*

ACT FOUR. SCENE TWO

Between the stocks and URSULA'S *booth*

Enter QUARLOUS *and* WINWIFE, *with their swords drawn, followed by* GRACE.

GRACE. Gentlemen, this is no way that you take; you do but breed one another trouble and offence, and give me no contentment at all. I am no she that affects to be quarrelled for, or have my name or fortune made the question of men's swords.

QUARLOUS. 'Sblood, we love you.

GRACE. If you both love me, as you pretend, your own reason will tell you but one can enjoy me; and to that point there leads a directer line than by my infamy, which must follow if you fight. 'Tis true, I have professed it to you ingenuously, that rather than to be yoked with this bridegroom is appointed me, I would take up any husband, almost upon any trust; though subtlety would say to me, I know, he is a fool, and has an estate, and I might govern him, and enjoy a friend beside. But these are not my aims. I must have a husband I must love, or I cannot live with him. I shall ill make one of these politic wives.

WINWIFE. Why, if you can like either of us, lady, say which is he, and the other shall swear instantly to desist.

QUARLOUS. Content, I accord to that willingly.

GRACE. Sure, you think me a woman of an extreme levity, gentlemen, or a strange fancy, that—meeting you by chance in such a place as this, both at one instant, and not yet of two hours' acquaintance, neither of you deserving afore the other of me—I should so forsake my modesty, though I might affect one more particularly, as to say, 'This is he,' and name him.

QUARLOUS. Why, wherefore should you not? What should hinder you?

GRACE. If you would not give it to my modesty, allow it yet to my wit; give me so much of woman and cunning as not to betray myself impertinently. How can I judge of you, so far as to a choice, without knowing you more? You are both equal, and alike to me yet, and so indifferently affected by me, as each of you might be the man, if the other were away. For you are reasonable creatures, you have understanding and discourse; and if fate send me an understanding husband, I have no fear at all but mine own manners shall make him a good one.

QUARLOUS. Would I were put forth to making for you, then!

GRACE. It may be you are, you know not what's toward you. Will you consent to a motion of mine, gentlemen?

WINWIFE. Whatever it be, we'll presume reasonableness, coming from you.

QUARLOUS. And fitness too.

GRACE. I saw one of you buy a pair of tables e'en now.

WINWIFE. Yes, here they be, and maiden ones too, unwritten in.

GRACE. The fitter for what they may be employed in. You shall write, either of you, here a word or a name, what you like best, but of two or three syllables at most; and the next person that comes this way, because destiny has a high hand in business of this nature, I'll demand which of the two words he or she doth approve; and according to that sentence fix my resolution and affection, without change.

QUARLOUS. Agreed, my word is conceived already.

WINWIFE. And mine shall not be long creating after.

GRACE. But you shall promise, gentlemen, not to be curious to know which of you it is, taken; but give me leave to conceal that till you have brought me either home or where I may safely tender myself.

WINWIFE. Why, that's but equal.

QUARLOUS. We are pleased.

GRACE. Because I will bind both your endeavours to work together, friendly and jointly, each to the other's fortune, and have myself fitted with some means to make him that is forsaken a part of amends.

QUARLOUS. These conditions are very courteous. Well, my word is out of the 'Arcadia,' then: 'Argalus.'

WINWIFE. And mine out of the play: 'Palemon.'

Enter TROUBLEALL.

TROUBLEALL. Have you any warrant for this, gentlemen?

QUARLOUS, WINWIFE. Ha!

TROUBLEALL. There must be a warrant had, believe it.

WINWIFE. For what?

TROUBLEALL. For whatsoever it is, anything indeed, no matter what.

QUARLOUS. 'Slight, here's a fine ragged prophet, dropped down i' the nick!

TROUBLEALL. Heaven quit you, gentlemen!

QUARLOUS. Nay, stay a little. Good lady, put him to the question.

GRACE. You are content, then?

WINWIFE, QUARLOUS. Yes, yes.

GRACE. Sir, here are two names written——

TROUBLEALL. Is Justice Overdo one?

GRACE. How, sir! I pray you read 'em to yourself, —it is for a wager between these gentlemen—and with a stroke, or any difference, mark which you approve best.

TROUBLEALL. They may be both worshipful names for aught I know, mistress, but Adam Overdo had been worth three of 'em, I assure you, in this place; that's in plain English.

GRACE. This man amazes me!—I pray you like one of 'em, sir.

TROUBLEALL. I do like him there, that has the best warrant, mistress, to save your longing, and—multiply him—it may be this. But I am still for Justice Overdo, that's my conscience; and quit you.   *Exit.*

WINWIFE. Is't done, lady?

GRACE. Ay, and strangely as ever I saw! What fellow is this, trow?

QUARLOUS. No matter what, a fortune-teller we ha' made him. Which is 't, which is 't?

GRACE. Nay, did you not promise not to inquire?

Enter EDGWORTH.

QUARLOUS. 'Slid, I forgot that, pray you pardon me. Look, here's our Mercury come; the licence arrives i' the finest time, too! 'Tis but scraping out Cokes's name, and 'tis done.

WINWIFE. How now, lime-twig, hast thou touched?

EDGWORTH. Not yet, sir, except you would go with me and see't, it's not worth speaking on. The act is nothing, without a witness. Yonder he is, your man with the box, fall'n into the finest company, and so transported with vapours! They ha' got in a northern clothier, and one Puppy, a western man, that's come to wrestle before my Lord Mayor anon, and Captain Whit, and one Val Cutting, that helps Captain Jordan to roar, a circling boy; with whom your Numps is so taken that you may strip him of his clothes, if you will. I'll undertake to geld him for you, if you had but a surgeon ready to sear him. And Mistress Justice there is the goodest woman! She does so love 'em all over in terms of justice and the style of authority, with her hood upright that —I beseech you come away, gentlemen, and see't.

QUARLOUS. 'Slight, I would not lose it for the Fair! What'll you do, Ned?

WINWIFE. Why, stay hereabout for you. Mistress Wellborn must not be seen. *Exit with* GRACE.

QUARLOUS. Do so, and find out a priest i' the meantime. I'll bring the licence.—Lead, which way is't?

EDGWORTH. Here, sir, you are o' the backside o' the booth already; you may hear the noise.

URSULA'S *booth is revealed, with* KNOCKEM, WHIT, NORTHERN, PUPPY, CUTTING, WASP, *and* MISTRESS OVERDO, *discovered drinking.*

KNOCKEM. Whit, bid Val Cutting continue the vapours for a lift, Whit, for a lift.

NORTHERN. I'll ne mare, I'll ne mare, the eale's too meeghty.

KNOCKEM. How now! my Galloway nag, the staggers, ha? Whit, gi' him a slit i' the forehead. Cheer up, man; a needle and thread to stitch his ears. I'd cure him now, an I had it, with a little butter and garlic, long pepper and grains. Where's my horn? I'll gi' him a mash presently, shall take away this dizziness.

PUPPY. Why, where are you, zurs? Do you vlinch, and leave us i' the zuds now?

NORTHERN. I'll ne mare, I's e'en as vull as a paiper's bag, by my troth, I.

PUPPY. Do my northern cloth zhrink i' the wetting, ha?

KNOCKEM. Why, well said, old flea-bitten! thou'lt never tire, I see. *They fall to their vapours again.*

CUTTING. No, sir, but he may tire if it please him.

WHIT. Who told dee sho, that he vould never teer, man?

CUTTING. No matter who told him so, so long as he knows.

KNOCKEM. Nay, I know nothing, sir, pardon me there.

EDGWORTH. —They are at it still, sir. This they call vapours.

WHIT. He shall not pardon dee, Captain, dou shalt not be pardoned. Pre'dee, shweetheart, do not pardon him.

CUTTING. 'Slight, I'll pardon him, an I list, whosoever says nay to't.

Here they continue their game of vapours, which is nonsense: every man to oppose the last man that spoke, whether it concerned him or no.

QUARLOUS. —Where's Numps? I miss him.

WASP. Why, I say nay to't.

QUARLOUS. O, there he is.

KNOCKEM. To what do you say nay, sir?

WASP. To anything, whatsoever it is, so long as I do not like it.

WHIT. Pardon me, little man, dou musht like it a little.

CUTTING. No, he must not like it at all, sir, there you are i' the wrong.

WHIT. I tink I bee, he musht not like it indeed.

CUTTING. Nay, then he both must and will like it, sir, for all you.

KNOCKEM. If he have reason, he may like it, sir.

WHIT. By no meensh, Captain, upon reashon; he may like nothing upon reashon.

WASP. I have no reason, nor I will hear of no reason, nor I will look for no reason, and he is an ass that either knows any, or looks for't from me.

CUTTING. Yes, in some sense you may have reason, sir.

WASP. Ay, in some sense, I care not if I grant you.

WHIT. Pardon me, dou ougsht to grant him

noting in no shensh, if dou do love dyshelf, angry man.

WASP. Why then, I do grant him nothing, and I have no sense.

CUTTING. 'Tis true, thou hast no sense indeed.

WASP. 'Slid, but I have sense, now I think on't better, and I will grant him anything, do you see?

KNOCKEM. He is i' the right, and does utter a sufficient vapour.

CUTTING. Nay, it is no sufficient vapour neither, I deny that.

KNOCKEM. Then it is a sweet vapour.

CUTTING. It may be a sweet vapour.

WASP. Nay, it is no sweet vapour neither, sir; it stinks, and I'll stand to't.

WHIT. Yes, I tink it dosh shtink, Captain. All vapour dosh shtink.

WASP. Nay, then it does not stink, sir, and it shall not stink.

CUTTING. By your leave, it may, sir.

WASP. Ay, by my leave it may stink, I know that.

WHIT. Pardon me, tou knowesht noting, it cannot by ty leave, angry man.

WASP. How can it not?

KNOCKEM. Nay, never question him, for he is i' the right.

WHIT. Yesh, I am i' de right, I confesh it; so ish de little man, too.

WASP. I'll have nothing confessed that concerns me. I am not i' the right, nor never was i' the right, nor never will be i' the right, while I am in my right mind.

CUTTING. Mind! why, here's no man minds you, sir, nor anything else.   *They drink again.*

PUPPY. Vriend, will you mind this that we do?

QUARLOUS. —Call you this vapours? This is such

belching of quarrel as I never heard. Will you mind your business, sir?

EDGWORTH. You shall see, sir.

NORTHERN. I'll ne mare, my waimb warks too mickle with this aueready.

EDGWORTH. Will you take that, Master Wasp, that nobody should mind you?

WASP. Why, what ha' you to do? Is't any matter to you?

EDGWORTH. No, but methinks you should not be unminded, though.

WASP. Nor I wu' not be, now I think on't.—Do you hear, new acquaintance? Does no man mind me, say you?

CUTTING. Yes, sir, every man here minds you, but how?

WASP. Nay, I care as little how as you do; that was not my question.

WHIT. No, noting was ty question. Tou art a learned man, and I am a valiant man, i' fait, la, tou shalt shpeak for me, and I vill fight for tee.

KNOCKEM. Fight for him, Whit? A gross vapour! He can fight for himself.

WASP. It may be I can, but it may be I wu' not, how then?

CUTTING. Why, then you may choose.

WASP. Why, and I'll choose whether I'll choose or no.

KNOCKEM. I think you may, and 'tis true; and I allow it for a resolute vapour.

WASP. Nay then, I do think you do not think, and it is no resolute vapour.

CUTTING. Yes, in some sort he may allow you.

KNOCKEM. In no sort, sir, pardon me, I can allow him nothing. You mistake the vapour.

WASP. He mistakes nothing, sir, in no sort.

WHIT. Yes, I pre'dee now, let him mishtake.

WASP. A turd i' your teeth, never pre'dee me, for I will have nothing mistaken.

KNOCKEM. Turd, ha, turd? a noisome vapour! Strike, Whit.

They fall by the ears, while EDGWORTH *steals the licence out of the box, and exit.*

MISTRESS OVERDO. Why, gentlemen, why, gentlemen, I charge you upon my authority, conserve the peace. In the King's name, and my husband's, put up your weapons, I shall be driven to commit you myself else.

QUARLOUS. Ha, ha, ha!

WASP. Why do you laugh, sir?

QUARLOUS. Sir, you'll allow me my Christian liberty. I may laugh, I hope.

CUTTING. In some sort you may, and in some sort you may not, sir.

KNOCKEM. Nay, in some sort, sir, he may neither laugh nor hope in this company.

WASP. Yes, then he may both laugh and hope in any sort, an't please him.

QUARLOUS. Faith, and I will then, for it doth please me exceedingly.

WASP. No exceeding neither, sir.

KNOCKEM. No, that vapour is too lofty.

QUARLOUS. Gentlemen, I do not play well at your game of vapours, I am not very good at it, but——

CUTTING. *Draws a circle on the ground.* Do you hear, sir? I would speak with you in circle.

QUARLOUS. In circle, sir? what would you with me in circle?

CUTTING. Can you lend me a piece, a Jacobus, in circle?

QUARLOUS. 'Slid, your circle will prove more costly than your vapours, then, sir. No, I lend you none.

CUTTING. Your beard's not well turned up, sir.

QUARLOUS. How, rascal, are you playing with my beard? I'll break circle with you.

They draw all, and fight.

PUPPY, NORTHERN. Gentlemen, gentlemen!

KNOCKEM. —Gather up, Whit, gather up, Whit, good vapours.

Exit, while WHIT *takes up the swords, cloaks, &c., and conceals them.*

MISTRESS OVERDO. What mean you, are you rebels, gentlemen? Shall I send out a sergeant-at-arms, or a writ o' rebellion against you? I'll commit you upon my womanhood, for a riot, upon my justice-hood, if you persist. *Exeunt* QUARLOUS *and* CUTTING.

WASP. Upon my justice-hood! marry, shit o' your hood, you'll commit! Spoke like a true Justice of Peace's wife indeed, and a fine female lawyer! Turd i' your teeth for a fee, now.

MISTRESS OVERDO. Why, Numps, in Master Overdo's name I charge you.

WASP. Good Mistress Underdo, hold your tongue.

MISTRESS OVERDO. Alas, poor Numps!

WASP. Alas! and why alas from you, I beseech you? or why poor Numps, Goody Rich? Am I come to be pitied by your tuft-taffeta now? Why, mistress, I knew Adam the Clerk, your husband, when he was Adam Scrivener, and writ for twopence a sheet, as high as he bears his head now, or you your hood, dame——

Enter BRISTLE *and others of the Watch.*

What are you, sir?

BRISTLE. We be men, and no infidels. What is the matter here, and the noises, can you tell?

WASP. Heart, what ha' you to do? Cannot a man quarrel in quietness, but he must be put out on't by you? What are you?

BRISTLE. Why, we be his Majesty's watch, sir.

WASP. Watch! 'Sblood, you are a sweet watch indeed. A body would think, an you watched well a-nights, you should be contented to sleep at this time a-day. Get you to your fleas and your flock-beds, you rogues, your kennels, and lie down close.

BRISTLE. Down! yes, we will down, I warrant you. —Down with him, in his Majesty's name, down, down with him, and carry him away to the pigeon-holes!

Some of the Watch seize WASP *and carry him off.*

MISTRESS OVERDO. I thank you, honest friends, in the behalf o' the Crown, and the peace, and in Master Overdo's name, for suppressing enormities.

WHIT. Stay, Bristle, here ish anoder brashe o' drunkards, but very quiet, special drunkards, will pay dee five shillings very well. Take 'em to dee, in de grashe o' God. One of 'em does change cloth for ale in the Fair here; te toder ish a strong man, a mighty man, my Lord Mayor's man, and a wrastler. He has wrashled so long with the bottle here, that the man with the beard hash almosht streek up his heelsh.

BRISTLE. 'Slid, the clerk o' the market has been to cry him all the Fair over here, for my Lord's service.

WHIT. Tere he ish, pre'dee take him hensh, and make ty best on him. *Exeunt* BRISTLE *and the rest of the Watch with* NORTHERN *and* PUPPY. How now, voman o' shilk, vat ailsh ty shweet fashe? Art tou melancholy?

MISTRESS OVERDO. A little distempered with these enormities. Shall I entreat a courtesy of you, Captain?

WHIT. Entreat a hundred, velvet voman, I vill do it, shpeak out.

MISTRESS OVERDO. I cannot with modesty speak it out, but—— *Whispers.*

WHIT. I vill do it, and more and more, for dee. What Ursula, an't be bitch, an't be bawd, an't be!

Enter URSULA.

URSULA. How now, rascal! what roar you for, old pimp?

WHIT. Here, put up de cloaks, Ursh, de purchase. Pre'dee now, shweet Ursh, help dis good, brave voman to a jordan, an't be.

URSULA. 'Slid, call your Captain Jordan to her, can you not?

WHIT. Nay, pre'dee leave dy consheits, and bring de velvet voman to de——

URSULA. I bring her? hang her! Heart, must I find a common pot for every punk i' your purlieus?

WHIT. O, good voordsh, Ursh, it ish a guest o' velvet, i' fait, la.

URSULA. Let her sell her hood and buy a sponge, with a pox to her! My vessel is employed, sir. I have but one, and 'tis the bottom of an old bottle. An honest proctor and his wife are at it within; if she'll stay her time, so. *Exit.*

WHIT. As soon ash tou cansht, shweet Ursh. Of a valiant man I tink I am te patientsh man i' the vorld, or in all Smithfield.

Re-enter KNOCKEM.

KNOCKEM. How now, Whit! close vapours, stealing your leaps? covering in corners, ha?

WHIT. No, fait, Captain, dough tou beesht a vishe man, dy vit is a mile hensh now. I vas procuring a shmall courtesy for a voman of fashion here.

MISTRESS OVERDO. Yes, Captain, though I am

Justice of Peace's wife, I do love men of war, and
the sons of the sword, when they come before my
husband.

KNOCKEM. Sayst thou so, filly? Thou shalt have a
leap presently, I'll horse thee myself else.

Re-enter URSULA, *followed by* LITTLEWIT *and*
MISTRESS LITTLEWIT.

URSULA. Come, will you bring her in now, and
let her take her turn?

WHIT. Gramercy, good Ursh, I tank dee.

MISTRESS OVERDO. Master Overdo shall thank her.
Exit.

LITTLEWIT. Good Gammer Urse, Win and I are
exceedingly beholden to you, and to Captain Jordan, and Captain Whit.—Win, I'll be bold to leave
you i' this good company, Win, for half an hour or
so, Win, while I go and see how my matter goes
forward, and if the puppets be perfect; and then I'll
come and fetch you, Win.

MISTRESS LITTLEWIT. Will you leave me alone with
two men, John?

LITTLEWIT. Ay, they are honest gentlemen, Win,
Captain Jordan and Captain Whit. They'll use you
very civilly, Win. God b'w'you, Win.   *Exit.*

URSULA. What, is her husband gone?

KNOCKEM. On his false gallop, Urse, away.

URSULA. An you be right Bartholomew birds, now
show yourselves so: we are undone for want of fowl
i' the Fair here. Here will be 'Zekiel Edgworth, and
three or four gallants with him at night, and I ha'
neither plover nor quail for 'em. Persuade this
between you two, to become a bird o' the game,
while I work the velvet woman within, as you call
her.

KNOCKEM. I conceive thee, Urse, go thy ways. *Exit*

URSULA. Dost thou hear, Whit? Is't not pity, my delicate dark chestnut here, with the fine lean head, large forehead, round eyes, even mouth, sharp ears, long neck, thin crest, close withers, plain back, deep sides, short fillets, and full flanks; with a round belly, a plump buttock, large thighs, knit knees, straight legs, short pasterns, smooth hoofs, and short heels, should lead a dull honest woman's life, that might live the life of a lady?

WHIT. Yes, by my fait and trot it is, Captain; de honesht voman's life is a scurvy dull life indeed, la.

MISTRESS LITTLEWIT. How, sir! is an honest woman's life a scurvy life?

WHIT. Yes, fait, shweetheart, believe him, de leef of a bondvoman! But if dou vilt hearken to me, I vill make tee a free voman and a lady. Dou shalt live like a lady, as te Captain saish.

KNOCKEM. Ay, and be honest, too, sometimes; have her wires and her tires, her green gowns and velvet petticoats.

WHIT. Ay, and ride to Ware and Rumford i' dy coash, shee de players, be in love vit 'em; sup vit gallantsh, be drunk, and cost dee noting.

KNOCKEM. Brave vapours!

WHIT. And lie by twenty on 'em, if dou pleash, shweetheart.

MISTRESS LITTLEWIT. What, and be honest still? that were fine sport.

WHIT. Tish common, shweetheart, tou mayst do it, by my hand. It shall be justified to ty husband's fashe, now. Tou shalt be as honesht as te skin between his hornsh, la.

KNOCKEM. Yes, and wear a dressing, top and top-gallant, to compare with e'er a husband on 'em all, for a foretop. It is the vapour of spirit in the wife to cuckold nowadays, as it is the vapour of fashion in the husband not to suspect. Your prying, cat-eyed citizen is an abominable vapour.

MISTRESS LITTLEWIT. Lord, what a fool have I been!

WHIT. Mend then, and do everyting like a lady, hereafter; never know ty husband from anoder man.

KNOCKEM. Nor any one man from another, but i' the dark.

WHIT. Ay, and then it ish no disgrashe to know any man.

URSULA. Help, help here!

KNOCKEM. How now! what vapour's there?

Re-enter URSULA.

URSULA. O, you are a sweet ranger, and look well to your walks! Yonder is your punk of Turnbull, ramping Alice, has fall'n upon the poor gentle-woman within, and pulled her hood over her ears, and her hair through it.

Enter ALICE, beating MISTRESS OVERDO.

MISTRESS OVERDO. Help, help, i' the King's name!

ALICE. A mischief on you, they are such as you are that undo us and take our trade from us, with your tuft-taffeta haunches!

KNOCKEM. How now, Alice!

ALICE. The poor common whores can ha' no traffic for the privy rich ones; your caps and hoods of velvet call away our customers, and lick the fat from us.

URSULA. Peace, you foul, ramping jade, you——

ALICE. 'Od's foot, you bawd in grease, are you talking?

KNOCKEM. Why, Alice, I say.

ALICE. Thou sow of Smithfield, thou!

URSULA. Thou tripe of Turnbull!

KNOCKEM. Cat-a-mountain vapours, ha!

URSULA. You know where you were tawed lately, both lashed and slashed you were in Bridewell.

ALICE. Ay, by the same token you rid that week, and broke out the bottom o' the cart, night-tub.

KNOCKEM. Why, lion-face, ha! do you know who I am? Shall I tear ruff, slit waistcoat, make rags of petticoat, ha? Go to, vanish for fear of vapours. Whit, a kick, Whit, in the parting vapour. *They kick out* ALICE. Come, brave woman, take a good heart, thou shalt be a lady too.

WHIT. Yes, fait, dey shall all both be ladies, and write madam. I vill do't myself for dem. Do is te vord, and D. is te middle letter of madam; D. D., put 'em together, and make deeds, vithout vich all vords are alike, la!

KNOCKEM. 'Tis true. Ursula, take 'em in, open thy wardrobe, and fit 'em to their calling. Green gowns, crimson petticoats, green women! my Lord Mayor's green women! guests o' the game, true bred! I'll provide you a coach to take the air in.

MISTRESS LITTLEWIT. But do you think you can get one?

KNOCKEM. O, they are common as wheelbarrows where there are great dunghills. Every pettifogger's wife has 'em; for first he buys a coach that he may marry, and then he marries that he may be made cuckold in't. For if their wives ride not to their cuckolding, they do 'em no credit. *Exeunt* URSULA, MISTRESS LITTLEWIT, *and* MISTRESS OVERDO. 'Hide and be hidden, ride and be ridden,' says the vapour of experience.

Enter TROUBLEALL.

TROUBLEALL. By what warrant does it say so?

KNOCKEM. Ha; mad child o' the Pie-powders, art

thou there? Fill us a fresh can, Urse, we may drink together.

TROUBLEALL. I may not drink without a warrant, Captain.

KNOCKEM. 'Slood, thou'lt not stale without a warrant, shortly. Whit, give me pen, ink, and paper; I'll draw him a warrant presently.

TROUBLEALL. It must be Justice Overdo's.

KNOCKEM. I know, man. Fetch the drink, Whit.

WHIT. I pre'dee now, be very brief, Captain, for de new ladies stay for dee.

KNOCKEM. O, as brief as can be, here 'tis already: 'Adam Overdo.'

TROUBLEALL. Why, now I'll pledge you, Captain.

KNOCKEM. Drink it off, I'll come to thee anon again. *Exeunt.*

ACT FOUR. SCENE THREE

The stocks

OVERDO, *as before. Enter* QUARLOUS *with the licence, and* EDGWORTH.

QUARLOUS. Well, sir, you are now discharged; beware of being spied hereafter.

EDGWORTH. Sir, will it please you enter in here at Ursula's, and take part of a silken gown, a velvet petticoat, or a wrought smock; I am promised such, and I can spare any gentleman a moiety.

QUARLOUS. Keep it for your companions in beastliness, I am none of 'em, sir. If I had not already forgiven you a greater tresspass, or thought you yet worth my beating, I would instruct your manners to whom you made your offers. But go your ways, talk not to me, the hangman is only fit to discourse with you; the hand of beadle is too merciful a punishment for your trade of life. *Exit* EDGWORTH. I am sorry I employed this fellow, for he thinks me such: 'facinus quos inquinat, aequat.' But it was for sport; and would I make it serious, the getting of this licence is nothing to me, without other circumstances concur. I do think how impertinently I labour, if the word be not mine that the ragged fellow marked; and what advantage I have given Ned Winwife in this time now, of working her, though it be mine. He'll go near to form to her what a debauched rascal I am, and fright her out of all good conceit of me. I should do so by him, I am sure, if I had the opportunity. But my hope is in her temper, yet; and it must needs be next to despair, that is grounded on any part of a woman's discretion. I would give, by my troth now, all I could spare, to my clothes and my sword, to meet my tattered soothsayer again, who was my judge i' the question, to know certainly whose word he has damned or saved; for till then, I live but under a reprieve. I must seek him. Who be these?

Enter BRISTLE *and some of the Watch, with* WASP.

WASP. Sir, you are a Welsh cuckold, and a prating runt, and no constable.

BRISTLE. You say very well.—Come, put in his leg in the middle roundel, and let him hole there.

WASP. You stink of leeks, metheglin, and cheese, you rogue.

BRISTLE. Why, what is that to you, if you sit sweetly in the stocks in the meantime? If you have a mind to stink, too, your breeches sit close enough to your bum. Sit you merry, sir.

QUARLOUS. How now, Numps?

WASP. It is no matter how; pray you look off.

QUARLOUS. Nay, I'll not offend you, Numps. I thought you had sat there to be seen.

WASP. And to be sold, did you not? Pray you mind your business, an you have any.

QUARLOUS. Cry you mercy, Numps. Does your leg lie high enough?

Enter HAGGIS.

BRISTLE. How now, neighbour Haggis, what says Justice Overdo's worship to the other offenders?

HAGGIS. Why, he says just nothing, what should he say, or where should he say? He is not to be found, man. He ha' not been seen i' the Fair here all this livelong day, never since seven o'clock i' the morning. His clerks know not what to think on't. There is no Court of Pie-powders yet. Here they be returned.

BRISTLE. What shall be done with 'em then, in your discretion?

HAGGIS. I think we were best put 'em in the stocks in discretion—there they will be safe in discretion—for the valour of an hour, or such a thing, till his worship come.

BRISTLE. It is but a hole matter if we do, neighbour Haggis.—Come, sir, here is company for you.—Heave up the stocks.

As they open the stocks, WASP *puts his shoe on his hand, and slips it in for his leg.*

WASP. —I shall put a trick upon your Welsh diligence perhaps.

BRISTLE. Put in your leg, sir.

They bring BUSY *and put him in.*

QUARLOUS. What, Rabbi Busy! is he come?

BUSY. I do obey thee. The lion may roar, but he cannot bite. I am glad to be thus separated from the heathen of the land, and put apart in the stocks, for the Holy Cause.

WASP. What are you, sir?

BUSY. One that rejoiceth in his affliction, and sitteth here to prophesy the destruction of fairs and May-games, wakes and Whitsun-ales, and doth sigh and groan for the reformation of these abuses.

WASP. —And do you sigh and groan, too, or rejoice in your affliction?

OVERDO. I do not feel it, I do not think of it; it is a thing without me. Adam, thou art above these batteries, these contumelies. 'In te manca ruit fortuna,' as thy friend Horace says; thou art one, 'quem neque pauperies, neque mors, neque vincula terrent.' And therefore, as another friend of thine says, —I think it be thy friend Persius—'Non te quaesiveris extra.'

QUARLOUS. What's here! a Stoic i' the stocks? The fool is turned philosopher.

BUSY. Friend, I will leave to communicate my spirit with you, if I hear any more of those superstitious relics, those lists of Latin, the very rags of Rome and patches of popery.

WASP. Nay, an you begin to quarrel, gentlemen, I'll leave you. I ha' paid for quarrelling too lately. Look you, a device: but shifting in a hand for a foot. God b' w' you.   *Gets out.*

BUSY. Wilt thou then leave thy brethren in tribution?

WASP. For this once, sir.   *Exit.*

BUSY. Thou art a halting neutral. Stay him there, stop him, that will not endure the heat of persecution!

BRISTLE. How now, what's the matter?

BUSY. He is fled, he is fled, and dares not sit it out.

BRISTLE. What, has he made an escape? Which way? Follow, neighbour Haggis.

Exeunt HAGGIS *and Watch.*

Enter DAME PURECRAFT.

DAME PURECRAFT. O me! in the stocks! Have the wicked prevailed?

BUSY. Peace, religious Sister, it is my calling, comfort yourself, an extraordinary calling; and done for my better standing, my surer standing, hereafter.

Enter TROUBLEALL.

TROUBLEALL. By whose warrant, by whose warrant, this?

QUARLOUS. —O, here's my man dropped in, I looked for.

OVERDO. Ha!

DAME PURECRAFT. O good sir, they have set the faithful here to be wondered at, and provided holes for the holy of the land.

TROUBLEALL. Had they warrant for it? showed they Justice Overdo's hand? If they had no warrant, they shall answer it.

Re-enter HAGGIS.

BRISTLE. Sure you did not lock the stocks sufficiently, neighbour Toby.

HAGGIS. No! see if you can lock 'em better.

BRISTLE. They are very sufficiently locked, and truly, yet something is in the matter.

TROUBLEALL. True, your warrant is the matter that is in question; by what warrant?

BRISTLE. Madman, hold your peace, I will put you in his room else, in the very same hole, do you see?

QUARLOUS. —How! is he a madman?

TROUBLEALL. Show me Justice Overdo's warrant, I obey you.

HAGGIS. You are a mad fool, hold your tongue.

Exeunt HAGGIS *and* BRISTLE.

TROUBLEALL. In Justice Overdo's name, I drink to you, and here's my warrant. *Shows his can.*

OVERDO. —Alas, poor wretch! how it yearns my heart for him!

QUARLOUS. If he be mad, it is in vain to question him. I'll try though.—Friend, there was a gentlewoman showed you two names some hour since, 'Argalus' and 'Palemon,' to mark in a book. Which of 'em was it you marked?

TROUBLEALL. I mark no name but Adam Overdo; that is the name of names. He only is the sufficient magistrate, and that name I reverence. Show it me.

QUARLOUS. This fellow's mad indeed. I am further off now than afore.

OVERDO. —I shall not breathe in peace till I have made him some amends.

QUARLOUS. Well, I will make another use of him, is come in my head: I have a nest of beards in my trunk, one something like his.

Re-enter BRISTLE *and* HAGGIS.

BRISTLE. This mad fool has made me that I know not whether I have locked the stocks or no. I think I locked 'em.

TROUBLEALL. Take Adam Overdo in your mind, and fear nothing.

BRISTLE. 'Slid, madness itself, hold thy peace, and take that!

TROUBLEALL. Strikest thou without a warrant? Take thou that!

TROUBLEALL fights with them, and they leave open the stocks.

BUSY. We are delivered by miracle! Fellow in fetters, let us not refuse the means; this madness was of the spirit. The malice of the enemy hath mocked itself. *Exeunt* BUSY *and* OVERDO.

DAME PURECRAFT. Mad do they call him? the world is mad in error, but he is mad in truth. I loved him o' the sudden—the cunning-man said all true—and shall love him more and more. How well it becomes a man to be mad in truth! O that I might be his yoke-fellow, and be mad with him, what a many should we draw to madness in truth with us! *Exit.*

BRISTLE. *Affrighted, missing them.* How now, all 'scaped! Where's the woman? It is witchcraft! her velvet hat is a witch, o' my conscience; or my key, t' one! The madman was a devil, and I am an ass; so bless me, my place, and mine office! *Exeunt.*

ACT FIVE

The puppet-booth

Enter LEATHERHEAD, *as puppet-master, with* FILCHER *and* SHARKWELL.

LEATHERHEAD. Well, luck and Saint Bartholomew! out with the sign of our invention, in the name of wit, and do you beat the drum the while. All the foul i' the Fair, I mean all the dirt in Smithfield,— that's one of Master Littlewit's carwhitchets now— will be thrown at our banner today, if the matter does not please the people. O the motions that I, Lantern Leatherhead, have given light to, i' my time, since my Master Pod died! Jerusalem was a stately thing, and so was Nineveh, and the City of Norwich, and Sodom and Gomorrah, with the rising o' the prentices, and pulling down the bawdy-houses there upon Shrove Tuesday; but the Gunpowder Plot, there was a get-penny! I have presented that to an eighteen- or twenty-pence audience, nine times in an afternoon. Your home-born projects prove ever the best; they are so easy and familiar. They put too much learning i' their things nowadays; and that, I fear, will be the spoil o' this. Littlewit? I say Micklewit! if not too mickle!—Look to your gathering there, Goodman Filcher.

FILCHER. I warrant you, sir.

LEATHERHEAD. An there come any gentlefolks, take twopence apiece, Sharkwell.   *Exit.*

SHARKWELL. I warrant you, sir, threepence an we can.

Enter OVERDO, *disguised as a porter.*

OVERDO. This latter disguise, I have borrowed of a porter, shall carry me out to all my great and good ends; which however interrupted, were never destroyed in me. Neither is the hour of my severity yet come, to reveal myself; wherein, cloud-like, I will break out in rain and hail, lightning and thunder, upon the head of enormity. Two main works I have to prosecute: first, one is to invent some satisfaction for the poor, kind wretch, who is out of his wits for my sake; and yonder I see him coming. I will walk aside and project for it.

Enter WINWIFE *and* GRACE.

WINWIFE. I wonder where Tom Quarlous is, that he returns not. It may be he is struck in here to seek us.

GRACE. See, here's our madman again.

Enter QUARLOUS, *in* TROUBLEALL's *habit, followed by*
DAME PURECRAFT.

QUARLOUS. —I have made myself as like him as his
gown and cap will give me leave.

DAME PURECRAFT. Sir, I love you, and would be
glad to be mad with you in truth.

WINWIFE. How! my widow in love with a madman?

DAME PURECRAFT. Verily, I can be as mad in spirit
as you.

QUARLOUS. By whose warrant? Leave your cant-
ing, gentlewoman, have I found you?—Save ye, quit
ye, and multiply ye! Where's your book? 'Twas a
sufficient name I marked; let me see't, be not afraid
to show't me.

GRACE. What would you with it, sir?

QUARLOUS. Mark it again and again, at your
service.

GRACE. Here it is, sir; this was it you marked.

QUARLOUS. 'Palemon'! Fare you well, fare you
well.

WINWIFE. How, Palemon!

GRACE. Yes, faith, he has discovered it to you now,
and therefore 'twere vain to disguise it longer: I am
yours, sir, by the benefit of your fortune.

WINWIFE. And you have him, mistress, believe it,
that shall never give you cause to repent her benefit,
but make you rather to think that in this choice she
had both her eyes.

GRACE. I desire to put it to no danger of protestation.   *Exeunt* GRACE *and* WINWIFE.

QUARLOUS. —Palemon the word, and Winwife the
man!

DAME PURECRAFT. Good sir, vouchsafe a yoke-fellow in your madness; shun not one of the sanctified sisters, that would draw with you in truth.

QUARLOUS. Away, you are a herd of hypocritical, proud ignorants, rather wild than mad; fitter for woods and the society of beasts, than houses and the congregation of men. You are the second part of the society of canters, outlaws to order and discipline, and the only privileged church-robbers of Christendom. Let me alone.—Palemon the word, and Winwife the man!

DAME PURECRAFT. I must uncover myself unto him, or I shall never enjoy him, for all the cunning-men's promises.—Good sir, hear me: I am worth six thousand pound; my love to you is become my rack; I'll tell you all and the truth, since you hate the hypocrisy of the parti-coloured Brotherhood. These seven years I have been a wilful holy widow, only to draw feasts and gifts from my entangled suitors. I am also by office an assisting sister of the Deacons, and a devourer, instead of a distributor, of the alms. I am a special maker of marriages for our decayed Brethren with our rich widows, for a third part of their wealth, when they are married, for the relief of the poor elect; as also our poor, handsome young virgins with our wealthy bachelors or widowers, to make them steal from their husbands, when I have confirmed them in the faith, and got all put into their custodies. And if I ha' not my bargain, they may sooner turn a scolding drab into a silent minister, than make me leave pronouncing reprobation and damnation unto them. Our elder, Zeal-of-the-Land, would have had me, but I know him to be the capital knave of the land, making himself rich by being made feoffee in trust to deceased Brethren, and cozening their heirs by swearing the absolute gift of their inheritance. And thus having eased my conscience, and uttered my heart with the tongue of my love, enjoy all my deceits together, I beseech you. I should not have revealed this to you, but that in time I think you are mad, and I hope you'll think me so too, sir?

QUARLOUS. Stand aside, I'll answer you presently. *Considers with himself.* Why should not I marry this six thousand pound, now I think on't, and a good trade too, that she has beside, ha? The tother wench Winwife is sure of; there's no expectation for me there. Here I may make myself some saver yet, if she continue mad—there's the question. It is money that I want. Why should I not marry the money when 'tis offered me? I have a licence and all; it is but razing out one name and putting in another. There's no playing with a man's fortune! I am resolved. I were truly mad an I would not!— Well, come your ways, follow me, an you will be mad, I'll show you a warrant.

Takes DAME PURECRAFT *along with him.*

DAME PURECRAFT. Most zealously, it is that I zealously desire.

OVERDO. *Calls* QUARLOUS. Sir, let me speak with you.

QUARLOUS. By whose warrant?

OVERDO. The warrant that you tender, and respect so: Justice Overdo's. I am the man, friend Trouble-all, though thus disguised—as the careful magistrate ought—for the good of the republic, in the Fair, and the weeding out of enormity. Do you want a house, or meat, or drink, or clothes? Speak whatsoever it is, it shall be supplied you. What want you?

QUARLOUS. Nothing but your warrant.

OVERDO. My warrant! for what?

QUARLOUS. To be gone, sir.

OVERDO. Nay, I pray thee stay. I am serious, and

have not many words, nor much time to exchange with thee. Think what may do thee good.

QUARLOUS. Your hand and seal will do me a great deal of good; nothing else in the whole Fair that I know.

OVERDO. If it were to any end, thou shouldst have it willingly.

QUARLOUS. Why, it will satisfy me, that's end enough to look on. An you will not gi' it me, let me go.

OVERDO. Alas, thou shalt ha' it presently. I'll but step into the scrivener's here by, and bring it. Do not go away. *Exit.*

QUARLOUS. —Why, this madman's shape will prove a very fortune one, I think. Can a ragged robe produce these effects? If this be the wise Justice, and he bring me his hand, I shall go near to make some use on't.

Re-enter OVERDO

He is come already!

OVERDO. Look thee: here is my hand and seal, Adam Overdo. If there be anything to be written above in the paper that thou want'st now, or at any time hereafter, think on't; it is my deed, I deliver it so. Can your friend write?

QUARLOUS. Her hand for a witness, and all is well.

OVERDO. With all my heart.

Urges DAME PURECRAFT.

QUARLOUS. —Why should not I ha' the conscience to make this a bond of a thousand pound now, or what I would else?

OVERDO. Look you, there it is, and I deliver it as my deed again.

QUARLOUS. Let us now proceed in madness.

Exeunt QUARLOUS *and* DAME PURECRAFT.

OVERDO. Well, my conscience is much eased. I ha' done my part, though it doth him no good, yet Adam hath offered satisfaction. The sting is removed from hence. Poor man, he is much altered with his affliction, it has brought him low! Now for my other work, reducing the young man I have followed so long in love, from the brink of his bane to the centre of safety. Here, or in some suchlike vain place, I shall be sure to find him. I will wait the good time.

Enter COKES, *followed by the Boys of the Fair.*

COKES. How now! what's here to do? Friend, art thou the master of the monuments?

SHARKWELL. 'Tis a motion, an't please your worship.

OVERDO. —My fantastical brother-in-law, Master Bartholomew Cokes!

COKES. A motion! what's that? *Reads the bill.* 'The ancient modern history of Hero and Leander, otherwise called the Touchstone of True Love, with as true a trial of friendship between Damon and Pythias, two faithful friends o' the Bankside.' Pretty, i' faith, what's the meaning on't? is't an interlude, or what is't?

FILCHER. Yes, sir, please you come near, we'll take your money within.

COKES. Back with these children! they do so follow me up and down!

Enter LITTLEWIT.

LITTLEWIT. By your leave, friend.

FILCHER. You must pay, sir, an you go in.

LITTLEWIT. Who, I! I perceive thou know'st not me. Call the master o' the motion.

SHARKWELL. What, do you not know the author,

fellow Filcher? You must take no money of him; he
must come in gratis. Master Littlewit is a voluntary;
he is the author.

LITTLEWIT. Peace, speak not too loud. I would not
have any notice taken that I am the author, till we
see how it passes.

COKES. Master Littlewit, how dost thou?

LITTLEWIT. Master Cokes! you are exceeding well
met. What, in your doublet and hose, without a
cloak or a hat?

COKES. I would I might never stir, as I am an
honest man, and by that fire; I have lost all i' the
Fair, and all my acquaintance too. Didst thou meet
anybody that I know, Master Littlewit? my man
Numps, or my sister Overdo, or Mistress Grace?
Pray thee, Master Littlewit, lend me some money to
see the interlude here. I'll pay thee again, as I am a
gentleman. If thou'lt but carry me home, I have
money enough there.

LITTLEWIT. O sir, you shall command it. What,
will a crown serve you?

COKES. I think it well. What do we pay for coming
in, fellows?

FILCHER. Twopence, sir.

COKES. Twopence? There's twelvepence, friend.
Nay, I am a gallant, as simple as I look now, if you
see me with my man about me, and my artillery
again.

LITTLEWIT. Your man was i' the stocks e'en now,
sir.

COKES. Who, Numps?

LITTLEWIT. Yes, faith.

COKES. For what, i' faith? I am glad o' that. Re-
member to tell me on't anon. I have enough now.
What manner of matter is this, Master Littlewit?
What kind of actors ha' you? Are they good actors?

LITTLEWIT. Pretty youths, sir, all children both old and young. Here's the master of 'em——

Enter LEATHERHEAD.

LEATHERHEAD. *Whispers to* LITTLEWIT. Call me not Leatherhead, but Lantern.

LITTLEWIT. Master Lantern, that gives light to the business.

COKES. In good time, sir, I would fain see 'em; I would be glad drink with the young company. Which is the tiring-house?

LEATHERHEAD. Troth, sir, our tiring-house is somewhat little. We are but beginners yet, pray pardon us. You cannot go upright in't.

COKES. No! not now my hat is off? What would you have done with me, if you had had me feather and all, as I was once today? Ha' you none of your pretty, impudent boys now, to bring stools, fill tobacco, fetch ale, and beg money, as they have at other houses? Let me see some o' your actors.

LITTLEWIT. Show him 'em, show him 'em. Master Lantern, this is a gentleman that is a favourer of the quality. *Exit* LEATHERHEAD.

OVERDO. —Ay, the favouring of this licentious quality is the consumption of many a young gentleman, a pernicious enormity.

Re-enter LEATHERHEAD *with a basket.*

COKES. What, do they live in baskets?

LEATHERHEAD. They do lie in a basket, sir, they are o' the small players.

COKES. These be players minors, indeed. Do you call these players?

LEATHERHEAD. They are actors, sir, and as good as any, none dispraised, for dumb shows; indeed, I am the mouth of 'em all.

COKES. Thy mouth will hold 'em all. I think one tailor would go near to beat all this company, with a hand bound behind him.

LITTLEWIT. Ay, and eat 'em all too, an they were in cake-bread.

COKES. I thank you for that, Master Littlewit, a good jest! Which is your Burbage now?

LEATHERHEAD. What mean you by that, sir?

COKES. Your best actor, your Field?

LITTLEWIT. Good, i' faith! you are even with me, sir.

LEATHERHEAD. This is he, that acts young Leander, sir. He is extremely beloved of the womenkind. They do so affect his action, the green gamesters that come here! And this is lovely Hero; this with the beard, Damon; and this, pretty Pythias. This is the ghost of King Dionysius, in the habit of a scrivener, as you shall see anon at large.

COKES. Well, they are a civil company—I like 'em for that. They offer not to fleer, nor jeer, nor break jests, as the great players do. And then, there goes not so much charge to the feasting of 'em, or making 'em drunk, as to the other, by reason of their little-ness. Do they use to play perfect? Are they never flustered?

LEATHERHEAD. No, sir, I thank my industry and policy for it. They are as well governed a company, though I say it——And here is young Leander, is as proper an actor of his inches, and shakes his head like an hostler.

COKES. But do you play it according to the printed book? I have read that.

LEATHERHEAD. By no means, sir.

COKES. No? How then?

LEATHERHEAD. A better way, sir. That is too learned and poetical for our audience. What do they know what Hellespont is, 'guilty of true love's blood'? or what Abydos is? or 'the other, Sestos hight'?

COKES. Th' art i' the right, I do not know myself.

LEATHERHEAD. No, I have entreated Master Little-wit to take a little pains to reduce it to a more familiar strain for our people.

COKES. How, I pray thee, good Master Littlewit?

LITTLEWIT. It pleases him to make a matter of it, sir, but there is no such matter, I assure you. I have only made it a little easy and modern for the times, sir, that's all. As for the Hellespont, I imagine our Thames here; and then Leander I make a dyer's son about Puddle Wharf; and Hero a wench o' the Bankside, who going over one morning to Old Fish Street, Leander spies her land at Trig Stairs, and falls in love with her. Now do I introduce Cupid, having metamorphosed himself into a drawer, and he strikes Hero in love, with a pint of sherry. And other pretty passages there are, o' the friendship, that will delight you, sir, and please you of judgment.

COKES. I'll be sworn they shall; I am in love with the actors already, and I'll be allied to them presently.—They respect gentlemen, these fellows.—Hero shall by my fairing; but which of my fairings? Le' me see—i' faith, my Fiddle; and Leander my Fiddlestick. Then Damon my Drum, and Pythias my Pipe, and the ghost of Dionysius, my Hobby-Horse. All fitted.

Enter WINWIFE *and* GRACE.

WINWIFE. Look, yonder's your Cokes gotten in among his playfellows. I thought we could not miss him at such a spectacle.

GRACE. Let him alone, he is so busy he will never spy us.

LEATHERHEAD. Nay, good sir!

COKES. *Handling the puppets.* I warrant thee I will not hurt her, fellow. What, dost think me uncivil? I pray thee be not jealous, I am toward a wife.

LITTLEWIT. Well, good Master Lantern, make ready to begin, that I may fetch my wife; and look you be perfect, you undo me else i' my reputation.

LEATHERHEAD. I warrant you, sir, do not you breed too great an expectation of it among your friends. That's the only hurter of these things.

LITTLEWIT. No, no, no.   *Exit.*

COKES. I'll stay here and see. Pray thee let me see.

WINWIFE. How diligent and troublesome he is!

GRACE. The place becomes him, methinks.

OVERDO. —My ward, Mistress Grace, in the company of a stranger! I doubt I shall be compelled to discover myself before my time.

Enter KNOCKEM, WHIT, *and* EDGWORTH, *with* MISTRESS
    OVERDO *and* MISTRESS LITTLEWIT, *masked.*

FILCHER. Twopence apiece, gentlemen, an excellent motion.

KNOCKEM. Shall we have fine fireworks and good vapours?

SHARKWELL. Yes, Captain, and waterworks too.

WHIT. I pre'dee take care o' dy shmall lady there, Edgworth; I vill look to dish tall lady myshelf.

LEATHERHEAD. Welcome, gentlemen; welcome, gentlemen.

WHIT. Pre'dee, mashter o' de monshtersh, help a very shick lady here to a chair to shit in.

LEATHERHEAD. Presently, sir.

           They bring MISTRESS OVERDO *a chair.*

WHIT. Good fait now, Ursula's ale and aqua-vitae ish to blame for't. Shit down, shweetheart, shit down and shleep a little.

EDGWORTH. *Courting* MISTRESS LITTLEWIT. Madam, you are very welcome hither.

KNOCKEM. Yes, and you shall see very good vapours.

OVERDO. —Here is my care come! I like to see him in so good company, and yet I wonder that persons of such fashion should resort hither!

EDGWORTH. This is a very private house, madam.

LEATHERHEAD. Will it please your ladyship sit, madam?

MISTRESS LITTLEWIT. Yes, goodman. They do so all-to-be-madam me, I think they think me a very lady!

EDGWORTH. What else, madam?

MISTRESS LITTLEWIT. Must I put off my mask to him?

EDGWORTH. O, by no means.

MISTRESS LITTLEWIT. How should my husband know me then?

KNOCKEM. Husband? an idle vapour! He must not know you, nor you him; there's the true vapour.

OVERDO. Yea, I will observe more of this.—Is this a lady, friend?

WHIT. Ay, and dat is anoder lady, shweetheart. If dou hasht a mind to 'em, give me twelvepence from tee, and dou shalt have eder-oder on 'em.

OVERDO. —Ay! this will prove my chiefest enormity. I will follow this.

EDGWORTH. Is not this a finer life, lady, than to be clogged with a husband?

MISTRESS LITTLEWIT. Yes, a great deal. When will they begin, trow, in the name o' the motion?

EDGWORTH. By and by, madam, they stay but for company.

KNOCKEM. Do you hear, puppet-master, these are tedious vapours; when begin you?

LEATHERHEAD. We stay but for Master Littlewit, the author, who is gone for his wife; and we begin presently.

MISTRESS LITTLEWIT. That's I, that's I.

EDGWORTH. That was you, lady, but now you are no such poor thing.

KNOCKEM. Hang the author's wife, a running vapour! Here be ladies will stay for ne'er a Delia o' 'em all.

WHIT. But hear me now, here ish one o' de ladish ashleep, shtay till she but vake, man.

Enter WASP.

WASP. How now, friends! what's here to do?

FILCHER. Twopence apiece, sir, the best motion in the Fair.

WASP. I believe you lie. If you do, I'll have my money again, and beat you.

MISTRESS LITTLEWIT. Numps is come!

WASP. Did you see a master of mine come in here, a tall young squire of Harrow o' the Hill, Master Bartholomew Cokes?

FILCHER. I think there be such a one within.

WASP. Look he be, you were best; but it is very likely. I wonder I found him not at all the rest. I ha' been at the eagle, and the black wolf, and the bull with the five legs and two pizzles,—he was a calf at Uxbridge Fair two years agone—and at the dogs that dance the morris, and the hare o' the tabor; and missed him at all these! Sure, this must needs be some fine sight that holds him so, if it have him.

COKES. Come, come, are you ready now?

LEATHERHEAD. Presently, sir.

WASP. Hoy-day, he's at work in his doublet and hose! Do you hear, sir, are you employed, that you are bare-headed and so busy?

COKES. Hold your peace, Numps, you ha' been i' the stocks, I hear.

WASP. Does he know that? Nay, then the date of my authority is out. I must think no longer to reign; my government is at an end. He that will correct another must want fault in himself.

WINWIFE. —Sententious Numps! I never heard so much from him before.

LEATHERHEAD. Sure, Master Littlewit will not come. Please you take your place, sir, we'll begin.

COKES. I pray thee do, mine ears long to be at it, and my eyes too. O Numps, i' the stocks, Numps? Where's your sword, Numps?

WASP. I pray you intend your game, sir, let me alone.

COKES. Well then, we are quit for all. Come, sit down, Numps, I'll interpret to thee. Did you see Mistress Grace? It's no matter neither, now I think on't, tell me anon.

WINWIFE. —A great deal of love and care he expresses.

GRACE. Alas, would you have him to express more than he has? That were tyranny.

COKES. Peace, ho! now, now.

LEATHERHEAD. 'Gentles, that no longer your expectations may wander,
Behold our chief actor, amorous Leander,
With a great deal of cloth, lapped about him like a scarf;
For he yet serves his father, a dyer at Puddle Wharf;
Which place we'll make bold with, to call it our Abydos,
As the Bankside is our Sestos; and let it not be denied us.
Now as he is beating, to make the dye take the fuller,

Who chances to come by, but fair Hero in a sculler;
And seeing Leander's naked leg and goodly calf,
Cast at him, from the boat, a sheep's eye and a half.
Now she is landed, and the sculler come back;
By and by you shall see what Leander doth lack.'

LEANDER. 'Cole, Cole, old Cole!'

LEATHERHEAD. 'That is the sculler's name, without control.'

LEANDER. 'Cole, Cole, I say, Cole!'

LEATHERHEAD.   'We do hear you.'

LEANDER.   'Old Cole!'

LEATHERHEAD. 'Old Cole! Is the dyer turned collier? How do you sell?'

LEANDER. 'A pox o' your manners, kiss my hole here, and smell.'

LEATHERHEAD. 'Kiss your hole and smell! there's manners indeed.'

LEANDER. 'Why, Cole, I say, Cole!'

LEATHERHEAD.   'It's the sculler you need?'

LEANDER. 'Ay, and be hanged.'

LEATHERHEAD.   'Be hanged? look you yonder.
Old Cole, you must go hang with Master Leander.'

COLE. 'Where is he?'

LEANDER.   'Here, Cole. What fairest of fairs
Was that fare that thou landedst but now a' Trig
    Stairs.'

COKES. What was that, fellow? Pray thee tell me,
I scarce understand 'em.

LEATHERHEAD. 'Leander does ask, sir, what fairest
    of fairs,
Was the fare that he landed but now at Trig Stairs?'

COLE. 'It is lovely Hero.'

LEANDER. 'Nero?'

COLE. 'No, Hero.'

LEATHERHEAD. 'It is Hero

Of the Bankside, he saith, to tell you truth without
    erring,
Is come over into Fish Street to eat some fresh
    herring.
Leander says no more, but as fast as he can,
Gets on all his best clothes, and will after to the
    Swan.'

    COKES. Most admirable good, is't not?

    LEATHERHEAD. 'Stay, sculler.'

    COLE.   'What say you?'

    LEATHERHEAD.   'You must stay for Leander,
And carry him to the wench.'

    COLE.   'You rogue, I am no pander.'

    COKES. He says he is no pander. 'Tis a fine lan-
guage, I understand it now.

    LEATHERHEAD. 'Are you no pander, Goodman
    Cole? Here's no man says you are.
You'll grow a hot Cole, it seems. Pray you stay for
    your fare.'

    COLE. 'Will he come away?'

    LEATHERHEAD. 'What do you say?'

    COLE. 'I'd ha' him come away.'

    LEATHERHEAD. 'Would you ha' Leander come
    away? Why, pray, sir, stay.
You are angry, Goodman Cole; I believe the fair
    maid
Came over wi' you o' trust. Tell us, sculler, are you
    paid?'

    COLE. 'Yes, Goodman Hogrubber o' Picthatch.'

    LEATHERHEAD.   'How, Hogrubber o' Picthatch?'

    COLE. 'Ay, Hogrubber o' Picthatch. Take you
    that.'   *Strikes him over the pate.*

    LEATHERHEAD. 'O my head!'

    COLE.   'Harm watch, harm catch.'

    COKES. 'Harm watch, harm catch,' he says. Very

good, i' faith. The sculler had like to ha' knocked you, sirrah.

LEATHERHEAD. Yes, but that his fare called him away.

LEANDER. 'Row apace, row apace, row, row, row, row, row.'

LEATHERHEAD. 'You are knavishly loaden, sculler, take heed where you go.'

COLE. 'Knave i' your face, Goodman Rogue.'

LEANDER.   'Row, row, row, row, row, row.'

COKES. He said, knave i' your face, friend.

LEATHERHEAD. Ay, sir, I heard him. But there's no talking to these watermen; they will ha' the last word.

COKES. God's my life! I am not allied to the sculler yet; he shall be Dauphin, my boy. But my Fiddlestick does fiddle in and out too much. I pray thee speak to him on't. Tell him I would have him tarry in my sight more.

LEATHERHEAD. I pray you be content, you'll have enough on him, sir.

'Now, gentles, I take it, here is none of you so stupid,
But that you have heard of a little god of love called Cupid;
Who, out of kindness to Leander, hearing he but saw her,
This present day and hour doth turn himself to a drawer.
And because he would have their first meeting to be merry,
He strikes Hero in love to him with a pint of sherry;
Which he tells her from amorous Leander is sent her,
Who after him into the room of Hero doth venture.'

LEANDER *goes into* HERO'S *room.*

JONAS. 'A pint of sack, score a pint of sack i' the Coney.'

COKES. Sack? you said but e'en now it should be sherry.

JONAS. 'Why, so it is: sherry, sherry, sherry!'

COKES. 'Sherry, sherry, sherry!' By my troth, he makes me merry. I must have a name for Cupid, too. Let me see, thou might'st help me now, an thou wouldst, Numps, at a dead lift; but thou art dreaming o' the stocks still. Do not think on't, I have forgot it. 'Tis but a nine days' wonder, man, let it not trouble thee.

WASP. I would the stocks were about your neck, sir; condition I hung by the heels in them till the wonder were off from you, with all my heart!

COKES. Well said, resolute Numps! But hark you, friend, where's the friendship all this while between my Drum Damon and my Pipe Pythias?

LEATHERHEAD. You shall see by and by, sir.

COKES. You think my Hobby-Horse is forgotten, too. No, I'll see 'em all enact before I go; I shall not know which to love best else.

KNOCKEM. This gallant has interrupting vapours, troublesome vapours. Whit, puff with him.

WHIT. No, I pre'dee, Captain, let him alone. He is a child, i' fait, la.

LEATHERHEAD. 'Now, gentles, to the friends, who in number are two,

And lodged in that alehouse in which fair Hero does do:

Damon, for some kindness done him the last week,

Is come, fair Hero in Fish Street this morning to seek.

Pythias does smell the knavery of the meeting;

And now you shall see their true-friendly greeting.'

PYTHIAS. 'You whoremasterly slave, you!'

COKES. 'Whoremasterly slave, you?' Very friendly and familiar, that.

DAMON. 'Whoremaster i' thy face;
Thou hast lain with her thyself, I'll prove 't i' this place.'

COKES. Damon says Pythias has lain with her himself, he'll prove 't in this place.

LEATHERHEAD. 'They are whoremasters both, sir, that's a plain case.'

PYTHIAS. 'You lie like a rogue.'

LEATHERHEAD. 'Do I lie like a rogue?'

PYTHIAS. 'A pimp and a scab.'

LEATHERHEAD. 'A pimp and a scab!
I say, between you, you have both but one drab.'

DAMON. 'You lie again.'

LEATHERHEAD. 'Do I lie again?'

DAMON. 'Like a rogue again.'

LEATHERHEAD. 'Like a rogue again!'

PYTHIAS. 'And you are a pimp again.'

COKES. And you are a pimp again, he says.

DAMON. 'And a scab again.'

COKES. And a scab again, he says.

LEATHERHEAD. 'And I say again, you are both whoremasters again,
And you have both but one drab again.'

DAMON, PYTHIAS. 'Dost thou, dost thou, dost thou?'

They fight.

LEATHERHEAD. 'What, both at once?'

PYTHIAS. 'Down with him, Damon.'

DAMON. 'Pink his guts, Pythias.'

LEATHERHEAD. 'What, so malicious?
Will ye murder me, masters both, i' mine own house?'

COKES. Ho! well acted, my Drum, well acted, my Pipe, well acted still!

WASP. Well acted, with all my heart.

LEATHERHEAD. 'Hold, hold your hands.'

COKES. Ay, both your hands, for my sake! for you ha' both done well.

DAMON. 'Gramercy, pure Pythias.'

PYTHIAS. 'Gramercy, dear Damon.'

COKES. Gramercy to you both, my Pipe and my Drum.

PYTHIAS and DAMON. 'Come, now we'll together to
  breakfast to Hero.'

LEATHERHEAD. ''Tis well you can now go to breakfast to Hero,
You have given me my breakfast, with a hone and
  honero.'

COKES. How is't, friend, ha' they hurt thee?

LEATHERHEAD.   O no,
Between you and I, sir, we do but make show.
'Thus, gentles, you perceive, without any denial,
'Twixt Damon and Pythias here, friendship's true
  trial.
Though hourly they quarrel thus, and roar each
  with other,
They fight you no more than does brother with
  brother;
But friendly together, at the next man they meet,
They let fly their anger, as here you might see't.'

COKES. Well, we have seen't, and thou hast felt it,
whatsoever thou sayest. What's next, what's next?

LEATHERHEAD. 'This while, young Leander with
  fair Hero is drinking,
And Hero grown drunk, to any man's thinking!
Yet was it not three pints of sherry could flaw her,
Till Cupid, distinguished like Jonas the drawer,
From under his apron, where his lechery lurks,
Put love in her sack. Now mark how it works.'

HERO. 'O Leander, Leander, my dear, my dear
    Leander,
I'll forever be thy goose, so thou'lt be my gander.'
    COKES. Excellently well said, Fiddle! She'll ever
be his goose, so he'll be her gander, was't not so?
    LEATHERHEAD. Yes, sir, but mark his answer now.
    LEANDER. 'And, sweetest of geese, before I go to
    bed,
I'll swim o'er the Thames, my goose, thee to tread.'
    COKES. Brave! he will swim o'er the Thames and
tread his goose tonight, he says.
    LEATHERHEAD. Ay, peace, sir, they'll be angry if
they hear you eavesdropping, now they are setting
their match.
    LEANDER. 'But lest the Thames should be dark,
    my goose, my dear friend,
Let thy window be provided of a candle's end.'
    HERO. 'Fear not, my gander, I protest I should
    handle
My matters very ill, if I had not a whole candle!'
    LEANDER. 'Well then, look to't,
And kiss me to boot.'
    LEATHERHEAD. 'Now here come the friends again,
    Pythias and Damon,
And under their cloaks they have of bacon a
    gammon.'
    PYTHIAS. 'Drawer, fill some wine here.'
    LEATHERHEAD.   'How, some wine there?
There's company already, sir, pray forbear.'
    DAMON. ''Tis Hero.'
    LEATHERHEAD.   'Yes, but she will not be taken,
After sack and fresh herring, with your Dunmow
    bacon.'
    PYTHIAS. 'You lie, it's Westfabian.'
    LEATHERHEAD.   'Westphalian, you should say.'

DAMON. 'If you hold not your peace, you are a coxcomb, I would say.

LEANDER and HERO are kissing.

What's here, what's here? kiss, kiss upon kiss.'

LEATHERHEAD. 'Ay, wherefore should they not? what harm is in this?
'Tis Mistress Hero.'

DAMON. 'Mistress Hero's a whore.'

LEATHERHEAD. 'Is she a whore? Keep you quiet, or, Sir Knave, out of door.'

DAMON. 'Knave out of door?'

HERO. 'Yes, knave out of door.'

DAMON. 'Whore out of door.'

HERO. 'I say knave out of door.'

DAMON. 'I say whore out of door.'

PYTHIAS. 'Yea, so say I, too.'

HERO. 'Kiss the whore o' the arse.'

LEATHERHEAD. 'Now you ha' something to do. You must kiss her o' the arse, she says.'

DAMON and PYTHIAS. 'So we will, so we will.'

They quarrel and fall together by the ears.

HERO. 'O my haunches, O my haunches! hold, hold!'

LEATHERHEAD. 'Stand'st thou still?
Leander, where art thou? stand'st thou still like a sot,
And not offer'st to break both their heads with a pot?
See who's at thine elbow there! puppet Jonas and Cupid.'

JONAS. 'Upon 'em, Leander, be not so stupid.'

They fight.

LEANDER. 'You goat-bearded slave!'

DAMON. 'You whoremaster knave!'

LEANDER. 'Thou art a whoremaster.'

JONAS. 'Whoremasters all.'

LEATHERHEAD. 'See, Cupid with a word has ta'en
    up the brawl.'

KNOCKEM. These be fine vapours!

COKES. By this good day, they fight bravely, do
they not, Numps?

WASP. Yes, they lacked but you to be their second
all this while.

LEATHERHEAD. 'This tragical encounter falling out
    thus to busy us,
It raises up the ghost of their friend Dionysius,
Not like a monarch, but the master of a school,
In a scrivener's furred gown, which shows he is no
    fool;
For therein he hath wit enough to keep himself
    warm.
"O Damon," he cries, "and Pythias, what harm
Hath poor Dionysius done you in his grave,
That after his death you should fall out thus, and
    rave,
And call amorous Leander whoremaster knave?"'

DIONYSIUS. 'I cannot, I will not, I promise you,
    endure it.'

Enter BUSY.

BUSY. Down with Dagon, down with Dagon! 'Tis
I will no longer endure your profanations.

LEATHERHEAD. What mean you, sir?

BUSY. I will remove Dagon there, I say, that idol,
that heathenish idol, that remains, as I may say, a
beam, a very beam; not a beam of the sun, nor a
beam of the moon, nor a beam of a balance, neither
a house-beam, nor a weaver's beam; but a beam in
the eye, in the eye of the Brethren; a very great
beam, an exceeding great beam; such as are your
stage-players, rhymers, and morris-dancers, who have
walked hand in hand, in contempt of the Brethren

and the Cause; and been borne out by instruments of no mean countenance.

LEATHERHEAD. Sir, I present nothing but what is licensed by authority.

BUSY. Thou art all licence, even licentiousness itself, Shimei!

LEATHERHEAD. I have the Master of the Revels' hand for't, sir.

BUSY. The master of rebels' hand thou hast, Satan's! Hold thy peace, thy scurrility shut up thy mouth! Thy profession is damnable, and in pleading for it thou dost plead for Baal. I have long opened my mouth wide and gaped, I have gaped as the oyster for the tide, after thy destruction; but cannot compass it by suit or dispute; so that I look for a bickering ere long, and then a battle.

KNOCKEM. Good Banbury vapours!

COKES. Friend, you'd have an ill match on't, if you bicker with him here. Though he be no man o' the fist, he has friends that will go to cuffs for him. Numps, will not you take our side?

EDGWORTH. Sir, it shall not need; in my mind, he offers him a fairer course, to end it by disputation. Hast thou nothing to say for thyself, in defence of thy quality?

LEATHERHEAD. Faith, sir, I am not well studied in these controversies between the hypocrites and us. But here's one of my motion, puppet Dionysius, shall undertake him, and I'll venture the cause on't.

COKES. Who, my Hobby-Horse? Will he dispute with him?

LEATHERHEAD. Yes, sir, and make a hobby-ass of him, I hope.

COKES. That's excellent! Indeed he looks like the best scholar of 'em all.—Come, sir, you must be as good as your word now.

BUSY. I will not fear to make my spirit and gifts known: assist me, zeal, fill me, fill me; that is, make me full!

WINWIFE. What a desperate, profane wretch is this! Is there any ignorance or impudence like his, to call his zeal to fill him against a puppet?

QUARLOUS. I know no fitter match than a puppet to commit with an hypocrite!

BUSY. First, I say unto thee, Idol, thou hast no calling.

DIONYSIUS. 'You lie, I am called Dionysius.'

LEATHERHEAD. The motion says you lie, he is called Dionysius i' the matter, and to that calling he answers.

BUSY. I mean no vocation, Idol, no present lawful calling.

DIONYSIUS. 'Is yours a lawful calling?'

LEATHERHEAD. The motion asketh if yours be a lawful calling.

BUSY. Yes, mine is of the spirit.

DIONYSIUS. 'Then idol is a lawful calling.'

LEATHERHEAD. He says, then idol is a lawful calling; for you called him idol, and your calling is of the spirit.

COKES. Well disputed, Hobby-Horse!

BUSY. Take not part with the wicked, young gallant. He neigheth and whinnieth; all is but whinnying sophistry. I call him idol again. Yet I say, his calling, his profession, is profane. It is profane, Idol.

DIONYSIUS. 'It is not profane.'

LEATHERHEAD. It is not profane, he says.

BUSY. It is profane.

DIONYSIUS. 'It is not profane.'

BUSY. It is profane.

DIONYSIUS. 'It is not profane.'

LEATHERHEAD. Well said, confute him with 'not,'

still. You cannot bear him down with your base noise, sir.

BUSY. Nor he me, with his treble creaking, though he creak like the chariot wheels of Satan. I am zealous for the cause——

LEATHERHEAD. As a dog for a bone.

BUSY. And I say it is profane, as being the page of Pride and the waiting-woman of Vanity.

DIONYSIUS. 'Yea? What say you to your tire-women then?'

LEATHERHEAD. Good.

DIONYSIUS. 'Or feather-makers i' the Friars, that are o' your faction of faith? Are not they, with their perukes and their puffs, their fans and their huffs, as much pages of Pride and waiters upon Vanity? What say you, what say you, what say you?'

BUSY. I will not answer for them.

DIONYSIUS. 'Because you cannot, because you cannot. Is a bugle-maker a lawful calling, or the comfit-makers? Such you have there. Or your French fashioner? You'd have all the sin within yourselves, would you not, would you not?'

BUSY. No, Dagon.

DIONYSIUS. 'What then, Dagonet? Is a puppet worse than these?'

BUSY. Yes, and my main argument against you is that you are an abomination; for the male among you putteth on the apparel of the female, and the female of the male.

DIONYSIUS. 'You lie, you lie, you lie abominably.'

COKES. Good, by my troth! he has given him the lie thrice.

DIONYSIUS. 'It is your old, stale argument against the players, but it will not hold against the puppets; for we have neither male nor female amongst us.

And that thou mayst see, if thou wilt, like a malicious, purblind zeal as thou art!'

> *Takes up his garment.*

EDGWORTH. By my faith, there he has answered
you, friend, by plain demonstration.

DIONYSIUS. 'Nay, I'll prove, against e'er a rabbin of
'em all, that my standing is as lawful as his; that I
speak by inspiration, as well as he; that I have as
little to do with learning as he, and do scorn her
helps as much as he.'

BUSY. I am confuted, the Cause hath failed me.

DIONYSIUS. 'Then be converted, be converted.'

LEATHERHEAD. Be converted, I pray you, and let
the play go on!

BUSY. Let it go on, for I am changed, and will
become a beholder with you.

COKES. That's brave, i' faith! Thou hast carried it
away, Hobby-horse. On with the play!

OVERDO. *Discovers himself.* Stay, now do I forbid,
I, Adam Overdo! Sit still, I charge you.

COKES. What, my brother-i'-law!

GRACE. My wise guardian!

EDGWORTH. Justice Overdo!

OVERDO. It is time to take enormity by the forehead and brand it, for I have discovered enough.

Enter QUARLOUS *disguised as* TROUBLEALL, *with*
DAME PURECRAFT.

QUARLOUS. Nay, come, mistress bride, you must do
as I do, now. You must be mad with me, in truth.
I have here Justice Overdo for it.

OVERDO. Peace, good Troubleall, come hither, and
you shall trouble none. I will take the charge of
you, and your friend, too. *To* EDGWORTH. You also,
young man, shall be my care; stand there.

EDGWORTH. Now, mercy upon me.

KNOCKEM. Would we were away, Whit, these are dangerous vapours. Best fall off with our birds, for fear o' the cage.

OVERDO. Stay, is not my name your terror?

WHIT. *Stealing away.* Yesh, fait, man, and it ish for tat ve vould be gone, man.

Enter LITTLEWIT.

LITTLEWIT. O gentlemen, did you not see a wife of mine? I ha' lost my little wife, as I shall be trusted, my little pretty Win. I left her at the great woman's house in trust yonder, the pig-woman's, with Captain Jordan and Captain Whit, very good men, and I cannot hear of her. Poor fool, I fear she's stepped aside. Mother, did you not see Win?

OVERDO. If this grave matron be your mother, sir, stand by her, 'et digito compesce labellum'; I may perhaps spring a wife for you anon. Brother Bartholomew, I am sadly sorry to see you so lightly given, and such a disciple of enormity, with your grave governor Humphrey. But stand you both there, in the middle place; I will reprehend you in your course. Mistress Grace, let me rescue you out of the hands of the stranger.

WINWIFE. Pardon me, sir, I am a kinsman of hers.

OVERDO. Are you so? of what name, sir?

WINWIFE. Winwife, sir.

OVERDO. Master Winwife! I hope you have won no wife of her, sir; if you have, I will examine the possibility of it, at fit leisure. Now to my enormities: look upon me, O London! and see me, O Smithfield! the example of justice, and mirror of magistrates, the true top of formality and scourge of enormity! Hearken unto my labours, and but observe my discoveries; and compare Hercules with me, if thou dar'st, of old; or Columbus, Magellan, or our countryman Drake, of later times. Stand forth, you weeds of enormity, and spread. First Rabbi Busy, thou superlunatical hypocrite. *To* LEATHERHEAD. Next, thou other extremity, thou profane professor of puppetry, little better than poetry. *To* KNOCKEM. Then thou strong debaucher and seducer of youth. *To* EDGWORTH. Witness this easy and honest young man. *To* WHIT. Now, thou esquire of dames, madams, and twelvepenny ladies.—Now, my green madam herself, of the price; let me unmask your ladyship. *Discovers* MISTRESS LITTLEWIT.

LITTLEWIT. O my wife, my wife, my wife!

OVERDO. Is she your wife? 'Redde te Harpocratem.'

Enter TROUBLEALL, *followed by* URSULA *and*
NIGHTINGALE.

TROUBLEALL. By your leave, stand by, my masters, be uncovered.

URSULA. O, stay him, stay him! Help to cry, Nightingale; my pan, my pan!

OVERDO. What's the matter?

NIGHTINGALE. He has stolen Gammer Ursula's pan.

TROUBLEALL. Yes, and I fear no man but Justice Overdo.

OVERDO. Ursula! where is she? O the sow of enormity, this! *To* URSULA. Welcome, stand you there. *To* NIGHTINGALE. You, songster, there.

URSULA. An't please your worship, I am in no fault. A gentleman stripped him in my booth, and borrowed his gown and his hat; and he ran away with my goods here for it.

OVERDO. *To* QUARLOUS. Then this is the true madman, and you are the enormity!

QUARLOUS. You are i' the right, I am mad but from the gown outward.

OVERDO. Stand you there.

QUARLOUS. Where you please, sir.

MISTRESS QUARLOUS. *Waking.* O, lend me a basin, I am sick, I am sick! Where's Master Overdo? Bridget, call hither my Adam.

OVERDO. How!

WHIT. Dy very own vife, i' fait, vorshipful Adam.

MISTRESS OVERDO. Will not my Adam come at me? Shall I see him no more, then?

She is sick and JUSTICE OVERDO *is silenced.*

QUARLOUS. Sir, why do you not go on with the enormity? Are you oppressed with it? I'll help you. Hark you, sir, i' your ear: your innocent young man, you have ta'en such care of all this day, is a cutpurse, that hath got all your brother Cokes's things, and helped you to your beating and the stocks. If you have a mind to hang him now, and show him your magistrate's wit, you may; but I should think it were better recovering the goods, and to save your estimation in him. I thank you, sir, for the gift of your ward, Mistress Grace. Look you, here is your hand and seal, by the way. Master Winwife, give you joy, you are 'Palemon,' you are possessed o' the gentlewoman; but she must pay me value, here's warrant for it. *To* TROUBLEALL. And, honest madman, there's thy gown and cap again; I thank thee for my wife. *To* DAME PURECRAFT. Nay, I can be mad, sweetheart, when I please still; never fear me. And careful Numps, where's he? I thank him for my licence.

WASP. How!

QUARLOUS. 'Tis true, Numps.

WASP. *Missing the licence.* I'll be hanged then.

QUARLOUS. Look i' your box, Numps.—Nay, sir, stand not you fixed here, like a stake in Finsbury to be shot at, or the whipping-post i' the Fair; but get your wife out o' the air, it will make her worse else. And remember you are but Adam, flesh and blood! you have your frailty. Forget your other name of Overdo, and invite us all to supper. There you and I will compare our discoveries, and drown the memory of all enormity in your bigg'st bowl at home.

COKES. How now, Numps, ha' you lost it? I warrant 'twas when thou wert i' the stocks. Why dost not speak!

WASP. I will never speak while I live again, for aught I know.

OVERDO. Nay, Humphrey, if I be patient, you must be so, too. This pleasant, conceited gentleman hath wrought upon my judgment, and prevailed. I pray you take care of your sick friend, Mistress Alice, and my good friends all——

QUARLOUS. And no enormities.

OVERDO. I invite you home with me to my house to supper. I will have none fear to go along, for my intents are 'ad correctionem, non ad destructionem; ad aedificandum, non ad diruendum.' So lead on.

COKES. Yes, and bring the actors along. We'll ha' the rest o' the play at home.   *Exeunt.*

THE EPILOGUE

Your Majesty hath seen the play, and you
Can best allow it from your ear and view.
You know the scope of writers, and what store
Of leave is given them, if they take not more,
And turn it into licence. You can tell
If we have used that leave you gave us well;
Or whether we to rage or licence break,
Or be profane, or make profane men speak.
This is your power to judge, great Sir, and not
The envy of a few. Which if we have got,
We value less what their dislike can bring,
If it so happy be t' have pleased the King.

III. MASQUE

III. MASQUE

Oberon,
the Fairy Prince

A Masque of Prince Henry's

*The first face of the scene appeared all obscure, and
     nothing perceived but a dark rock with trees
     beyond it, and all wildness that could be pre-
     sented; till at one corner of the cliff, above the
     horizon, the moon began to show, and rising, a
     SATYR was seen by her light to put forth his head
     and call.*

1ST SATYR. Chromis! Mnasil! none appear?
    See you not who riseth here?
    You saw Silenus late, I fear!
    I'll prove if this can reach your ear.

*He wound his cornet and thought himself answered,
     but was deceived by the echo.*

O, you wake then! Come away,
    Times be short are made for play;
    The hum'rous moon too will not stay.
    What doth make you thus delay?
Hath his tankard touched your brain?
    Sure, they're fall'n asleep again;
    Or I doubt it was the vain
    Echo, did me entertain.
Prove again—

He wound the second time and found it.
> I thought 'twas she!
> Idle nymph, I pray thee, be
> Modest, and not follow me;
> I nor love myself, nor thee.

*Here he wound the third time and was answered by
another* SATYR, *who likewise showed himself.
To which he spoke:*

> Ay, this sound I better know;
> List! I would I could hear mo.

*At this they came running forth severally from
divers parts of the rock, leaping and making
antic action and gestures, to the number of ten,
—some of them speaking, some admiring—and
amongst them a* SILENE *who is ever the prefect
of the* SATYRS, *and so presented in all their
Chori and meetings.*

2ND SATYR. Thank us, and you shall do so.
3RD SATYR. Ay, our number soon will grow.
2ND SATYR. See Silenus!
3RD SATYR.   Cecrops too!
4TH SATYR. Yes. What is there now to do?
5TH SATYR. Are there any nymphs to woo?
4TH SATYR. If there be, let me have two.
SILENUS. Chaster language! These are nights
> Solemn to the shining rites
> Of the Fairy Prince and knights,
> While the moon their orgies lights.

2ND SATYR. Will they come abroad anon?
3RD SATYR. Shall we see young Oberon?
4TH SATYR. Is he such a princely one
> As you spake him long agone?

SILENUS. Satyrs, he doth fill with grace
    Every season, every place;
    Beauty dwells but in his face;
    He's the height of all our race.
Our Pan's father, god of tongue,
    Bacchus, though he still be young,
    Phoebus, when he crownèd sung,
    Nor Mars, when first his armour rung,
Might with him be named that day.
    He is lovelier, than in May
    Is the spring, and there can stay
    As little, as he can decay.

CHORUS. O that he would come away!

3RD SATYR. Grandsire, we shall leave to play
With Lyaeus now, and serve
Only Oberon.

SILENUS.   He'll deserve
All you can, and more, my boys.

4TH SATYR. Will he give us pretty toys,
To beguile the girls withal?

3RD SATYR. And to make 'em quickly fall?

SILENUS. Peace, my wantons! he will do
More than you can aim unto.

4TH SATYR. Will he build us larger caves?

SILENUS. Yes, and give you ivory staves,
When you hunt; and better wine——

1ST SATYR. Than the master of the vine?

2ND SATYR. And rich prizes, to be won
When we leap or when we run?

1ST SATYR. Ay, and gild our cloven feet?

3RD SATYR. Strew our heads with powders sweet?

1ST SATYR. Bind our crookèd legs in hoops
Made of shells, with silver loops?

2ND SATYR. Tie about our tawny wrists
Bracelets of the fairy twists?

4TH SATYR. And, to spite the coy nymphs' scorns,
Hang upon our stubbèd horns
Garlands, ribands, and fine posies——
   3RD SATYR. Fresh as when the flower discloses?
   1ST SATYR. Yes, and stick our pricking ears
With the pearl that Tethys wears.
   2ND SATYR. And to answer all things else,
Trap our shaggy thighs with bells,
That as we do strike a time,
In our dance shall make a chime——
   3RD SATYR. Louder than the rattling pipes
Of the wood gods——
   1ST SATYR.   Or the stripes
Of the tabour, when we carry
Bacchus up, his pomp to vary.
   CHORUS. O that he so long doth tarry!
   SILENUS. See, the rock begins to ope!
Now you shall enjoy your hope;
'Tis about the hour, I know.

*There the whole scene opened, and within was dis-
   covered the frontispiece of a bright and glorious
   palace, whose gates and walls were transparent.
   Before the gates lay two* SYLVANS, *armed with
   their clubs, and dressed in leaves, asleep. At
   this the* SATYRS *wondering,* SILENUS *proceeds:*

Look! does not his palace show
Like another sky of lights?
Yonder with him live the knights
Once the noblest of the earth,
Quickened by a second birth;
Who for prowess and for truth
There are crowned with lasting youth,
And do hold, by Fate's command,
Seats of bliss in Fairyland.
But their guards, methinks, do sleep!

Let us wake 'em.—Sirs, you keep
Proper watch, that thus do lie
Drowned in sloth!

    1ST SATYR.   They ha' ne'er an eye
To wake withal.

    2ND SATYR.   Nor sense, I fear;
For they sleep in either ear.

    3RD SATYR. Holla, Sylvans!—Sure they're caves
Of sleep, these, or else they're graves!

    4TH SATYR. Hear you, friends, who keeps the
      keepers?

    1ST SATYR. They're the eighth and ninth sleepers!

    2ND SATYR. Shall we cramp 'em?

    SILENUS.   Satyrs, no.

    3RD SATYR. Would we'd Boreas here, to blow
Off their leafy coats, and strip 'em.

    4TH SATYR. Ay, ay, ay—that we might whip 'em!

    3RD SATYR. Or that we had a wasp or two
For their nostrils!

    1ST SATYR.   Hairs will do
Even as well. Take my tail.

    2ND SATYR. What d' you say t' a good nail
Through their temples?

    2ND SATYR.   Or an eel,
In their guts, to make 'em feel?

    4TH SATYR. Shall we steal away their beards?

    3RD SATYR. For Pan's goat, that leads the herds?

    2ND SATYR. Or try whether is more dead
His club or th' other's head?

    SILENUS. Wags, no more; you grow too bold.

    1ST SATYR. I would fain now see 'em rolled
Down a hill, or from a bridge
Headlong cast, to break their ridge-
Bones; or to some river take 'em,
Plump; and see if that would wake 'em.

2ND SATYR. There no motion yet appears.
SILENUS. Strike a charm into their ears.

At which the SATYRS *fell suddenly into this catch:*

Buzz, quoth the blue fly,
Hum, quoth the bee;
Buzz and hum they cry,
And so do we.
In his ear, in his nose,
Thus, do you see?—
He ate the dormouse,
Else it was he.

The two SYLVANS *starting up amazed, and betaking
themselves to their arms, were thus questioned
by* SILENUS:

How now, Sylvans! can you wake?
I commend the care you take
I' your watch! Is this your guise,
To have both your ears and eyes
Sealed so fast, as these mine elves
Might have stol'n you from yourselves?

3RD SATYR. We had thought we must have got
Stakes, and heated 'em red-hot,
And have bored you through the eyes,
With the Cyclops, ere you'd rise.

2ND SATYR. Or have fetched some trees to heave
Up your bulks, that so did cleave
To the ground there.

4TH SATYR.   Are you free
Yet of sleep, and can you see
Who is yonder up aloof?

1ST SATYR. Be your eyes yet moon-proof?

1ST SYLVAN. Satyrs, leave your petulance,
And go frisk about and dance;
Or else rail upon the moon.

Your expectance is too soon.
For before the second cock
Crow, the gates will not unlock;
And till then we know we keep
Guard enough, although we sleep.

   1st SATYR. Say you so? then let us fall
To a song or to a brawl.
Shall we, grandsire? Let us sport,
And make expectation short.

   SILENUS. Do, my wantons, what you please.
I'll lie down and take mine ease.

   1st SATYR. Brothers, sing then, and upbraid,
As we use, yon seeming maid.

SONG.

   Now, my cunning lady, Moon,
   Can you leave the side so soon
     Of the boy you keep so hid?
   Midwife Juno sure will say
   This is not the proper way
     Of your paleness to be rid.
   But perhaps it is your grace
   To wear sickness i' your face,
     That there might be wagers laid
     Still, by fools, you are a maid.

   Come, your changes overthrow
   What your look would carry so;
     Moon, confess then what you are.
   And be wise, and free to use
   Pleasures that you now do lose;
     Let us Satyrs have a share.
   Though our forms be rough and rude,
   Yet our acts may be endued
     With more virtue. Everyone
     Cannot be Endymion.

The song ended they fell suddenly into an antic dance, full of gesture and swift motion, and continued it till the crowing of the cock; at which they were interrupted by SILENUS.

SILENUS. Stay, the cheerful chanticleer
Tells you that the time is near.
See, the gates already spread!
Every Satyr bow his head.

There the whole palace opened and the nation of fays were discovered, some with instruments, some bearing lights, others singing; and within, afar off in perspective, the knights masquers sitting in their several sieges; at the further end of all, OBERON, *in a chariot which, to a loud triumphant music, began to move forward, drawn by two white bears, and on either side guarded by three* SYLVANS, *with one going in front.*

SONG.

Melt earth to sea, sea flow to air,
  And air fly into fire,
Whilst we in tunes to Arthur's chair
  Bear Oberon's desire;
Than which there's nothing can be higher,
  Save James, to whom it flies:
But he the wonder is of tongues, of ears, of eyes.

Who hath not heard, who hath not seen,
  Who hath not sung his name?
The soul that hath not, hath not been;
  But is the very same
With buried sloth, and knows not fame,
  Which doth him best comprise:
For he the wonder is of tongues, of ears, of eyes.

*By this time the chariot was come as far forth as the
face of the scene; and the* SATYRS *beginning to
leap, and express their joy for the unused state
and solemnity, the foremost* SYLVAN *began to
speak:*

1ST SYLVAN. Give place, and silence; you were rude
    too late.
This is a night of greatness and of state,
Not to be mixed with light and skipping sport;
A night of homage to the British court,
And ceremony due to Arthur's chair,
From our bright master, Oberon the fair;
Who with these knights attendants, here preserved
In Fairyland, for good they have deserved
Of yon high throne, are come of right to pay
Their annual vows; and all their glories lay
At feet, and tender to this only great,
True Majesty, restorèd in this seat;
To whose sole power and magic they do give
The honour of their being, that they live
Sustained in form, fame, and felicity,
From rage of fortune or the fear to die.
    SILENUS. And may they well. For this indeed is
    he,
My boys, whom you must quake at when you see.
He is above your reach; and neither doth
Nor can he think within a Satyr's tooth;
Before his presence you must fall or fly.
He is the matter of virtue, and placed high.
His meditations to his height are even;
And all their issue is akin to Heaven.
He is a god o'er kings; yet stoops he then
Nearest a man, when he doth govern men,
To teach them by the sweetness of his sway,
And not by force. He's such a king as they

Who are tyrants' subjects, or ne'er tasted peace,
Would, in their wishes, form for their release.
'Tis he that stays the time from turning old,
And keeps the age up in a head of gold;
That in his own true circle still doth run,
And holds his course as certain as the sun.
He makes it ever day and ever spring
Where he doth shine, and quickens everything
Like a new nature; so that true to call
Him by his title is to say, he's all.

　　1ST SYLVAN. I thank the wise Silenus for this praise.
Stand forth, bright fays and elves, and tune your lays
Unto his name. Then let your nimble feet
Tread subtle circles that may always meet
In point to him, and figures to express
The grace of him and his great Empress;
That all that shall tonight behold the rites
Performed by princely Oberon and these knights,
May without stop point out the proper heir
Designed so long to Arthur's crowns and chair.

　　　　　　　　The SONG *by two* FAYS.

1ST FAY.	Seek you majesty, to strike?
	Bid the world produce his like.
2ND FAY.	Seek you glory, to amaze?
	Here let all eyes stand at gaze.
CHORUS.	Seek you wisdom, to inspire?
	Touch then at no other's fire.

1ST FAY.	Seek you knowledge, to direct?
	Trust to his without suspect.
2ND FAY.	Seek you piety, to lead?
	In his footsteps only tread.
CHORUS.	Every virtue of a king,
	And of all, in him, we sing.

Then the lesser FAYS *dance forth their dance, which ended, a full* SONG *follows by all the voices:*

> The solemn rites are well begun;
> And though but lighted by the moon,
> They show as rich as if the sun
> Had made this night his noon.
> But may none wonder that they are so bright;
> The moon now borrows from a greater light.
> Then, princely *Oberon,*
> Go on,
> This is not every night.

There OBERON *and the knights dance out the first masque dance, which was followed with this*

SONG.

> Nay, nay,
> You must not stay,
> Nor be weary yet;
> This 's no time to cast away,
> Or for fays so to forget
> The virtue of their feet.
> Knotty legs and plants of clay
> Seek for ease, or love delay,
> But with you it still should fare
> As with the air of which you are.

After which they danced forth their second masque dance, and were again excited by a

SONG.

1ST FAY. Nor yet, nor yet, O you in this night blest,
> Must you have will or hope to rest.

2ND FAY.   If you use the smallest stay,
            You'll be overta'en by day.
1ST FAY.   And these beauties will suspect
            That their forms you do neglect,
            If you do not call them forth.
2ND FAY.   Or that you have no more worth
            Than the coarse and country fairy,
            That doth haunt the hearth or dairy.

Then followed the measures, corrantos, galliards, &c., till PHOSPHORUS, *the day star, appeared and called them away; but first they were invited home by one of the* SYLVANS *with this*

SONG.

Gentle knights,
Know some measure of your nights.
Tell the high-graced *Oberon*
It is time that we were gone.
    Here be forms so bright and airy,
    And their motions so they vary,
    As they will enchant the fairy,
    If you longer here should tarry.

PHOSPHORUS. To rest, to rest! The herald of the day,
Bright Phosphorus, commands you hence; obey.
The moon is pale and spent, and wingèd Night
Makes headlong haste to fly the Morning's sight,
Who now is rising from her blushing wars,
And with her rosy hand puts back the stars;
Of which myself the last, her harbinger,
But stay to warn you that you not defer
Your parting longer. Then do I give way,
As Night hath done, and so must you, to Day.

*After this they danced their last dance into the work;
and with a full song the Star vanished, and the
whole machine closed.*

SONG.

O, yet how early, and before her time,
The envious Morning up doth climb,
    Though she not love her bed!
What haste the jealous Sun doth make,
His fiery horses up to take,
    And once more show his head!
Lest, taken with the brightness of this night,
The world should wish it last, and never miss his
    light.

The Vision of Delight

Presented at Court in Christmas, *1617*

THE SCENE: *A street in perspective of fair build-ing discovered*

DELIGHT *is seen to come as afar off, accompanied with* GRACE, LOVE, HARMONY, REVEL, SPORT, LAUGHTER; WONDER *following.* DELIGHT *spake in song (stilo recitativo):*

Let us play and dance and sing,
  Let us now turn every sort
O' the pleasures of the spring
  To the graces of a court;
From air, from cloud, from dreams, from toys,
To sounds, to sense, to love, to joys;

Let your shows be new as strange,
  Let them oft and sweetly vary;
Let them haste so to their change,
  As the seers may not tarry;
Too long t' expect the pleasing'st sight
Doth take away from the delight.

Here the first ANTIMASQUE *entered.*

A she-monster delivered of six BURRATINES, *that dance with six* PANTALOONS; *which done,* DELIGHT *spoke again:*

Yet hear what your Delight doth pray:
  All sour and sullen looks away,
  That are the servants of the day;

Our sports are of the humorous Night,
   Who feeds the stars that give her light,
   And useth, than her wont more bright,
   To help the vision of Delight.

Here the NIGHT *rises and took her chariot bespangled
with stars.*

               DELIGHT *proceeds:*

See, see, her sceptre and her crown
   Are all of flame, and from her gown
   A train of light comes waving down.
This night, in dew she will not steep
   The brain, nor lock the sense in sleep;
   But all awake with phantoms keep,
   And those to make delight more deep.

By this time the NIGHT *and* MOON *being both risen,*
  NIGHT, *hovering over the place, sang:*

NIGHT.   Break, Fancy, from thy cave of cloud,
       And spread thy purple wings;
         Now all thy figures are allowed,
       And various shapes of things.
       Create of airy forms a stream,
       It must have blood, and naught of phlegm;
       And though it be a waking dream——
THE CHOIR. Yet let it like an odour rise
       To all the senses here,
         And fall like sleep upon their eyes,
       Or music in their ear.

The Scene here changed to cloud, and FANCY, *breaking forth, spake:*

Bright Night, I obey thee, and am come at thy call,
But it is no one dream that can please these all;
Wherefore I would know what dreams would de-
    light 'em;

For never was Fancy more loath to affright 'em.
And Fancy, I tell you, has dreams that have wings,
And dreams that have honey, and dreams that have
    stings;
Dreams of the maker, and dreams of the teller,
Dreams of the kitchen, and dreams of the cellar;
Some that are tall, and some that are dwarfs,
Some that were haltered, and some that wear scarfs;
Some that are proper, and signify o' thing,
And some another, and some that are nothing.
For say the French farthingale and the French hood
Were here to dispute—must it be understood
A feather for a wisp were a fit moderator?
Your ostrich, believe it, 's no faithful translator
Of perfect Utopian. And then it were an odd piece
To see the conclusion peep forth at a cod-piece.
  The politic pudding hath still his two ends,
Though the bellows and bagpipe were ne'er so good
    friends;
And who can report what offence it would be
For the squirrel to see a dog climb a tree?
If a dream should come in now to make you afeard,
With a windmill on 's head and bells at his beard,
Would you straight wear your spectacles here at
    your toes,
And your boots o' your brows, and your spurs o'
    your nose?
Your whale he will swallow a hogshead for a pill;
But the maker o' the mousetrap is he that hath skill.
And the nature of the onion is to draw tears,
As well as the mustard. Peace, pitchers have ears,
And shuttlecocks wings; these things do not mind
    'em.
If the bell have any sides, the clapper will find 'em.
There's twice so much music in beating the tabour,
As i' the stockfish, and somewhat less labour.

Yet all this while, no proportion is boasted
'Twixt an egg and an ox, though both have been
    roasted;
For grant the most barbers can lay o' the cittern,
Is it requisite a lawyer should plead to a gittern?
    You will say now the morris-bells were but bribes
To make the heel forget that e'er it had kibes;
I say let the wine make ne'er so good jelly,
The conscience o' the bottle is much i' the belly.
For why? do but take common counsel i' your way,
And tell me who'll then set a bottle of hay
Before the old usurer, and to his horse
A slice of salt butter, perverting the course
Of civil society? Open that gap,
And out skip your fleas, four and twenty at a clap,
With a chain and a trundle-bed following at th'
    heels,
And will they not cry then, the world runs a-wheels?
As for example, a belly and no face,
With the bill of a shoveller may here come in place;
The haunches of a drum, with the feet of a pot,
And the tail of a Kentishman to it—why not?
Yet would I take the stars to be cruel
If the crab and the rope-maker ever fight duel,
On any dependence, be it right, be it wrong;
But mum! a thread may be drawn out too long.

Here the second ANTIMASQUE *of* PHANTASMS *came*
    forth, which danced.
        FANCY *proceeded*:

Why, this you will say was fantastical now,
As the cock and the bull, the whale and the cow;
But vanish away! I have change to present you,
And such as I hope will more truly content you.—
    Behold the gold-haired Hour descending here,
      That keeps the gate of Heaven, and turns the year!

Already with her sight how she doth cheer,
And makes another face of things appear!

Here one of the HOURS *descending, the whole scene*
changed to the bower of ZEPHYRUS, *whilst* PEACE
sung as followeth:

PEACE.   Why look you so, and all turn dumb,
To see the opener of the New Year come?
My presence rather should invite,
And aid, and urge, and call, to your de-
    light;
The many pleasures that I bring
Are all of youth, of heat, of life and spring,
And were prepared to warm your blood,
Not fix it thus, as if you statues stood.
THE CHOIR.   We see, we hear, we feel, we taste,
We smell the change in every
    flower;
We only wish that all could last,
And be as new still as the hour.
                    The Song ended,

WONDER *spake:*

Wonder must speak or break: what is this? grows
The wealth of Nature here, or Art? it shows
As if Favonius, father of the spring,
Who in the verdant meads doth reign sole king,
Had roused him here, and shook his feathers, wet
With purple swelling nectar; and had let
The sweet and fruitful dew fall on the ground
To force out all the flowers that might be found;
    Or a Minerva with her needle had
Th' enamoured earth with all her riches clad,
And made the downy Zephyr, as he flew,
Still to be followed with the spring's best hue.
    The gaudy peacock boasts not in his train

So many lights and shadows, nor the rain-
Resolving Iris, when the Sun doth court her,
Nor purple pheasant while his aunt doth sport her
To hear him crow, and with a perchèd pride
Wave his discoloured neck and purple side.
　I have not seen the place could more surprise;
It looks, methinks, like one of Nature's eyes,
Or her whole body set in Art. Behold!
How the blue bindweed doth itself enfold
With honeysuckle, and both these entwine
Themselves with bryony and jessamine,
To cast a kind and odoriferous shade.

FANCY.

How better than they are, are all things made
By Wonder! But awhile refresh thine eye;
I'll put thee to thy oftener what and why.

Here, to a loud music, the bower opens, and the
　　MASQUERS *are discovered as the glories of the*
　　spring

WONDER *again spake:*

Thou wilt indeed. What better change appears?
Whence is it that the air so sudden clears,
And all things in a moment turn so mild?
Whose breath or beams have got proud earth with
　　child
Of all the treasure that great Nature's worth,
And makes her every minute to bring forth?
How comes it winter is so quite forced hence,
And locked up under ground? that every sense
Hath several objects? trees have got their heads,
The fields their coats? that now the shining meads
Do boast the paunce, the lily, and the rose;
And every flower doth laugh as Zephyr blows?
That seas are now more even than the land?

The rivers run as smoothèd by his hand;
Only their heads are crispèd by his stroke?
How plays the yearling with his brow scarce broke
Now in the open grass? and frisking lambs
Make wanton salts about their dry-sucked dams,
Who to repair their bags do rob the fields?
   How is't each bough a several music yields?
The lusty throstle, early nightingale,
Accord in tune, though vary in their tale?
   The chirping swallow called forth by the sun,
And crested lark doth his division run?
The yellow bees the air with murmur fill?
The finches carol, and the turtles bill?
Whose power is this? what god?

FANCY.   Behold a king,
Whose presence maketh this perpetual spring,
The glories of which spring grow in that bower,
And are the marks and beauties of his power.

To which the CHOIR *answered:*

'Tis he, 'tis he, and no power else,
That makes all this what Fancy tells;
The founts, the flowers, the birds, the bees,
The herds, the flocks, the grass, the trees,
Do all confess him; but most these
Who call him Lord of the Four Seas,
King of the Less and Greater Isles,
And all those happy when he smiles.
Advance, his favour calls you to advance,
And do your this night's homage in a dance.

Here they danced their ENTRY, *after which they sung
again:*

Again! again! you cannot be
Of such a true delight too free,

Which, who once saw, would ever see;
And if they could the object prize,
Would, while it lasts, not think to rise,
But wish their bodies all were eyes.

Here they danced their MAIN DANCE, *after which
they sung:*

CHOIR. In curious knots and mazes so
The Spring at first was taught to go;
And Zephyr, when he came to woo
His Flora, had their motions too;
And thence did Venus learn to lead
Th' Idalian brawls, and so to tread
As if the wind, not she, did walk;
Nor pressed a flower, nor bowed a stalk.

They danced with LADIES *and the whole* REVELS
followed; after which AURORA *appeared, the*
NIGHT *and* MOON *being descended, and this*
EPILOGUE *followed:*

I was not wearier where I lay
By frozen Tithon's side tonight,
Than I am willing now to stay,
And be a part of your delight.
But I am urgèd by the Day,
Against my will, to bid you come away.

THE CHOIR

They yield to time, and so must all.
As night to sport, day doth to action call;
Which they the rather do obey,
Because the Morn with roses strews the way.

Here they danced their going off
AND ENDED

The Fortunate Isles

AND THEIR UNION

———

*Celebrated in a Masque designed for the Court,
on the Twelfth Night, 1625*

HIC CHOREAE, CANTUSQUE VIGENT

His Majesty being set,

Entreth in, running, JOHPHIEL, *an airy spirit, and
(according to the Magi) the intelligence of
Jupiter's sphere, attired in light silks of several
colours, with wings of the same, bright yellow
hair, a chaplet of flowers, blue silk stockings,
and pumps, and gloves, with a silver fan in his
hand.*

JOHPHIEL. Like a lightning from the sky,
  Or an arrow shot by Love,
  Or a bird of his let fly,
   Be't a sparrow or a dove;
  With that wingèd haste come I,
   Loosèd from the sphere of Jove,
    To wish good-night
    To your delight.

*To him enters a melancholic student, in bare and
worn clothes shrouded under an obscure cloak,
and the eaves of an old hat, fetching a deep
sigh, his name* MASTER MEREFOOL.

MEREFOOL. O! O!

JOHPHIEL. In Saturn's name, the father of my lord,
What overchargèd piece of melancholy

843

Is this, breaks in between my wishes thus
With bombing sighs?

MEREFOOL.   No! no intelligence!
Not yet? and all my vows now nine days old!
Blindness of fate! Puppies had seen by this time;
But I see nothing that I should, or would see!
What mean the Brethren of the Rosy Cross,
So to desert their votary?

JOHPHIEL.   O! 'tis one
Hath vowed himself unto that airy order,
And now is gaping for the fly they promised him.
I'll mix a little with him for my sport.

MEREFOOL. Have I both in my lodging and my
    diet,
My clothes, and every other solemn charge,
Observed them! made the naked boards my bed!
A faggot for my pillow, hungred sore!

JOHPHIEL. And thirsted after 'em!

MEREFOOL.   To look gaunt and lean!

JOHPHIEL. Which will not be.

MEREFOOL.   Who's that?—Yes, and outwatched,
Yea, and outwalkèd any ghost alive
In solitary circle, worn my boots,
Knees, arms, and elbows out!

JOHPHIEL.   Ran on the score!

MEREFOOL. That have I—who suggests that?—and
    for more
Than I will speak of, to abate this flesh,
And have not gained the sight—

JOHPHIEL.   Nay, scarce the sense.

MEREFOOL. Voice, thou art right—of anything but
    a cold
Wind in my stomach——

JOHPHIEL.   And a kind of whimsy——

MEREFOOL. Here in my head, that puts me to the
    staggers,

Whether there be that brotherhood or no.

JOHPHIEL. Believe, frail man, they be; and thou
    shalt see.

MEREFOOL. What shall I see?

JOHPHIEL.   Me.

MEREFOOL.   Thee! where?

JOHPHIEL.   Here, if you
Be Master Merefool.

MEREFOOL.   Sir, our name is Merryfool,
But by contraction Merefool.

JOHPHIEL.   Then are you
The wight I seek; and, sir, my name is Johphiel,
Intelligence to the sphere of Jupiter,
An airy jocular spirit, employed to you
From father Outis.

MEREFOOL.   Outis! who is he?

JOHPHIEL. Know ye not Outis? then you know
    nobody.
The good old hermit, that was said to dwell
Here in the forest without trees, that built
The castle in the air, where all the Brethren
Rhodostaurotic live. It flies with wings,
And runs on wheels; where Julian de Campis
Holds out the brandished blade.

MEREFOOL.   Is't possible
They think on me?

JOHPHIEL.   Rise, be not lost in wonder,
But hear me, and be faithful. All the Brethren
Have heard your vows, salute you, and expect you,
By me, this next return. But the good father
Has been content to die for you.

MEREFOOL.   For me?

JOHPHIEL. For you. Last New Year's day, which
    some give out,
Because it was his birthday, and began
The year of jubilee, he would rest upon it,

Being his hundred five and twentieth year;
But the truth is, having observed your genesis,
He would not live, because he might leave all
He had to you.

MEREFOOL.   What had he?

JOHPHIEL.   Had? an office,
Two, three, or four.

MEREFOOL.   Where?

JOHPHIEL.   In the upper region;
And that you'll find. The farm of the great customs
Through all the ports of the air's intelligences,
Then Constable of the Castle Rosy-Cross,
Which you must be, and keeper of the keys
Of the whole Kabal, with the seals; you shall be
Principal secretary to the stars:
Know all the signatures and combinations,
The divine rods, and consecrated roots—
What not? Would you turn trees up like the wind,
To show your strength? march over heads of armies,
Or points of pikes, to show your lightness? force
All doors of arts with the petard of your wit?
Read at one view all books? speak all the languages
Of several creatures? master all the learnings
Were, are, or shall be? or, to show your wealth,
Open all treasures hid by nature, from
The rock of diamond to the mine of sea-coal?
Sir, you shall do it.

MEREFOOL.   But how?

JOHPHIEL.   Why, by his skill,
Of which he has left you the inheritance,
Here in a pot: this little gallipot
Of tincture, high rose tincture. There's your order;
You will have your collar sent you ere't be long.

MEREFOOL. I looked, sir, for a halter; I was
        desperate.

JOHPHIEL. Reach forth your hand.

MEREFOOL.   O sir, a broken sleeve
Keeps the arm back, as 'tis i' the proverb.
    JOHPHIEL.   Nay,
For that I do commend you; you must be poor
With all your wealth and learning. When you ha'
        made
Your glasses gardens in the depth of winter,
Where you will walk invisible to mankind,
Talked with all birds and beasts in their own lan-
        guage;
When you have penetrated hills like air,
Dived to the bottom of the sea like lead,
And ris' again like cork, walked in the fire,
An 'twere a salamander, passed through all
The winding orbs like an Intelligence,
Up to the Empyreum; when you have made
The world your gallery, can dispatch a business
In some three minutes with the Antipodes,
And in five more negotiate the globe over;
You must be poor still.
    MEREFOOL.   By my place, I know it.
    JOHPHIEL. Where would you wish to be now, or
        what to see,
Without the fortunate purse to bear your charges,
Or wishing hat? I will but touch your temples,
The corners of your eyes, and tinct the tip,
The very tip o' your nose, with this collyrium,
And you shall see i' the air all the ideas,
Spirits, and atoms, flies, that buzz about
This way, and that way, and are rather admirable,
Than any way intelligible.
    MEREFOOL.   O, come, tinct me,
Tinct me! I long,—save this great belly—I long!
But shall I only see?
    JOHPHIEL.   See, and command
As they were all your varlets or your footboys.

But first you must declare—your Greatness must,
For that is now your style—what you would see,
Or whom.

    MEREFOOL. Is that my style? my Greatness, then,
Would see King Zoroastres.

    JOHPHIEL.   Why, you shall;
Or any one beside. Think whom you please:
Your thousand, your ten thousand, to a million;
All's one to me, if you could name a myriad.

    MEREFOOL. I have named him.

    JOHPHIEL.   You've reason?

    MEREFOOL.   Ay, I have reason;
Because he's said to be the father of conjurors,
And a cunning man i' the stars.

    JOHPHIEL.   Ay, that's it troubles us
A little for the present; for, at this time,
He is confuting a French almanac;
But he will straight have done, ha' you but pa-
    tience.
Or think but any other in meantime,
Any hard name.

    MEREFOOL.   Then Hermes Trismegistus.

    JOHPHIEL. O, ὁ τρισμέγιστος! why, you shall see him,
A fine hard name. Or him, or whom you will,
As I said to you afore. Or what do you think
Of Howleglass, instead of him?

    MEREFOOL.   No, him
I have a mind to.

    JOHPHIEL.   O, but Eulenspiegel
Were such a name! but you shall have your long-
    ing.
What luck is this, he should be busy too!
He is weighing water but to fill three hour-glasses,
And mark the day in penn'orths like a cheese,
And he has done. 'Tis strange you should name him
Of all the rest! there being Iamblichus,

Or Porphyry, or Proclus, any name
That is not busy.

    MEREFOOL.   Let me see Pythagoras.

    JOHPHIEL.   Good.

    MEREFOOL.   Or Plato.

    JOHPHIEL.   Plato is framing some ideas,
Are now bespoken, at a groat a-dozen,
Three gross at least; and for Pythagoras,
He's rashly run himself on an employment
Of keeping asses from a field of beans,
And cannot be staved off.

    MEREFOOL.   Then Archimedes.

    JOHPHIEL. Yes, Archimedes!

    MEREFOOL.   Ay, or Aesop.

    JOHPHIEL.   Nay,
Hold your first man, a good man, Archimedes,
And worthy to be seen; but he is now
Inventing a rare mouse-trap with owl's wings
And a cat's-foot, to catch the mice alone.
And Aesop, he is filing a fox-tongue
For a new fable he has made of court.
But you shall see 'em all, stay but your time,
And ask in season; things asked out of season
A man denies himself. At such a time
As Christmas, when disguising is afoot,
To ask of the inventions and the men,
The wits and the engines that move those orbs!
Methinks you should inquire now after Skelton,
Or Master Scogan.

    MEREFOOL.   Scogan? what was he?

    JOHPHIEL. O, a fine gentleman, and Master of Arts,
Of Henry the Fourth's times, that made disguises
For the King's sons, and writ in ballad-royal
Daintily well.

    MEREFOOL. But wrote he like a gentleman?

JOHPHIEL. In rhyme, fine tinkling rhyme, and
    flowand verse,
With now and then some sense! and he was paid
    for't,
Regarded and rewarded; which few poets
Are nowadays.
    MEREFOOL.   And why?
    JOHPHIEL.   'Cause every dabbler
In rhyme is thought the same. But you shall see him.
Hold up your nose.
    MEREFOOL.   I had rather see a Brahman,
Or a Gymnosophist yet.
    JOHPHIEL.   You shall see him, sir,
Is worth them both; and with him Dominie Skelton,
The worshipful Poet Laureate to King Harry,
And Tityre-tu of those times. Advance, quick Scogan,
And quicker Skelton, show your crafty heads
Before this heir of arts, this lord of learning,
This master of all knowledge in reversion!

Enter SCOGAN *and* SKELTON, *in like habits as they
    lived.*

    SCOGAN. Seemeth we are called of a moral intent,
If the words that are spoken as well now be meant.
    JOHPHIEL. That, Master Scogan, I dare you insure.
    SCOGAN. Then, son, our acquaintance is like to
    endure.
    MEREFOOL. A pretty game! like Crambo. Master
    Scogan,
Give me thy hand. Thou'rt very lean, methinks;
Is't living by thy wits?
    SCOGAN.   If it had been that,
My worshipful son, thou hadst ne'er been so fat.
    JOHPHIEL. He tells you true, sir. Here's a gentle-
    man,
My pair of crafty clerks, of that high carat

As hardly hath the age produced his like;
Who not content with the wit of his own times,
Is curious to know yours, and what hath been.
    MEREFOOL. Or is, or shall be.
    JOHPHIEL.   Note his latitude.
    SKELTON.   O vir amplissimus,
                  Ut scholis dicimus,
                  Et gentilissimus!
    JOHPHIEL.   The questionissimus
Is, should he ask a sight now, for his life;
I mean a person he would have restored
To memory of these times, for a playfellow,
Whether you would present him with an Hermes,
Or with an Howleglass?
    SKELTON.   An Howleglass
                  To come to pass
                  On his father's ass;
                  There never was,
                  By day nor night,
                  A finer sight;
                  With feathers upright
                  In his hornèd cap,
                  And crooked shape,
                  Much like an ape,
                  With owl on fist,
                  And glass at his wrist.
    SCOGAN. Except the four knaves entertained for
    the guards
Of the kings and the queens that triumph in the
    cards.
    JOHPHIEL. Ay, that were a sight and a half, I con-
    fess,
To see 'em come skipping in, all at a mess!
    SKELTON.   With Elinor Rumming
                  To make up the mumming,
                  That comely gill

That dwelt on a hill,
But she is not grill;
Her face all boozy,
Droopy and drowsy,
Scurvy and lousy,
Comely crinkled,
Wond'rously wrinkled,
Like a roast pig's ear
Bristled with hair.

SCOGAN. Or, what do you say to Ruffian FitzAle?

JOHPHIEL. An excellent sight, if he be not too stale.
But then we can mix him with modern vapours,
The child of tobacco, his pipes, and his papers.

MEREFOOL. You talked of Elinor Rumming; I had
rather
See Ellen of Troy.

JOHPHIEL.　　　　Her you shall see.
　　　　　　　　　But credit me,
　　　　　　　　　That Mary Ambree
　　　　　　　　　Who marched so free
　　　　　　　　　To the siege of Gaunt,
　　　　　　　　　And death could not daunt,—
　　　　　　　　　As the ballad doth vaunt—
　　　　　　　　　Were a braver wight,
　　　　　　　　　And a better sight.

SKELTON.　　　　Or Westminster Meg,
　　　　　　　　　With her long leg,
　　　　　　　　　As long as a crane;
　　　　　　　　　And feet like a plane;
　　　　　　　　　With a pair of heels
　　　　　　　　　As broad as two wheels,
　　　　　　　　　To drive down the dew,
　　　　　　　　　As she goes to the stew;
　　　　　　　　　And turns home merry,
　　　　　　　　　By Lambeth Ferry.
　　　　　　　　　Or you may have come

In, Thomas Thumb,
In a pudding fat
With Doctor Rat.

JOHPHIEL.   Ay, that! that! that!
We'll have 'em all,
To fill the hall.

The ANTIMASQUE *follows,*

Consisting of these twelve persons: HOWLEGLASS, *the four* KNAVES, *two* RUFFIANS (FITZALE *and* VAPOUR), ELINOR RUMMING, MARY AMBREE, LONG MEG *of Westminster,* TOM THUMB, *and* DOCTOR RAT.

Which done,

MEREFOOL. What, are they vanished! where is skipping Skelton?
Or moral Scogan? I do like their show,
And would have thanked them, being the first grace
The Company of the Rosy Cross hath done me.

JOHPHIEL. The Company o' the Rosy Cross, you widgeon!
The company of players. Go, you are,
And will be still yourself, a Merefool! In,
And take your pot of honey here, and hogs'-grease;
See who has gulled you, and make one. *Exit* MEREFOOL.   Great King,
Your pardon, if desire to please have trespassed.
This fool should have been sent to Anticyra,
The isle of hellebore, there to have purged,
Not hoped a happy seat within your waters.
Hear now the message of the Fates and Jove,
On whom these Fates depend, to you, as Neptune,
The great commander of the seas and isles.
That point of revolution being come
When all the Fortunate Islands should be joined,
Macaria, one, and thought a principal,

That hitherto hath floated, as uncertain
Where she should fix her blessings, is tonight
Instructed to adhere to your Britannia;
That where the happy spirits live, hereafter
Might be no question made by the most curious,
Since the Macarii come to do you homage,
And join their cradle to your continent.

Here the scene opens, and the MASQUERS *are discovered sitting in their several sieges. The air opens
above, and* APOLLO, *with* HARMONY *and the*
SPIRITS *of Music, sing, the while the island
moves forward,* PROTEUS *sitting below and hearkening.*

SONG.

Look forth, the Shepherd of the Seas,
And of the ports that keep the keys,
And to your Neptune tell,
Macaria, prince of all the isles,
Wherein there nothing grows but smiles,
Doth here put in to dwell.

The winds are sweet and gently blow,
But Zephyrus no breath they know,
The Father of the Flowers;
By him the virgin violets live,
And every plant doth odours give,
As new as are the hours.

CHORUS. Then think it not a common cause
That to it so much wonder draws,
And all the heavens consent
With harmony to tune their notes,
In answer to the public votes
That for it up were sent.

By this time, the island having joined itself to the
shore, PROTEUS, PORTUNUS, *and* SARON *come*
forth, and go up singing to the State, while the
MASQUERS *take time to rank themselves.*

SONG.

PROTEUS.   Ay, now the heights of Neptune's hon-
       ours shine,
       And all the glories of his greater style
       Are read, reflected in this happiest isle.

PORTUNUS.   How both the air, the soil, the seat
       combine
       To speak it blessèd!

SARON.   These are the true groves
       Where joys are born.

PROTEUS.   Where longings.

PORTUNUS.   And where loves!

SARON.   That live!
       That last!

PORTUNUS.   No intermitted wind
       Blows here, but what leaves flowers or
       fruit behind.

CHORUS.   'Tis odour all that comes!
       And every tree doth give his gums.

PROTEUS.   There is no sickness, nor no old age
       known
       To man, nor any grief that he dares
       own.
       There is no hunger there, nor envy of
       state,
       Nor least ambition in the magistrate.
       But all are even-hearted, open, free,
       And what one is another strives to be.

PORTUNUS.   Here, all the day, they feast, they
       sport, and spring;

Now dance the Graces' hay, now
    Venus' ring;
To which the old musicians play and
    sing.

SARON. There is Arion, tuning his bold harp,
    From flat to sharp.

PORTUNUS.   And light Anacreon,
    He still is one!

PROTEUS.   Stesichorus there too,
That Linus and old Orpheus doth
    outdo
To wonder.

SARON.   And Amphion, he is there.

PORTUNUS. Nor is Apollo dainty to appear
In such a choir, although the trees be
    thick.

PROTEUS. He will look in, and see the airs be
    quick,
And that the times be true.

PORTUNUS.   Then, chanting,

PROTEUS.   Then,
Up, with their notes, they raise the
    Prince of Men.

SARON. And sing the present prophecy that
    goes,
Of joining the bright lily and the rose.

CHORUS. See! all the flowers—

PROTEUS.   That spring the banks along,
Do move their heads unto that under
    song.

CHORUS. Saron, Portunus, Proteus, help to
    bring
Our primrose in, the glory of the
    spring!
And tell the daffodil, against that day,

> That we prepare new garlands fresh
> as May,
> And interweave the myrtle and the
> bay.

This sung, the island goes back, whilst the UPPER
CHORUS *takes it from them, and the* MASQUERS
prepare for their figure.

CHORUS.   Spring all the graces of the age,
> And all the loves of time;
> Bring all the pleasures of the stage,
> And relishes of rhyme.
> Add all the softnesses of courts,
> The looks, the laughters, and the
> sports;
> And mingle all their sweets and salts,
> That none may say the triumph
> halts.

The MASQUERS *dance their* ENTRY *or first dance.*

*Which done, the first prospective, a maritime palace,
or the house of* OCEANUS, *is discovered, to loud
music.*

The other above is no more seen.

JOHPHIEL. Behold the palace of Oceanus!
Hail, reverend structure! boast no more to us
Thy being able all the gods to feast;
We saw enough, when Albion was thy guest.

The MEASURES.

*After which, the second prospective, a sea, is shown
to the former music.*

JOHPHIEL. Now turn, and view the wonders of
the deep,

Where Proteus' herds and Neptune's orcs do keep,
Where all is ploughed, yet still the pasture's green;
New ways are found, and yet no paths are seen.

Here PROTEUS, PORTUNUS, SARON, *go up to the* LADIES
with this SONG.

PROTEUS.   Come, noble nymphs, and do not hide
        The joys for which you so provide.
SARON.   If not to mingle with the men,
        What do you here? Go home again.
PORTUNUS.   Your dressings do confess,
        By what we see, so curious parts
        Of Pallas' and Arachne's arts,
           That you could mean no less.

PROTEUS.   Why do you wear the silk-worm's toils,
        Or glory in the shell-fish' spoils;
        Or strive to show the grains of ore
        That you have gathered on the shore,
           Whereof to make a stock
        To graft the greener emerald on,
        Or any better-watered stone?
SARON.   Or ruby of the rock?

PROTEUS.   Why do you smell of ambergris,
        Of which was formèd Neptune's niece,
        The Queen of Love; unless you can,
        Like sea-born Venus, love a man?
SARON.   Try, put yourselves unto't.
CHORUS.   Your looks, your smiles, and thoughts
          that meet,
        Ambrosian hands, and silver feet,
           Do promise you will do't.

The REVELS *follow.*

Which ended, the Fleet is discovered, while the three cornets play.

JOHPHIEL. 'Tis time your eyes should be refreshed at length
With something new, a part of Neptune's strength:
See yond' his fleet, ready to go or come,
Or fetch the riches of the Ocean home;
So to secure him, both in peace and wars,
Till not one ship alone, but all, be stars.

Then the last

SONG.

PROTEUS.   Although we wish the glory still might last
            Of such a night, and for the causes past;
            Yet now, great Lord of Waters and of Isles,
            Give Proteus leave to turn unto his wiles.

PORTUNUS.   And whilst young Albion doth thy labours ease,
            Dispatch Portunus to the ports.

SARON.   And Saron to the seas,
            To meet old Nereus with his fifty girls,
            From agèd Indus laden home with pearls
            And orient gums, to burn unto thy name.

CHORUS.   And may thy subjects' hearts be all on flame,
            Whilst thou dost keep the earth in firm estate,

And 'mongst the winds dost suffer no
    debate;
But both at sea and land our powers
    increase,
With health and all the golden gifts
    of peace.

After which, their last dance.

THE END

IV. VERSE

IV. VERSE

Verse

FROM *Cynthia's Revels*

ECHO'S SONG

Slow, slow, fresh fount, keep time with my salt
    tears;
  Yet slower, yet, O faintly gentle springs.
List to the heavy part the music bears;
  Woe weeps out her division, when she sings.
      Droop herbs and flowers,
      Fall grief in showers;
      Our beauties are not ours.
        O, I could still,
Like melting snow upon some craggy hill,
    Drop, drop, drop, drop,
Since nature's pride is now a withered daffodil.

HYMN TO CYNTHIA

  Queen and huntress, chaste and fair,
  Now the sun is laid to sleep,
  Seated in thy silver chair,
  State in wonted manner keep.
      Hesperus entreats thy light,
      Goddess excellently bright.

  Earth, let not thy envious shade
  Dare itself to interpose;
  Cynthia's shining orb was made
  Heaven to clear, when day did close.
      Bless us then with wishèd sight,
      Goddess excellently bright.

Lay thy bow of pearl apart,
And thy crystal-shining quiver;
Give unto the flying hart
Space to breathe, how short soever;
    Thou that mak'st a day of night,
    Goddess excellently bright.

FROM *Poetaster*

HERMOGENES' SONG

If I freely may discover
What would please me in my lover:
    I would have her fair and witty,
    Savouring more of court than city,
    A little proud, but full of pity.
    Light and humorous in her toying,
    Oft building hopes and soon destroying,
    Long, but sweet in the enjoying;
Neither too easy nor too hard—
All extremes I would have barred.

She should be allowed her passions,
So they were but used as fashions:
    Sometimes froward, and then frowning;
    Sometimes sickish, and then swooning;
    Every fit with change still crowning.
    Purely jealous I would have her,
    Then only constant when I crave her;
    'Tis a virtue should not save her.
Thus, nor her delicates would cloy me,
Neither her peevishness annoy me.

HORACE'S DRINKING SONG

Swell me a bowl with lusty wine,
Till I may see the plump Lyaeus swim
    Above the brim.

I drink as I would write,
In flowing measure, filled with flame and sprite.

FROM *The New Inn*

LOVEL'S SONG

It was a beauty that I saw,
    So pure, so perfect, as the frame
    Of all the universe was lame,
To that one figure, could I draw,
Or give least line of it a law!

A skein of silk without a knot!
    A fair march made without a halt!
    A curious form without a fault!
A printed book without a blot!
All beauty, and without a spot!

*The Just Indignation the Author took at the Vulgar
Censure of his Play by some Malicious Spectators
begat this following*

ODE TO HIMSELF

Come, leave the loathèd stage,
And the more loathsome age,
Where pride and impudence, in faction knit,
    Usurp the chair of wit,
Indicting and arraigning every day
    Something they call a play.
    Let their fastidious, vain
    Commission of the brain
Run on, and rage, sweat, censure, and condemn;
They were not made for thee, less thou for
    them.

Say that thou pour'st them wheat,
And they will acorns eat;
'Twere simple fury still thyself to waste
On such as have no taste;
To offer them a surfeit of pure bread,
Whose appetites are dead.
No, give them grains their fill,
Husks, draff to drink and swill.
If they love lees and leave the lusty wine,
Envy them not; their palate's with the swine.

No doubt some mouldy tale
Like 'Pericles', and stale
As the Shrieve's crusts, and nasty as his fish-
Scraps out of every dish,
Thrown forth and raked into the common tub,
May keep up the Play Club.
There sweepings do as well
As the best ordered meal;
For who the relish of these guests will fit,
Needs set them but the alms-basket of wit.

And much good do't you then;
Brave plush and velvet men
Can feed on orts; and safe in your stage-clothes,
Dare quit, upon your oaths,
The stagers, and the stage-wrights too, your peers,
Of larding your large ears
With their foul comic socks,
Wrought upon twenty blocks;
Which if they are torn and turned and patched
enough,
The gamesters share your guilt, and you their
stuff.

Leave things so prostitute,
And take th' Alcaic lute,
Or thine own Horace' or Anacreon's lyre;
 Warm thee by Pindar's fire.
And though thy nerves be shrunk and blood be
 cold
  Ere years have made thee old,
 Strike that disdainful heat
 Throughout, to their defeat;
As curious fools, and envious of thy strain,
May blushing swear no palsy's in thy brain.

 But when they hear thee sing
 The glories of thy King,
His zeal to God and his just awe o'er men;
 They may, blood-shaken, then
Feel such a flesh-quake to possess their powers,
 As they shall cry, like ours,
 In sound of peace or wars,
 No harp e'er hit the stars;
In tuning forth the acts of his sweet reign,
And raising Charles's chariot 'bove his Wain.

FROM *The Sad Shepherd*

AEGLAMOUR'S SOLILOQUY

Here she was wont to go, and here, and here,
Just where those daisies, pinks, and violets grow!
The world may find the spring by following her,
For other print her airy steps ne'er left.
Her treading would not bend a blade of grass,
Or shake the downy blow-ball from his stalk.
But like the soft west wind she shot along;
And where she went, the flowers took thickest root,
As she had sowed 'em with her odorous foot.

SHEPHERD'S SONG

Though I am young, and cannot tell
Either what Death or Love is well;
Yet I have heard they both bear darts,
And both do aim at human hearts.
And then again, I have been told
Love wounds with heat, as Death with cold;
So that I fear they do but bring
Extremes to touch, and mean one thing.

As in a ruin, we it call
One thing to be blown up or fall,
Or to our end like way may have
By flash of lightning or a wave;
So Love's enflamèd shaft, or brand,
May kill as soon as Death's cold hand;
Except Love's fires the virtue have
To fright the frost out of the grave.

FROM *The Golden Age Restored*

DIALOGUE

PALLAS.   Already do not all things smile?

ASTRAEA.   But when they have enjoyed a while
The Age's quick'ning power,——

GOLDEN AGE. That every thought a seed doth bring,
And every look a plant doth spring,
And every breath a flower——

PALLAS.   Then Earth unploughed shall yield
her crop,
Pure honey from the oak shall drop,
The fountain shall run milk;
The thistle shall the lily bear,
And every bramble roses wear,
And every worm make silk.

CHOIR.

The very shrub shall balsam sweat,
And nectar melt the rock with heat,
    Till Earth have drunk her fill;
That she no harmful weed may
    know,
Nor barren fern, nor mandrake low,
    Nor mineral to kill.

FROM *Pleasure Reconciled to Virtue*

HYMN TO THE BELLY

Room! room! make room for the bouncing Belly,
First father of sauce and deviser of jelly;
Prime master of arts and the giver of wit,
That found out the excellent engine, the spit,
The plough and the flail, the mill and the hopper,
The hutch and the boulter, the furnace and copper,
The oven, the bavin, the mawkin, the peel,
The hearth and the range, the dog and the wheel.
He, he first invented the hogshead and tun,
The gimlet and vice too, and taught 'em to run;
And since, with the funnel and hippocras bag,
He's made of himself that now he cries swag;
Which shows, though the pleasure be but of four
    inches,
Yet he is a weasel, the gullet that pinches
Of any delight, and not spares from his back
Whatever to make of the belly a sack.
Hail, hail, plump paunch! O the founder of taste,
For fresh meats or powdered, or pickle or paste!
Devourer of broiled, baked, roasted or sod!
And emptier of cups, be they even or odd!
All which have now made thee so wide i' the waist,
As scarce with no pudding thou art to be laced;
But eating and drinking until thou dost nod,
Thou break'st all thy girdles and break'st forth a
    god.

FROM *The Gypsies Metamorphosed*

PATRICO'S SONG

The fairy beam upon you,
The stars to glister on you;
    A moon of light,
    In the noon of night,
Till the fire-drake hath o'ergone you!

The wheel of Fortune guide you,
The boy with the bow beside you
    Run aye in the way,
    Till the bird of day
And the luckier lot betide you!

II

To the old, long life and treasure;
To the young, all health and pleasure;
    To the fair, their face
    With eternal grace;
And the foul, to be loved at leisure!

To the witty, all clear mirrors;
To the foolish, their dark errors;
    To the loving sprite,
    A secure delight;
To the jealous his own false terrors!

FROM *The Masque of Augurs*

APOLLO'S SONG

Which way and whence the lightning flew,
Or how it burnèd bright and blue,
Design and figure by your lights.
Then forth, and show the several flights
Your birds have made, or what the wing

Or voice in augury doth bring;
Which hand the crow cried on, how high
The vulture or the erne did fly;
What wing the swan made, and the dove,
The stork, and which did get above.
Show all the birds of food or prey,
But pass by the unlucky jay,
The night-crow, swallow, or the kite;
  Let these have neither right——
CHORUS.   Nor part,
        In this night's art.

FROM *Pan's Anniversary*

DIALOGUE

1ST NYMPH

Thus, thus begin the yearly rites
Are due to Pan on these bright nights;
His morn now riseth, and invites
To sports, to dances, and delights.
      All envious and profane, away,
      This is the shepherds' holiday.

2ND NYMPH

Strew, strew the glad and smiling ground
With every flower, yet not confound
The primrose drop, the Spring's own spouse,
Bright day's-eyes, and the lips of cows,
      The garden star, the Queen of May,
      The rose, to crown the holiday.

3RD NYMPH

Drop, drop your violets, change your hues,
Now red, now pale, as lovers use,
And in your death go out as well

As when you lived unto the smell;
　　That from your odour all may say,
　　This is the shepherds' holiday.

FROM *Epigrams*

TO MY BOOK

It will be looked for, book, when some but see
Thy title, 'Epigrams,' and named of me,
Thou should'st be bold, licentious, full of gall,
Wormwood, and sulphur, sharp and toothed withal;
Become a petulant thing, hurl ink and wit,
As madmen stones, not caring whom they hit.
Deceive their malice, who could wish it so.
And by thy wiser temper, let men know
Thou art not covetous of least self-fame,
Made from the hazard of another's shame;
Much less with lewd, profane, and beastly phrase,
To catch the world's loose laughter or vain gaze.
He that departs with his own honesty
For vulgar praise, doth it too dearly buy.

ON THE UNION

When was there contract better driven by Fate,
　Or celebrated with more truth of state?
The world the temple was, the priest a king,
　The spousèd pair two realms, the sea the ring.

TO ALCHEMISTS

If all you boast of your great art be true,
Sure, willing poverty lives most in you.

TO WILLIAM CAMDEN

Camden, most reverend head, to whom I owe
All that I am in arts, all that I know,—
How nothing's that!—to whom my country owes
The great renown and name wherewith she goes;

Than thee the age sees not that thing more grave,
More high, more holy, that she more would crave.
What name, what skill, what faith hast thou in
          things!
What sight in searching the most antique springs!
What weight and what authority in thy speech!
Man scarce can make that doubt, but thou canst
          teach.
Pardon free truth, and let thy modesty,
Which conquers all, be once overcome by thee.
Many of thine this better could than I,
But for their powers, accept my piety.

ON COURTWORM

All men are worms; but this no man. In silk
'Twas brought to court first wrapped, and white as
          milk;
Where, afterwards, it grew a butterfly,
Which was a caterpillar. So 'twill die.

TO JOHN DONNE

Donne, the delight of Phoebus and each Muse,
Who, to thy one, all other brains refuse;
Whose every work, of thy most early wit,
Came forth example and remains so yet;
Longer a-knowing than most wits do live;
And which no affection praise enough can give!
To it, thy language, letters, arts, best life,
Which might with half mankind maintain a strife;
All which I meant to praise, and yet I would,
But leave, because I cannot as I should!

ON SIR JOHN ROE

What two brave perils of the private sword
     Could not effect, not all the Furies do,
That self-divided Belgia did afford;
     What not the envy of the seas reached, too;

The cold of Moscow and fat Irish air,
  His often change of clime—though not of mind—
What could not work; at home in his repair
  Was his blest fate, but our hard lot to find.
    Which shows wherever death doth please
      t'appear,
    Seas, sèrenes, swords, shot, sickness, all are there.

TO THE GHOST OF MARTIAL

Martial, thou gav'st far nobler epigrams
To thy Domitian, than I can my James.
But in my royal subject I pass thee;
Thou flatter'dst thine, mine cannot flattered be.

ON MY FIRST SON

Farewell, thou child of my right hand, and joy,
My sin was too much hope of thee, loved boy;
Seven years th' wert lent to me, and I thee pay,
Exacted by thy fate, on the just day.
O, I could lose all father now. For why
Will man lament the state he should envy?
To have so soon 'scaped world's and flesh's rage,
And, if no other misery, yet age?
Rest in soft peace, and, asked, say here doth lie
Ben Jonson his best piece of poetry;
For whose sake, henceforth, all his vows be such
As what he loves may never like too much.

TO SIR COD

Leave, Cod, tobacco-like, burnt gums to take,
Or fumy clysters, thy moist lungs to bake;
Arsenic would thee fit for society make.

TO FRANCIS BEAUMONT

How I do love thee, Beaumont, and thy Muse,
That unto me dost such religion use!

How I do fear myself, than am not worth
The least indulgent thought thy pen drops forth!
At once thou mak'st me happy, and unmak'st;
And giving largely to me, more thou tak'st.
What fate is mine, that so itself bereaves?
What art is thine, that so thy friend deceives?
When even there, where most thou praisest me,
For writing better, I must envy thee.

ON POET-APE

Poor Poet-Ape, that would be thought our chief,
 Whose works are e'en the frippery of wit,
From brokage is become so bold a thief,
 As we, the robbed, leave rage, and pity it.
At first he made low shifts, would pick and glean,
 But the reversion of old plays; now grown
To a little wealth and credit in the scene,
 He takes up all, makes each man's wit his own.
And told of this, he slights it. Tut, such crimes
 The sluggish, gaping auditor devours;
He marks not whose 'twas first, and after-times
 May judge it to be his as well as ours.
  Fool, as if half-eyes will not know a fleece
  From locks of wool, or shreds from the whole
   piece!

ON SPIES

Spies, you are lights in state, but of base stuff,
Who, when you've burnt yourselves down to the
 snuff,
Stink, and are thrown away. End fair enough.

TO ROBERT, EARL OF SALISBURY

Upon the accession of the Treasurership to him

Not glad, like those that have new hopes or suits,
With thy new place, bring I these early fruits

Of love, and what the Golden Age did hold
A treasure, art, contemned in th'age of gold;
Nor glad as those that old dependents be,
To see thy father's rites new laid on thee;
Nor glad for fashion; nor to show a fit
Of flattery to thy titles; nor of wit.
But I am glad to see that time survive,
Where merit is not sepulchred alive;
Where good men's virtues them to honours bring,
And not to dangers; when so wise a King
Contends t' have worth enjoy from his regard,
As her own conscience, still the same reward.
These, noblest Cecil, laboured in my thought;
Wherein what wonder see thy name hath wrought!
That whilst I meant but thine to gratulate,
I have sung the greater fortunes of our state.

ON LUCY, COUNTESS OF BEDFORD

This morning, timely rapt with holy fire,
   I thought to form unto my jealous Muse
What kind of creature I could most desire,
    To honour, serve, and love, as poets use.
I meant to make her fair and free and wise,
    Of greatest blood, and yet more good than great;
I meant the day-star should not brighter rise,
    Nor lend like influence from his lucent seat.
I meant she should be courteous, facile, sweet,
    Hating that solemn vice of greatness, pride;
I meant each softest virtue there should meet,
    Fit in that softer bosom to reside.
Only a learnèd and a manly soul
    I purposed her; that should, with even powers,
The rock, the spindle, and the shears control
    Of Destiny, and spin her own free hours.
      Such when I meant to feign, and wished to see,
      My Muse bade 'Bedford' write, and that was
        she.

ON ENGLISH MONSIEUR

Would you believe, when you this Monsieur see,
That his whole body should speak French, not he?
That so much scarf of France, and hat and feather,
And shoe and tie and garter should come hither,
And land on one whose face durst never be,
Toward the sea, farther than half-way tree?
That he, untravelled, should be French so much,
As Frenchmen in his company should seem Dutch?
Or had his father, when he him did get,
The French Disease, with which he labours yet?
Or hung some Monsieur's picture on the wall,
By which his dam conceived him, clothes and all?
Or is it some French statue? No, 't doth move,
And stoop, and cringe. O, then it needs must prove
The new French tailor's motion, monthly made,
Daily to turn in Paul's and help the trade.

TO LUCY, COUNTESS OF BEDFORD
With Master Donne's 'Satires'

Lucy, you brightness of our sphere, who are
Life of the Muses' day, their morning star!
  If works—not th'authors—their own grace should
    look,
  Whose poems would not wish to be your book?
  But these, desired by you, the maker's ends
  Crown with their own. Rare poems ask rare
    friends.
Yet satires, since the most of mankind be
Their unavoided subject, fewest see;
For none e'er took that pleasure in sin's sense,
But, when they heard it taxed, took more offence.
They, then, that, living where the matter is bred,
Dare for these poems yet both ask and read,
And like them too, must needfully, though few,
Be of the best; and 'mongst those, best are you.

Lucy, you brightness of our sphere, who are
The Muses' evening as their morning star.

TO SIR HENRY SAVILE

If, my religion safe, I durst embrace
That stranger doctrine of Pythagoras,
I should believe the soul of Tacitus
In thee, most weighty Savile, lived to us;
So hast thou rendered him, in all his bounds
And all his numbers, both of sense and sounds.
But when I read that special piece, restored,
Where Nero falls and Galba is adored,
To thy own proper I ascribe then more,
And gratulate the breach I grieved before;
Which Fate, it seems, caused in the history,
Only to boast thy merit in supply.
O wouldst thou add like hand to all the rest!
Or—better work—were thy glad country blest,
To have her story woven in thy thread!
Minerva's loom was never richer spread.
For who can master those great parts like thee,
That liv'st from hope, from fear, from faction free;
That hast thy breast so clear of present crimes,
Thou need'st not shrink at voice of after-times;
Whose knowledge claimeth at the helm to stand,
But, wisely, thrusts not forth a forward hand,
No more than Sallust in the Roman state?
As, then, his cause, his glory emulate.
Although to write be lesser than to do,
It is the next deed, and a great one, too.
We need a man that knows the severall graces
Of history, and how to apt their places;
Where brevity, where splendour, and where height,
Where sweetness is required, and where weight.
We need a man can speak of the intents,
The councils, actions, orders, and events

Of state, and censure them. We need his pen
Can write the things, the causes, and the men.
But most we need his faith—and all have you—
That dares nor write things false nor hide things
    true.

TO JOHN DONNE

Who shall doubt, Donne, where I a poet be,
When I dare send my epigrams to thee?
That so alone canst judge, so alone dost make;
And, in thy censures, evenly dost take
As free simplicity to disavow,
As thou hast best authority t' allow.
Read all I send, and if I find but one
Marked by thy hand, and with the better stone,
My title's sealed. Those that for claps do write,
Let puisnes', porters', players' praise delight,
And, till they burst, their backs like asses load.
A man should seek great glory, and not broad.

INVITING A FRIEND TO SUPPER

Tonight, grave sir, both my poor house and I
Do equally desire your company;
Not that we think us worthy such a guest,
But that your worth will dignify our feast
With those that come, whose grace may make that
    seem
Something, which else could hope for no esteem.
It is the fair acceptance, sir, creates
The entertainment perfect; not the cates.
Yet you shall have, to rectify your palate,
An olive, capers, or some better salad
Ush'ring the mutton; with a short-legged hen,
If we can get her, full of eggs, and then
Lemons and wine for sauce; to these a coney
Is not to be despaired of, for our money;

And though fowl now be scarce, yet there are clerks,
The sky not falling, think we may have larks.
I'll tell you of more, and lie, so you will come:
Of partridge, pheasant, woodcock, of which some
May yet be there; and godwit, if we can;
Knat, rail, and ruff too. Howsoe'er, my man
Shall read a piece of Virgil, Tacitus,
Livy, or of some better book to us,
Of which we'll speak our minds, amidst our meat.
And I'll profess no verses to repeat;
To this, if aught appear which I not know of,
That will the pastry, not my paper, show of.
Digestive cheese and fruit there sure will be;
But that which most doth take my Muse and me
Is a pure cup of rich Canary wine,
Which is the Mermaid's now, but shall be mine;
Of which had Horace or Anacreon tasted,
Their lives, as do their lines, till now had lasted.
Tobacco, nectar, or the Thespian spring
Are all but Luther's beer to this I sing.
Of this we will sup free, but moderately,
And we will have no Polly or parrot by;
Nor shall our cups make any guilty men,
But at our parting we will be as when
We innocently met. No simple word
That shall be uttered at our mirthful board,
Shall make us sad next morning, or affright
The liberty that we'll enjoy tonight.

EPITAPH ON SALATHIEL PAVY

A Child of Queen Elizabeth's Chapel

Weep with me, all you that read
This little story;
And know, for whom a tear you shed
Death's self is sorry.

'Twas a child that so did thrive
    In grace and feature,
As Heaven and Nature seemed to strive
    Which owned the creature.

Years he numbered scarce thirteen
    When Fates turned cruel,
Yet three filled zodiacs had he been
    The stage's jewel;

And did act—what now we moan—
    Old men so duly,
As, sooth, the Parcae thought him one,
    He played so truly.

So, by error, to his fate
    They all consented;
But viewing him since, alas, too late,
    They have repented,

And have sought—to give new birth—
    In baths to steep him;
But being so much too good for earth,
    Heaven vows to keep him.

EPITAPH ON ELIZABETH, LADY H——

Wouldst thou hear what man can say
In a little? Reader, stay.
Underneath this stone doth lie
As much beauty as could die,
Which in life did harbour give
To more virtue than doth live.
If at all she had a fault,
Leave it buried in this vault.
One name was Elizabeth;
Th' other let it sleep with death,

Fitter where it died to tell,
Than that it lived at all. Farewell.

TO WILLIAM ROE

Roe, and my joy to name, th' art now to go
Countries and climes, manners and men to know,
T' extract and choose the best of all these known,
And those to turn to blood, and make thine own.
May winds as soft as breath of kissing friends
Attend thee hence; and there, may all thy ends,
As the beginnings here, prove purely sweet,
And perfect in a circle always meet.
So, when we, blest with thy return, shall see
Thyself, with thy first thoughts, brought home by
    thee,
We each to other may this voice inspire:
This is that good Aeneas, passed through fire,
Through seas, storms, tempests; and, embarked for
    Hell,
Came back untouched. This man hath travelled
    well.

FROM *The Forest*

TO PENSHURST

Thou art not, Penshurst, built to envious show
Of touch or marble, nor canst boast a row
Of polished pillars, or a roof of gold;
Thou hast no lantern whereof tales are told,
Or stair or courts; but stand'st an ancient pile,
And these grudged at, art reverenced the while.
Thou joy'st in better marks, of soil, of air,
Of wood, of water; therein thou art fair.
Thou hast thy walks, for health as well as sport;
Thy mount, to which the dryads do resort,
Where Pan and Bacchus their high feasts have made

Beneath the broad beech, and the chestnut shade,
That taller tree, which of a nut was set
At his great birth, where all the Muses met.
There in the writhèd bark are cut the names
Of many a sylvan, taken with his flames;
And thence the ruddy satyrs oft provoke
The lighter fauns to reach thy Lady's Oak.
Thy copse too, named of Gamage, thou hast there,
That never fails to serve thee seasoned deer,
When thou wouldst feast or exercise thy friends.
The lower land, that to the river bends,
Thy sheep, thy bullocks, kine, and calves do feed;
The middle grounds thy mares and horses breed.
Each bank doth yield thee conies; and the tops
Fertile of wood, Ashore, and Sidney's Copse,
To crown thy open table, doth provide
The purpled pheasant, with the speckled side.
The painted partridge lies in every field,
And for thy mess is willing to be killed.
And if the high swol'n Medway fail thy dish,
Thou hast thy ponds, that pay thee tribute fish,
Fat, agèd carps that run into thy net.
And pikes, now weary their own kind to eat,
As loath the second draught or cast to stay,
Officiously, at first, themselves betray;
Bright eels, that emulate them, and leap on land
Before the fisher, or into his hand.
Then hath thy orchard fruit, thy garden flowers,
Fresh as the air and new as are the hours.
The early cherry, with the later plum,
Fig, grape, and quince, each in his time doth come;
The blushing apricot and woolly peach
Hang on thy walls, that every child may reach.
And though thy walls be of the country stone,
They're reared with no man's ruin, no man's groan;

There's none that dwell about them wish them
    down,
But all come in, the farmer and the clown,
And no one empty-handed, to salute
Thy Lord and Lady, though they have no suit.
Some bring a capon, some a rural cake,
Some nuts, some apples. Some that think they make
The better cheeses, bring 'em; or else send
By their ripe daughters, whom they would commend
This way to husbands, and whose baskets bear
An emblem of themselves in plum or pear.
But what can this, more than express their love,
Add to thy free provisions, far above
The need of such; whose liberal board doth flow
With all that hospitality doth know?
Where comes no guest but is allowed to eat,
Without his fear, and of thy Lord's own meat;
Where the same beer and bread, and self-same wine
That is his Lordship's, shall be also mine,
And I not feign to sit—as some, this day,
At great men's tables—and yet dine away.
Here no man tells my cups, nor, standing by,
A waiter doth my gluttony envy,
But gives me what I call, and lets me eat;
He knows below he shall find plenty of meat;
Thy tables hoard not up for the next day.
Nor, when I take my lodging, need I pray
For fire or lights or livery; all is there,
As if thou then wert mine, or I reigned here.
There's nothing I can wish, for which I stay.
That found King James when, hunting late this way
With his brave son, the Prince, they saw thy fires
Shine bright on every hearth, as the desires
Of thy Penates had been set on flame
To entertain them, or the country came,
With all their zeal, to warm their welcome here.

What great I will not say, but sudden cheer
Didst thou then make 'em! and what praise was
    heaped
On thy good Lady, then, who therein reaped
The just reward of her high housewifery:
To have her linen, plate, and all things nigh,
When she was far; and not a room but dressed
As if it had expected such a guest!
These, Penshurst, are thy praise, and yet not all.
Thy Lady's noble, fruitful, chaste withal;
His children thy great Lord may call his own,
A fortune in this age but rarely known.
They are, and have been taught religion; thence
Their gentle spirits have sucked innocence.
Each morn and even, they are taught to pray
With the whole household, and may every day
Read in their virtuous parents' noble parts
The mysteries of manners, arms, and arts.
Now, Penshurst, they that will proportion thee
With other edifices, when they see
Those proud, ambitious heaps, and nothing else,
May say their lords have built, but thy Lord dwells.

TO SIR ROBERT WROTH

How blest art thou, canst love the country, Wroth,
    Whether by choice or fate or both;
And though so near the city and the court,
    Art ta'en with neither's vice nor sport:
That at great times art no ambitious guest
    Of Sheriff's dinner or Mayor's feast;
Nor com'st to view the better cloth of state,
    The richer hangings, or crown plate;
Nor throng'st, when masquing is, to have a sight
    Of the short bravery of the night,
To view the jewels, stuffs, the pains, the wit
    There wasted, some not paid for yet!

But canst at home, in thy securer rest,
   Live, with unbought provision blest;
Free from proud porches or their gilded roofs,
   'Mongst lowing herds and solid hoofs;
Alongst the curlèd woods and painted meads,
   Through which a serpent river leads
To some cool, courteous shade which he calls his,
   And makes sleep softer than it is!
Or, if thou list the night in watch to break,
   Abed canst hear the loud stag speak,
In spring oft rousèd for thy Master's sport,
   Who, for it, makes thy house his court;
Or with thy friends, the heart of all the year,
   Div'st upon the lesser deer;
In autumn at the partridge mak'st a flight,
   And giv'st thy gladder guests the sight;
And in the winter hunt'st the flying hare,
   More for thy exercise than fare,
While all that follow their glad ears apply
   To full greatness of the cry;
Or hawking at the river or the bush,
   Or shooting at the greedy thrush,
Thou dost with some delight the day outwear,
   Although the coldest of the year!
The whilst the several seasons thou hast seen
   Of flow'ry fields, of copses green,
The mowèd meadows with the fleecèd sheep,
   And feasts that either shearers keep;
The ripened ears yet humble in their height,
   And furrows laden with their weight;
The apple harvest that doth longer last;
   The hogs returned home fat from mast;
The trees cut out in log, and those boughs made
   A fire now, that lent a shade!
Thus Pan and Sylvan having had their rites,
   Comus puts in for new delights;

And fills thy open hall with mirth and cheer,
    As if in Saturn's reign it were.
Apollo's harp and Hermes' lyre resound,
    Nor are the Muses strangers found.
The rout of rural folk come thronging in,—
    Their rudeness then is thought no sin—
Thy noblest spouse affords them welcome grace;
    And the great heroes of her race
Sit mixed, with loss of state or reverence.
    Freedom doth with degree dispense.
The jolly wassail walks the often round,
    And in their cups their cares are drowned;
They think not then which side the cause shall leese,
    Nor how to get the lawyer fees.
Such, and no other, was that age of old
    Which boasts t' have had the head of gold;
And such since thou canst make thine own content,
    Strive, Wroth, to live long innocent.
Let others watch in guilty arms, and stand
    The fury of a rash command;
Go enter breaches, meet the cannon's rage,
    That they may sleep with scars in age,
And show their feathers shot and colours torn,
    And brag that they were therefore born.
Let this man sweat and wrangle at the bar,
    For every price, in every jar,
And change possessions oft'ner, with his breath,
    Than either money, war, or death;
Let him than hardest sires more disinherit,
    And eachwhere boast it as his merit
To blow up orphans, widows, and their states,
    And think his power doth equal Fate's.
Let that go heap a mass of wretched wealth,
    Purchased by rapine, worse than stealth,
And brooding o'er it sit, with broadest eyes,
    Not doing good scarce when he dies.

Let thousands more go flatter vice, and win
    By being organs to great sin;
Get place and honour, and be glad to keep
    The secrets that shall break their sleep;
And, so they ride in purple, eat in plate,
    Though poison, think it a great state.
But thou, my Wroth, if I can truth apply,
    Shalt neither that nor this envy.
Thy peace is made, and when man's state is well,
    'Tis better if he there can dwell.
God wisheth none should wrack on a strange shelf;
    To Him man's dearer than t'himself.
And, howsoever we may think things sweet,
    He always gives what He knows meet;
Which who can use is happy. Such be thou.
    Thy morning's and thy evening's vow
Be thanks to Him, and earnest prayer, to find
    A body sound, with sounder mind;
To do thy country service, thyself right;
    That neither want do thee affright,
Nor death; but when thy latest sand is spent,
    Thou may'st think life a thing but lent.

TO THE WORLD

A Farewell for a Gentlewoman, Virtuous and Noble

False world, good-night! since thou hast brought
    That hour upon my morn of age,
Henceforth I quit thee from my thought;
    My part is ended on thy stage.

Do not once hope that thou canst tempt
    A spirit so resolved to tread
Upon thy throat, and live exempt
    From all the nets that thou canst spread.

I know thy forms are studied arts,
　　Thy subtle ways be narrow straits;
Thy courtesy but sudden starts,
　　And what thou call'st thy gifts are baits.

I know, too, though thou strut and paint,
　　Yet thou art both shrunk up and old;
That only fools make thee a saint,
　　And all thy good is to be sold.

I know thou whole art but a shop
　　Of toys and trifles, traps and snares,
To take the weak, or make them stop;
　　Yet thou art falser than thy wares.

And, knowing this, should I yet stay,
　　Like such as blow away their lives,
And never will redeem a day,
　　Enamoured of their golden gyves?

Or, having 'scaped, shall I return,
　　And thrust my neck into the noose
From whence so lately I did burn,
　　With all my powers, myself to loose?

What bird or beast is known so dull,
　　That fled his cage or broke his chain,
And, tasting air and freedom, wull
　　Render his head in there again?

If these, who have but sense, can shun
　　The engines that have them annoyed,
Little for me had reason done,
　　If I could not thy gins avoid.

Yes, threaten, do. Alas, I fear
   As little as I hope from thee;
I know thou canst nor show nor bear
   More hatred than thou hast to me.

My tender, first, and simple years
   Thou didst abuse, and then betray;
Since, stirred'st up jealousy and fears,
   When all the causes were away.

Then, in a soil hast planted me,
   Where breathe the basest of thy fools;
Where envious arts professèd be,
   And pride and ignorance the schools;

Where nothing is examined, weighed,
   But, as 'tis rumoured, so believed;
Where every freedom is betrayed,
   And every goodness taxed or grieved.

But what we're born for, we must bear;
   Our frail condition it is such,
That what to all may happen here,
   If 't chance to me, I must not grutch.

Else I my state should much mistake,
   To harbour a divided thought
From all my kind: that for my sake,
   There should a miracle be wrought.

No, I do know that I was born
   To age, misfortune, sickness, grief;
But I will bear these with that scorn
   As shall not need thy false relief.

Nor for my peace will I go far,
  As wand'rers do, that still do roam;
But make my strengths, such as they are,
  Here in my bosom, and at home.

TO CELIA

Kiss me, sweet. The wary lover
Can your favours keep, and cover,
When the common courting jay
All your bounties will betray.
Kiss again; no creature comes.
Kiss, and score up wealthy sums
On my lips, thus hardly sundered
While you breathe. First give a hundred,
Then a thousand, then another
Hundred, then unto the tother
Add a thousand, and so more;
Till you equal with the store,
All the grass that Rumney yields,
Or the sands in Chelsea fields,
Or the drops in silver Thames,
Or the stars that gild his streams,
In the silent summer nights,
When youths ply their stol'n delights;
That the curious may not know
How to tell 'em, as they flow,
And the envious, when they find
What their number is, be pined.

SONG

To the same

Drink to me only with thine eyes,
  And I will pledge with mine;

Or leave a kiss within the cup,
 And I'll not look for wine.
The thirst that from the soul doth rise,
 Doth ask a drink divine;
But might I of Jove's nectar sup,
 I would not change for thine.

I sent thee late a rosy wreath,
 Not so much honouring thee,
As giving it a hope that there
 It could not withered be.
But thou thereon didst only breathe,
 And sent'st it back to me;
Since when it grows, and smells, I swear,
 Not of itself, but thee.

EPODE

Not to know vice at all, and keep true state,
 Is virtue and not fate;
Next to that virtue is to know vice well,
 And her black spite expel.
Which to effect—since no breast is so sure
 Or safe, but she'll procure
Some way of entrance—we must plant a guard
 Of thoughts, to watch and ward,
At th' eye and ear, the ports unto the mind,
 That no strange or unkind
Object arrive there, but the Heart, our spy,
 Give knowledge instantly
To wakeful Reason, our affections' king,
 Who, in th' examining,
Will quickly taste the treason, and commit
 Close, the close cause of it.
'Tis the securest policy we have
 To make our sense our slave;

But this true course is not embraced by many.
  By many? scarce by any.
For either our affections do rebel,
  Or else the sentinel
That should ring 'larum to the heart, doth sleep;
  Or some great thought doth keep
Back the intelligence, and falsely swears
  They're base and idle fears
Whereof the loyal Conscience so complains.
  Thus, by these subtle trains,
Do several passions invade the mind,
  And strike our Reason blind.
Of which usurping rank, some have thought Love
  The first, as prone to move
Most frequent tumults, horrors, and unrests
  In our inflamèd breasts.
But this doth from the cloud of error grow,
  Which thus we overblow:
The thing they here call Love is blind Desire,
  Armed with bow, shafts, and fire,
Inconstant like the sea, of whence 'tis borne,
  Rough, swelling, like a storm;
With whom who sails rides on the surge of fear,
  And boils as if he were
In a continual tempest. Now, true Love
  No such effects doth prove;
That is an essence far more gentle, fine,
  Pure, perfect, nay divine.
It is a golden chain let down from Heaven,
  Whose links are bright and even;
That falls like sleep on lovers, and combines
  The soft and sweetest minds
In equal knots. This bears no brands nor darts,
  To murder different hearts;
But in a calm and godlike unity,
  Preserves community.

O, who is he that, in this peace, enjoys
  Th' elixir of all joys?
A form more fresh than are the Eden bowers,
  And lasting as her flowers;
Richer than Time, and as Time's virtue rare;
  Sober as saddest care;
A fixèd thought, an eye untaught to glance.
  Who, blest with such high chance,
Would, at suggestion of a steep desire,
  Cast himself from the spire
Of all his happiness? But soft, I hear
  Some vicious fool draw near,
That cries we dream, and swears there's no such
    thing
  As this chaste love we sing.
Peace, Luxury, thou art like one of those
  Who, being at sea, suppose,
Because they move, the continent doth so.
  No, Vice, we let thee know,
Though thy wild thoughts with sparrows' wings do
    fly,
  Turtles can chastely die.
And yet—in this t'express ourselves more clear—
  We do not number here
Such spirits as are only continent
  Because lust's means are spent;
Or those who doubt the common mouth of fame,
  And for their place or name,
Cannot so safely sin. Their chastity
  Is mere necessity.
Nor mean we those whom vows and conscience
  Have filled with abstinence;
Though we acknowledge who can so abstain
  Makes a most blessèd gain.
He that for love of goodness hateth ill
  Is more crown-worthy still,

Than he which for sin's penalty forbears:
   His heart sins, though he fears.
But we propose a person like our dove,
   Graced with a phoenix' love;
A beauty of that clear and sparkling light,
   Would make a day of night,
And turn the blackest sorrows to bright joys;
   Whose od'rous breath destroys
All taste of bitterness, and makes the air
   As sweet as she is fair.
A body so harmoniously composed,
   As if Nature disclosed
All her best symmetry in that one feature!
   O, so divine a creature
Who could be false to? chiefly, when he knows
   How only she bestows
The wealthy treasure of her love on him,
   Making his fortunes swim
In the full flood of her admired perfection?
   What savage, brute affection
Would not be fearful to offend a dame
   Of this excelling frame?
Much more a noble and right generous mind,
   To virtuous moods inclined,
That knows the weight of guilt; he will refrain
   From thoughts of such a strain,
And to his sense object this sentence ever:
'Man may securely sin, but safely never.'

FROM *Underwoods*

A CELEBRATION OF CHARIS

In Ten Lyric Pieces

I

His Excuse for Loving

Let it not your wonder move,
Less your laughter, that I love.
Though I now write fifty years,
I have had, and have my peers.
Poets, though divine, are men;
Some have loved as old again.
And it is not always face,
Clothes, or fortune gives the grace,
Or the feature, or the youth;
But the language and the truth,
With the ardour and the passion,
Gives the lover weight and fashion.
If you then will read the story,
First prepare you to be sorry
That you ever knew till now
Either whom to love or how.
But be glad as soon, with me,
When you know that this is she
Of whose beauty it was sung,
She shall make the old man young;
Keep the middle age at stay,
And let nothing high decay;
Till she be the reason why
All the world for love may die.

2

How He Saw Her

I beheld her, on a day,
When her look outflourished May,
And her dressing did outbrave
All the pride the fields then have.
Far I was from being stupid,
For I ran and called on Cupid,
'Love, if thou wilt ever see
Mark of glory, come with me.
Where's thy quiver? Bend thy bow.
Here's a shaft; thou art too slow!'
And withal I did untie
Every cloud about his eye.
But he had not gained his sight
Sooner, than he lost his might
Or his courage; for away
Straight he ran, and durst not stay,
Letting bow and arrow fall;
Nor for any threat or call,
Could be brought once back to look.
I, foolhardy, there uptook
Both the arrow he had quit,
And the bow, which thought to hit
This my object. But she threw
Such a lightning, as I drew,
At my face, that took my sight
And my motion from me quite;
So that there I stood a stone,
Mocked of all, and called of one—
Which with grief and wrath I heard—
Cupid's statue with a beard,
Or else one that played his ape
In a Hercules's shape.

3

What He Suffered

After many scorns like these,
Which the prouder beauties please,
She content was to restore
Eyes and limbs, to hurt me more;
And would, on conditions, be
Reconciled to Love and me:
First, that I must kneeling yield
Both the bow and shaft I held
Unto her; which Love might take
At her hand, with oath to make
Me the scope of his next draught,
Aimèd with that self-same shaft.
He no sooner heard the law,
But the arrow home did draw,
And—to gain her by his art—
Left it sticking in my heart;
Which when she beheld to bleed,
She repented of the deed,
And would fain have changed the fate,
But the pity comes too late.
Loser-like now, all my wreak
Is that I have leave to speak,
And, in either prose or song,
To revenge me with my tongue;
Which how dexterously I do,
Hear, and make example, too.

4

Her Triumph

See the chariot at hand here of Love,
    Wherein my lady rideth!
Each that draws is a swan or a dove,
    And well the car Love guideth.
As she goes, all hearts do duty
        Unto her beauty;
And enamoured, do wish, so they might
        But enjoy such a sight,
That they still were to run by her side,
Through swords, through seas, whither she would
        ride.

Do but look on her eyes; they do light
    All that Love's world compriseth!
Do but look on her hair; it is bright
    As Love's star when it riseth!
Do but mark, her forehead's smoother
        Than words that soothe her!
And from her archèd brows, such a grace
        Sheds itself through the face,
As alone there triumphs to the life
All the gain, all the good of the elements' strife.

Have you seen but a bright lily grow,
    Before rude hands have touched it?
Ha' you marked but the fall o' the snow,
    Before the soil hath smutched it?
Ha' you felt the wool of bever,
        Or swan's-down ever?
Or have smelt o' the bud o' the briar,
        Or the nard in the fire?
Or have tasted the bag of the bee?
O so white! O so soft! O so sweet is she!

5

His Discourse with Cupid

Noblest Charis, you that are
Both my fortune and my star,
And do govern more my blood
Than the various moon the flood,
Hear what late discourse of you
Love and I have had, and true!
'Mongst my Muses finding me,
Where he chanced your name to see
Set, and to this softer strain;
'Sure,' said he, 'if I have brain,
This here sung can be no other,
By description, but my Mother!
So hath Homer praised her hair;
So Anacreon drawn the air
Of her face, and made to rise
Just above her sparkling eyes,
Both her brows, bent like my bow.
By her looks I do her know,
Which you call my shafts. And see!
Such my Mother's blushes be,
As the bath your verse discloses
In her cheeks, of milk and roses,
Such as oft I wanton in.
And, above her even chin,
Have you placed the bank of kisses,
Where you say men gather blisses,
Ripened with a breath more sweet
Than when flowers and west-winds meet.
Nay, her white and polished neck,
With the lace that doth it deck,
Is my Mother's! Hearts of slain
Lovers made into a chain!

And between each rising breast,
Lies the valley called my nest,
Where I sit and prune my wings
After flight, and put new stings
To my shafts. Her very name
With my Mother's is the same.'
'I confess all,' I replied,
'And the glass hangs by her side,
And the girdle 'bout her waist;
All is Venus, save unchaste.
But alas, thou seest the least
Of her good, who is the best
Of her sex; but couldst thou, Love,
Call to mind the forms that strove
For the apple, and those three
Make in one, the same were she.
For this beauty yet doth hide
Something more than thou hast spied;
Outward grace weak love beguiles.
She is Venus when she smiles,
But she's Juno when she walks,
And Minerva when she talks.'

6

Claiming a Second Kiss by Desert

Charis, guess, and do not miss,
Since I drew a morning kiss
From your lips, and sucked an air
Thence, as sweet as you are fair,
What my Muse and I have done:
　　Whether we have lost or won,
If by us the odds were laid
That the bride, allowed a maid,
Looked not half so fresh and fair,
With th'advantage of her hair

And her jewels, to the view
Of th'assembly, as did you?
 Or that, did you sit or walk,
You were more the eye and talk
Of the Court today, than all
Else that glistered in Whitehall;
So as those that had your sight
Wished the bride were changed tonight,
And did think such rites were due
To no other Grace but you?
 Or, if you did move tonight
In the dances, with what spite
Of your peers you were beheld,
That at every motion swelled,
So to see a lady tread
As might all the Graces lead,
And was worthy, being so seen,
To be envied of the Queen?
 Or, if you would yet have stayed,
Whether any would upbraid
To himself his loss of time;
Or have charged his sight of crime,
To have left all sight for you?
 Guess of these which is the true;
And if such a verse as this
May not claim another kiss.

7

Begging Another, on Colour of Mending the Former

For Love's sake, kiss me once again;
I long, and should not beg in vain.
 Here's none to spy or see;
  Why do you doubt or stay?
I'll taste as lightly as the bee,
That doth but touch his flower, and flies away.

Once more, and faith, I will be gone.
Can he that loves ask less than one?
    Nay, you may err in this,
    And all your bounty wrong;
This could be called but half a kiss.
What we're but once to do, we should do long.

I will but mend the last, and tell
Where, how it would have relished well;
    Join lip to lip, and try;
    Each suck other's breath.
And whilst our tongues perplexèd lie,
Let who will think us dead or wish our death.

8

Urging Her of a Promise

Charis one day, in discourse
Had of Love, and of his force,
Lightly promised she would tell
What a man she could love well;
And that promise set on fire
All that heard her with desire.
With the rest, I long expected
When the work would be effected;
But we find that cold delay
And excuse spun every day,
As until she tell her one,
We all fear she loveth none.
Therefore, Charis, you must do't,
For I will so urge you to't,
You shall neither eat nor sleep;
No, nor forth your window peep,
With your emissary eye,
To fetch in the forms go by,
And pronounce which band or lace

Better fits him than his face.
Nay, I will not let you sit
'Fore your idol glass a whit,
To say over every purl
There, or to reform a curl;
Or with Secretary Cis
To consult, if fucus this
Be as good as was the last.
All your sweet of life is past;
Make account, unless you can—
And that quickly—speak your man.

9

Her Man Described by her own Dictamen

Of your trouble, Ben, to ease me,
I will tell what man would please me.
　I would have him, if I could,
Noble, or of greater blood.
Titles, I confess do take me;
And a woman God did make me.
French to boot, at least in fashion,
And his manners of that nation.
　Young I'd have him, too, and fair,
Yet a man; with crispèd hair
Cast in thousand snares or rings
For Love's fingers or his wings;
Chestnut colour, or more slack
Gold, upon a ground of black;
Venus' or Minerva's eyes,
For he must look wanton-wise.
　Eyebrows bent like Cupid's bow,
Front an ample field of snow,
Even nose, and cheek withal
Smooth as is the billiard ball;
Chin as woolly as the peach,

And his lip should kissing teach,
Till he cherished too much beard,
And make Love or me afeard.

   He would have a hand as soft
As the down, and show it oft;
Skin as smooth as any rush,
And so thin to see a blush
Rising through it ere it came.
All his blood should be a flame
Quickly fired, as in beginners
In love's school, and yet no sinners.

   'Twere too long to speak of all;
What we harmony do call
In a body should be there.
Well he should his clothes to wear,
Yet no tailor help to make him
Dressed; you still for man should take him,
And not think h' had eat a stake,
Or were set up in a brake.

   Valiant he should be as fire,
Showing danger more than ire;
Bounteous as the clouds to earth,
And as honest as his birth.
All his actions to be such
As to do nothing too much:
Nor o'erpraise nor yet condemn,
Nor outvalue nor contemn,
Nor do wrongs nor wrongs receive,
Nor tie knots nor knots unweave;
And from baseness to be free,
As he durst love Truth and me.

   Such a man, with every part,
I could give my very heart;
But of one, if short he came,
I can rest me where I am.

10

Another Lady's Exception, Present at the Hearing

> For his mind, I do not care;
> That's a toy that I could spare.
> Let his title be but great,
> His clothes rich, and band sit neat;
> Himself young, and face be good;
> All I wish is understood.
> What you please you parts may call;
> 'Tis one good part I'd lie withal.

A SONG

O, do not wanton with those eyes,
  Lest I be sick with seeing;
Nor cast them down, but let them rise,
  Lest shame destroy their being.

O, be not angry with these fires,
  For then their threats will kill me;
Nor look too kind on my desires,
  For then my hopes will spill me.

O, do not steep them in thy tears,
  For so will sorrow slay me;
Nor spread them, as distract with fears;
  Mine own enough betray me.

THE HOUR-GLASS

Do but consider this small dust, here running in the
    glass,
      By atoms moved.
Could you believe that this the body was
      Of one that loved?

And in his mistress' flame playing like a fly,
　　Turned to cinders by her eye?
Yes, and in death as life unblest,
　　To have't expressed,
Even ashes of lovers find no rest.

MY PICTURE

Left in Scotland

I now think Love is rather deaf than blind;
　　For else it could not be
　　　　That she
Whom I adore so much, should so slight me,
　　And cast my love behind.
I'm sure my language to her was as sweet,
　　And every close did meet
　　In sentence of as subtle feet,
　　　As hath the youngest he
That sits in shadow of Apollo's tree.
　　O, but my conscious fears,
　　　That fly my thoughts between,
　　　Tell me that she hath seen
　　My hundreds of grey hairs;
　　Told seven and and forty years;
Read so much waste, as she cannot embrace
My mountain belly and my rocky face;
And all these through her eyes have stopped her ears.

THE DREAM

　　Or scorn or pity on me take,
　　I must the true relation make;
　　　I am undone tonight.
　　Love, in a subtle dream disguised,
　　Hath both my heart and me surprised,
Whom never yet he durst attempt t'awake.
　　Nor will he tell me for whose sake

He did me the delight,
    Or spite;
But leaves me to inquire,
In all my wild desire
Of Sleep again, who was his aid;
And Sleep so guilty and afraid,
As since he dares not come within my sight.

AN ODE

To Himself

Where dost thou careless lie,
    Buried in ease and sloth?
Knowledge that sleeps doth die;
And this security,
    It is the common moth,
That eats on wits and arts, and destroys them both.

Are all th' Aonian springs
    Dried up? Lies Thespia waste?
Doth Clarius' harp want strings,
That not a nymph now sings?
    Or droop they, as disgraced,
To see their seats and bowers by chatt'ring pies defaced?

If hence thy silence be,
    As 'tis too just a cause,
Let this thought quicken thee:
Minds that are great and free
    Should not on fortune pause;
'Tis crown enough to virtue still, her own applause.

What though the greedy fry
    Be taken with false baits
Of worded balladry,

And think it poesy?
   They die with their conceits,
And only piteous scorn upon their folly waits.

   Then take in hand thy lyre,
     Strike in thy proper strain;
   With Japhet's line, aspire
   Sol's chariot for new fire
     To give the world again;
Who aided him, will thee, the issue of Jove's brain.

   And since our dainty age
     Cannot endure reproof,
   Make not thyself a page
   To that strumpet, the stage;
     But sing high and aloof,
Safe from the wolf's black jaw and the dull ass's hoof.

A FIT OF RHYME AGAINST RHYME

   Rhyme, the rack of finest wits,
   That expresseth but by fits
      True conceit;
   Spoiling senses of their treasure,
   Cozening judgment with a measure,
      But false weight;

   Wresting words from their true calling,
   Propping verse, for fear of falling
      To the ground;
   Jointing syllabes, drowning letters,
   Fast'ning vowels, as with fetters
      They were bound!

   Soon as lazy thou wert known,
   All good poetry hence was flown,
      And are banished.

For a thousand years together,
All Parnassus' green did wither,
 And wit vanished.

Pegasus did fly away;
At the wells no Muse did stay,
 But bewailed.
So to see the fountain dry,
And Apollo's music die,
 All light failed.

Starveling rhymes did fill the stage;
Not a poet in an age,
 Worth crowning;
Not a work deserving bays,
Nor a line deserving praise,
 Pallas frowning.

Greek was free from rhyme's infection,
Happy Greek, by this protection,
 Was not spoiled.
Whilst the Latin, queen of tongues,
Is not yet free from rhyme's wrongs,
 But rests foiled.

Scarce the hill again doth flourish,
Scarce the world a wit doth nourish,
 To restore
Phoebus to his crown again,
And the Muses to their brain,
 As before.

Vulgar languages, that want
Words and sweetness, and be scant
 Of true measure,
Tyrant rhyme hath so abusèd,
That they long since have refusèd
 Other caesure.

He that first invented thee,
May his joints tormented be,
  Cramped forever;
Still may syllabes jar with time,
Still may reason war with rhyme,
  Resting never.

May his sense, when it would meet
The cold tumour in his feet,
  Grow unsounder;
And his title be long fool,
That in rearing such a school
  Was the founder.

AN ELEGY

Let me be what I am: as Virgil cold,
As Horace fat, or as Anacreon old;
No poet's verses yet did ever move,
Whose readers did not think he was in love.
Who shall forbid me, then, in rhyme to be
As light and active as the youngest he
That from the Muses' fountains doth endorse
His lines, and hourly sits the poets' horse?
Put on my ivy garland; let me see
Who frowns, who jealous is, who taxeth me.
Fathers and husbands, I do claim a right
In all that is called lovely; take my sight,
Sooner than my affection, from the fair.
No face, no hand, proportion, line, or air
Of beauty, but the Muse hath interest in;
There is not worn that lace, purl, knot, or pin,
But is the poet's matter; and he must,
When he is furious, love, although not lust.
But then content, your daughters and your wives
If they be fair, and worth it—have their lives

Made longer by our praises; or if not,
Wish you had foul ones and deformèd got,
Curst in their cradles, or there changed by elves,
So to be sure you do enjoy yourselves.
Yet keep those up in sackcloth, too, or leather,
For silk will draw some sneaking songster thither.
It is a rhyming age, and verses swarm
At every stall; the City cap's a charm.
But I who live, and have lived twenty year,
Where I may handle silk as free and near
As any mercer, or the whale-bone man
That quilts those bodies, I have leave to span;
Have eaten with the beauties and the wits
And braveries of court, and felt their fits
Of love and hate, and came so nigh to know
Whether their faces were their own, or no.
It is not likely I should now look down
Upon a velvet petticoat, or a gown
Whose like I have known the tailor's wife put
      on,
To do her husband's rites in, ere 'twere gone
Home to the customer—his lechery
Being the best clothes still to preoccupy.
Put a coach-mare in tissue, must I horse
Her presently? Or leap thy wife of force,
When, by thy sordid bounty, she hath on
A gown of that was the caparison?
So I might dote upon thy chairs and stools,
That are like clothed; must I be of those fools,
Of race accounted, that no passion have,
But when thy wife, as thou conceiv'st, is brave?
Then ope thy wardrobe, think me that poor groom
That from the footman when he was become
An officer there, did make most solemn love
To every petticoat he brushed, and glove

He did lay up; and would adore the shoe
Or slipper was left off, and kiss it, too;
Court every hanging gown, and after that,
Lift up some one, and do I tell not what.
Thou didst tell me, and wert o'erjoyed to peep
In at a hole, and see these actions creep
From the poor wretch; which though he played in
    prose,
He would have done in verse with any of those
Wrung on the Withers by lord Love's despite,
Had he the faculty to read and write!
Such songsters there are store of; witness he
That chanced the lace laid on a smock to see,
And straightway spent a sonnet; with that other,
That, in pure madrigal, unto his mother
Commended the French hood and scarlet gown
The Lady May'ress passed in through the town,
Unto the Spittle sermon. 'O, what strange
Variety of silks were on th' Exchange,
Or in Moorfields, this other night!' sings one.
Another answers, ' 'Las, those silks are none,'
In smiling l'envoy, as he would deride
Any comparison had with his Cheapside;
And vouches both the pageant and the day
When not the shops, but windows do display
The stuffs, the velvets, plushes, fringes, lace,
And all the original riots of the place.
Let the poor fools enjoy their follies; love
A goat in velvet, or some block could move
Under that cover, an old midwife's hat,
Or a close-stool, so cased, or any fat
Bawd in a velvet scabbard! I envy
None of their pleasures, nor will ask thee why
Thou art jealous of thy wife's or daughter' case,
More than of either's manners, wit, or face

AN EPISTLE

Answering to One that Asked to be Sealed of the Tribe of Ben

Men that are safe and sure, in all they do,
Care not what trials they are put unto;
They meet the fire, the test, as martyrs would,
And though opinion stamp them not, are gold.
I could say more of such, but that I fly
To speak myself out too ambitiously;
And showing so weak an act to vulgar eyes,
Put conscience and my right to compromise.
Let those that merely talk and never think,
That live in the wild anarchy of drink,
Subject to quarrel only, or else such
As make it their proficiency how much
They've glutted in and lechered out that week,
That never yet did friend or friendship seek,
But for a sealing—let these men protest.
Or th' other on their borders, that will jest
On all souls that are absent, even the dead,
Like flies or worms which man's corrupt parts fed;
That to speak well, think it above all sin,
Of any company but that they are in;
Call every night to supper in these fits,
And are received for the covey of wits;
That censure all the town, and all th' affairs,
And know whose ignorance is more than theirs—
Let these men have their ways, and take their times
To vent their libels and to issue rhymes.
O, have no portion in them, nor their deal
Of news they get, to strew out the long meal;
I study other friendships, and more one
Than these can ever be, or else wish none.
What is't to me whether the French design
Be, or be not, to get the Valtelline?

Or the States' ships sent forth belike to meet
Some hopes of Spain in their West Indian fleet?
Whether the dispensation yet be sent,
Or that the match from Spain was ever meant?
I wish all well, and pray high Heaven conspire
My Prince's safety and my King's desire;
But if for honour we must draw the sword,
And force back that which will not be restored,
I have a body yet that spirit draws,
To live or fall a carcase in the cause.
So far, without inquiry what the States,
Brunsfield, and Mansfield do this year, my fates
Shall carry me at call; and I'll be well,
Though I do neither hear these news, nor tell
Of Spain or France; or were not pricked down one
Of the late mystery of reception—
Although my fame to his not underhears,
That guides the motions and directs the bears.
But that's a blow by which, in time, I may
Lose all my credit with my Christmas clay
And animated porcelain of the court;
Ay, and for this neglect, the coarser sort
Of earthen jars there may molest me, too.
Well, with mine own frail pitcher what to do,
I have decreed: keep it from waves and press,
Lest it be jostled, cracked, made naught, or less.
Live to that point I will, for which I am man,
And dwell as in my centre as I can;
Still looking to, and ever loving, Heaven;
With reverence using all the gifts then given.
'Mongst which if I have any friendships sent,
Such as are square, well-tagged, and permanent,
Not built with canvas, paper, and false lights,
As are the glorious scenes at the great sights;
And that there be no fev'ry heats, nor colds,
Oily expansions, or shrunk, dirty folds,

But all so clear, and led by reason's flame,
As but to stumble in her sight were shame;
These will I honour, love, embrace, and serve,
And free it from all question to preserve.
So short you read my character, and theirs
I would call mine, to which not many stairs
Are asked to climb. First give me faith, who know
Myself a little; I will take you so,
As you have writ yourself. Now stand, and then,
Sir, you are sealèd of the Tribe of Ben.

To the Immortal Memory and Friendship of that Noble Pair

SIR LUCIUS CARY AND SIR HENRY MORISON

The Turn

Brave infant of Saguntum, clear
Thy coming forth in that great year,
When the prodigious Hannibal did crown
His rage, with razing your immortal town.
Thou, looking then about,
Ere thou wert half got out,
Wise child, didst hastily return,
And mad'st thy mother's womb thine urn.
How summed a circle didst thou leave mankind,
Of deepest lore, could we the centre find!

The Counterturn

Did wiser Nature draw thee back,
From out the horror of that sack,
Where shame, faith, honour, and regard of right
Lay trampled on; the deeds of death and night
Urged, hurried forth, and hurled
Upon th' affrighted world;

Sword, fire, and famine with fell fury met;
    And all on utmost ruin set;
As could they but life's miseries foresee,
No doubt all infants would return like thee?

The Stand

For what is life, is measured by the space,
      Not by the act?
Or maskèd man, if valued by his face,
      Above his fact?
    Here's one outlived his peers,
    And told forth fourscore years;
He vexèd time, and busied the whole state;
    Troubled both foes and friends,
    But ever to no ends;
    What did this stirrer, but die late?
How well at twenty had he fall'n, or stood!
For three of his four score, he did no good.

The Turn

    He entered well, by virtuous parts,
    Got up and thrived with honest arts;
He purchased friends and fame and honours then,
And had his noble name advanced with men.
      But weary of that flight,
      He stooped in all men's sight
    To sordid flatteries, acts of strife,
    And sunk in that dead sea of life
So deep, as he did then death's waters sup;
But that the cork of title buoyed him up.

The Counterturn

    Alas, but Morison fell young!
    He never fell; thou fall'st, my tongue.
He stood, a soldier to the last right end,

A perfect patriot and a noble friend,
    But most a virtuous son.
    All offices were done
  By him, so ample, full, and round
  In weight, in measure, number, sound,
As though his age imperfect might appear;
His life was of humanity the sphere.

The Stand

Go now, and tell out days summed up with fears,
    And make them years;
Produce thy mass of miseries on the stage,
    To swell thine age;
    Repeat of things a throng
    To show thou hast been long,
Not lived; for Life doth her great actions spell,
    By what was done and wrought
    In season, and so brought
To light; her measures are how well
Each syllabe answered, and was formed how fair;
These make the lines of life, and that's her air.

The Turn

    It is not growing like a tree
    In bulk, doth make man better be;
Or standing long an oak, three hundred year,
To fall a log at last, dry, bold, and sear.
    A lily of a day
    Is fairer far, in May,
    Although it fall and die that night;
    It was the plant and flow'r of light.
In small proportions we just beauties see;
And in short measures life may perfect be.

The Counterturn

Call, noble Lucius, then, for wine,
    And let thy looks with gladness shine;
Accept this garland, plant it on thy head,
And think, nay know, thy Morison's not dead.
        He leaped the present age,
        Possessed with holy rage,
    To see that bright eternal day,
    Of which we priests and poets say
Such truths as we expect for happy men;
And there he lives with memory, and Ben

The Stand

Jonson, who sung this of him, ere he went
        Himself to rest,
Or taste a part of that full joy he meant
        To have expressed
        In this bright asterism;
        Where it were friendship's schism,
Were not his Lucius long with us to tarry,
        To separate these twi-
        Lights, the Dioscuri,
    And keep the one half from his Harry.
But Fate doth so alternate the design,
Whilst that in Heav'n, this light on earth must
    shine.

The Turn

    And shine as you exalted are,
    Two names of friendship, but one star;
Of hearts the union—and those not by chance
Made, or indenture, or leased out t'advance
        The profits for a time.
        No pleasures vain did chime,

Of rhymes or riots at your feasts,
  Orgies of drink or feigned protests;
But simple love of greatness and of good,
That knits brave minds and manners more than
    blood.

The Counterturn

This made you first to know the why
  You liked, then after to apply
That liking, and approach so one the tother
Till either grew a portion of the other;
    Each stylèd by his end,
    The copy of his friend.
  You lived to be the great surnames
  And titles, by which all made claims
Unto the virtue. Nothing perfect done,
But as a Cary or a Morison.

The Stand

And such a force the fair example had,
    As they that saw
The good, and durst not practise it, were glad
    That such a law
    Was left yet to mankind;
    Where they might read, and find
Friendship, indeed was written not in words,
    And with the heart, not pen,
    Of two so early men,
  Whose lines her rolls were, and records;
Who, ere the first down bloomèd on the chin,
Had sowed these fruits and got the harvest in.

*The Humble Petition of Poor Ben
To th' Best of Monarchs, Masters, Men,*

KING CHARLES

Doth most humbly show it
To your Majesty, your poet:
 That whereas your royal father,
 James the Blessèd, pleased the rather
 Of his special grace to letters,
 To make all the Muses debtors
 To his bounty, by extension
 Of a free poetic pension,
 A large hundred marks' annuity,
 To be given me in gratuity
 For done service, and to come.
  And that this so accepted sum,
 Or dispensed in books or bread,—
 For with both the Muse was fed—
 Hath drawn on me, from the times,
 All the envy of the rhymes,
 And the rattling pit-pat noise
 Of the less poetic boys;
 When their pot-guns aim to hit,
 With their pellets of small wit,
 Parts of me they judged decayed;
 But we last out, still unlaid.
  Please your Majesty to make,
 Of your grace, for goodness' sake,
 Those your father's marks, your pounds;
 Let their spite, which now abounds,
 Then go on and do its worst;
 This would all their envy burst,
 And so warm the poet's tongue,
 You'd read a snake in his next song.

AN ELEGY ON THE LADY ANNE PAWLET

Marchioness of Winchester

What gentle ghost, besprent with April dew,
Hails me so solemnly to yonder yew?
And beck'ning woos me, from the fatal tree
To pluck a garland for herself or me?
I do obey you, beauty, for in death
You seem a fair one. O that you had breath
To give your shade a name! Stay, stay, I feel
A horror in me! All my blood is steel.
Stiff! stark! my joints 'gainst one another knock.
Whose daughter? ha! great Savage of the Rock!
He's good, as great. I am almost a stone!
And ere I can ask more of her, she's gone!
Alas, I am all marble! write the rest
Thou wouldst have written, Fame, upon my breast;
It is a large, fair table, and a true,
And the disposure will be something new,
When I, who would the poet have become,
At least may bear th' inscription to her tomb.
She was the Lady Jane, and Marchioness
Of Winchester; the heralds can tell this.
Earl Rivers' grandchild—serve not forms, good
          Fame,
Sound thou her virtues, give her soul a name.
Had I a thousand mouths, as many tongues,
And voice to raise them from my brazen lungs,
I durst not aim at that; the dotes were such
Thereof, no notion can express how much
Their carat was! I or my trump must break,
But rather I, should I of that part speak!
It is too near of kin to Heaven, the soul,
To be described. Fame's fingers are too foul

To touch these mysteries. We may admire
The blaze and splendour, but not handle fire.
What she did here, by great example, well,
T'enlive posterity her fame may tell;
And calling truth to witness, make that good
From the inherent graces in her blood.
Else, who doth praise a person by a new,
But a feigned way, doth rob it of the true.
Her sweetness, softness, her fair courtesy,
Her wary guards, her wise simplicity
Were like a ring of virtues, 'bout her set,
And piety the centre, where all met.
A reverend state she had, an awful eye,
A dazzling, yet inviting majesty;
What nature, fortune, institution, fact
Could sum to a perfection was her act.
How did she leave the world? with what contempt?
Just as she in it lived! and so exempt
From all affection! When they urged the cure
Of her disease, how did her soul assure
Her suff'rings, as the body had been away!
And to the torturers, her doctors, say:
'Stick on your cupping-glasses, fear not, put
Your hottest caustics too, burn, lance, or cut;
'Tis but a body which you can torment,
And I into the world all soul was sent!'
Then comforted her Lord and blessed her son,
Cheered her fair sisters in her race to run,
With gladness tempered her sad parents' tears,
Made her friends' joys to get above their fears;
And, in her last act, taught the standers-by
With admiration and applause to die!
Let angels sing her glories, who did call
Her spirit home to her original!
Who saw the way was made it, and were sent

To carry and conduct the compliment
'Twixt death and life, where her mortality
Became her birthday to Eternity.
And now, through circumfusèd light, she looks
On Nature's secrets there, as her own books;
Speaks Heaven's language, and discovereth free
To every order, every hierarchy;
Beholds her Maker, and in Him doth see
What the beginnings of all beauties be,
And all beatitudes, that thence do flow,
Which they that have the crown are sure to know!
Go now, her happy parents, and be sad,
If you not understand what child you had;
If you dare grudge at Heaven, and repent
T'have paid again a blessing was but lent,
And trusted so as it deposited lay,
At pleasure to be called for every day;
If you can envy your own daughter's bliss,
And wish her state less happy than it is;
If you can cast about your either eye,
And see all dead here, or about to die:
The stars, that are the jewels of the night,
And day, deceasing with the prince of light,
The sun! great kings and mightiest kingdoms fall!
Whole nations, nay, mankind, the world, with all
That ever had beginning there, t'have end!
With what injustice should one soul pretend
T'escape this common known necessity;
When we were all born, we began to die.
And but for that contention and brave strife
The Christian hath, t'enjoy the future life,
He were the wretched'st of the race of men;
But as he soars at that, he bruiseth then
The Serpent's head, gets above Death and Sin,
And, sure of Heaven, rides triumphing in.

EUPHEME

The Picture of her Mind

Painter, you're come, but may be gone,
    Now I have better thought thereon;
    This work I can perform alone,
    And give you reasons more than one:

Not that your art I do refuse,
    But here I may no colours use;
    Beside, your hand will never hit,
    To draw a thing that cannot sit.

You could make shift to paint an eye,
    An eagle tow'ring in the sky,
    The sun, a sea, or soundless pit;
    But these are like a mind, not it.

No, to express mind to sense
    Would ask a Heaven's intelligence;
    Since nothing can report that flame,
    But what's of kin to whence it came.

Sweet Mind, then speak yourself, and say,
    As you go on, by what brave way
    Our sense you do with knowledge fill,
    And yet remain our wonder still.

I call you Muse, now make it true;
    Henceforth may every line be you,
    That all may say, that see the frame,
    This is no picture, but the same.

A mind so pure, so perfect fine,
    As 'tis not radiant, but divine;
    And so disdaining any tryer;
    'Tis got where it can try the fire

There, high exalted in the Sphere,
    As it another Nature were,
    It moveth all, and makes a flight
    As circular as infinite.

Whose notions when it will express
    In speech, it is with that excess
    Of grace, and music to the ear,
    As what it spoke it planted there.

The voice so sweet, the words so fair,
    As some soft chime had stroked the air,
    And, though the sound were parted thence,
    Still left an echo in the sense.

But that a mind so rapt, so high,
    So swift, so pure, should yet apply
    Itself to us, and come so nigh
    Earth's grossness—there's the how and why.

Is it because it sees us dull,
    And stuck in clay here, it would pull
    Us forth, by some celestial sleight,
    Up to her own sublimèd height?

Or hath she here, upon the ground,
    Some paradise or palace found,
    In all the bounds of beauty fit
    For her t'inhabit? There is it.

Thrice happy house, that hast receipt
    For this so lofty form, so straight,
    So polished, perfect, round, and even,
    As it slid moulded off from Heaven!

Not swelling like the ocean proud,
    But stooping gently as a cloud,
    As smooth as oil poured forth, and calm
    As showers, and sweet as drops of balm.

Smooth, soft, and sweet; in all, a flood,
    Where it may run to any good;
    And where it stays, it there becomes
    A nest of odorous spice and gums.

In action, wingèd as the wind;
    In rest, like spirits left behind
    Upon a bank, or field of flowers,
    Begotten by that wind and showers.

In thee, fair Mansion, let it rest,
    Yet know with what thou art possessed;
    Thou entertaining in thy breast
    But such a mind, mak'st God thy guest.

A FRAGMENT OF PETRONIUS TRANSLATED

Foeda est in coitu et brevis voluptas

Doing a filthy pleasure is, and short;
And done, we straight repent us of the sport.
Let us not then rush blindly on unto it,
Like lustful beasts, that only know to do it;
For lust will languish, and that heat decay.
But thus, thus, keeping endless holiday,
Let us together closely lie, and kiss;
There is no labour nor no shame in this.

This hath pleased, doth please, and long will
    please; never
Can this decay, but is beginning ever.

FROM CHAPMAN'S *Hesiod*

To my Worthy and Honoured Friend

MASTER GEORGE CHAPMAN

On his Translation of Hesiod's 'Works and Days'

Whose work could this be, Chapman, to refine
Old Hesiod's ore, and give it us, but thine,
Who hadst before wrought in rich Homer's mine?

What treasure thou hast brought us! and what store
Still, still dost thou arrive with at our shore,
To make thy honour and our wealth the more!

If all the vulgar tongues that speak this day
Were asked of thy discoveries, they must say,
To the Greek coast thine only knew the way.

Such passage hast thou found, such returns made,
As now, of all men, it is called thy trade;
And who make thither else, rob or invade.

FROM THE SHAKESPEARE *Folio*

To the Memory of my Beloved the Author

MASTER WILLIAM SHAKESPEARE

And What He Hath Left Us

To draw no envy, Shakespeare, on thy name,
Am I thus ample to thy book and fame;

While I confess thy writings to be such
As neither man nor Muse can praise too much.
'Tis true, and all men's suffrage. But these ways
Were not the paths I meant unto thy praise;
For silliest ignorance on these may light,
Which, when it sounds at best, but echoes right;
Or blind affection, which doth ne'er advance
The truth, but gropes, and urgeth all by chance;
Or crafty malice might pretend this praise,
And think to ruin where it seemed to raise.
These are as some infamous bawd or whore
Should praise a matron. What could hurt her more?
But thou art proof against them, and indeed
Above th' ill fortune of them, or the need.
I therefore will begin. Soul of the age!
The applause, delight, the wonder of our stage!
My Shakespeare, rise; I will not lodge thee by
Chaucer or Spenser, or bid Beaumont lie
A little further, to make thee a room.
Thou art a monument, without a tomb,
And art alive still, while thy book doth live,
And we have wits to read and praise to give.
That I not mix thee so, my brain excuses,—
I mean with great, but disproportioned Muses—
For if I thought my judgment were of years,
I should commit thee surely with thy peers,
And tell how far thou didst our Lyly outshine,
Or sporting Kyd, or Marlowe's mighty line.
And though thou hadst small Latin and less Greek,
From thence to honour thee I would not seek
For names, but call forth thund'ring Aeschylus,
Euripides, and Sophocles to us,
Pacuvius, Accius, him of Cordova dead,
To life again, to hear thy buskin tread
And shake a stage; or, when thy socks were on,
Leave thee alone for the comparison

Of all that insolent Greece or haughty Rome
Sent forth, or since did from their ashes come.
Triumph, my Britain, thou hast one to show,
To whom all scenes of Europe homage owe.
He was not of an age, but for all time!
And all the Muses still were in their prime,
When like Apollo he came forth to warm
Our ears, or like a Mercury to charm.
Nature herself was proud of his designs,
And joyed to wear the dressing of his lines,
Which were so richly spun, and woven so fit,
As since, she will vouchsafe no other wit.
The merry Greek, tart Aristophanes,
Neat Terence, witty Plautus now not please,
But antiquated and deserted lie,
As they were not of Nature's family.
Yet must I not give Nature all: thy art,
My gentle Shakespeare, must enjoy a part;
For though the poet's matter nature be,
His art doth give the fashion; and that he
Who casts to write a living line, must sweat—
Such as thine are—and strike the second heat
Upon the Muses' anvil; turn the same,
And himself with it, that he thinks to frame;
Or, for the laurel, he may gain a scorn,
For a good poet's made, as well as born;
And such wert thou. Look how the father's face
Lives in his issue; even so, the race
Of Shakespeare's mind and manners brightly shines
In his well-turnèd and true-filèd lines;
In each of which he seems to shake a lance,
As brandished at the eyes of ignorance.
Sweet swan of Avon! what a sight it were
To see thee in our waters yet appear,
And make those flights upon the banks of Thames

That so did take Eliza, and our James!
But stay, I see thee in the hemisphere
Advanced, and made a constellation there!
Shine forth, thou star of poets, and with rage
Or influence, chide or cheer the drooping stage;
Which since thy flight from hence, hath mourned
　　like night,
And despairs day, but for thy volume's light.

FROM FILMER'S *French Court-Airs*

To My Worthy Friend

MASTER EDWARD FILMER

On his Work Dedicated to the Queen

What charming peals are these,
That, while they bind the senses do so please?
　　They are the marriage rites
Of two, the choicest pair of man's delights,
　　Music and poesy;
French air and English verse here wedded lie.

Who did this knot compose
Again hath brought the lily to the rose;
　　And, with their chainèd dance,
Recelebrates the joyful match with France.
　　They are a school to win
The fair French daughter to learn English in;
　　And, gracèd with her song,
To make the language sweet upon her tongue.

FROM BROME'S *Northern Lass*

*To my Old Faithful Servant
and by his Continued Virtue my Loving Friend*

MASTER RICHARD BROME

I had you for a servant once, Dick Brome,
    And you performed a servant's faithful parts;
Now you have got into a nearer room
    Of fellowship, professing my old arts.
And you do do them well, with good applause,
    Which you have justly gainèd from the stage,
By observation of those comic laws
    Which I, your master, first did teach the age.
You learned it well, and for it served your time,
    A prenticeship which few do nowadays;
Now each court hobby-horse will wince in rhyme,
    Both learned and unlearned, all write plays.
It was not so of old. Men took up trades
    That knew the crafts they had been bred in right:
An honest bilbo-smith would make good blades,
    And the physician teach men spew or shite;
        The cobbler kept him to his nawl; but now,
        He'll be a pilot, scarce can guide a plough.

V. CRITICISM

Criticism

––––––––

from EVERY MAN
OUT OF HIS HUMOUR

Induction

After the second sounding,

GREX.

Enter CORDATUS, ASPER, *and* MITIS.

CORDATUS. Nay, my dear Asper,—

MITIS.   Stay your mind.

ASPER.   Away!
Who is so patient of this impious world
That he can check his spirit, or rein his tongue?
Or who hath such a dead, unfeeling sense,
That Heaven's horrid thunders cannot wake,
To see the earth cracked with the weight of sin,
Hell gaping under us, and o'er our heads
Black, rav'nous ruin, with her sail-stretched wings,
Ready to sink us down, and cover us?
Who can behold such prodigies as these,
And have his lips sealed up? Not I; my language
Was never ground into such oily colours,
To flatter vice, and daub iniquity.
But, with an armèd and resolvèd hand,
I'll strip the ragged follies of the time,
Naked, as at their birth——

CORDATUS.   —Be not too bold.

ASPER. You trouble me—and with a whip of steel,

935

Print wounding lashes in their iron ribs.
I fear no mood stamped in a private brow,
When I am pleased t'unmask a public vice.
I fear no strumpet's drugs nor ruffian's stab,
Should I detect their hateful luxuries;
No broker's, usurer's, or lawyer's gripe,
Were I disposed to say they're all corrupt.
I fear no courtier's frown, should I applaud
The easy flexure of his supple hams.
Tut, these are so innate and popular,
That drunken custom would not shame to laugh
In scorn, at him that should but dare to tax 'em.
And yet, not one of these, but knows his works,
Knows what damnation is, the devil, and Hell;
Yet hourly they persist, grow rank in sin,
Puffing their souls away in perj'rous air,
To cherish their extortion, pride, or lusts.

   MITIS. Forbear, good Asper, be not like your name.

   ASPER. O, but to such, whose faces are all zeal,
And with the words of Hercules invade
Such crimes as these! that will not smell of sin,
But seem as they were made of sanctity!
Religion in their garments, and their hair
Cut shorter than their eyebrows! when the con-
     science
Is vaster than the ocean, and devours
More wretches than the Counters.

   MITIS.   Gentle Asper,
Contain your spirit in more stricter bounds,
And be not thus transported with the violence
Of your strong thoughts.

   CORDATUS.   Unless your breath had power
To melt the world, and mould it new again,
It is in vain to spend it in these moods.

   ASPER. I not observed this throngèd round till
     now.   *Making address to the people.*
Gracious and kind spectators, you are welcome;

Apollo and the Muses feast your eyes
With graceful objects, and may our Minerva
Answer your hopes, unto their largest strain!
Yet here mistake me not, judicious friends.
I do not this to beg your patience,
Or servilely to fawn on your applause,
Like some dry brain, despairing in his merit.
Let me be censured by th' austerest brow,
Where I want art or judgment, tax me freely.
Let envious censors, with their broadest eyes,
Look through and through me; I pursue no favour.
Only vouchsafe me your attentions,
And I will give you music worth your ears.
O, how I hate the monstrousness of time,
Where every servile, imitating spirit,
Plagued with an itching leprosy of wit,
In a mere halting fury, strives to fling
His ulc'rous body in the Thespian spring,
And straight leaps forth a poet! but as lame
As Vulcan, or the founder of Cripplegate.

   MITIS. In faith, this humour will come ill to some;
You will be thought to be too peremptory.

   ASPER. This humour? good! And why this hu-
      mour, Mitis?
Nay, do not turn, but answer.

   MITIS.   Answer, what?

   ASPER. I will not stir your patience, pardon me,
I urged it for some reasons, and the rather
To give these ignorant, well-spoken days
Some taste of their abuse of this word 'humour.'

   CORDATUS. O, do not let your purpose fall, good
      Asper,
It cannot but arrive most acceptable,
Chiefly to such as have the happiness
Daily to see how the poor, innocent word
Is racked and tortured.

   MITIS.   Ay, I pray you proceed.

ASPER. Ha, what? what is't?

CORDATUS.   For the abuse of humour.

ASPER. O, I crave pardon, I had lost my thoughts.
Why, humour, as 'tis 'ens,' we thus define it
To be a quality of air or water,
And in itself holds these two properties,
Moisture and fluxure; as, for demonstration,
Pour water on this floor, 'twill wet and run.
Likewise the air, forced through a horn or trumpet,
Flows instantly away, and leaves behind
A kind of dew; and hence we do conclude
That whatsoe'er hath fluxure and humidity,
As wanting power to contain itself,
Is humour. So in every human body,
The choler, melancholy, phlegm, and blood,
By reason that they flow continually
In some one part, and are not continent,
Receive the name of humours. Now thus far
It may, by metaphor, apply itself
Unto the general disposition:
As when some one peculiar quality
Doth so possess a man, that it doth draw
All his affects, his spirits, and his powers,
In their confluxions, all to run one way,
This may be truly said to be a humour.
But that a rook, in wearing a pied feather,
The cable hat-band, or the three-piled ruff,
A yard of shoe-tie, or the Switzer's knot
On his French garters, should affect a humour—
O, it is more than most ridiculous!

CORDATUS. He speaks pure truth. Now, if an idiot
Have but an apish or fantastic strain,
It is his humour!

ASPER.   Well, I will scourge those apes;
And to these courteous eyes oppose a mirror,
As large as is the stage whereon we act,
Where they shall see the time's deformity

Anatomized in every nerve and sinew,
With constant courage and contempt of fear.

MITIS. Asper, I urge it as your friend, take heed.
The days are dangerous, full of exception,
And men are grown impatient of reproof.

ASPER. Ha, ha!
You might as well have told me, yond' is heaven;
This, earth; these, men; and all had moved alike.
Do not I know the time's condition?
Yes, Mitis, and their souls, and who they be,
That either will or can except against me:
None but a sort of fools, so sick in taste,
That they contemn all physic of the mind,
And, like galled camels, kick at every touch.
Good men and virtuous spirits, that loathe their
    vices,
Will cherish my free labours, love my lines,
And, with the fervour of their shining grace,
Make my brain fruitful to bring forth more objects,
Worthy their serious and intentive eyes.
But why enforce I this? as fainting? No.
If any here chance to behold himself,
Let him not dare to challenge me of wrong;
For, if he shame to have his follies known,
First he should shame to act 'em. My strict hand
Was made to seize on vice, and with a gripe,
Squeeze out the humour of such spongy natures
As lick up every idle vanity.

CORDATUS. Why, this is right Furor Poeticus!
Kind gentlemen, we hope your patience
Will yet conceive the best, or entertain
This supposition: that a madman speaks.

ASPER. What! are you ready there?—Mitis, sit
    down,
And my Cordatus.—Sound ho! and begin.—
I leave you two, as censors, to sit here.
Observe what I present, and liberally

Speak your opinions upon every scene,
As it shall pass the view of these spectators.—
Nay, now you're tedious, sirs, for shame, begin.—
And, Mitis, note me, if, in all this front,
You can espy a gallant of this mark:
Who, to be thought one of the judicious,
Sits with his arms thus wreathed, his hat pulled
    here;
Cries mew, and nods, then shakes his empty head;
Will show more several motions in his face
Than the new London, Rome, or Nineveh;
And, now and then, breaks a dry biscuit jest,
Which, that it may more easily be chewed,
He steeps in his own laughter.

    CORDATUS.   Why? will that
Make it be sooner swallowed?

    ASPER.   O, assure you.
Or if it did not, yet as Horace sings,
'Jejunus raro stomachus vulgaria temnit,'
Mean cates are welcome still to hungry guests.

    CORDATUS. 'Tis true, but why should we observe
      'em, Asper?

    ASPER. O, I would know 'em, for in such assemblies
They're more infectious than the pestilence:
And therefore I would give them pills to purge,
And make 'em fit for fair societies.
How monstrous and detested is't to see
A fellow that has neither art nor brain
Sit like an Aristarchus, or stark ass,
Taking men's lines, with a tobacco face,
In snuff, still spitting, using his wryed looks,
In nature of a vice, to wrest and turn
The good aspect of those that shall sit near him,
From what they do behold! O, 'tis most vile.

    MITIS. Nay, Asper.

    ASPER.   Peace, Mitis, I do know your thought;
You'll say your guests here will except at this.

Pish! you are too timorous, and full of doubt.
Then he, a patient, shall reject all physic,
'Cause the physician tells him, 'You are sick.'
Or, if I say that he is vicious,
You will not hear of virtue. Come, you're fond.
Shall I be so extravagant to think
That happy judgments and composèd spirits
Will challenge me for taxing such as these?
I am ashamed.

    CORDATUS.   Nay, but good pardon us,
We must not bear this peremptory sail,
But use our best endeavours how to please.

    ASPER. Why, therein I commend your careful
        thoughts,
And I will mix with you in industry
To please—but whom? attentive auditors,
Such as will join their profit with their pleasure,
And come to feed their understanding parts.
For these I'll prodigally spend myself,
And speak away my spirit into air;
For these I'll melt my brain into invention,
Coin new conceits, and hang my richest words
As polished jewels in their bounteous ears.
But stay, I lose myself, and wrong their patience;
If I dwell here, they'll not begin, I see.
Friends, sit you still, and entertain this troop
With some familiar and by-conference;
I'll haste them sound.—Now, gentlemen, I go
To turn an actor, and a humourist;
Where, ere I do resume my present person,
We hope to make the circles of your eyes
Flow with distillèd laughter. If we fail,
We must impute it to this only chance:
Art hath an enemy called Ignorance.   *Exit*.

    CORDATUS. How do you like his spirit, Mitis?

    MITIS. I should like it much better, if he were less
confident.

CORDATUS. Why, do you suspect his merit?

MITIS. No, but I fear this will procure him much envy.

CORDATUS. O, that sets the stronger seal on his desert. If he had no enemies, I should esteem his fortunes most wretched at this instant.

MITIS. You have seen his play, Cordatus? Pray you, how is't?

CORDATUS. Faith, sir, I must refrain to judge. Only this I can say of it: 'tis strange, and of a particular kind by itself, somewhat like Vetus Comoedia; a work that hath bounteously pleased me, how it will answer the general expectation I know not.

MITIS. Does he observe all the laws of comedy in it?

CORDATUS. What laws mean you?

MITIS. Why, the equal division of it into acts, and scenes, according to the Terentian manner; his true number of actors; the furnishing of the scene with Grex, or chorus; and that the whole argument fall within compass of a day's business.

CORDATUS. O no, these are too nice observations.

MITIS. They are such as must be received, by your favour, or it cannot be authentic.

CORDATUS. Troth, I can discern no such necessity.

MITIS. No?

CORDATUS. No, I assure you, signior. If those laws you speak of had been delivered us, ab initio, and in their present virtue and perfection, there had been some reason of obeying their powers. But 'tis extant that that which we call Comoedia was at first nothing but a simple and continued song, sung by one only person, till Susario invented a second; after him, Epicharmus a third; Phormus and Chionides devised to have four actors, with a prologue and chorus; to which Cratinus, long after, added a fifth and sixth; Eupolis, more; Aristophanes, more than they; every man, in the dignity of his spirit and judgment, supplied something. And though that in him this kind of poem appeared absolute and fully perfected, yet how is the face of it changed since, in Menander, Philemon, Cecilius, Plautus, and the rest; who have utterly excluded the chorus, altered the property of the persons, their names and natures, and augmented it with all liberty, according to the elegancy and disposition of those times wherein they wrote. I see not, then, but we should enjoy the same licence, or free power, to illustrate and heighten our invention as they did; and not be tied to those strict and regular forms, which the niceness of a few—who are nothing but form—would thrust upon us.

MITIS. Well, we will not dispute of this now. But what's his scene?

CORDATUS. Marry, Insula Fortunata, sir.

MITIS. O, the Fortunate Island! Mass, he has bound himself to a strict law there.

CORDATUS. Why so?

MITIS. He cannot lightly alter the scene, without crossing the seas.

CORDATUS. He needs not, having a whole island to run through, I think.

MITIS. No? how comes it, then, that in some one play we see so many seas, countries, and kingdoms passed over with such admirable dexterity?

CORDATUS. O, that but shows how well the authors can travail in their vocation, and outrun the apprehension of their auditory. But, leaving this, I would they would begin once; this protraction is able to sour the best settled patience in the theatre.

MITIS. They have answered your wish, sir, they sound. *The third sounding.*

CORDATUS. O, here comes the Prologue.

from POETASTER,
OR HIS ARRAIGNMENT

Final Scene

AUGUSTUS CAESAR, MAECENAS, GALLUS, VIRGIL, TIBUL-
LUS, HORACE, CRISPINUS, DEMETRIUS, TUCCA, LICTORS.

LICTOR. In the name of Caesar, silence!

TIBULLUS. Let the parties, the accuser and the
accused, present themselves.

LICTOR. The accuser, and the accused, present
yourselves in court.

CRISPINUS, DEMETRIUS. Here.

VIRGIL. Read the indictment.

TIBULLUS. 'Rufus Laberius Crispinus, and Demetrius Fannius, hold up your hands. 'You are
before this time jointly and severally indicted, and
here presently to be arraigned upon the statute of
calumny, or Lex Remmia, the one by the name of
Rufus Laberius Crispinus, alias Crispinas, poetaster
and plagiary; the other by the name of Demetrius
Fannius, play-dresser and plagiary. That you,—not
having the fear of Phoebus, or his shafts, before your
eyes—contrary to the peace of our liege lord, Augustus Caesar, his crown and dignity, and against
the form of a statute in that case made and provided, have most ignorantly, foolishly, and—more
like yourselves—maliciously, gone about to deprave
and calumniate the person and writings of Quintus
Horatius Flaccus, here present, poet and priest to
the Muses; and to that end have mutually conspired
and plotted, at sundry times, as by several means
and in sundry places, for the better accomplish-

ing your base and envious purpose; taxing him
falsely of self-love, arrogancy, impudence, railing,
filching by translation, &c. Of all which calumnies,
and every of them, in manner and form aforesaid, what answer you? Are you guilty or not
guilty?'

TUCCA. —Not guilty, say.

CRISPINUS, DEMETRIUS. Not guilty.

TIBULLUS. How will you be tried?

TUCCA. —By the Roman gods and the noblest
Romans.

CRISPINUS, DEMETRIUS. By the Roman gods and the
noblest Romans.

VIRGIL. Here sits Maecenas and Cornelius Gallus.
Are you contented to be tried by these?

TUCCA. —Ay, so the noble Captain may be joined
with them in commission, say.

CRISPINUS, DEMETRIUS. Ay, so the noble Captain
may be joined with them in commission.

VIRGIL. What says the plaintiff?

HORACE. I am content.

VIRGIL. Captain, then take your place.

TUCCA. Alas, my worshipful praetor! 'tis more of
thy gent'ness than of my deserving, I wuss. But
since it hath pleased the court to make choice of
my wisdom and gravity, come, my calumnious
varlets: let's hear you talk for yourselves now, an
hour or two. What can you say? Make a noise. Act,
act!

VIRGIL. Stay, turn, and take an oath first. 'You
    shall swear,
By thunder-darting Jove, the King of Gods,
And by the genius of Augustus Caesar,
By your own white and uncorrupted souls,
And the deep reverence of our Roman justice,

To judge this case with truth and equity,
As bound by your religion and your laws.'
Now read the evidence; but first, demand
Of either prisoner, if that writ be theirs.

TIBULLUS. Show this unto Crispinus.—Is it yours?

TUCCA. Say ay.—What! dost thou stand upon it,
pimp? Do not deny thine own Minerva, thy Pallas,
the issue of thy brain.

CRISPINUS. Yes, it is mine.

TIBULLUS. Show that unto Demetrius. Is it yours?

DEMETRIUS. It is.

TUCCA. There's a father will not deny his own
bastard now, I warrant thee.

VIRGIL. Read them aloud.

TIBULLUS. 'Ramp up, my genius, be not retro-
    grade;
But boldly nominate a spade a spade.
What, shall thy lubrical and glibbery Muse
Live, as she were defunct, like punk in stews?'

TUCCA. —Excellent!

TIBULLUS. 'Alas! that were no modern conse-
    quence,
To have cothurnal buskins frighted hence.
No, teach thy incubus to poetize;
And throw abroad thy spurious snotteries,
Upon that puffed-up lump of barmy froth——'

TUCCA. —Aha!

TIBULLUS. 'Or clumsy, chilblained judgment; that,
    with oath,
Magnificates his merit, and bespawls
The conscious time with humourous foam and
    brawls,
As if his organons of sense would crack
The sinews of my patience. Break his back,
O poets, all and some! for now we list

Of strenuous vengeance to clutch the fist.

> Subscribit Crispinus.'

TUCCA. Ay, marry, this was written like a Hercules in poetry, now.

CAESAR. Excellently well threatened!

VIRGIL. Ay, and as strangely worded, Caesar.

CAESAR. We observe it.

VIRGIL. The other now.

TUCCA. This 's a fellow of a good, prodigal tongue, too; this 'll do well.

TIBULLUS. 'Our Muse is in mind for th' untrussing
a poet;
I slip by his name, for most men do know it:
A critic, that all the world bescumbers
With satirical humours and lyrical numbers——'

TUCCA. —Art thou there, boy?

TIBULLUS. 'And, for the most part, himself doth
advance,
With much self-love and more arrogance.'

TUCCA. —Good again!

TIBULLUS. 'And, but that I would not be thought
a prater,
I could tell you he were a translator.
I know the authors from whence he has stole,
And could trace him, too, but that I understand
'em not full and whole.'

TUCCA. —That line is broke loose from all his fellows; chain him up shorter, do.

TIBULLUS. 'The best note I can give you, to know
him by,
Is that he keeps gallants' company;
Whom I would wish in time should him fear,
Lest after they buy repentance too dear.

> Subscribit Demetrius Fannius.'

TUCCA. Well said! This carries palm with it.

HORACE. And why, thou motley gull, why should
    they fear?
When hast thou known us wrong or tax a friend?
I dare thy malice to betray it. Speak.
Now thou curl'st up, thou poor and nasty snake,
And shrink'st thy pois'nous head into thy bosom.
Out, viper, thou that eat'st thy parents, hence!
Rather, such speckled creatures as thyself
Should be eschewed and shunned. Such as will bite
And gnaw their absent friends, not cure their fame;
Catch at the loosest laughters, and affect
To be thought jesters; such as can devise
Things never seen or heard, t'impair men's names,
And gratify their credulous adversaries;
Will carry tales, do basest offices,
Cherish divided fires, and still increase
New flames, out of old embers; will reveal
Each secret that's committed to their trust—
These be black slaves. Romans, take heed of these.

TUCCA. Thou twang'st right, little Horace, they
be indeed a couple of chap-fall'n curs. Come, we of
the bench, let's rise to the urn, and condemn 'em
quickly.

VIRGIL. Before you go together, worthy Romans,
We are to tender our opinion,
And give you those instructions that may add
Unto your even judgment in the cause:
Which thus we do commence. First, you must know
That where there is a true and perfect merit,
There can be no dejection; and the scorn
Of humble baseness, oftentimes, so works
In a high soul, upon the grosser spirit,
That to his bleared and offended sense,
There seems a hideous fault blazed in the object;
When only the disease is in his eyes.

Here hence it comes, our Horace now stands taxed
Of impudence, self-love, and arrogance,
By these, who share no merit in themselves,
And therefore think his portion is as small.
For they, from their own guilt, assure their souls,
If they should confidently praise their works,
In them it would appear inflation;
Which, in a full and well-digested man,
Cannot receive that foul, abusive name,
But the fair title of erection.
And, for his true use of translating men,
It still hath been a work of as much palm,
In clearest judgments, as t' invent or make.
His sharpness, that is most excusable,
As being forced out of a suffering virtue,
Oppressèd with the licence of the time.
And howsoever fools or jerking pedants,
Players or suchlike buffoon, barking wits,
May, with their beggarly and barren trash,
Tickle base vulgar ears, in their despite;
This, like Jove's thunder, shall their pride control:
'The honest satyr hath the happiest soul.'
Now, Romans, you have heard our thoughts. With-
draw when you please.

TIBULLUS. Remove the accused from the bar.

TUCCA. Who holds the urn to us, ha?—Fear
nothing, I'll quit you, mine honest pitiful stinkards.
I'll do't.

CRISPINUS. Captain, you shall eternally girt me to
you, as I am generous.

TUCCA. Go to.

CAESAR. Tibullus, let there be a case of vizards
privately provided. We have found a subject to
bestow them on.

TIBULLUS. It shall be done, Caesar.

CAESAR. Here be words, Horace, able to bastinado a man's ears.

HORACE. Ay. Please it, great Caesar, I have pills
    about me,
Mixed with the whitest kind of hellebore,
Would give him a light vomit, that should purge
His brain and stomach of those tumorous heats;
Might I have leave to minister unto him.

CAESAR. O, be his Aesculapius, gentle Horace!
You shall have leave, and he shall be your patient.
Virgil, use your authority, command him forth.

VIRGIL. Caesar is careful of your health, Crispinus,
And hath himself chose a physician
To minister unto you. Take his pills.

HORACE. They are somewhat bitter, sir, but very
    wholesome.
Take yet another. So. Stand by, they'll work anon.

TIBULLUS. Romans, return to your several seats.
Lictors, bring forward the urn, and set the accused
at the bar.

TUCCA. Quickly, you whoreson egregious varlets,
come forward! What, shall we sit all day upon you?
You make no more haste now than a beggar upon
pattens, or a physician to a patient that has no
money, you pilchers.

TIBULLUS. 'Rufus Laberius Crispinus, and Demetrius Fannius, hold up your hands. You have,
according to the Roman custom, put yourselves
upon trial to the urn, for divers and sundry calumnies, whereof you have before this time been indicted, and are now presently arraigned. Prepare
yourselves to hearken to the verdict of your tryers.
Caius Cilnius Maecenas pronounceth you, by this
handwriting, guilty. Cornelius Gallus, guilty. Pan-
tillus Tucca——'

TUCCA. Parcel-guilty, I.

DEMETRIUS. He means himself; for it was he indeed
Suborned us to the calumny.

TUCCA. I, you whoreson cantharides, was't I?

DEMETRIUS. I appeal to your conscience, Captain.

TIBULLUS. Then you confess it now?

DEMETRIUS. I do, and crave the mercy of the court.

TIBULLUS. What saith Crispinus?

CRISPINUS. O, the Captain, the Captain——

HORACE. My physic begins to work with my patient, I see.

VIRGIL. Captain, stand forth and answer.

TUCCA. Hold thy peace, poet-praetor, I appeal from thee to Caesar, I. Do me right, royal Caesar.

CAESAR. Marry, and I will, sir.—Lictors, gag him, do.
And put a case of vizards o'er his head,
That he may look bi-fronted, as he speaks.

TUCCA. Gods and fiends! Caesar! thou wilt not, Caesar, wilt thou? Away, you whoreson vultures, away. You think I am a dead corpse now, because Caesar is disposed to jest with a man of mark, or so. Hold your hooked talons out of my flesh, you inhuman harpies. Go to, do't. What, will the royal Augustus cast away a gentleman of worship, a captain and a commander, for a couple of condemned, caitiff, calumnious cargos?

CAESAR. Dispatch, lictors.

TUCCA. Caesar!

CAESAR. Forward, Tibullus.

VIRGIL. Demand what cause they had to malign Horace.

DEMETRIUS. In troth, no great cause, not I, I must confess; but that he kept better company, for the

most part, than I; and that better men loved him,
than loved me; and that his writings thrived better
than mine, and were better liked and graced; nothing else.

VIRGIL. Thus envious souls repine at others' good.

HORACE. If this be all, faith, I forgive thee freely.
Envy me still, so long as Virgil loves me,
Gallus, Tibullus, and the best, best Caesar,
My dear Mecaenas. While these, with many more,
Whose names I wisely slip, shall think me worthy
Their honoured and adored society,
And read and love, prove and applaud my poems;
I would not wish but such as you should spite them.

CRISPINUS. O!

TIBULLUS. How now, Crispinus?

CRISPINUS. O, I am sick!

HORACE. A basin, a basin, quickly! Our physic
works. Faint not, man.

CRISPINUS. O——'retrograde'——'reciprocal——'incubus.'

CAESAR. What's that, Horace?

HORACE. 'Retrograde,' reciprocal,' and 'incubus'
are come up.

GALLUS. Thanks be to Jupiter!

CRISPINUS. O——'glibbery' — 'lubrical' — 'defunct' —
O——

HORACE. Well said. Here's some store.

VIRGIL. What are they?

HORACE. 'Glibbery,' 'lubrical' and 'defunct.'

GALLUS. O, they came up easy.

CRISPINUS. O— O——

TIBULLUS. What's that?

HORACE. Nothing yet.

CRISPINUS. 'Magnificate.'

MAECENAS. 'Magnificate'? That came up somewhat hard.

HORACE. Ay. What cheer, Crispinus?

CRISPINUS. O, I shall cast up my—'spurious'—'snotteries'——

HORACE. Good. Again.

CRISPINUS. 'Chilblained'——O——O——'clumsy'——

HORACE. That 'clumsy' stuck terribly.

MAECENAS. What's all that, Horace?

HORACE. 'Spurious snotteries,' 'chilblained,' 'clumsy.'

TIBULLUS. O Jupiter!

GALLUS. Who would have thought, there should ha' been such a deal of filth in a poet?

CRISPINUS. O——'barmy froth'——

CAESAR. What's that?

CRISPINUS. 'Puffy'—'inflate'—'turgidous'—'ventositous.'

HORACE. 'Barmy froth,' 'puffy,' 'inflate,' 'turgidous,' and 'ventositous' are come up.

TIBULLUS. O terrible, windy words!

GALLUS. A sign of a windy brain.

CRISPINUS. O——'oblatrant'——'furibund'——'fatuate'——'strenuous'——

HORACE. Here's a deal: 'oblatrant,' 'furibund,' 'fatuate,' 'strenuous.'

CAESAR. Now all's come up, I trow. What a tumble he had in his belly!

HORACE. No, there's the often 'conscious damp' behind still.

CRISPINUS. O——'conscious'——'damp.'

HORACE. It is come up, thanks to Apollo and Aesculapius. Yet there's another; you were best take a pill more.

CRISPINUS. O no. O——O——O——O!

HORACE. Force yourself then a little, with your finger.

CRISPINUS. O——O——'prorumpèd.'

TIBULLUS. 'Prorumpèd'? What a noise it made! as if his spirit would have prorumped with it.

CRISPINUS. O——O——O!

VIRGIL. Help him. It sticks strangely, whatever it is.

CRISPINUS. O——'clutched.'

HORACE. Now it's come: 'clutched.'

CAESAR. 'Clutched'? It's well that's come up! It had but a narrow passage.

CRISPINUS. O——

VIRGIL. Again, hold him; hold his head there.

CRISPINUS. 'Snarling gusts'——'quaking custard.'

HORACE. How now, Crispinus?

CRISPINUS. O——'obstupefact.'

TIBULLUS. Nay, that are all we, I assure you.

HORACE. How do you feel yourself?

CRISPINUS. Pretty and well, I thank you.

VIRGIL. These pills can but restore him for a time;
Not cure him quite of such a malady,
Caught by so many surfeits, which have filled
His blood and brain thus full of crudities.
'Tis necessary, therefore, he observe
A strict and wholesome diet. Look you take,
Each morning, of old Cato's principles
A good draught, next your heart; that walk upon,
Till it be well digested; then come home,
And taste a piece of Terence, suck his phrase
Instead of liquorice; and, at any hand,
Shun Plautus, and old Ennius—they are meats
Too harsh for a weak stomach. Use to read,
But not without a tutor, the best Greeks:
As Orpheus, Musaeus, Pindarus,

Hesiod, Callimachus, and Theocrite,
High Homer; but beware of Lycophron—
He is too dark and dangerous a dish.
You must not hunt for wild, outlandish terms,
To stuff out a peculiar dialect;
But let your matter run before your words.
And if, at any time, you chance to meet
Some Gallo-Belgic phrase, you shall not straight
Rack your poor verse to give it entertainment;
But let it pass, and do not think yourself
Much damnified, if you do leave it out,
When nor your understanding nor the sense
Could well receive it. This fair abstinence,
In time, will render you more sound and clear.
And this have I prescribed to you, in place
Of a strict sentence.—Which till he perform,
Attire him in that robe.—And henceforth, learn
To bear yourself more humbly; not to swell,
Or breathe your insolent and idle spite
On him whose laughter can your worst affright.

   TIBULLUS. Take him away.

   CRISPINUS.   Jupiter guard Caesar!

   VIRGIL. And for a week or two, see him locked up
In some dark place, removed from company;
He will talk idly else after his physic.—
Now, to you, sir. Th' extremity of law
Awards you to be branded in the front,
For this your calumny. But, since it pleaseth
Horace, the party wrong'd, t' entreat of Caesar
A mitigation of that juster doom,
With Caesar's tongue thus we pronounce your sen-
   tence:
Demetrius Fannius, thou shalt here put on
That coat and cap, and henceforth think thyself
No other than they make thee; vow to wear them

In every fair and generous assembly,
Till the best sort of minds shall take to knowledge
As well thy satisfaction, as thy wrongs.

HORACE. Only, grave praetor, here, in open court,
I crave the oath for good behaviour
May be administered unto them both.

VIRGIL. Horace, it shall.—Tibullus, give it them.

TIBULLUS. 'Rufus Laberius Crispinus, and Demetrius Fannius, lay your hands on your hearts. You shall here solemnly attest and swear: that never after this instant, either at booksellers' stalls, in taverns, twopenny rooms, tiring-houses, noblemen's butteries, puisnes' chambers, the best and farthest places where you are admitted to come, you shall once offer or dare—thereby to endear yourself the more to any player, ingle, or guilty gull in your company—to malign, traduce, or detract the person or writings of Quintus Horatius Flaccus, or any other eminent man, transcending you in merit, whom your envy shall find cause to work upon, either for that, or for keeping himself in better acquaintance, or enjoying better friends. Or if, transported by any sudden and desperate resolution, you do, that then you shall not, under the baton, or in the next presence, being an honourable assembly of his favourers, be brought as voluntary gentlemen to undertake the forswearing of it. Neither shall you, at any time, ambitiously affecting the title of the untrussers or whippers of the age, suffer the itch of writing to overrun your performance in libel, upon pain of being taken up for lepers in wit, and, losing both your time and your papers, be irrecoverably forfeited to the hospital of fools. So help you our Roman gods, and the genius of great Caesar.'

VIRGIL. So! now dissolve the court.

HORACE, TIBULLUS, GALLUS, MAECENAS, VIRGIL. And
    thanks to Caesar,
That thus hath exercised his patience.
    CAESAR. We have, indeed, you worthiest friends
    of Caesar.
It is the bane and torment of our ears,
To hear the discords of those jangling rhymers,
That, with their bad and scandalous practices,
Bring all true arts and learning in contempt.
But let not your high thoughts descend so low
As these despisèd objects; let them fall,
With their flat grovelling souls. Be you yourselves.
And as with our best favours you stand crowned,
So let your mutual loves be still renowned.
Envy will dwell where there is want of merit,
Though the deserving man should crack his spirit.

SONG.

 'Blush, folly, blush! Here's none that fears
   The wagging of an ass's ears,
   Although a wolfish case he wears.
   Detraction is but baseness' varlet;
    And apes are apes, though clothed in scarlet.'
Exeunt.

from VOLPONE

Dedicatory Epistle

TO

THE MOST NOBLE AND MOST EQUAL SISTERS,

THE TWO FAMOUS UNIVERSITIES,

FOR THEIR LOVE AND ACCEPTANCE

SHOWN TO HIS POEM IN THE PRESENTATION,

BEN JONSON,

THE GRATEFUL ACKNOWLEDGER,

DEDICATES BOTH IT AND HIMSELF.

There follows an epistle, if you dare venture on the length:

Never, most equal Sisters, had any man a wit so presently excellent as that it could raise itself, but there must come both matter, occasion, commenders, and favourers to it. If this be true, and that the fortune of all writers doth daily prove it, it behoves the careful to provide well toward these accidents, and, having acquired them, to preserve that part of reputation most tenderly, wherein the benefit of a friend is also defended. Hence is it that I now render myself grateful, and am studious to justify the bounty of your act; to which, though your mere authority were satisfying, yet, it being an age wherein poetry and the professors of it hear so ill on all sides, there will a reason be looked for in the subject. It is certain, nor can it with any forehead be opposed, that the too much licence of poetasters in this time hath much deformed their mistress; that every day their manifold and manifest ignorance doth stick unnatural reproaches upon her. But, for their petulancy, it were an act of the greatest injustice, either to let the learned suffer, or so divine a skill (which, indeed, should not be attempted with unclean hands) to fall under the least contempt.

For if men will impartially, and not asquint, look toward the offices and function of a poet, they will easily conclude to themselves the impossibility of any man's being the good poet, without first being a good man. He that is said to be able to inform young men to all good disciplines, inflame grown men to all great virtues, keep old men in their best and supreme state, or, as they decline to childhood, recover them to their first strength; that comes forth the interpreter and arbiter of nature, a teacher of things divine, no less than human, a master in manners; and can alone, or with a few, effect the business of mankind—this, I take him, is no subject for pride and ignorance to exercise their railing rhetoric upon. But it will here be hastily answered that the writers of these days are other things; that not only their manners but their natures are inverted, and nothing remaining with them of the dignity of poet but the abused name, which every scribe usurps; that now, especially in dramatic, or—as they term it—stage poetry, nothing but ribaldry, profanation, blasphemy, all licence of offence to God and man, is practised. I dare not deny a great part of this, and am sorry I dare not, because in some men's abortive features (and would they had never boasted the light!) it is over-true. But that all are embarked in this bold adventure for Hell, is a most uncharitable thought and, uttered, a more malicious slander.

For my particular, I can, and from a most clear conscience, affirm that I have ever trembled to think toward the least profaneness; have loathed the use of such foul and unwashed bawdry as is now made the food of the scene. And howsoever I cannot escape, from some, the imputation of sharpness, but that they will say I have taken a pride, or lust, to be bitter, and not my youngest infant but hath come into the world with all his teeth; I would ask of these supercilious politics, what nation, society, or general order, or state I have provoked? what public person? whether I have not, in all these, preserved their dignity, as mine own person, safe? My works are read, allowed—I speak of those that are entirely mine. Look into them. What broad reproofs have I used? Where have I been particular? Where personal, except to a mimic, cheater, bawd, or buffoon, creatures for their insolencies worthy to be taxed? Yet to which of these so pointingly, as he might not either ingenuously have confessed or wisely dissembled his disease? But it is not rumour can make men guilty, much less entitle me to other men's crimes. I know that nothing can be so innocently writ or carried, but may be made obnoxious to construction. Marry, whilst I bear mine innocence about me, I fear it not. Application is now grown a trade with many; and there are, that profess to have a key for the deciphering of everything. But let wise and noble persons take heed how they be too credulous, or give leave to these invading interpreters to be over-familiar with their fames, who cunningly, and often, utter their own virulent malice under other men's simplest meanings.

As for those that will (by faults which charity hath raked up, or common honesty concealed) make themselves a name with the multitude, or, to draw their rude and beastly claps, care not whose living faces they intrench with their petulant styles; may they do it without a rival, for me. I choose rather to live graved in obscurity, than share with them in so preposterous a fame. Nor can I blame the wishes of those severe and wiser patriots who, providing the hurts these licentious spirits may do in a state, desire rather to see fools and devils and those antique relics of barbarism retrieved, with all other ridiculous and exploded follies, than behold the wounds of private men, of princes, and nations. For, as Horace makes Trebatius speak, among these

. . . *sibi quisque timet, quamquam est intactus, et odit.*

And men may justly impute such rages, if continued, to the writer, as his sports. The increase of which lust in liberty, together with the present trade of the stage in all their misc'line interludes, what learned or liberal soul doth not already abhor? where nothing but the filth of the time is uttered, and that with such impropriety of phrase, such plenty of solecisms, such dearth of sense, so bold prolepses, so racked metaphors, with brothelry able to violate the ear of a pagan, and blasphemy to turn the blood of a Christian to water. I cannot but be serious in a cause of this nature, wherein my fame, and the reputations of divers honest and learned, are the question; when a name so full of authority, antiquity, and all great mark is, through their insolence, become the lowest scorn of the age; and those men subject to the petulancy of every vernaculous orator, that were wont to be the care of kings and happiest monarchs.

This it is that hath not only rapt me to present indignation, but made me studious heretofore, and by all my actions, to stand off from them. Which may most appear in this my latest work (which you, most learned arbitresses, have seen, judged, and, to my crown, approved) , wherein I have laboured, for their instruction and amendment, to reduce not only the ancient forms, but manners of the scene: the easiness, the propriety, the innocence, and last the doctrine, which is the principal end of poesy, to inform men in the best reason of living. And though my catastrophe may, in the strict rigour of comic law, meet with censure, as turning back to my promise; I desire the learned and charitable critic to have so much faith in me, to think it was done of industry. For with what ease I could have varied it nearer his scale, but that I fear to boast my own faculty, I could here insert. But my special aim being to put the snaffle in their mouths, that cry out we never punish vice in our interludes, &c., I took the more liberty; though not without some lines of example drawn even in the ancients themselves, the goings-out of whose comedies are not always joyful, but oft-times the bawds, the servants, the rivals, yea, and the masters are mulcted. And fitly, it being the office of a comic poet to imitate justice and instruct to life, as well as purity of language, or stir up gentle affections. To which I shall take the occasion elsewhere to speak.

For the present, most reverenced Sisters, as I have cared to be thankful for your affections past, and here made the understanding acquainted with some ground of your favours, let me not despair their continuance to the maturing of some worthier fruits. Wherein, if my Muses be true to me, I shall raise the despised head of Poetry again, and, stripping her out of those rotten and base rags wherewith the times have adulterated her form, restore her to her

primitive habit, feature, and majesty, and render
her worthy to be embraced and kissed of all the
great and master spirits of our world. As for the
vile and slothful, who never affected an act worthy
of celebration, or are so inward with their own
vicious natures, as they worthily fear her, and think
it a high point of policy to keep her in contempt,
with their declamatory and windy invectives; she
shall, out of just rage, incite her servants (who are
genus irritabile) to spout ink in their faces, that
shall eat farther than their marrow, into their fames.
And not Cinnamus the Barber, with his art, shall be
able to take out the brands, but they shall live and
be read, till the wretches die, as things worst deserving of themselves in chief, and then of all mankind.

From my house in the Blackfriars, this eleventh of
February, 1607(8).

from THE SAD SHEPHERD

The Prologue

He that hath feasted you these forty years,
And fitted fables for your finer ears,—
Although at first he scarce could hit the bore,
Yet you, with patience heark'ning more and more,
At length have grown up to him, and made known
The working of his pen is now your own—
He prays you would vouchsafe, for your own sake,
To hear him this once more, but sit awake.
And though he now present you with such wool

As from mere English flocks his Muse can pull,
He hopes when it is made up into cloth,
Not the most curious head here will be loath
To wear a hood of it, it being a fleece
To match or those of Sicily or Greece.
His scene is Sherwood, and his play a tale
Of Robin Hood's inviting from the Vale
Of Belvoir, all the shepherds to a feast;
Where, by the casual absence of one guest,
The mirth is troubled much, and in one man
As much of sadness shown, as passion can.

THE SAD SHEPHERD *passeth silently over the stage.*

The sad young shepherd, whom we here present,
Like his woe's figure, dark and discontent,
For his lost love, who in the Trent is said
To have miscarried,—'las, what knows the head
Of a calm river, whom the feet have drowned?—
Hear what his sorrows are; and if they wound
Your gentle breasts, so that the end crown all
Which in the scope of one day's chance may fall,
Old Trent will send you more such tales as these,
And shall grow young again as one doth please.

Here the PROLOGUE, *thinking to end, returns on a
new purpose, and speaks on.*

But here's an heresy of late let fall,
That mirth by no means fits a pastoral;
Such say so who can make none, he presumes,
Else there's no scene more properly assumes
The sock. For whence can sport in kind arise,
But from the rural routs and families?
Safe on this ground then, we not fear today
To tempt your laughter by our rustic play;
Wherein if we distaste, or be cried down,
We think we therefore shall not leave the town;

Nor that the fore-wits, that would draw the rest
Unto their liking, always like the best.
The wise and knowing critic will not say
This worst or better is, before he weigh
Where every piece be perfect in the kind;
And then, though in themselves he difference find,
Yet if the place require it where they stood,
The equal fitting makes them equal good.
You shall have love and hate and jealousy,
As well as mirth and rage and melancholy,
Or whatsoever else may either move
Or stir affections, and your likings prove.
But that no style for pastoral should go
Current, but what is stamped with Ah! and O!—
Who judgeth so may singularly err;
As if all poesy had one character,
In which what were not written, were not right;
Or that the man who made such one poor flight
In his whole life, had with his wingèd skill
Advanced him upmost on the Muses' hill;
When he like poet yet remains, as those
Are painters who can only make a rose.
From such your wits redeem you, or your chance,
Lest to a greater height you do advance
Of folly, to contemn those that are known
Artificers, and trust such as are none!

from
TIMBER
or
Discoveries Made Upon Men and Matter

AS THEY HAVE FLOWED OUT OF HIS DAILY READINGS
OR HAD THEIR REFLUX TO HIS PECULIAR NOTION
OF THE TIMES

Opinio

Opinion is a light, vain, crude, and imperfect thing, settled in the imagination, but never arriving at the understanding, there to obtain the tincture of reason. We labour with it more than truth. There is much more holds us, than presseth us. An ill fact is one thing, an ill fortune is another. Yet both often-times sway us alike, by the error of our thinking.

Impostura

Many men believe not themselves what they would persuade others; and less, do the things which they would impose on others; but least of all, know what they themselves most confidently boast. Only they set the sign of the cross over their outer doors, and sacrifice to their gut and their groin in their inner closets.

Iactura vitae

What a deal of cold business doth a man mis-spend the better part of life in! in scattering compliments, tendering visits, gathering and venting news, following feasts and plays, making a little winter-love in a dark corner.

Natura non effeta

I cannot think Nature is so spent and decayed that she can bring forth nothing worth her former years. She is always the same, like herself; and when she collects her strength, is abler still. Men are decayed, and studies; she is not.

Non nimium credendum antiquitati

I know nothing can conduce more to letters than to examine the writings of the ancients, and not to rest in their sole authority or take all upon trust from them; provided the plagues of judging and pronouncing be away, such as are envy, bitterness, precipitation, impudence, and scurrile scoffing. For to all the observations of the ancients, we have our own experience, which, if we will use and apply, we have better means to pronounce. It is true they opened the gates and made the way, that went before us, but as guides, not commanders: *non domini nostri, sed duces fuere.* Truth lies open to all; it is no man's several. *Patet omnibus veritas, nondum est occupata. Multum ex illa etiam futuris relictum est.*

Censura de poetis

Nothing in our age, I have observed, is more preposterous than the running judgments upon poetry and poets; when we shall hear those things commended, and cried up for the best writings, which a man would scarce vouchsafe to wrap any wholesome drug in; he would never light his tobacco with them. And those men almost named for miracles, who yet are so vile that, if man should go about to examine and correct them, he must make all they have done but one blot. Their good is so entangled with their bad, as forcibly one must draw on the other's death with it. A sponge, dipped in ink, will do all:

> . . . *comitetur Punica librum*
> *spongea.*

Et paulo post,

> *Non possunt . . . multae, . . . una litura potest.*

Yet their vices have not hurt them. Nay, a great many they have profited, for they have been loved for nothing else. And this false opinion grows strong against the best men, if once it take root with the ignorant. Cestius, in his time, was preferred to Cicero, so far as the ignorant durst. They learned him without book, and had him often in their mouths. But a man cannot imagine that thing so foolish or rude, but will find and enjoy an admirer, at least a reader or spectator. The puppets are seen now, in despite of the players. Heath's epigrams and the Sculler's poems have their applause. There are never wanting, that dare prefer the worst preachers, the worst pleaders, the worst poets; not that the better have left to write or speak better, but that they that hear them judge worse. *Non illi peius dicunt, sed hi corruptius iudicant.* Nay, if it were put to the question of the Water-Rhymer's works against Spenser's, I doubt not but they would find more suffrages; because the most favour common vices, out of a prerogative the vulgar have, to lose their judgments and like that which is naught.

Poetry, in this latter age, hath proved but a mean mistress to such as have wholly addicted themselves to her, or given their names up to her family. They who have but saluted her on the by, and now and then tendered their visits, she hath done much for, and advanced in the way of their own professions (both the law and the gospel) beyond all they could have hoped, or done for themselves, without her favour. Wherein she doth emulate the judicious but preposterous bounty of the time's grandees, who accumulate all they can upon the parasite or fresh-man in their friendship, but think an old client or honest servant bound, by his place, to write and starve.

Indeed, the multitude commend writers as they do fencers or wrestlers, who, if they come in ro-bustiously, and put for it with a deal of violence, are received for the braver fellows; when many times their own rudeness is a cause of their disgrace, and a slight touch of their adversary gives all that boisterous force the foil. But in these things the unskilful are naturally deceived, and, judging wholly by the bulk, think rude things greater than polished, and scattered more numerous than composed. Nor think this only to be true in the sordid multitude, but the neater sort of our gal-lants; for all are the multitude, only they differ in clothes, not in judgment or understanding.

De Shakespeare nostrati

I remember, the players have often mentioned it as an honour to Shakespeare, that in his writing, whatsoever he penned, he never blotted out line. My answer hath been, 'Would he had blotted a thousand!' Which they thought a malevolent speech. I had not told posterity this, but for their ignor-ance, who choose that circumstance to commend their friend by, wherein he most faulted; and to justify mine own candour, for I loved the man, and do honour his memory (on this side idolatry) as much as any. He was, indeed, honest, and of an open and free nature; had an excellent fancy, brave notions, and gentle expressions; wherein he flowed with that facility, that sometime it was necessary he should be stopped. *Sufflaminandus erat,* as Augustus said of Haterius. His wit was in his own power; would the rule of it had been so, too. Many times he fell into those things, could not escape laughter: as when he said in the person of Caesar, one speaking to him, 'Caesar, thou dost me wrong'; he replied, 'Caesar did never wrong, but with just cause'; and suchlike, which were ridiculous. But he redeemed his vices with his virtues. There was ever more in him to be praised than to be pardoned.

Ingeniorum discrimina

In the difference of wits, I have observed, there are many notes. And it is a little mastery to know them, to discern what every nature, every disposition will bear. For, before we sow our land, we should plough it. There are no fewer forms of minds than of bodies, amongst us. The variety is incredible, and therefore we must search. Some are fit to make divines, some poets, some lawyers, some physicians; some to be sent to the plough, and trades.

Nota 1. There is no doctrine will do good, where nature is wanting. Some wits are swelling and high, others low and still; some hot and fiery, others cold and dull. One must have a bridle, the other a spur.

Nota 2. There be some that are forward and bold, and these will do every little thing easily—I mean that is hard by, and next them; which they will utter unretarded, without any shamefastness. These never perform much, but quickly. They are what they are, on the sudden. They show presently like grain that, scattered on the top of the ground, shoots up, but takes no root; has a yellow blade, but the ear empty. They are wits of good promise at first, but there is an *ingenistitium*; they stand still at sixteen, they get no higher.

Nota 3. You have others that labour only to ostentation, and are ever more busy about the colours and surface of a work, than in the matter and foundation. For that is hid, the other is seen.

Nota 4. Others that in composition are nothing but what is rough and broken. *Quae per salebras altaque saxa cadunt.* And if it would come gently, they trouble it of purpose. They would not have it run without rubs, as if that style were more strong and manly, that struck the ear with a kind of unevenness. These men err not by chance, but knowingly and willingly. They are like men that affect a fashion by themselves; have some singularity in a ruff, cloak, or hat-band; or their beards specially cut, to provoke beholders and set a mark upon themselves. They would be reprehended while they are looked on. And this vice, one that is in authority with the rest, loving, delivers over to them to be imitated; so that oft-times the faults which he fell into, the others seek for. This is the danger, when vice becomes a precedent.

Nota 5. Others there are that have no composition at all, but a kind of tuning and rhyming fall in what they write. It runs and slides and only makes a sound. Women's poets they are called, as you have women's tailors.

'They write a verse as smooth, as soft as cream,
In which there is no torrent, nor scarce stream.'

You may sound these wits, and find the depth of

them with your middle finger. They are cream-bowl, or but puddle-deep.

Nota 6. Some that turn over all books, and are equally searching in all papers; that write out of what they presently find or meet, without choice; by which means it happens, that what they have discredited and impugned in one work, they have before or after extolled the same in another. Such are all the essayists, even their master, Montaigne. These, in all they write, confess still what books they have read last; and therein their own folly, so much that they bring it to the stake raw and undigested; not that the place did need it neither, but that they thought themselves furnished, and would vend it.

Nota 7. Some again, who—after they have got authority or (which is less) opinion, by their writings, to have read much—dare presently to feign whole books and authors, and lie safely. For what never was, will not easily be found; not by the most curious.

Nota 8. And some, by a cunning protestation against all reading, and false vendition of their own naturals, think to divert the sagacity of their readers from themselves, and cool the scent of their own fox-like thefts; when yet they are so rank, as a man may find whole passages together usurped from one author. Their necessities compelling them to read for present use, which could not be in many books; and so come forth more ridiculously and palpably guilty than those who, because they cannot trace, they yet would slander their industry.

Nota 9. But the wretcheder are the obstinate contemners of all helps and arts, such as, presuming on their own naturals (which, perhaps, are excellent), dare deride all diligence; and seem to mock at the terms, when they understand not the things, thinking that way to get off wittily with their ignorance. These are imitated often by such as are their peers in negligence, though they cannot be in nature. And they utter all they can think, with a kind of violence and indisposition, unexamined, without relation either to person, place, or any fitness else. And the more wilful and stubborn they are in it, the more learned they are esteemed of the multitude, through their excellent vice of judgment, who think those things the stronger that have no art; as if to break were better than to open, or to rend asunder gentler than to loose.

Nota 10. It cannot but come to pass that these men, who commonly seek to do more than enough, may sometimes happen on something that is good and great; but very seldom. And when it comes, it doth not recompense the rest of their ill. For their jests and their sentences (which they only and ambitiously seek for) stick out and are more eminent, because all is sordid and vile about them; as lights are more discerned in a thick darkness than a faint shadow. Now, because they speak all they can, however unfitly, they are thought to have the greater copy. Where the learned use ever election and a mean; they look back to what they intended at first, and make all an even and proportioned body. The true artificer will not run away from Nature as if he were afraid of her, or depart from life and the likeness of truth; but speak to the capacity of his hearers. And though his language differ from the vulgar somewhat, it shall not fly from all humanity with the Tamburlaines and Tamar Chams of the late age, which had nothing in them but the scenical strutting and furious vociferation to warrant them to the ignorant gapers.

He knows it is his only art so to carry it, as none but artificers perceive it. In the meantime, perhaps, he is called barren, dull, lean, a poor writer, or by what contumelious word can come in their cheeks, by these men who, without labour, judgment, knowledge, or almost sense, are received or preferred before him. He gratulates them, and their fortune. Another age or juster men will acknowledge the virtues of his studies: his wisdom in dividing, his subtlety in arguing; with what strength he doth inspire his readers, with what sweetness he strokes them; in inveighing, what sharpness, in jest what urbanity he uses; how he doth reign in men's affections, how invade and break in upon them; and makes their minds like the thing he writes. Then in his elocution to behold what word is proper; which hath ornament, which height; what is beautifully translated; where figures are fit; which gentle, which strong, to show the composition manly. And how he hath avoided faint, obscure, obscene, sordid, humble, improper, or effeminate phrase; which is not only praised of the most, but commended, which is worse; especially for that it is naught.

Scriptorum catalogus

Cicero is said to be the only wit that the people of Rome had equalled to their empire. *Ingenium par imperio.* We have had many, and in their several ages—to take in but the former seculum— Sir Thomas More, the elder Wyatt, Henry, Earl of Surrey, Chaloner, Smith, Elyot, Bishop Gardiner were, for their times, admirable; and the more because they began eloquence with us. Sir Nicholas Bacon was singular and almost alone, at the beginning of Queen Elizabeth's times. Sir Philip Sidney and Master Hooker, in different matter, grew great masters of wit and language, and in whom all vigour of invention and strength of judgment met. The Earl of Essex, noble and high; and Sir Walter Raleigh, not to be contemned, either for judgment or style. Sir Henry Savile, grave and truly lettered; Sir Edwin Sandys, excellent in both; Lord Egerton, the Chancellor, a grave and great orator, and best when he was provoked. But his learned and able, though unfortunate, successor is he who hath filled up all numbers, and performed that in our tongue, which may be compared, or preferred, either to insolent Greece or haughty Rome. In short, within his view and about his times were all the wits born, that could honour a language or help study. Now things daily fall, wits grow downward, and eloquence grows backward; so that he may be named, and stand, as the mark and acme of our language.

De augmentis scientiarum

I have ever observed it to have been the office of a wise patriot, among the greatest affairs of the state, to take care of the commonwealth of learning. For schools, they are the seminaries of state; and nothing is worthier the study of a statesman than that part of the republic which we call the advancement of letters. Witness the care of Julius Caesar, who, in the heat of the Civil War, writ his books of analogy, and dedicated them to Tully. This made the late Lord Saint Albans entitle his work 'Novum Organum.' Which though by the most of superficial men, who cannot get beyond the title of nominals, it is not penetrated nor understood; it really openeth all defects of learning whatsoever, and is a book

Qui longum noto scriptori prorogat aevum.

My conceit of his person was never increased toward him by his place or honours. But I have, and do reverence him for the greatness that was only proper to himself, in that he seemed to me ever, by his work, one of the greatest men, and most worthy of admiration, that had been in many ages. In his adversity, I ever prayed that God would give him strength, for greatness he could not want. Neither could I condole, in a word or syllable, for him; as knowing no accident could do harm to virtue, but rather help to make it manifest.

De stultitia

What petty things they are we wonder at, like children that esteem every trifle, and prefer a fairing before their fathers! What difference is between us and them, but that we are dearer fools, coxcombs at a higher rate? They are pleased with cockle-shells, whistles, hobby-horses and suchlike; we, with statues, marble pillars, pictures, gilded roofs where underneath is lath and lime, perhaps loam. Yet we take pleasure in the lie, and are glad we can cozen ourselves. Nor is it only in our walls and ceilings, but all that we call happiness is mere painting and gilt; and all for money. What a thin membrane of honour that is! And how hath all true reputation fallen, since money began to have any! Yet the great herd, the multitude, that in all other things are divided, in this alone conspire and agree: to love money. They wish for it, they embrace it, they adore it; while yet it is possessed with greater stir and torment than it is gotten.

Poesis et pictura

Poetry and picture are arts of a like nature, and both are busy about imitation. It was excellently said of Plutarch, poetry was a speaking picture, and picture a mute poesy. For they both invent, feign, and devise many things, and accommodate all they invent to the use and service of nature. Yet, of the two, the pen is more noble than the pencil. For that can speak to the understanding, the other but to the sense. They both behold pleasure and profit as their common object; but should abstain from all base pleasures, lest they should err from their end, and, while they seek to better men's minds, destroy their manners. They both are born artificers, not made. Nature is more powerful in them than study.

De pictura

Whosoever loves not picture, is injurious to truth, and all the wisdom of poetry. Picture is the invention of Heaven, the most ancient, and most akin to Nature. It is itself a silent work, and always of one and the same habit. Yet it doth so enter and penetrate the inmost affection, being done by an excellent artificer, as sometimes it o'ercomes the power of speech and oratory. There are diverse graces in it; so are there in the artificers. One excels in care, another in reason, a third in easiness, a fourth in nature and grace. Some have diligence and comeliness, but they want majesty. They can express a human form in all the graces, sweetness, and elegancy; but they miss the authority. They can hit nothing but smooth cheeks; they cannot express roughness or gravity. Others aspire to truth so much, as they are rather lovers of likeness, than beauty. Zeuxis and Parrhasius are said to be contemporaries: the first found out the reason of lights and shadows in picture; the other more subtly examined the lines.

De stilo

In picture, light is required no less than shadow; so in style, height as well as humbleness. But beware they be not too humble, as Pliny pronounced of Regulus' writings. You would think them written, not on a child, but by a child. Many, out of their own obscene apprehensions, refuse proper and fit words, as 'occupy,' 'nature,' and the like. So the curious industry in some, of having all alike good, hath come nearer a vice than a virtue.

Praecipiendi modi

I take this labour in teaching others, that they should not be always to be taught; and I would bring my precepts into practice. For rules are ever of less force and value than experiments. Yet with this purpose: rather to show the right way to those that come after, than to detect any that have slipped before, by error; and I hope it will be more profitable. For men do more willingly listen, and with more favour, to precept, than reprehension. Among diverse opinions of an art, and most of them contrary in themselves, it is hard to make election. And therefore, though a man cannot invent new things after so many, he may do a welcome work yet to help posterity to judge rightly of the old. But arts and precepts avail nothing, except nature be beneficial and aiding. And therefore these things are no more written to a dull disposition, than rules of husbandry to a barren soil. No precepts will profit a fool; no more than beauty will the blind, or music the deaf. As we should take care that our style in writing be neither dry nor empty, we should look again it be not winding, or wanton with far-fetched descriptions. Either is a vice; but that is worse which proceeds out of want, than that which riots out of plenty. The remedy of fruitfulness is easy, but no labour will help the contrary. I will like and praise some things in a young writer, which yet if he continue in, I cannot but justly hate him for the same. There is a time to be given all things for maturity; and that even your country husbandman can teach, who to a young plant will not put the pruning-knife, because it seems to fear the iron, as not able to admit the scar. Nor more would I tell a green writer all his faults, lest I should make him grieve and faint, and at last despair. For nothing doth more hurt than to make him so afraid of all things, as he can endeavour nothing. Therefore youth ought to be instructed betimes, and in the best things; for we hold those longest, we take soonest, as the first scent of a vessel lasts, and that tint the wool first receives. Therefore a master should temper his own powers, and descend to the other's infirmity. If you pour a glut of water upon a bottle, it receives little of it; but with a funnel, and by degrees, you shall fill many of them, and spill little of your own; to their capacity they will all receive and be full. And as it is fit to read the best authors to youth first, so let them be of the openest and clearest. As Livy before Sallust, Sidney before Donne; and beware of letting them taste Gower or Chaucer at first, lest, falling too much in love with antiquity, and not apprehending the weight, they grow rough and barren in language, only. When their judgments are firm, and out of danger, let them read both, the

old and the new. But no less take heed that their
new flowers and sweetness do not as much corrupt
as the others' dryness and squalor, if they choose
not carefully. Spenser, in affecting the ancients,
writ no language. Yet I would have him read for
his matter, but as Virgil read Ennius. The reading
of Homer and Virgil is counselled by Quintilian,
as the best way of informing youth and confirming
man. For besides that, the mind is raised with the
height and sublimity of such a verse; it takes spirit
from the greatness of the matter, and is tincted with
the best things. Tragic and lyric poetry is good,
too; and comic, with the best, if the manners of
the reader be once in safety. In the Greek poets,
as also in Plautus, we shall see the economy and
disposition of poems better observed than in Terence, and the later, who thought the sole grace
and virtue of their fable the sticking in of sentences, as ours do the forcing in of jests.

Praecepta elementa

It is not the passing through these learnings that
hurts us, but the dwelling and sticking about them.
To descend to those extreme anxieties and foolish
cavils of grammarians is able to break a wit in
pieces, being a work of manifold misery and vain-
ness, to be *elementarii senes*. Yet even letters are,
as it were, the bank of words, and restore themselves
to an author as the pawns of language. But talking
and eloquence are not the same: to speak, and to
speak well, are two things. A fool may talk, but
a wise man speaks, and out of the observation,
knowledge, and use of things. Many writers perplex
their readers and hearers with mere nonsense. Their
writings need sunshine. Pure and neat language I
love, yet plain and customary. A barbarous phrase

hath often made me out of love with a good sense, and doubtful writing hath wracked me beyond my patience. The reason why a poet is said that he ought to have all knowledges, is that he should not be ignorant of the most, especially of those he will handle. And indeed, when the attaining of them is possible, it were a sluggish and base thing to despair. For frequent imitation of anything becomes a habit quickly. If a man should prosecute as much as could be said of everything, his work would find no end.

Consuetudo

Custom is the most certain mistress of language, as the public stamp makes the current money. But we must not be too frequent with the mint, every day coining. Nor fetch words from the extreme and utmost ages; since the chief virtue of a style is perspicuity, and nothing so vicious in it as to need an interpreter. Words borrowed of antiquity do lend a kind of majesty to style, and are not without their delight sometimes. For they have the authority of years, and, out of their intermission, do win to themselves a kind of grace-like newness. But the eldest of the present and newest of the past language is the best. For what was the ancient language, which some men so dote upon, but the ancient custom? Yet when I name custom, I understand not the vulgar custom—for that were a precept no less dangerous to language than life, if we should speak or live after the manners of the vulgar—but that I call custom of speech, which is the consent of the learned; as custom of life, which is the consent of the good. Virgil was most loving of antiquity; yet how rarely doth he insert *aquai* and *pictai*! Lucretius is scabrous and rough in these; he seeks 'em, as some do Chaucerisms with us, which were better expunged and banished. Some words are to be culled out for ornament and colour, as we gather flowers to strew houses or make garlands; but they are better when they grow to our style, as in a meadow, where though the mere grass and greenness delights, yet the variety of flowers doth heighten and beautify. Marry, we must not play or riot too much with them, as in paronomasies; nor use too swelling or ill-sounding words, *quae per salebras altaque saxa cadunt*. It is true, there is no sound but shall find some lovers, as the bitter'st confections are grateful to some palates. Our composition must be more accurate in the beginning and end, than in the midst; and in the end more than in the beginning; for through the midst the stream bears us. And this is attained by custom, more than care and diligence.

Oratio imago animi

Language most shows a man: speak, that I may see thee. It springs out of the most retired and inmost parts of us, and is the image of the parent of it, the mind. No glass renders a man's form or likeness so true as his speech. Nay, it is likened to a man; and as we consider feature and composition in a man, so words in language, in the greatness, aptness, sound, structure, and harmony of it. Some men are tall and big; so some language is high and great. Then the words are chosen, their sound ample, the composition full, the absolution plenteous and poured out, all grave, sinewy, and strong. Some are little, and dwarfs; so of speech it is humble and low, the words poor and flat, the members and periods thin and weak, without knitting or number. The middle are of a just stature. There the language is plain and pleasing; even without stopping, round without swelling; all well turned, composed, elegant, and accurate. The vicious language is vast and gaping, swelling and irregular; when it contends to be high, full of rock, mountain, and pointedness; as it affects to be low, it is abject, and creeps, full of bogs and holes. And according to their subject, these styles vary and lose their names. For that which is high and lofty, declaring excellent matter, becomes vast and tumorous, speaking of petty and inferior things. So that which was even and apt in a mean and plain subject, will appear most poor and humble in a high argument. Would you not laugh to meet a great councillor of state in a flat cap, with his trunk hose and a hobby-horse cloak, his gloves under his girdle; and yon haberdasher in a velvet gown, furred with sables? There is a certain latitude in these things, by which we find the degrees. The next thing to the stature is the figure and feature in language: that is, whether it be round and straight, which consists of short and succinct periods, numerous and polished; or square and firm, which is to have equal and strong parts, everywhere answerable and weighed. The third is the skin and coat, which rests in the well-joining, cementing, and coagmentation of words, whenas it is smooth, gentle, and sweet,—like a table, upon which you may run your finger without rubs, and your nail cannot find a joint—not horrid, rough, wrinkled, gaping, or chapped. After these, the flesh, blood, and bones come in question. We say it is a fleshy style when there is much periphrasis and circuit of words, and when, with more than enough, it grows fat and corpulent: *arvina orationis,* full of suet and tallow. It hath blood and juice when the words are proper and apt, their sound sweet, and the phrase neat and picked. *Oratio uncta et bene pasta.* But where there is redundancy, both the blood and juice are faulty and vicious. *Redundat sanguine, quae multo plus dicit quam necesse est.* Juice, in language, is somewhat less than blood; for if the words be but becoming and signifying, and the sense gentle, there is juice. But where that wanteth, the language is thin, flagging, poor, starved, scarce covering the bone; and shows like stones in a sack. Some men, to avoid redundancy, run into that; and while they strive to have no ill blood, or juice, they lose their good. There be some styles again, that have not less blood, but less flesh and corpulence. These are bony and sinewy: *ossa habent et nervos.*

Poesis

A poem, as I have told you, is the work of the poet, the end and fruit of his labour and study. Poesy is his skill, or craft of making: the very fiction itself, the reason or form of the work. And these three voices differ as the thing done, the doing, and the doer; the thing feigned, the feigning, and the feigner; so the poem, the poesy, and the poet. Now, the Poesy is the habit, or the art— nay, rather the Queen of Arts, which had her original from Heaven, received thence from the Hebrews, and had in prime estimation with the Greeks, transmitted to the Latins, and all nations that professed civility. The study of it, if we will trust Aristotle, offers to mankind a certain rule and pattern of living well and happily, disposing to us all civil offices of society. If we will believe Tully, it nourisheth and instructeth our youth, delights our age, adorns our prosperity, comforts our adversity, entertains us at home, keeps us company abroad, travels with us, watches, divides the times of our earnest and sports, shares in our country recesses and recreations; insomuch as the wisest and best learned have thought her the absolute mistress of manners, and nearest of kin to Virtue. And, whereas they entitle Philosophy to be a rigid and austere Poesy, they have, on the contrary, styled Poesy a dulcet and gentle Philosophy, which leads on and guides us by the hand to Action, with a ravishing delight and incredible sweetness. But before we handle the kinds of poems, with their special differences, or make court to the art itself, as a mistress, I would lead you to the knowledge of our poet by a perfect information, what he is, or should be, by nature, by exercise, by imitation, by study; and so bring him down through the disciplines of grammar, logic, rhetoric, and the ethics, adding somewhat, out of all, peculiar to himself, and worthy of your admittance or reception.

1. Ingenium. First, we require in our poet, or maker (for that title our language affords him elegantly with the Greek), a goodness of natural wit. For, whereas all other arts consist of doctrine and precepts, the poet must be able, by nature and instinct, to pour out the treasure of his mind; and, as Seneca saith, *Aliquando secundum Anacreontem insanire iucundum esse:* by which he understands the poetical rapture. And according to that of Plato: *Frustra poeticas fores sui compos pulsavit.* And of Aristotle: *Nullum magnum ingenium sine mixtura dementiae fuit. Nec potest grande aliquid et supra ceteros loqui, nisi mota mens.* Then it riseth higher, as by a divine instinct, when it contemns common and known conceptions. It utters somewhat above a mortal mouth. Then it gets aloft, and flies away with his rider, whither before it was doubtful to ascend. This the poets understood by their Helicon, Pegasus, or Parnassus; and this made Ovid to boast,

> *Est deus in nobis; agitante calescimus illo;*
> *Sedibus aethereis spiritus ille venit.*

And Lipsius to affirm, *Scio poetam neminem prae-stantem fuisse sine parte quadam uberiore divinae aurae.* And hence it is that the coming up of good poets (for I mind not *mediocres* or *imos*) is so thin and rare among us. Every beggarly corporation affords the state a mayor, or two bailiffs, yearly; but *solus rex aut poeta non quotannis nascitur.*

2. *Exercitatio.* To this perfection of nature in our poet, we require exercise of those parts, and frequent. If his wit will not arrive suddenly at the dignity of the ancients, let him not yet fall out with it, quarrel, or be over-hastily angry, offer to turn it away from study, in a humour; but come to it again upon better cogitation, try another time, with labour. If then it succeed not, cast not away the quills yet, nor scratch the wainscot, beat not the poor desk; but bring all to the forge and file again, turn it anew. There is no statute law of the king-dom, bids you be a poet against your will, or the first quarter. If it come in a year or two, it is well. The common rhymers pour forth verses, such as they are, extempore, but there never come from them one sense worth the life of a day. A rhymer and a poet are two things. It is said of the incom-parable Virgil that he brought forth his verses like a bear, and after formed them with licking. Scaliger the Father writes it of him, that he made a quantity of verses in the morning, which afore night he reduced to a less number. But that which Valerius Maximus hath left recorded of Euripides,

the tragic poet, his answer to Alcestis, another
poet, is as memorable as modest; who—when it
was told to Alcestis that Euripides had in three
days brought forth but three verses, and those with
some difficulty and throes, Alcestis glorying he
could with ease have sent forth a hundred in the
space—Euripides roundly replied, 'Like enough,
but here is the difference: thy verses will not last
those three days; mine will to all time.' Which
was as to tell him he coud not write a verse. I have
met many of these rattles, that made a noise and
buzzed. They had their hum, and no more. Indeed, things wrote with labour deserve to be so
read, and will last their age.

3. *Imitatio*. The third requisite in our poet, or
maker, is imitation: to be able to convert the substance or riches of another poet to his own use. To
make choice of one excellent man above the rest,
and so to follow him till he grow very he, or so
like him as the copy may be mistaken for the
principal. Not as a creature that swallows what
it takes in, crude, raw, or undigested; but that
feeds with an appetite, and hath a stomach to con-
coct, divide, and turn all into nourishment. Not to
imitate servilely, as Horace saith, and catch at vices
for virtue; but to draw forth out of the best and
choicest flowers, with the bee, and turn all into
honey; work it into one relish and savour; make
our imitation sweet; observe how the best writers
have imitated, and follow them. How Virgil and
Statius have imitated Homer; how Horace, Archi-
lochus; how Alcaeus and the other Lyrics; and so
of the rest.

4. *Lectio*. But that which we especially require in
him is an exactness of study and multiplicity of

reading, which maketh a full man; not alone enabling him how to know the history or argument of a poem, and to report it; but so to master the matter and style as to show he knows how to handle, place, or dispose of either with elegancy, when need shall be. And not think he can leap forth suddenly a poet by dreaming he hath been in Parnassus, or having washed his lips—as they say—in Helicon. There goes more to his making than so. For to nature, exercise, imitation, and study, art must be added, to make all these perfect. And, though these challenge to themselves much, in the making up of our maker, it is art only can lead him to perfection, and leave him there in possession, as planted by her hand.

To judge of poets is only the faculty of poets; and not of all poets, but the best. *Nemo infelicius de poetis iudicavit quam qui de poetis scripsit.* 'But,' some will say, 'critics are a kind of tinkers, that make more faults than they mend ordinarily. See their diseases, and those of grammarians.' It is true, many bodies are the worse for the meddling with, and the multitude of physicians hath destroyed many sound patients with their wrong practice. But the office of a true critic, or censor, is not to throw by a letter anywhere, or damn an innocent syllabe, but lay the words together and amend them; judge sincerely of the author and his matter, which is the sign of solid and perfect learning in a man. Such was Horace, an author of much civility, and (if anyone among the heathen can be) the best master both of virtue and wisdom; an excellent and true judge, upon cause and reason; not because he thought so, but because he knew so, out of use and experience.

from

INFORMATIONS BY BEN JONSON
TO W. D., WHEN HE CAME
TO SCOTLAND UPON FOOT
1619

*Certain Informations and Manners of Ben Jonson's
to William Drummond*

1

That he had an intention to perfect an epic poem
entitled 'Heroölogia,' of the worthies of his country roused by fame, and was to dedicate it to his
country. It is all in couplets, for he detesteth all
other rhymes. Said he had written a discourse of
poesy both against Campion and Daniel, especially
this last; where he proves couplets to be the bravest
sort of verses, especially when they are broken, like
hexameters; and that cross-rhymes and stanzas (because the purpose would lead him beyond eight lines
to conclude) were all forced.

2

He recommended to my reading Quintilian (who,
he said, would tell me the faults of my verses as if
he had lived with me) and Horace, Plinius Secundus' epistles, Tacitus, Juvenal, Martial, whose epigram, *'Vitam quae faciunt beatiorem,* &c.,' he hath
translated.

3

His censure of the English poets was this:

That Sidney did not keep a decorum, in making everyone speak as well as himself. Spenser's stanzas pleased him not, nor his matter; the meaning of which allegory he had delivered in papers to Sir Walter Raleigh.

Samuel Daniel was a good, honest man; had no children; but no poet.

That Michael Drayton's 'Polyolbion,' if he had performed what he had promised (to write the deeds of all the worthies) had been excellent. His long verses pleased him not.

That Sylvester's translation of Du Bartas was not well done, and that he wrote his verses before it, ere he understood to confer. Nor that of Fairfax his.

That the translations of Homer and Virgil in long alexandrines were but prose.

That John Harington's Ariosto, under all translations, was the worst.

That when Sir John Harington desired him to tell the truth of his epigrams, he answered him that he loved not the truth, for they were narrations and not epigrams.

That Warner, since the King's coming to England, had marred all his 'Albion's England.'

That Donne's 'Anniversary' was profane and full of blasphemies. That he told Master Donne if it had been written of the Virgin Mary, it had been something; to which he answered that he described the idea of a woman, and not as she was.

That Donne, for not keeping of accent, deserved hanging.

That Shakespeare wanted art.

That Sharpham, Day, Dekker were all rogues, and that Minsheu was one.

That Abraham Fraunce, in his English hexameters, was a fool.

That, next himself, only Fletcher and Chapman could make a masque.

4

His judgment of stranger poets was:

That he thought not Bartas a poet, but a verser, because he wrote not fiction. He cursed Petrarch for redacting verses to sonnets, which he said were like that tyrant's bed, where some who were too short were racked, others too long cut short.

That Guarini, in his 'Pastor Fido,' kept not decorum, in making shepherds speak as well as himself could.

That Lucan, taken in parts, was good divided; read altogether, merited not the name of a poet.

That Bonifonius' 'Vigilium Veneris' was excellent.

That he told Cardinal Duperron, at his being in France, Anno 1613, who shew him his translations of Virgil, that they were naught.

That the best pieces of Ronsard were his odes.

All this was to no purpose, for he neither doth understand French nor Italian.

7

He esteemeth John Donne the first poet in the world in some things. His verses of the lost chain he hath by heart, and that passage of 'The Calm,' that dust and feathers do not stir, all was so quiet. Affirmeth Donne to have written all his best pieces ere he was twenty-five years old.

Sir Henry Wotton's verses of a happy life he hath by heart, and a piece of Chapman's translation of the thirteenth of the Iliads, which he thinketh well done.

That Donne said to him he wrote the epitaph on Prince Henry, 'Look to me, Faith,' to match Sir Edward Herbert in obscureness.

He hath by heart some verses of Spenser's 'Calendar,' about wine, between Cuddie and Percie.

8

The conceit of Donne's transformation, or 'Metempsychosis,' was that he sought the soul of that apple which Eve pulled, and thereafter made it the soul of a bitch, then of a she-wolf, and so of a woman. His general purpose was to have brought in all the bodies of the heretics from the soul of Cain, and at last left it in the body of Calvin. Of this he never wrote but one sheet; and now, since he was made Doctor, repenteth highly, and seeketh to destroy all his poems.

9

That Petronius, Plinius Secundus, Tacitus speak best Latin.

That Quintilian's sixth, seventh, eighth books were not only to be read, but altogether digested. Juvenal, Perse, Horace, Martial for delight, and so was Pindar; for health, Hippocrates.

Of their nation, Hooker's ecclesiastical history (whose children are now beggars) for church mat-

ters; Selden's 'Titles of Honour' for antiquities here,
and one book of the gods of the Gentiles, whose
names are in the Scripture, of Selden's.

Tacitus, he said, wrote the secrets of the council
and senate, as Suetonius did those of the cabinet and
court.

10

For a heroic poem, he said there was no such
ground as King Arthur's fiction, and that Sir Philip
Sidney had an intention to have transformed all
his 'Arcadia' to the stories of King Arthur.

11

His acquaintance and behaviour with poets living
with him:

Daniel was at jealousies with him.

Drayton feared him, and he esteemed not of him.

That Francis Beaumont loved too much himself
and his own verses.

That Sir John Roe loved him; and when they two
were ushered by my Lord Suffolk from a masque,
Roe wrote a moral epistle to him, which began,
that next to plays the court and the state were the
best.

'God threatens kings, kings lords, as lords do us.'

He beat Marston, and took his pistol from him.

Sir William Alexander was not half kind unto him,
and neglected him, because a friend to Drayton.

That Sir Robert Aytoun loved him dearly.

Nat Field was his scholar, and had read to him the
satires of Horace and some epigrams of Martial.

That Markham (who added his 'English Arcadia')

was not of the number of the faithful, i.e., poets, but a base fellow.

That such were Day and Middleton.

That Chapman and Fletcher were loved of him.

Overbury was first his friend, then turned his mortal enemy.

12

Particulars of the actions of other poets, and apothegms:

That the Irish having robbed Spenser's goods, and burnt his house and a little child new born, he and his wife escaped; and after, he died for lack of bread in King Street, and refused twenty pieces sent to him by my Lord of Essex, and said he was sorry he had no time to spend them.

That in that paper Sir Walter Raleigh had of the allegories of his 'Faery Queen,' by the Blatant Beast the Puritans were understood; by the false Duessa, the Queen of Scots.

That Southwell was hanged; yet, so he had written that piece of his, 'The Burning Babe,' he would have been content to destroy many of his.

Francis Beaumont died ere he was thirty years of age.

Sir John Roe was an infinite spender, and used to say when he had no more to spend he could die. He died in his arms of the pest, and he furnished his charges, twenty pounds, which was given him back.

That Drayton was challenged for entitling one book 'Mortimeriados.'

That Sir John Davies played, in an epigram, on Drayton, who in a sonnet concluded his mistress might been the tenth worthy; and said he used a phrase like Dametas, in 'Arcadia,' who said for wit his mistress might be a giant.

Donne's grandfather, on the mother side, was Heywood the Epigrammatist.

That Donne himself, for not being understood, would perish.

That Sir Walter Raleigh esteemed more of fame than conscience.

The best wits of England were employed for making of his history. Ben himself had written a piece to him of the Punic War, which he altered and set in his book.

Sir Walter hath written the life of Queen Elizabeth, of which there is copies extant.

Sir Philip Sidney had translated some of the Psalms, which went abroad under the name of the Countess of Pembroke.

Marston wrote his father-in-law's preachings, and his father-in-law his comedies.

Shakespeare, in a play, brought in a number of men saying they had suffered shipwreck in Bohemia, where there is no sea near by some hundred miles.

Daniel wrote 'Civil Wars,' and yet hath not one battle in all his book.

The Countess of Rutland was nothing inferior to her father, Sir Philip Sidney, in poesy. Sir Thomas Overbury was in love with her, and caused Ben to read his 'Wife' to her; which he, with an excellent grace, did, and praised the author. That the morn thereafter he discorded with Overbury, who would have him to intend a suit that was unlawful. The lines my Lady kept in remembrance:

'He comes too near, that comes to be denied.'

Beaumont wrote that elegy on the death of the Countess of Rutland; and in effect, her husband wanted the half of his —— in his travels.

Owen is a pure pedantic schoolmaster, sweeping his living from the posteriors of little children, and hath nothing good in him, his epigrams being bare narrations.

Chapman hath translated Musaeus in his verses, like his Homer.

Fletcher and Beaumont, ten years since, hath written 'The Faithful Shepherdess,' a tragicomedy, well done.

Dyer died unmarried.

Sir Philip Sidney was no pleasant man in countenance, his face being spoiled with pimples, and of high blood, and long. That my Lord Lisle, now Earl of Leicester, his eldest son resembleth him.

13

Of his own life, education, birth, actions:

His grandfather came from Carlisle, and he thought from Annandale to it; he served King Henry VIII, and was a gentleman. His father lost all his estate under Queen Mary, having been cast in prison and forfeited, at last turned minister; so he was a minister's son. He himself was posthumous born a month after his father's decease, brought up poorly, put to school by a friend (his master, Camden); after, taken from it and put to another craft (I think was to be a wright or bricklayer), which he could not endure. Then went he to the Low Countries, but, returning soon, he betook himself to his wonted studies. In his service in the Low Countries, he had, in the face of both the camps, killed an enemy and taken Opima Spolia from him; and since his coming to England, being appealed to the fields, he had killed his adversary, which had hurt him in the arm, and whose sword was ten inches longer than his; for the which he was imprisoned, and almost at the gallows. Then took he his religion by trust, of a priest who visited him in prison. Thereafter he was twelve years a papist.

He was Master of Arts in both the Universities, by their favour, not his study.

He married a wife who was a shrew, yet honest. Five years he had not bedded with her, but remained with my Lord Aubigny.

In the time of his close imprisonment under Queen Elizabeth, his judges could get nothing of him, to all their demands, but ay and no. They placed two damned villains, to catch advantage of him, with him; but he was advertised by his keeper. Of the spies he hath an epigram.

When the King came in England, at that time the pest was in London, he being in the country at Sir Robert Cotton's house with old Camden, he saw in a vision his eldest son (then a child and at London) appear to him with the mark of a bloody cross on his forehead, as if it had been cutted with a sword; at which amazed, he prayed unto God, and in the morning he came to Master Camden's chamber to tell him, who persuaded him it was but an apprehension of his fantasy, at which he should not be disjected. In the meantime comes there letters from his wife, of the death of that boy in the plague. He appeared to him, he said, of a manly shape, and of that growth that he thinks he shall be at the resurrection.

He was delated by Sir James Murray to the King,

for writing something against the Scots in a play, 'Eastward Ho,' and voluntarily imprisoned himself with Chapman and Marston, who had written it amongst them. The report was that they should then had their ears cut, and noses. After their delivery, he banqueted all his friends; there was Camden, Selden, and others. At the midst of the feast, his old mother drank to him, and shew him a paper which she had (if the sentence had taken execution) to have mixed in the prison among his drink, which was full of lusty, strong poison. And that she was no churl, she told, she minded first to have drunk of it herself.

He had many quarrels with Marston, beat him and took his pistol from him, wrote his 'Poetaster' on him. The beginning of them were that Marston represented him in the stage.

In his youth, given to venery. He thought the use of a maid nothing, in comparison to the wantonness of a wife, and would never have another mistress. He said two accidents strange befell him: one, that a man made his own wife to court him, whom he enjoyed two years ere he knew of it, and one day finding them by chance, was passingly delighted with it; one other, lay divers times with a woman who shew him all that he wished, except the last act, which she would never agree unto.

Sir Walter Raleigh sent him governor with his son, Anno 1613, to France. This youth, being knavishly inclined, among other pastimes (as the setting of the favour of damosels on a codpiece) caused him to be drunken and dead drunk, so that he knew not where he was; thereafter laid him on a car, which he made to be drawn by pioneers through the streets, at every corner showing his governor stretched out, and telling them that was a more lively image of the crucifix than any they had. At which sport young Raleigh's mother delighted much, saying his father young was so inclined, though the father abhorred it.

He can set horoscopes, but trusts not in them. He, with the consent of a friend, cozened a lady, with whom he had made an appointment to meet an old astrologer in the suburbs; which she kept, and it was himself disguised in a long gown and a white beard, at the light of a dim-burning candle, up in a little cabinet reached unto by a ladder.

Every first day of the new year, he had twenty pounds sent him from the Earl of Pembroke to buy books.

After he was reconciled with the Church and left off to be a recusant, at his first communion, in token of true reconciliation, he drank out all the full cup of wine.

Being at the end of my Lord Salisbury's table with Inigo Jones, and demanded by my Lord why he was not glad, 'My Lord,' said he, 'you promised I should dine with you, but I do not.' For he had none of his meat; he esteemed only that his meat which was of his own dish.

He hath consumed a whole night in lying looking to his great toe, about which he hath seen Tartars and Turks, Romans and Carthaginians, fight in his imagination.

Northampton was his mortal enemy, for brawling, on a Saint George's day, one of his attenders. He was called before the Council for his 'Sejanus,' and accused both of popery and treason by him.

Sundry times he hath devoured his books, i.e. sold them all for necessity.

He hath a mind to be a churchman; and so he might have favour to make one sermon to the King, he careth not what thereafter should befall him. For he would not flatter, though he saw Death.

At his hither coming, Sir Francis Bacon said to him, he loved not to see poesy go on other feet than poetical dactylus and spondaeus.

14

His narration of great ones:

He never esteemed of a man for the name of a lord.

Queen Elizabeth never saw herself, after she became old, in a true glass. They painted her, and sometimes would vermilion her nose. She had always, about Christmas Evens, set dice, that threw sixes or five, and she knew not they were other, to make her win and esteem herself fortunate. That she had a membrana on her which made her incapable of man, though for her delight she tried many. At the coming over of Monsieur, there was a French chirurgeon who took in hand to cut it; yet fear stayed her, and his death. King Philip had intention, by dispensation of the Pope, to have married her.

Sir Philip Sidney's mother, Leicester's sister, after she had the little pox, never shew herself in Court thereafter, but masked.

The Earl of Leicester gave a bottle of liquor to his lady, which he willed her to use in any faintness; which she, after his return from Court, not knowing it was poison, gave him, and so he died.

Salisbury never cared for any man longer nor he could make use of him.

My Lord Lisle's daughter, my Lady Wroth, is unworthily married on a jealous husband.

Ben one day being at table with my Lady Rutland, her husband coming in, accused her that she kept table to poets; of which she wrote a letter to him, which he answered. My Lord intercepted the letter, but never challenged him.

My Lord Chancellor of England wringeth his speeches from the strings of his band, and other councillors from the picking of their teeth.

Pembroke and his lady discoursing, the Earl said the women were men's shadows, and she maintained them. Both appealing to Jonson, he affirmed it true; for which my Lady gave a penance, to prove it in verse. Hence his epigram.

Essex wrote that epistle, or preface, before the translation of the last part of Tacitus, which is A. B. The last book the gentleman durst not translate, for the evil it contains of the Jews.

The King said Sir Philip Sidney was no poet; neither did he see ever any verses in England, to the Sculler's.

It were good that the half of the preachers of England were plain ignorants, for that either in their sermons they flatter, or strive to show their own eloquence.

15

His opinion of verses:

That he wrote all his first in prose, for so his master, Camden, had learned him.

That verses stood by sense, without either colours or accent; which yet other times he denied.

A great many epigrams were ill, because they expressed in the end what should have been understood by what was said.

Some loved running verses. *Plus mihi comma placet.*

He imitated the description of a night from Boni-fonius's 'Vigilium Veneris.'

He scorned such verses as could be transponed; that of Sir John Davies:

'Where lives the man that never yet did hear
 Of chaste Penelope, Ulysses' Queen?'

'Of chaste Penelope, Ulysses' Queen,
 Where lives the man that never yet did hear?'

18

Miscellanies:

John Stow had monstrous observations in his 'Chronicle,' and was of his craft a tailor.

He and I walking alone, he asked two cripples what they would have to take him to their order.

In his 'Sejanus' he hath translated a whole oration of Tacitus.

The first four books of Tacitus ignorantly done in English.

John Selden liveth on his own; is the law-book of the judges of England, the bravest man in all languages. His book, 'Titles of Honour,' written to his chamber-fellow, Heyward.

Taylor was sent along here to scorn him.

Camden wrote that book, 'Remains of Britain';
Joseph Hall 'The Harbinger' to Donne's 'Anniversary.'

The epigram of Martial, XI, *'In Verpum,'* he vaunts to expone.

Lucan, Sidney, Guarini make every man speak as

well as themselves, forgetting decorum; for Dametas sometimes speaks grave sentences.

Lucan, taken in parts, excellent; altogether, naught.

He dissuaded me from poetry, for that she had beggared him, when he might have been a rich lawyer, physician, or merchant.

Questioned about English, 'them,' 'they,' 'those.' 'They' is still the nominative, 'those' accusative, 'them' neuter collective; not 'them men,' 'them trees,' but 'them' by itself referred to many.

'Which,' 'who' be relatives; not 'that.'

'Floods,' 'hills' he would have masculines.

He was better versed, and knew more in Greek and Latin, than all the poets in England, and quintessenceth their brains.

He made much of that epistle of Plinius, where *'ad prandium, non ad notam'* is; and that other, of Messalinus, who Pliny made to be removed from the table; and of the gross turbot.

One wrote an epigram to his father, and vaunted he had slain ten. The quantity of *decem* being false, another answered the epigram, telling that *decem* was false.

Sir John Davies' epigram of the whore's c—— compared to a cowl.

Of all styles, he loved most to be named honest, and hath of that an hundred letters so naming him.

He had this oft:

> 'Thy flattering picture, Phryne, is like thee
> Only in this, that you both painted be.'

In his merry humour, he was wont to name himself 'The Poet.'

He went from Leith homeward, the twenty-fifth of January, 1619, in a pair of shoes which, he told, lasted him since he came from Darlington, which he minded to take back that far again. They were appearing like Coryat's; the first two days he was all excoriate.

If he died by the way, he promised to send me his papers of this country, hewn as they were.

I have to send him descriptions of Edinburgh borough-laws, of the Lomond.

That piece of the Pucelle of the Court was stolen out of his pocket by a gentleman who drank him drowsy, and given Mistress Bulstrode; which brought him great displeasure.

He is a great lover and praiser of himself, a contemner and scorner of others; given rather to lose a friend than a jest, jealous of every word and action of those about him (especially after drink, which is one of the elements in which he liveth). A dissembler of ill parts which reign in him, a bragger of some good that he wanteth; thinketh nothing well but what either he himself, or some of his friends and countrymen, hath said or done. He is passionately kind and angry, careless either to gain or keep; vindictive, but—if he be well answered—at himself.

For any religion, as being versed in both.

Interpreteth best sayings and deeds often to the worst.

Oppressed with fantasy, which hath ever mastered his reason, a general disease in many poets. His inventions are smooth and easy, but above all he excelleth in a translation.

When his play of a silent woman was first acted,

there was found verses after on the stage against him, concluding that that play was well named 'The Silent Woman'; there was never one man to say 'plaudite' to it.

FINIS

INDEX OF VERSE